STUDIES PRESENTED TO
DAVID MOORE ROBINSON

David M. Robinson

STUDIES PRESENTED TO
DAVID MOORE ROBINSON

PH.D., LL.D., L.H.D., LITT.D., D.PHIL. (HON.)

PROFESSOR EMERITUS OF ART AND ARCHAEOLOGY
THE JOHNS HOPKINS UNIVERSITY

PROFESSOR OF CLASSICS AND ARCHAEOLOGY
THE UNIVERSITY OF MISSISSIPPI

ON HIS SEVENTIETH BIRTHDAY

VOLUME I

Edited by

GEORGE E. MYLONAS

Professor of History of Art and Archaeology
Washington University

WASHINGTON UNIVERSITY
SAINT LOUIS, MISSOURI
1951

DAVID MOORE ROBINSON

MAGISTRO CLARISSIMO

DOCTORI ERUDITO

AMICO BENIGNO

LITTERARUM UTRIUSQUE LINGUAE

ET RERUM ANTIQUARUM

LUMINI

DISCIPULI   COMITES   AMICI

NATALI LXX

BIOGRAPHICAL SKETCH

DAVID MOORE ROBINSON was born at Auburn, N. Y., September 21, 1880. He obtained his A.B. degree at the University of Chicago in 1898 and his Ph.D. in 1904. He was fellow in Greek, 1898-1901, and studied at the American School of Classical Studies in Athens (1901-1902, as a fellow 1902-1903), at Halle (1902), Berlin (1903-1904) and Bonn (1909).

After a year of teaching at Illinois College, 1904-1905, as head of the Department of Classics, he associated himself with the Johns Hopkins University to which he gave a life-time of devoted and inspired service. Successively he attained the various academic positions of Associate in Classical Archaeology (1905-1908), Associate Professor (1908-1912), Professor of Greek Archaeology and Epigraphy (1912-1913), Professor of Classical Archaeology and Epigraphy (1913-1920), W. H. Collins Vickers Professor of Archaeology and Epigraphy, lecturer in Greek Literature (1911-1947) and chairman of the Department of Art and Archaeology (1913-1947). He also served as chairman of the Latin Department, 1944-1945. He retired in 1947 but for 1947-1948 he remained at the Johns Hopkins as Research Professor in Classics.

His learning, his warm personality, his contagious enthusiasm for classical studies, his inspired teaching, his genuine interest in his students, and his devotion to his work attracted nation-wide attention, brought to the Johns Hopkins an ever-increasing number of serious students, and earned for his department national and international reputation. With justified pride he can point to the numerous scholars who earned their degrees under him and who are trying to continue the tradition he established of learning, teaching, and research in the many institutions of higher learning which they serve all over the nation. The names of these scholars form a very impressive list, a list which will enable the reader to surmise the influence of the Master at work today.

It will prove impossible, however, to fathom his influence on the students he met in his lecture tours and in his teaching in Universities and Colleges other than the Johns Hopkins. For although his main efforts were exerted on behalf of that institution, he also served as Professor of Greek at Notre Dame College, Baltimore (1921-1935), as acting director and Professor of the Greek Language and Literature at the American School of Classical Studies at Athens (1909-1910), and again as Librarian and Professor of Greek and Archaeology in 1946-1947. He was lecturer at Bryn Mawr College (1911-1912), Professor of Classical Philology in the summer sessions of Columbia University (1919) and the University of California at Berkeley (1927). He taught Sociology and Anthropology at the University of California at Los Angeles (summer of 1941). He was visiting Professor of Art at the University of Chicago (1930), Professor of Latin at Syracuse University (in the summers of 1929, 1931-1933), and at the College of William and Mary (summer of 1941). He further served as C. L. Moore lecturer at Trinity College (1935), McBride lecturer at Western Reserve University (1930), Lecturer in Fine Arts at New York University (1926-1931), and Larwill lecturer at Kenyon College (1932). His work at the various universities was supplemented by the lectures he delivered on behalf of a great number of learned societies. Especially, however, he lectured for the Archaeological Institute of America. It can be definitely stated that scarcely a chapter of that Institute exists before which Professor Robinson has not lectured repeatedly. In recognition of this contribution, the Institute appointed him Charles Eliot Norton Lecturer for the years 1924, 1925, 1928, and 1929.

His teaching and lecturing were enriched by his personal achievement in the field of excavating. He started as a member of the excavation staff at Corinth in 1902 and 1903 and at Sardis in 1910. In 1924 he directed the excavation of Pisidian Antioch and of Sizma for the University of Michigan. His greatest achievement in the field is his discovery, excavation, and publication of Olynthus, to which site he devoted four campaigns from 1928-1938, and a good part of his life.

His brilliant record as a teacher, lecturer, and excavator is matched by his voluminous publications. These will be appreciated through even a casual perusal of his Bibliography collected in this volume. There exists no field of Greek and Roman Archaeological research which has not been enriched by Professor Robinson's scholarly writings. He has also published books or articles on Greek and Roman Literature, History, Epigraphy, Philology, Linguistics, Fine Arts, and even poetry, having translated poems of Sappho, Horace, and others into verse. This immense accomplishment was supplemented by editorial work faithfully carried out over a number of years. He served as an Associate Editor of the *Classical Weekly* from 1913-1936, of the *American Journal of Philology* since 1920 (honorary editor since 1943). He was the founder and first Editor-in-chief of *Art and Archaeology* from 1914-1918, Associate Editor from 1918-1934. He was the founder and first Editor-in-chief of the *Art Bulletin* from 1919-1921, and chairman of the editorial board until 1934, Associate Editor since 1934. He served as the Editor of News, Discussions and Bibliography of the *American Journal of Archaeology* from 1932-

1938, and as the author of its Bibliography since 1938; now he serves as an Associate Editor. For many years he was the American representative for the *Supplementum Epigraphicum,* and the International Journal *Litteris.* He was the Editor of the *Johns Hopkins Studies in Archaeology,* a series already comprising thirty-eight volumes. With Professor Hadzsits he is the co-editor of the series *Our Debt to Greece and Rome* in which appeared forty-five volumes. He served as a member of the Publications Committee of the American School of Classical Studies at Athens from 1931 to 1938.

It will be too long to list the fifty or more learned Societies and Associations in which Professor Robinson is a member, including the American Philosophical Society, the American Academy of Arts and Sciences, the Archaeological Society of Greece (honorary member), the German Archaeological Institute, the Royal Numismatic Society of England (fellow). But it should be noted that he served on the Executive Committees and as an officer in a number of our leading societies. Thus he served as the General Secretary of the Archaeological Institute of America from 1921-1923, as Vice President from 1921-1930 and as First Vice President from 1930-1935. He has also served twice as a member of the Executive Committee of the American Council of Learned Societies and of the American School of Classical Studies at Athens and for a long time he was on the Academic Council of the Johns Hopkins University and the Council of the American and British Commonwealth. He was President of the College Art Association, 1919-1923, a director, 1923-1943, and since then honorary director. He has been President of the Classical Association of the Atlantic States, 1920-1921, chairman of the Advisory Council of the American School of Classical Studies at Rome, 1920-1921, and Vice President of the American Classical League (1945-1950).

Greece naturally became the special object of his varied philanthropic activity. We find him serving as the President of the Maryland Branch of the Greek War Relief Association, since 1940, as a member of the Council for the Restoration of Greece, of the National Council of the Dodecanesian Society, as President of the Society of Byzantine and Modern Greek Studies, as honorary President of the Pan-Macedonian Association and of the Helleno-American Society of Northern Greece.

This biographical sketch would be incomplete without the mention of his marriage to Helen Haskell on August 31, 1910. His many students will cherish forever the picture of Mrs. Robinson as the graceful hostess who brightened so many of their days, and those who were privileged to participate in the excavations of Olynthus will never forget her kindness, her efficiency and cheerfulness in the midst of adverse conditions, and her understanding of the failings of human nature. To this faithful companion of his life Professor Robinson owes much of his success.

For his great activity and contribution to his chosen field Professor Robinson was honored by a number of institutions. In 1915 he was awarded an LL.D. degree by Jamestown College; in 1925 an L.H.D. degree by Trinity College and an Litt.D. degree by Syracuse University in 1933. The University of Thessalonike in 1951 awarded him an honorary degree of Doctor of Philosophy for his excavations of Olynthus and his important researches in Macedonia. His own Alma Mater, the University of Chicago, in 1941 cited him as a "useful citizen."

In 1947 Professor Robinson retired from the Johns Hopkins with the title of Professor emeritus of Art and Archaeology. But for him retirement from one institution meant but a life dedicated anew to the course of teaching at another. The University of Mississippi became the fortunate Institution of Higher Learning in whose Halls the voice of the great teacher, a modern παγὰ λαλέουσα, continues to open the fonts of learning and research to the youth of America. As Professor of Classics and Archaeology in that Institution he carries on the lighted torch of knowledge and truth to new heights.

For his past, present, and future achievement and on the occasion of his seventieth birthday, the scholarly world acclaims the great teacher and scholar and wishes him many more years of fruitful life devoted to scholarship and ΕΥΤΥΧΙΑΝ ΚΑΛΗΝ.

G. E. M.

LIST OF SCHOLARS WHO STUDIED UNDER DAVID M. ROBINSON AND ON WHOM DEGREES WERE CONFERRED BY HIM

MASTERS OF ART

Fraser, Alexander David, 1919. Essay: "The Greek Helmet." Professor of Classical Archaeology and History, University of Virginia, 1930——.

Harrison, Mary Ella, 1919. Essay: "Childhood and Youth in Roman Art." Died, 1941.

Beardsley, Mrs. Wilfred A. (Grace Hadley), 1921. Essay: "The Negro Type in Greek and Roman Art." Manager and Co-owner, St. Lucie Colony Hotel, 1946——.

Persons, Elizabeth, 1921. Essay: "Caryatids and the Use of the Human Figure as a Support in Art." Head of the Department of Archaeology and Art History, Florida Southern College, 1937——.

Dulac, Mrs. Victor (Hilda North), 1922. Essay: "Old Age and Maturity in Greek and Roman Art."

Skalet, Charles Hannord, 1922. Essay: "Chapters in the History of Ancient Sicyon." Professor of Greek, Latin, Classical History, and Archaeology, Head of the Department, Concordia College, 1923——.

Metour, Eugene Paul, 1924. Essay: "The Art of the Catacombs and the Beginning of Christian Painting." Died, 1929.

Rusk, William Sener, 1924. Essay: "William Henry Rinehart and the Influence of Classical Sculpture." Professor of History of Art, Wells College, 1928——.

Suhr, Elmer George, 1925. Essay: "Sculptured Portraits of Greek Statesmen." Professor of Archaeology, University of Rochester, 1948——.

Carroll, Charles Borromeo, 1926. Essay: "Caves and Their Ancient Uses." Epiphany College.

Cooper, Ethel, 1926. Essay: "Praxiteles and His Influence." Teacher of English, Western High School, 1928——.

Couch, Herbert Newell, 1926. Essay: "Sources for the Study of Sardis." Member of staff at Olynthus, 1928; Professor of Greek and Latin Classics, Brown University, 1945——.

Couch, Mrs. Herbert N. (Eunice Burr Stebbins), 1926. Essay: "The Letters of Augustus Preserved in Greek Inscriptions and in the Greek Writers." Member of staff at Olynthus, 1928.

Gallagher, Mary Teresa, 1926. Essay: "The Representation of Armor in Hellenistic and Roman Sculpture." Retired Public School Teacher, 1947.

McGehee, Mary Wilson, 1926. Essay: "Replicas of Scenes on Attic Red-figured Vases." Member of staff at Olynthus, 1928; Assistant Professor of Art, Vassar College, 1927——.

Canfield, Lillian Caroline, 1930. Essay: "Minoan-Mycenaean Survivals in Eastern Greek Pottery." Resident in Far Eastern Department, University of Washington, 1944——.

McDermott, William Coffman, 1930. Essay: "The Ape in Classical Art and Literature." Associate Professor of Classics and Classical History, Assistant Dean of University of Pennsylvania, 1942——.

Medford, Richard Carl, 1931. Essay: "Achilles, Some Scenes from His Life as Painted on Greek Vases." Director of Fine Arts Museum in Hagerstown, Maryland, 1932-1940. Now research fellow in Algiers.

Ellingson, Mrs. Rudolph Conrad (Helen Madeline Mary Ross; 1932. Essay: "The Terra-Cotta Industry at Olynthus." Instructor in Classics, Mt. Royal College, 1932-38; Director of Archaeology, Museum, Evansville, Ind.; Olynthus staff member, 1931.

Fluck, Edward James, 1932. Essay: "Studies in Love Names on Greek Vases." Instructor at Muhlenberg College, Allentown, Pa., 1936——.

Schulz, Alexander Heinrich Gottfried, 1935. Essay: "The Burials and Burial Customs of Prehistoric Greece." Member of Olynthus staff, 1931; Custodian of the Classical, Oriental, and Egyptian Museum at the University of Illinois, Urbana, Illinois.

Albright, Frank Phidias, 1936. Essay: "Red-figured Vases of Olynthus Found in 1934." Member of Olynthus staff, 1938; Assistant Professor of Greek and Latin and Chairman of the Art Department, Union College, 1948——.

Edwards, George Roger, 1937. Essay: "Attic Black-glazed Pottery." Instructor in Art and Classics, Bowdoin College; Special Fellow of the American School of Classical Studies at Corinth, Athens, Greece, 1947-48, and in the Agora, 1948-1949. Assistant Professor of Classical Archaeology, University of Pennsylvania, 1949——.

Vestling, Mrs. Carl S. (Christina Brungate Meredith), 1937. Essay: "The Finger-rings Found at Olynthus in 1931 and 1934."

Prakken, Donald Wilson, 1937. Essay: "Demetrius of Phalerum." Assistant Professor of Classics, Franklin and Marshall College, 1946——.

Craft, John Richard, 1939. Essay: "The City Drainage at Olynthus." Member of staff at Olynthus, 1938. Director of Washington County Museum of Fine Arts, 1940-1949. Director of Art Museum, Columbia S. C., 1949——.

Grossberg, Herbert, 1941. Essay: "The Influence of the Pantheon and Its Relation to Domed Buildings in the History of Architecture." Instructor and Chairman of Department of Humanities, Herzel Junior College.

Caldwell, Robert Wallace, 1942. Essay: "The Chimaera." Vice-Consul in Athens, now in Dublin.

MacDonald, William Allan, 1942. Essay: "The History and Culture of Abdera." Assistant Professor of Art and Chairman of the Department, Western Maryland College, 1947-1948. Associate Professor, University of Minnesota, 1948——.

Macht, Mrs. Martin Benzyl (Carol Hortense Malisoff), 1942. Essay: "The Origin and Development of the Pagan Basilica."

Palmer, Hazel, 1943. Essay: "A Catalogue of Italic and Corinthian Pottery." Fellow in the Institute for Advanced Study, Princeton, 1949——.

Voelkel, Laura Bennett, 1943. Essay: "The Coinage of the Roman Republic Considered from an Historical Point of View." Assistant Professor of Latin, Greek and Archaeology, Mary Washington College, 1948——; Secretary of the Advisory Committee of the American School of Classical Studies in Rome, 1948——.

Cazel, Mrs. Fred A. (Annarie Jane Peters), 1944. Essay: "Pre-Hellenic and Archaic Greek Propylaea."

Benedict, Stewart Hurd, 1945. Essay: "Arretium, Its History, Its Pottery, and a Contribution to the Chronology of the Ware." Master in French and German, DeVeaux School, 1946——.

McIntosh, Edith Roberts, 1945. Essay: "Oriental Influences in Early Greek Sculpture." Librarian, Naval Medical Field Res. Laboratory, 1949——.

Parks, Mrs. John H. (Betty Jean Hite), 1945. Essay: "A Discussion of Selected Roman Kitchen Utensils." Instructor in Classics, Kent State College, Ohio.

Eckels, Claire Wittler, 1946. Essay: "The Representation of Children in Classical Sculpture." Teacher of Art, Greenwood School.

Potter, Mrs. James Harry (Emma Josephine Hill), 1946. Essay: "Delian Houses." Teacher of French and Art, Baltimore High Schools, 1943-49.

Fay, Ladislas Ernest Michael, 1948. Essay: "Early Greek Religion." Fellow, New York University.

Wooden, Howard Edmund, 1948. Essay: "Geometric Pottery." Master at St. Paul's School.

Rubright, James, 1950, University of Mississippi. Essay: "Methods of Illumination as illustrated by the Robinson Collection of Lamps at the University of Mississippi." Robinson fellow in the American School of Classical Studies at Athens.

A total of forty-one students on whom was conferred the Degree of Master of Arts.

DOCTORS OF PHILOSOPHY[1]

Magoffin, Ralph van Deman, 1908. Dissertation: *"A Study of the Topography and Municipal History of Praeneste,"* published in the Johns Hopkins University Studies in History and Political Sciences, series xxvi, nos. 9-10, Johns Hopkins Press, Baltimore, 1908, 101 pp. President of Archaeological Institute of America, 1922-32; Professor of Classics, New York University, 1923-1942. Died, 1942.

*Johnson, Allan Chester, 1909. Dissertation: *"A Comparative Study in Selected Chapters in the Syntax of Isaeus, Isocrates, and the Attic Psephismata preceding 300 B. C.,"* published by C. Meisner and N. Kargaduris, Athens, 1911, 78 pp. Musgrave Professor of Latin, 1933-43; West Professor of Classics, Princeton University, 1943-49.

Wagener, Anthony Pelzer, 1909. Dissertation: *"Popular Associations of Right and Left in Roman Literature,"* published by J. H. Furst Co., Baltimore, 1912, 58 pp. Professor and Head of Department of Ancient Languages, William and Mary College, 1929———.

Fox, William Sherwood, 1911. Dissertation: *"The Johns Hopkins Tabellae Defixionum,"* published by the Johns Hopkins Press, Baltimore, 1912, 32 pp. Professor of Classics, University of Western Ontario, 1917-27, Dean, 1919-27, President 1927-47.

Harcum, Cornelia Gaskins, 1913. Dissertation: *"Roman Cooks,"* published by J. H. Furst Co., Baltimore, 1914, 84 pp. Keeper of the Classical Section of the Royal Ontario Museum and Assistant Professor of History of Industrial Art, University of Toronto, 1914-1927. Founder of Harcum scholarships for women in archaeology. Died, 1927.

---

1. Those nineteen marked with a star have won by examination fellowships at the American School of Classical Studies in Athens. John Day won fellowships in both Athens and Rome. Magoffin and Wagener won fellowships at the American Academy in Rome.

Bourne, Ella, 1913. Dissertation: *"A Study of Tibur—Historical, Literary, and Epigraphical—from the Earliest Times to the Close of the Roman Empire,"* published by George Banta Co., Menasha, Wisconsin, 1916, 74 pp. Professor of Latin, Mills College. Died, 1947.

*Edwards, John Bowen, 1913. Dissertation: *"The Demesman in Attic Life,"* published by George Banta Co., Menasha, Wisconsin, 1916, 63 pp. Professor of Greek, Wells College, 1924-31; Manager, Friendly Inn, Baltimore, 1941——.

Armstrong, Mary Emma, 1915. Dissertation: "The Significance of Color in Roman Ritual." Instructor, Goucher College, 1915-20; Professor of Latin and Greek, Olivet College, 1920——.

Shields, Emily Ledyard, 1915. Dissertation: *"Cults of Lesbos,"* published by George Banta Co., Menasha, Wisconsin, 1917, 100 pp. Professor of Latin, Smith College, 1923——.

*Johnson, Franklin Plotinos, 1921. Dissertation: *"Lysippus,"* published by Duke University Press, 1927, 334 pp., 61 pls. Associate Professor of Art, University of Chicago, 1930——.

Beardsley, Mrs. Wilfred A. (Grace Hadley), 1922. Dissertation: *"The Ethiopian in Greek and Roman Civilization,"* published by Johns Hopkins Press, Baltimore, 1929, 41 pp. Professor at Goucher College. Manager and Co-owner, St. Lucie Colony Hotel, 1946——.

Highbarger, Ernest Leslie, 1923. Dissertation: *"Chapters in the History and Civilization of Ancient Megara,"* published by Johns Hopkins Press, Baltimore, 1927, 65 pp. Professor of Classical Languages, Northwestern University, 1927——.

Skalet, Charles Hannord, 1923. Dissertation: *"Sicyon: An Archaeological and Historical Study with a Prosopographia Sicyonia,"* published in the Johns Hopkins Studies in Archaeology, No. 3, Johns Hopkins Press, Baltimore, 1928, 223 pp., 16 pls. Professor of Greek, Latin, Classical History, and Archaeology, Concordia College, 1923——, Head of Department.

Wilson, Lillian May, 1924. Dissertation: *"A Study of the Roman Toga,"* published by Johns Hopkins Press, Baltimore, 1924, 132 pp., 75 illustrations. Member of Olynthus Staff, 1928.

*Comber, Mrs. Thomas Francis, Jr. (Adele Madeline Wildes), 1925. Dissertation: "Coordinations in Ancient Greek and Roman Temple Plans."

*Day, John, A.B. Ohio State University, 1925. Dissertation: "Chapters in the History of the Pireaus." Associate Professor of Greek and Latin, Barnard College, 1940——.

Suhr, Elmer George, 1926. Dissertation: *"Sulptured Portraits of Greek Statesmen,"* published by Johns Hopkins Press, Baltimore, 1931, 25 pp. Professor of Archaeology, University of Rochester, 1948———.

Couch, Herbert Newell, 1927. Dissertation: *"Treasuries of the Greeks and Romans,"* published by George Banta Co., Menasha, Wisconsin, 1929, 112 pp. Member of Olynthus Staff, 1928; Professor of Greek and Latin, Brown University, 1945———, and Chairman of the Department, 1948———.

*Couch, Mrs. Herbert N. (Eunice Burr Stebbins), 1927. Dissertation: *"The Dolphin in the Literature and Art of Greece and Rome, Including Pre-Hellenic Civilizations,"* published by George Banta Co., Menasha, Wisconsin, 1929, 136 pp. Member of Olynthus Staff, 1928.

Mylonas, George Emmanuel, 1929. Dissertation: *"The Neolithic Settlement at Olynthus,"* published as Excavations at Olynthus, vol. I, J. H. Furst Co., Baltimore, 1929, 108 pp. Member of Olynthus Staff, 1928, 1931; Field Director, 1938; Director of Excavations at Haghios Kosmas, Eleusis, 1930-34, Akropotamos, 1938; Professor of Art and Archaeology, Head of Department, 1940———, Washington University.

Tanzer, Helen H., 1929. Dissertation: *"The Common People of Pompeii, A Study of the Graffiti,"* published in the Johns Hopkins Studies in Archaeology, No. 29, Johns Hopkins Press, Baltimore, 1939, 139 pp., 49 figs. Professor of Classics Brooklyn College, 1929-37; originator and editor of Latin Visualized (films illustrating Roman Civilization), 1930; Received Pompeii Medal in 1949; Retired.

Clement, Paul A., Jr., 1930. Dissertation: "The Cults of Thessaly." Member of the staff at Olynthus, 1934; Managing Editor, Publications of American School of Classical Studies, Athens, Institute for Advanced Study, Princeton, 1938-1949; Assistant Professor of Classics and Archaeology, University of California, Los Angeles, 1949———.

Gude, Mabel, 1930. Dissertation: *"The History of Olynthus,"* published by Johns Hopkins Press, Baltimore, 1933, 23 pp. Correspondence Supervisor, Scott, Foresman, and Co.

*Carpenter, Mrs. James Saltonstall (Marian Elizabeth Allen Guptill), 1931. Dissertation: "The Influence of Pergamene Sculpture." Editorial Assistant, George Washington University, 1937———.

Richardson, Bessie Ellen, 1931. Dissertation: *"The Greek Portrayal of Old Age,"* published by Johns Hopkins Press, Baltimore, 1933, 376 pp., 26 figs. Associate Professor of Classics and English, Madison College, 1946———.

McGehee, Mary Wilson, 1932. Dissertation: "Replica Scenes on Attic Red-figured Vases." Member of Olynthus Staff, 1928.

*Graham, James Walter, 1933. Dissertation: *"Domestic Architecture in Classical Greece,"* published by Johns Hopkins Press, Baltimore, 1938, 25 pp. Member of Olynthus Staff, 1931; Assistant Professor of Archaeology, University of Toronto, 1947———; Keeper of Classical Collection, Royal Ontario Museum of Archaeology, 1947———.

Hicks, Ruth Ilsley, 1933. Dissertation: "Theseus." Assistant Professor of Classics, Wilson College, 1933———.

*Hill, Dorothy Kent, 1933. Dissertation: "Conventions of Attic Black-figured Drawing." Curator of Ancient Art, Walters Art Gallery, 1935———.

Loomis, Bertha Lillian, 1933. Dissertation: "The Elephant in the Literature and Art of Greece and Rome." Professor, Head of Department of Classical Languages, Hood College, 1926———.

Martin, Susan Hutchinson, 1933. Dissertation: "Ancient Melos." Professor of Classical Languages, Mt. St. Vincent College, 1935———.

Rusk, William Sener, 1933. Dissertation: *"Thornton, Latrobe, and Walter and the Classical Influence on Their Works,"* published by Johns Hopkins Press, Baltimore, 1939. Professor of History of Art, Head of Department, Wells College, 1928———.

Raymond, Doris, 1933. Dissertation: "Macedonian Regal Coinage before Philip II." Professor of Classics, St. Mary's College, Leavenworth, Kansas; on staff of Agora Excavation in Athens, 1935. Assistant Professor of Classics, University of Mississippi, 1951———.

Wolf, George Carl, 1933. Dissertation: "The Peacock in the Literature and Art of the Greeks and Romans." Clergyman.

*Fluck, Edward James, 1934. Dissertation: *"A Study of the Greek Love Names,"* published by Johns Hopkins Press, Baltimore, 1937, 25 pp. Instructor in Classics at Muhlenberg College.

*Freeman, Sarah Elizabeth, 1934. Dissertation: *"The Excavation of a Roman Temple at Corinth,"* published by Johns Hopkins Press, Baltimore, 1941, 70 pp. Member of Olynthus Staff, 1931; Curator of Fine Arts, Johns Hopkins University, 1944———.

McDermott, William Coffman, 1934. Dissertation: *"The Ape in Classical Literature and Art,"* published by Johns Hopkins Press, Baltimore, 1938, 34 pp. Associate Professor of Classics and Classical History, University of Pennsylvania, 1948——; Assistant Dean of University of Pennsylvania, 1942——.

Hanfmann, George Maxim Anossov, 1935. Dissertation: "Metal Objects from Olynthus." Associate Professor and tutor of Fine Arts, Harvard University, 1948——; Curator of Classical Art, Fogg Museum, 1948——.

*Weinberg, Mrs. Saul S. (Gladys Rachel Davidson), 1935. Dissertation: "Miscellaneous Finds from Corinth," to be published in the Corinth Series. Member of Olynthus Staff, 1934.

Ross, Mrs. Arthur (Eleanore Burnham Lay), 1936. Dissertation: "Terra-cottas Found at Olynthus in 1934." Member of Olynthus Staff, 1934; Instructor in Latin, Syracuse University, 1936——.

*Wallace, William Pitkin, 1936. Dissertation: "The History of Eretria to 98 B. C." Assistant Professor of Greek and Roman History, University College, Toronto, 1946——.

*Weinberg, Saul S., 1936. Dissertation: "The Prehistoric House of the Mainland of Greece." Member of Olynthus Staff, 1938; Fellow, Guggenheim Foundation, 1946-47; Associate Professor of Archaeology, University of Missouri, 1948——.

Wolfe, Ruby Luella, 1936. Dissertation: "Studia Corinthia and a Prosopographia Corinthia." Died, 1938.

West, Mildred Georgia, 1937. Dissertation: "Pegasus in Classical Literature and Art." Teacher, Adult Evening School, Baltimore Polytechnic Institute, 1947——.

Alexander, John Aleck, 1939. Dissertation: *Potidaea.* Published by the University of Georgia, 1951. Member of Olynthus Staff, 1938; Associate Professor of History, University of Georgia, 1947——.

*Edwards, George Roger, 1939. Dissertation: "Attic Black-glazed Pottery." Special Fellow in the American School of Classical Studies at Corinth, Athens, Greece, 1947-48, and in the Agora, 1948-1950. Assistant Professor of Classical Archaeology, University of Pennsylvania, 1950——.

Ellingson, Mrs. Rudolph Conrad (Helen Madeline Ross), 1939. Dissertation: "Terra-cotta Figurines of Macedonia and Thrace." Member of Olynthus Staff, 1931; Head of Department of Archaeology, Evansville Museum, 1947——.

Young, Judy (Thelma Judith Yanofsky), 1939. Dissertation: "Early Boeotian Figurines of Terra-cotta." Advertising Copy Writer, Bamberger and Co., 1948——.

Albright, Frank Phidias, 1940. Dissertation: "Funeral Customs of the Greeks." Member of Olynthus Staff, 1938; Assistant Professor of Greek and Latin and Chairman of the Art Department, Union College, 1948——.

Cook, William Hoyt, 1940. Dissertation: "Boxing in Greek Literature and Art." Professor of Greek, College of Charleston, 1928——.

Craft, John Richard, 1940. Dissertation: "The Civic Water Supply of Ancient Greece." Member of Olynthus Staff, 1938. Director of Washington County Museum of Fine Arts, 1940-1949. Director of Art Museum, Columbia, S. C., 1949——.

McDonald, William Andrew, 1940. Dissertation: *"The Political Meeting Places of the Greeks,"* published in the Johns Hopkins Studies in Archaeology, No. 34, Johns Hopkins Press, Baltimore, 1943, 35 pp. Member of Olynthus Staff, 1938; Associate Professor of Classics and Archaeology, University of Minnesota, 1948——.

Kinsey, Robert Samuel, 1941. Dissertation: "The Bovine Elements in Greek Art and Literature." Associate Professor of Classics and Archaeology, Thiel College, 1946——.

Mayhew, Edgar deNoailles, 1941. Dissertation: *"English Baroque: Sir John Vanburgh and the Baroque County House,"* published by Johns Hopkins Press, Baltimore, 1943, 39 pp. Assistant Professor of Art, Connecticut College, 1949——.

Armstrong, Jane, 1942. Dissertation: "Florentine Headdresses: 1300-1500." Lecturer at National Gallery of Art, 1946.

Grossberg, Herbert Elkan, 1942. Dissertation: "The Influence of the Pantheon and Its Relation to Domed Buildings in the History of Architecture." Instructor and Chairman of Department of Humanities, Herzel Junior College.

*Parsons, Arthur Wellesley, 1942. Dissertation: *"Klepsydra and the Paved Court of the Pythion,"* published in *Hesperia,* XII, 1943, 56 pp. Member of Olynthus Staff, 1931, 1934; Director, American School of Classical Studies, 1940-1941 and 1945-46; Professor of Archaeology, 1947-48; Liaison Officer and U. S. Representative of U. N. Security Council International Investigating Committee in Athens, 1946-48. Died, September 29, 1948.

Yavis, Constantine George, 1942. Dissertation: *"Greek Altars,"* published by the St. Louis University Press, 1949. Assistant Professor of Classics and Archaeology, St. Louis University, 1948——.

*Young, John Howard, 1942. Dissertation: "Sunium: An Historical Survey of an Attic Deme." Member of Excavation Staff of University of Pennsylvania, at Curium, Cyprus, 1946-48; Assistant Professor of Archaeology, Johns Hopkins University, 1948——.

Caldwell, Robert Wallace, 1943. Dissertation: "The Chimaera." Vice-Consul in Athens, now in Dublin.

MacDonald, William Allan, 1943. Dissertation: "A History of Abdera, with a Prosopographia and Testimonia." Assistant Professor of Art and Chairman of the Department, Western Maryland College, 1947——.

Medford, Richard Carl, 1943. Dissertation: "Achilles, A Study in Ancient Painting." Director of Fine Arts Museum in Hagerstown, Maryland, 1932——; Special Traveling Fellow of the Johns Hopkins University in Algiers, 1945-46.

*Palmer, Hazel, 1944. Dissertation: "Italo-Corinthian Pottery." Fellow in the Institute for Advanced Study, Princeton, 1949——.

Macht, Mrs. Martin Benzyl (Carol H. Malisoff), 1945. Dissertation: "Wedgwood, a Neo-Classic Expression."

Voelkel, Laura Bennett, 1945. Dissertation: "The Coin Types of the Emperor Domitian." Assistant Professor of Latin, Greek, and Archaeology, Mary Washington College, 1948——; Secretary of the Advisory Committee of the American School of Classical Studies in Rome, 1948——.

Callaway, Joseph Sevier, 1946. Dissertation: *Sybaris.* Published in Johns Hopkins Studies in Archaeology, No. 37, 1950. Professor and Head of Department of Classics, University of Chattanooga, 1946——.

Cazel, Mrs. Fred A. (Annarie Jane Peters), 1946. Dissertation: "Greek Propylaea." Research Assistant in archaeology, Johns Hopkins University, 1944-46.

Duke, Theodore Thomas, 1946. Dissertation: "A History of Laodicea Under the Seleucids and Romans with Prosopographia and Testimonia Epigraphica." Professor of Classics, University of Akron, 1946——.

Ellinger, Mrs. Ilona E. (Ilona Deak-Ebner), 1946. Dissertation: "Winged Human Figures in the Pre-Christian Era." Teacher of Art, McCoy College, Johns Hopkins University, 1948-49; Professor of Art, Trinity College, Washington, D. C.

George, John Emmanuel, 1946. Dissertation: "Ancient Cydonia." Assistant Professor in Classics, Notre Dame College of Staten Island, 1948——.

*Howland, Richard Hubbard, 1946. Dissertation: "Greek Lamps." Agora Fellow at Athens, 1936-38; Assistant Professor of Art, Johns Hopkins University, 1947——.

Aratowsky, Bernard, 1947. Dissertation: "Ancient Salamis." Assistant Professor of Greek and Archaeology, Stanford University, 1949-50; University of Florida, 1950——.

Kapsalis, Peter Tryphonios, 1947. Dissertation: "Gestures in Greek Art and Literature." Assistant Professor, Loyola University, Chicago, 1946——.

Wiencke, Matthew Immanuel, 1947. Dissertation: "Greek Household Religion." Instructor in Classics, Yale University, 1947——.

A total of SEVENTY-FOUR Scholars on whom was conferred the degree of Doctor of Philosophy.

When acting as Professor of Classical Archaeology at Bryn Mawr College in 1911-12, Professor Robinson was a referee on the dissertations of the following and helped examine them for the Ph.D. degree:

Bowerman, Helen, A.B. Mt. Holyoke College, 1901, Student at Bonn and Rome, 1910-11, Ph.D. Bryn Mawr College, 1912; Dissertation: *Roman Sacrificial Altars*, published 1913, 103 pp. Formerly Professor of Latin, Wilson College.

Rambo, Eleanor Ferguson, A.B. Bryn Mawr College, 1908, Ph.D. 1918; Dissertation: *"Lions in Greek Art,"* published 1920, 56 pp.

Swindler, Mary H., Ph.D. Bryn Mawr College, 1912. Dissertation: *"Cretan Elements in the Cult and Ritual of Apollo,"* published 1913, 77 pp. Formerly editor of the *American Journal of Archaeology* and Professor of Classical Archaeology at Bryn Mawr College; now at the University of Pennsylvania Museum, Philadelphia.

Taylor, Lily, A.B. Wisconsin, 1906, Ph.D. Bryn Mawr College, 1912; Dissertation: *"The Cults of Ostia,"* published 1912, 98 pp.

A LIST OF THE PUBLISHED WRITINGS OF DAVID MOORE ROBINSON*

1904 - 1950

BOOKS AND ARTICLES

1904

"A New Sinopean," *BPW* 24, 1566-7.

"Notes on the Delian Choregic Inscriptions," *AJP* 25, 184-191.

1906

Ancient Sinope. An Historical Account, with a Prosopagraphia Sinopensis and an Appendix of Inscriptions. Reprinted with *corrigenda* from *AJP* 27, 125-153, 245-279; *AJA* 9, 294-333; The Johns Hopkins Press. See also PAPA 36, xxv-xxvii (abstract).

"New Inscriptions from Sinope," *AJP* 27, 447-450.

"Ointment Vases from Corinth," *AJA* 10, 420-426.

"Notes on Inscriptions from Sinope," *ib.* 429-443.

"Terra-Cottas from Corinth," *ib.* 159-173.

1907

"Notes on some κιονίσκοι in Athens," *CP* 2, 100.

"New Inscriptions in Athens," *AJP* 28, 424-433.

"Corrections to A.J.A., ix, 328," *AJA* 11, 446.

1908

"Fragment of a Panathenaic Amphora with the Name of the Archon Neaechmus," *AJA* 12, 47-48.

"Recent Archaeological Work in Greece," *AJA* 12, 67-68.

"Notes on Vases in Philadelphia," *ib.* 431-435.

1909

"An *Oenophorus* belonging to the Johns Hopkins University," *AJA* 13, 30-38.

1910

"New Greek Inscriptions from Attica, Achaia, Lydia," *AJP* 31, 377-403.

"A Panathenaic Amphora with the Archon's Name Asteius," *AJA* 14, 422-425.

"Greek and Latin Inscriptions at Sardes," *ib.* 414-416.

---

* Scholarly reviews are listed separately. More than a hundred articles and reviews in the daily and Sunday newspapers and popular magazines and many abstracts and items of news published when he was editor of News, Discussions, and Bibliography of the *AJA* 36 (1932) to 41 (1937) are here omitted. A total of 257 articles and books published are included in the present list.

"Important Excavations at Pergamum, Sardis, and Didyma," *CW* 4, 99-100.

"The Life of the Ancient Greek," *ib.* 5, 58-61, 66-70.

1911

"The Panathenaic Amphora with the Archon's Name Asteius," *AJA* 15, 504-506.

"Two Corinthian Copies of the Head of the Athena Parthenos," *ib.* 482-503.

Article on the Greek Drama in Hastings' *Dictionary of Religion and Ethics* IV, 879-883.

1912

"Inscriptions from Sardes, I," (with W. H. Buckler) *AJA* 16, 10-82.

"The History of Art in Our Colleges," *Nation*, Dec. 19, 587.

1913

"Inscriptions from Sardes, II," (with W. H. Buckler) *AJA* 17, 290-352.

"Inscriptions from the Cyrenaica," *ib.* 157-200.

"Inscriptions from Sardes, III," (with W. H. Buckler) *ib.* 17, 353-370.

1914

"Greek Inscriptions from Sardes, IV," (with W. H. Buckler) *AJA* 18, 35-74; "V," *AJA* 18, 321-362.

"Corrigenda and Addenda to Inscriptions from the Cyrenaica," *AJA* 17, 504-505.

"Discovery of the Tomb of Osiris in Egypt," A&A 1, 85.

1915

"Statuette from Crete," A&A 1, 211-212.

"Recent Discoveries at Cyrene," *ib.* 212-214.

"Bronze Statue of a Roman Boy," *ib.* 214-215.

"Mosque of St. Sophia at Constantinople," *ib.* 258.

"Two Unpublished Vase Illustrations from Homer," *AJA* 19, 78-79.

"Greek Literature in English Translations," *CW* 8, 153-156.

1916

"The Place of Archaeology in the Teaching of the Classics," *CW* 10, 2-8.

"An Important Egyptian Collection for the Brooklyn Museum," A&A 5, 122.

"The Altoviti Venus," *ib.* 181-183.

1917

"More Modern Versions of the Harmodius Hymn," *CW* 10, 138-142.

"Reproductions of Classical Art," *ArtB* 5, 221-234.

"The Cervantes Monument in Golden Gate Park," *ib.* 247.

"The Theft of a Greek Head," *ib.* 309.

"The Pallaiuolo Madonna Recently Acquired by Martin A. Ryerson," *ib.* 305-307.

"Portraits by Van Dyck Which Have Come to America," *ib.* 6, 253-256.

"The College Museum of Reproductions," *B. College Art Ass'n of Am.* 2, 27-29.

"Some Greek Vases at the Johns Hopkins University," *AJA* 21, 86-87.

"A Vase Fragment in the Style of Oltos Used in Restoring a Cylix with a Reminiscence of a Satyr-play," *ib.* 159-168.

1918

"A Note on the So-called Sappho Bust," A&A 6, 285-286.

"Reproductions for the College Museum and Art Gallery," *B. College Art Ass'n of Am.* 3, 15-21.

"Caricature in Ancient Art," *ib.* 65-68.

1919

"Archaeology in the Schools," *U. of Penn. Bulletin (Sixth Ann. Schoolmen's Week Proc.)* 20, 377-385.

1920

"The War Memorial at Hopkins," *Johns Hopkins News Letter,* 23 (No. 16), 5.

"An Unpublished Greek Decree from Sardis," *Johns Hopkins University Circular* No. 316, 13-14.

"A Roman Terra-cotta Savings Bank at the Johns Hopkins University," *AJA* 24, 78.

"Pergamum and Ephesus," *A&A* 9, 157-170.

1921

"A Cylix in the Style of Duris," *AJA* 25, 1-17.

"Etruscan and Later Terra-cotta Antefixes at the Johns Hopkins University," *ib.* 79-80.

"Discovery of a new Prehistoric Site in Greece at Zygouries," *A&A* 12, 38-39.

1922

"Lost at Sea, a Poetical Elaboration of a Greek Epigram," *Independent,* July 8; *Literary Digest,* Aug. 12.

"Notes on Two Inscriptions from Sinope," *AJP* 43, 71-73.

"An Amphora of Nikosthenes in Baltimore," *AJA* 26, 54-58.
"A New Epitaph from Sinope and a New Epitaph in Dialogue Form from Sardis," *ib*. 80-81.
"General Meeting of the Archaeological Institute," *ib*. 12, 41-42.
"The College Art Association of America," *ib*. 12, 240.

1923

"Etruscan-Campanian Antefixes and Other Terra-cottas from Italy at the Johns Hopkins University," *AJA* 27, 1-22.
"An Addendum to the Article on Antefixes," *ib*. 340.
"Notes on the Statue of Aphrodite in the Royal Ontario Museum," *ArtB* 4, 50-58.
"Note on the So-called Hockey Reliefs from Athens," *ib*. 140.
"An Original Greek Bronze Statuette in Munich," *ib*. 109-110.
"Note on the So-called Ludovisi Throne," *ib*. 102.
"Notes on Strikes in Antiquity," in Abbott's *Roman Politics*, 173.
"Fourteenth Annual Report of the Archaeological Institute," *Bull. Arch. Inst.* 13, 16-24.
"Two New Epitaphs from Sardis," in *Anatolian Studies Presented to Sir William Ramsay*, 341-353.
"Report of Revue de Philologie xlvi," *AJP* 44, 180-183.

1924

Sappho and Her Influence, 271 pp., 30 plates; Boston: Marshall Jones Co. Now New York: Longmans, Green and Co.
"Some Roman Terra-cotta Saving-banks," *AJA* 28, 239-250.
"Preliminary Report on the Excavations at Pisidian Antioch and at Sizma," *ib*. 434-444.
"Note on the Place of Ancient History in the Curriculum," *ER* 67, 102.
"Report as General Secretary of the Archaeological Institute," *Bull. Arch. Inst. of Am.* 24, 19-24.
The Songs of Sappho (with M. M. Miller), *Greek Text of all Sappho and of Poems about Sappho and of Erinna Prepared and Translated by D. M. Robinson who also Contributes an Introduction on "The Recovery and Restoration of the Egyptian Relics" and a "Critical Memoir of Sappho."* xvi, 435 pp., 10 plates; Lexington, Ky.: The Maxwelton Co.
"A New Latin Economic Edict from Pisidian Antioch," *TAPA* 55, 5-20.
"Notes on Herodotus II, 135," *CP* 20, 343-344.

1925

"Poem: A Dialogue between a Tombstone and a Wayfarer," *The Literary Supplement, Johns Hopkins News Letter,* I, June 8, 4.

"The Light Archaeology Throws on Acts xiii and xiv," *Helps to the Study of the Bible,* N. Y.

"The Archaeological Museum at the Johns Hopkins University," *A&A* 19, 265-267.

"Archaeology and Art," *JHU Alumni Mag.* 14, 25-33.

1926

The Deeds of Augustus as recorded on the Monumentum Antiochenum, AJP 48, 1-54. Also published as a book by the Johns Hopkins Press, Baltimore.

"Important Discoveries at Antioch," *Through the Ages,* II, 1-9.

"A New Portrait Head of Menander," *Bull. Royal Ontario Museum,* Jan., 1-6.

"Where Paul Turned to the Gentiles," *Christian Herald,* Dec. 5.

"Roman Sculptures from Pisidian Antioch," *AJA* 30, 80.

"A New Procurator in the Latin Inscription from Antioch," *ib.* 79.

"Two New Heads of Augustus," *ib.* 124-136.

"The Greek Bucolic Triad; Theocritus, Bion, and Moschus; Their Lives, Works and Influence," Part of Miller-Robinson *The Greek Idyls,* 1-24.

"Notes on Inscriptions from Antioch in Pisidia," *JRS* 15, 253-262.

"A Head of Sappho," *A&A* 12, 147.

"Notes on Inscriptions of Sardis," *REG* 38, 70-72.

"The Discovery of a Prehistoric Site at Sizma," *AJA* 31, 26-50.

Greek and Latin Inscriptions from Asia Minor, TAPA 57, 195-237, reprinted as a monograph.

Roman Sculptures from Colonia Caesarea (Pisidian Antioch), ArtB 9, 5-69, reprinted as a monograph.

"Where Paul Combatted Diana of Ephesus," *Christian Herald,* Jan. 9.

"Among the Seven Churches of Asia," *ib.* Feb. 13.

"Where the Seat of Satan Was," *ib.* March 13.

"Beth-Shan," *ib.* May 15.

"Uncovering the Secrets of Ur," *ib.* June 26.

1927

"Inscriptions at Dineir, Ancient Apamea," *AJP* 48, 29-33.

"A Graeco-Parthian Portrait Head of Mithradates," *AJA* 31, 338-344.

"Notes from Rome," *A&A* 24, 239-240.

"Entgegnung," *PW* 47, 603-604.

1928

"Eine Nike aus Antiochia in Pisidien," *Antike Plastik, Walther Amelung zum sechzigsten Geburtstag,* 200-205.

"Four Unpublished Vases in the Style of the Brygos Painter," *AJA* 32, 33-55.

"Notes from Rome," *A&A* 24, 239-240; 25, 157, 203-204.

"Notes on the Augusteum in Rome," *ib.* 25, 107-108.

"Notes from North Africa," *ib.* 22, 2, 1.

"Monumentum Antiochenum," *Klio* 22, 169-172.

"The Discovery and Excavation of Olynthus," *Johns Hopkins Circular No. 396,* 26-29.

"Cornelia G. Harcum. Obituary notice," *AJA* 31, 356.

"Francis Willey Kelsey. Obituary notice," *ib.* 357-358.

1929

"A Preliminary Report on the Excavations at Olynthus," *AJA* 33, 53-76.

"A Deed of Sale at Olynthus," *TAPA* 59, 225, 232.

Foreword, Mylonas, *The Neolithic Settlement at Olynthus,* vi-x.

1930

"The Lasso on a Pyxis in the Style of the Penthesilea Painter," *AJA* 34, 177-181.

"The Life of Prof. James W. Bright," *Dict. of Amer. Biography III,* 45.

A Catalogue of the Greek Vases in the Royal Ontario Museum of Archaeology, in Toronto, 2 vols., 288 pp., 108 plates, Toronto.

Ἀνασκαφαὶ τῆς Ἀρχαίας Ὀλύνθου *Deltion*—Parartema 12, 1-6.

Excavations at Olynthus, II. Architecture and Sculpture. Houses and Other Buildings. XXII, 155 pp., 307 figs., 4 plates, Baltimore.

1931

Excavations at Olynthus, III. The Coins Found at Olynthus in 1928. 143 pp., 28 plates. Baltimore.

Excavations at Olynthus, IV. The Terra-cottas of Olynthus found in 1928. 119 pp., 62 plates. Baltimore.

"New Light on Classical Greece; Olynthos," (with Seltman). London, *Illustrated News,* May 26, 1928, 948-9.

"Parthenon Described," *Johns Hopkins News Letter,* Nov. 18, 1930.

"An Illustration of Hesiod on a Black-figured Plate by the Strife Painter, With a New Poetical Version of a Part of Hesiod," *AJA* 34, 353-359.

"Second Campaign at Olynthos," *Johns Hopkins Circular,* 44.

"Sappho, the World's Greatest Poetess," *Educ. Radiograms,* Syracuse, 24-31.

"Excavations at Olynthos," *Johns Hopkins News Letter,* Nov. 13.

"Bouzyges and the First Plough on a Krater by the Painter of the Naples Hephaistos," *AJA* 35, 152-160.

Sardis VII, 1. Greek and Latin Inscriptions. (with Buckler) 198 pp., 12 plates, Leyden.

1932

"New Treasure from the City of Demosthenes' Olynthiacs," *London Illustrated News* 180, 117-119, 174-175.

"Fresh Revelations of the Art and Life of Classical Greece," *Gardens, Houses and People* 7, Jan. 1-3, 25; Feb. 4, 14; Mar. 4, 14; April 4-5.

"Excavations at Olynthos," *The American Scholar* 1, 113-115.

"Mosaics from Olynthos," *AJA* 36, 16-24.

"The Residential Districts and the Cemeteries at Olynthos," *ib.* 118-138.

"Illustrations of Aeschylus' Choephoroi and of a Satyr-play on Hydrias by the Niobid Painter," *ib.* 401-406.

"New Inscriptions from Olynthos and Environs," *TAPA* 62, 40-56.

"Excavation of Olynthus," *Bull. of Amer. Council of Learned Societies,* No. 18, 111-115 (Annex No. 27, 347-351).

1933

Excavations at Olynthus, V. Mosaics, Vases and Lamps of Olynthus Found in 1928 and 1931. xxi, 297 pp., 209 plates, Baltimore.

Excavations at Olynthus, VI. The Coins Found at Olynthus in 1931. xiv, 111 pp., 30 plates, Baltimore.

Excavations at Olynthus, VII. The Terra-Cottas of Olynthus Found in 1931. xii, 111 pp., 61 plates, Baltimore.

"A Typical Block of Houses at Olynthos; With an Account of Three Hoards of Coins," *AJA* 37, 111-113.

"A New Greek Inscription from Macedonia," *AJA* 37, 602-604.

"Bibliography of Archaeological Books of 1933," *ib.* 363-375.

1934

Corpus Vasorum Antiquorum, The Robinson Collection, fasc. 1; 57 pp., 48 plates, Cambridge, Mass.

"A Red-figured Vase Influenced by the Parthenon Frieze," *AJA* 38, 45-48.

"Some Unpublished Vases in Baltimore," *ib.* 188.

"The Bronze State Seal of Larissa Kremaste," *ib.* 219-222.

"The Villa of Good Fortune at Olynthos," *ib.* 501-510.

"The Resurrection of an Ancient City," *Parnassus* 6, 36-39.

"Bilder von der neuesten Ausgrabung in Olynthos," (Abstract of German lecture given at Berlin) *Arch. Anz.,* 3/4, 497-506.

"A Greek Pompeii: Excavations at Olynthus," *Illustrated London News* 185, Nov. 10, 766-769.

"The Villa of Good Fortune. Superb Pebble Mosaics," *ib.* 767.

"Household Utensils of Classical Greece," *ib.* 769-780.

"Inscriptions from Olynthus, 1934," *TAPA* 65, 103-137.

1935

"Where the Saint George and the Dragon Legend Originated," *American Weekly,* Jan. 27.

"Die Ausgrabungen in Olynth in Mazedonien," (Abstract of lecture at Berlin) *Forschungen und Fortschritte,* 11. Apr. 10, 137-139.

"A New Fragment of the Athenian Decree on Coinage," *AJP* 39, 149-154.

"The Third Campaign at Olynthos," *AJA* 39, 210-247.

"Report of the Third Campaign of Excavation at Olynthus," *American Council of Learned Societies, Bulletin* No. 23, 141-144. (Annex 35, 507-510.)

"Poetical Translation of Horace III, 13," *Johns Hopkins Alumni Magazine,* XXIII, No. 2, January.

1936

A Short History of Greece. xi, 227 pp., New York.

Pindar, a Poet of Eternal Ideas. vii, 118 pp., Baltimore.

"Die Ausgrabungen in Olynthos," *Die Antike* 11, 274-292.

"Bibliography of Archaeological Books 1933 and 1934," *AJA* 39, 284-292.

"Pindar and His Influence," *TAPA* 66 xxx.

"The Cyniscus of Polyclitus," *ArtB* 18, 133-149.

"Unpublished Greek Vases in Baltimore," *AJA* 40, 117-118.

"The Lewis Painter—Polygnotus II," (with Sarah E. Freeman) *ib.* 215-227.

"A New Lebes Gamikos With a Possible Representation of Apollo and Daphne," *ib.* 507-519.

"A State Seal-matrix from Panticapaeum," *Classical Studies,* presented to Edward Capps, 306-313.

"Evan Taylor Sage," *CJ* 32, 61-62.

"Bibliography of Archaeological Books, 1935," *AJA* 40, 296-300.

1937

A Study of Greek Love-names, Including a Discussion of Paederasty and a Prosopographia (with E. J. Fluck). viii, 204 pp., Baltimore.

Corpus Vasorum Antiquorum, U. S. A., the Robinson Collection, fasc. 2. 40 pp., 57 pls., Cambridge, Mass.

"A New Fragment of the Fifth-century Athenian Naval Catalogues," *AJA* 41, 292-299.

"Bibliography of Archaeological Books, 1936," *ib.* 354-359.

"An Unpublished Inscription from the Collection of David M. Robinson," *Hesperia,* Suppl. 1, 158-160, No. 92.

"A New Fragment of an Attic Treasure-record," *AJP* 58, 38-44.

1938

Excavations at Olynthus, VIII: The Hellenic House. (With J. W. Graham.) xiv, 370 pp., 110 pls., Baltimore.

Excavations at Olynthus IX: The Chalcidic Mint and the Excavation Coins Found in 1928-1934 . (With P. A. Clement.) xxi, 413 pp., 36 pls., Baltimore.

Corpus Vasorum Antiquorum: The Robinson Collection, fasc. 3. 62 pp., Cambridge, Mass.

"Olynthus," *RE* 18, 325-342.

Prähistorische und griechische Häuser. RE, supplement, 7, 224-278 (reprinted as a monograph).

"A Magical Text from Beroea in Macedonia," *Classical and Mediaeval Studies in Honor of Edward Kennard Rand,* 245-253.

"The Greek City Wiped Out in a Day by Philip of Macedon," *Illustrated London News,* 103, 846-850, 862.

"Bibliography of Archaeological Books, 1937," *AJA* 42, 324-329.

1939

"The Fourth Campaign at Olynthus," (with G. E. Mylonas) *AJA* 43, 48-77.

"Remigio Alarum," *CJ* 34, 543.

"Three Marble Heads from Anatolia," *Anatolian Studies, presented to William Hepburn Buckler,* 249-268.

"Bibliography of Archaeological Books, 1938," *AJA* 43, 371-377.

Inscriptions from Macedonia, 1938. TAPA 69, 43-76 (reprinted as monogragh with 27 plates).

"The Greek Chlamys not Rectangular," *Greece and Rome* 8, No. 24, 190.

"Addenda to T.A.P.A., LXIX, 43-76 (Greek and Latin Inscriptions from Macedonia)," *TAPA* 70, 62-63.

1940

"Bibliography of Archaeological Books, 1939," *AJA* 44, 286-292.

"A New Marble Bust of Menander, Wrongly Called Vergil," *Proceedings of the American Philosophical Society* 83, 465-477.

1941

Excavations at Olynthus, Part X: Metal and Minor Miscellaneous Finds. An Original Contribution to Greek Life (with a new up-to-date map of Olynthus). xxvii, 593 pp., 171 pls., Baltimore.

"Edward Theodore Newell," *AJA* 45, 284-285.

"Bibliography of Archaeological Books, 1940," *AJA* 45, 329-332.

"The Glory That Was and Is Greece," *Greece 1821-1941*, 43-45.

1942

Excavations at Olynthus, Part XI: Necrolynthia. A Study in Greek Burial Customs and Anthropology. xxvii, 279 pp., 71 pls., Baltimore. (Assisted by F. P. Albright.)

"New Greek Bronze Vases, A Commentary on Pindar," *AJA* 46, 172-197.

"Bibliography of Archaeological Books, 1941," *AJA* 46, 314-316.

"Poetical Translations" in *The Songs of Sappho*, Peter Pauper Press.

1943

"Bibliography of Archaeological Books, 1942," *AJA* 47, 261-263.

"A New Arcadian Inscription," *CP* 38, 191-199.

"Palamas and Phoutrides," *Athene* 4, 38-39.

1944

The Great Glory and Glamor of the Dodecanese. 30 pp., 20 figs., New York.

Lizette Woodworth Reese. 32 pp., Baltimore, Enoch Pratt Free Library

"Greek Horoi and a New Attic Mortgage Inscription," *Hesperia* 13, 16-21.

"A Plea for Pausanias," *CW* 37, 165.

"Reminiscences and Remarks," *ib.* 234.

"The Greek Dodecanese," Symposium, published by the Dodecanesian National Council, New York, 93.

"Bibliography of Archaeological Books, 1943," *AJA* 48, 226-28.

1945

"A New Attic Onos or Epinetron," *AJA* 49, 480-490.

"Bibliography of Archaeological Books, 1944," *ib.* 205-208.

"Gordon J. Laing," *ib.* 583-5.

"Julia R. Rogers," *Bulletin of Arch. Institute*, 35, 37-38.

"Report of the Delegate to the American Classical League," *ib.* 54.

"The Wheel of Fortune," *Proceedings of the American Philological Association* 76, xxxvii-xxxviii.

1946

Excavations at Olynthus, XII. Domestic and Public Architecture (with excursus I on pebble mosaics with colored plates, excursus II on the oecus unit, testimonia, list of Greek words, etc.). 519 pp., 272 plates, 12 figs., Baltimore, The Johns Hopkins Press.

Baalbec and Palmyra. 140 pp., 66 plates, 2 plans (photographs by Hoyningen-Huene), New York, J. J. Augustin Publishers Corp.

"Bibliography of Books, 1945," *AJA* 50, 335-340.

"Report on the American Classical League," *Bull. of Arch. Inst.* 37, 53.

"The Wheel of Fortune," *CP* 41, 207-216.

1947

"Report of the Professor of Greek Literature and Archaeology and Librarian," American School of Classical Studies at Athens, 66th Annual Report, 1946-1947, 38-40.

"Two New Grave Stelae from the Deme of Demosthenes," *AJA* 51, 366-369. Cf. also *AJA* 53 (1949) 452.

"Bibliography of Books, 1946," *ib.* 211-217.

1948

"News from Greece," *CO* 25, No. 5, 46.

"Three New Mortgage Inscriptions from Attica," *AJP* 69, 201-204.

"The Crisis and Conditions in Greece, Key Point in Contest Contra Communision," *Athene* 9, 3-12 (reprinted as a monograph).

"Archaeology in Greece Today," *CO* 25, 58-59.

"Grave Stele from Paeania," *AJA* 52, 452.

"Addendum," *ib.* 68.

"John Adams Scott, Ph.D. '97 (Greek)," *Johns Hopkins Alumni Magazine* 36, 70-71.

America in Greece, a Traditional Policy. 200 pp., New York, Anatolia Press.

"Archaeology, Remmants of the Past," *The American People's Encyclopedia* 2, Chicago, The Spencer Press, 194-239.

"A New Heracles Relief," *Hesperia* 17, 137-140.

"Three New Inscriptions from the Deme of Ikaria," *ib.* 141-143.

"Bibliography of Archaeological Books, 1947," *AJA* 52, 534-544.

"New Attic Sculptures and Inscriptions," *ib.* 380-381.

1949

"The Robinson Collection of Greek Gems, Seals, Rings, Earrings," *Hesperia*, Supplement 8, 305-323.

"An Inscribed Kouros Base, Supplementary Note," *ib.* 363-364.

"A New Fifth Roman Copy of the Orpheus Relief at the University of Mississippi," *Hommages à Joseph Bidez et à Franz Cumont*, 303-311.

1950

Excavations at Olynthus, XIII. The Vases Found in 1934 and 1938. xv, 465 pp., 267 plates. Baltimore, Md.

"A Small Hoard of Mycenaean Vases and Statuettes," *AJA* 54, 1-9, 7 plates, 1 colored.

"A Hoard of Alexander Coins from Megalopolis," *American Numismatic Society, Museum Notes*, 4 (1950) 13-28.

"A New Mortgage Inscription from Ikaria," *Hesperia* 19 (1950) 23-24.

"The Perfect Female," *CJ* 45, 182.

Some twenty articles in the *American Educator Encyclopedia,* 1948-1950.

Several articles in the *American People's Encyclopedia.*

"P. N. Ure," *AJA* 54 (1950) 429.

REVIEWS

Waldstein, *Argive Heraeum, AJP* 26 (1905) 457-466.

Baumgarten, Poland and Wagner, *Die Hellenische Kultur, ib.* 27 (1906) 112-114.

Poulsen, *Die Dipylongraeber und die Dipylonvasen, ib.* 28 (1907) 240-241.

Chabert, *Histoire sommaire des études d'épigraphie grecque, ib.* 358-359.

Tucker, *Life in Ancient Athens, ib.* 359-360.

Janell, *Ausgewaehlte Inschriften, ib.* 360-361.

Powell, *Erichthonius and the Three Daughters of Cecrops, CP* 2 (1907) 350-351.

Farnell, *The Cults of the Greek States, AJP* 29 (1908) 93-98.

Von Mach, *Greek Sculpture, CW* 1 (1908) 147-149.

Weir, *The Greek Painters, ib.* 229-230.

D'Ooge, *The Acropolis of Athens, AJP* 30 (1909) 331-337.

Prentice, *Greek and Latin Inscriptions (in Syria), ib.* 199-207.

Carroll, *The Attica of Pausanias, CW* 2 (1909) 134-135.

Robert, *Pausanias als Schriftsteller, Studien und Beobachtungen, AJP* 31 (1910) 213-222, also *CW* 3 (1910) 205-206.

Fowler and Wheeler, *A Handbook of Greek Archaeology, AJP* 31 (1910) 331-334.

Gardiner, *Greek Athletic Sports and Festivals, AHR* 16 (1911) 589-591.

Zippelius, *Priene nach den Ergebnissen der Ausgrabungen der Kgl. Preuss. Museen, 1895-1898, rekonstruiert, AJP* 32 (1911) 487-488.

Baur, *Centaurs in Art, ib.* 33 (1912) 465-467.

Elderkin, *Problems in Periclean Buildings, CW* 6 (1913) 206-207.

Fournier, *Inscriptions de Sardes, REA* 16 (1914) 438-440.

Besnier, *Lexique de Géographie Ancienne, AHR* 19 (1914) 918-919.

Seaton, *Apollonius Rhodius, the Argonautica, CW* 7 (1914) 172-173.

Mooney, *The Argonautica of Apollonius, ib.* 173-176.

Powers, *The Message of Greek Art, A&A* 1 (1914) 44-45; *CW* 7 (1914) 29-32.

Gardner, *Principles of Greek Art, ib.* 88-89.

Smith, *Greek Art and National Life, ib.* 89-90.

Waldstein, *Greek Sculpture and Modern Art, ib.* 135.

Clark, *Holy Land of Asia Minor, ib.* 176.

Whiting, *Athens the Violet Crowned, CW* 8 (1915) 101-103.

Manatt, *Aegean Days, A&A* 1 (1915) 264; *CW* 8 (1915) 150-151.

Goodyear, *Greek Refinements: Studies in Temperamental Architecture, A&A* 2 (1915) 33.

Hall, *Aegean Archaeology, AJP* 36 (1915) 345-346.

Davis, *Readings in Ancient History, I. Greece and the East, CW* 9 (1915) 53.

Davis, *Readings in Ancient History, II. Rome and the West, ib.* 53-54.

Davis, *A Day in Old Athens, ib.* 263-264.

Bosanquet, *Days in Attica, A&A* 1 (1915) 263.

Beggs, *The Four in Crete, ib.* 3 (1916) 123.

Myres, *Handbook of the Cesnola Collection of Antiquities from Cyprus, ib.* 124.

Richter, *The Metropolitan Museum of Art: Greek, Etruscan and Roman Bronzes, ib.* 247.

Fairbanks, *Greek Gods and Heroes as Represented in the Classical Collections of the Museum of Fine Arts, Boston, ib.* 244.

Thomson, *The Greek Tradition. Essays in the Reconstruction of Ancient Thought, ib.* 126.

Wolfson, *Ancient Civilization, ib.* 189.

Carus, *The Venus of Milo, ib.* 190.

Pennell, *Pictures in the Land of Temples, CW* 9 (1916) 216.

Droop, *Archaeological Excavation, A&A* 3 (1916) 124.

Fox, *Greek and Roman Mythology, ib.* 126-127; *CW* 11 (1917) 22-23.

Fowler, *History of Sculpture, A&A* 4 (1916) 252-253.

Holborn, *The Need for Art in Life, ib.* 5 (1917) 186.

Rider, *The Greek House, ib.* 186-187.

Watts, *The Renaissance of the Greek Ideal, ib.* 251.

Barstow, *Famous Sculpture, ib.* 315-316.

Seachrest, *Greek Photoplays, ib.* 316.

Tatlock, *Greek and Roman Mythology, ib.* 124.

Babcock, *Greek Wayfarers and Other Poems, ib.* 220.

Wolfson, *Ancient Civilization, CW* 10 (1917) 111-112.

Carus, *Venus of Milo, ib.* 216.

Jardé, *La Grèce antique et la vie grecque, ib.* 175.

Stobart, *The Glory That Was Greece, ib.* 11 (1918) 21-22.

Fox, *Greek and Roman Mythology, ib.* 22-23.

Chase, *Museum of Fine Arts, Boston: Catalogue of Arretine Pottery, ib.* 282-283.

Moore, *Religious Thought of the Greeks, ib.* 344.

Banks, *Seven Wonders of the Ancient World, CW* 11 (1918) 150-151.

Dawkins, *Modern Greek in Asia Minor, ib.* 175.

Cagnat and Chapot, *Manuel d'archéologie romaine, ib.* 12 (1919) 44-46.

Gardner, *History of Ancient Coinage, ib.* 46-47.

Flickinger, *Greek Theater and Its Drama, ib.* 69-71.

Walters, *Classical Dictionary of Greek and Roman Antiquities, Biography, Geography, and Mythology,* A&A 8 (1919) 62.

Bell, *Philosophy of Paintings, ib.* 62.

Hamlin, *History of Ornament, ib.* 63.

Goodyear, *History of Art, ib.* 63.

Dennison, *Gold Treasure of the Late Roman Period, ib.* 63-64.

Robinson, *Days of Alcibiades, ib.* 125.

White, *Unwilling Vestal, ib.* 125.

Robinson, *Domestic Architecture, ib.* 125-126.

Gardner, *History of Ancient Coinage, ib.* 127.

Emmanuel, *Antique Greek Dance, ib.* 127.

Richter, *Handbook of the Classical Collection, Metropolitan Museum of Art, ib.* 240; *ArtB* 2 (1919) 39-41.

Dempsey, *Delphic Oracle. Its Early History, Influence and Fall,* A&A 8 (1919) 242.

Hawley, *Asia Minor, ib.* 242.

Clark, *Japan at First Hand, ib.* 304.

Latourette, *Development of Japan, ib.* 304.

Kirtland, *Samurai Trails, ib.* 304.

Brooks, *Great Artists and Their Works by Great Authors, ib.* 370.

Memoirs of the American Academy in Rome, I, AJP 11 (1920) 108-109.

Harris, *Origin and Meaning of Apple Cults,* A&A 9 (1920) 98.

Memoirs of the American Academy in Rome, II ib. 98-99; *AJP* 12 (1921) 87.

Pennell, *Etchers and Etchings,* A&A 10 (1920) 157.

Dana, E., *Story of Jesus; Pictures and Paintings by Giotto, Angelico, Duccio, Ghirlandaio, etc., ib.* 203.

Hill, *Medals of the Renaissance, ib.* 246.

Beazley, *The Lewes House Collection of Ancient Gems, ib.* 247-248.

Beazley, *Attic Red-figured Vases in American Museums, ib.* 251; 11 (1921) 77-78.

Hoppin, *Handbook of Attic Red-figured Vases, ib.* 157; *ArtB* 2 (1920) 123-128.

Kimball and Edgell, *History of Architecture, ArtB* 2 (1920) 176-178.

Herford, *Handbook of Greek Vase Painting, ib.* 178-181.

Warren, *Foundations of Classic Architecture, ib.* 225-227.

Vaughan, *Madness in Greek Thought and Custom,* CW 14 (1921) 150-151.

McClees, *A Study of Women in Attic Inscriptions, ib.* 197-199.

Marshall, *Discovery in Greek Lands, ib.* 166-167; *A&A* 11 (1921) 267.

Allen, *The Greek Theatre of the Fifth Century Before Christ, CW* 15 (1921) 29-30; *A&A* 11 (1921) 268.

Poulsen, *Delphi, CW* 15 (1921) 45-48; *A&A* 12 (1921) 45-46.

Frank, *Economic History of Rome to the End of the Republic, A&A* 11 (1921) 79.

Hambidge, *Dynamic Symmetry, ib.* 123-125.

Havell, *Ideals of Indian Art, ib.* 125.

Ferguson, *Outlines of Chinese Art, ib.* 125-126.

Richter, *Catalogue of Engraved Gems of the Classical Style, Metropolitan Museum of Art, ib.* 173.

O'Connor, *Charm of Kashmir, A&A* 12 (1921) 46-47.

Nutting, *Furniture of the Pilgrim Century,* 1620-1720, *ib.* 282-283.

Robert, *Die griechische Heldensage, AJP* 43 (1922) 90-92.

Buschor, *Greek Vase Painting, A&A* 13 (1922) 193-194.

Mooney, *Travel Among the Ancient Romans, ib.* 45-46.

Van Buren, *Figurative Terra-cotta Revetments in Etruria and Latium, ib.* 14 (1922) 110.

Oswald and Pryce, *An Introduction to the Study of Terra Sigillata Treated from a Chronological Standpoint, ib.* 110-111.

Phoutrides, *Kostes Palamas' Life Immovable, CW* 15 (1922) 92-94.

Dickins, *Hellenistic Sculpture, ib.* 118-120.

Wendell, *Traditions of European Literature, ib.* 16 (1923) 13-16.

Blegen, C. W., *Korakou, a Prehistoric Settlement Near Corinth, AHR* 27 (1922) 810-811; *A&A* 13 (1922) 285-286.

Scott, *Unity of Homer, CW* 16 (1923) 212-214.

Hyde, *Olympic Victor Monuments and Greek Athletic Art, ib.* 17 (1923) 59-62.

Jardé, *L'evolution de l'humanité, AHR* 29 (1923) 112-113.

Rostovtzeff, *Iranians and Greeks in South Russia, ib.* 114-116; *ArtB* 5 (1923) 48-50.

Bode-Oldenbourg, *Peter Paul Rubens, A&A* 16 (1923) 128.

Jardé, *La formation du peuple grec, AHR* 31 (1924) 112-113.

Glotz, *La civilisation Égéenne, ib.* 588-589.

Baur, *Catalogue of the Stoddard Collection of Greek and Italian Vases in Yale University, ArtB* 6 (1924) 64-66.

MacDonald, *Uses of Symbolism in Greek Art, ib.* 66-67.

Hoppin, *Handbook of Greek Black-figured Vases, A&A* 20 (1925) 229.

Williams, *Catalogue of Egyptian Antiquities, ib.* 280.

Chase, G., *Greek and Roman Sculpture in American Collections, ib.* 281.

Speleers, *Les Figurines funeraires Égyptiennes, ib.* 148.

Chase and Post, *History of Sculpture, ArtB* 7 (1926) 162-163.

Caskey, *Catalogue of Greek and Roman Sculpture, ib.* 163-164.

Poulsen, *Greek and Roman Portraits, ib.* 8 (1927) 50-51.

Pfuhl, *Malerei and Zeichnung der Greichen, ib.* 51-52.

Pfuhl, *Meisterwerke Griechischer Zeichnung und Malerei, ib.* 52.

Richter, *Ancient Furniture, ArtB* 9 (1927) 80-81.

Rostovtzeff, *Social and Economic History of the Roman Empire, ib.* 81-82.

Cambridge Ancient History, V, AHR 32 (1927) 93.

Bruck, *Totenteil und Seelgeraet im Griechischen Recht, AJA* 31 (1927) 132-133.

Kjellberg, *Studien zu den Attischen Reliefs des fuenften Jahrhunderts, ib.* 273-274.

Jones, *Geography of Strabo, CJ* 24 (1929) 541-543.

Flaccus, *The Spirit and Substance of Art, A&A* 24 (1928) 196.

Cambridge Ancient History, V, AHR 33 (1928) 93-95.

Genouillac, *Céramique Cappadocienne, I and II, AJA* 32 (1928) 131-132.

Eichler and Kris, *Publikationen aus den Kunsthistorischen Sammlungen in Wien, II, Die Kameen, ArtB* 11 (1929) 115.

Stevens, *Erechtheum, ib.* 115-116.

Duncan, *Introduction to Biblical Archaeology, A&A* 27 (1929) 94.

Tonks, *History of Italian Painting, AJA* 33 (1929) 337-338.

Ath. Mitteilungen XLIX, A&A 27 (1929) 143.

Swindler, *Ancient Painting, A&A* 30 (1930) 50-51.

Mozley, *Statius, CJ* 35 (1930) 147-148.

Jahrbuch des deut. Arch. Inst. Bd. 43, *A&A* 28 (1929) 148.

Grose, *Catalogue of McClean Collection of Greek Coins, ib.* 29 (1930) 96.

Strong, *Catalogue of Greek and Roman Antiques in the Possession of Lord Melchett, ib.* 46.

Goldman, *Excavations at Eutresis, ArtB* 14 (1931) 277.

Jones, *Geography of Strabo, VI, CJ* 26 (1931) 241.

Blegen, *Zygouries, AJA* 34 (1931) 109.

Beyen, *Ueber Stilleben aus Pompeii, Litteris* 7 (1931) 84-85.

Baur and Rostovtzeff, *Excavations at Dura-Europos, AJA* 34 (1931) 398.

Jacobsthal and Langsdorff, *Die Bronze-Schnabelkannen, ib.* 400.

Robertson, *Handbook of Greek and Roman Architecture, CJ* 26 (1931) 147-150.

Beazley, *Attic Black Figure, ArtB* 12 (1931) 302-304.

Ashmole, *Catalogue of Ancient Marbles at Ince Blundell Hall, ib.* 304.

Howard, *Pheidias, A&A* 30 (1930) 148.

Schmidt-Degener, *Rembrandt, ib.* 193.

Lamb, *Greek and Roman Bronzes, ib.* 29 (1930) 285.

Sydow, *Handbuch der West-Afrikanischen Plastik, ib.* 31 (1931) 143.

Obermaier and Heiss, *Iberische Prunk-Keramik, ib.* 192.

Mueller, *Fruehe Plastik in Griechenland und Vorderasien, ib.* 238.

Broneer, *Corinth, Terracotta Lamps, ib.* 286.

Hill and King, *Corinth, Decorated Architectural Terracottas, ib.* 337.

Duncan, *Prehistoric Man, ib.* 32 (1933) 46.

Gallatin, *Syracusan Dekadrachms of the Euainetos Type, AJA* 35 (1932) 359.

Memoirs of the American Academy in Rome, AJA 36 (1932) 209.

Baur and Rostovtzeff, *Excavations at Dura-Europos, Prelim. Report of Second Season, A&A* 33 (1932) 279.

Deonna, *Dédale ou la Statue de la Grèce archaique, ib.* 55.

Bellinger, *Catalogue of the Coins Found at Corinth, ib.* 111.

Jones, *Geography of Strabo, VII, CJ* 27 (1932) 304.

Richter, *The Metropolitan Museum of Art, Handbook of the Classical Collection, ib.* 618.

Boak-Peterson, *Karanis, JAOS* 52 (1932) 63-65.

Memoirs of the American Academy at Rome, X, AJA 38 (1933) 188.

Drachmann, *Ancient Oil Mills and Presses, AJP* 37 (1933) 636.

Berard, *Did Homer Live?, CJ* 29 (1934) 306-308.

Ruediger, *Sappho, ihr Ruf und Ruhm in der Nachwelt, ib.* 465-466.

Jones, *Strabo's Geography, VIII, ib.* 30 (1934) 43-44.

Debevoise, *Parthian Pottery, CJ* 31 (1936) 258-259.

Lyde, *Contexts in Pindar with Reference to the Meaning of* Φώς, *CP* 31 (1936) 267.

Snell, *Bacchylidis Carmina cum Fragmentis, ib.* 268.

Greek Poetry and Life, CW 30 (1936) 23-25.

Chamberlain, *A Translation of Theocritus, ib.* 70-72.

Fyfe, *Hellenistic Architecture, ib.* 101-102.

Bowra, *Pindari Carmina, CP* 32 (1937) 280-283.

Amundsen, *Greek Ostraca in the University of Michigan Collection, Part I, ib.* 33 (1938) 231-232.

Bowra, *Greek Lyric Poetry from Alcman to Simonides, ib.* 210-216.

Carpenter-Bon-Parsons, *Corinth, III, Part II. The Defenses of Acrocorinth and the Lower Town, ib.* 34 (1939) 80-82

Diehl, *Anthologia Lyrica Graeca, ib.* 72-73.

Smith, *Corpus Vasorum Antiquorum, U. S. Fasc.* 5, *ib.* 75-78.

Smith and Moorhead, *A Short History of the Ancient World, CW* 32 (1939) 273-274.

Pendlebury, *The Archaeology of Crete, CW* 33 (1939) 112-114.

Jeanmaire, *La Sibylle et le retour de l'age d'or, AJP* 62 (1941) 367-370.

Roussel, *Sparte, CW* 34, (1941) 233-234.

Meritt, *Epigraphica Attica, ib.* 35 (1941) 101-102; *AHR* 47 (1942) 404.

Van Gulik, *Catalogue of the Bronzes in the Allard Pierson Museum at Amsterdam, Part I, AJA* 46 (1942) 149-150.

Webster, *Greek Art and Literature, CJ* 37 (1942) 429-433.

Trevelyan, *Goethe and the Greeks, CW* 36 (1942) 76-82.

Lehmann-Hartleben and Olsen, *Dionysiac Sarcophagi in Baltimore, ib.* 137-139.

Bates, *Sophocles, Poet and Dramatist, AJP* 44 (1942) 120-121.

Ryberg, *An Archaeological Record of Rome from the Seventh to the Second Century B. C., CP* 38 (1942) 140-144.

Campbell, *The Agamemnon of Aeschylus Translated, AJP* 64 (1943) 369-370.

Macurdy, *The Quality of Mercy, ib.* 371-373.

Prentice, *The Ancient Greeks, ib.* 365-368.

Couch, *Classical Civilization: Greece, ib.* 480-484.

Geer, *Classical Civilization: Rome, ib.* 484-485.

Allan-Mattingly-Robinson, *Transactions of the International Numismatic Congress, London 1936, AJP* 65 (1944) 283-285.

Weber, *Schliemann's First Visit to America, 1850-1851, ib.* 285-286.

Richter, *Etruscan Art in the Metropolitan Museum, ib.* 410-412.

Classical Studies in Honor of William Abbott Oldfather, AJA 48 (1944) 397-398.

Rostovtzeff - Bellinger - Brown - Welles, *The Excavations at Dura-Europos. Preliminary Report of the Ninth Season of Work, 1935-1936, Part I, AJP* 66 (1945) 430-433.

Lattimore, *Themes in Greek and Latin Epitaphs, CJ* 41, (1945) 38-41.

Friedlaender, *Documents of Dying Paganism, U. S. Quart. Book List, I, No. 2, 1.*

Feyel, *Polybe et l'Histoire de Béotie au III Siècle avant notre Ère, AJA* 49 (1945) 618-619.

Feyel, *Contribution à l'Épigraphie Béotienne, ib.* 619-620.

Bérard, *La Colonisation Grecque de l'Italie Méridionale et de la Sicile dans l'Antiquité, ib.* 621-622.

Waltz, *La Question d'Orient dans l'Antiquité, ib.* 622.

Meautis, *Mythes Inconnus de la Grèce Antique, ib.* 622-623.

Croiset, *La Civilisation de la Grèce Antique, ib.* 623-624.

Norwood, *Pindar, AJP* 68 (1947) 332-334.

Weitzmann, *Illustrations in Roll and Codex, U. S. Quart. Book List,* Dec. 1947, 333-334.

Kerenyi, *Die Geburt der Helena, CW* 41 (1948) 138-139.

Kerenyi, *Prometheus, Die Griechische Mythologie von der Menschlichen Existenz, ib.* 139.

Toll, *The Excavations at Dura-Europos. Preliminary Report of the Ninth Season of Work, 1935-36, Part II. The Necropolis, AJP* 69 (1948) 459-460.

Olmstead, *History of the Persian Empire, U. S. Quart. Book List, IV,* (1948) 324-325.

Pritchett-Neugebauer, *The Calendars of Athens, ib.* 405-406.

Weitzmann, *The Joshua Roll, ib.* 406.

Karo, *Greek Personality in Archaic Sculpture, ib.* (1949) 8.

Dumbarton Oaks Papers, IV, ib. 207-208.

McDaniel, *Conception, Birth and Infancy in Ancient Rome and Modern Italy, CW* 42 (1949) 238-239.

Creaghan-Raubitschek, *Early Christian Epitaphs, AHR* 44 (1949) 408.

Feytmans, *Les Vases Grecs de la Bibliothèque Royale de Belgique, AJA* 53 (1949) 411-412.

Rodenwaldt, *Köpfe von den Südmetopen des Parthenons, ib.* 53 (1949) 415-416.

Hoffleit-Friedländer, *Epigrammata, CW* 43 (1950) 155-157.

Raubitschek, *Dedications from the Athenian Akropolis, AHR* 45 (1950) 405-406.

Richter, *Roman Portraits, AJA* 54 (1950) 89-90.

Bellinger, *Excavations at Dura-Europos. The Coins.* Frisch-Toll, *The Bronze Objects.* Cox, *The Greek and Roman Pottery, AHR* 45 (1950) 572-573.

Jucker, *Vom Verhältnis der Römer zur Bildenden Kunst der Griechen, Archaeology* 3 (1950) 252-253.

Richter, *Archaic Greek Art, U. S. Quarterly Book Review,* 6, 146.

Reviews of: *Ancient Sinope and Excavations at Olynthus*

Ancient Sinope.

REA 1907, 96; DLZ 1907, 622; NJ 1907, 224; WKP 1907, 998-1001; NPR 1907, 344; RC 1907, 159; LCB 1907, 1109-1112; BFC 1908, 14-15; *Riv. d. Fil.* 1907, 195; 1908, 151; CJ 1907, 190; *Records of Past* 1907, 65; CP 1908, 463-465; *Riv. d. Storia Ant.* 1907, 167; *Listy Filologické* 1907, 395; 1908, 142-147; RA 1906, 372; BCH 1906, 138-139; BPW 1907, 334; AHR 1907, 687-688; *EngHistRev* 1907, 821; REG 1907, 86-87; *Annales d. Geog.* 1908, 50; *Am. Ant. & Orient. Jour.* 1907, 259; *JRAsiatSoc* 1908, 256-257; *Mélanges de la Fac. Orient. de Beyrouth* 1909, 47-48.

Excavations at Olynthus, II.

List of 29 reviews was published in *Olynthus, XII,* 472-473.

Excavations at Olynthus, III.

CP 1931, 339; *Am. Magazine of Art* 1931, 327; *Bilychnis* 1931, 195; *Spink's Numism. Circular* 1931, 251; *Athenaeum* 1931, 328; RH 1931, 153-155; *Liverpool Annals* 1931, 150; ZfN 1931, 127-130; *Parnassus* 1931, 34; AHR 1931, 301; NumChronicle 1931, 39; 1933, 253; *Year's Work in Cl.Studies* 1931, 92; JHS 1931, 303-304; RA 1931, 216; RevNum 1931, 258-259; CR 1932, 86; 1933, 94; A&A 1932, 329; PW 1933, 46; RevPhil 1933, 111-113; REA 1932, 200-204; *Acropole* 1932, 179-180; *Deutsche Literatur-Zeichnung* 1933, 1368; CW 1935, 160; *il Mondo Classico* 1932, 207-209; *L'Antiquité Classique* 1933, 490-491; *Antiquity* 1932, 254-256.

Excavations at Olynthus, IV.

CP 1931, 339; *Am. Magazine of Art* 1931, 327; *Bilychnis* 1931, 195; *Spink's* 1931, 413-414; PW 1932, 236-239; REG 1932, 458; 1936, 173; *il Mondo Classico* 1932, 207-208; 1933, 32-34; *Boll. Bibliografico* 1931, 259; CR 1932, 21; *L'Antiquité Classique* 1933, 490-492; *Athenaeum* 1931, 563-566; *Acropole* 1932, 87-88; RH 1931, 153-155; *Liverpool Annals* 1931, 150; AHR 1931, 301; *Antiquity* 1932, 254-256; AntiquariesJ 1932, 458; JHS 1931, 307; RA 1931, 217; *London Times Suppl.* 1932, 366; RevPhil 1932, 390-398; AJA 1932, 207; A&A 1932, 328; EngHistRev 1932, 480; *Gnomon* 1933, 105; *Boll Filologia* 1933, 81; CW 1935, 166; *Bull Arch d'Aléxandrie* 1934, 371-374; *Bull de l'Assoc. Budé* 1932, 40-43.

Excavations at Olynthus, V.

List of reviews was published in *Olynthus, XIII,* 436.

Excavations at Olynthus, VI.

DLZ 1933, 1610; CJ 1933, 143; CP 1935, 82-84; *Spink's Num. Circ.* 1933, 334; PW 1933, 1262-1263; BollFilClass 1933, 9-15; *Schweizerische Num. Rundschau* 1933, 410-412; AHR 1933, 299; *Antiquité Classique* 1934, 347-348; *Literarische Anzeiger* 1934, 2; NZ 1933, 332-333; 1934, 127; A&A 1934, 48; REA 1933, 250; *Athenaeum* 1934, 169; JHS 1934, 92; *Rivista di Filologia* 1934, 271; RH 1933, 133; *Bull.Soc.Arch.d'Aléxandrie* 1934, 22, 374; RN 1934, 144; EHR 1934, 733; HistZeit 1934, 390; RA 1934, 211-213; CW 1935, 160; RevBelge 1934; 858; BullBudé 1932, 38; CR 1934, 85; LAAA 1934, 42; *Acropole* 1935, 46.

Excavations at Olynthus, VII.

BollFilologia 1934, 237; DLZ 1934, 698-700; RH 1934, 159; *Athenaeum* 1934, 171; BulSocArchAléxandrie 1934, 371-374; *Greece & Rome* 1934, 191; AHR 1934, 759; AJA 1934, 497; PW 1934, 1284-1286; CJ 1934, 173-174; CR 1934, 132; EngHistRev 1934, 733; HZ 1934, 390; JHS 1934, 216-217; RevPhil 1935, 94-95; CW 1935, 166; *Gnomon* 1935, 162-164; REG 1935, 170-173; *Acropole* 1935, 45-46; RevBelge 1935, 139; LAAA 1934, 42; RA 1935, 290-291; CP 1936, 93-95; *L'Antiquité Class.* 1935, 472-473; REA 1936, 230.

Excavations at Olynthus, VIII.

List of 31 reviews published in *Olynthus XII,* 473-474.

Excavations at Olynthus, IX.

Spink's Num. Chron. 1938, 393; *DLZ* 1939, 204; *CW* 1939, 174-175; 1941, 222; *Études Class.* 1939, 308; *Tijdschrift voor Geschiedenes* 1939, 79; *RH* 1938, 317-319; *AHR* 1939, 582; *Athenaeum* 1938, 302-303; *PW* 1939, 540-542; *RevBelgeNum* 1939, 126-127; *L'Antiquité Class.* 1939, 269-297; *il Mondo Classico* 1938, 3-4; *Boll Filolog* 1939, 178; *Woch.* 1939, 119-123; 1940, 123, 939; *LAAA* 1939, 78-79; *Rev Phil* 1939, 308; *AJA* 1940, 162-164; *AJP* 1940, 102-105; *CP* 1940, 210; *EngHist Rev* 1939, 522-523; *BCH* 1939, 121-122, 202; *Rivista di Filologia* 1940; fasc. III, 1-2; *Antiquity* 1941, 302; *JHS* 1939, 319-320; *CR* 1939, 143-144.

Excavations at Olynthus, X.

CW 1941, 63-64; *Johns Hopkins Alumni Magazine* 1942, 63-64; *AJA* 1942, 150-152; *AmYearBook* 1941, 902; *AHR* 1942, 824-825; *CP* 1943, 150-151; *CR* 1943, 52; *AJP* 1943, 457-458; *Greece and Rome* 1942, 95; *JHS* 1942, 103; *CJ* 1944, 543; *Antiquity* 1944, 168; *REA* 1948, 138; *RivFil* 1949, 290-295.

Excavations at Olynthus, XI.

AJA 1943, 138-139; *CP* 1943, 220-221; *CW* 1943, 64-66; *Antiquity* 1943, 217-218; *JHS* 1942, 163; *CR* 1943, 86; *CJ* 1944, 180-182; *ClOutlook* 1943, 51; *AHR* 1943, 303-305; *AmAnthropologist* 1943, 137-139; *Johns Hopkins Alumni Magazine* 1943, 60-61; *Man* 1943, 94-95; *Greece & Rome* 1943, 98.

Excavations at Olynthus, XII.

CW 1948, 94-96; *Antiquité Class.* 1947, 430-432; *BCH* 1947-1948, 379-381; *Mercure de France* 1948, 722-724; *Umschau* 1943, 197-199; *Polemon* 1947-1948, 10-11; *ClOutlook* 1947, 72-73; *CP* 1947, 199-201; *Études Class.* 1946, 303-304; *AHR* 1947, 145; *CJ* 1947, 91-95; *Athenaeum* 1947, 105-107; *Tijdschrift voor Geschiedenis* 1948, 189-190; *Athene* 1948, 19-20; *Greece & Rome* 1942, 140-141; *EHR* 1947, 552; *U.S.Quart.Book List* 1947, 126; *Johns Hopkins Alumni Magazine* 1947, 142-143; *RevPhil* 1948, 73-76; *JHS* 1946, 134-135; *Rivista di Filologia* 1947, 278-285; *AJA* 1947, 332-336; *Antiquitas* 1948, 208-209; *AJP* 1948, 396-407; *Boethius in Goetesborg Hoegskolas Aisshrift* 1948; 3-22; *AntJ* 1947, 187; *Mélanges de l'Université St. Joseph*, 1948, 343-345; *Mercure de France*, 1948, 722-724.

EDITOR'S NOTE

This note should be started with a word of apology for the late appearance of this volume. Our original intentions were to have the *Studies* appear on September 21, 1950, the seventieth anniversary of the birthday of Professor David M. Robinson. However, the great enthusiasm for and interest in the project shown by colleagues the world over, followed by an avalanche of articles, made impossible the materialization of those intentions. Indeed, it proved physically impossible to prepare for the printer and to publish within eight months some two hundred and fifty learned discussions which are to be included in the project nor was it feasible to include them all in one volume.

The wealth and variety of the material submitted posed another problem, the problem of arrangement. The articles could have been published in the order of their submission, or they could have been arranged in an alphabetical sequence. But these arrangements would have resulted in a wild mixture of content which would have made very difficult the use of the *Studies*. And so it was decided to publish the articles in groups and in accordance with their subject matter. Thus in the first volume are included articles dealing with Prehistoric Greece, Egypt and the Near East, Architecture and Topography, Sculpture, Monumental Painting and Mosaics. In the second volume, which will appear shortly, are included articles dealing with Vase Painting, Coins, Inscriptions, Literature, History and the Private Life of the Greeks and the Romans, Mythology, Religion, Philosophy, and Miscellaneous subjects. This arrangement will explain the tardy appearance of a number of articles which had been submitted at an early date. I take this opportunity to express my heartfelt thanks to all our collaborators for their cooperation and assistance without which the work of the Editor would have proved an impossible task. I am especially indebted to those of our collaborators whose articles were kept for so long, in some cases for over a year, for their understanding and patience.

I take great pleasure in acknowledging my indebtedness to the members of the Committee for their help. Especially I am grateful to my old friend and classmate Professor William C. McDermott, of the University of Pennsylvania, for his ever ready help and advice. To my colleagues Professor William Willis, of the University of Mississippi, and Professor Constantine G. Yavis, of the St. Louis University, I want to express my heartfelt thanks. Professor Willis undertook to direct the campaign for raising funds and the appearance of this volume is largely due to his enthusiastic efforts. In this connection I wish to express the gratitude of the members of the Committee to all those who with their generous contributions made possible the publication of the *Festschrift*. Professor Yavis undertook the task of soliciting and filling subscriptions, a task which he is carrying out with great success. To Professor Ilona Ellinger, of Trinity College, we are indebted for the vignette which graces the title page of the *Studies*. To my assistants, Mrs. Jean Child Haldiman, Miss June Olson, Mr. Frederick Burford and Mr. Richard W. Burke of Washington University, and to Dr. Doris Raymond of the University of Mississippi, I am under deep obligation for their wholehearted help.

I wish also to acknowledge my indebtedness to Professor Glanville Downey, Editor-in-chief of the *American Journal of Archaeology*, for his many suggestions and his permission to use "the style sheet" prepared under his direction for contributors to the *American Journal of Archaeology* even when it was in its typewritten stage. For a project like ours containing such a variety of subject matter published in many languages, the task of uniformity becomes a Herculean one. We have attempted to maintain such a uniformity, but we are conscious of the many lapses which seemed impossible to avoid and for which we ask the indulgence of the readers. Often we have sacrificed uniformity to clarity. Abbreviations used are listed in the pages which follow, but here we may mention that references to Greek authors are as a rule given in Roman numerals, while such to Latin authors in Arabic numerals.

To the syndics of the Eden Publishing House, and especially to Messrs. Otto Ehlers, Joseph A. Hausladen, and Ralph Meng I want to express my sincere thanks for their help and achievement in publishing this volume in record time.

ABBREVIATIONS

AA:	Archäologischer Anzeiger.
A & A:	Art and Archaeology.
AASOR:	Annual of the American School of Oriental Research.
AFO:	Archiv für Orientforschung.
AHR:	American Historical Review.
AJA:	American Journal of Archaeology.
AJNum:	American Journal of Numismatics.
AJP:	American Journal of Philology.
AM:	Athenische Mitteilungen.
Annuario:	Annuario della R. Scuola Archeologica de Atene.
AntDenk:	Antike Denkmäler.
AntJ:	Antiquaries' Journal.
ArtB:	Art Bulletin.
AZ:	Archäologische Zeitung.
BCH:	Bulletin de correspondence hellénique.
BSA:	Annual of the British School of Archaeology at Athens.
BollComm:	Bollettino della Commissione Archeologica Comunale di Roma.
CAH:	Cambridge Ancient History.
CIA:	Corpus Inscriptionum Atticarum.
CIG:	Corpus Inscriptionum Graecarum.
CIL:	Corpus Inscriptionum Latinarum.
CJ:	Classical Journal.
ClMed:	Classica et Mediaevalia.
CO:	Classical Outlook.
CP:	Classical Philology.
CQ:	Classical Quarterly.
CVA:	Corpus Vasorum Antiquorum.
CW:	Classical Weekly.
Deltion:	Ἀρχαιολογικὸν Δελτίον.
Ephemeris:	Ἀρχαιολογικὴ Ἐφημερίς and Ἐφημερὶς Ἀρχαιολογική.
FHG:	Müller, Fragmenta Historicorum Graecorum.
HThR:	Harvard Theological Review.
IG:	Inscriptiones Graecae.
JAOS:	Journal of the American Oriental Society.
JDAI and JdI:	Jahrbuch des K. deutschen archäologischen Instituts.

JEA:	Journal of Egyptian Archaeology.
JHS:	Journal of Hellenic Studies.
JOAI:	Jahreshefte des österreichischen archäologischen Instituts.
LAAA:	Liverpool Annals of Archaeology and Anthropology.
MonAnt:	Monumenti Antichi.
NSc:	Notizie degli Scavi di Antichita.
NumChron:	Numismatic Chronicle.
OLZ:	Orientalische Literaturzeitung.
PAPA:	Proceedings of the American Philological Society.
PAPS:	Proceedings of the American Philosophical Society.
PhilWoch:	Philologische Wochenschrift.
Praktika:	Πρακτικὰ τῆς ἐν ᾿Αθήναις ᾿Αρχαιολογικῆς ῾Εταιρείας.
RA:	Revue archéologique.
RE:	Pauly-Wissowa, Real-Encyclopädie der class. Altertumswissenschaft.
REA:	Revue des études anciennes.
RendLinc:	Rendiconti della R. Accademia dei Lincei.
RevNum:	Revue numismatique.
RM:	Römische Mitteilungen.
SEG:	Supplementum Epigraphicum Graecum.
StEtr:	Studi Etruschi.
TAPA:	Transactions of the American Philological Association.
ZfN:	Zeitschrift für Numismatik.

TABLE OF CONTENTS

LIST OF ILLUSTRATIONS

FIGURES IN THE TEXT

PLATES

PLATE 1
a. Sling bullets from Olynthus. b. Clay sling bullets from Hassuna. "Neolithic phase." c. Front and side views of Bull's Head "O" as restored.

PLATE 2
a, c, d. The Olive Bull's head (= O); b, the head from Knossos (= K).

PLATE 3
a. Ossuary at Agios Kosmas. b. Round pit beyond grave 11. c, d. An Early Helladic kitchen utensil.

PLATE 4
Objects from a grave at Charvati in Attica.
a, b. Terra cotta figurine of a female figure on horse back. c. Terra cotta figurine of a rider. d. Tripod of stone with a bull's head.

PLATE 5
a. Stone Tripod from the grave at Charvati in Attica. b. Sherds found below the archaic basis of the Temple of Artemis.

PLATE 6
a. Stone axes from Sardis in the Sturge Collection of the British Museum. b. Sherds found below the archaic basis of the Temple of Artemis. c. Heads from an Assyrian relief, Paris. d. Side view of the door-figure from Boghazköy.

PLATE 7
a. Part of the Gudea stele in Berlin. b. Relief of the Hammurabi stele. c. Detail (Head) of the door-figure from Boghazköy. d. Heads from the relief of the Magi from Ergili (now in Istanbul).

PLATE 8
a, b, c. Egyptian and Cypriot figured-capitals.

PLATE 9
a, b, c, d, e, f. Roman, Egyptian, and Cypriot figured-capitals.

PLATE 10
a, b, c. Cypriot and Roman figured-capitals. d. Double capital in the Egyptian Museum at Florence.

PLATE 11
a. Building model from the Argive Heraeum after Müller. b. Building model from the Argive Heraeum after Oikonomos. c. Building model from the Argive Heraeum after Oikonomos. d. Building model from Perachora after Payne.

PLATE 12
a. Building model from Perachora. b. Blocks between the pedestal of the Promachos and the North Wall of the Acropolis. c. Block at the south end of the long flight of steps to the West of the Parthenon.

ing cramp-hole. e. Section through waist showing junction of both legs and cramp-holes. From above.

PLATE 80

a. Left leg and thigh, showing cramp-hole. b. Interior of abdomen fragment shown in c. c, d, e. Fragments of a youthful figure; c. abdomen, d. arm, e. foot. f. Left foot, showing repair. g. Left leg and thigh, showing puntello.

PLATE 81

Marble head at Union College.

PLATE 82

a. Gold stater, Ptolemy I Soter. b. Silver tetradrachm, Ptolemy I Soter. c. Gold stater bearing jugate heads of Ptolemy I and Berenike. d. Plaster plaque from Memphis at Hildesheim. e, f. Marble head from Egypt at Copenhagen.

PLATE 83

a, b. Marble head from Greece in the Louvre. c, d. Marble head in the Pergamon Museum at Berlin.

PLATE 84

a, b. Head from Cairo. c, d. Head from Thera.

PLATE 85

Jugate heads of Ptolemy I Soter and Berenike in Alexandria. a, b. Engraved carnelian in the Metropolitan Museum, inscribed Aspasiou. c. Amethyst ring stone in the Metropolitan Museum.

PLATE 86

a. Amethyst ringstone in the Metropolitan Museum. b. Gem with herm of Dionysos. c. Fragment of a gem by Aspasios in Florence. d. Red jasper with the head of Athena Parthenos by Aspasios. e. Red jasper with herm of Dionysos in the British Museum. f. Marble disk in the Metropolitan Museum.

PLATE 87

a. Ape riding on a donkey. b. Ape (or man) riding on a donkey. c. Seated ape holding a large pot.

PLATE 88

Foot of a Thymiaterion from Olympia. (Inv. B 1001). Front and side views.

PLATE 89

Foot of a Thymiaterion in the Metropolitan Museum. Front and side views.

PLATE 90

a, b. Terra cotta figurines from the Tyre region. c. Shield fragment from Olympia. (Inv. B. 1799.)

PLATE 91

a. Bronze statuette in Brussels. b. Bronze statuette from Monte Falterona in the Louvre. c. Bronze statuette from Monte Guragazza in Bologna.

PLATE 92

a. Bronze figure of Turms in the Ashmolean Museum. b. Bronze statuette from Monte Falterona in Florence. c. Bronze statuette in Florence.

PLATE 93

a. The Capitoline wolf. b. Bronze lion medallion from Tarquinia.

PLATE 94

a. Lion water spout from Himera. b. Relief from a house on block Ds at Dura-Europos.

THE SIGNIFICANCE OF THE SLING FOR GREEK PREHISTORY

V. GORDON CHILDE
University of London, Institute of Archaeology

PLATE 1

It might almost seem impertinent for one whose academic office confines him to the barbarous products of preliterate societies, to offer a written tribute to a colleague who has so greatly enriched our knowledge of classical peoples by uncovering and interpreting the concrete remains of their civilization. But not the least of Prof. Robinson's contributions to classical archaeology was to recognize the importance and organize the scientific excavations of Olynthus, and these carried the history of the site back beyond the bounds of literary tradition to its prehistoric foundations in a peasant village of the New Stone Age. Now among other relics there discovered were sling bullets of stone and baked clay—the first to be recorded in prehistoric Macedonia (pl. 1a).[1] Some consequences of this discovery might then appropriately be considered in a volume devoted to the excavations' organizer and director.

In classical times the significance of the sling as a weapon of war and of the chase, both among the Greeks and Romans and among their barbarian neighbors, has been fully recognized thanks to plentiful literary references. Prehistorians, however, have been inclined to neglect this weapon or even ignore it altogether.[2] One excuse is, of course, the fact that any pebble from the brook will serve as a bullet. Such pebbles are not artifacts and can only be recognized as ammunition when found in a significant context in the course of excavation, as by R. E. M. Wheeler at Maiden Castle, Dorset.[3] However, some prehistoric barbarians did make sling bullets of baked clay, giving them the standard form subsequently reproduced in the lead *glandes* so familiar from classical times, or shaped—or at least selected— stone sling bullets of like form.

Among these barbarians were the neolithic peoples of Greece. Tsountas' excavations in Thessaly and Central Greece already brought

---

1. Mylonas, *Excavations at Olynthus*, I, 79, fig. 86a-c; fig. 92, drawing of c.

2. Note for instance the paucity of references under *"Schleuder,"* "Schleudersteine," etc. in the index of Ebert's *Reallexikon der Vorgeschichte*.

3. Wheeler, *Maiden Castle, Dorset* (Society of Antiquaries, Research Committee Reports, No. 12, London, 1943), 49-50.

to light many neolithic sling bullets. Wace and Thompson[4] substantially increased the collections and established that they went back to the earlier neolithic phase, Tsountas' period A. Olynthus then extended the neolithic sling province to Macedonia. At the same time it was noticed that recognizable arrow-heads of flint or obsidian were conspicuously rare in neolithic Greece. In view of the relatively large mass of material subsequently gathered from systematic excavations in Arcadia, Corinthia, Messenia, and the Vardar Valley, it is permissible to assert that stone arrow-heads were not used on the Greek Mainland or Macedonia during the local neolithic period; they are explicitly attested first in the "Early Bronze Age"[5] as if their use were introduced with the Early Helladic culture and its relative, the Early Macedonian. Of course, arrows may end in bone, or even in hardened wood, points so that the absence of stone arrow-heads does not disprove the use of the bow. Nevertheless in view of the universal popularity of "flint" arrow-heads wherever the bow was used and suitable material was available, not only in the Old World, but also in America, one may legitimately infer that in neolithic Greece the sling was the principal propulsive weapon while the bow played a very minor role, if any, in hunting and fighting.

In this respect neolithic Greece is contrasted strikingly with the peninsula that occupies the opposite extremity of the Mediterranean, since Spain abounds in arrow-heads and even pictures of prehistoric archers. Greece by the same token is united to a large Asiatic province which is similarly contrasted with Egypt. The sling was never an Egyptian weapon. Though it is represented in paintings since the Middle Kingdom, it is always being used by foreigners. Thousands of flint arrow-heads on the other hand from the earliest predynastic sites (Merimde, Fayum, Badari, Armant, etc.) as from all subsequent periods attest the predominant importance of the bow. In Mesopotamia[6] and Iran the position is reversed.

Clay sling pellets of standard form have been collected from the earliest horizons yet reached at Hassuna in Assyria[7] (pl. 1b) and at

---

4. Wace and Thompson, *Prehistoric Thessaly*, 43, 72, 73, 125, 201; add now Mrs. Walker Kosmopoulos, *The Prehistoric Inhabitation of Corinth*, fig. 23, h-i ("period II").

5. e.g., Blegen, *Zygouries*, 199; Froedin and Persson, *Asine*, 243: Goldman *Eutresis*, 206. The two arrow-heads assigned to "period III" at Corinth (Walker Kosmopoulos, *op. cit.*, 52) are not derived from a satisfactorily closed find while it is now recognized that the Dimini culture, even in Thessaly, overlaps with Early Helladic.

6. i.e., the whole area between the Tigris and Euphrates together with the Assyrian *doab*.

7. *JNES* 4 (1945) 267.

Sialk in western Iran.[8] Then they are associated with all the early chalcolithic cultures of Mesopotamia, characterized by Hassuna,[9] Halaf,[10] and allied wares as well as Hissar I in northern Iran[11] and at Anau (I or II)[12] and Shah-tepe[13] on the steppes still further north. On the contrary flint or obsidian arrow-heads are conspicuously missing from all the Mesopotamian assemblages named, from Sialk I and II and from Bakun A.[14] There are a couple of specimens from Hissar I, but they only become common in Hissar III and Anau III while in Mesopotamia they are hardly known before the Uruk period. Here again the evidence is not merely negative and could not be explained by assuming that the prehistoric peoples of Mesopotamia and Iran were ideal peasants who abstained both from the "savage" activity of hunting and the "civilized" one of war. The inference must be the same as in the case of neolithic Greece.

Accordingly it appears that round either extremity of the Fertile Crescent where literate civilizations originated, the neolithic economy is manifested in two cycles contrasted in armaments. The Nilotic horn lies in a province where the bow was the principal propulsive engine; that position was occupied by the sling at the opposite end of the Crescent. Of course the contrast is not confined to armament. In Egypt arrow-heads are associated from the first with a ceramic tradition aiming at producing dark-faced self-colored (red or black) wares. The Asiatic "sling stone cultures" on the contrary unanimously preferred pale fabrics, painted in darker colors, however much the patterns thus executed differ among the several cultures; and even the very coarse storage jars of Hassuna "neolithic" are light-colored.

It would be tempting to deduce from these and other contrasts the existence of two distinct and independent cycles of neolithic culture, best characterized by the sling and the bow respectively. One might then go on to speculate on their independent origins in palaeolithic or mesolithic culture-cycles or provinces, already contrasted in late pleistocene times. Such speculations would be inappropriate in the present context save to make plain that the preference for the sling

8. Ghirshman, *Fouilles de Sialk*, I, 33, 103.

9. Besides the type site the association is also attested at Matarrah according to information kindly supplied by the excavator, Dr. Robert Braidwood.

10. e.g., Von Oppenheim, *Tell Halaf*, I (1943), 110; Mallowan, "Excavations at Arpachiya," *Iraq* 2 (1935) 88.

11. *Museum Journal, Pennsylvania*, 23 (1933) 36.

12. Pumpelly, *Explorations in Turkestan* (Carnegie Institute Publications, 73), 157.

13. Arne, *Excavations at Shah-tepe, Iran* (Sino-Swedish Expedition, Publication, 27), 261.

14. Langsdorff and McCown, *Tall-i-Bakun A* (Oriental Institute Publication, 59), 76.

can be treated as a significant link between "neolithic" Greece and the Mesopotamian province and added to the long familiar common traits of dark-on-light vase-painting, use of stamp seals and so on.

On the other hand the exact connection between the Asiatic sling-stone province and its extension in Peninsular Greece is made still more obscure. The intervening Levantine littoral has always been a frontier region influenced both by Egypt and by Mesopotamia. But in the earliest neolithic levels of Palestine,[15] characterized by Tahunian flints at Jericho, arrow-heads already abundant proved the preference for the bow. Further north neither sling bullets nor arrow-heads were found in the chalcolithic graves of Byblos, but flint arrow-heads did turn up on virgin rock at several points.[16] Then in the Amouq plain on the Orontes[17] the earliest levels, phases A and B of Dr. Braidwood's classification, yielded plenty of arrow-heads, apparently associated with self-colored wares, but two well formed stone sling bullets are attributed to phase A too. Clay sling bullets become abundant first in phase C when, significantly enough, Halafian painted sherds also appear.

In Cilicia and on the Anatolian plateau the evidence is still quite ambiguous. Neither undoubted arrow-heads nor recognizable sling bullets[18] are explicitly associated with the self-colored neolithic pottery of Mersin. Stone arrow-heads are extremely rare on the plateau; none has been recorded from the early levels of Troy or Thermi, but there were a few in the chalcolithic site of Alishar.[19] On the other hand sling bullets have been reported from Boz-eüyük and Troy (II—V)[20] and one is illustrated from Alaca Höyük.[21]

Finally there are no certain sling bullets from "neolithic" Cyprus. A couple of arrow-heads were collected at the early site of Khirokitia[22] where the lowest levels contained a little ill-baked dark-faced pottery, the later no pottery at all till the very latest when the first painted sherds began. At the later site of Erimi, characterized by painted ware with strong affinities to Thessalian A fabrics, arrow-heads were

15. Neuville, "L'Age de la pierre en Palestine," *Revue biblique* (1934) 255; cf. *LAAA* 22 (1935) 168 and 176.

16. Dunand, *Fouilles de Byblos, 1926-1932*, 404.

17. Information kindly supplied by Dr. Braidwood; cf. *AJA* 41 (1937) 8-13.

18. Burkitt, "The Earlier Cultures at Mersin," *LAAA* 26 (1939), describes three obsidian implements as "typologically transverse arrow-heads" but admits doubt that they were ever so used (p. 63); slate "marbles" found lower down (p. 71) might conceivably have been sling bullets.

19. Von der Osten, *Excavations at Alishar Hüyük, 1930-32* (Oriental Institute Publications, 28), 82.

20. Dörpfeld, *Troia und Ilion*, 370.

21. Remzi Ogiz Arik, *Les Fouilles de Alaca Höyük*, pl. CL. 823.

22. Report in the press; information kindly supplied by Dr. Dikaios.

conspicuously absent.[23] Conversely Evans[24] denied that the sling was a Minoan weapon. Indeed though early evidence for the use of the bow is equally lacking, Cretan neolithic pottery has more in common with the dark-faced wares of the Levant coasts than with Mesopotamian painted wares.

The available data then would accord with the hypothesis that a bow-and-arrow province extended all along the East Mediterranean coast from Egypt to Cilicia if not further north and embraced Crete and presumably Cyprus (Khirokitia) as insular offshoots. Later, in Halaf times, this continuum would have been interrupted to allow a linkage between Mesopotamia and Mainland Greece, presumably by way of North Syria and Cyprus (Erimi).

To avoid ending with a pure speculation let me recall one further fact that emerges. Neolithic Greece is notoriously linked with the great "Danubian" neolithic province, north of the Balkans, by significant traits such as the carpenters' use of adzes to the exclusion of axes,[25] and the popularity of *Spondylus* shell ornaments, that serve to contrast the latter with the contemporary West European province. To the list of traits we may now probably add a preference for the sling; for though no early sling bullets have been recorded north of Bulgaria,[26] arrow-heads are conspicuously missing in pure early neolithic Danubian cultures while universal in the west.

---

23. *Report of the Department of Antiquities, Cyprus*, 1936, 52; a hoard of pebbles which was found may well represent sling ammunition.

24. *The Palace of Minos*, II, 344.

25. I am discussing the wood-working tools in a forthcoming study.

26. Gaul, *The Neolithic Period in Bulgaria* (American School of Prehistoric Research Bulletin No. 16) 45, 93.

A MINOAN BULL'S HEAD

CHARLES SELTMAN
Queens' College, Cambridge

Plates 1-2

The fascination which bulls exercised even on primitive artists among the dwellers by the shores of the Aegean can be traced back to neolithic times. A small object, but one of the most interesting of objects found in the first year of David Moore Robinson's excavations at Olynthus, was a white marble fragment with reddish veins discovered at a depth of 1.25 metres in the neolithic settlement, and possibly made about 3,000 B.C. It is part of a vase, or bowl, with a lug shaped as the head of a bull, a unique specimen which is called "a testimony to the high ability of the Olynthian prehistoric stone-cutters."[1] Nearly a thousand years later an ivory cylinder seal from Crete of E.M. date was engraved with three magnificent bulls,[2] and this was a precursor of many other Minoan seals with such pictures. An intense admiration of bulls, possibly veneration of them, grew apace in Crete.

The evidence at our disposal indicates that a kind of acme of the depiction of bulls in art was reached during the first half of the fifteenth century B.C.; for it was then that Minoan artists produced certain curious objects which served apparently as firkins, or decanters. They were also—as works of art—much sought after by great personages in Crete itself, in Egypt, and in the Peloponnesos. These were the so-called Bull's-head Rhytons. Proof of the extent of their popularity is: first, the famous (though incomplete) black bull's head (pl. 2, b); second, several paintings in the tombs of great Egyptian nobles of the reign of Thothmes III; and third, some very small fragments—a horn-socket here, and an ear or a dewlap there—of six other bulls' heads. To these can now be added another, more complete than the celebrated black bull's head from the Little Palace at Knossos.

Few sculptures in stone have survived from the Minoan civilization; but of those that have the most brilliant by far was the black steatite bull's head discovered by Sir Arthur Evans at Knossos and first fully published by him in 1914.[3] In the whole history of European art the

1. Robinson, D. M., *Excavations at Olynthus*: Part I, by Mylonas, G. E., *The Neolithic Settlement*, 76, fig. 81a.
2. Matz, F., *Fruehkretische Siegel*, 8, No. 38, Pl. XIII, 18.
3. *Archaeologia* 65 (1914) 79 ff; *P.M. II*, 527 ff; *CAH, Plates* i, 168; Bossert, *Ancient Crete*, 176 fig. 308; Rodenwaldt, *Kunst d. Antike*, 1927, Pl. 123. However, Karo, *JDAI* (1911) 252, points out that it is "zur Haelfte verloren."

bull's head of Knossos must rank as one of the famous creations of
mankind. The other specimen, of even greater merit, was rescued
from oblivion twenty-three years ago, and is the subject of this paper[4]
(pl. 2, a, c, d; pl. 1, c).

This head of dark, olive-green, mottled steatite, formed part of a
collection of Egyptian antiquities made during the nineteenth century
by a French amateur archaeologist who did not appear to have owned
any Greek things. There is, therefore, some probability that it was
found in Egypt and taken thence with certain limestone figurines,
bronzes, canopic jars, and ushabtiu to a château in France. Let us call
it the "Olive Bull's Head." It is slightly smaller than the black Knossos
head, for the latter is 20.6 centimetres (8.1 inches) from crown to
chin, the former 18 centimetres (7.1 inches). Other broken bits show
that dark green steatite was more popular than black or grey.[5]

Those very small fragments of other similar heads which have been
found both in Crete and at Mycenae are, for the sake of completeness,
described at the end of this paper (see *Appendix*). Pictures of the
Knossos head—only half of which is original—and descriptions of it
are familiar to students of Minoan art; accordingly it seems best to
consider the "Olive head" and the Knossos head together and to record
in what respects they differ.

For the sake of brevity I will call the Knossian head "K" and the
other "O".

i) Back plate which seals the rhyton: partly preserved for K, missing from O. On the back-plate of K is the graffito[6] of a facing
bull's head with long horns, and this is in part responsible for
the reconstruction of the horns of K by Sir Arthur Evans. Our
O has also a graffito, for within the inside curvature on the right
side of the neck are three symbols of Minoan Linear Script A:
ϸ𐘍𐘇. Considering that the scribe who wrote them had to
scratch them in a place none too easy to reach, the first and
second are very clear examples of the Script, the third less
distinct. A convenient table of signs peculiar to Linear Script A
has recently been prepared and published by Sir John Myres[7] in
which letters there numbered 75, 59, and 61 will be found to
correspond to those on the O bull's head.

---

4. Information about provenience is meager. It was found in a shop off the
rue Lafayette, Paris, in association with Egyptian antiquities. The proprietor
stated that the collection came from a château to the south of Paris—"assez loin."
The collector who acquired the head in 1926 died nine years later.
5. Like the four little fragments of bull's heads from Mycenae: see *Appendix*,
items 5 to 8.
6. *Archaeologia, ibid.* 82, fig. 89; *P.M.* II, 527, fig. 329.
7. *JHS* 66 (1946) "The Minoan Signary," table on p. 3, first four columns;
Kober, A., *AJA* 52 (1948) 95 (after Myres).

ii) Horns. None of these has been preserved, either for the surviving two heads, or for the little fragments. But at Mycenae in the fourth shaft-grave there was discovered a bull's head rhyton of silver with gold-encased horns[8] which serves as an indicator. Within the gold casing for the horns was some disintegrating material which the excavators took to be wood, but which was more probably ivory, as Wace has conjectured.[9] On the evidence of this silver bull's head and of a famous passage in the *Odyssey*[10] Sir Arthur Evans restored K with gilt horns. O has been fitted with plaster horns of a natural color (pl. 1, c). The sockets into which ivory (or wood) horns were fitted prove to have been generally square in section, but once at least, round.[11] Sometimes the sculptor pegged the horns into their sockets by means of pins plugged through approximately at right-angles to the axis of the horn as it passed into its socket. But sometimes he managed to assure stability without resort to this excessive precaution.

iii) Ears. Both K and O have lost their ears. Sir Arthur Evans restored them for K in plaster. It is likely that they, like the horns, were of ivory or wood.[12] However, there was found in the Tomb of the Double-axes at Knossos a pair of steatite ears for a bull's head of much smaller dimensions,[13] but not the head to which they belonged.

iv) Eyes. The right eye of K was found with it, a lens of rock-crystal on the hollowed under-surface of which are painted pupil and iris.[14]

v) Muzzle. On K a white shell inlay, only partly preserved, curves over the nostrils. On O this area is marked with parallel lines and was doubtless painted white. The maker of O used no shell-inlay because he was making a slightly less expensive article, probably for export; or because inlay had proved unsatisfactory.

vi) Markings. Incurved angular designs are present on the face and neck of both K and O, and these too will have been painted (white or red-brown?) to represent the markings of a bull's hide. Long hairs, as of a shaggy breed of bull are, in both

---

8. Karo, *JDAI* 26 (1911) 249 ff.; *Schachtgraeber von Mykenai*, 33, No. 384, Pls. 119-121; Evans *P.M.* II, 530 ff.
9. *BSA* 24 (1919-1920, 1920-1921) 203.
10. 3, 430 ff.
11. See *Appendix*, item 8.
12. The silver head from the fourth shaft-grave had ears of a different material—bronze. Karo, *JDAI ibid.* and *Schachtgraeber, ibid.*
13. See *Appendix*, item 4. The head itself may in this case have been of wood.
14. Evans, *Archaeologia, ibid.*, 8. Removable eyes have been made for O to give a similar effect.

examples, engraved over cheeks, brows and nose, while the tightly-curled locks over the forehead and between the horns, and two engraved roundels—one central and high between the eyes, one higher among the locks—are there both on K and on O. Markings and locks are differently disposed on the two heads.

vii) Openings. Both heads have a small opening in the lower lip from which liquid could escape in a thin stream. K has a large opening on the top of the neck into which the liquid was poured, and this would have to be kept corked with a bung, like the bung of a cask, the cork being taken out when liquid was to be drawn off at the little lip-hole.[15] But such a bung was rather unsightly; and the carver of O, with that ingenuity so characteristic of an inventive Minoan, thought of something neater. The left ear-socket does not go right through into the head and is comparatively shallow, though an ear could have been easily wedged into it. But the right ear-socket goes right through into the interior; it served as the opening for pouring in liquid, and the right ear became the bung. Here is an additional reason in support of the view expressed above that the ears were probably of ivory or wood; and since the mechanism of O is an improvement on that of K, it is probable that O was made somewhat later than K. The neatness of the "ear-bung" device is apparent when the employment of such a rhyton as this is considered. The silver bull's head from the Mycenaean fourth shaft-grave is fitted on the top of the neck near the truncation with a strong wire loop, by means of which it could be hung in a wall.[16] And though the material of the steatite heads made them heavier than the silver one, these stone heads when in use as decanters must either have been hung on a fitted rack, or placed on a shaped stand which supported them in a nearly upright position. Then, when the owner called for a drink, the serving-boy took in his right hand a cup and held it under the bull's mouth while, with his left hand, he twiddled the bull's right ear and pulled it free from its socket to let some air in. When he pushed back the ear the flow was stopped. Other evidence abounds to show that the Minoans were prone to invent neat gadgets such as this. This very neatness—as well as the exceptional artistic quality which we perceive in these heads—was probably responsible for their popularity among the great nobles of Egypt.

15. There is a bung-hole in one fragment, *Appendix*, item 6, and in the silver head from the fourth shaft-grave, Karo, *JDAI ibid.*

16. Karo, *ibid.* 249 and *Schachtgraeber*, 276, 3.

viii) It remains to summarize precisely what is missing and what survives of these two heads, K and O. Both are without their original horns and ears, since perishable materials were employed to make these adjuncts. One eye of K has been preserved; neither eye of O. K has part of its back-plate; O has not. But, except for the lack of an eye and a piece of back-plate, O is far more complete, since half of K, as Karo pointed out in 1911, is missing; whereas O is a complete head but for the lost point of the dewlap.[17] For this reason the "Olive" Bull's-head must be given pride of place among the numerous works of art carved out of steatite by the artists of Minoan Crete.

The Olive head is, indeed, to be preferred, not only for its greater completeness, but also because it is a better work of art. When the fingers are passed over the Olive head it is as though the actual bony skull of the animal can be felt underneath. The whole anatomy seems to come near to perfection; so do the curve of the neck with its huge muscles, the great bone ridge between the two horn-sockets, the smooth cheeks, and the almost soft muzzle and mouth. He is proportionally wider between the horns and a more powerful beast than the Black Bull of Knossos, and when you turn to a good cast of the latter you suddenly realize the Black Bull to be more summarily—even more carelessly—made. This is most apparent from a study of the locks of hair and the two roundels of hair which on the Olive head are more finely and carefully carved than on the black. Accordingly, while the Olive head is evidently a little later in date than the other, it is the work of a more accomplished artist.[18]

Since it seems possible that this head was found in Egypt, it will be well to recapitulate in proper chronological form the evidence for the import into the empire of Thothmes III of such works of art as Minoan bulls' heads.

The long reign, 1501 to 1447 B.C., of that monarch coincided with the height of Egyptian prosperity as well as power. "He was the first," as J. H. Breasted pointed out,[19] "to build an empire in any real sense. He was the first world-hero." This commanding and versatile personage had an interest in fine art which was shared by the nobles

---

17. There are certain minor injuries, such as chips off the left lower eye-lid and the right horn-socket. These are very ancient breaks; whereas the dewlap break has the appearance and feel of a somewhat more recent injury—perhaps a century old. The back-plate was possibly flanged, tight-fitting and pegged at the dewlap's back; but mechanisms varied for the various heads and we cannot be sure.

18. It has not been subjected to the evidence-effacing restorations customary forty years ago. The eyes of jet and wax can be lifted out; the plaster horns can be withdrawn; the plaster piece of dewlap is separate.

19. In *CAH*, II, 87.

a   b

Figure 1. Paintings of Keftiu from Egyptian tombs.

who were nearest to him; and in their tomb-paintings they recorded gifts of works of art as well as objects of high value brought from foreign lands to them as representatives of the Pharaoh who ruled over such vast territories. You could not offer to Thothmes III, or to his viziers, anything but the very best, for the Pharaoh in his spare time was an artist himself.[20] It seems clear that no country in the world of that day could produce anything half so fine or delicate as could Minoan Crete, and the presents brought from that island by the Keftiu—the Egyptian name for the Cretans—were recorded with satisfaction by their recipients. Apart from bullion the presents were mainly of the following kinds: metal jugs and amphorae, cups of the "Vaphio" shape, helmets, strings of beads—probably seal-stones— pointed rhytons, statuettes of bulls, and a variety of animal-head rhytons in the form of lions', griffins', wolves', and especially bulls' heads. The last are represented in paintings within the tombs at Thebes of three of the great nobles of the reign of Thothmes III.

User-amon was grand-vizier in the early part of the reign, perhaps about 1500 B.C. In his tomb is the figure of a Keftian holding in his right hand a splendid Bull's head, supporting it gently with his left (fig. 1,a).[21] This official was succeeded in office about 1471 B. C. by

20. *Ibid.* 81.
21. Evans, *P.M.* II, figs. 340a, 471.

his nephew, the celebrated Rekhmara, in whose tomb appear paintings
of many Cretans and their presents. Here, upon the ground-line, over
a set of three metal ingots, rests just such another Bull's-head rhyton
(fig. 2)[22] Rekhmara had a son, Men-kheper'ra-senb, who was Trea-
surer, High-Priest of Amon, Architect and Chief of the Office of
Works in the latter part of the reign. In his tomb is the painting of a
Keftian youth holding upon a dish yet another Bull's-head rhyton of
similar proportions (fig. 1, b).[23]

With such evidence before us it would occasion no surprise if a
steatite bull's head like the Olive one had been discovered in Egypt,
where, indeed, other Minoan imports have frequently been found.[24]
And when we conclude that it was made between 1500 and 1450 B.C.,
we find this corresponds to the period known as Late Minoan I, to
which the Black Bull's head of Knossos is likewise assigned.

The purpose which these heads were meant to serve (apart from
their value in the Minoan export trade to Egypt) has been much discussed, and emphasis has in the past always been laid on their sup-

Figure 2. Painting of a Bull's head rhyton from the tomb of Rekhmara.

posedly "sacral" or ritual character. It is thought that they were
libation vessels employed in the cult of a Bull-god. If, however, that
had been their sole or primary purpose, would they have been quite
so readily exported to Egypt and to Mycenae? Are sacred vessels not
meant to be kept at home? Or, if exported, should they pass to people
other than one's co-religionists? We do not know what answers a
Minoan would have given to these questions. It may be wiser to suppose that, although the bull had its religious associations, vessels
shaped as Bull's heads may nevertheless have been employed at royal
or aristocratic feasts as decanters devoid of any precise cult significance.

Yet the outstanding splendor of these works of art proves that they

22. *Ibid.* fig. 339.
23. *Ibid.* figs. 340b, 482; *CAH Plates* i, 150a. Concerning other Minoan rhytons,
lion-heads, see Karo, *JDAI* 26, 253 ff.
24. See Fimmen, D., *Die Kretisch-mykenische Kultur*, 152 ff.; Bossert, *Ancient
Crete*, figs. 557-560.

were, without doubt, made for a society which had a profound passion for bulls and the excitement of the Ring. In the history of mankind the most terrifying and perhaps the most daring of sports was that which took place in the Bull-rings of Crete and Mycenae 3,500 years ago. The remote descendant of the ancient Minoan Ring is the Spanish Bull-ring; but the Greek and Cretan youths and girls—unarmed and depending on nothing but precision in timing and exquisite muscular perfection—might claim in their brief day more glory than the most brilliant Matador of Spain or Spanish America. No one will deny that the sculptural remains of the Minoan civilization attain their perfection in those monuments which are concerned with this greatest of all sports, since one has but to recall the Vaphio and Dendra cups,[25] the Toronto and the Oxford girl and boy, and the Spencer-Churchill bronze,[26] to recognize this fact.

But the most splendid are the Bull's heads themselves. Indeed, it may fairly be said that the two heads—one of black, one of dark olive-green steatite—are the earliest surviving masterpieces of European sculpture in the grand manner.

---

25. Bossert, *op. cit.* figs. 70-75; Seltman, *Approach to Greek Art*, Pl. 4.
26. *Ibid.* Pls. 7-9, Pl. 10b.

ADDENDUM

Since this article was written a fresh piece of evidence, concerning the importance of Bulls' heads as rhytons in the Bronze Age, has come to light. The London "Times" of November 8, 1949, carries a report from its Correspondent at Istanbul concerning the excavations made by Mr. and Mrs. Tashin Ozgüç, Professors in the Department of Archaeology in the University of Ankara. During the past summer their excavations at Kültepe, on the site of the old Hittite city of Kanes, have secured brilliant results, and it is reported that "perhaps the best find is a bull-headed rhyton used for ritual libations at official and religious ceremonies," and two photographs of this black rhyton are shown in the "Times" of the date cited above. It appears to measure about 17 centimetres from crown to chin, and is therefore only a little smaller than No. 1 above—the "olive Bull's head." Moreover, it is in about the same state of completeness: eye and horn-sockets are empty, the horns having been made of some perishable material; and the actual eyes having been lost. From the illustration it does not seem likely that this is an actual import from Crete, since it is evidently coarser than any of the Minoan specimens listed above. Therefore it may well be a local Hittite imitation of some vanished imported Minoan Bull's head.

APPENDIX

STEATITE MINOAN BULLS' HEADS AND FRAGMENTS OF BULLS' HEADS

1. The "Olive Bull's Head," possibly from Egypt; more complete than No. 2.

2. The Black half-head from the Little Palace, Knossos (see footnote 3 above for references in *Archaeologia, P. M. II*, etc.)

3. Half a horn-socket from drain of Royal Road, Knossos (*P. M. II*, p. 531). Figure 3.

4. Two ears and some schist inlays, from the Tomb of the Double Axes at Knossos (*Archaeologia* 65 [1914] 58). Figure 4.

5. The point of a dewlap from the acropolis of Mycenae (Karo, *JDAI* 26 [1911] 251 f.; Wace in *BSA* 24, p. 203 and Pl. XIII, 3 a, b, c). Figure 5.

6. Piece of neck, right side top, from closet under stairs to N.W. of court of palace, Mycenae (Wace, *ibid.* 203 f. and Pl. XIII, 3d, e). Figure 6.

7. Piece of forehead with right and part of left horn-socket from the Rhyton Well, Mycenae (Wace, *ibid.* 202 and Pl. XIII, 1C, c, d). Figure 7.

8. Piece upper left side of face with one eye and one horn-socket, found with No. 7 (Wace, *ibid.* and Pl. XIII, 1D, a, b). Figure 8.[27]

9. An ear from Palaikastro, Crete, may or may not belong to a lost head. Information inadequate (Karo, *JDAI* 26, 252, footnote 2).

Color of Steatite	Size, True or Approximate, Crown to Chin	Socket-holes Horns	Ears	Remarks
1. Dark green	18 cm. true	Square	Round	Complete but for dewlap; right ear-hole is bung-hole
2. Black	20.6 cm. true	Square	Round	Left half of head missing; bung-hole on nape
3. Dark grey	———	Square	——	Tiny fragment of biggish head
4. No record	11-12 cm. approx.	——	——	Two ears. Head itself was perhaps of wood
5. Dark green	———	——	——	Point of dewlap only with extreme tip missing
6. Dark green	18 cm. approx.	——	Round	Piece; shows bung-hole on nape
7. Dark green	25 cm. approx.	Square	——	Piece; hair naturalistic
8. Dark green	21 cm. approx.	Round	——	Piece; hair finer and more formal

---

27. Nos. 5, 6, 7, 8 are published anew by Wace, *Mycenae* (1949) 68, figs. 26, 27 a. b.

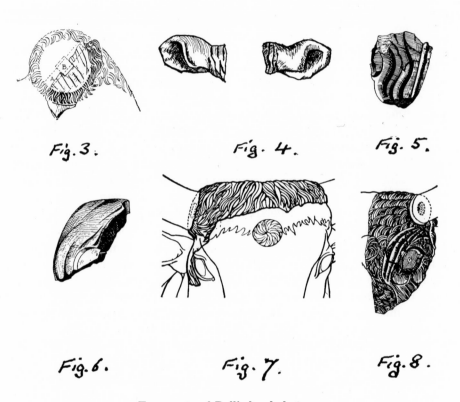

Fig. 3.   Fig. 4.   Fig. 5.

Fig. 6.   Fig. 7.   Fig. 8.

Fragments of Bull's head rhytons.

DIE KNOSSISCHEN WAGENINVENTARE

Johannes Sundwall

Åbo Akademi, Finland

Zu den in bezug auf Inhalt am leichtesten zu deutenden Urkunden des knossischen Palastes gehören diejenigen, die von Evans
in *Palace of Minos* IV, 786 — 825, § 114 Deposits of Tablets depicting Chariots (von Kober in ihrer Klassifikation unter N aufgenommen) veröffentlicht und besprochen werden. Diese Täfelchen
verzeichnen Kriegswagen, Pferde, Räder, Brustpanzer, Peitsche
u.a. Es scheint, daß das Archiv der Inventardokumente mit einem
Gebäude administrativ zusammenhing, das Evans als "Armory"
bezeichnen möchte (on the Northern border of the paved "Via
Sacra"). Auf alle Fälle ist eine Scheidung der Dokumente in
solche, die Wagen, Pferde, Panzer u.dgl., und solche, die Räder
verzeichnen, aufrechtzuhalten, denn die ersteren zeigen ganz niedrige Zahlen, 1 u. 2, wie Evans a.O.S. 787 bemerkt, die anderen
"large numbers". Zu den Ausführungen von Evans möchte ich
hier einige Bemerkungen beisteuern, die sich bei der Durcharbeitung
des verzeichneten Sachmateriales dieser Täfelchen ergeben.

Wir können unter den in Frage kommenden Urkunden eine Klasse
unterscheiden, wo nach einer einleitenden Zeichengruppe das von
Evans unzweifelhaft richtig (a.O.S. 803) als Brustpanzer (Breast-
plate) gedeutete Bild mit der Zahl 1 oder 2 steht (wenn 2 folgt,
dürfte dies nach einer sehr ansprechenden Vermutung von Evans
a.O.S. 806 bedeuten, daß die Bemannung des Wagens aus zwei
Personen bestand), ferner das vollständig wiedergegebene Bild des
Wagens mit der Zahl 1 und schließlich ein Pferdekopf nebst nach-
folgendem Zeichen (vgl. *Fig. 1 a* unten) mit der Zahl 1 zu erkennen
sind. Leider ist von solchen Urkunden keine intakt vorhanden.
Eine ähnliche Anordnung haben einige andere Täfelchen, nur folgt
dort nach der einleitenden Zeichengruppe erst der Wagen mit 1,
und dann Brustpanzer und Pferdekopf mit 1 und als drittes eine
Zweizeichengruppe mit 1. Auch hier ist der Wagen vollständig
abgebildet und über die Bedeutung der anderen Sachzeichen kann
ebenfalls kein Zweifel bestehen (vgl. die Ausführungen von Evans
a.O.). Das oben erwähnte, nach dem Pferdekopf folgende und
damit zusammengehörende Zeichen ist nun näher zu bestimmen,
denn die Deutung ist nicht ohne weiteres gegeben. Am besten ist
es in den Täfelchen Evans a.O. 795 Fig. 768 zu erkennen. Daß es
in allen diesen Wagen- und Wagenteilurkunden als Ideogramm

steht, ist offenbar, während es in einigen anderen knossischen Tex-
ten auch als Schriftzeichen (als Anfangszeichen oder in der Gruppen-
mitte) zu belegen ist. Für uns kommt es nur auf die Sachbedeutung
an, wir wollen also alle diejenigen Kombinationen mustern, wo es
sich in dieser Stellung feststellen läßt (vgl. *Fig. 1 a — d*). Evans
hat (a.O.S. 497 f.) in dem zweiten Zeichen aller dieser Gruppen
ein Sägezeichen vermutet und dieses als "Carpenter's Sign" gedeutet, m.a.W. als die Bezeichnung einer Wagenfabrik oder dgl.
("a conclusion supported by the fact that the number following
it — only consists of a single unit.") Mir leuchtet diese Erklärung
nicht ganz ein, denn die Verknüpfung mit den Pferdezeichen (siehe

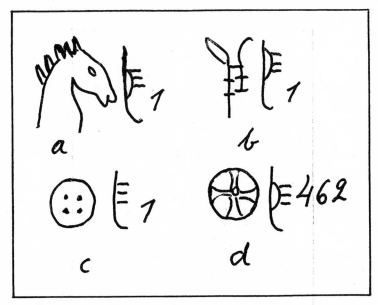

Figure 1

darüber noch unten) wäre dann doch schwer zu verstehen. Daß
wir hier das Sägezeichen vor uns haben, wie Evans angenommen
hat, dürfte allerdings richtig sein. Es ist nun auffallend, daß
sowohl das Pferde- wie das Radzeichen auch mit einem anderen
Zeichen kombiniert stehen kann, wie *Fig. 2* zeigt, das Evans (a.O.S.
807 Fig. 786) als "Whip"-Zeichen mit aller Wahrscheinlichkeit
richtig deutet. Die Peitsche, bei den Aegyptern besonders kostbar
mit Silber, Gold, Ebenholz und wertvollen Steinen besetzt, sym-
bolisierte dort die Würde hoher Hofchargen, wie der Wagenlenker
des Pharao (vgl. Erman, Aegypten S.654 f.). Etwas ähnliches kann
auch für das minoische Kreta angenommen werden (vgl. über

den ägyptischen Einfluß Evans a.O.S 803 f.). Sowohl das Säge-
wie das Peitschenzeichen daß dieses Zeichen auch als Schriftzeichen
und besonders häufig, als Endzeichen zu belegen ist, kommt hier
nicht in Betracht) wäre demnach ideographisch zu verstehen und
etwa auf das Ressort zwei verschiedener Palastfunktionäre oder
Palastdepartemente zu beziehen.

Eine völlig andere Erscheinung als diejenigen Täfelchen, die
einen ganzen Wagen abbilden, bieten die Urkunden, auf denen ein
Wagengestell ohne Räder aber mit Deichsel und Oberriemen (oder
Nebendeichsel, wie man diese Hilfskonstruktion nennen will) zu
sehen ist. Die nachfolgende Zahl ist klein, 1 — 3, aber der Text
um so länger (abgebildet Evans a.O. Fig. 764, 766ᵃ). Die Zeichen-

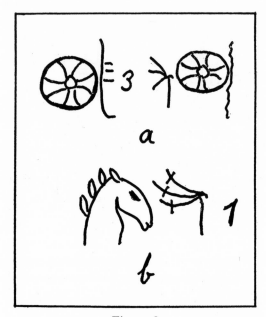

Figure 2

gruppen werden sicherlich noch für die phonetische Deutung von
grossem Wert sein.   Leider sind mehrere Exemplare solcher Urkunden recht fragmentarisch erhalten.   An diese Urkundengruppe
schließen sich diejenigen Täfelchen an, die nur leere Wagenkasten-
gestelle nebst Deichsel als Inventarobjekt abbilden (Evans a.O.S.
793 Fig. 766 b-e). Die Zahlen (in einem Ex. 100 Stück) zeigen
uns, daß es Inventarverzeichnisse manufakturartig hergestellter
Gegenstände sind, wie wir solche auch aus ägyptischen Abbildungen
kennen (vgl. Evans a.O. Fig. 765), die etwa gleichzeitig mit den

knossischen Täfelchen sind. Die vorangehenden Zeichengruppen (der Text) sind ebenfalls zahlreich, in allen Exemplaren begegnet dieselbe Hauptzeichengruppe. Werkstattmäßig werden auch Räder hergestellt, wie eine andere Kategorie von Täfelchen lehrt (vgl. Evans a.O.S. 793 f. Fig. 767 — 8), die mitunter hohe Zahlen (vgl. hier *Fig. 1 d*) aufweist. Die Fabrikation verteilt sich auf die beiden Palastfunktionäre oder Departemente, die mit dem Säge- bzw. Peitschenzeichen symbolisch bezeichnet werden.

Es gibt nun auch Inventartexte, die nur Panzer und Pferde verzeichnen (vgl. Evans a.O.S. 803 f.; vgl. auch das Täfelchen Fig. 763 i, wo nach Evans' Ansicht, S.787, der Pferdekopf auch für Wagen stünde, was ich nicht glauben kann). Diese Urkunden zeigen dieselbe kurze Fassung wie die vollständigen Wagenverzeichnisse, nur durch eine Hauptzeichengruppe eingeleitet. Auch hier sind kleine Zahlen, meistens 2 Brustharnische und 1 Pferd. Insofern sind sie im Großen und Ganzen inhaltlich verständlich, weisen aber einige rätselhafte ideographische Einzelheiten auf. Auf den Abbildungen der Brustpanzer steht mitunter das "Korn"zeichen ("Foddersign" nach Evans a.O.S. 801 f.), das Evans mit dem Futtern der Pferde in Verbindung setzt, das den "Knights" obliegt. Dasselbe Zeichen, als Endzeichen einer Gruppe bekannt, die als ein offizieller Titel aufzufassen sei (Evans a.O.S. 802), stünde demnach dort auch als Schriftzeichen ideographisch. Die Bedeutung ergibt sich, meiner Vermutung nach, aus der mit den Pferdeideogrammen parallelen Stellung, die wir in *Fig. 1 a b c* sehen können (daß in *b* eine stilisierte Pferdefigur gezeichnet wird, hat Evans klar nachgewiesen, a.O.S. 800). Statt also das Kornzeichen (*Fig. 1 c*) als Bezeichnung für "feeding of the horses in the royal stables" zu deuten, möchte ich darin ein ideographisches Equivalent für "Pferd" sehen, und eine Bestätigung in dem aus dem Aegyptischen übernommenen phonetischen Wert des Zeichens *sp* (vgl. meine Schrift der Ursprung d. kret. Schrift 1920, S.5 nr 5) finden. Es ist nämlich denkbar, daß die Minoer auch das Fremdwort mit der Uebernahme des Pferdes entliehen hatten, welches sie mit dem phonetischen Wert dieses Zeichens in ägyptischer Fassung wiedergaben (vgl. über das Wort für Pferd im Lykischen "esbe" Kretschmer, *Glotta* 27, 257).

Wo nun das in Frage kommende Zeichen auf dem Brustpanzer abgebildet wird, könnte es sich meines Erachtens auf besondere Persönlichkeiten oder Chargen des Palastes beziehen, die mit den Pferden zu tun hatten, unzweifelhaft hohe Palastbeamte. In denjenigen Zeichengruppen, wo das betreffende Zeichen deutlich als Determinativ steht, wären solche zu erkennen. Auf diejenigen Urkunden, in denen auf dem Panzer das Gefäßzeichen eingezeichnet ist, und die zu einer ganz anderen Kategorie von Inventaren als die oben besprochenen gehören, will ich hier nicht eingehen. Sie wären mit den Verzeichnissen der Vorratshäuser zusammen zu besprechen.

SAPPHO*

Immortal Sappho, maid divine,
Thou sharest with the heavenly nine
All honor. Shout through all the town
That on her head we place a crown.
Hasten with the chaplet green,
Greet her one and all as queen;
The Lesbian, a tenth muse we name,
And prophesy that her bright fame
Shall spread o'er all the world.
This title till the stars do fall,
Nations yet unborn shall call
And glorify her name.

Lucy Milburn

* The vignette, representing Sappho and designed by Professor Ilona Ellinger, very appropriately graces the title page of a volume honoring Professor Robinson whose work and verses on the great poetess are well known. The poem of Lucy Milburn is also offered in recognition of his contribution to our appreciation of Sappho.

A MINOAN NAME

CONST. D. KTISTOPOULOS
Athens

I would like to offer some suggestions relative to a hypothetical reading of a Minoan name as my contribution to the volume dedicated to the celebration of the seventieth anniversary of Professor David M. Robinson.

Sundwall cites the sign-groups ⟨signs⟩ and ⟨signs⟩.[1] I think, that the first of these is the same with the sign-group ⟨signs⟩ cited by Aug. Mosso,[2] which represents very probably a personal name. Its second sign is peculiar to Linear Script B.[3] According to the hypothetical phonetic values assigned provisionally by me to signs of the Linear Script B,[4] the sign-group ⟨signs⟩ should be read: "mu-ke/ki-še-še," so that we could get the hypothetical Minoan name "muke/i šeše."

Now, I notice that Bossert, in his article "Sur quelques problèmes historiques des inscriptions de Karatepé" [*Revue hittite et asianique*, 9 (1948-1949) 5] writes that a name "Muksas" occurs in the Hittite hieroglyphic texts, which name could also be read "Moksas," while in the Phoenician texts of Karatepé the same name is read "M-p-š" (= Mopsos). Furthermore, Bossert identifies the name "Mu/oksas" with the name "*Μόψος*" known from the Greek tradition, and which name is also cited as "*Μόξος*." On the other hand, "*Μόψος*," the founder of "*Μαλλός*" (Cilicia), is said to be the son of the Cretan "*Ῥάκιος*"; Bossert remarks on the point that ". . . . dans la tradition grecque transparaisse l' origine crétoise de la famille de Mopsos."

If my hypothetical reading of a Minoan name "Muke/išeše" should eventually be proved as acceptable, the identification or the near connection of this name with the Hittite "Mu/oksas" and the Phoenician "M-p-š," as well as with the names "*Μόψος*"-"*Μόξος*," would appear to be probable; in such event, another name might be added to the list of personal and place-names known as common to both Crete and Asia Minor.

*   *   *   *   *   *   *

Evans[5] cites the sign-group ⟨signs⟩ while, on the other hand, Sundwall cites the sign-group ⟨signs⟩.[5a] I had primarily assigned to

---

1. *Altkretische Urkundenstudien*, 2, No. 16.
2. *The Dawn of Mediterranean Civilization*, 30, fig. 7.
3. Evans, *P.M.*, IV, fig. 666, No. 37; Myres, J. L., "The Minoan Signary," *JHS* 66 (1946) 2, under No. II.
4. *A contribution to the problem of the Minoan Script*, and *Παρατηρήσεις τινὲς ἐπὶ τῆς Μινωϊκῆς γλώσσης*.
5. *P.M.*, IV, fig. 690, 708.
5a. *op. cit.*, fig. 26, p. 44.

the first sign, which is peculiar to Linear Script B,[6] the hypothetical phonetic value "o", but, after some elaborations of the material, I am led to the conclusion that this value appears as inadmissible; I now hesitate between two other values, one of which would be "mo." On the basis of that new hypothetical value the first of the above sign-groups should be read: "mo-ke/ ki-šo-*si* (?)," and the second: "mo-pe-šo-*si* (?)." In these hypothetical words "moke/kišo*si* (?)-mopešo*si* (?)" one sees an *enallage* of the sounds "k" and "p," exactly as in "Moksas-Moposos" (cf. also the Ionic use of "$\varkappa$" instead "π" : ὅχως = ὅπως, etc.).

The above-mentioned sign-groups are associated with the sign-groups ⏾⏦ and ⏾⏚ , which seem to have the hypothetical meaning of male and female children;[7] in such event, one might suppose, on the basis of my aforesaid hypothetical readings, that they indicate "children" relative, one way or another, to "*Μόψος-Μόξος*"-(line?, worship?, service?).

Finally, let me add that my hypothetical reading "-ke/ ki šo" of the termination "- ⏚⏦," occurring in some Minoan words, presents a similarity with the termination "kiš" of Hittite names, as for example: Khalkiš, Zulkiš, Mi/ unkiš, etc. (Cf. Hrozný, article "Hittites," Encyclopaedia Britannica, 1947, vol. II).

*   *   *   *   *   *   *

Certainly, the above conjectures are precarious. The Minoan γραμμάτων συνθέσεις persevere to keep their secrets. In my article "L' énigme Minoenne"[8] I have alluded to the heavy task which is in store for the scholars interested in the problem and which will have to be faced after the publication of the whole material of the Minoan inscriptions. Miss Kober, in her study "The Minoan Scripts: Fact and Theory,"[9] which is a fair and full statement of the question of the Minoan script, and of the problems and difficulties arising in the efforts for its decipherment, seemed to be pessimistic as to a quick success in this field. Possibly, the future will prove that Miss Kober is right. At any rate, with my optimistic disposition, I do not like to overlook the possibility that the work of scholars may also be favored by good fortune. Perhaps, besides human endeavors, πάντα ταῦτα θεῶν βοηθῶν καὶ τύχης δεῖται.

6. Evans, *P.M.*, IV, fig. 666, No. 31; Myres, *op. cit.*, under No. 60.

7. Evans, *P.M.*, IV, 708; Sundwall, *op. cit.*, 23, 44; *Weitere Bemerkungen zu den Hagia Triada Täfelchen III*, 26; Hrozný, *Les inscriptions Crétoises*, 130.

8. *Archiv Orientálni*, 17 (1949), No. I

9. *AJA* 52 (1948) 82-103.

THE DANCE IN ANCIENT CRETE

LILLIAN B. LAWLER

Hunter College of the City of New York

Among practically all peoples on the face of the earth today, dancing as an art is very old. As scholars learn more and more about the civilizations of ancient races, the antiquity of the dance seems to grow greater and greater; and indeed some students have called the dance the oldest of all the arts of man.

The Greeks, being a people of great intellectual curiosity, constantly strove to discover the origin or the "inventor" of this or that phase of their culture, and, naturally, included in their speculations much conjecture as to how the dance began. In general they seem to have come to the conclusion that the dance was divinely inspired— a direct creation of the gods, by them revealed to chosen mortals, who then taught it to their fellow men;[1] and the mortals most often named by the Greeks as those who had developed the art of the dance under divine inspiration and transmitted it to others were the Minoan Cretans.[2]

The persistent tradition among the Greeks that the Minoans had "invented" the dance would lead us to three conclusions: (1) that the Cretans were especially fond of, and skilled in, the dance; (2) that the Greeks knew of no ancient people whose dances antedated those of the Cretans; and (3) that the dances of the Cretans were highly developed even before the Heroic Age of the Greek mainland. Archaeological and literary evidence tends to substantiate all three of these conclusions. Sir Arthur Evans found evidence of habitation in Crete as early as the Neolithic period—that is, about 5,000 B. C.; and there is no reason to question the possibility that the neolithic Cretans had simple ceremonial dances. Even the Egyptian dance could hardly be of greater antiquity. In the earliest surviving literary work of the Greeks, the *Iliad*, with its memories of the Mycenaean Age, the skill of the Cretans in the dance and the fame of their ancient "dancing-place" at Knossos are accepted (*Iliad*, XVI, 617; XVIII, 590-606). From Homer to Athenaeus (XIV, 630 b) the idea that "the Cretans are dancers" is a literary commonplace; it is expressed with reference to both the prehistoric and the historic dwellers in the island. The physical characteristics of the Minoan Cretans, as we observe them in their art, are consistent with their reputed agility and dancing

---

1. Plato, *Legg.* II, 672-3; Libanius, *De Salt.* 56; *Anth. Plan.*, 286.
2. Athenaeus, V, 181 b; Lucian, *Salt.* 8; Strabo, X, 4, 18 and 16.

skill, and their love of rhythm and bodily activity. Temperamentally
(if we may judge from the material remains of their civilization) they
were a spirited, happy, alert, intelligent people, fond of life and color
and movement, and possessed of a keen sense of beauty. Furthermore,
Minoan art, even as early as about 1500 B. C., abundantly attests the
fact that at that time the Cretan dance was highly developed in choreography, in figures, and in steps; that it was refined out of all early
crudity; that it was on occasion vivacious or stately, solemn or
ecstatic; and that it was strikingly beautiful to look upon. It is
evident also that the dance was of the greatest importance in Crete,
not only as an amusement and spectacle, but, even more, as an integral
part of the state religion.

Of the actual dances performed by the Cretans, we have specific,
detailed information on some, and we can make reasonable inferences
about others. Certainly many of their dances must have vanished
without leaving a trace; but it is possible that we have a fair idea
of the nature of some of those which were most impressive and
distinctive.

Oldest of all the Cretan dances, according to the literary tradition,
were those of the Curetes (Lucian, *Salt.* 8). These were noisy,
frenzied, leaping dances of men, with much attendant shouting and
clashing of weapons. Their effect upon spectators was marked; we
are told (Strabo, X, 3, 7 and 11) that they inspired terror. The legend
that they were taught to the Curetes by the goddess Rhea, and were
first used to drown the cries of the infant Zeus, associates them from
the beginning with religion; and the preservation and repetition of
the dances through the centuries, by Curetes and others, including
even nobles and members of the royal family (Lucian, *Salt.* 8), em-
phasizes their great importance in the culture of Crete.

The identity of the Curetes has been a puzzle from the time of the
Greeks (cf. Strabo, X, 3, 6-8, 11, 19-23) to the present. Space forbids
a detailed discussion of this complicated problem. However, similar
dances are ascribed to the Corybantes of Asia Minor; to the Dactyli
of Mount Ida in Phrygia and Mount Ida in Crete; to the Cabiri on
Samothrace; and to the Telchines of Crete, Cyprus, and Rhodes
(Strabo, X, 3, 7, 19-23; cf. Eustathius, 771-2, on *Iliad,* IX, 525). The
actual dances would, of course, be performed by trained human
dancers, who would claim real or ritualistic descent from the legendary beings of the same name. All of these semi-mythical groups are
regarded as of great antiquity—the Curetes were, indeed, called the
sons of Earth (Strabo, X, 3, 19). All of them are associated, in one
way or another, with the worship of a great mother goddess; and

to all of them is ascribed skill in sorcery, in music and the dance, in invention, and, later, in the smelting of metals. They all come to be thought of as supernatural beings, *daimones,* or even minor deities. It is tempting to recognize as the basis in fact for each of them a hieratic family or tribe of "medicine men," cultural and religious leaders among their people in remote prehistoric times. A common Anatolian origin for both priesthood (if it may be so designated) and dance would definitely seem to be indicated.

A leaping dance, accompanied by as much noise as the dancers can possibly make, is common among many primitive peoples, in all parts of the world.[3] It is not essentially a war dance. Dances of this type are used by primitive peoples for two purposes: (1) to quicken the growing force in nature by restless activity, particularly by young dancers, and thereby to induce fertility in food plants, the high leaps serving as sympathetic magic to produce tall stalks; and (2) to frighten away evil spirits with loud and startling sounds. It is, then, a *magic* and *apotropaic* dance—i. e., in it the performers endeavor by magic to effect something desirable, and to ward off something evil, at the same time.

In its first form, the dance of the Curetes consisted undoubtedly of random, uncouth leaps, executed with as much energy as possible, and accompanied by blood-curdling yells. It is interesting to note that even in classical times certain Cretan dance-songs were notoriously loud (Strabo, X, 3, 16). As time went on, the dancers probably beat sticks together to add to the noise;[4] we may compare here the use of clappers as fertility magic at Egyptian vintage celebrations.[5] When the tribe learned the use of metals, the superior noise-making qualities of metallic objects would instantly become evident; the tradition that the Curetes and their Anatolian counterparts had a part in the invention of smelting is significant in this connection. There was certainly a phase of the dance in which any metal objects—cooking utensils, tools, double axes,[6] or weapons—would be used indiscriminately as noise-makers. The peculiar handiness of weapons would easily lead to their frequent use in the dance. Soon thereafter would come the wearing of armor by the dancers; and before long the old dance of fertility would become an armed dance. Lines of dancers would rush against each other, clashing shield on shield (Lucian, *Salt.,* 8); and individual dancers would beat their own shields with spears or swords.

---

3. Sachs, Curt, *World History of the Dance,* 26, 33, 87-8, and *passim.*
4. Lawler, Lillian B., "The Dance of the Pinakides," *TAPA* 71 (1940) 230-8.
5. Sachs, Curt, *Geist und Werden der Musikinstrumente,* 16.
6. Hall, H. R., *The Civilization of Greece in the Bronze Age,* Fig. 353, p. 276— a representation of "clashing double axes," according to Hall.

There is no evidence, however, that the dance of the Curetes, as performed in prehistoric Crete, was ever a combat or war dance; apparently it remained, as it began, a dance of fertility and a noise-making dance (Strabo, X, 3, 11). This is emphasized by the fact that cymbals and tympana began to be used to accompany the dance, and to increase its metallic noisiness.[7] The flute, too, served as accompaniment.

Greek writers, particularly Strabo, give us a few casual references to other aspects of the dance of the Curetes. Whether these are to be interpreted as features of the Minoan dance, or of an armed dance of the historical period, we cannot say; but presumably the Greeks thought of them in connection with the early form of the dance. We are told, for instance, that the dances sometimes formed a part of a mystery ritual (Strabo, X, 3, 7 and 9), and were performed in secret; and that in these mysteries the dances portrayed, mimetically, the story of the birth of Zeus and the attempt of Cronus to find and devour the child (Strabo, X, 3, 11). This association of the dance with a mystery cult would recall, incidentally, the connection of the dance with Samothrace. We are told also (Strabo, X, 3, 13) that the dance was sometimes performed in caves in Crete. The importance of caves in the religion of Minoan Crete,[8] not to mention the fact that a cave figures in the story of the birth of Zeus, would render this statement not inherently impossible; and votive cymbals have, in fact, been found in the Idaean cave in Crete. However, an outdoor locale, with forests and mountains (Diodorus, V, 66; Strabo, X, 3, 23), is more usually associated with these dances. Further, we are told (Strabo, X, 3, 21) that in these dances the performers "walked with a butting of their heads." This would seem to be an instance of popular etymology—an attempt to seek the origin of the word *Corybantes* in *koryttein*, "butt with the head," and *bainein*. However, if the dance did on occasion, as we are informed, set forth mimetically the story of the birth of Zeus, there may have been in it some portrayal of Amaltheia, the goat which suckled the divine child. It is an odd fact that among the names of dances which have come down to us from Greek times there is one, *nibatismos* or *nibadismos*, which has been interpreted[9] as denoting a goat dance. This dance is said to

---

7. Eustathius, 771-2, on *Iliad*, IX, 525. Cf. Nilsson, Martin P., *The Minoan-Mycenaean Religion*, 507; Evans, Sir Arthur, *The Palace of Minos*, III, 471-2 and Figs. 328, 329 a; Glotz, Gustave, *Aegean Civilization*, 296. The Corybantes are said to have invented tympana—Strabo, X, 3, 13.

8. Marinatos, Spyridon, N., "The Cult of the Cretan Caves," *Rev. of Relig.*, 5 (1941) 129-136; cf. Nilsson, *op. cit.*, 53, 471 and *passim*.

9. Meursius, Johannes, "Orchestra," in Vol. VIII of Jacobus Gronovius' *Thesaurus Graecarum Antiquitatum*, Venice, Typis Bartholomaei Javarina, 1732-37, s.v. *nibatismos*.

have been of "barbaric" origin (Hesychius, s.v.) ; it may have been Phrygian (Athenaeus, XIV, 629 d).

The Greeks associated their own Pyrrhic dance with that of the Curetes (Proclus, 246; Eustathius, 771-2, on *Iliad*, IX, 525). The word *pyrrhichē* troubled them. They explained it variously as from the name of Pyrrhus, son of Achilles, who is sometimes called the "inventor" of the Pyrrhic dance;[10] or from the name of one Pyrrhichus, who is called now a Cretan,[11] now a Lacedaemonian (Athenaeus, XIV, 630 e, f). Actually, the name is probably to be associated with the Greek *pyr*, "fire"[12]—not with reference to a funeral pyre (cf. Schol. Pind., *Pyth*. II, 127; Aristotle, frag. 519), but probably because the vigorous leaps of the dancers were thought of by the early Greeks as resembling leaping tongues of flame, shooting into the air (Marius Plotius, *De Metris*, 498). The Pyrrhic dance of the Greeks, as it changed character over the centuries, is somewhat outside the scope of the present discussion.[13]

Occasionally, in the literature of the Greeks, we come upon mention of other armed dances of Crete. We know very little about these dances; indeed, we do not know whether they were thought to be Minoan, or whether they were dances of Dorian Greeks living in Crete in the Hellenic period. If they were pre-Greek dances, it is possible that most of them were simply variants of the leaping dance of the Curetes. Among these dances are those called by the Greeks the *orsitēs*, the *epikrēdios*, and the *telesias*. The first two of these are mentioned by Athenaeus (XIV, 629 c) as being in the same category as the Pyrrhic dance; apart from this we know nothing of them. Some scholars, notably Meursius and Scaliger,[14] have regarded the *orsitēs* and the *epikrēdios* as the two principal subdivisions of the Cretan dance. There seems to be no ancient authority for this theory; and it is, in fact, probably the result of a misreading of a passage in Athenaeus (XIV, 629 c). Etymologically the *orsitēs* might denote a "stirring," "rousing," "inspiring" dance (from the Greek verb *ornymi*), and the *epikrēdios* a "brandishing" dance (from the Greek verb *kradaō*). Pollux (IV, 99) definitely calls the *telesias* an armed dance, says it was named for the Cretan dancer Telesias, and links it with the Pyrrhic. Hesychius (s.v. *telesias*) says it was done with a

---

10. Lucian, *Salt.* 9; Schol. Pind., *Pyth.* II, 127; Proclus, 246; Hesychius, s.v. *pyrrhichizein; Et. Mag.*, 699, 1; Marius Plotius, *De Metris*, pp. 497-8, Keil.

11. Pollux, IV, 99; Marius Plotius, *loc. cit.*; Hesychius, *loc. cit.*

12. Cf. Hesychius, *loc. cit.; Et. Mag.*, 699, 1.

13. See Latte, Kurt, "De Saltationibus Graecorum Capita Quinque," *Religionsgeschichtliche Versuche und Vorarbeiten*, 13 (1913), 27-63.

14. Meursius, *op. cit.*, s.v. *Krētikē;* Julius Caesar Scaliger, "De Comoedia et Tragoedia," in same volume of Gronovius, 1535 E, F.

sword. Whether the Macedonian *telesias* (Athenaeus, XIV, 629 d, 630 a) was identical with that of Crete or not, we do not know. Some scholars have associated the name of the dance with the Greek word *teletē,* "mystery ritual," and think it had a connection with the "passion plays" of the Cretans.[15] It is probable that all three of the names may denote dances of the Classical period, and not those of the Minoans at all.

In addition to these dances, there is some mention in Greek literature of a Cretan funeral dance, performed by men in armor. This dance was called the *prylis*—a word which we are told meant "footsoldier" in the speech of the people of Gortyn, "as say the men of old."[16] Some writers, both ancient and modern, have called this a dance of the island of Cyprus; but it is probable that this theory is the result of an error in the transmission of the text of a fragment of Aristotle.[17] The word *prylis* is used in Greek literature to denote an armed dance in general—that of the Curetes, for instance, or that of the Amazons, in honor of Artemis (Callimachus, *Hymn. Iov.,* 52; *Hymn. Art.,* 240). Armed dances around a corpse, a funeral pyre, or a burial mound seem to have been known to the Homeric Greeks. In classical and post-classical antiquity there was a tradition (Schol. Pind., *Pyth.* II, 127; Marius Plotius, *De Metris,* p. 498 Keil) that Achilles was the "inventor" of such armed dances. There is no confirmation of this in the *Iliad;* however, from various passages in the epic (*Iliad,* XXIII, 8-14, 130-4, 224-5; 259-897) we know that encircling processions of chariots or of men in armor were features of funeral ceremonies in the Heroic Age. Such processions are found among many peoples. Their chief purpose, aside from the primary one of honoring the dead, would seem to be either to endeavor, magically, by the display of physical activity, to infuse life again into the corpse, or to drive off evil spirits from the dead man, so that his spirit may rest, and not haunt the living. As the rhythmic processions develop, they usually take on the character of mimetic dances, portraying the valiant deeds performed in life by the dead man. Often they are transformed into actual armed combats, in which the flow of blood serves as a libation to the dead. We know little of the exact nature of the *prylis.* However, the solemn procession of men and women on the Hagia Triada sarcophagus, unarmed and bearing offerings, to the music of lyre and double flute, is evidence that the Minoans did actually have processional funeral dances of a sort.

15. Cf. Latte, *op. cit.,* 31.
16. Eustathius, 893, 37, on *Iliad,* XII, 77; Schol. Pind., *Pyth.* II, 127; Hesychius, s.v. *prylin.*
17. Frag. 519. Cf. Latte, *op. cit.,* 31-32.

Although the famous armed dances of Crete bulk large in the literature of the Greeks, they were by no means the only outstanding dances of the prehistoric inhabitants of the island. Certainly very old in Crete, as in all lands, were simple circle dances, closed and unclosed. A fragment of Sappho (Frag. 114, Edmonds) says: "Thus once upon a time the Cretan women danced rhythmically with delicate feet around a lovely altar, treading upon the soft, smooth flowers of the meadow." With this should perhaps be associated another fragment of the poetess,[18] which describes a sacred grove of apple trees, with a cool spring and blooming roses, and a flowery meadow nearby. In such lovely settings, apparently, did many of the Cretan dances take place.

Circle dances, and especially those with hands clasped, have, for all their simplicity, a highly mystical significance among all ancient peoples. They are often performed around an altar, a tree, a pillar or other sacred object, or around a musician. They enclose an object or person or place in a magic circle, purify it, and keep off evil influences. Some remnant of this thought and practice continues down from antiquity through all the centuries to modern times.

Perhaps the best-known example of a circle dance in Crete is that furnished by the famous terra cotta group from Palaikastro.[19] It depicts three small female figures moving in an unclosed circle around a lyre-player. The dance described in *Iliad*, XVIII, 590-606, is often taken as another example of a Cretan circle dance.[20] There youths and maidens, holding one another's wrists, run around lightly and rapidly, much as a vase spins on a potter's wheel, as the epic poet puts it. A cithara-player accompanies them, and two tumblers perform along with them. There is some doubt that the poet is here referring to a Cretan dance. What he actually seems to say is that the dancing-floor upon which the performance takes place is "like that which once in wide Cnossus Daedalus made for fair-haired Ariadne." Furthermore, there is evidence that the arrangement of dancers *anamix*, or men and women in alternation, was not used until after the fall of Crete, when somebody (traditionally Theseus) first used it on the island of Delos, in the *geranos* dance instituted to celebrate the end of Athenian subserviency to the Cretan Minotaur.[21] Even more

18. Page, D. L., *Greek Literary Papyri*, I, Poetry, 374-379; Turyn, *TAPA* 73 (1942) 308-318.

19. Dawkins, R. M., "Excavations at Palaikastro, III," *BSA* 10 (1903-4) 216-220; Evans, *op. cit.*, III, 72. Fig. 41.

20. Evans, *op. cit.*, III, 74-80.

21. Eustathius, 1166, on *Iliad*, XVIII, 590; cf. Pollux, IV, 101; Lawler, L. B., "The Geranos Dance—A New Interpretation," *TAPA* 77 (1946) 112-130.

important is the fact that, as we shall see in a moment, the dance of the *Iliad* is not a simple circle dance at all. However, there is no reason to doubt that the Cretans did have light, swift, circle dances, performed by either men or women dancers, but probably not by both together.

If we consider more carefully the dance described in the *Iliad*, it becomes evident that it has two basic figures. Immediately after the circular movement the dancers form two lines, which dance toward and away from each other (line 602). Such a dance may well have been found in ancient Crete—although it, too, would in all probability not be performed by men and women together. Dances of two opposing lines occur among most peoples. They range from simple advancing and retreating movements to the complicated "country dances" and "figure dances" of the nineteenth century, and include our own Virginia reel and other "square dances" which are at present enjoying a resurgence of popularity in this country.

It is known that the Egyptians had a dance mimetic of the movements of the heavenly bodies;[22] and many scholars think that the Minoans had one also. Such a dance could be performed by a group of dancers each of whom moved individually, representing a particular planet in its orbit; or it could have a choreography exactly like that of the dance described in the *Iliad*—a rapid circle, representing the movements of the planets through the skies, followed by a dance of two lines in opposition, representing the apparent approach of the various planets to the earth and to one another, and their subsequent separation. Oddly enough, Euripides, in the *Electra* (467), speaking of the very shield of Achilles which forms the basis for the description of the dance in the *Iliad*, says there were depicted on it "ethereal dances of stars." If there was an astronomic or celestial dance in prehistoric Greece or Crete, it may well have been similar to the dance of the *Iliad*. The author of the *Etymologicum Magnum* (690, 47) describes a "zodiacal" dance in which the group of dancers runs rapidly around an altar, first from right to left and then from left to right, finishing with a complete circling of the altar. In this connection it may be interesting to recall that among the Greeks Urania, patroness of astronomy, is also one of the Muses, patronesses of the dance; and that the Greeks saw in the movements of the planets a cosmic form of dance (Lucian, *Salt.* 7; Libanius, *De Salt.* 12).

Duncan Mackenzie, Sir Arthur Evans' associate in his excavations in Crete, expressed the opinion[23] that at times the circle dance became

22. Oesterley, W. O. E., *The Sacred Dance*, 69-70.
23. In "Cretan Palaces and the Aegean Civilization," *BSA* 12 (1905-1906) 249.

a sort of "skirt dance." In view of the prevailing costume of the Cretan women, it is entirely possible that Mackenzie was correct, and that on occasion a circle dance of women might be interrupted as the performers released one another's hands and slowly turned, each upon her own axis, while the full skirts swung out in the manner of a "nautch" dance. As a matter of fact, some definite evidence for a dance of this sort has been found. On a fresco of about 1500 B. C., from the queen's living-room in the palace at Knossos,[24] there is a delicate figure—a charming little lady, in the costume of the day, with left arm bent at the elbow, the forearm across the breast, and the right arm curving out low from the shoulder. Her long hair swings up from her shoulders on either side, forming the arc of a circle. It seems fairly certain that the figure is a dancer, whirling so rapidly that her hair flies out and up from her shoulders.

The circle dance also seems to have become at times an invocation dance, in which women dancers moved in a circle, and, with arms raised, besought the Great Goddess to appear to them.[25] There is evidence that in these cases they sometimes formed patterns or designs, and then stood still in formation, so that the goddess and the spectators might see them.[26] The "pictures" so made would, naturally, have a symbolical significance. In the northwestern part of the palace at Knossos, Sir Arthur Evans found bits of a miniature fresco which proved to be a representation of a ritual dance, performed in a theatral area filled with a gala crowd of excited spectators of both sexes.[27] Evans believed that the dance so depicted was identical with that of *Iliad* XVIII, 590-606; but the dancers are women only, and a close scrutiny of the fresco hardly substantiates Evans' belief. There is no circle formation, no formation of two opposing lines. The dancers perform individually, with hands free. The painting is not complete; nevertheless, the fourteen dancers who remain, on the right side of the composition, give some indication of a choreographic alignment similar to the pattern of a conventionalized lily, as it appears in fleur-de-lis form in Cretan art. The pattern is seen from the side, and a little aslant. We know that the lily was sacred to the Cretan

24. Evans, *op. cit.*, III, frontispiece; Plate xxv, facing page 370; Fig. 40, page 71.

25. For example, on the Isopata ring: Nilsson, *op. cit.*, Fig. 85, page 296; Evans, *op. cit.*, III, Fig. 38, page 68; Persson, Axel W., *The Religion of Greece in Prehistoric Times*, figs. 8a and 8b, page 173.

26. Lawler, Lillian B., "The Lily in the Dance," *AJP* 65 (1944) 75-80; Libanius, *De Salt.* 116, 118.

27. Evans, *op. cit.*, III, Plate xviii, facing page 66; also, pp. 66-80, and Fig. 38; II, 776.

goddess; and in Greek literature[28] "the lily" is mentioned as a figure in the dance. Another pattern which seems to have been used in the dance is that of a bunch of grapes—e.g., one woman in the first row, three in the second row, five in the third row, etc.[29] Such "living pictures" were evidently of great beauty.

There seem to have been invocation dances of another type in Crete. Nilsson[30] has set forth well the evidence pointing to a belief in bird epiphanies of deities on the part of the Minoans. To them, apparently, any bird descending from the sky might indicate the approach of the goddess. To invoke a deity, peoples in all parts of the world, in a form of sympathetic magic, employ dances mimetic of a sacred bird or animal, particularly one in whose form the deity is believed most likely to appear. Accordingly, it is not surprising to find bird motifs in the invocation dances of Crete. In the Palaikastro group, mentioned above, the three dancing women hold their arms out and up from the shoulders in a "wing" pose. Terra cotta doves, found with the figures, and apparently belonging to the group, confirm the bird-like impression given by the little dancers.[31]

One thinks in this connection of the large numbers of Late Helladic figurines depicting women, with both arms covered by the upper garment and raised in a winglike manner,[32] which have been found in various parts of the Greek mainland. The attitude is usually regarded as one of supplication; I would like to add the possibility of invocation, as in the Palaikastro group. The fact that the face is beaklike, as in other figurines of the period, is probably not significant. It is interesting to note that in Greek ceramic art there is a parallel to these figurines in the "wing-sleeved" dancers in Dionysiac settings—women dancers with arms outspread in a winglike manner, and with one or both hands covered by, or twisted into, the garment.[33] These figures are, in fact, one of the most characteristic features of the Dionysiac dance as portrayed for us on Greek vases.

This brings us to dances of a different type—those in which the

---

28. Athenaeus, III, 114 f; Hesychius, s.v. *krinon;* cf. Lawler (see note 26). 75-80.

29. Riess, Ernst, "Hesychiana," *CW* 37 (1944) 240-1; cf. Hesychius, s.v. *botrydon.*

30. *Op. cit.,* 285-293.

31. Lawler, Lillian B., "The Dancing Figures from Palaikastro," abstracted in the *AJA* 44 (1940) 106; also, "The Dance of the Holy Birds," *CJ* 37 (1941-42) 351-361.

32. Robinson, David M., "A Small Hoard of Mycenaean Vases and Statuettes," *AJA* 54 (1950) 6-9 and Plate VII. In note 29, page 6, Dr. Robinson lists many of the more famous of these figurines.

33. Lawler, Lillian B., "The Maenads," *Memoirs of the American Academy in Rome* 6 (1927) 69-112 and Plates 14, No. 2; 16, Nos. 2 and 3; 17, No. 1.

dancers wear bird or animal costumes or masks, and think of themselves as partaking of the nature of sacred animals. In all the lands around the Mediterranean there is evidence from earliest times of ritualistic animal dances or mummery; and Crete seems no exception to the rule. Animal dances are customarily undertaken for a variety of purposes—e.g., to honor a supposed animal ancestor, to secure communion with an animal god, to worship a sacred animal, to invoke or win the support of a deity to whom the animal in question is sacred, to induce fertility by the imitation of a fertile animal, to secure to the worshipper some characteristic of the animal imitated, etc. Garbed in skins or in animal costumes, and masked, the dancers think of themselves as partaking of the nature of the sacred animals. Primitive dances of this type are often preserved for centuries, and kept from deteriorating into uproarious burlesque, by means of the secrecy and rigorous prescription of detail of a mystery cult—as e.g., in that of Mithras.[34] Sometimes they become formalized into symbolic rituals, in which the garment of skin worn by the worshipper is the sole visible link with the primitive animal dance. In this connection we recall the importance of garments of skin in Cretan religion.[35]

In 1901, D. G. Hogarth found in Crete a large number of moulds for seals,[36] on many of which appears a single figure of the type which both Evans and Hogarth call the "Eagle-Lady." In its most striking form it is seen as a bird-headed, winged woman, apparently engaged in a vigorous dance step. The breasts are prominent, and the dress is typically Cretan. Other moulds show what appear to be bird-masks. Hogarth (p. 91) did not believe that the figures represented any cult ritual, but held that they were purely fanciful. However, some scholars believe it highly probable that these representations portray a real cult dance, performed in hood-like masks and elaborate winged costumes. I am inclined to agree with them, and to see in the sealings a portrayal of a ritual dance requiring great speed and vigor, and making use of violent arm *schēmata* suggesting the movement of wings.[37] It may have been performed by solo dancers; or, on the other hand, the single figure of a small mould may have been representative of a group of cult dancers.

Much disputed, but not to be ignored, is the possibility that the Minoans may have had a ritual dance in which a male dancer wore

---

34. Lawler, Lillian B., "Pindar and Some Animal Dances," *CP* 41 (1946) 155-9.

35. Nilsson, *op. cit.*, 132-3; Persson, *op. cit.*, 43, 161; Cook, A. B., "Animal Worship in the Mycenaean Age," *JHS* 14 (1894) 161-169.

36. "The Zakro Sealings," *JHS* 22 (1902) 76-93.

37. Lawler, Lillian B., "The Dance of the Holy Birds," *CJ* 37 (1941-42) 355-7.

a headdress representing a bull[38]—thereby giving rise to the story of the Minotaur. If this was indeed so—and there is some evidence that it may have been—the dancer would perhaps be the king or his son. We know that among the Egyptians[39] and the ancient Hebrews[40] the king sometimes performed a solemn dance in important religious ceremonies.

There is considerable evidence of a cumulative nature for a pig or boar dance, common to Crete and prehistoric Thrace.[41] It is probable also that the Minoans had masked dances in which the dancer portrayed a bee, a fish, a lion,[42] a stag, a goat, or an ass.[43] One writer even believes he has found evidence for a mask that looks like the face of a fly![44]

On Cretan rings and other art objects there are frequently seen creatures which are usually called "daemons."[45] They look like strange animals, walking erect, and wearing the skins of other animals over their heads and upon their backs. Frequently the skin so worn ends in a long tail. Many of these composite figures have human hands and feet, and all of them wear girdles, which seem to hold the skin which is worn upon the back. These facts lead many writers to believe that the figures are really masked dancers, although a few still look upon them as completely imaginary. Often they carry something —water-jugs, for instance, or, sometimes, dead animals. Their association with religious ritual seems certain; some of them, for instance, appear in connection with the double axe and other sacred symbols. They would seem to be votaries, performing in a processional dance, sometimes perhaps in connection with the ceremonial watering of a sacred tree, sometimes in a ritual of offering or libation, sometimes in the consecration of the first wine of the season. Similar figures are to be found in Assyrian and Babylonian art.

Among later writers there is a persistent tradition of a maze or labyrinth dance among the Cretans, in which the dancers pursued a

---

38. Cf. Cook, A. B., *Zeus*, I, 472-495.

39. Kees, Herman, *Der Opfertanz des ägyptischen Königs*, Hinrichs, Leipzig, 1912.

40. II Samuel, VI, 14-16; cf. Oesterley, *op. cit.*, 31-42, 54-8 and *passim*.

41. Lawler, Lillian B., and Kober, Alice E., "The Thracian Pig Dance," *CP* 40 (1945) 98-107.

42. Lawler, Lillian B., "Ichthyes Choreutai," *CP* 36 (1941) 142-155: "A Lion among Ladies," *TAPA* 78 (1947) 88-98.

43. Cook, A. B., "Animal Worship in the Mycenaean Age" (see note 35), 81-169. This, although rendered obsolete in some details by later discoveries, yet remains a challenging paper, of deep interest to students of the ancient dance.

44. Herkenrath, Emil, "Mykenische Kultszenen," *AJA* 41 (1937) 419.

45. Nilsson, *op. cit.*, 317-330; Cook, "Animal Worship" (see note 35), 81-169; Persson, *op. cit.*, 76-9 and Plate 24, p. 179.

winding course suggestive of the devious passages of a maze. Some scholars have tried to associate this dance with the one mentioned in *Iliad*, XVIII, 590-606. However, as we have seen, that dance consists of a crisp, rapid circle movement, followed by forward and backward motions of two lines; and the essence of a maze or labyrinth dance is not the attaining of any goal, but rather a continuous, never-ending twisting and untwisting. Dances of the maze type are common to all early peoples, in all parts of the earth, whether they have labyrinthine buildings and caves or not;[46] and many historians of the dance trace them all to a very primitive dance form which is nothing but an imitation of the crawling of a snake.

It is highly probable that the Cretans may have had a snake dance as a part of the ritual of their goddess.[47] We know that dancing played a vital part in their rituals. Also, the importance of the snake in their religion is well attested. Among them the snake was semi-divine; some scholars even think that in primitive days their goddess herself was a sacred snake—perhaps a python, brought from Egypt, where a great snake was regarded as the embodiment of the fertility goddess Rannut. Certainly we hear a great deal about giant serpents in sacred spots in Crete and Greece;[48] and the snake is frequently portrayed in Cretan art. Also, many archaeologists see in the art motifs of the maze, the meander, the chevron, and the spiral a conventionalization of a snake; and Sir Arthur Evans[49] detected in a Cretan design frequently seen at Knossos a conventionalization of the markings on an adder.

There is reason to believe that the Minoans had a solemn snake dance, performed at night, by torchlight. The long line of worshippers, carrying a snake or a replica of one, or with hands crossed in front of the body to represent a snake, seem to have wandered in a sinuous path. Some students of the ancient dance think that a dance of this type was performed in the gloom of the many caves in the mountains near Knossos. It may have been climaxed by the exhibition of a living python. Certainly such a performance would have been weird and spectacular in the highest degree. It is highly prob-

46. Space does not permit a discussion of the problem of the labyrinth itself; see Lillian B. Lawler, "The Geranos Dance," *TAPA* 77 (1946) 119, note 19.

47. *Ibid.*, 112-130.

48. Aelian, *Nat. Animal.* 11, 2; Schol. Aristoph. *Nub.* 508; Herodotus, VIII, 41; Aristophanes, *Lys.* 758; Philostratus the Elder, II, 17, 6; Pindar, *Pyth.* IV, 244; Apollodorus I, 9, 16; Hesiod, *Theog.* 333; Apollon. Rhod., IV, 1396 ff. Cf. Küster Erich, *Die Schlange in der griechischen Kunst und Religion*, Giessen, Töpelmann, 1913, *passim*.

49. *P.M.*, IV, 178-192.

able that the *geranos* dance of Delos, which was not a "crane" dance but a chthonic maze dance used originally as a victory celebration, was derived from a Minoan dance of this nature;[50] however, the alternation of male and female dancers so characteristic of the *geranos* would not be a feature of the Minoan prototype.

Cretan figurines attest the fact that there were in Crete snake-handling rituals, in which women votaries or priestesses of the Cretan goddess carried small, living snakes in their hands, or allowed the reptiles to coil about their necks and shoulders.[51] Snake-handling in religious rituals is a very ancient practice. It is almost always accompanied with shouts or hymns, and with a shuffling sort of dance. It is attended with a considerable amount of religious frenzy, and is always profoundly horrible to look upon. (Observers have often commented upon the fierce intensity of the expression on the faces of the Cretan figurines.) Similar dances are found in many other civilizations. They may be seen among the Hopi Indians, and also among the devotees of the various snake-handling cults in the mountains of Tennessee today. Usually snake-handling is found among primitive or retarded peoples. In Crete the early practice seems to have become fixed in cult ritual and preserved, probably through the agency of special priestesses, down into the era of high civilization.[52]

In the wild dances of the Dionysiac rituals of Thrace and Phrygia, which have a recognizable connection with some of the Cretan rites, snakes were sometimes torn to pieces by frenzied women votaries (Galen, *De antid.*, 1, 6, 14). Whether the Cretan dancers went to this extreme or not we do not know. There is a tradition of the tearing to pieces of a live bull in certain Cretan ceremonies.[53] In such cases, it is highly probable that the dancers were under the influence of narcotics. In Greek times, there were "snake mysteries," apparently with snake-handling, in honor of the goddess Athena, on the Acropolis at Athens, down to a late period; and the Christian St. Cyprian speaks (*Confess.* 1; cf. Eudocia, *De S. Cypr.*, II, 20-1) of having been initiated into these "mysteries" at the age of ten.

Sometimes, in Greek rites, snakes were carried in covered baskets during ceremonial dances and processions, especially those connected with mystery rituals. In all likelihood this custom was of Cretan origin.

---

50. Lawler, L. B., "The Geranos Dance," *TAPA* 77 (1946).

51. Evans, *P.M.*, IV, Fig. 139, p. 177; Figs. 149 and 150, pp. 194-5; also, Bossert, H. T., *The Art of Ancient Crete*, Figs. 289 and 290.

52. Lawler, L. B., "Snake Dances," *Archaeology* 1 (1948) 110-113.

53. Firmicus Maternus 84; cf. Johannes Leipoldt, "Dionysos," *Angelos*, Beiheft 3, Leipzig, Pfeiffer, 1931, 2, 39-40.

Similar, in appearance, at least, to the dance in which the replica of a great serpent is carried is a garland-carrying dance.[54] There is specific evidence[55] that in ancient Crete there was celebrated a festival called the Hellotia, in which a huge garland of myrtle was borne in procession. Inside the garland, we are told, were "the bones of Europa, whom they call Hellotis." The garland is said to have been thirty feet "in circumference." This probably refers not to the circumference of the strand of the garland, but to the perimeter of the garland when carried in a closed circle formation; for in a well-known account of a similar ritual (Athenaeus, V, 202 d, e) a garland three feet high has a "perimeter" of twenty-four feet.

Europa, or Hellotis, as she seems to have been called on occasion, (one writer — *Et. Mag*, s.v. *Hellotia* — says that the word *hellotia* means "maiden" in the Phoenician tongue) was apparently a lesser divinity or spirit of the Cretans, a personification of the vegetation which dies and is reborn each year. There is some hint that fire is important in her cult.[56] The large garland carried in her festival has been connected by several scholars[57] with the May garlands of Europe, which are burned on bonfires at the Midsummer festival. Such a ceremony is both a "sun charm" and a vegetation rite. Worshippers believe that it increases mystically the life-giving power of the sun, and ensures the rebirth in the new season of the dead food-plants. The effect of the garland-carrying ceremony would have been not unlike that of the "daisy chains" and similar processions at Commencement exercises in various colleges today. As Cook and Nilsson point out,[58] the garland carried in procession at the Hellotia must have had a puppet inside it, perhaps "the relic of a dead heroine." The garland-carrying dance or procession of the Hellotia was taken over by the Greeks, and perpetuated, notably at Corinth. A variant of it, in both Crete and Greece, seems to have been a dance in which green or flowering branches were carried in honor of a divinity of vegetation or of flowers.[59]

A garland-carrying dance seems to have been performed also in honor of the goddess or spirit of childbirth, Eileithyia, both in ancient Crete and later on the island of Delos. A garland was sacred to her

---

54. Lawler, Lillian B., "A Necklace for Eileitthyia," *CW* 42 (1948) 2-6.

55. Athenaeus, XV, 678 a, b; *Et. Mag.*, s.v. *Hellotia;* Schol. Pind., *Ol.* XIII, 40; Hesychius, s.vv. *Hellotia* and *hellotis.*

56. Nilsson, Martin P., *Griechische Feste*, 94-6.

57. Cook, A. B., *Zeus* I, 525-530; 338-9; Farnell, Lewis R., *Cults of the Greek States*, II, 479.

58. Cook, A. B., *op. cit.*, I, 525; Nilsson, *Griech. Feste*, 96.

59. Cf. Persson, *Religion of Greece in Prehistoric Times*, 57, pl. 13.

from remote antiquity; and the carrying of a large one would serve
to thank her for past kindnesses to the community, to please her,
and to move her to renewed beneficence. In Greek times this changes
from a garland-carrying dance to one in which a "chain" of the
joined or crossed hands of the dancers represents the garland—
whence the Greek name for the dance, *hormos*, a "chain." At this
point it is danced by youths and maidens alternating, in the arrangement of the *geranos* (Lucian, *Salt*. 12). Ultimately (Apuleius, *Met*.
10) vigorous warlike motifs, for the youth, at least, seem to have
been introduced into the dance.[60]

Another Cretan dance in which objects were carried in procession
is the one depicted in low relief on the famous "Harvester Vase,"
found at Hagia Triada.[61] Archaeologists have differed in their interpretation of the scene;[62] but the most plausible explanation would
seem to be that it is a harvest festival, a ceremonial gathering of the
crops, accompanied with song and dance and general merriment.
With consummate skill, and with a great deal of vividness, the Cretan
artist has shown us the happy villagers. They swing along four
abreast, in step, their legs raised high at every stride. Their heads
are thrown back, and some of them have their mouths open in song.
Over their shoulders they carry long objects which have been variously interpreted as sheaves of wheat, reaping tools, pitchforks,
weapons, or even "tridents for spearing fish," but which are probably flails. Their leader, an elderly man, is clad in a rough, heavy
cloak, so stiff that it is almost bell-like. Small as the scale of the cup
is, the man's beard and facial expression are quite clear. Behind him
are three cloaked figures which are often interpreted as "girl chor-
isters"; their mouths are open wide, and they seem to sing. A second
man, his head back and his mouth open, shakes a sistrum, an Egyptian
musical instrument which is in essence a metal rattle with vibrating
wires. Evans compares him with a representation on a seal, an intense, ecstatic face of Libyan type. He calls him a "Dervish priest,"
and thinks the vase is evidence that the orgiastic dances of North
Africa had a marked influence upon Crete.[63] One of the men dancers
on the vase, apparently carried away in the excitement of the occasion,
stoops down and dances in a crouching position. It has been pointed

---

60. Lawler, Lillian B., "A Necklace for Eileithyia," *CW* 42 (1948) 2-6.

61. Evans, *Palace of Minos*, II, Plate xvii; Bossert, *op. cit.*, Figs. 276-281, incl.

62. Glotz, *op. cit.*, 274; Hall, H. R., *Aegean Archaeology*, 62-3; Plate xvii; C. H.
and H. B. Hawes, *Crete the Forerunner of Greece*, 128-9; Mosso, Angelo, *The
Palaces of Crete and Their Builders*, 166-172 and Fig. 75; Baikie, James, *Sea
Kings of Crete*, 124-5, 226-7, and Plate xxvii, facing p. 209; Evans, *Palace of
Minos*, II, 47-8, 278, Fig. 22 a and b, and Plate xvii; IV, 217-220.

63. *P.M.*, IV, 217-220.

out[64] that even today in Crete, during the village festivals, a dancer will, from time to time, stoop and strike the earth, then rise again, all in rhythm. Striking the earth is fertility magic from the earliest days of man—an effort to stir the earth to renewed production. No two of the figures on the vase are alike, and the whole scene gives a convincing illusion of reality.

Somewhat akin to the harvest dance is the dance of the first fruits —a ceremony in which the first few grains of the food crops are carefully garnered, placed in ritual vessels, carried in procession to the altar of the goddess of vegetation, and offered to her in thanksgiving. The vessel used, taken over later by the Greeks and by them called a *kernos*, was of a distinctive type—a pan-like receptacle for smaller vessels, the whole set upon a sort of pedestal or ring. In each of the tiny cups was placed a different kind of grain, or a little milk, oil, wine, or water. The *kernos* had a place in the Greek mysteries at Eleusis—mysteries which many scholars regard as of Cretan origin.[65] A vessel of the same type is still used today, for the blessing of the first fruits, in the Greek Orthodox Church.[66] Cretan *kernoi* have been found in abundance by excavators.[67] One late example, from the Cretan town of Kourtes, is especially interesting.[68] In consists of a ring of stout red clay, upon which are set six small cups. Three little human figures are placed upon the ring, alternating with cups; of these, one holds its hands to the head, one holds its hands to its breast, and one takes hold of the cups next to him (or her—the sex is indeterminate). The excavator, Xanthoudides, associated the figures with the later Greek dance known as the "kernos-carrier"—*kernophoros* or *kernophoron orchēma* (Pollux, IV, 103). Athenaeus (XIV, 629 d) tells us that this dance was ecstatic, thereby implying a ritual of joy and exuberance similar to that on the Harvester Vase—and also, perhaps, the use of wine in the ritual. The dancers of the kernos-carrying dance may have been women; they may have accompanied a priestess or attendant who carried the *kernos* upon her head. The excavator sees a parallel in the fact that in the Greek Orthodox Church the priests carry the Eucharist in vessels upon their heads.

Not unlike the dance of the first fruits is the gift-bearing procession. In the entrance corridor of the west porch of the palace at Knossos, Evans found remains of a great mural painting representing

---

64. Mosso, *op. cit.*, 170.
65. Cf. Persson, *op. cit.*, 79.
66. Xanthoudides, S., "Cretan Kernoi," *BSA* 12 (1905-6) 9-23.
67. Evans, *Palace of Minos* I, 75-6, and Figs. 43 and 44; Nilsson, *Minoan-Mycenaean Religion*, 387.
68. Xanthoudides, *op. cit.*, Fig. 3, p. 16.

such a procession.[69] He believed that originally the painting continued for some distance on adjacent walls, and that it contained at least 356 life-sized figures. The ceremony so portrayed must have been of considerable importance. Extant fragments of the painting show, for the most part, young men of high station and aristocratic bearing, carrying cups and vases, apparently as offerings. One section of the fresco, however, depicts the lower portions of six men clad in the long robe that is characteristic of musicians and singers. One woman, in the Cretan flounced skirt, accompanies them. The presence of musicians attests the formal nature of the procession, and stamps it as a dance, in the ancient sense of the word. Farther along is seen an elaborately dressed female figure, toward which four pairs of youths move, two pairs on either side. Evans thinks this is a representation of the goddess, and believes that the whole procession is a ritual dance in her honor. Other gift-bearing processions have been found in Cretan art, but none so fine as this. Also, Egyptian art sometimes shows gift-bearing processions of Cretans, making offerings to the Egyptian king;[70] but these paintings contain no musicians, and we cannot be sure they are to be considered as representing processional dances.

As we have seen, rites in honor of a vegetation deity, and of other deities as well, sometimes become ecstatic—that is, the dancer passes into a sort of delirium or trance, and believes that the deity has taken possession of his body and mind. In this state dancers often utter strange sounds and words that are taken as prophecies and other messages from the divinity. It is practically certain that ecstatic dances were well known in Crete, as they were among the Egyptians, Assyrians, Hittites, and Hebrews,[71] and among the Greeks and the peoples of Asia Minor in classical times. Among the Cretans they were apparently performed by men or by women. As we have already noted, wine or narcotics may have been a contributory agency in the production of the ecstatic state in the dancer.

Ecstatic dances are often associated with "mystery" plays and sacred dramas; and we know from many sources[72] that the Cretans were famous for such rituals. At the cave on Mount Ida, as we have noted, they enacted in pantomimic dance the birth of the son of the Great Goddess and the way in which he was saved and protected by

---

69. *P.M.*, II, 720-5 and Plate xii.

70. *Ibid.*, II, Figs. 470-4, 482.

71. *Ibid.*, III, 68-70, and Fig. 39; II, 614 and Fig. 386; Persson, *op.cit., passim;* Oesterley, *op. cit.*, 108-9; cf. I Samuel, X, 5.

72. Strabo, X, 3, 11; Diodorus, V, 77, 3; cf. Nilsson, *op. cit.*, 403, 504-8; Persson, *op. cit.*, 148-150.

the Curetes.[73] It is perhaps in this connection that one armed dance came to be called *telesias*. In similar dances they portrayed the death and rebirth of a divinity representing vegetation, and in so doing held out a hope of immortality to man, with a life of eternal happiness in the "Isles of the Blest" across the seas.[74] Some of these "passion plays" may have been part of a solemn initiation, in the manner of the later "mystery" cults; but it is certain that some of them, at least, were open to all who cared to view them.[75] In some of them there appears to have been a sort of "throne dance" the exact nature of which is undetermined. It may have been a dance around a throne believed to be occupied by the spirit of the deity, or actually occupied by an image of the deity; or, on the other hand, it may have been a mystic circle dance around a person to be initiated — perhaps to purify him symbolically.[76] In any case, the Cretan "passion plays" were undoubtedly of spectacular beauty, and were awe-inspiring in the extreme, with their wild accompaniment of flutes, cymbals, and hand-drums, and the loud outcries of the worshippers.

We have noted the fact that many rhythmic activities which we should hardly call dances were so considered by the peoples of the ancient world. In this category should be included the ritual swinging of young girls. In a small domestic shrine in the Cretan city of Phaestos, Evans found a terra cotta figurine which could be interpreted only as a girl swinging.[77] With it were found two side posts, each surmounted by a dove, the symbol of the presence of the Great Goddess. As Evans pointed out, swinging is "a religious rite the world over," to drive away demons, to draw inspiration from the spirits in the air, and to ensure good (i.e., high) crops. The ritual was part of the Athenian festivals of the Aiora and the Anthesteria, and is portrayed on Greek vases[78]. It is practiced to this day in Greece, on holy days, notably Easter and St. George's day. Undoubtedly the Greeks derived the swinging "dance" ultimately from the Minoans.

On several gold rings found in Crete and in the neighborhood of

73. Strabo, X, 3, 7; cf. Swindler, Mary H., *Cretan Elements in the Cults and Ritual of Apollo*, 9.

74. Nilsson, *op. cit.*, 512, 542-559; Cook, *Zeus* I, 673.

75. Diodorus, V, 77, 3; Porphyry, *De antro nymph.* 20; Hoeck, Karl, *Kreta*, Göttingen, Rosenbusch, 1823-29, III, 308-9; Persson, *op. cit.*, 148-150.

76. Nock, A. D., "A Cabiric Rite," *AJA* 45 (1941) 577-581; "Notes on Reliefs and Myths—II, Thronosis," *JHS* 46 (1926) 47-8; Cook, *Zeus* II, 120, 838, 852, 893, 940; Latte, *op. cit.*, 95-6; Dio Chrysostom XII, 33, 388 R; Manetho, IV, 104; Plato, *Euthyd.* 227 D; Hesychius, s.v. *perichorizein*; cf. Persson, *op. cit.*, 56.

77. *P.M.*, IV, 24-7; Bossert, *op. cit.*, Fig. 291.

78. F.-Reichhold, *Griechische Vasenmalerei*, Pl. 125; text, pp. 28-9.

Mycenae, there are represented ritual scenes which apparently involve a group of related dances.[79] In the scenes, a man or a woman is depicted as shaking or pulling down a branch or the trunk of what is obviously a sacred tree, growing in an enclosure. In most cases the tree is laden with fruit; and Evans has conjectured[80] that in such representations a votary is offering sacred sustenance to the mother goddess, whom he recognizes in the large female figure seen on most of the rings, usually in the center of the composition. Glotz[81] regards the scenes as representing a seasonal and ceremonial plucking of sacred fruit from a consecrated tree. However, it is noteworthy that in several cases the large female figure (whether goddess or attendant of the shrine) definitely looks as if she might be striking, or threatening to strike, the man or woman seizing the sacred branch. In most of these representations the figure grasping the tree is evidently moving stealthily or cautiously. Frequently the scene looks very much like an attempted theft of sacred fruit. Many scholars have expressed their feeling that various figures on the rings seem to be taking part in a dance; but interpretations of the nature of the dance have varied widely—e.g., "mourning," "joy," "frenzy," "sacred communion," etc. It seems not unreasonable to see in the representations a Cretan prototype for the food-stealing and beating dances performed, for example, at the shrine of Artemis Orthia in Sparta and other Greek cities, in classical times.[82] In these dances, young men endeavored to steal food from an altar, and were ceremonially beaten with clubs or whips by attendants at the shrine. It is interesting to observe that sometimes the large female figure on the Cretan rings has her arms markedly akimbo, in a gesture which Evans interpreted as symbolizing hunger; it looks more like a raising of the arms in a threatening gesture against the real or ritualistic intruder.[83] The same gesture is seen frequently on Cretan figurines; they are always female figures, be it noted, and they are probably representations of the Great Goddess.

---

79. Persson, *op. cit.*, Ring No. 3, pp. 37-8; No. 4, p. 39; No. 17, pp. 64-5; Evans (see note 7), III, Fig. 91, p. 140; Furtwaengler, *Antike Gemmen*, Pl. VI, 3; Nilsson (see note 7), Pl. I, 2.

80. *P.M.*, I, 162; III, 142-3.

81. *Aegean Civilization*, 274.

82. *Pollux*, IV, 105; Athenaeus, XIV, 621 d, e; Herodotus, III, 48, 2; Hesychius, s.v. *klōpeia;* Plutarch, *Arist.* 17; Plato, *Legg.* I, 633 B; Xenophon, *Lac.* II, 9. See also Bosanquet, R. C., "Excavations at Sparta, 1906," *BSA* 12 (1905-6) 338-343; Rose, H. J., in R. M. Dawkins, *The Sanctuary of Artemis Orthia at Sparta*, 405; Rose, H. J., "Greek Rites of Stealing," *HThR* 34 (1941) 1-5; Lillian B. Lawler, "The Dance of the Ancient Mariners," *TAPA* 75 (1944) 20-33; "Four Dancers in the *Birds* of Aristophanes," *TAPA* 73 (1942) 61-3.

83. Evans, *Palace of Minos* I, 161 and Fig. 116. Bossert, *op. cit.*, Fig. 399 f. Lawler, Lillian B., "Dancing with the Elbows," *CJ* 38 (1942) 161-3.

Further light on the rings is, I believe, to be found in the Greek writer Callimachus (*Hymn. Del.* 316-324). He tells us that on the island of Delos, in Greek times, mariners landed briefly to perform an ancient dance, in which they "whirled around the altar," and "bit the sacred trunk of the olive, holding their hands behind their backs." From other sources (Hesychius, s.v. **Dēlkakos bōmos*, which should be emended to *Deliakos*) we learn that in the dance the sailors were beaten. Biting a sacred tree or piece of wood is an old charm to avert evil; and food-stealing and beating dances are common in purificatory and fertility rites, among many primitive peoples.[84] Connections between Delos and ancient Crete are close; and it is probable that there is a relationship between the Delian ceremonies and the Cretan rings. The importance of ritualistic scourging in the cult of the great Cretan goddess has often been pointed out.[85] As for the movements of the beaten men, as they twisted and wriggled to avoid the scourging, there is some likelihood that they formed a dance similar to that known in Greek times as the *mothōn*—a contorted, writhing dance which survived down into classical times among the Helots of Sparta.[86]

Among other dances specifically associated with prehistoric Crete by Greek writers is the acrobatic dance or dance of the tumblers. To the modern reader, activity of this sort hardly seems to be real dancing; we regard the field of tumbling and that of dancing as essentially distinct. To the Greek and the Cretan, however, there seems to have been no such hard and fast distinction. Tumbling was regularly performed to music, rhythmically, and that made it a dance. Associated with juggling and magic, it was regarded as related to religious frenzy (Strabo, X, 3, 23).

Athenaeus tells us definitely (V, 180 f-181 b) that the use of tumblers for entertainment, at festivals and at dinners, is a borrowing from the Cretan dance; and he goes on to say that both dancing and tumbling are indigenous to the Cretans. In making these remarks, Athenaeus is commenting on a passage in the *Odyssey* (IV, 15-19) and one in the *Iliad* (XVIII, 590-606), the latter of which we have considered above. In each, two tumblers perform, whirling among dancers. There has been much discussion of the epic passages. Some

---

84. Lawler, Lillian B., "Beating Motifs in the Greek Dance," *CO* 21 (1944) 59-61; " 'Flat Hand' in the Greek Dance," *CO* 19 (1942) 58-60. Nilsson, *Griechische Feste*, 192-4, 466.

85. Persson, *op. cit.*, 110, 122; Lawler, "The Dance of the Ancient Mariners," *TAPA* 75 (1944) 20-33.

86. Schol. Aristoph., *Plut.* 279; Pollux, IV, 101; Athenaeus, XIV, 618 d; Aristophanes, *Eq.* 697 and schol. ad loc.; Photius, s.v. *mothōn; Et. Mag.*, s.vv. *mothōn, mothōnia;* Hesychius, s.v. *mothōnas;* Plutarch, *Lyc.* 28; Lawler, "The Dance of the Ancient Mariners," *TAPA* 75 (1944) 31-3.

critics believe they are later interpolations, perhaps actually by a
Cretan writer, living in an age long after the period of Crete's great-
ness, but still aware of some of the glories of the past civilization of
his native land. However that may be, it seems entirely likely that
Athenaeus is correct in his statement that the ancient Cretans had
a highly developed tumbling dance.

From archaeological and literary sources we know something of
the figures or *schēmata* practiced by Minoan and Mycenaean acrobats,
both men and women. They were, for instance, adept at front and
back somersaults, flying leaps resembling dives, and perhaps also cart-
wheels (witness the repeated mention of "whirling")[87] and rapid
kicking of their own backs or heads. They stood on their heads; they
stood and walked on their hands or forearms, sometimes over and
around various obstacles. They knew and used what is sometimes
called the "bridge"—a bend far backward, until the fingers of the
performer touch the ground. On the pommel of a sword found at
Mallia, in Crete,[88] there is a fine representation of an acrobat bent
backwards into the form of a wheel, the soles of his feet almost
touching the back of his head. A similar pose is seen on a sealing
from Mallia.[89] Chapouthier, who found the sword, believes that the
tumbler is to be interpreted as taking this pose among swords, as
in the famous representation from Southern Italy, now in the Naples
Museum;[90] and that the Cretan sword so decorated is thereby designated as "for sport, not war." D. M. Robinson has pointed out[91] that
the wheel formed in this way by tumblers is akin to the "wheel of
fortune," originally a solar symbol; and that it was believed to have
"beneficent prophylactic powers." This and other acrobatic movements and poses are probably of Oriental origin. Chapouthier (52-4)
has adduced parallels from Cappadocia and Egypt. The "wheel" is
seen in Egyptian funeral dances, as well as at joyous festivals of the
gods, and at feasts; and it is definitely associated with the cult of the
dead as well as with the cult of the gods. It may be that one of the
original purposes of the tumbling exhibitions, as of armed dances at
funerals, was the desire to rout death by a display of violent physical
activity. It is interesting in view of this possibilty that Pollux
(IV, 105) lists *kybistēsis* as a *schēma* of the tragic dance. All of the

---

87. *Iliad*, XVIII, 606; *Odyssey*, IV, 19.

88. Chapouthier, Fernand, "Deux épées d'apparat découvertes en 1936 au
palais de Mallia," *Études crétoises*, Vol. V, Paris, 1938, 1-62, with frontispiece and
Plates X-XX, incl.

89. *Ibid.*, Fig. 23, p. 54.

90. *Ibid.*, Fig. 31, p. 60; cf. Xenophon, *Symp.* II, 1; Athenaeus, IV, 129 d.

91. "The Wheel of Fortune," *CP* 41 (1946) 207-216.

figures which we have mentioned are found later, in Greek tumbling.[92] It is highly possible that Cretan performers used even more spectacular acrobatic and juggling figures, as did the "wonder-workers," the *thaumatourgoi* and *thaumatopoioi* of the Greek banquet-rooms and theaters (Athenaeus, IV, 129 d) ; but on this point evidence is lacking.

A tumbling dance presupposes long and rigorous training, and inevitably suggests the matter of professionalism. We know that trained acrobats were sometimes attached to temples in Egypt.[93] Whether the Minoans had highly-trained, professional or semi-professional acrobatic dancers or jugglers or not, we do not know; but on the analogy of the ritual bull-play, we may surmise that they did. One aspect of the Great Goddess, as Evans has conjectured with much plausibility, is that of the "Lady of Sport"; and the charming figurine depicting her in that guise, published by Evans,[94] is fitting for a patroness of tumbling as for a presiding divinity of the bull-arena.

There are several other dances and figures which are attested for prehistoric Crete, by literary or archaeological evidence, but of the exact nature of which we are not sure. We are informed repeatedly, for instance, that the *hyporcheme* was native to Crete (Plutarch, *De Mus.* 9; Athenaeus, V, 181 b). Apparently in pre-Hellenic times this was a song or hymn sung to flute or lyre, by a group of singers, men or women, boys or girls, while a separate chorus of dancers interpreted the song by means of much movement and much gesture.[95] It was thus a combination of instrumental music, song, dance, and pantomime. Writers stress the fact that it was "lively" and rapid,[96] and even "sportive" (Athenaeus, I, 15 d; XIV, 630 d). The effect may have been similar in general to that of some of our modern dance performances, especially the opera-pantomime versions of Rimsky-Korsakov's *Le Coq d'Or*, in which the singers actually sit on benches while the dancing cast performs.[97]

The *hyporcheme* was important in the cult of the Great Mother and her son in Crete. It seems to have been taken over by the Dorian Greeks, and used chiefly in the worship of Apollo,[98] sometimes in "tetragonal" choruses (Athenaeus, V, 181 b). Its later development in Greece is something of a puzzle. It is variously said to have been akin to the Pyrrhic dance (Schol. Pind., *Pyth.* II, 127) ; to have been

---

92. Xenophon, *Symp.* II, 1, 8, 11, 22; VII, 2, 3.
93. Chapouthier, *op. cit.,* 52.
94. *P.M.,* frontispiece to Vol. IV.
95. Callimachus, *Hymn. Del.* 304-5; Lucian, *Salt.* 16; Heliodorus, III, 2.
96. Athenaeus, I, 15 d; Plutarch, *Quaest. conv.* IX, 15, 2; *Et. Mag.* 690, 47.
97. Robert, Grace, *The Borzoi Book of Ballets,* 95-96.
98. Swindler, *op. cit.,* 54-57, 65.

like the dance of comedy, the *kordax* (Athenaeus, XIV, 630 d) ; to
have been concerned with mythological tales.[99] The author of the
Etymologicum Magnum (690, 47) equates it with the "zodiacal" circle
dance discussed above. On occasion it is Dionysiac (Athenaeus, XIV,
617 b). Whether in Greece the singers and dancers finally came to
form one and the same group, we do not know. Several portions of
hyporchemes are extant (cf., e.g., Athenaeus, XIV, 617 b), but they
do not solve the problem of the exact nature of the genre. All that we
can say with assurance is that from first to last the *hyporcheme* was
essentially a lyric with strong musical, orchestic, and mimetic accompaniment.[100]

Another Cretan dance of mimetic nature seems to have been similar
to that performed by the Greeks to the hymn called the *nomos*.[101]
In it a solemn ode or song recounting the adventures of a deity was
apparently sung, to the accompaniment of flute or lyre, by singers
who at the same time executed dignified steps and interpretative gestures. The *nomos* had recognizable divisions or sections (Strabo, IX,
3, 10). It evidently was less violent than the hyporcheme—of necessity; for simultaneous singing and dancing uses up a great deal of
breath! The Greek *nomos* was used at Delphi, among other places, to
set forth Apollo's slaying of the Pythian serpent (Proclus, *Chrest.*
320; Strabo, IX, 3, 10). In the early Pythian *nomos*, the lyre-player,
a Cretan, is said to have sung a solo part, impersonating the god
himself (Proclus, *Chrest.* 320). Miss Swindler has expressed the
opinion (p. 58) that this may point to a Minoan usage.

Still another type of Cretan dance, the *paean* (Strabo, X, 4, 18),
seems to have been a rhythmic procession in honor of a divinity, with
the dancers chanting a solemn hymn, accompanied by the cithara, as
they marched with stately step. It may have been used particularly
in time of epidemic or other crisis, or in connection with an occasion
of great solemnity. The author of the *Homeric Hymn to the Pythian
Apollo* (III, 514-523) tells how a band of Cretans came to Delphi to
establish the shrine there, singing and marching to the paean, with
Apollo himself as their leader. The god plays the cithara, and "steps
high and handsomely" (516)—phraseology that recalls the figures on
the Harvester Vase. Some scholars have conjectured that a feature
of a Minoan religion was a pilgrimage, at regular times of the year,
to a sacred grove, cave, mountain, tree, or other hallowed spot.[102] If

---

99. *Ibid.,* 54.
100. Proclus, *Chrest.* 242; Athenaeus, XIV, 628 d, 631 c; Diehl, in *RE,* s.v.
"Hyporcheme"; Latte, *op. cit.,* 14-15; Hoeck, *op. cit.,* III, 345-352.
101. Swindler, *op. cit.,* 57-8.
102. Hall, *op. cit.,* 156.

this is true, it is reasonable to suppose that those making the pilgrimage sang the paean as they marched. We may adduce as a parallel the singing lines of modern pilgrims who approach such shrines as those of St. Anne de Beau Pré, Lourdes, etc. The paean was adopted by the Greeks, and used particularly in the cult of Apollo, at Delphi, Delos, and other centers. Among the Greeks it was used[103] as a ceremony of prayer and supplication in time of pestilence or other trouble; before a battle or other important undertakings; as a religious processional on festal days; as a dance at or around an altar or a temple; as a wedding procession; as a victory procession (cf. *Iliad*, XXII, 391-2); and as a general expression of joy. Also, it came to be used with libations and sacrifices on many occasions, even at symposia. It was especially important at the Hyacinthia and the Gymnopaedia in Sparta.[104] It was extended to the worship of deities other than Apollo, and the flute was substituted for or added to the cithara as accompaniment to the dance. It was often imitated in tragedy — as, e.g., in Sophocles' *Trachiniae* (205-223), Euripides' *Hercules Furens* (685-700), Euripides' *Ion* (111-143), and elsewhere. Throughout its history, the distinctive refrain "Iē Paian!" seems to have been retained; it may be of pre-Greek origin.

Several Greek paeans are extant, complete or in fragments,[105] and even musical notes have been preserved for some of these. Written in the Dorian mode, the music suggests the dignity and stateliness which we should expect of the paean; and the rhythms of the verse are harmonious also. However, we can only conjecture as to the nature of the music and verse used by the Minoans in their form of the paean.

The Greeks tell us[106] that the *sikinnis*, characteristic dance of their satyr play, was of Cretan origin. We know of the Greek *sikinnis* that it was spirited, and involved a great deal of swift leg motion—apparently kicks, leaps, "splits," and dizzy turns and whirlings. It was performed by male dancers, garbed as satyrs; and it was often lewd. There is a persistent tradition connecting it with "priests" and with the dance of the Curetes. It may actually have been originally a representation of the characteristic steps of the dance of the Curetes, which, as we have seen, was closely connected with religious ritual.

---

103. Fairbanks, Arthur, "*A Study of the Greek Paean*," *Cornell Studies in Classical Philology*, 12 (1900).

104. Xenophon, *Hell.* IV, 5, 11; cf. *Anab.* VI, 1, 11. Athenaeus, XV, 678 c; *Et. Mag.* 243, 3.

105. Fairbanks, *op. cit.*, 139-153.

106. Athenaeus, I, 20 f; XIV, 630 b, c. Meursius, *op. cit.*, s.vv. *sikinnis* and *sikinnotyrbē*, assembles the Greek references to the dance.

The more vulgar aspects may have been later additions, the result of the absorption of the dance into the cult of Dionysus; for there is no evidence pointing to lewdness in the dances of the Minoans.

Perhaps to be associated with the *sikinnis* is a gesture frequently seen in Cretan art—something which looks like the modern military salute.[107] A variant of the gesture is the pressing of both hands to the face.[108] It is used by both men and women. Evans calls it a gesture of adoration, and says its use on a dedicated statuette put the dedicator under the special protection of the deity. It seems to be a ritualistic shading or shielding of the eyes from the radiance of a deity. Interestingly enough, among the *schēmata*, or figures, specifically associated with the dance of the Greek satyr play is one usually called *skopos* (sometimes *skōps, skōpeuma,* or *cheir hyposkopos*), in which the dancer shields his eyes with his hand. It seems entirely possible that this is the Cretan gesture.[109] In the Greek satyr play it seems to have been used as a gesture of peering or seeking. It is, indeed, an odd fact that in the satyr plays there are a great many plots or situations involving searching, seeking, and peering, and that such peering can be recognized as one of the commonplaces of the genre.[110] The *schēma* spreads to comedy, and is present even in tragedy. There may even be some connection with the mystic searches at the Thesmophoria and at Eleusis.[111]

There are other ritualistic gestures in Cretan art, some of which we can recognize and understand, but many of which are obscure to us. In the former group is the gesture of the palms turned toward an object—up, or on a level with the shoulders, or down, according as the object is placed above, in front of, or below the person using the gesture. This gesture, which continued down into classical Greek times, indicates reverence, worship, supplication, and is used with reference to a sacred object or a deity.[112] In the obscure group is the attitude of a male figure[113] which, with both arms curved in a circle

---

107. Evans, I, 682, Fig. 501; III, Fig. 313, p. 449; Fig. 320, p. 459; Fig. 323, p. 463; Supplementary Plate xxxix; Bossert, *op. cit.*, Figs. 311 a, 312, 315, 320, 321 a; *Études crétoises* (see note 88), III, 1934, Plate xxvi, facing p. 94.

108. Evans, *op cit.*, III, Fig. 322, p. 462.

109. Athenaeus, XIV, 629 f; Hesychius, s.v. *hyposkopon chera;* Photius, *Lexicon*, p. 527, 7; Pliny, *Hist. Nat.* 35, 138; cf. Lillian B. Lawler, "Blinding Radiance and the Greek Dance," *CJ* 37 (1941-42) 94-6. For the *episkopon chera* and the horned owl dance cf. D. M. Robinson, *CVA, Robinson Collection,* 2, p. 57, pl. 48, and especially 498-9.

110. Lawler, Lillian B., "The Dance of the Owl," *TAPA* 70 (1939) 482-502, and especially 498-9.

111. Farnell, *op. cit.*, III, 87, 92.

112. Sittl, Karl, *Die Gebärden der Griechen und Römer*, Leipzig, Teubner, 1890, Chapter X, "Gebärden des Gebetes."

113. Evans, *op. cit.*, II, 235 and Fig. 132.

before him, touches its fingertips together. Evans says he is "saluting his divine mother." The same gesture is seen in female figures,[114] sometimes with the curving arm suggesting snakes. In another gesture both hands are raised, with one palm toward the front, the other palm turned to the side.[115] Further studies of Cretan gestures will undoubtedly be made in the future; and they will illuminate considerably our concept of the Cretan dance.

We have record of a dance called simply *Krētikon*, "Cretan" (Hesychius, s.v.). We know nothing of its nature; we are not even sure it is not one of the Cretan dances already mentioned. However, there is one curious coincidence in our record of it: The lexicographer Hesychius, in mentioning it, speaks of the same word as denoting a soft, short garment. Representations in Greek art show dances in honor of the goddess Artemis, performed by maidens in short, delicate dresses, sometimes with their breasts uncovered in a manner reminiscent of the Minoan fashion.[116] There may be a connection between the two types of dance.

In the *Ecclesiazousae* of Aristophanes, toward the end of the play (1165-6), the chorus bids Blepyrus (or some of their own number, according to a few editors) "move your feet in the Cretan manner (*krētikōs*)." Blepyrus agrees to do so, and the play moves on to a joyous conclusion, as the chorus, the serving-maids, and Blepyrus dance out to dinner. There has been much discussion as to the significance of *krētikōs* in this passage. Some of the suggestions that have been made are: (1) It is a jest, "because the Cretans were great eaters, and sat down to table early in the morning" (Schol. ad loc.); (2) that it refers to a hyporcheme;[117] (3) that it is a metrical reference, and calls for a dance in cretic rhythms.[118] In all probability the meaning is none of these, but merely "lightly," "rapidly," "stepping high," as in the paean of the *Homeric Hymn to the Pythian Apollo*, which we have considered above. I expect to discuss the significance of *krētikōs*, as a term descriptive of dancing, in a forthcoming study.

We have had occasion from time to time in this paper to mention the musical accompaniment to the Cretan dance. Earliest accompani-

---

114. Cook, *Zeus*, II, Fig. 406 b, p. 536.

115. *Ibid.*, II, 406 c, p. 536.

116. Séchan, Louis, *La danse grecque antique*, Plate viii, facing p. 140; Emmanuel, Maurice, *Essai sur l'Orchestique Grecque*, Figs. 584-588, p. 305.

117. White, J. W., *The Verse of Greek Comedy*, 148; J. van Leeuwen, *Aristophanis Ecclesiazusae*, p. 155.

118. White, *op. cit.*, 148; Anon., *Aristophanes—The Eleven Comedies*, II, p. 403, and note 1; W. J. Oates and Eugene O'Neill, Jr., *The Complete Greek Drama*, II, 1053; Suidas, s.v. *krētikōs*.

ments must have been furnished by the human voice, and also by hand-clapping, finger-snapping, foot-stamping, and the beating together of sticks or small pieces of wood; these are all used by early peoples. Beginning in the Bronze Age, as we have seen, metal objects, particularly weapons, were used as percussion instruments, so to speak; and soon metal cymbals were introduced. There is evidence for a conch shell and for tiny hand-bells as musical instruments in Crete.[119] Also, we have noted that the Minoans had the hand-drum or tympanum. In addition, archaeological finds have proved that they used a syrinx, or Pan-pipe; the single flute; the double flute; the seven-stringed lyre; the sistrum, or metal rattle; and the bagpipe.[120]

A great many of the Cretan dances were undoubtedly performed by the rank and file of the people. However, there must have been a great many trained dancers in the island. We have noted above the possibility that there were professional or semi-professional tumbling dancers. It is practically certain also that there were bands of votaries or attendants at various shrines, who by long practice had become adept in particular rituals and dances. They were apparently not professionals, as we know the term. Reasonable modern parallels would be modern Greek villagers who, year after year, excel in dances in the public square on religious holidays; or a group of "Eagle dancers" or "Snake Dancers" within an American Indian tribe— people who during the greater part of the year are ordinary members of the community. A parallel from a different point of view would be a group of altar boys associated with a parish church. Some scholars think the singers and dancers of the paean may have formed such a highly trained group.[121] The successors of the mythical Curetes would be another example, as would also the dancers of the "mystery plays," and the dancers who handled snakes. In Greek days such a band of dancers was called a *thiasos*. The word is not Greek; presumably both the word and the institution which it denotes were handed down to the Greeks by the Minoans and Mycenaeans.

Such are the bits of information which we have, or are able to deduce, about the Cretan dance. It was colorful, rich, spectacular; and it influenced the Greek dance tremendously—probably more than we can even conjecture. It is possible that a large number of Greek dances and figures not here mentioned are ultimately Cretan, although evidence of that fact is no longer to hand. Even in classical antiquity,

119. Glotz, *op. cit.*, 273.
120. Mosso, *op. cit.*, 322.
121. Fairbanks, *op. cit.*, 66.

the Cretans boasted that most of the Greek religion (which would, of course, include the Greek dance) was of Cretan origin.[122] The Greeks called them liars;[123] but the discoveries of modern scholars are proving that they spoke the truth.

122. Hoeck, *op. cit.*, III, 143.
123. Callimachus, *Hymn. Iov.* 8; cf. the Epistle of St. Paul to Titus, I, 12.

LIFE IMMOVABLE

.   .   .   .

Sky everywhere; and sunbeams on all sides;
Something about like honey from Hymettus;
The lilies grow of marble witherless;
Pentele shines, birthgiver of Olympus.

The digging pick on Beauty stumbles still;
Cybele's womb bears gods instead of mortals;
And Athens bleeds with violet blood abundant
Each time the Afternoon's arrows pour on her.

The sacred olive keeps its shrines and fields;
And in the midst of crowds that slowly move
Like caterpillars on a flower white,
The people of the relics lives and reigns
Myriad-souled; and in the dust, the spirit
Glitters; I feel it battling in me with Darkness.

.   .   .   .

Kostes Palamas
Translated by
Aristides E. Phoutrides

SCHERIA - SANTORIN

J. P. Droop
Liverpool

Once the Ægean sea was the scene of a stupendous cataclysm. The volcanic island that the classical Greeks knew as Thera and the moderns call Santorin was destroyed by an eruption which rent the crater and let in the sea engulfing half the land. All that is left is the eastern half of the island and the sea to the west; the ancient crater is practically bottomless. Ships must moor to buoys attached to the land, for their anchors are useless.[1]

Now pottery of the first Late Cycladic period has been found in the island and there are plentiful remains of the post-Mycenaean Geometric age. But nothing has been found that can be ascribed to the years between, a gap that suggests that the island was desolate for something like seven centuries. It is reasonable to suppose that the L. C. I pottery dates the catastrophe to about 1700 B. C.

It is generally agreed that the Homeric poems, though composed later and reflecting a different state of society, embody details that belong to the civilization of the preceding age, and this whether Agamemnon is thought on the modern view to have ruled the Mycenae of L. H. III, or, as used to be thought, was a king among later invaders, a view that is still supported by the absence of any trace in L. H. III remains of the worship of the Homeric Olympians. No one in fact supposes that there was a complete break between the Homeric age and the preceding time.

If then traditions of the earlier age survived to the time of the Homeric poems, it would not be surprising to find in Homer a reference to the stupendous catastrophe of Santorin; and, since earthquakes and tidal waves were in the Homeric theology the prerogative of Poseidon, the Earthshaker, a reference to it as the work of Poseidon. And this I submit is exactly what we do find in the thirteenth book of the Odyssey in the description of Poseidon's meditated punishment of the Phaeacians for the safe conduct they gave Odysseus to his home, thereby cheating the god of his vengeance for the blinding of his son, the Cyclops.

"Now I fain would smite a fair ship of the Phaeacians, as she comes home from a convoy on the misty deep, that thereby they may learn to hold their hands, and cease from giving escort to men; and *I would overshadow their city with a great mountain*."[2]

---

1. See Fouqué, "Santorin et ses éruptions"; Washington, *AJA* 9 (1894) 504.
2. *Odyssey*, XIII, 149-152, Butcher, T., and Lang.

I submit that it was the catastrophe of Santorin dimly remembered through the ages that gave rise to this tale of the vengeance of Poseidon on the Phaeacians.

Santorin, then, and not the traditional Corfu, was Scheria, the land of the Phaeacians. It is true that the Odyssey does not say that the city was actually overwhelmed, only that Poseidon accomplished the first part of his vengeance on the ship that had carried Odysseus. "He smote the ship into a stone and rooted her far below with the downstroke of his hand."[3] Yet he had threatened to complete his vengeance and had obtained Zeus' sanction for it, and if we remember his vengeful character and the very real provocation he had received, we need not suppose that the prayers and sacrifices of Alcinous would have been likely to turn him from his purpose, "to overshadow their city with a great mountain." Moreover, to suppose so would be to suppose that a prophecy was unfulfilled. Homer is much too artistic to suggest anything of the kind.

There would seem to be little against the identification of Scheria with Santorin. Santorin is, of course, a good deal further than Corfu from the traditional Ithaca, and Victor Bérard did note with satisfaction that Corfu is in fact a night's sail from Ithaca. That, however, need not worry us, for in the first place, we do not know that the traditional Ithaca is Ithaca (Dörpfeld thought it was not), and in the second place, the general impression that we get is that there was a touch of magic about the Phaeacian ships. Did they not go to Euboea "which certain of our men say is the furthest of lands and accomplished the journey on the self same day and won home again and were not weary?"[4]

It may, however, be objected that "to overshadow their city with a great mountain"—is a better description of the destruction of Pompeii than of the blowing up of the Ægean island. But we ought not to expect a reference to a catastrophe centuries old to be very exact. The essential fact handed down was the awful destruction of the city carried out in a way that to the Homeric mind could only have been the work of Poseidon. The poet's tale is woven to account for it.

---

3. *Odyssey*, XIII, 163, Butcher, T., and Lang.
4. *Odyssey*, VII, 325.

PREHISTORIC SKYROS

HAZEL D. HANSEN

Stanford University

Skyros played no prominent part in the history of Greek lands. Only in three instances did the island come into notice—in her legendary past with the sojourn of Achilles and the treacherous death of Theseus at the hands of Lykomedes, and in the Athenian conquest in the fifth century when Kimon added to his reputation by bringing home to Athens the bones of Theseus. The picture of prehistoric Skyros is as fragmentary as her past but from available miscellaneous material the early history of the island is gradually emerging. For in addition to the meagre finds which have had only slight notice in publications, there is a mass of unpublished material in the local museum, various objects in private collections, and a heterogeneous group of surface finds. Perhaps it is not too premature at this time to make a general review of the material and to note the indications for future investigation.

Skyros is one of the most solitary islands in the Aegean for nearly all the other islands are nearer to one another or to the mainland.[1] It is about twenty-one miles distant to the nearest isle of the Northern Sporades and about twenty-three miles northeast of Euboea. It is not a large island,[2] and it is composed of two mountain ranges united by a narrow isthmus about two miles wide which divides Skyros into two nearly equal parts with the Bay of Achilli (the ancient Achilleion) on the east and that of Kalamitsa on the west. Thus Skyros somewhat resembles the figure eight. At present the isthmus is largely covered with sand drifts and cultivated only at the western end, but in antiquity this fertile area was planted more extensively (fig. 1).

The southern half of the island is almost completely deserted; it is mountainous and rocky, intersected by steep ravines, and barren except for an occasional clump of trees in some isolated glen. Its highest peak is Kochylas, 793 meters. Although this half of the island

---

1. Its isolation and the capricious sea between it and the mainland and Euboea are the reasons why Skyros is far less frequently visited than the other islands of the Northern Sporades which have been described many times by travelers. In the early part of the fifteenth century Bondelmonte was the first modern traveler to visit Skyros; then after a long interval Tournefort came for a brief visit in 1702; a century later Pouqueville; and then Leake introduced the era of travelers who were concerned with the antiquities rather than the tales of the miraculous image in the Monastery of St. George. See Girard, "Antiquités des Sporades Septentrionales," *BCH* 3 (1879) 59 ff.

2. Skyros is about sixteen miles long, varies in width from two to eight and a half miles, and has a circumference of sixty miles and an area of about eighty square miles. See map.

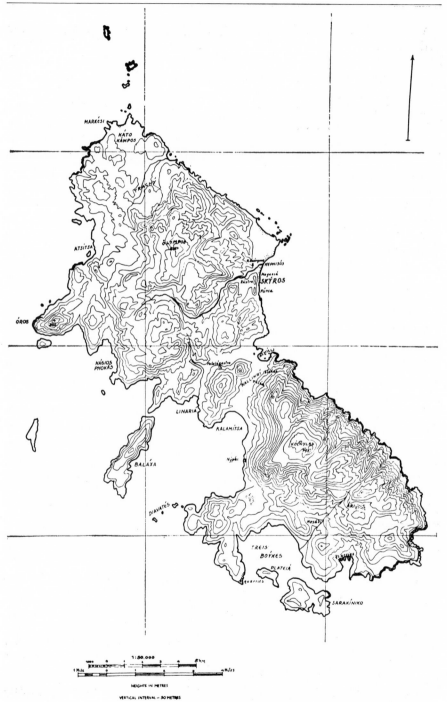

Figure 1. The Island of Skyros.

is uncultivated it affords in spots good pasturage for the goats for which Skyros has always been famous. The plateau of Ari is barren but rain water collects in the hollows and is useful in summer for the herds and flocks there. The long winding coastline of jagged cliffs rising abruptly from the sea, the mountainous nature of the island and especially the rocky abruptness of the southern part justify the Homeric Σκῦρον . . . . αἰπεῖαν.[3]

Beside the level area of the isthmus there are two notable plains in the northern part of the island which are fertile and well-watered;[4] one extending for about five miles north of the town of Skyros, the other comprising the rich valley of Trachy and the plain of Kato Kampos. The northern part of Skyros is not so mountainous but it has several peaks of considerable height of which Olympos (525 meters) and the Oros (320 meters) are the best known. The hills are covered with pine forests.

The best and safest harbor, Treis Boukes, lies at the southern end;[5] it has good anchorage along the eastern and western shores, its triple entrances (hence its name) being formed by two small islands, Plateia and Sarakiniko. On the western coast is Kalamitsa Bay, somewhat protected from the force of the west wind by the island of Balaxa and the Diavates group, and its harbor of Linaria serves today as the chief port since it faces the mainland. It has always been a main line of communication across the island to the town site. On the eastern side of Skyros the town itself has no good anchorage for today's ships with only twelve fathoms of depth of water but it is serviceable for fishing boats. Along the northwestern coastline there are coves and sheltered landing places such as Agios Phokas and Atsitsa but they lead into sparsely settled areas.

The most obvious place for a settlement on Skyros is the site of the modern town which extends up the slopes of the steep acropolis, the Kastro in modern parlance, and spreads out fan-shaped at its base.

---

3. *Iliad*, IX, 668. In the stricter sense the adjective applies only to the lofty perch of the town itself, a dominating feature of the landscape, for the acropolis rock rises to 400 meters above sea level. Other deserving epithets are αἰγίλιψ (Lycophr., *Alex.*, 1325); scopulosa Skyros (Stat., *Achill.*, I ,691-2); while ἠνεμόεσσα (Dionys. Perieg. 521) and ἀνεμώδης (Soph. frg. 553, ed. Pearson) are especially fitting because the winds at certain seasons do blow violently. Skyros situated in the open sea and isolated is exposed to all winds. For other descriptions see Graindor, *Histoire de l'île de Skyros jusqu'en 1538*, 11, n. 1.

4. For the cultivation of the olive and vine note the picture of Philostratos who describes Skyros as a woman of severe countenance, her hair entwined with reeds, dressed in dark blue, holding in one hand an olive branch, in the other a shoot of the vine (*Imag.*, I); and Galen who recommends the wine of Skyros for fever (*Medici Graeci*, 15, p. 648. ed. Kuhn). The fig leaf appears on Skyrian coins. See Svoronos in *Journ d' Arch. Numismatique*, 3 (1900) 39.

5. According to Leake it has about twenty fathoms depth in the middle, *Travels in Northern Greece*, III, 106, n. 1.

The ancient acropolis was an easily protected height, within easy communication of both the east and west coasts, with arable land adjoining it, watered by the river Kephisos, a small perennial stream which meanders across the valley and empties into the sea not far north of the town.[6] At all times the narrow strip on either side of the river served any settlement in this area and today the inhabitants refer to this rich land simply as "the gardens" *(περιβόλια)*. It is natural that this acropolis became the chief site in antiquity and has remained so throughout all the succeeding centuries. Immediately to the north and east of it the first archaeological discoveries in Skyros were made.

The graves of Skyros first attracted attention. In November 1860 some workmen digging near the river in land belonging to the Monastery of St. George uncovered a tomb of four poros slabs with a fifth for a covering. The abbot, Nicodemos Lavriotes, reported this discovery to the president of the Archaeological Society in Athens and sent the finds there, listing them as follows:[7] fourteen clay vases, glass bottles, pieces of a helmet, a metal mirror and a piece of a sword. It seems as if the skeleton had some sort of fine gold-like covering which fell to pieces when touched.

In 1893 Max Mayer noted along the shore a line "of pre-Attic tombs" which had suffered much through time.[8] He found pottery which he described as brown pottery with geometric decorations and vases of reddish glaze with a peculiar decoration, some Mycenaean vases, and an abundance of a very primitive red ware. Unfortunately Mayer did not publish the results before his death.

Four years later Paul Girard mentioned the tombs to the northeast of the town but it is not clear to which discovery he is referring.[9] No digging took place then until 1918, but in the interval some light was shed upon the material from Skyros for in March 1905 when Dawkins made a brief visit to the island he was shown some vases from two tombs which had been discovered accidentally by men digging for clay for bricks at a place called Peramata not far from the sea near the right bank of the river.[10] They were cist graves made of slabs of stone. One grave contained a number of vases and un-

---

6. Strabo, IX, 3, 16. Today the river is nameless for the Skyrians refer to it as "the river"; occasionally it takes a name from a given district through which it flows.

7. *Μιχαὴλ Κωνσταντινίδης, Ἡ Νῆσος Σκῦρος,* 70.

8. *BCH* 17 (1893) 207-8; *RA* 21 (1893) 86.

9. *BCH* 3 (1879) 62. He wrote that the gaves contained bones, vases, bottles, broken weapons, and some spindle whorls.

10. *BSA* 11 (1904-5) 78-80. Peramata is part of the rich garden area along the banks of the river.

fortunately some gold wire over which a quarrel arose and as a result most of the vases were broken, including a kernos with about fifteen small vases attached. The surviving whole vases include a jug with a cutaway neck and lugs on the upper part of the body, a two-handled cup with a high base, and a jug with a Mycenaean decoration on the shoulder and vertical bands marking the handle. The two latter vases were decorated with a reddish brown glaze paint. This tomb Dawkins considered as belonging to the end of the Mycenaean period.[11] From the other tomb came four vases of geometric style.

In 1918 D. Evangelides dug in the cliffs along the sea near the place called Magazia and uncovered some handmade vases and sherds of the Bronze Age and some graves of the Geometric Period.[12] The pottery resembling Γ 3 ware of Thessaly included: (1) red sherds of good clay, thin, with a polished surface. One sherd has light red lines on it; another is from the base of a bowl. (2) red sherds with ash-grey fabric, for the most part of poor quality. The surface is polished and has a mottled effect in buff, red, and black. Shapes are bowls or open flat dishes. (3) good black sherds, with a highly polished surface. (4) vases of poor fabric and workmanship; thick red, black or reddish black sherds with a rough surface. (5) sherds of coarse-grained thick fabric, reddish brown clay. One sherd of this category has two conical lugs. At the top level Evangelides found one sherd of L.H.III. The four graves were of the usual type, each having four slabs for the sides and a fifth for the cover.[13] One grave was that of a child, another of an adult and the remaining two, smaller than the first, contained nothing but earth. In the second grave were a piece of bronze and four vases: a jug with a cutaway neck, of red clay with incised lines on the lip; a one-handled jug or pitcher of grey-black clay with a slightly polished surface and incised lines on the handle; two one-handled cups with a high base, apparently made by the same potter, one of grey-black clay with a black coating inside and out, the other of very red clay with a thin reddish brown coating inside and out. Such is his meagre report.

In August 1935 when Ioannis Papadimitriou was visiting his native island at the request of the Ministry of Education he undertook a small trial excavation in the place called Themis, on the northwest bank of the river, north of the town, in lands owned by the

---

11. But Wace pointed out that the beaked jug was similar to vases from cist tombs at Sesklo and Dimeni and from Tomb A at Theotoku which belong to the Early Iron Age. *Prehistoric Thessaly*, 208-9.

12. *Deltion*, 1918, 41-45.

13. Cf. *Prehistoric Thessaly*, 208-216; *BSA* 18 (1911-12) 4 ff.; Frödin and Persson, *Asine*, 422 ff.

Monastery of St. George.[14] On the slopes of the hill where the little
church of St. George stands and in the adjoining fields good Mycenaean sherds may be picked up. Here were found five tombs of the
usual type, made of four poros slabs for the sides and two more for
the top and bottom. Throughout the area sherds and pieces of blue
glass were scattered. The contents of one tomb are deserving of
notice. Outside this tomb were some vases: one of reddish brown
clay of poor workmanship, a vase which had been mended in antiquity and within which were eight to ten one-handled cups, most of
them broken, and a jug decorated in protogeometric style and similar
to vases which Dawkins published. Of great interest are the objects
within the tomb which included a bronze bowl containing one hundred blue glass beads, four bronze fibulae (two broken and two well
preserved), a bronze buckle with a high profiled center, armbands,
and a piece of a bronze ring and iron sword, and ten gold discs belonging to a garment. These discs were pressed from a mould and
the design is made of pricked dots;[15] the edge of the disc is bent down
a little so that if it were used on cloth it could be clamped down on the
material. There seems no other way of attaching them. When compared with the well known discs from Shaft Grave III at Mycenae
the similarity of design is at once apparent—double circles with
knobs, running spirals, rosettes of six petals, and groups of half
circles—but the discs from Skyros seem poorer in design executed
with a monotonous regularity and displaying little of the rich variety
shown in the examples from Mycenae.[16] This grave is dated in the
period of transition from sub-Mycenaean to the protogeometric period
and its contents indicate that the Mycenaean tradition lingered on
into the succeeding period. It is interesting that it shows the custom
of putting funeral objects outside the grave, a very ancient practise
which has been observed at Agios Kosmas.[17]

In February 1938 along the shore in the district called Magazia
four graves in the side of the cliffs were exposed to view during the
winter rains. Mr. Ph. Stavropoullos dug them and recovered more
than fifty vases, necklaces, bronze rings, fibulae, bronze bracelets,
and a few objects of gold.[18] They are apparently of the same date as
the preceding graves.

---

14. *AA*, 1936, 228-234 and p. 156.
15. For patterns in gold and silver in this technique see *Ephemeris*, 1899,
Pl. X, no. 1. Tsountas found similar designs on objects from Amorgos and Syra
and Seager likewise in E.M. tombs at Mochlos.
16. Karo, *Die Schachtgräber von Mykenai*, Pl. XXIX.
17. Mylonas in Πρακτ. 'Ακαδ. 'Αθηνῶν, 5 (1930) 322, and *AJA* 38 (1934)
271.
18. *AJA* 43 (1939) 131. Only part of these finds is in the one-room museum
in the local town hall. As yet they are not published. Unfortunately during the

Lastly in 1945 D. P. Theochares dug in a cliff east of the city near the place called τοῦ παππᾶ τὸ χῶμα where he found more than a hundred neolithic sherds of monochrome ware.[19] They include (1) sherds of a very red and brownish red ware, of well baked clay, having a polished surface. The probable shape is a bowl. (2) red and brown sherds belonging to bowls with and without bases. These pieces were rather carefully made and most of them have a polished surface. Two sherds have lugs. (3) grey sherds whose surface is sometimes mottled grey to black. (4) sherds of coarse ware, red or brownish black, with an unpolished surface. Some of these examples have lugs. The smaller finds from this same place include some obsidian blades and a bone needle, and in the area around the city were found some celts of Thessalian *B* and *Γ* types and arrowheads.

On the northeast lower slopes of the acropolis in the district called Krokos there are traces of rockcut tombs, most of them being almost completely ruined, but one is preserved enough to show part of a dromos.[20] The plan of the others is problematical but the number (five) and vague traces of half a dozen more in the same region naturally lead to the suggestion of a Mycenaean cemetery.

Such is the list of reported graves. Before we leave the town area one other place needs to be mentioned. Southwest of the Kastro is the conical hill, Furca, the site of Deffner's investigation in 1923.[21] He found traces of prehistoric dwellings, partly destroyed by ignorant quarrymen, a cave probably having served as a shelter for workmen, some potsherds which he did not identify, and the prehistoric quarries.[22]

Thus there is an accumulating mass of evidence clearly pointing to the existence of a prehistoric cemetery in the area north and east of the town of Skyros, a cemetery which was in use from the Bronze Age into the Early Iron Age. A total of sixteen graves have been

war and occupation the museum suffered damage. When I visited Skyros in 1947 I undertook to have the room and the cases repaired and I washed and put together as many of the vases as possible.

19. Προϊστορικαὶ Ἔρευναι ἐν Σκύρῳ καὶ Εὐβοίᾳ, *Ephemeris*, 1945-47, Ἀρχαιολογικὰ Χρονικά, 1-12.

20. Here in 1891 Mayer started some excavations because he thought the necropolis would yield abundant results but his work was stopped by the local authorities. *BCH* 15 (1891) 669.

21. *Ephemeris* 1923, 102-116. Not only at Furca but also at Markesi he found a quarry from which apparently the blocks of poros were cut for the neighboring temple.

22. He described the method of working as follows. The projecting pieces of rock were severed by means of a rope which was wet and dipped in sand and then strengthened by weaving into it pieces of flint. Workmen on either side of the rock drew the rope back and forth and when a channel of sufficient depth was obtained wedges of wood were inserted at intervals and wet until the rock was completely cut.

opened over a period of ninety years, their contents reported, but none have been thoroughly studied nor completely published. Added to these are the rockcut tombs on the slope of the acropolis.

Besides the area around the town there are three other places on the island which deserve mention. One is midway along the isthmus, Kallikri, which is somewhat sandy but it is inhabited and remarkably watered by many springs which flow down the western slope of the mountain.[23] On the slope where are the springs of Phlea and Slenas[24] arrowheads and obsidian blades may be picked up. The whole embankment along this side has caves and rocky shelters which invite exploration and one is inclined to think that here may be found other traces of prehistoric habitation.[25]

At the northern end of the island there is the fertile area of Trachy and Kato Kampos, a large well-watered plain, but the northern coastline is rocky and surrounded by shoal water and affords no good landing place. At Markesi, which marks the northern extremity of the island, during the classical era there was a temple there, and graves and the quarry already mentioned. The great wealth of this plain could hardly have been overlooked by prehistoric settlers in Skyros and the finding of obsidian blades there makes it another place inviting investigation.

From the great harbor of Treis Boukes to the small and arid plain of Mesadi obsidian blades are found. Long ago Mayer mentioned some prehistoric remains in this area but if a settlement existed here it probably would have been sparse because of the nature of the plain.[26] Yet despite the aridness the region has always been in use. Near the harbor are reservoirs for use of those sailing there which date from the Venetian occupation, for at that time the Venetians kept a fleet in the harbor of Treis Boukes. During the Roman era the neighboring quarries were worked extensively and the colored marble of Skyros became widely known.[27] Here possibly the

---

23. They include Agios Mamas, Loutro, Nyphi, Platania, Soteras.

24. A corruption of Σωλῆνας.

25. For such traces near Agios Mamas see Deffner, Τοπωνυμίαι τῆς νήσου Σκύρου, Λαογραφία, θ', p. 570. See uder Ἅγιος Μάμας.

26. BCH 17 (1893) 207; RA 21 (1893) 86. Mayer mentioned prehistoric fortifications, dwellings, three pelasgic walls on the crest of the mountains and some Cyclopean roads which aided communication between scattered areas. All this means little or nothing. What Frederich observed elsewhere may be applied here: "Mauerreste dieser vorgriechischen Bewohner haben sich auf dem Stadtberge natürlich nicht erhalten, und was Max. Mayer sonst auf der Insel gefunden haben, will bleibt nach dem, was darüber bekannt geworden ist, ganz problematisch." AM 31 (1906) 259.

27. Pliny. N. H. 2. 106; 36, 26.

ancient Kresion is to be located.[28] In this area are still to be seen
remains of ancient round towers.[29] The importance of such a safe
harbor cannot be overlooked in prehistoric times for it may have been
a station on the road from Melos with its obsidian trade, and such
contact as Skyros had with the Cyclades and Crete was aided by this
line of communication.[30]

It is clear that from the earliest period Skyros was closely related
to northern Greece. It is an established fact that the area around the
acropolis became the chief settlement. Here the depth of half a meter
of a neolithic deposit, even though only in one place, suggests that the
earliest period of habitation may prove to be one of considerable importance. These neolithic sherds verify the dependence of Skyros
upon northern Greece for the similarity to Thessalian A1 ware is
apparent[31] and so the island becomes a part of the larger neolithic
area which extended south into the Peloponnesos.[32] The rarity of the
black wares need not be stressed unduly,[33] for all the published neolithic sherds come from a single spot, but there are other examples in
the museum whose exact location is not recorded. When there has
been so little excavation it seems imprudent to emphasize the absence
of archaeological material. Conversely the finding of one neolithic
deposit is most gratifying for it may be equally true of Skyros as of
Mycenae when Schliemann wrote with scarcely any exaggeration that
each potsherd was a new page of history.

The close connection of Skyros with northern Greece continued in
the Bronze Age. The thick handmade vases resemble Γ 3 ware in
Thessaly, while the finding of the L. H. III sherd among these vases

28. Plut., *Kimon*, 8. See Graindor, *op. cit.*, 13. According to others Kresion is
located on the western end of the isthmus on Kalamitsa Bay where there is a
large flat sandy beach and the place was watered by the spring Nyphi, lying
to the south, which today supplies Linaria. Among the ancient remains found
here are parts of Ionic columns, three sarcophagi, fortification walls, silver coins
and vases; Deffner, *op. cit.*, 582. See under *Κρῆσιον; Δ. Παπαγεωργίου, Ἱστορία
τῆς Σκύρου*, 7-8.

29. In 1893 Mayer reported a dozen of them which seemed to have escaped the
notice of earlier travelers. One was twenty-five meters in diameter. *BCH* 15
(1891) 669; 17 (1893) 207; *RA* 21 (1893) 86. For towers elsewhere on Skyros
see *Παπαγεωργίου, op. cit.*, 3 ff.

30. Bosanquet, "The Obsidian Trade" in *Excavations at Phylakopi in Melos*,
216 ff. Early connections with Crete should not be forgotten, nor the presence
of Cretan Theseus and Lykomedes on Skyros. See Fredrich, *AM* 31 (1906) 258.

31. Cf. *Τσούντας, Αἱ Προϊστορικαὶ Ἀκροπόλεις Διμηνίου καὶ Σέσκλου*, 159 ff.
Prehistoric Thessaly 13 ff.; Grundmann, "Aus neolithischen Siedlungen bei
Larisa," *AM* 57 (1932) 102 ff.; and "Magula Hadzimissiotiki," *AM* 62 (1937)
56-69; Heurtley, *Prehistoric Macedonia*, 63 ff.

32. For bibliography see Weinberg, "Aegean Chronology: Neolithic Period and
Early Bronze Age," *AJA* 51 (1947) 166, n. 4.

33. Theochares, *op. cit.*, 5, n. 1.

leads to the suggestion that the making of such ware continued in Skyros, as it did in Thessaly, into the Mycenaean period, and so the island remained within the sphere of northern influence. Skyros was drawn into the Mycenaean orbit with the north, but how extensive that influence was or how long it lasted we do not know. As yet the only indications are the few Mycenaean vases in the museum, the Mycenaean tombs at the foot of the acropolis, and the wealth of one grave with its gold objects. Also, I myself have seen several pieces of Mycenaean gold jewelry in private collections on Skyros but the exact places of their finding no longer are known.

It is clear that Mycenaean ware continued side by side with the local pottery until both wares were supplanted by protogeometric ware. When the vases from the graves excavated by Papadimitriou and Stavropoullos are published the picture of Skyros in the protogeometric period will become clearer, for this period was a flourishing one for the island. The richness of these graves compares favorably with the quantity of vases from tombs of the Early Iron Age in Thessaly, especially with those of the tholos tomb at Marmariane. The protogeometric vases of Skyros show a combination of various elements including a small amount of Mycenaean influence, borrowings from the earlier and long established tradition of handmade pottery, and some influence from Attica at a time when the protogeometric style there was well advanced. But to fully evaluate this protogeometric style and period we must also know about the succeeding geometric period and for Skyros the first examples have come recently to the museum.

Throughout the protogeometric period the greatest influence in Skyros was exerted from Thessaly. This relationship is natural because of the proximity of the island to that area rather than to the more distant south. This too is in keeping with the tradition which made the early inhabitants of Skyros kinsfolk of the Thessalians and called the island Magnesia. But it remains for the spade of the excavator to bring to light a more complete record.

THE CULT OF THE DEAD IN HELLADIC TIMES

GEORGE E. MYLONAS
Washington University

PLATE 3

The discovery of the circular altar in the Grave Circle of Mycenae by Schliemann seemed to prove that a cult of the dead was practiced in prehistoric times by the people of continental Greece. Subsequent discoveries seem to have provided additional evidence favoring the belief in such a practice, and today the existence of that cult is accepted by all. It seems to me, however, that the evidence on which that belief is based is not as conclusive as it is assumed to be and that it can stand re-examination in the light of the many discoveries of the last decades and our greater knowledge of the arts and practices of the prehistoric inhabitants of Greece.*

Before we begin our re-examination of the available evidence, we must pause to recognize two important aspects of our problem. Firstly: we must note that the available evidence is purely archaeological, that because of its nature it is rather scanty and difficult to recognize, that often it is not only meagre but obscure and yields to varied interpretations; on the other hand we must recognize that it is subject to additional discoveries and that unless proved by repeated instances it cannot be used with confidence and with finality. To disregard the limitation, imposed by the nature of our evidence, is to embark upon speculation and its uncertain course. Secondly: we must be certain of what we mean by the term cult of the dead. A great many misunderstandings have been developed, because the cult of the dead has been confused with the burial rites and many an element belonging to the latter has been taken to be part of the former. Dr. Farnell was first to point out that "we should distinguish, and mark the distinction with precision, between ancestor-cult, hero-cult, and thirdly the general religious tendance of the dead."[1]

Professor Nilsson, in his monumental work on Minoan-Mycenaean religious practices, has pointed out that the burial rites are performed only once and on the occasion of a man's death; the cult of the dead results from the "tendance" of the dead, from the "bringing of gifts,

---

* A discussion of the Minoan practices, already in manuscript, will appear shortly we hope. The inclusion of the Minoan material in the present study would have made it entirely too long. Perhaps it should be added that I was a firm believer in the existence of a cult of the dead in Helladic times and on the mainland of Greece. In fact, the desire to bring together the evidence proving that belief motivated the present study. Cf. Mylonas, in *Ephemeris* 1937, 43.

1. Farnell, L. R., *Greek Hero Cults and Ideas of Immortality*, 2.

the offering of sacrifices etc. to the dead and to his tomb on certain days or on certain occasions" in the years that follow the burial.[2] The term "tendance" was introduced by Farnell, who explains that "tendance long maintained is likely to engender actual worship."[3] In the performance of the cult, rites held at the time of the burial may again be repeated, but, if they are to prove the existence of a cult, such rites must be proved as held not at the time of the burial but sometime afterwards and repeatedly.

We must further differentiate the cult of the dead and the hero cult. The former has as its object the dead in general, while the latter a particular person. The cult of the dead is a family cult, we may even call it an ancestor-cult; the cult of a hero is that exercised around a person and shared by all the people. According to Nilsson, the latter evolved out of the former: "The cult of ancestors is the service of the dead moulded into regular and fixed forms and repeated at fixed intervals; it is performed by the members of the family and prolonged for generations. When such a regular cult of the dead is severed from the family and becomes a concern of the public in general, a hero cult arises."[4] Farnell denies this development when he states that "often the hero cult reveals no ancestral character at all; and that it originally was ancestral is merely the presupposition of the theorist who holds that all worship of heroes was originally worship of ancestors."[5] No matter what conception is the correct one, the fact remains that a clear distinction between the cult of the dead in general and the cult of a particular dead or hero is essential. Finally we may note that a cult presupposes free access at all times and over the years to the place it is to be held.

It is now generally recognized that the Mycenaen cultural period was not an isolated phenomenon but that it had its roots in the developments of the eras that preceded it. Consequently a discussion of the cult of the dead in Mycenaean times will actually have to begin with the study of the available evidence for the earlier periods, beginning with the Early Helladic period. Neolithic graves are indeed rare.[5a] From the Peloponnesus we have the sepulchral deposits in the ridges of the East and West Yerogalaro excavated by Blegen. They

2. Nilsson, M. P., *The Minoan-Mycenaean Religion and its Survival in Greek Religion,*[2] 585-586
3. Farnell, *op. cit.,* 5
4. Nilsson, *op. cit.,* 586
5. Farnell, *op. cit.,* 284
5a. Blegen, C. W., *Prosymna. The Helladic Settlement Preceding the Argive Heraeum,* 25-29. Heurtley, W. A., *Prehistoric Macedonia,* 54-55. *Hesperia* 5 (1936) 20-21. Perhaps it should be noted that the Athenian neolithic grave presents strong structural similarities to the Early Helladic graves discovered at Chalkis and Corinth.

belong to the two divisions of the Neolithic period and contrast sharply. While the skeletal remains belonging to the first Neolithic period exhibit evidence of burning, those of the second period show no signs of fire. In the earlier period we seem to have individual burials, while in the later the bones found were in an ossuary. In both periods, however, articles seem to have been deposited with the body. From northern Greece we have but one grave from the late Neolithic period discovered by Heurtley at the site of Servia. At the bottom of a shaft, 1.20 m. in diameter, a skeleton was found in the contracted position. Over it a number of vases were found, and among these a zoomorphic pot. In central Greece and in the Agora of Athens, about two meters east of the Metroön, was uncovered a neolithic grave containing a skeleton in a contracted position and equipped with two vases. No other neolithic graves are known from the mainland of Greece. Our material therefore is too scanty to allow definite conclusions as to the burial habits, etc., of the neolithic inhabitants of Greece.

I. EARLY HELLADIC PERIOD

Comparatively few Early Helladic graves have thus far been discovered in the mainland of Greece. In the typical Early Helladic sites of Korakou and Eutresis no graves were found.[6] A rock-cut tomb was found in Corinth in 1896 but it offers no clear evidence as to the burial habits of the period.[7] At Zygouries and on the Ambelakia hill Blegen excavated four Early Helladic graves.[8] They are in the form of roughly oval cavities in the rock—mostly natural cavities below projecting ledges augmented by cutting the rock further— and each contained a number of dead, ranging from 3 to 15. No evidence of a cult of the dead was discovered at the site. At Prosymna Blegen found five well made shafts cut in the rock varying in diameter from 1.40-1.65 m. and in depth from 90 cm. to 1.30 m. These perhaps were used originally as graves but were opened and "thoroughly rifled" of their contents in later and perhaps Byzantine times.[9] At Asine the members of the Swedish expedition explored two and possibly three Early Helladic graves which yielded a number of vases but no evidence of a cult.[10]

6. Blegen, C. W., *Korakou, a Prehistoric Settlement Near Corinth*, 100. Goldman, H., *Excavations at Eutresis in Boeotia*, 221. The infant burial, grave 20, found at Eutresis and in Pit II that has been attributed to this period most probably belongs to Middle Helladic times.

7. AJA 1 (1897) 313 ff.

8. Blegen, C. W., *Zygouries, a Prehistoric Settlement in the Valley of Cleonae*, 43-55

9. Blegen, C. W., *Prosymna*, 47.

10. Frödin, O, Persson, A., *Asine. Results of the Swedish Excavations 1922-1930*, 338, 341.

The greatest number of Early Helladic graves in the mainland of Greece were found at Agios Kosmas in Attica.[11] At a short distance from the settlement and along the shore-line twenty-two graves have been explored thus far forming part of an extensive cemetery of Early Helladic III times. These are either quatrilateral cists made of upright slabs or built and oval in shape; both find parallels in the Cycladic graves explored by Tsountas in the island of Syros. The graves apparently were family sepulchers and the remains of a number of bodies were found in each of them; some (pl. 3a) are ossuaries recalling the burials of Zygouries and those of the island of Crete.[12] With the dead funeral gifts were laid either in the grave or outside of it in areas marked by stones. Graves especially made for children were also found, and the examples explored have a quatrilateral shape and in all details are similar to the graves of the adults. By the NW. corner of grave 11 we uncovered a small circular pit, averaging 44 cm. in diameter, two thirds of the opening of which were lined with slabs as shown in plate 3b. It was found covered with a single slab, and to a depth of 40 cm. contained small stones and pebbles. Below the stones and pebbles a layer of earth 15 cm. in depth was found, and below this the rock.

Neither skeletal remains nor ashes nor other objects were found in this pit and its function must remain problematical. Its size will only make it a grave for an infant; and yet its shape is so different from that of the explored children's graves. Because of that it has been suggested that it was a "bothros" or a sacrificial pit where offerings to the dead were made.[13] However, the lack of any remains proving that function and the fact that no other evidence was uncovered in the cemetery or in any other suggesting a cult of the dead will make this suggestion very tenuous. We are inclined to accept this circular pit as a grave of an infant. That no skeletal remains were found in it is not unusual; very rarely bones of infants from that early era are preserved and in only one of the other graves of children in the cemetery were found badly decayed bones. The shape can also be

---

11. For a preliminary report cf. Mylonas, G. E., *AJA* 38 (1934) 258-279. The final study of the site has been completed thanks to grants awarded for the purpose by the American Philosophical Society to which the author wishes to express his appreciation.

12. For the Cretan ossuaries cf. *Zygouries*, 42-55, 211, 214; Marinatos in *Deltion* 12 (1929) 102 ff. Pendlebury, J. D. S., *The Archaeology of Crete*, 47, 63-65, 80, 101-102, 133, etc.

13. For sacrificial bothroi, cf. Oikonomos, G. P., *De Profusionum receptaculis sepulcralibus*, Athens, 1921. Bulle assumes the sacred character of the "bothroi" found at Orchomenos (*Orchomenos* I, 34). However, they are now recognized as typical elements of one of the architectural phases of the Early Helladic period and perhaps served as storage pits. Cf Marinatos, *BCH* 70 (1946) 337-351.

accounted for; perhaps that grave was made in imitation of the built, oval graves of adults in the same way as the rectangular graves for children were built in imitation of the cist graves. Consequently we cannot place any importance in the shape and the contents of the pit near grave 11. We can therefore conclude that at Agios Kosmas we have no evidence of a cult of the dead and in this our remains on that site are in agreement with the evidence obtained at other sites where graves were found.

Three more graves of Early Helladic times were found by Valmin at the site of Malthi-Dorion. But since these were associated by their discoverer with remains of the later period we shall include them in our discussion of the Middle Helladic remains.[14]

The survey of the Early Helladic graves found thus far in the mainland of Greece makes possible the following conclusions: It seems that the interment was the only mode of burial in Early Helladic times; that the graves were family sepulchers and often assumed the form of ossuaries; that they were grouped together in well-defined cemeteries located beyond the boundaries of the settlements; that the practice of burial within the confines of the settlement seems not to have been known; that grave furnitures were buried with the bodies in the graves or placed around the graves in areas lined with stones; that we have no evidence thus far of a cult of the dead in Early Helladic times.

II. MIDDLE HELLADIC PERIOD

Our knowledge of the Middle Helladic times is more complete because more graves of that period have been explored and also because the available evidence was organized and fully discussed in a fundamental study by Professors Blegen and Wace.[15] In that study, which appeared in 1930, it was stated that "altogether .... several hundred examples of these graves are now available for study, and their distribution is seen to be widespread throughout continental Greece." Since then more graves have been found and the known list includes examples from the following districts: *Thessaly:* Sesklo, Dimini, Volos, Rini, Phthiotic Thebes, Rachmani, Tsangli and Zerelia; *Malis:* Lianokladi; *Boeotia and Phocis:* Orchomenos, Pyrgos, Drachmani, Agia Marina, Eutresis; *Attica:* Aphidna, Eleusis, Acropolis of Athens;

14. Outside continental Greece, graves belonging to the Early Bronze Age were found in *Crete*, cf. note 12 *supra*; in the *Cyclades* cf. Tsountas, Chr., *Ephemeris* 1898, 137 ff. and 1899, 73 ff.; Dümmler, *AM* (1886), 15 ff.; Varoucha, Eir., *Ephemeris* 1925-1926, 107 ff.; *Congres International* (1905), 216 ff. In *Euboea* cf. Papavasileiou, Περὶ τῶν ἐν Εὐβοίᾳ ἀρχαίων τάφων, Athens, 1910 and *Leucas* (cf. Dörpfeld, A., *Alt-Ithaka, München*, 1927).

15. Blegen, C. W., and Wace, A. J. B., "Middle Helladic Tombs," *Symbolae Osloenses* 9 (1930) 28-37.

Corinthia: Korakou, Corinth, Gonia, Zygouries; *Argolis:* Mycenae, Tiryns, Asine, Prosymna, Karakasi; *Lakonia:* Geraki; *Messenia:* Malthi-Dorion; *Elis:* Pisa and Olympia.

The distribution of these graves is wide, their numbers substantial, and their evidence clear and well published.[16] They present rather homogeneous burial customs: the universal mode of burial is interment; most of the graves contained but one body with none or very few furnishings and it seems that the graves in which furnishings were found do not belong to the earlier part of the period; the custom of intra-mural burials seems to be universal and so are pithos burials. The evidence for the burial customs of the period which these graves provide is definite and clear, the indications for a cult of the dead in contrast are few and indefinite and yet the existence of a cult of the dead in Middle Helladic times has been postulated and advanced on the basis of data provided by some excavations. The data can stand a re-examination.

Perhaps the most striking remains that have been connected with the cult of the dead have been uncovered at Malthi-Dorion.[17] In the Middle Helladic strata of that site Valmin found thirty-two graves, the overwhelming majority of which belonged to children. In addition to these, three earlier graves were found and these gave rise to the belief in the practice of a cult of the dead in Middle Helladic times at that site. Apparently the three graves belong to the Early Helladic period and perhaps to its closing years. One of them, grave XXXIX, contained but one skeleton (pp. 190-191) and was considered as "the centre and nucleus of the three found inside and below the 'grave ring.'" Grave XXXVII, a mere crevice in the rock (p. 180), contained the remains of at least three skeletons lying in disorder. Grave XXXVIII (p. 189) was merely cut in the earth and had a roughly circular shape about two meters in diameter. It was found filled with bones piled without any order. A "solid wall of heavy blocks placed in a double row" (p. 18) was associated with these graves; its relation to them could be interpreted in various ways. Valmin in places suggests that perhaps the wall was part of a fence enclosing the area in which the three Early Helladic graves are located, and thus postulates a grave circle similar to that of Mycenae. But elsewhere he states that the

---

16. In some sites only a few graves were found, in others a great many. Thus, at Sesklo 160 graves were explored, at Prosymna 32, at Asine 103, and at Malthi-Dorion 32. For pertinent bibliography cf. Blegen-Wace, *loc. cit.* and *infra.*

17. The results of the excavations at Malthi-Dorion have been published in a splendid monograph by Valmin, M. N., *The Swedish Messenia Expedition, Part I: Malthi-Dorion. Prehistoric Acropolis in Western Messenia,* 1938 The graves are discussed on pages 186-207.

"double row of heavy blocks" may well belong to "the northern side of the thickened 'head' of the town wall," that it belongs to a tower which flanked the southern, main gate of the settlment. Again (p. 188 note 2) he expresses the belief that the "fence" to which the double row of stones belongs, "cannot have been constructed in order to enclose them (the graves), ... since one of the graves is for the most part outside it." In his last statement he is perfectly correct, as a glance at his plans will prove. If, then, the double row of stones was not built to enclose the graves we cannot have a grave circle, and the fact that its west end rests over the earth-cut Grave XXXVIII seems to indicate that the builders of that wall were ignorant of the existence of that grave at that point. Again no special meaning could be attached to the accumulated bones in the two graves;[17a] because these are typical Early Helladic ὀστεοθῆκαι and find close parallels in the graves of Zygouries especially.

The study of the plans of the site will leave no doubt that the town wall covered grave XXXVII and at least more than half of grave XXXIX. (cf. fig. 1) And if we assume that at that point the town wall was thickened to form a tower that protected the south gate, then of necessity we have to conclude that all the graves were covered by the fortification works guarding that gate. The town walls, the tower, and the gate were built in Middle Helladic II times; the graves belong to the Early Helladic period, perhaps to its closing years. If the Early Helladic graves were known to the Middle Helladic people of the site and were considered sacred, then we would expect the builders to construct the city walls in such a way as to enclose the graves in the fortified area without trespassing upon their ground. Such was the case at Mycenae and its royal graves.[18] At Malthi-Dorion, however, the wall was extended right over the graves. Now we may note that in other parts of the settlement of Dorion the city wall was

17a. For example, Klaffenbach, G., in *Gnomon* 13 (1907) 76, starting from the preliminary report of the excavations, suggested that the contents of these graves were formed from the collected remains of earlier graves built over by the town wall.

18. Wace, A. J. B., *Mycenae. An Archaeological History and Guide*, 62 plan 3 opposite p. 62 and figure 22; *BSA* 25 (1921-1922; 1922-1923) 108 ff. cf. Belger, Ch., *Die myk. Lokalsage von den Gräbern Agamemnons und der Seinen*, 26. cf. Lorimer's review in *Cl. Rev.* 1940, 50-57, and especially: "the comparison . . . of the E.H. with the shaft-grave Circle of Mycenae is misleading, for none of the shaft-graves is an ossuary, and the fortification wall far from being built over them, was manifestly designed to enclose and protect them and to leave accessible the soil beneath which they lay." Yet Thompson, G., *Studies in Ancient Greek Society. The Prehistoric Aegean*, 249, states that "near the main gate was a large cemetery enclosed by monoliths like the grave circle at Mycenae." The graves at Dorion are neither a large cemetery nor are they enclosed by monoliths.

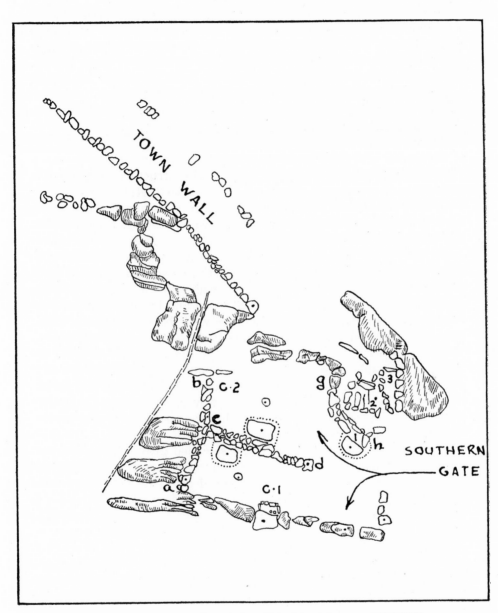

Fig. 1. The Southern Gate (after Valmin). 1 is grave XXXVIII,
2 is grave XXXIX, 3 is grave XXXVII.

built over the remains of the earlier period without any regard;[19] in a similar way the south gate and its walls were built over the graves and their area without any regard as to their existence. It is probable that the builders did not even suspect the existence of those graves. To maintain therefore that these graves were the center of special veneration does not seem to be warranted by the evidence. Again to maintain that the "double row of heavy blocks" was part of a fence surrounding the graves and forming a grave circle is contrary to the evidence.

We are on uncertain grounds again when we turn to the so-called "sanctuary for the cult of the dead." The structure so named is located inside the main, southern gate of the fortified site and at present is formed by two walls arranged in a T-shaped form.[20] The wall corresponding to the horizontal bar, wall "a-b" fig. 1, runs almost east and west and is built carefully and of large well-hewn stones while wall "c-d," corresponding to the vertical bar of the letter T, apparently a cross wall, runs almost north and south and is also built of stones. On either side of the cross wall were found two slabs in a thick layer of ashes and carbonized wood and beyond them on each of the sections a column base. No other walls belonging to the structure have survived and Valmin admits that no other walls might have existed. However, he is inclined to believe that two side walls on the east and west sides perhaps existed originally, that they were made of perishable material, and were possibly based on the "projecting rocks" that are to be seen on those sides. However, no traces of such side walls have been found. It is assumed that the structure opened toward its fourth, southern side, because no traces of a wall were found on that side; that it opened toward the so-called grave-circle, and that consequently the structure was connected with the graves in that circle and was given to the veneration of the dead. I do not believe that these assumptions are justified by the evidence. No traces of a south wall have survived, but in a similar manner no traces of an eastern or western wall have survived. The structure could not have opened to a "grave-circle", because such a grave circle did not exist as we have seen. We cannot assume that the structure was built to be used for the cult of the dead after the graves were covered by the fortifications, because we have to prove first that such a cult was venerated over

---

19. Valmin, *op. cit.*, 23, where it is stated: "As this wall (the Middle Helladic town wall) runs above some of the Early Helladic houses we may conclude that most of them were ruined and perhaps hidden below the surface when the Middle Helladic town was planned." Certainly this reasoning should apply to graves which were even below the last Early Helladic level.

20. Valmin, *op. cit.*, 126-131.

the graves before the construction of the gate. No evidence proving
the existence of such a cult is forthcoming. Finally we may assume
that the structure opened not to a grave-circle, but to the southern gate
and this is indicated by the remains uncovered there. That the structure was in some way connected with the arrangements of the southern
gate, and thus had no religious or other significance, is indicated by
the study of the gates of the settlement.

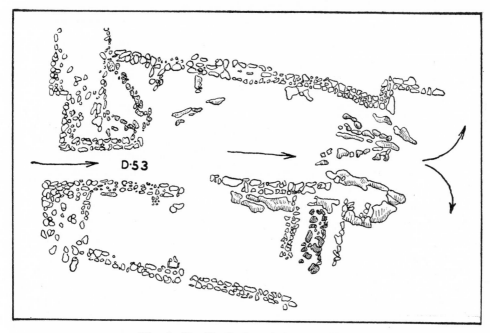

Fig. 2. The North Gate (after Valmin).

That fortified site had three main gates and at least two other
"outlets"[21]. The best preserved gate (D 53) is on the north side
(figure 2). It is only 1.55 m. in width, but its opening, framed on
both sides by walls, is 4.50 m. long and leads to a rectangular space
12 m. in length and 5 m. in width. This space to the south is termi-
nated by a passageway that "leads to both the two large areas left
open in the north-eastern and the north-western part of the town."

Gate B 18 is in the south-west corner of the town wall (figure 3).
The gate opening leads to a triangular space, surrounded by walls,
which through a narrow passage communicates with the interior.
Opening D 77 (figure 4), at the north-west corner of the wall, is very

21. *Ibid.*, 17-22.

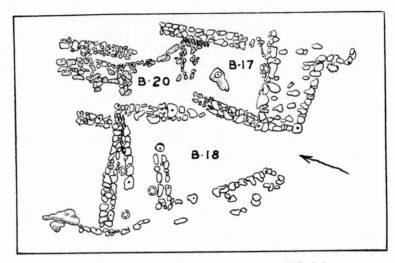

Fig. 3. The South-Western Gate (after Valmin).

instructive. It gives access to a "sort of court (D 76)" which is immediately beyond the gate opening. Limiting that court to the eastward we find a wall that runs almost parallel to the gate opening and to the city wall (figure 4 m-n). It thus blocked the forward movement of persons entering and forced them to "take a more winding route", as indicated by the arrow in figure 4.

Opening D 8 on the north-eastern corner presents a circuitous arrangement. Beyond the opening, a wall blocks the forward move-

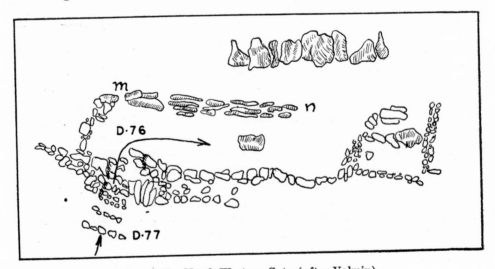

Fig. 4. The North-Western Gate (after Valmin).

ment and contributes to the formation of an angular passage that leads to a wider space surrounded by walls (figure 5).

Thus, in three out of four openings we find a wall built beyond the entrance and parallel to the city wall blocking the forward advance and forcing the "traffic" to proceed sidewise. Only in Gate D 53, on the north side, one could proceed directly at some distance before he was forced to turn to one or the other side. But on the north side the ground was such that extra caution was not necessary. Valmin states that "the slope of the mountain outside the northern gate" was so abrupt that it made it impossible for vehicles to enter the settlement through that side.

In the main, southern gate, that is of interest to us, we would expect an arrangement similar to that used in the gates and openings more exposed to the attack of an enemy. We should expect a small court beyond its opening, and a wall beyond it blocking the forward advance and deflecting traffic to the side. That is exactly what we find, and that seems to be the meaning of our T-shaped structure. Wall "a-b" corresponds exactly to the court wall "m-n" of opening D 77 (figures 1 and 4). It was there to break the forward advance, to hinder a direct access to the interior of the fortified area. Cross wall "c-d" was there perhaps to divide the "traffic" in accordance to its destination; those who were destined for the southwestern section of the settlement would go through C 1, those for the northeastern sec-

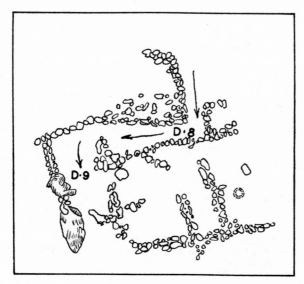

Fig. 5. The North-Eastern Gate (after Valmin).

tion would go through C 2. The slabs could have been mere hearths,[22] and the bases along with other bases that have not survived could have supported a roof covering part of this structure that was open on three sides and closed only on the one.[23] The structure must have looked like an inner portico or pavilion. As part of the gate arrangements, the structure could be explained adequately.

Of course, no importance could be assigned to the cist grave XXXV, and the bothros-like groove found in area D 15.[24] The "bothros" belongs to the Early Helladic settlement, and, though it may have been used in Middle-Helladic times in connection with a hearth that was built near it, it could have no relation to the grave that was constructed away from it and at some distance. The fact that Early Helladic sherds were found in the grave[25] seems to indicate that it was laid accidentally in an Early Helladic setting. Furthermore the bottom of that grave is level with the edge (opening?) of the "groove" and that seems to exclude any relation between the two.

The interesting remains of Dorion do not seem to prove the existence of a cult of the dead at that site and in Middle Helladic times.

The study of the remains of Asine will lead us to the same conclusion. At that site the members of the Swedish expedition found and explored a total of 103 Middle Helladic graves; of these at least 58 belonged to children and 23 to adults[26]. The preponderance of children's graves has with reason been attributed to the existence of regular cemeteries for the adults at some distance from the settlement similar to those found by Blegen at the Argive Heraeum. We can therefore maintain that the graves of Asine are all intramural burials. The graves uncovered present a variety of forms; 3 were rock-cut, 66 were earth-cut, 5 were indicated by a stone enclosure, 25 were cists and only 6 were of the variety known as pithos burials. A stratigraphic differentiation of the varieties and consequently a chronological distinction of the graves from their form proved impossible; yet Persson believes that the simple stone-enclosed graves could be placed at the beginning of the period. Very few furnishings were found in the graves and no finds were discovered over them.

However, at least four stone enclosures were found which Persson interprets as grave-altars, "direct predecessors of the tomb-altar found by Schliemann over the Fourth Shaft-grave at Mycenae."[27] As

---

22. cf. Yavis, C. G., *Greek Altars*, 39.
23. Fragments of what seemed to have been roof tiles were found indicating the existence of such a roof.
24. Valmin, *op. cit.*, 33, 205.
25. *Ibid.*, 25.
26. *Asine*, 115-128 and 341-354.
27. *Ibid.*, 347.

a result of this interpretation, these tomb-altars are taken to "speak unhesitatingly and unmistakably in favor of a real burial cult" existing at Asine. In that Persson finds himself in complete agreement "with Blegen's and Wace's belief that a cult of the dead was practiced" in continental Greece in Middle Helladic times.

Unfortunately the evidence at Asine is neither so definite nor so abundant as to prove the existence of such altars. Let us review that evidence. The first example of these so-called tomb-altars was found "close to" grave 14. Its location is not indicated on the plan of the site, but its dimensions are given as 90 cm. in length and 50 cm. in width. Within this enclosure no skeletal remains were found and it is recorded that "ashes were found in the vicinity." The dimensions of this enclosure compare with those of regular graves of children and even those of adults, and we would expect to find more proof within the enclosure and not in its vicinity of its sacrificial nature. That no bones were found within it cannot be a decisive proof against its use as a grave because often bones of infants decay completely, leaving no traces behind. As a matter of fact no bones were found in grave 54 of Asine and because of that it was characterized as a cenotaph. But a cenotaph for an infant and in an intramural burial does not seem to have any meaning. The enclosure could have been a grave for a child, and it is found in the vicinity of graves 12, 13, 14 all of which are children's graves. We may further note that close by the stone enclosure were found some "skeletal remains, possibly those of a child" merely lying in the earth, and these constitute grave No. 14[28]. With this child burial the so-called altar is apparently associated. But is it probable to believe that such an elaborate altar would have been built for a child which was not considered important enough to be laid in a regularly constructed grave?

Just north of Grave 21 another enclosure was found. Unfortunately no dimensions of that enclosure are given, but from the statement "it should have been a tomb," we may deduce that its size was similar to that of the first example. No bones were found within the enclosure, nor any other objects, but "charcoal and ashes were present in the soil around it." If we trace grave 21, an earth-cut grave of an adult, on the plan we find that it and the enclosure were found near walls. The third "stone-enclosure" was found close to grave 59, in which were found the skeletal remains of a woman 40 to 50 years old. Again the dimensions of the enclosure are not given, but, since it was assumed to be a tomb at the beginning, it must be at least of the size

28. *Ibid.*, 116.

of the first example. Within it no bones were found, or anything else, but "among the stones were discovered charcoal and ashes."

A small square of stones was found in the vicinity of Grave 63, an earth-cut sepulcher within which was found a "rather defective and disturbed skeleton of a child." We do not have the dimensions of the "square," but it also was found empty. "Close by were traces of charcoal and ashes."

Thus, two examples of the so-called altar enclosures were found near graves of children and two by graves of adults. At least three of the enclosures had the dimensions and the form of regular graves; one of them was found near an earth-cut grave and the other near a few bones (grave 14). Their size and form and the sharp contrast which they exhibit to the simple graves which they are assumed to have served give rise to a number of questions. Why were they made in the form and size of a grave if they were to serve as altars? Why have no traces of offerings survived? Why are traces of charcoal and ashes found in their vicinity and not within them? On the other hand, the charcoal and ashes found in their vicinity could be accounted for by the fact that these enclosures were lowered in the burnt layer which separates the Early Helladic from the Middle Helladic level and which is to be found below the Middle Helladic floors. We must recall that all the graves of the Middle Helladic period of Asine were found within the area of the settlement that succeeded an earlier settlement which was destroyed by fire. That this explanation of the ashes is probable is also indicated by the discovery of Early Helladic sherds below some of the stones of enclosure No. 3, while Middle Helladic sherds were found above them.[29] The fact that no skeletal remains were found in these enclosures does not necessarily prove that they were not used as graves. Bones of infants quite often decay completely, and many a child grave was found entirely empty in a number of sites and even at Asine (grave 54).[30]

There is another reason, a very important one, that will force us to reject the identification of these enclosures as altars. From the evidence presented in the final publication of the site it seems that these stone enclosures were found at the same level as the rest of the graves. Their openings were on the same level as the openings of the other graves. As the Middle Helladic graves were naturally lowered below the floor levels of the contemporary settlement, it follows that the stone-enclosures too were below the level of the settlement and

---

29. *Ibid.*, 347.

30. Cf. *supra* p. 67. Wace, A. J. B., *Chamber Tombs at Mycenae*, 129. Valmin, *op. cit.*, 204, 206. *Prosymna*, 43. *AM* 59 (1934) 160.

were covered over by that level in the same way as were the graves. How then could they have served as altars? If they were altars, in which the people of the Middle Helladic settlement and their descendents offered sacrifices to their dead, these enclosures would have been found on a higher level, above the graves, on the level of the actual settlement. That was the case with the famous altar at the Grave Circle of Mycenae. It was placed above the graves it had to serve. That is not the case in Asine. The levels in which these enclosures were found prove definitely that they too served as graves.

The survey of the evidence obtained at Asine seems not to be sufficient to prove the existence of a cult of the dead at that site and in the Middle Helladic period.

From Asine we shall have to go to Phocis for our next evidence. Near the village of Drachmani, and in 1905, Professor Soteriades explored a mound almost three meters in height and "of small diameter." It was found to enclose the Middle Helladic grave of a woman. By the grave he found a "bothros" containing ashes, charcoal, and the charred remains of wheat. The skeleton was lying simply on the earth in a contracted position and with it were found a bronze knife, few pieces of bronze, two pairs of earrings made of coiled gold wire, five Minyan, and two matt-painted vases. A little under the surface of the top of the mound Soteriades found a large jar, 60 cm. in height, decorated with matt-painted geometric designs.[31]

Blegen and Wace were the first to point out the importance of that find. In the jar found on top of the τύμβος they saw "an offering placed over the tomb after the burial." The "bothros" near the grave led them to conclude that at Drachmani and in the Middle Helladic times there existed an "established cult of the dead in which burnt sacrifices were made and offerings were deposited over the tomb." According to them, the "bothros" at Drachmani finds its analogy in the altar discovered by Schliemann in the Grave Circle of Mycenae.[32]

It is unfortunate that we have so few details regarding the find at Drachmani, and some of these are pretty vague. For example: it is stated that the "bothros" was found παρὰ τὸν τάφον. But how near? Was the "bothros" covered by the mound? It seems that it was. Did its opening reach the top or the side surface of the mound? If its opening was under the mound and at a level with the grave proper, then it could not have been used for a "cult" because we have seen that a cult requires the performance of rites to the dead, on certain days or on certain occasions, over the years; its use was limited

31. *Ephemeris* 1908, 93-94.
32. Blegen-Wace, *op. cit.*, 34.

to the time of burial and its contents were formed during the burial and therefore formed part of the burial rites. In a similar manner the single jar on the top of the mound is not conclusive. If a cult was practiced we would expect to find more traces of it in a greater number of offerings. The single jar might have been laid there immediately after the burial and the erection of the mound, and formed part of the furnishings supplied to the deceased. Soteriades compared it to the vase-markers placed over the Geometric graves. The jar does not seem to have a hole through its base; it could not therefore have served as a means through which libations and offerings were channeled into the grave; it did not serve as a "bothros," as an altar. Perhaps we should add that the "bothros" of Drachmani differs basically from that of Mycenae; the latter was above ground, always visible, always accessible, while the former seems to have been covered by a mound and after the burial was no longer accessible.

At most, the evidence from the Drachmani grave seems to indicate that the person buried in it was treated with greater respect and splendor than usual, that perhaps in his honor a special ritual was held at the time of the burial or shortly afterwards; a ritual that culminated with the erection of the mound and the placing of the jar on its top.

At the site of the Argive Heraeum Blegen excavated 32 Middle Helladic graves grouped in seven different groups and forming an extensive cemetery beyond the actual settlement.[33] Three of the excavated graves seem to offer evidence of interest. Grave I, in Group I, was a simple unlined cist which, according to the excavator, was originally covered with slabs. On the floor of the grave in the space "which must have been directly before the face" an unbroken small jug was found. But outside of the cist, on the west, many fragments of vessels were found which made four almost complete pots, which "certainly belong to the original furniture of the grave." The bones in the grave were found "shattered and disrupted" and this as well as the disappearance of the covering slabs proves that the grave was entered into and disturbed. Blegen states that "the original position of the four vessels, which had been thrust out to the west, could not be certainly determined" but suggests that they may have been placed "above the cover-slabs and not beneath them."[34]

"Close-beside" grave III, group III, two yellow Minyan goblets were found. And these could also be considered as originally "deposited above instead of within the cist." In the cist no furnishings

33. Blegen, C. W., *Prosymna*, 30-50.
34. *Ibid.*, 31.

were found, but the remnants of the upper section "of the skeleton lay collected in a heap beside the lower legs in the Northwest extremity of the cist."[35] This disarrangement of the bones remains unexplained especially since Blegen sees no molestation from the outside that might have caused the disturbance. However, the vases found outside the cist in this instance also were not over the covering slabs. The floor of the cist was 1.05 m. from the surface.

The third example is more important. Above the slabs of Grave IV, Group IV, and about 1 m. below the present surface of the soil, a "mass of small stones and earth" was found and upon it were found a matt-painted jug with a tall spout, two small cups, and a goblet of yellow Minyan ware. A dagger and a tweezer were found in the cist with the bones. Again these were not in proper arrangement. "Most of the upper part of the skeleton was actually found in disorder in the southeasterly part of the cist, a puzzling phenomenon like that already noted in Graves III and VIII." Blegen suggests that perhaps the body was placed "in a position with head and trunk considerably raised, so that when the connecting tissues decayed the skull rolled down toward the feet, dislocating some of the other bones in its fall."[36] However, the depth of the grave, only 35 cm., would not permit a posture raised enough to bring about these results.

On the basis of the discovery of the vases outside the three graves Blegen concludes that the "offerings were sometimes deposited above the Middle Helladic graves, after the burial, not merely within the cist itself." With this statement we are in agreement in spite of the paucity of the evidence, especially since we have a similar practice at Drachmani and at Agios Kosmas in an earlier period. This does not mean that the Middle Helladic placing of vases over the graves was developed from an Early Helladic custom; it merely indicates that such a practice could have developed in an area for specific reasons that apply to that area.

However, Blegen continues: "these offerings need not have been placed over the graves at the actual moment of the funeral; indeed they suggest rather a continuing cult of the dead in which offerings and sacrifices were made above the place of burial." And this conclusion he bases, along with Wace, on the Drachmani mound. But we have seen that the evidence at Drachmani is not conclusive; the same we can say for the Heraeum. At least one of the graves outside of which vases were found, Grave I, Group I, was disturbed badly at a later period. One could assume that the shattered vessels were thrown

35. *Ibid.*, 34.
36. *Ibid.*, 37-38.

out of the grave at the time of the disturbance. Even grave IV was somewhat touched by later people. But there is an additional argument. To believe that the vases were placed over the graves at a later time we have to assume that the covering slabs were lying on or near the surface. Since the cists are cut in hard, clay-like *stereo*, they must have been sunk below the surface of the soil. How deep over the *stereo* was that soil in Middle Helladic times is impossible to determine. Today the covering slabs were found from 75 cm. to one meter below the surface; but in Middle Helladic times they must have been covered with soil of undetermined depth. On top of that earth, quite above the cover-slabs, we would expect to find the vases if they were later offerings to the dead, for otherwise we would assume that every time an offering was to be made the earth over the slabs was removed. That seems doubtful, and the position in which the vases were found does not indicate that they were lying on a substantial layer of earth extending over the slabs. This observation cannot be conceived as definite evidence, but it seems to indicate that perhaps the vases were originally in the cist itself from which at a later time they were thrown out, or at the most that they were placed over the graves perhaps at the time of burial. We may finally note that out of some three hundred and fifty graves excavated thus far only in the one instance at the Argive Heraeum and the one at Drachmani we can be positive that vases were placed outside the graves. But even in those two instances we cannot prove that they were deposited sometime after the burial. At any rate two instances and four graves out of three hundred and fifty are not sufficient to warrant the conclusion that a cult of the dead was in existence in the Middle Helladic period.

Summarizing our evidence we can state: 1) that a great number of graves belonging to the Middle Helladic period have been excavated to date in a wide area of continental Greece. 2) Most of these graves are within the confines of the settlement, and only in one instance—at Prosymna—they were grouped into cemeteries beyond the settlement. 3) The indications for the existence of a cult of the dead in this period are neither definite nor conclusive. Perhaps only the grave at Drachmani may indicate special ritual, but unfortunately the details of that excavation are so meager that they do not allow any definite conclusions. 4) The indications from Malthi-Dorion, Asine, and Prosymna do not seem to prove the existence of a cult. 5) It is possible to maintain that as far as we know to date we have no definite evidence proving the existence of a cult of the dead practiced by the people in general over the graves of their families in the Middle Helladic period.

III. LATE HELLADIC PERIOD

The last period of the Prehistoric Age is represented by a great number of graves excavated over a wide area in continental Greece. The following list, without any claims to completeness, will help to illustrate this broad diffusion of the explored graves:

Thessaly: Dimini, Sesklo, Marmariani, Rakhmani, Kapakli, Goura.

Boeotia and Phocis: Delphi, Agios Theodoros, Thisbe, Orchomenos, Thebes.

Attica: Spata, Menidi, Thorikos, Ligori, Kopreza, Brauron, Sphettos, Steiria, Porto-Rafti, Marathon, Athens, Eleusis, Salamis, Aegina.

Corinthia and Argolis: Korakou, Zygouries, Mycenae, Prosymna, Dendra, Agios Elias, Nauplia, Asine, Argos, Berbati, Palaeokhori, Skhoenokhori.

Laconia: Vaphio, Campos.

Triphylia and Messenia: Bodia, Kakovatos, Pylos, Malthi-Dorion.

Achaea: Anthia, Gourzoumisa, Bodia, Prostovitsa, Chalandritsa, Koutreika, Agios Vasileios.[37]

The careful exploration of so many graves has established almost in complete detail the elaborate and impressive burial rites of the Mycenaean world. These have been discussed recently by Professors Nilsson, Wace, Blegen, Persson, and Mylonas. The question which, we be-

---

37. THESSALY: Tsountas, Ch., *Αἱ προϊστορικαὶ ἀκροπόλεις Διμηνίου καὶ Σέσκλου*, 115, 121, 150. Wace-Thompson, *Prehistoric Thessaly*, 40, 53-54, 68, 82, 206. *AM* 1886, 435 ff.; 1887, 136 ff.; 1896, 247. *Ephemeris* 1906, 81. Tsountas-Manatt, *The Mycenaean Age*, 385, 395.
BOEOTIA-PHOCIS: *Fouilles de Delphes* V, 6 ff. Schliemann, *Orchomenos*, 1881. Pausanias, IX, 38, 2. *Ephemeris* 1909, 57 ff.; 1910, 209 ff.; *Praktika* 1910, 152 ff. *Deltion*, 1917, 124 ff.
ATTICA: *AM* 1877, 82 ff., 261 ff.; 35 (1910) 17 ff. *BCH* 1878, 185 ff. *'Αθήναιον* 1877, 167 ff. Lolling, H. G., et al. *Das Kuppelgrab bei Menidi*, 1880. *Ephemeris* 1895, 193 ff. *Mycenaean Age*, 383 ff. *Hesperia* 4 (1935) 318 ff.; 9 (1940) 274 ff.; 17 (1948) 155 ff.; 18 (1949) 318 ff. *AJA* 36 (1932) 110; 40 (1936) 424; 43 (1939) 518 ff. Mylonas, G. *Προϊστορικὴ 'Ελευσίς*, 57-59, BSA 42 (1947) 1 ff. *Praktika* 1933, 36; 1934, 8-10, 29-38; 1935, 7-9.
CORINTHIA-ARGOLIS: Blegen, C. W., *Korakou*, 100 ff.; *Zygouries*, 57 ff.; *Prosymna*, 51 ff. *BSA* 25 (1921-1922; 1922-1923) 284 ff. Wace, A. J. B., *Mycenae*, 13-19; *Chamber Tombs at Mycenae*. *AM* 3 (1878) 271 ff.; 5 (1880) 143 ff.; 38 (1913) 347 ff. *BCH* 28 (1904) 364ff. *Ephemeris* 1878, 17-18; 1880, 21; 1888, 127 ff.; 1892, 52 ff.; 1895, 221 ff. Frödin-Persson, *Asine*. Persson, A., *The Royal Tombs at Dendra Near Midea; New Tombs at Dendra Near Midea. AJA* 32 (1928) 113 ff. *BCH* 1923, 214 ff.
TRIPHYLIA-MESSENIA: *AM* 1907, xv; 1908, 295 ff.; 1909, 269 ff. *AJA* 35 (1931) 199; 32 (1928) 113. *Ephemeris* 1912, 268 ff.; 1914, 99 ff. *Praktika* 1909, 65, 274-292; 1926, 91, 140-141. *AA* 1928, 596; 1930, 20 ff. Valmin, *op. cit.*, 207 ff.
LACONIA: *Ephemeris* 1888, 197; 1889, 129 ff.; 1891, 189 ff. *Praktika* 1889, 21; 1890, 37; 1891, 23. *Mycenaean Age*, 160, 230.
ACHAEA: *Praktika* 1928, 114-119; 1929, 87, 89; 1930, 81-87; 1931, 71-73; 1932, 57-61; 1933, 90-93; 1934, 114-115; 1936, 21; 1937, 84-93.

lieve, still remains unanswered is whether or not these graves have provided sufficient and definite evidence proving the existence of a cult of the dead among the Mycenaean people. Our authorities leave the impression that such a cult was practiced, and Nilsson, in his monumental work, has discussed the relics on which such an impression could be founded. They include niches, cists, and the remains of fires that have been found in a number of Mycenaean graves. These relics we shall consider briefly in our effort to reach a definite conclusion on the matter.

A. *Niches*

In a number of graves rock-cut niches are found not only in the burial chambers but also in the dromoi. The niches in the chambers could not very well have served for a cult that requires tendance on definite days and occasions in the years that followed burial, because it is definitely established that the door openings of the graves were walled up after every interment and thus free access to the chambers and their niches was impossible. The niches in the dromoi must be considered individually because, according to Professor Nilsson, some only served for burial purposes while others were used in the cult for the dead.[38]

The most definite evidence for the use of niches was secured by Blegen at Prosymna, by Wace at Mycenae, and by Persson at Asine and Dendra. At Prosymna niches were found cut in the lateral walls of the dromoi in tombs VI, XXX, and XXXVII.[39] The opening of all three niches was closed either by a wall of small stones (in 2 cases: tombs VI and XXX) or by a thin slab (tomb XXXVII). Niches in tombs VI and XXXVII were found packed with bones, presumably carried out from the chamber; in the niche of tomb XXX the remains of a child were found. Thus the niches of Prosymna served either as ὀστεοθῆκαι or for infant burials.

At Mycenae Wace found a niche closed by a stone slab at the beginning of the dromos of tomb 529. It contained no remains. An irregular carving in the stone was found 90 cm. above the floor of the dromos and toward the top of the right door jamb of tomb 523. In it were found L.H. III sherds, "mostly pieces of plain kylikes."[40] No cult significance was attributed to these by Wace who concluded: "The use of such niches for the burial of infants is a satisfactory ex-

---

38. Nilsson, *The Minoan-Mycenaean Religion*₂, 587-588 and 589 for conclusions.
39. *Prosymna*, 234-235.

planation of them and is not inconsistent with lack of bones because an infant's bones are apt to decay completely."[41]

Additional evidence was obtained by the members of the Swedish expedition at Asine. Rock-cut niches were found in the dromoi of tombs 3, 4, and 5. The niche of tomb 3 was only 30-35 cm. above the floor of the dromos and its opening had been closed by a stone wall. Many decayed bones were found on its floor proving that the niche served either as a burial place or as a bone depository.[42] In the dromos of tomb 4 a burial niche was cut only 10 cm. above the floor of the dromos. Its opening was closed with a stone packing and in it were found three bone fragments badly preserved. On the opposite wall and slightly above the level of the first, another niche of smaller dimensions was found and this is believed to have been built to serve as a place where sacrifices or some ritual could be held in connection with the tomb in the opposite wall. However, no evidence was found to indicate such a use, and no "palpable evidence of sacrifices" was found.[43] More interesting is the niche found in the dromos of tomb 5. It was cut in the rock only 60 cm. below the top edge of the side. Its opening was found closed with a rubble packing and within it were found 3 post-Mycenaean or Proto-Geometric vases. One of these vases, a crater, was half filled with burnt earth and calcined animal bones. Persson, who discussed the grave and the niche, concludes: "clearly a sacrifice to persons buried in the chamber. The niche was cut after the grave was walled up and the dromos was either partially or fully filled. . . . Probably, part of the dromos fill was cleared away, the niche cut, and the offerings placed in it, after which the pit was again filled up." The same conclusion is reached by Nilsson: "It is evident that this find, which does not contain any human remains, is an offering made after the tomb was closed."[44]

One of the details of the niche, however, remains puzzling. If it served as a place of cult why was its opening closed by a wall? This was a characteristic feature of the Mycenaean graves; so characteristic indeed that the wall blocking the door of tomb 3 at Asine was brought forth as a proof that the tomb was actually used. To the assumption that tomb 3 "had never been used as a tomb," Persson

---

40. *Chamber Tombs at Mycenae*, 35.

41. *Ibid.*, 129. cf. *supra*, p. 78. Tsountas has reported four niches from Mycenae. All were found in the chambers and were used for burials: *Ephemeris* 1888, 129.

42. *Asine*, 172-173. It is interesting to remark that this niche as well as that of Tomb 4 took the place of the chamber: *ibid.* 357.

43. *Asine*, 175. The niches in the dromos of this tomb are called "burial niches" by Persson on page 357.

44. Nilsson, *op. cit.*, 588. *Asine*, 178-179 and 357.

counters: "but to this the objection must be made that the stone packing of the door, which was partly in *situ* and partly collapsed, would
not have been put into position except in connection with a burial,
that is to say immediately after such had taken place." We find such
a wall closing the niches in tombs 3 and 4 at Asine, which are proved
to have been used for burial or as depositories of bones, and in the
niches of the tombs at Prosymna which were used for the same purpose.[45] Why should a place for sacrifices be walled up after the rites?
It seems to us more probable that this niche too served for the burial
of an infant. The ashes in the crater may indicate that the infant
was cremated; that toward the end of the Mycenaean Age cremation
was practiced in continental Greece is indicated by the graves of
Salamis and the burial of Prosymna.[46] It may be interesting to note
that Blegen has recently suggested that the well-known Mycenaean
terra-cotta figurines were placed in graves of children; the "small
clay idol in the shape of a cow's head" found in this niche will give
added weight to the suggestion that the niche served for the burial
of an infant.[47]

In the dromos of a chamber tomb at Nauplia, and about a meter
above its floor, a niche was found containing a few bones, "a fragmentary idol, a plate and some glass-like splinters." Similar niches
were found in the chambers of other tombs in the same district. Both
Staes and Kavvadias consider these as sepulchral niches "because they
were found blocked by a slab or by a stone wall and contained earth,
bones, and *kterismata*."[48]

The survey of the niches found in the dromoi of the explored graves,
and of their contents has indicated that in general such niches were
used either as ὀστεοθῆκαι or as the places for infant burials. The niche
in the dromos of tomb 5, at Asine, which has been taken to indicate
a cult, seems to us most probably to have served as a place where the
remains of a cremated child were placed along with its kterismata;
the niche of grave 523 at Mycenae obtained its deposit when the
dromos was filled. It should be noted that stems of kylikes were found

---

45. *Asine*, 173. *Prosymna*, 51-52, 113, 186-188.

46. *Prosymna*, Tomb XLI page 242. Kavvadias, P., Προϊστορικὴ Ἀρχαιολογία,
310-311. Wide, S. *AM* 1910, 17 ff. For a discussion of post-Mycenaean-Geometric
examples of cremation see Lorimer, H. L., "*Pulvis et Umbra*," *JHS* 53 (1933)
161 ff. Also, Myres, J. L., *Who Were the Greeks*, 380 ff.

47. *Prosymna*, 256: "Both animals and figurines might conceivably be play-
things, the cherished possession of children who died." Persson, *The New Tombs
at Dendra*, 33, objects to this interpretation and considers the figurines as the
"counterparts of the *ushebtis* of the Egyptian tombs."

48. Kavvadias, *op. cit.*, 290. *Ephemeris* 1892, 73. *AM* 5 (1880) 143 ff. Ἀθήναιον
7 (1878) 183, 515 ff.

mostly in that niche, and Blegen and Wace have suggested that one of the last acts of the burial ritual was the drinking of a toast in honor of the dead after which the kylix used for that purpose was broken and left in front of the door.[49] Stems of such vases are commonly found before the doors and naturally were mixed with the earth-filling that was poured into the dromos after each successive burial.

We may perhaps end our discussion by drawing attention to another important fact. With the exception of the niche in tomb 5 at Asine, all the known niches are located a little above the floor of the dromos. And the Asine niche is not on the surface, but 60 cm. below the edge of the rock that formed the side of the dromos. It is now generally accepted that after each interment not only the door of the chamber was well packed, but also the dromos itself was filled with loose earth.[50] The earth filling the dromos and the packing of the door were removed every time a body had to be buried in the chamber, and were replaced after that was accomplished. It is evident that normally the niches were buried below the filling of the dromos and were inaccessible. And the question naturally arises: If they were inaccessible normally how could they have served a cult of the dead?

At the beginning of our discussion we noted that niches were found in chambers of tombs; that these niches, because of their inaccessibility, could not be considered as serving a cult of the dead. Examples of niches in chambers are known from Mycenae, Prosymna, Nauplia, and Dendra. Certainly, the most complete information for the use of the "chamber niches" has been recorded by Blegen in his discussion of the Prosymna examples and it might prove profitable to review briefly his conclusions.

Six tombs in the Prosymna cemetery yielded niches cut in their chamber walls. Three of the niches were found with their openings blocked by a wall (Tombs XVI, XXXIV, XLIII). In these walled up niches bones were found proving that they served for burials or as depositories. This observation is interesting since it again underscores the meaning of the walls closing the openings of niches. Extensive heaps of bones were found in the niches of tombs VIII and XXIX proving their funeral use. The niche in Tomb IX seems to have been used in Geometric and later times for a cult in honor of the dead

---

49. *Prosymna*, 238. *Chamber Tombs at Mycenae*, 131. Such stems were also found at Asine: cf. *Asine*, 165, 358.

50. *The Mycenaean Age*, 139. *Chamber Tombs at Mycenae*, 127 ff. *Prosymna*, 236, 241. *New Tombs at Dendra*, 154. *Royal Tombs at Dendra*, 26. *Asine*, 357. *Ephemeris* 1895, 218; 1888, 129. Mylonas, G., "Homeric and Mycenaean Burial Customs," *AJA* 52 (1948) 69.

and therefore its original contents were not preseved. Thus the evidence obtained by Blegen is conclusive: it proves that at Prosymna such niches cut in the chambers were used for burials or as bone depositories. The same conclusion was reached by Tsountas for the tombs at Mycenae and by Staes and Kavvadias for the Nauplia group.[51]

In the chamber of tomb 9 at Dendra a niche was discovered which, according to Persson, its excavator, "must be considered from all appearances as a sacrificial niche with a slaughter table hewn from the rock." The niche was found 40 cm. above the floor and measured 1.85 in length, 65 cm. in depth, and 1.10 m. in height. The only indications that helped Persson to reach his conclusion were "two square sinkings about 10 cm. deep" that "occurred in the two inner corners" and which "bore a distinct resemblance to the sinkings for the blood in the freestanding slaughter-table that was found in Chamber Tomb No. 2, the so-called Cenotaph, at Dendra."[51a] Since no other corroborative evidence was uncovered, we believe that this "resemblance" which is neither so pronounced nor definite, is inadequate to support his conclusion. The cuttings in the floor of the niche may be another elaboration, and the chamber of this tomb presents definite instances of such elaboration, or an accented area for the placing of the kterismata or even for the placing of the bodies of infants. We may recall that below the floor of the niche of Tomb XVI at Prosymna a shallow cist, only 15 cm. deep, was found filled with human bones. Had the contents of that cist disappeared we could very well have assumed that the cist was used for sacrificial purposes. And since no other evidence is forthcoming we would hesitate to attribute to the Dendra example a function different from that of other "chamber niches" whose funeral use is attested.

The survey of the niches found in Mycenaean graves has failed to bring forth any evidence that will indicate that these niches had anything to do with a cult held in honor of the dead. On the contrary it proved that they served either as ὀστεοθῆκαι or as burial niches.

B. Cists

Pits or cists cut in the rock are very common in Mycenaean tombs

---

51. *Prosymna*, 52, 75, 113, 162, 164, 186, 245: Tombs VIII, IX, XVI, XXXIV, XXIX, XLIII. Tsountas, *Ephemeris* 1888, 129. Kavvadias, *op. cit.*, 290.

51a. *New Tombs at Dendra*, 55, 159. *Royal Tombs at Dendra*, 100 and 109 ff. Pl. XXIX. We may note that at Asine niches in the chambers were not found: *Asine*, 357. We may also note that the depth of the Dendra niche, 65 cm. is almost identical with that of the following three burial niches of Prosymna: Tomb XXIX, depth of niche 64 cm. (p. 75); XXXIV, depth 65 cm. (p. 173); XLIII depth 67 cm. (p. 186).

and their use seems to be clear. Some are to be found in the chamber proper, others in the stomion, still others in the dromos, and others near the tombs. Tsountas observed that some of these cists served "to secure an inviolable repose to individuals of peculiar distinction in the family."[52] Blegen has pointed out that the majority of the cists he found in the tombs at Prosymna (85 out of a total of 87) were used for the secondary burials of assembled remains and as bone depositories, and only two served for primary interments.[53] Wace also observed that the majority of the "pits" were for the *disiecta membra* and that a few were used for primary burials. Only two pits, in graves 502 and 520, because of their small size, "may have been sacrificial pits." The pit in grave 520 was a mere diamond-shaped depression about 25 cm. deep in which nothing was found. But in grave 521, "a shallow shapeless pit" only 15 cm. deep was found and another round in shape and only 20 cm. deep; both contained bones and apparently served as depositories.[54] Evidently then, neither the shape nor the dimensions of such pits were prohibitive of their use as depositories and they could not be construed as evidence indicating their use as sacrificial pits. Nilsson and Persson further have pointed out that some cists were used for burials, others for storing gifts, and still others as sacrificial pits.[55]

At least the pit in the chamber of the tholos at Menidi and one of the pits in the chamber of the unrifled beehive tomb at Dendra have been considered as sacrificial pits. Sometime during the use of the chamber the former was covered up by a terrace or bench and consequently it could not have served a cult that continued through the ages.[56] In the pit of Dendra the remains of burned offerings were found.[57] If these offerings were burned during the burial, that act formed part of the burial rites and consequently it does not prove the existence of a cult. This seems to be indicated by the position of the pit in the chamber whose door was packed after each burial so that no one could enter at a later time to indulge in a cult. If the offerings were burned after the burial, then they must have been burned at a

---

52. *Mycenaean Age*, 137.

53. *Prosymna*, 246.

54. *Chamber Tombs at Mycenae*, 136-137, 23, 28.

55. Nilsson, *op. cit.*, 589-595. For sacrificial pits in general cf. Oiconomos, G. P., *De profusionum receptaculis sepulcralibus*, 8. *New Tombs at Dendra* 31-32; *Royal Tombs at Dendra*, 73 ff. "Cists" are found in two Minoan graves in the Mavro Spileo cemetery, Nilsson, *op. cit.*, 592, and *BSA* 28 (1928) 246. They are used for burial in the late and post Mycenaean cemeteries of Cephallonia: Kavvadias, *op. cit.*, 355 ff. Marinatos, *Ephemeris* 1932, 17 ff. and 1933, 68 ff.

56. Lolling, H., et al., *Das Kuppelgrab bei Menidi*, 37 ff. Nilsson, *op. cit.*, 590. Wolters, *JDAI* 13 (1898) 13 ff.; 14 (1899) 103 ff.

57. *Royal Tombs at Dendra*, 13 ff.

later time when the grave was re-opened for re-use. In that case, the deposit was formed because of the death of another member of the family and not as a result of repeated offerings made at specified times and occasions as the cult would require. Consequently it cannot prove the existence of a cult of the dead. As a matter of fact such a cult is not indicated by these pits.

C. *Fire*

It is a well established fact that traces of fire have been found in a number of Mycenaean graves. The idea that they prove cremation has been abandoned and a good many scholars believe that fire was used to fumigate and purify the graves when they were re-opened to be used for new interments.[58] Professor Nilsson in addition believes that fire was used in connection with the burial rites and the cult of the dead. The graves at Dendra have provided the strongest basis for such a belief.

In the chamber of the tholos tomb at Dendra Persson discovered four pits. In one of these the remains of a maiden (a princess?) were found. In the other the bodies of a man and a woman (the king and the queen?) were discovered. Human and animal bones and the skull of a dog were found in the third, while the fourth contained ashes, charcoal, and burned objects. On the floor of the chamber were found, along with sherds and a variety of beads, some bones which perhaps belonged originally to at least three individuals. According to Persson the burned objects found in the pit were the remnants of funeral gifts that were burned in a pyre lighted in the tholos and later swept in the pit.[59] We must add that the tholos tomb at Dendra is not the only one in which burned objects were found. As early as 1888 Tsountas had reported the discovery of various burned "ornaments of gold leaf and of glass paste . . . . trinkets and toilet accessories" mixed with ashes and charcoal in Mycenaean graves, and attributed these to the burning of personal belongings in honor of the dead.[60] Thus, with reason Professor Nilsson remarks that in "the Mycenaean age a curious mixture of inhumation and burning of offerings is found in many and important instances. The corpses were inhumed with rich gifts, but other gifts were burned in or before the

---

58. *The Mycenaean Age*, 138. *Ephemeris* 1888, 131, 134. Nilsson, *op. cit.*, 595 ff. *Chamber Tombs at Mycenae*, 140 ff. *Prosymna*, 250 ff. *Asine*, 159 ff. *New Tombs at Dendra*, 23, 32, 53, 59. Evans, Sir A., *The Shaft Graves and Beehive Tombs of Mycenae*, 3 ff. Mylonas. *op. cit.*, 68. Dörpfeld's theory of scorching has found no favor among scholars: *Mélanges Nicole*, 1905, 95 ff. and *Comptes rendus du congres international d'Archéologie* 1905, 161 ff. Cf. Gercke-Norden, *Einleitung in die Klassische Altertumswiss.* II, I⁴, 1930, 66 ff. for bibliography.

59. *Royal Tombs at Dendra*, 13 ff. Nilsson, *op. cit.*, 590, 597.

tomb. This mixture, which is recorded nowhere else, presents a fresh problem and requires an explanation." In my study of the burial customs of the Homeric and Mycenaean world I emphasized this problem when I stated: "if the burning of the belongings of the dead was customary, it will remain unexplained why some of the κτέρεα were burned, while others, the majority indeed, were laid out around the corpse." Now Professor Nilsson in explanation suggests that this resulted from the survival of the custom of burning gifts to the dead together with his corpse. He further suggests that "this implies that the Greeks, when they immigrated used cremation, but having settled in Greece succumbed to Minoan culture in burial customs as well as in other habits of life and in art, though they sometimes kept the burning of gifts to the dead as a survival of their old custom."[61]

This explanation, however, does not seem to agree with the available evidence. It is generally believed that the first wave of the Indo-European inhabitants of Greece, i. e. the first so-called Greeks, immigrated to the Hellenic peninsula at the end of the Early Helladic Era.[62] If Nilsson's suggestion is correct then we should find graves with cremated remains at least in the early part of the Middle Helladic period, at a time when the contact of continental Greece with Crete seems to have been interrupted. Not a single example of cremation has been found as yet, although a good many graves from that early period have been explored both in the Peloponnesus and in northern Greece.[63] There must be another explanation that will account for this burning of the κτέρεα.

---

60. *Ephemeris* 1888, 134. *Mycenaean Age*, 147.

61. Nilsson, *op. cit.*, 599.

62. Cf. especially J. B. Haley—C. W. Blegen, "The Coming of the Greeks," *AJA* 32 (1928) 141-154. Blegen, "Athens and the Early Age of Greece," in *Athenian Studies Presented to W. S. Ferguson, Harvard Studies in Classical Philology*. Suppl. Vol. I, 1-9. Buck, C. D., "The Language of Greece, 2000-1000," *Cl.Phil.* 21 (1926) 1 ff. Mylonas, *Ephemeris* 1930, 6 ff. Nilsson, *op. cit.*, 12-13, points out that Persson, *Asine*, 433, has suggested that the Ionians were the first wave of Indo-Europeans to reach Greece. Long before Persson, Kretschmer, in *Glotta* 1 (1909) 9 ff. argued that to be the case on linguistic grounds and his arguments were accepted as possible by Buck, *op. cit.*, 24. In my article on the prehistoric inhabitants of Greece, *Ephemeris* 1930, 17-20, I maintained that the Ionians were the first Indo-Europeans to reach the Greek peninsula and that they were followed by the Aeolians and the Achaeans.

63. It is true that Professor Nilsson suggests (*op. cit.* 11) that the first Indo-European tribes invaded and were established in Greece at the end of the Middle Helladic Period. But in that case we shall have to postulate an abrupt abandonment of their traditional, according to Nilsson, custom of cremation and the adoption of that of interment. When we recall how tenaciously people hold on to their burial habits the world over this sudden change seems doubtful. In Greece itself we find that when cremation was introduced in Geometric times it did not displace interment, but it was practiced side by side with the latter. The same is true in Italy where down to Imperial times some families, following their tradi-

We cannot of course, be positive about the ideas which underlie the burial customs of the Mycenaean people but the relics recovered thus far seem to indicate that they, like the Homeric heroes, believed that the "psyche" or "spirit" of the deceased remained in the grave as long as the flesh was preserved. To keep it in the grave until the complete decay of the flesh, the door of the chamber was packed and the dromos was filled in after the interment; but after the flesh had decomposed the "spirit" no longer remained in the grave but descended, as Homer would say, to the realm of the shades. Sometimes, however, a grave had to be re-used before the body of the previously buried was completely decomposed, and consequently while his "spirit" was assumed still to be in that grave. Then the earth from the dromos and the packing from the door had to be removed, the chamber itself had to be fumigated and made ready for the later occupant. To placate the "spirit" still in the grave and to induce it to stay in it, even though the door was wide open and fumigation made the stay in the chamber unpleasant, gifts had to be offered to it. Perhaps the partial decay of the body suggested the rite of burning these gifts; consumed by fire, by fire that helped to purify the grave itself, they could be acceptable offerings to "the spirit" which perhaps could no longer use gifts in actuality since its body was so far spent. Thus the burning of the gifts could prove instrumental in propitiating the disturbed "spirit" and served to reassure the relatives who had to open and enter its chamber. In this connection we may recall Odysseus' promise to the shades that on his return to Ithaka he would not only sacrifice to them a barren heifer, but that he would also fill the sacrificial fire ἐσθλῶν.[64]

This explanation will account for the finds in the chamber of the tholos tomb at Dendra. Whether or not we believe that the man and the woman, the king and the queen of Persson, were buried at the same time, we shall have to admit that the grave was re-opened at

---

tional customs, buried their dead, while others cremated them. And this dualism seems to go all the way back to the prehistoric times when races with different burial customs established themselves in the peninsula and gradually mixed. Even if we assumed that the first Indo-European tribes came into Greece at the end of the Middle Helladic period and that until then they practiced cremation only to abandon it as they came under Cretan influence, still we should expect to find some cases of cremation in the early years of their establishment in continental Greece. Such cases of cremation have not been found as yet. Even the graves of cemeteries "S" and "F" at Nidri in Leucas contained interments only: Dörpfeld, W., *Alt-Ithaka*, 207. As for the traces of fire in cemetery "R", which were attributed by Dörpfeld to crematory pyres, their extent and depth do not warrant his supposition. And then the body found in the pithos will remain unexplained. However, Myres accepts the existence of cremation at Leukas, *Who Were the Greeks*, 395 ff.

64. *Odyssey* XI, 30-31.

least once after its initial use, since another complete skeleton, that
of the princess (?), was found in another cist; and this is further
indicated by the traces of fire found on the floor of the chamber, fire
that was used for the purification and fumigation of the grave. It is
not impossible to assume that the re-opening of the grave occurred
soon after the initial burial and before the body or bodies of those
buried first were completely decomposed. That, according to our explanation, would call for the burning of gifts to appease the "spirit"
or "spirits" which were disturbed. Thus the burned gifts found in
one of the cists could be explained as the remnants of the offerings
made to appease the disturbed "spirits." When graves were re-opened
at long intervals that allowed the complete decomposition of the
bodies previously placed in them the need of appeasing disturbed
"spirits" did not exist and consequently it was not necessary to burn
gifts. Thus the burning of some offerings in a limited number of
graves can be explained without doing violence to any evidence to
date.

We may recall that Schliemann found ashes and burned animal
bones at the foot of the stelai he unearthed in the Grave Circle of
Mycenae, and that at the foot of the third stele he found a gold plated
button among the grey ashes.[65] Wace and his colleagues have proved
that these stelai originally were standing at a lower level; that during
the re-arrangement of the Circle, in late Heladic III times, they were
removed from that position and were erected at the higher level that
was then established.[66] The burned remains therefore found at their
bases resulted from sacrifices made not at the time of their initial
erection, but at the time of the re-arrangement. The limited amount
of the ashes found would further indicate that the rites were held
but once and did not result from a repeated practice. It seems reasonable to suggest that at the foot of the stelai offerings were burned,
and not placed, as a propitiation for the disturbance caused by the
removal of the stelai from their original position. It is a well-known
fact that a cult was practiced over the shaft graves, a cult which indicated the belief in the presence of "the spirits" in those graves in
spite of the decomposition of their bodies. It was natural that those
"spirits" were disturbed by the removal of their stelai and had to be
appeased. This could be accomplished by offerings, offerings which
were burned. In the finds made by the stelai of the Grave Circle
therefore, we may see another indication favoring our interpretation
of the burned offerings.

---

65. *Mykenai*, 104 and 99.
66. *BSA* 25 (1921-1922; 1922-1923) 108 ff. Wace, *Mycenae*, 62 plan 3 opposite
page 62 and figure 22.

Chamber tomb No. 2 at Dendra was assumed to offer another example of burned offerings made in pursuance of a cult of the dead.
In that chamber were found a stone slaughtering block, a sacrificial
table, a hearth, two menhirs, and two pits cut in the stereo. One of
these, located in front of the hearth, contained animal bones, while
the other was found empty; a third pit in the stomion was found
packed with large and small bronze vessels. Persson has proved that
the grave was a cenotaph of two persons who had died abroad and,
in my study of the burial customs, I have attributed this unique
funeral equipment to the special rites required for the "calling" of
the spirits of the two to a grave in the homeland.[67] These rites recall
those performed by Odysseus at the edge of Hades when he was trying to lure the "psyche" of Teiresias and learn from it about his
journey homeward.[68] That these rites had no relation to a cult of the
dead is indicated by the fact, pointed out by Persson, that this tomb
in every respect was treated like any other Mycenaean tomb—its door
was carefully blocked, and its dromos was properly filled up; and
these acts apparently took place after the unique rites in the chamber
were completed.

Unfortunately we have no complete information for the grave of
Marathon in whose floor was found a thick layer of ashes mixed
with animal bones.[69] Until the final report is published no conclusions
can be based on its remains. Nor should undue importance be attributed to sherds blackened by fire that are found in and out of the
chambers of Mycenaean graves. Vessels would be blackened by fires
lighted in chambers for its fumigation. Again many vases were
shattered and thrown out of the chamber during the re-opening of
graves, and very often sherds picked in chambers fit others gathered
in the dromos.[70] It is natural to assume that among the shattered
vases occasionally were some that were blackened or burned by the
fires lighted for purification and fumigation.

Traces of fire were found in practically all the Chamber Tombs at
Dendra but those discovered in the stomion of tomb 10 are of especial
interest and have been considered as a "sure evidence of a repeated
cult of the dead." Persson, in his usual thorough way, has recorded
the various layers of the filling of the stomion that was found without

---

67. *Royal Tombs at Dendra*, 73 ff. and 108 ff. Nilsson, *op. cit.*, 600. Mylonas,
op. cit., 75.

68. *Odyssey*, XI, 25 ff.

69. *Praktika*, 1933, 36; 1934, 8-10, 29-38. Cf. *AA* 1935, 179. The same could
be stated for the tholos tomb at Berbati in Argolis excavated by Persson, cf.
Nilsson, *op. cit.*, 597.

70. *Prosymna*, 237. *Asine*, 170, 357. *New Tombs at Dendra*, 63, 66, 94.

packing. The entire height of the stomion amounted to 3.30 m.; to a height of 1.20 m. above its floor the filling consisted of "crumbled, yellowish rock; then followed a layer of charcoal about 5 cm. thick, in which several sherds of the two large vases were found in addition to a number of ivory fragments and remains of animal bones. This deposit was covered by a layer of ash, about 25 cm. thick and on top of this another, blacker layer of charcoal, 10 cm. thick occurred."[71] Thus the traces of fire and ashes stop completely at a height of 1.60 m. above the floor of the stomion, and the filling itself stops shortly afterwards leaving an opening of about 1.65 m. in height. Through that opening access to the chamber could be obtained without difficulty. Ashes and charcoal were also found in the chamber and they could be attributed to the fires lighted in the course of the preparation of the chamber to receive new comers. That the chamber was used for burial more than once is also indicated by the "dromos fill and the blocking wall in front of the stomion." Yet only one skeleton was found lying in a shaft along the rear wall of the chamber. To account for this, Persson suggested that the remains in the chamber were removed to another grave when the roof of the chamber started to collapse. This will explain the lack of packing that as a rule blocks the doorway; there was no need for such a packing since no bodies were left on the floor of the chamber.

The time of the removal of the remains from the chamber is indicated by the fragments of two large vessels of the Palace style that were found in the chamber, in the stomion, and in the dromos. Apparently they were dropped there when the contents of the grave were being removed. In the stomion these fragments were found "in levels up to a height of 1.60 m. above the floor," although some of them were discovered in the first layer of charcoal that followed the filling of the "crumbled, yellowish rock," i. e. only 1.25 above level. This discovery of fragments of the same vases in the various burned layers seems to indicate that these layers were formed almost at the same time, since the dropping of the sherds in these layers must have occurred at one and the same time, on the occasion of the clearing of the chamber. If the layers were formed in one and the same occasion then these burned layers do not indicate a repeated practice of a cult of the dead. Fires in front of the stomion and even animal bones are not uncommon and Tsountas attributed the latter to funeral feasts

71. *New Tombs at Dendra*, 59-95: for the vases from the chamber, stomion, and dromos, see figs. 77 and 78; see p. 64, for the levels in which fragments of these vases were found.

held at the time of burial in honor of the departed.[72] To similar acts, and to the use of fire for purification and fumigation should be attributed the ashes and charcoal and even the animal bones found in the stomion of Chamber Tomb 10 at Dendra; especially so since the contents of that tomb were removed and thus the supposed object of the cult. Consequently the evidence from this tomb also does not seem to prove the existence of a cult of the dead.

Our survey of the evidence supplied by the traces of fire common in Mycenaean graves seems to lead to the following conclusions: 1) Fires were lighted to fumigate and purify the graves when they were re-opened. 2) The span of time that elapsed determined the few or the many traces of fire or the lack of such traces in a grave. 3) Occasionally offerings were burned in the graves. It is suggested that this occurred only when a grave had to be re-opened before the previously interred corpse had decayed completely. The burnt offerings were made to "the spirit" of the partly decomposed occupant. 4) No evidence can clearly point to a cult of the dead in which fire was used.

The only real evidence that we have for a cult of the dead in Mycenaean times comes from the Royal cemetery of Mycenae. In the Grave Circle of its citadel and over the fourth shaft grave Schliemann uncovered the famous circular altar of Mycenae that could have served only a cult of the dead.[73] That altar was placed in the position in which it was found during the re-arrangement of the Grave Circle in Late Helladic III times, and certainly proves that at least in those times a cult in honor of the princes buried in the shaft graves was held at Mycenae. That the cult was practiced even before the late Mycenaean era seems to be indicated by the fact that the area of the graves was protected against encroachment by the city walls, and also by the discovery of Professor Keramopoullos.[74] In 1913 a caving in of the rock within the circle disclosed almost at its center a cavity with two openings to graves I and IV. Within it were found, with earth, ashes and traces of a hearth. The ashes seem to be stratified in at least three layers proving the repeated use of the area. The finds and the position of the hollow led Keramapoullos to suggest that it was used for a cult held in honor of the dead, that the hollow was filled when the Grave Circle was re-arranged, that it was replaced by the round altar placed over the fourth Grave. This suggestion seems very probable and the remains in the middle of the circular

72. *Ephemeris* 1888, 130, 134. *Royal Tombs at Dendra* 10. *New Tombs at Dendra*, 23, 53.

73. Schliemann, *Mycenae and Tiryns*, 212 ff. Nilsson, *op. cit.*, 608.

74. *Ephemeris* 1918, 52 ff. Wace, *Mycenae*, 61.

area seem to indicate that a cult was held there from the beginning of the Late Helladic period.[75]

No definite evidence is forthcoming that will prove the practice of a cult over or in front of the other tholos tombs at Mycenae. Sherds and even vases of Late Helladic and even earlier dates have been found in the dromoi of a number of tholos tombs; those of Klytaimnestra and of Aegisthos being the best known.[76] It is a well known fact that shattered pots were thrown in the dromoi quite often when the graves were re-used. Their existence in various levels can be attributed to another well-established fact; to the clearing and refilling of the dromoi before and after every successive interment; and to this could be attributed the discovery of earlier pottery that was brought with the earth used to fill the dromoi.

Beyond Mycenae some evidence favoring the idea of a cult was revealed in the dromos of Menidi. That evidence has again been set forth by Professor Nilsson and there can be no doubt that a cult of the dead was held there in early archaic times.[77] Whether or not sherds of "Mycenaean vases and large fragments of coarse pottery and pithoi" found in front of the door of the tholos prove the existence of a cult in Mycenaean times will remain uncertain. The fragments of pottery were blackened by smoke even in their interior; but we have seen above how that could have resulted from the fires kindled within the chamber for purification and fumigation. The fragments of bones noted could be attributed to the funeral feasts that apparently were held at the time of the burial and the traces of fire find parallels to such found in front of the doors of other Mycenaean graves. These traces of fire can be accounted for in two ways: 1) they may have resulted from the activities of the funeral feasts; 2) they may have been the remains of a propitiating service imposed by the necessity of re-opening the grave before the completed decomposition of the newly buried. They may also be the result of both these factors. Even if we are willing to admit the relics found before the door of the Menidi tomb as evidence indicating the existence of a cult, still we have to note that between these Late Helladic remains and those of the early archaic period there is a break and a long gap that will remain unaccounted for and that will prohibit the acceptance of a development of the later archaic from the earlier Mycenaean cult and the

---

75. Nilsson, *op. cit.*, 610. Perhaps we should note that there is no definite proof for the uninterrupted practice of the cult from Mycenaean to late historic times, but that is generally accepted.

76. For these graves cf. Nilsson, *op. cit.*, 604-605.

77. Cf. *Das Kuppelgrab bei Menidi*, for the complete report of the excavations and finds. Also Wolters, *JDAI* 13 (1898) 13 ff.; 14 (1899), 103 ff.

belief of an uninterrupted continuation of the cult from late Helladic to early archaic years.

Summarizing our remarks we can state that: 1) There can be no doubt that a cult of the dead was held within the Grave Circle of Mycenae and in honor of the kings buried there at least in Late Helladic III times. We must bear in mind, however, that the cemetery was a royal cemetery and the dead honored there were leaders, perhaps of some distinction. A similar cult could be assumed for the tholos tomb at Menidi, although the evidence there is not conclusive. That tomb, however, seems also to be that of a leader or prince. 2) No evidence whatsoever is known which will prove that a cult of the dead was practiced by the masses in Late Helladic times in connection with the family graves.

The non-existence of a general cult of the dead is further indicated by indirect evidence: by the attitudes of the Late Helladic people toward the remains of the dead. Tsountas, Blegen, Wace, and Persson have observed repeatedly that remains of previous burials were unceremoniously swept aside or thrown in the dromoi. This occurred so often as to form a characteristic feature of the burial customs of the Mycenaeans. "If when the tomb was re-opened for a fresh burial," observed Wace, "the remains of the immediately preceding burial were not packed into a pit in the dromoi or chamber, or even thrown out into the dromoi as in Tomb 515, they were simply swept up in a heap to the sides or corners of the chamber." To this Blegen has added: "It is evident that the actual physical remains of the dead were held in little respect, when the time came for subsequent burial."[78]

This disrespectful attitude toward the earlier remains, indicating the belief that it could be indulged without fear of retribution, contrasts very pointedly with the meticulous care with which the body was treated at the time of burial, with the careful packing of the doors, and the filling of the dromoi. I believe that this could only be explained, as I pointed out in my study of the burial customs of the Mycenaeans, if we assume that the Late Helladic inhabitants of continental Greece believed that "the 'spirit' of the departed was sentient and was around the grave as long as the flesh was in existence; then the corpse had to be treated with respect, it had to be provided with supplies, it had to be given favorite objects that in life belonged to it; it had to be kept in the grave by walled doors" and filled to the top dromoi. "The moment the body was dissolved and was transformed into a pile of bones, it no longer had need of anything; there was no

---

78. *Chamber Tombs at Mycenae*, 137. *Prosymna*, 247.

danger that its spirit would reappear; the spirit had descended into
its final abode never to return; and so the bones could be swept aside
or even thrown out."[79] In a few instances the bones were packed
carefully in cists; in others, they were never disturbed. But the fact
still remains that as a rule the remains of previous burials were
treated summarily and unceremoniously. And the question arises:
how could a cult of the dead exist among people who treated the remains of their ancestors with such disrespect? The very disrespectful
treatment of the remains seems to indicate that these were without
significance, and the "spirit," to which once they belonged, was without the power to influence the life of the living. Such conceptions
held by the masses could not bring about a cult of the dead.

All explorers of graves have observed that in the opening of a grave
vases which formed part of the kterismata of ancestors were shattered and thrown out of the chamber; that valuable objects were removed by the living relatives.[80] If a cult of the dead was practiced by
the masses, this little habit will remain unexplained. How could people
be assumed to bring gifts and offerings to the departed—as the cult
will require—when they indulged in the breaking and pilfering of the
gifts and offerings already in the grave?

These indications by themselves may not be decisive, but when they
are added to the non-existence of clear evidence proving a cult of the
dead, they become decisive. And the only conclusion that could be
drawn is that a general cult of the dead was not practiced in Mycenaean times by the masses. The words "general" and "masses" are
intentionally used and become essential when we recall that a cult
was practiced over the graves of the kings buried in the shaft graves
of Mycenae and perhaps over other royal graves. How can we account for that cult?

In answer, I may be allowed to repeat what I have stated in my
study of the burial customs of the Mycenaean age. There I suggested
that the "Mycenaeans could have believed that a few chosen individuals were fated not to end the same way as the common man, but
were allowed to have an interest and to influence the life of the living
even after their bodies had decomposed. It was not difficult, perhaps,
to assume that an exceptional prince, with a life filled with benevolent
acts or mighty deeds, a prince who in actual life was so different and
so much above the average man, would be treated differently after
death, that he would be allowed to come to the help of the people to

---

79. *AJA* 52 (1948) 70-71. Cf. *Chamber Tombs at Mycenae*, 144.
80. *Asine*, 357, 358. *Prosymna*, 237. *Chamber Tombs at Mycenae*, 131, 138,
145. *Mycenaean Age*, 147, and Tsountas' personal communication to Wace.

whose service he had devoted his life. Such a belief, perhaps, is reflected in the Homeric poems in a few instances. The Dioskouroi were favored with a special arrangement, and Menelaos was not fated to end in Hades, but was to be transported to the Elysian plains. To Erechtheus, the benevolent ruler of Athens, sacrifices were offered. In modern times too, popular imagination has developed many a story about an exceptional person keeping active after death."

We may even assume with confidence that the cult was helped, if it was not brought about, by beliefs and practices held by neighboring peoples with whom the Mycenaeans came in contact toward the end of the Middle Helladic period. The shaft graves over which the cult was practiced can be considered, as Blegen and Wace have pointed out, as "elaborate versions of the Middle Helladic graves."[81] Their built walls find parallel in the built grave No. 6 of Eleusis,[82] and the extended positions of the bodies found in them is anticipated by the semi-contracted position current in the latter part of the Middle Helladic period.[83] As a rule the graves of that period contain but one body; however, in a number of cases two, three, and even more bodies were found in the same grave. Thus the shaft graves are not unique in this respect.[84] Comparatively few furnishings are found in Middle Helladic sepulchers, and this contrasts rather sharply with the rich-in-gold shaft graves of Mycenae.[85] Nor are the shaft graves unique in this respect. Rich kterismata were laid in the rock-cut chamber tombs which appear at the beginning of the Late Helladic I period. The origin of this type of grave has not beeen definitely established. Wace finds their prototypes in the rock-cut graves of Zygouries, while Sir Arthur Evans has pointed out that in Crete this type of grave antedates its appearance in the mainland by almost two centuries.[86] Persson now argues with success that in the construction of their chamber tombs the Mycenaeans followed Egyptian prototypes.[87] Both Persson and Marinatos look to Egypt as the source of the gold found in the shaft graves and point out a number of elements which could have been borrowed from that land directly and without the inter-

81. *Symbolae Osloenses* 9 (1930) 31. *Chamber Tombs at Mycenae*, 125.
82. Mylonas, G. E., *Προϊστορικὴ Ἐλευσίς* (= *ΠΕ*), 54.
83. *Asine*, 343. *ΠΕ*, 152 and personal communication of Professor Karo regarding his excavations at Tiryns.
84. Tsountas, Ch., *Αἱ προϊστορικαὶ ἀκροπόλεις Διμηνίου καὶ Σέσκλου* (= *ΔΣ*), 74 f. and 125 ff. *AJA* 37 (1933) 278, fig. 8. Blegen, *Gonia*, 64; *Zygouries*, 55-57. *Asine*, 122, fig. 100.
85. *ΔΣ*, 74. *Ephemeris* 1908, 94. *ΠΕ*, 55 f. *AJA* 34 (1930) 406 f. *Prosymna*, 30-50. *Asine*, 345. Valmin, *op. cit.*, 195-207.
86. *Chamber Tombs at Mycenae*, 125. Perhaps the rock-cut tombs of the Early Helladic period found at Corinth and Chalkis should also be considered as possible sources. *Palace of Minos*, II, 557. Cf. Pendlebury, *The Archaeology of Crete*, 133.
87. *New Tombs at Dendra*, 164-175.

mediacy of Crete. This is strengthened by the direct commercial intercourse vouched for by Late Helladic I and II vases found in Egypt
which, as Wace and Blegen have established, are "more than eight
times as many" as those imported into Egypt from the island of Crete
in those early years.[88]

From Egypt we can derive the cult of the Minoan princes indicated
not only by the sarcophagus of Agia Triada,[89] but also by the temple-
tomb of Knossos.[90] Persson compares that temple-tomb with
Kekemet's tomb at Assuan;[91] but I think that its basement plan could
be compared more advantageously with the Egyptian temple of the
simple type (fig. 6). It is natural to expect that the Minoans would

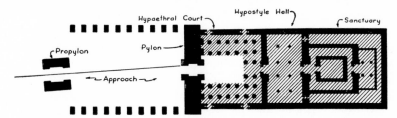

Fig. 6. A. The South Temple at Karnak (= J. Ferguson, *A History
of Architecture*, fig. 25).

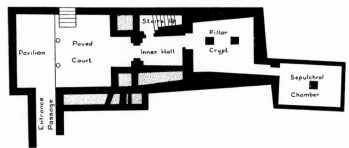

B. The Basement Plan of the Temple-Tomb at Knossos (= *P.M.*, IV,
part II, plan).

88. *Ibid.*, 176-196. Persson even suggests, p. 195, the possibility that "the
peoples of Argolis had taken part in the great war of liberation fought by the
Egyptians against the Hyksos"; and from this war they returned well-equipped
with gold and with cultural ideas. Marinatos, *infra*, p. 127. Wace and Blegen,
in *Klio*, 1937, 147. Persson, p. 195, recalls in this connection the story of Danaos
and Aegyptos. It is interesting to note that Tsountas, *The Mycenaean Age*, 344 f.,
suggested that the Danaans were the builders of the shaft graves. That Egypt
was rich in gold is attested from many sources; but see especially Tel-el-Amarna
letter no. XIX where Tushratta states: "in my brother's land [Egypt] gold is as
common as dust."

89. For a complete, up-to-date discussion of the sarcophagus cf. Nilsson, *op. cit.*,

modify the type borrowed, as it was their habit, yet the similarities are striking: the pavilion of the Minoan structure could be equated with the Egyptian propylon; the paved court with the avenue of approach; the inner hall with the hypaethral court; the pillar crypt with the hypostyle hall, and the sepulchral chamber of the Minoan tomb with the sanctuary of the Egyptian temple. All these elements are to be found in the same relation and in the same axial arrangement. The rectangular bastions on either side of the door to the inner hall of the temple-tomb, unique in Minoan architecture, find their closest parallel in the massive bastions of the Egyptian pylons. It seems very probable that the basement plan of the temple-tomb at Knossos was drawn after that of the Egyptian temple in its simpler form.

In discussing the Minoan structure and its contents, Sir Arthur remarked: "Evidently the Priest-kings of Knossos in some sort regarded themselves as Pharaohs overseas."[92] It would not be surprising if the kings of Knossos, in their effort to act the role of the Pharaoh, introduced the idea of their deification after death. The same could be maintained for the chieftains of Mycenae and the princes of the mainland, who, following the Egyptian pattern and along with the gold and artistic concepts, introduced from Egypt the cult practiced in the Grave Circle at Mycenae and over royal graves elsewhere. Thus the cult at Mycenae could be considered as influenced by the Egyptian worship of the Pharaoh or as developed independently out of the love and respect in which a prince was held during his lifetime;[93] or as a result of both these factors.

A cult of the dead was practiced in some Mycenaean graves but in post-Mycenaean, historic times. The evidence for the existence of such a cult has been brought together by Nilsson and has been added to by Blegen. We have already noted the evidence proving the practicing of a cult in post-Mycenaean times in the dromos of the tholos tomb at Menidi. A similar cult perhaps was held in the dromos of the tomb of Klytaemnestra, where a mass of Geometric pottery was found, and above tomb 520 of Mycenae where Wace found a deposit of Geometric pottery.[94] But there can be no doubt that we have a cult of the dead in the cemetery of Prosymna. In that cemetery, and in thirteen out of the fifty explored tombs, Blegen found

426-443, where are found the pertinent bibliography and views of scholars. I regret that I was unable to find and use for this study Professor Picard's recent book *Les religions préhelléniques*.

90. *P.M.*, IV, 964 ff.

91. *New Tombs at Dendra*, 166.

92. *P.M.*, IV, 987. Perhaps we should recall that outside the rock chamber was found a "cupped block" with clear Egyptian affinities.

93. Cf. Farnell, *op. cit.*, 17-18.

94. Nilsson, *op. cit.*, 604. Wace, *Chamber Tombs at Mycenae*, 23.

definite evidence proving the existence of a "wide-spread cult of the dead carried on in the late Geometric period." The evidence is in the form of deposits that contained pottery especially, and a few bronze objects. Interestingly enough a small bell-shaped cup (No. 1218), from one of those deposits, finds an exact duplicate among the finds made in the dromos of the tomb at Menidi. Based on this substantial evidence Blegen has interpreted his finds as good evidence for the survival of a hero cult or a cult of the dead at Prosymna.[95] There can be no doubt that we have a cult of the dead at Prosymna in late Geometric times which perhaps was continued into later years, but I doubt that we have a survival of such a cult.

A survival would imply the existence of a cult in Mycenaean times. Nothing was found in or around the graves in which Geometric deposits were discovered, (in graves II, III, VIII, IX, X, XIX, XXV, XXVI, XXXIV, XXXVII, XL, XLIII, XLIX, and L) to indicate that such a cult was practiced there in Late Helladic times. These graves have yielded substantially the same remains as all the others at Prosymna. In a number of them bones were swept unceremoniously to the side walls[96] and in one instance[97] bones and pottery were dispersed and crushed; this dispersal, according to Blegen, occurred in the Mycenaean period when the recess of the tomb was "rifled and most of its contents removed." I submit that a tomb treated in such a fashion could not have been the center of a cult. It seems therefore probable that the cult, whose evidence is undisputable, was started at the Heraeum sometime in the latter part of the Geometric period. That also seems to be the case with the cult at Menidi and the possible cults at the tomb of Klytaimnestra and Tomb No. 520 at Mycenae. However, we have no evidence taking the cult of the dead to proto-Geometric times and consequently to the end of the Mycenaean period. Blegen pointed that out when he emphasized that the Prosymna deposits are characterized by a total absence of Protogeometric objects, "a circumstance which might appear to indicate a clear break between the period of the burials and that of the votive deposits."[98] In view of the fact that a cult in Mycenaean times does not seem to be indicated by the Prosymna tombs, I am inclined to believe that such a clear break does exist and that consequently we do not have a survival of a cult, but a cult which began in late Geometric times.

---

95. "Post-Mycenaean Deposits in Chamber Tombs," *Ephemeris* 1937, 377-390.
96. *Prosymna*, Tombs, III (p. 182), VIII, X (p. 199), XIII (p. 195), XXV (p. 89), XXXIV (p. 113) and XXXVII (p. 126).
97. Tomb XLIII, *Prosymna*, 186-189.
98. *Ephemeris* 1937, 389.

How can we account for the beginning of such a cult at that time and after the break? Perhaps the evidence obtained from the Mycenaean graves at Delos will help to point toward an explanation.

It is now definitely proved that the island of Delos was inhabited during the Bronze Age, and from the closing phase of that Age, from the Mycenaean period, two graves have survived. One of these, before the hall of Antigonos, at least in Hellenistic times was surrounded by a circular wall and transformed into an *abaton*. But as Nilsson, has again pointed out, the tomb was visible in earlier than the Hellenistic times, since its door-jambs stood more than half-a-meter above the floor of the classical period; and yet the grave was not removed during the purification of the island by Peisistratos and by the Athenians. Apparently already in the days of the tyrant it was a "holy place." F. Courby very aptly has identified the tomb as the θήκη, or the grave of the two Hyperborean maidens, Opis and Arge, mentioned by Herodotus (IV, 35).[99]

The second grave was discovered by Professor Picard "in the precinct of the temple of Artemis" at precisely the spot in which, according to Herodotus (IV, 34) stood the σῆμα of the other two Hyporborean maidens, Hyperoche and Laodike. That tomb too was transformed into an *abaton* in historic times.[100] In and around it were found numerous fragments of pottery which were grouped by the excavator in the following classes: 1) Sherds belonging to types and styles of pottery current in M.M.II-III times. 2) Sherds called "myceniens" and placed in L.M.I.-II times. 3) Sherds belonging to the archaic period among which are to be found some Corinthian pieces and the fragments of a bronze cauldron. There can be no doubt that the sherds of the historic period belong to votive offerings. Thus they prove that the place was venerated, as Herodotus has described, from archaic times down. But it will be noticed that no finds belonging to the Geometric period were made. At Delos again we have the same break in the sacred use of the graves which has been noticed at Prosymna, at Menidi, and elsewhere. That break will seem to indicate that the cult at Delos began only early in the archaic period and it was not a survival. By that period the tradition of the existence of the graves of the Hyperborean maidens in the island perhaps had become current. The tradition would naturally claim that their death had occurred at a very remote period, beyond the pale of memory of the living. Then, perhaps by accident through the caving in of

99. *Exploration de Délos*, V, 65 ff., plans opposite p. 64. Nilsson, *op. cit.*, 611-614.

100. Picard-Replat, "Hérodote, l' Artémision délien, et les deux tombeaux des Vierges hyperboréennes," *BCH* 48 (1924) 247 ff.

their roof, the Mycenaean tombs were revealed to the people of the
island. The peculiar type of the graves, their strange contents, their
position, perhaps excited the imagination and it was natural for the
people to associate the graves with the maidens, to assume that these
strange and very old sepulchers, so different from those current, were
the ones in which the legendary maidens were buried.[101] This was
naturally followed by a cult established in the supposed graves of the
maidens.

In a similar manner perhaps the post-Mycenaean cults were established at Prosymna, at Menidi, and elsewhere. A casual event or
an accident, in the case of the graves at the Heraeum the caving in of
the roof, revealed to the people the existence of the graves. Perhaps
the accident happened at a time of stress and difficulty; but the graves
so revealed could certainly have been associated with the traditions
of the site and as a result of that the cult was started. Since a survival of a cult from Mycenaean times does not seem possible, it is
probable to suggest that the post-Mycenaean cults were developed in
this manner.

The general conclusions which can be adduced from our discussion
are apparent. There seems to be no definite evidence that will prove
or even indicate the existence of a general cult of the dead in Helladic
times and on the mainland of Greece. The elements noted by scholars
thus far belong to the rites performed during burial and in no way
indicate a cult. The existence of a hero-cult, however, is very
limited and thus far can be proved to have existed only at Mycenae.
It does not seem to have developed from an ancestral cult, but rather
from the belief in the superhuman qualities of a king that were continued even after his death. It is also probable that the cult was pat-
terned after the Egyptian worship of the Pharaoh. The cult of the
dead seems to have become popular in post-Mycenaean, late Geometric
times. But then it was not a continuation of an older, existing cult,
but rather a new cult which perhaps sprang out of the need to im-
mortalize a leader and out of the desire to rationalize and substantiate
legends by associating them with ancient relics, especially with prehistoric graves. Of course, due to the nature of the evidence conclusions on this problem can only be advanced with reservations and new
evidence may in the future force a modification of the expressed
views. But it is safe to maintain that our evidence to date does not
favor the view of the existence of a cult of the dead in Helladic times
and on the mainland of Greece.

---

101. Cf. Farnell, *op. cit.*, 284.

AN EARLY HELLADIC KITCHEN UTENSIL

J. PENROSE HARLAND
University of North Carolina

PLATE 3

In excavating the Bronze Age site at Nemea, the writer came upon a terracotta object which was at first here as well as elsewhere classified as a Spit Holder (pl. 3 c). Subsequent examination of the object revealed that this was an improbable identification.

The object had been broken into three pieces which have been put together with no part missing. The three parts were found close together by the east arc of a pithos (#3), the lower and preserved part of which was sunken into the beaten clay floor of a house in area R. This house on stratigraphic evidence may be dated with certainty not later than Early Helladic III (ca. 2200-2000 B. C.).

The support, as the object may well be called, is made up of a curved, downward sloping and tapering flat member, the end of which forms a rear base, and of two cylindrical legs set at the two upper and front corners. In the center of the flat body of the object, near the top, is a round loop-handle, set at a right angle to the front and parallel with the sloping part. The front has a slight downward curve and is concave in plan.

The clay is unlevigated and brick-red in color, the biscuit being uniformly of this color. It is unpolished and is without slip and decoration. The dimensions are: 0.10 m., height of each front corner; 0.092 m., height in center of the concave and slightly dipping front; 0.11 m., width across the front from corner to corner; 0.065 m., width of "tail-piece" or flat base; 0.13 m., length of left side of the sloping flat piece, 0.135 m. of its right side.

There are several objections to the identification of this object as a spit holder. For steadiness a spit should rest in the center of so narrow a support. But the little loop-handle rises above the level of the front edge and so a spit would have to be placed to either side of the handle. And one would expect the surface on which rested the end of a spit to be flat, but in this example there is a sharp front edge and this edge shows absolutely no wear at all. Further, it is to be noted that the front of the object, the front of the left leg (as one faces it), all of the right leg, and the top of the handle, are brown in color, while the rest of the support is brick-red, all of which indicates that the front was turned toward the heat, whether the fire or a heated vessel.

It seems only reasonable to suppose that the clay object is a *Pot Support*, not a spit holder, and by trial it was found to fit snugly against the cooking vessel, as shown in plate 3, d. The vessel shown here was found in House "P", almost contiguous with House "R", and in the same stratum, which may be equated with Early Helladic III. This vessel (No. 12)—of rather coarse ware, red and reddish brown in color, and measuring 0.152 in height, 0.185 and 0.175 m. in diameter of rim and body respectively—was one of several such domestic vessels found on the hill (called Tsoungiza) at Nemea. With its crudely flattened base, the pot rocks on a table and it and other such vessels might well require a support to avoid its tipping over, when on or off the fire.

The Pot Support, for such it clearly is, might have been used for other ceramic shapes as well. The sauceboat, when not filled, is quite unsteady. However, considering the popularity of the sauceboat in the Early Helladic period, the paucity of pot supports and their crudeness of fabric may argue against their being used with the more numerous and often finely made sauceboats. It seems more reasonable to associate the pot support with the cooking pots and other domestic vessels used for holding food or liquids.

Incidentally, three weeks later the right leg with adjoining top corner belonging to a similar pot support was found in the same area (R) but at a slightly lower level. This one was of black, coarse clay and its height, 0.085 m., was just 1.5 cm. less than that of our entire pot support. The part of the second support, along with a loom weight, some sherds, and flakes of obsidian, seemed to be lying on the floor of House "B" which may be dated in E.H. II.

The two levels, represented by the two pot supports, may be associated with two sub-periods of the Early Helladic period, namely II and III, or possibly we have to deal with two different levels of habitation in E.H. III or—less probably—in E.H. II. Then, too, we may have a case of intrusive evidence: the disturbance of the strata, caused by the sinking of Pithos #3 into the floor of an E.H. III house may have brought the fragmentary support down into the previous stratum of E.H. II. Of course, the pot support may have been a feature of both sub-periods.

One thing, however, is quite clear and that is that in the later part of the Early Helladic period the pot support was in use in this settlement at Nemea. That a people at so early a period and in a back-country, mountain valley, should have made and used so convenient, but not so necessary, a utensil, is not surprising in the light of the extraordinary number of different shapes represented by the pottery found entire or in part in the Early Helladic level at Nemea.

LA DEA MICENEA A CAVALLO

Doro Levi
Scuola Archeologica Italiana di Atene

Tavole 4-5

Le due statuette in terracotta riprodotte alla tav. 4, a, b, c sono state rinvenute questa primavera in una tomba fra Kharvati e Spata, nella Mesogeia attica,[1] e sono entrate a far parte della Collezione di Madame Helène A. Stathatos, che, col consueto acume, ne ha intuito l'eccezionale interesse.

La prima rappresenta una figura femminile seduta di fianco sul dorso di un cavallo.[2] L'argilla è giallina-chiara, farinosa, ben depurata, coperta di ingubbiatura crema e decorata a vernice bruno-scura, metallica-opaca, con sbavature bruno-chiare e rossicce. Il corpo femminile, rappresentato nella sagoma "lunata" indicante le braccia sollevate, è piatto, ma il tronco si allarga in basso sempre più verso la sezione cilindrica, presentando una leggiera prominenza sulla parte posteriore seduta. Le gambe tubolari, informi, sono piegate ad angolo retto ai ginocchi, non sembrano coperte da alcun panno, con piedi appiattiti dalle punte un po' ricadenti in basso. I seni sono a prominenze globulari accentuate. Il volto è indicato da una sola presa tagliente, assai sporgente in avanti; sulla testa posa un berretto o polos troncoconico allargato verso l'alto e incavato a scodella superiormente. Il cavallo ha il dorso molto allungato, le gambe corte cilindriche legger-

---

1. La provenienza è stata indicata da prima come Kharvati, poiché in questa località — nel centro dell'Attica, a Nord-Est dell'Imetto e Sud del Pentelico, sulla strada Atene-Vafina, a circa quattro chilometri dal bivio di questa strada, di cui il ramo che piega verso Sud-Est si avvia verso Spata — è la residenza del rinvenitore. In realtà informazioni successive indicherebbero come località del rinvenimento un punto distante circa 3-4 chilometri da Kharvati verso Spata, quindi più vicino a quest'ultima località che dista dalla prima meno di sei chilometri in linea retta. Si tratta dunque probabilmente di una tomba appartenente al già noto centro miceneo ubicato nei pressi di Spata, il villaggio che anzi ha dato la prima importante scoperta di relitti micenei in Attica, la scoperta di due tombe a camera scavate nel calcare fatta dallo Stamatakis nel 1877 (v. Curtius — Kaupert, *Karten von Attika*, foglio VII; per le scoperte micenee in Attica, cfr. la piantina data dallo Stubbings, "The Mycenaean Pottery of Attica," *BSA* 42 (1947) 3. Durante la publicazione del presente lavoro la statuetta femminile a cavallo, come pure il tripode in pietra sotto nominato, sono riprodotti nella Cronaca degli scavi e trovamenti del *BCH* 73 (1949) 521, fig. 3 e tav. XXIX, 2.

2. Naturalmente la donna e il cavallo sono stati da prima modellati in due pezzi separati di argilla; questi però sono stati attaccati insieme crudi, e l'argilla della donna è stata rimodellata nella parte posteriore unendola in un tutto con la sella sottostante: cosicché il gruppo dopo la cottura non palesa nessuno stacco di dietro, e neppure un gradino o un dislivello tra le due sue parti costitutive. Davanti invece due zolle di argilla sono state incastrate tra i fianchi della donna e i bracciuoli della sella per una più stabile saldatura delle due parti, zolle che non sono state accuratamente spalmate negli interstizi, e di cui si può scorgere il netto distacco dalla parte originariamente modellata.

mente affusolate verso le estremità; la coda è lunga e folta, pure schiacciata dietro a orlo molto tagliente; egualmente la criniera è modellata a breve cresta tagliente; il muso è appuntito, con una scanalatura lungo l'orlo superiore, e con gli orecchi a due piccoli mezzi dischi. La donna siede su una sella fornita di due altissimi bracciuoli quasi verticali, con orlo superiore tondeggiante, a quanto sembra fornita posteriormente di una bassa spalliera leggermente obliqua verso l'esterno; pure sotto ai piedi della donna v'è una sporgenza, che sembra indicare uno sgabellino per la posa dei piedi. La decorazione dipinta è a grosse fasce arcuate e ondulate, distribuite irregolarmente sulla parte anteriore della donna, dalla punta delle braccia sollevate in giù e fra i seni, fasce che continuano verticalmente lungo le gambe, dove il colore è in parte scomparso; colore è applicato sui due lati della presa che indica la faccia, e su gran parte del polos superiormente. Sulla parte posteriore della donna una grossa fascia verticale indica la treccia, cadente dall'orlo del polos, e da essa si dipartono tratti più sottili lateralmente. Un'altra fascia dipinta corre lungo tutto l'orlo della sella. Sul cavallo, fasce di colore partono dalla froge lungo i lati del muso, scendono lungo le zampe anteriori fino alle estremità, accompagnate da linee più sottili; sulla parte posteriore del gruppo inoltre una fascia ondulata si diparte dal collo del cavallo e, lungo il dorso, scende alle estremità della zampa posteriore. Vernice era applicata anche sulla scanalatura superiore del muso e sulla coda.

La zampa posteriore destra è di restauro; è scheggiato inoltre un minusculo trattino del polos di dietro. Lungh. dalla punta della froge alla coda del cavallo m. 0.11; alt. totale della statuetta m. 0.126; dalla punta dei piedi della donna m. 0.105; ampiezza del torso della donna m. 0.04.

La seconda statuetta rappresenta un cavaliere. L'argilla è rossiccia-arancione, ben ingubbiata e levigata sulla superficie crema-arancio; la decorazione è in vernice rossiccia semi-lucente. Il corpo del cavallo è schiacciato ai lati, restringendosi quasi a spigolo sulla groppa; pure qui la criniera sporge a cresta tagliente. Le gambe sono soddisfacentemente proporzionate, solo che le anteriori sono più lunghe delle posteriori, e tutte sono divaricate verso le estremità; il muso è piuttosto corto. Il torso dell'uomo è a cilindro allungato; le sue gambe sono avanzate e schiacciate contro i fianchi del cavallo, con le punte dei piedi ritorte indietro come stringendosi ai fianchi stessi. Le braccia si allargano quasi a intero cerchio, assottigliandosi e schiacciandosi verso le mani, che continuano in un nastro ininterrotto con le orecchie del cavallo a cui sembrano afferrarsi. La testa dell'uomo è superiormente a bassa callotta, che sembra indicare una copertura a berretto perchè decorata da una serie di sottilissimi tratti a raggiera; sotto al berretto si distingue solo una sporgenza adunca per il naso, separato da una rientranza a unghiata da un'appendice appuntita inferiore, che più che il mento sembra indicare l'estremità di una barba, apparentemente modellata in una bassa e piatta prominenza anche ai lati sulle guance. La decorazione dipinta sul dorso dell'uomo è a due larghe fasce orizzontali racchiudenti due nastri sottili; la fascia superiore si prolunga lungo tutte le braccia; un largo anello circonda il collo; una macchia tondeggiante è al posto della fronte sopra al naso, due dischetti sono sulle guance. Dal mento una fascia verticale scende sul mezzo della parte anteriore dell'uomo, altri nastri seguono le sue gambe esternamente, un anello circonda le cosce, e altre fascette vanno internamente dai ginocchi ai piedi. Fasce simili corrono sul dorso del cavallo, ai lati in basso sopra al ventre, lungo le zampe esternamente, dalla froge ai lati del collo e fino alle estremità anteriori; sottili nastri si dipartono dalla criniera verso il collo e dalla fascia del dorso a quelle del ventre.

La coda è rotta; la zampa anteriore destra, spezzata a metà, è riincollata. Lungh. dalla froge al resto della coda, m. 0.09; alt. m. 0.115; largh. dell'apertura delle braccia m. 0.045.

A quanto risulta dalla succinta descrizione del rinvenitore, nella tomba di Kharvati, scavata nella roccia naturale, oltre ai due oggetti sopra descritti si sarebbero rinvenuti, assieme a scarsi resti di uno scheletro, solamente gli altri tre oggetti sotto descritti:

Tripode in steatite verdastra chiara ben levigata (tav. 4d, 5a, b). Coppa a sezione di sfera, sorretta da tre piedi verticali, a parete piatta anteriormente e curva, semi-elissoidale, posteriormente. A metà distanza tra due piedi sporge dall'orlo una rozza testa taurina, schematicamente modellata, con froge tagliata via netta, a superficie circolare piatta, due bassi cornetti appena iniziati, e due occhi a dischetti in rilievo, limitati da un solco circolare e con una minuscola scodelletta scavata nel centro. Decorazione incisa. L'orlo superiore della coppa, orizzontale, è decorato da una riga a zig-zag, piuttosto irregolare; la parte inferiore esterna della coppa, da ampie duplici o triplici linee a zig-zag pendenti da una riga orizzontale sotto l'orlo, e formanti precisamente due molteplici angoli fra piede e piede; dalla parte dov'è la protome taurina, un angolo su ogni parte della testa; sulla nuca taurina, spina di pesce. La decorazione delle superfici piatte esterne dei piedi presenta nella parte inferiore di ogni piede due rettangoli scavati su un piano leggermente inferiore a quello degli orli e di un listello mediano; entro i rettangoli è un'incisione di molteplici zig-zag; sulla parte superiore dei piedi, lasciata a livello degli orli e del listello mediano, in basso sono due cerchi affiancati con un punto nel centro, e sopra zig-zag orizzontali molteplici, o semplici ma separati da una riga rettilinea. La decorazione complessiva di ogni piede era chiusa entro un rettangolo inciso.

Tutti i tre piedi sono leggermente scheggiati in basso, e quello a sinistra della testa è inoltre parzialmente spezzato in basso e scrostato. Un cornetto della protome è spuntato; piccole scrostature e incrinature qua e là. Diametro esterno dell'orlo della coppa, m. 0.13; alt. m. 0.075.

Spiralina d'oro a filo sottile (fig. 1, b) girato cinque volte su sè

Figure 1. Atene, Coll. Stathatos: Nastro e anellino in oro da una tomba micenea presso Kharvati in Attica.

stesso, col filo tutto unito. Diam. m. 0.018; largh. complessiva m. 0.004.

Nastrino a sottile foglia d'oro (fig. 1a), formante un largo anellino con le estremità arrotondate; le estremità si incrociano appena. Diam. m. 0.037 x 0.032; largh. della foglia m. 0.006.

I due oggetti d'oro potrebbero appartenere a qualsiasi età e civiltà; molte obbiezioni sono state invece opposte alla contemporaneità del tripode con le statuette — queste, come vederemo, di evidente tecnica e decorazione micenea —, tripode del quale è stata da qualcuno perfino dubitata l'autenticità, della creazione o almèno della decorazione.

Anzitutto va constatato invece che la sua forma è spiccatamente minoica, e precisamente della più tarda fase di sviluppo di questa civiltà. Basti rammentare numerosi esemplari provenienti da Gournià,[3] e anche altri, inediti, conservati al Museo di Candia, talora provvisti di un beccuccio aperto. Tipicamente cretese-micenea è, di più, la stilizzazione del muso taurino, a sagoma sommariamente delineata, con la froge tagliata piatta e formante spigolo su tutto il contorno, corna corte e tronche: stilizzazione che appare essenzial-

<hr>

3. *Gournià*, tav. III, nn. 64-66; Maraghiannis, *Antiquités crétoises*, 1, tav. XXXVII, 17. Vedi inoltre l'esemplare dal Palazzo di Midea, Persson, *New Tombs at Dendra near Midea*, 11, fig. 8, più grande e in pietra vulcanica. Per gli esemplari da Jaliso v. sotto, nota 12.

mente identica, perfino con gli occhi a dischetti in rilievo, già nel rhytòn medio-minoico a forma di toro da Mochlos,[4] e perdura giù giù fino all'avanzata epoca micenea, nel rhytòn a testa taurina da Gourniá,[5] nei buoi in terracotta e bronzo da Phaistòs[6] e dall' Antro di Psychrò,[7] in quello frammentario, col pelame indicato a rametti stilizzati, dal medesimo Antro,[8] nella protome taurina sporgente da un vaso di Micene,[9] e via dicendo.[10] Talora la parte anteriore della froge, invece di essere perfettamente liscia come nel nostro tripode, ha una schematica indicazione di bocca e narici, di solito mediante un tratto orizzontale sormontato da due punti o cerchielli, sostituiti in altri casi — come a es. nel frammento ceramico da Micene testé menzionato — da una decorazione geometrica.

La perplessità riguardo l'autenticità del tripode, o almeno la sua appartenenza al medesimo complesso tombale delle due statuette, è stata suggerita evidentemente dagli elementi della sua decorazione: elementi che per verità sono più caratteristici del repertorio geometrico che di quello cretese-miceneo, ma che per altro nello stile geometrico risalgono fino ai primi inizi del protogeometrico, per es., nella medesima associazione di zig-zag e cerchielli e nella medesima tecnica di incisione, in numerosi vasi del Ceramico di Atene.[11] Ma oramai per togliere ogni dubbio sull'autenticità del nostro oggetto ci soccorre un tripode si può dire gemello al nostro — solo che privo della testa taurina e più riccamente decorato, benché coi medesimi elementi — rinvenuto nella Tomba LXVII della necropoli di Moschù Vunara nei recenti scavi di Jaliso. E' anch'esso in steatite, e provvisto di un pestello troncoconico che ne determina l'uso di mortaio.[12] Anche prima di tale decisiva scoperta, del resto, era da tempo ben stabilito e pacifico che entrambi i suddetti elementi derivano allo stile geometrico dal precedente reper-

---

4. Evans, *The Palace of Minos at Knossos*, II, 259, fig. 154 a.
5. *Gourniá*, tav. XI, n. 20; Maraghiannis, *op. cit.*, 1, tav. XXXIX, 6.
6. *Mon. Ant.* 12 (1902) col. 127, fig. 54; Maraghiannis, 1, tav. XV.
7. *BSA* 6 (1899) 108, fig. 39; Maraghiannis, 1, tav. XXIX, 12-25.
8. *BSA* 6 (1899) 104, fig. 103; Maraghiannis, 1, tav. XXIX, 34.
9. Schliemann, *Mykenae*, 118 e, fig. 160, p. 119.
10. Cfr. tra i rozzi tori e buoi fittili dal "Piazzale dei Sacelli" di H. Triada, Banti, *Annuario*, N. S. 3-5, 53, fig. 31 ss. Palesano in parte una struttura affine e affini elementi compositivi pure i due rhytà a testa taurina da Karpathos e da Jaliso, Bossert, *Altkreta*[3], figg. 466-467. Simile stilizzazione a quella del nostro tripode ha una testa taurina in steatite nella medesima Collezione Stathatos, che sarà pubblicata da C. T. Seltman: da considerarsi verisimilmente un "peso" minoico, similmente alla testa bronzea dall'Antro di Psychrò identificata come un peso da Sir Arthur Evans, *Corolla Numismatica B. V. Head*, 353, fig. 9; *Palace of Minos*, IV, 655, fig. 639.
11. Vedi Kübler, *Kerameikos*, IV, tav. 30, ecc.ecc.
12. *Annuario* 13-14, Tomba LXVII, n. 5, p. 276 ss., figg. 21-22 e tav. a colori XX. Cfr. anche un altro tripode in steatite, senza decorazione incisa, dalla medesima necropoli di Moschù Vunara, Tomba XLIV, *Annuario* 6-7, 199, fig. 123.

torio dell'arte cretese-micenea. Lo zig-zag, familiare a Creta dai tempi
più remoti, usato quale decorazione incisa di materiali duri, come
vassoini in pietra, tavole da offerta, altarini e simili, fino dall'epoca
delle tholoi della Messarà,[13] rimane in vita attraverso i secoli per consimili oggetti[14] come anche sulla ceramica dipinta, dove lo troviamo
come motivo dominante — per citare uno dei tanti possibili esempi tra
i materiali poco innanzi rammentati di Gournià —, applicato in fasce
orizzontali, solo o alternato a rosette, sul corpo di due rhytà conici
ancora appartenenti al "periodo della Città" (Tardo-Minoico I), come
pure a tratti orizzontali tra fasce verticali sulla vasta superficie delle
tardissime larnakes.[15] Sul continente ellenico può essere tanto cospicuo
quale decorazione architettonica quanto lo è — sia pure associato ad
altri motivi curvilinei — sulle colonne della porta del "Tesoro di
Atreo," fa la sua apparizione come decorazione incisa o sbalzata, per
es. sugli ori delle Tombe a fossa,[16] ed è profuso in tutte le sue varietà
— singolo, a fasce molteplici, internamente striato, alternato ad altri
motivi, formante triangoli striati, ecc.ecc. — nella ceramica, fino alle
sue più tarde categorie.[17] Tra i vari esempi venuti in luce a Micene
fino dai primi scavi dello Schliemann, il motivo appare anche sul frammento con protome taurina poco sopra citato.[18] Dalla medesima ceramica di Micene possiamo addurre anche un paio di esempi del secondo
ovvio elemento, il cerchiello, che nella ceramica, come negli ori sbalzati,
si presenta nei suoi vari aspetti, semplice, molteplice, con o senza
punto nel centro, alternato ad anellini, dischi o sfere:[19] su un frammento da Micene tutta una vasta zona è occupata da cerchielli, irregolarmente disegnati e senza punto centrale; mentre duplici cerchielli
con punto centrale appaiono alternati alle figure umane sulla parte posteriore dell' "Anfora dei guerrieri," anfora pur essa decorata a protomi taurine sporgenti nel mezzo delle duplici anse a cestello.[20]

Gli ultimi confronti vengono a ricordarci — se ve n'era bisogno —
quanto prediletta e profusa sia questa protome taurina nell'arte cretese-
micenea e in quella delle regioni da essa influenzate: essa non manca

---

13. Cfr. Evans, *Palace*, II, 44 s., fig. 20 e-f.

14. Per es. a Phaistòs, cfr. *Mon. Ant.* 12 (1902) col. 101, fig. 35.

15. *Gournià*, tav. VIII, nn. 19-20; tav. X, n. 45.

16. Karo, *Schachtgräber von Mykenai*, 262 ss., v. per es. il diadema, tav.
XXXVI.

17. Furumark, *The Mycenaean Pottery*, 386 ss., cfr. p. 383, fig. 67, motivo 61.
Assai frequente è il motivo nella decorazione a metope, *ibid.*, 414, fig. 72, motivo 75.

18. Schliemann, *Mykenae*, 119, fig. 160; cfr. altri esempi, tav. X, nn. 40-41;
tav. XII, n. 55; a spina di pesce o su anse, p. 79, nn. 85, 86, 89; ecc.ecc.

19. V. Furumark, *op. cit.*, 355 ss., cfr. p. 343, fig. 57, motivo 41.

20. Schliemann, *op. cit.*, 161, fig. 214. Fra gli oggetti in steatite con questa
decorazione possiamo ricordare l'impugnatura di pugnale o testa di mazza da
Jaliso, *Annuario* 6-7, 126, fig. 45.

tra i rinvenimenti di Ras-Shamra e Minet-el Beida, donde provengono
i due bei rhytà fittili a corpo allungato e scanalato con testa taurina
sulla spalla;[21] rhytà a testa taurina si alternano a quelli in forma di
teste di animali diversi e a vasi, evidentemente metallici, con protomi
animali, nelle pitture della tomba tebana di Rekhmire.[22] Non può
dunque far sorpresa la protome sul nostro tripode — sia essa motivo
decorativo o abbia valore religioso — benché l'oggetto nel suo aspetto
complessivo rimanga per ora unico nell'arte micenea — come lo
sarebbe del resto pure per quella geometrica. Puramente ipotetico
sarebbe qualsiasi suggerimento sul suo uso: se cioè sia stato semplice
oggetto d'uso quotidiano, come i tripodi di Gournià e quelli di Jaliso,
o se la testa taurina gli abbia aggiunto un valore rituale, e il tripode
abbia servito da coppa di libazione, da altarino votivo, o per scopi
consimili. Né è determinabile se sia intenzionale un certo aspetto
zoomorfico che la testa taurina conferisce all'insieme dell'oggetto, pure
essendo conservato in esso il canonico numero dei tre piedi usuali negli
utensili minoici del genere.

Nonché meritare sospetti, dunque, il tripode di steatite al contrario
conferma la veridicità dei dati sopra riferiti sul rinvenimento di
Kharvati, e anzi, per la strettissima affinità col tripode miceneo di
Rodi — rinvenuto questo in una tomba singola e associato con materiali approssimativamente databili — ci permetterà una precisazione
cronologica su tutto il complesso del rinvenimento stesso.

La figurina femminile seduta a cavallo, per forma, argilla e vernice
si classifica immediatamente nella categoria più numerosa e più conosciuta degli "idoli" micenei, di cui hanno restituito svariati esemplari
già gli scavi dello Schliemann a Micene, e che si sono moltiplicati per
gli abbondanti ritrovamenti di quasi tutti i successivi scavi preistorici
nell'area della civiltà micenea, nel Peloponneso, ad Asine, Dendra,
Zygouries, Argo, nelle necropoli rodiote a Jaliso, come anche sul
continente greco, a Delfi, Tebe, pure ad Eleusi, ad Atene stessa ecc.[23]
In molti dei citati scavi se ne sono trovati gruppi compatti entro tombe,
e qui gli "idoli" possono aver avuto uno dei tanti significati funerari
suggeriti per essi, di immagini di schiave offerte in sacrifizio per il
servizio d'oltretomba al le padrone, o di balie per i bambini morti
(perchè ad Argo sono stati rinvenuti con particolare frequenza in

21. V. *Syria*, 13 (1932) 4, tav. IV, 1, 3; Evans, *Palace*, IV, 777, fig. 756.

22. Evans, II, 534 ss., p. 736 ss.; Bossert, *Altkreta*[3], fig. 536 ss., fig. 548.

23. Su questi idoli v. soprattutto le trattazioni complessive di Winter *Typen
der figürlichen Terrakotten*, 1, 2-3; Müller, Val., *Frühe Plastik in Griechenland
und Vorderasien*, 55 ss., fig. 249 ss.; Furumark, *Chronology of Mycenaean Pottery*,
86 ss. Per Atene vedi i numerosi frammenti provenienti dagli scavi sulle pendici
settentrionali dell'Acropoli, Broneer, *Hesperia* 8 (1939) 407, fig. 89.

tombe di bambini), o di giuocattoli;[24] ma che il tipo "a crescente di luna" rappresenti primariamente ed essenzialmente la dea con le braccia sollevate nell'atto di accogliere l'adorazione dei devoti è stato dimostrato dal rinvenimento di una figurina strettamente imparentata a questo tipo, entro alla sua cappellina pure in terracotta, nel santuarietto tardo-minoico della "Camera della Sorgente" (Spring-Chamber) del Palazzo di Cnosso:[25] atteggiamento che si ritrova infatti nella "dea della colomba" dal "Sacello delle Bipenni" nella medesima Cnosso,[26] che sembra risalire lontanissimo, fino a tempi neolitici,[27] e tramandarsi giù fino all'età di transizione e a quella post-minoica con le dee di Gazi, di Karphi, della Messarà e di Prinias.[28] La parte inferiore degli idoli a crescente di luna — come del resto quella delle altre due forme spesso associate o alternate ad essi nei ritrovamenti, il tipo a corpo discoidale e quello con le mani portate ai seni — è generalmente a fusto conico o campanato; almeno un esemplare per altro è ricordato con le gambe rozzamente modellate come nella nostra statuetta;[29] ma un esemplare di immagine femminile con le braccia ai seni, e seduta per di più, proviene appunto dal sacello delle Doppie Asce, che ci ha già palesato la dea con le braccia sollevate ad accogliere gli adoranti.[30] La sagomatura del corpo del nostro idolo è accuratamente trattata, con la parte centrale massiccia, i seni ben marcati e giusta-

24. Vedi Blegen, *Prosymna*, 255 s., 358 ss.; cfr. Persson, *The Royal Tombs at Dendra near Midea*, 88 s.

25. Vedi Evans, II, 128 s., fig. 63.

26. *Ibid.*, II, 340, fig. 193. E' interessante far osservare che l'idolo in terracotta, col ben noto simbolo divino della colomba posata sulla testa, è qui fiancheggiato da due ancelle che invece portano le mani ai seni, e che ricordano l'altro tipo di "idoli" micenei che si rinvengono così spesso associati al tipo nostro.

27. Vedi Evans, *op. cit.*, II, 129.

28. *Ibid.*, IV, 140 ss., fig. 110; Demargne, P., *La Crète dédalique*, 245 s. La datazione di tutte queste figurine è ancora un po' fluttuante: Pendlebury, *The Archaeology of Crete*, 312, considera geometrica la dea della "Camera della Sorgente." L'atteggiamento si conserva anche nel post-miceneo della periferia del mondo egeo, per es. nella bella dea con braccia sollevate da Efestia di Lemno, cfr. Della Seta, *Ephemeris* 1937, 2, 651 ss., tav. III.

29. Müller, Val., *op. cit.*, 58 s. L'esemplare é nel Museo di Atene, e quindi momentaneamente irreperibile.

30. Evans, I, 52, fig. 14. Questa ricorrenza di una figurina di tipo seduto e modellata separatamente dal sedile (sedili o troni lavorati a parte sono stati assai spesso trovati in associazione agli idoli, cfr. per es. a Tebe, *Deltion* 3 [1917] 190, fig. 135, a Dendra, Persson, *op. cit.*, 88, fig. 61, ecc.ecc.; v. anche le dee assise sul trono, per es. Winter, *op. cit.*, 2, nn. 4-5, quella con bambino in braccio esposta al Louvre, marcata *ca.* 1872, nonché il più raro tipo della divinità ignuda sul trono, *Fouilles de Delphes*, II, 3, p. 27, fig. 32; V, 14, fig. 60), e la rarità del tipo a gambe modellate, confermano, se ve n'era bisogno, la genuinità dell'oggetto da noi trattato. Fra le statuette di dee sedute sul trono dobbiamo ricordare quella della Tomba LXXIX da Moschù Vunara a Jaliso (*Annuario* 13-14, 306, fig. 52 e tav. a colori XXIII), benché della dea non si conservino che i piedi, perché questi palesano la medesima modellatura della nostra statuetta attica; sotto ai piedi, inoltre, anche in quella notiamo una specie di sgabello. Il trono è sorretto da tre gambe, decorate a spina di pesce.

mente collocati, l'arco del crescente ben delineato e le incavature fra collo e braccia assai profonde; il polos sul capo è nettamente profilato: tutti elementi questi che, aggiunti alla levigatezza della superficie dell'argilla e alla relativa lucentezza del colore, permettono di classificare il nostro prodotto in un gruppo più antico e di migliore fattura, anteriore a un secondo gruppo in cui si palesano una crescente trascuratezza di forme, con una meno sentita divisione strutturale delle varie parti del corpo, e un deterioramento nella qualità della vernice e dell'argilla. La lunga treccia cadente sulle spalle *(πλόκαμος μακρός)*, che si può notare già nella sopra citata dea della colomba, è in questa modellata in rilievo, ma si trova alternatamente modellata o dipinta nei nostri idoli, dove curiosamente si diparte per lo più, come nel nostro esemplare, dall'orlo del polos, quando questo esiste.[31] Differenzia solo lievemente la nostra dalla maggior parte delle statuette consimili del migliore periodo la decorazione dipinta — che con probabilità rappresenta il vestito, precisamente un chitone di tipo continentale, a maniche corte e ricoprente il petto fino al collo:[32] in queste ultime è infatti per lo più indicato a sottili e fitte lineette ondulate verticali tanto sul lato anteriore che su quello posteriore. La data della nostra figura può essere fissata approssimativamente fra il XIIIe il XII secolo a.C.[33]

---

31. Si diparte invece dalla sommità o dal mezzo della nuca in qualche esemplare ove il polos manca.

32. Cfr. Rodenwaldt, *Tiryns*, II, 7, nota 6. Il tipo a immagine femminile nuda, quale ci è già apparso nella dea della "Camera della Sorgente" di Cnosso e nelle dee sedute di Delfi, è assai raro, e forse indica l'introduzione di motivi dall'Oriente (cfr. Müller, V., *op. cit.*, 58; anche Demargne, *op. cit.*, 272 ss.).

33. Il gruppo più antico è datato dal Furumark precisamente — forse un po' troppo precisamente! — fra il 1300 e il 1230 a.C. (Miceneo III B). Negli esemplari più rozzi, generalmente appartenenti al gruppo più recente, troviamo spesso una decorazione dipinta schematica a reticolato sulla parte anteriore (cfr. *Fouilles de Delphes*, II, 3, tav. III, fig. 21, 2; p. 19, fig. 22), oppure anche a spina di pesce con la linea centrale fra i seni (*ibid.*, 21, fig. 24, 1). L'irregolarità della decorazione del nostro esemplare può essere parzialmente dovuta anche all'inconsueta posizione della donna.

Il tipo dell'idolo con le mani ai seni sembra risalire a un periodo lievemente anteriore a quello degli altri, cioè ancora al sec. XIV.

La datazione della nostra statuetta secondo la classificazione dei consimili idoli dovrebbe dunque essere nel XIII sec. Ma contrasta con questa datazione l'associazione del tripode in steatite — associazione che dobbiamo considerare stretta, se prestiamo fede alle notizie dei rinvenitori che parlano di una piccola tomba scavata nella roccia, contenente i pochi nostri oggetti e scarsi resti probabilmente di un solo scheletro. La somiglianza del nostro tripode con quello della tomba LXVII di Moschù Vunara, sopra citata (v. nota 12), è così perfetta che si deve ammettere trattarsi di due oggetti pressoché contemporanei, probabilmente di una medesima fabbrica. Ora questa tomba, con un singolo seppellimento, contiene oggetti che debbono appartenere alla più avanzata fase del periodo Miceneo III C del Furumark, cioè al sec. XII (la seconda fase del quale si estenderebbe precisamente dal 1200 al 1125). Il vaso più significativo di detta tomba è un'anfora ovale (*Annuario* 13-14, p. 278, fig. 23) con decorazione metopale sulle spalle, consistente in serie verticali di archi concentrici opposti a gruppi fra linee verticali: decorazione appunto attribuita dallo stesso Furumark alla fase sviluppata del

La statuetta della Collezione Stathatos, dunque, rappresenta una dea a cavallo. Riprendendo recentemente in esame[34] una bella quanto misteriosa cretula di Haghia Triada (fig. 2) ho cercato di dimostrare che il motivo della divinità a cavallo di un animale, vero o fantastico, è uno dei non pochi assai presto penetrati e adattati nel repertorio dell'arte minoica dal mondo religioso orientale. In Babilonia da tempo immemorabile è stato espresso, e tramandato alle

Figure 2. Cretule cretese da H. Triada: La dea a cavallo di un mostro fantastico.

vicine civiltà asiatiche giù giù fino ai tempi storici, il concetto del dominio della divinità sulle forze della natura mediante la rappresentazione di dèi sovrastanti svariati tipi di mostri e animali, in piedi, o su un trono posato sul dorso degli animali, o anche, sebbene più raramente, seduti in groppa agli animali stessi. Nella cretula di Haghia Triada ho creduto di vedere importato dall'Oriente assieme a questo motivo religioso anche il tipo del mostro, su cui siede graziosamente la dea minoica col suo elegante vestito a kaunakes: cioè il serpente-grifo, meglio conosciuto sotto il nome di "drago di Babele." Al tempo della mia prima pubblicazione della cretula, questa immagine della dea-cavallerizza era ancora unica nel mondo cretese-miceneo, fatta eccezione per un'altra cretula proveniente da Gournià, rubata

Miceneo III C (v. *Mycenaean Pottery*, p. 348 ss., motivo 44, n. 14, fig. 58 a, p. 345; cfr. anche consimili motivi ad archi concentrici a proposito della decorazione metopale, *ibid.*, 416 ss., motivo 75, fig. 72, nn. 32-33 a, p. 414). Gli altri vasi dalla Tomba di Moschù Vunara or ora citata palesano ugualmente un carattere estremamente avanzato: così una seconda anfora, grezza, decorata solamente a due fasce, e tre anfore a staffa con la medesima semplicissima ornamentazione.

Una decorazione assai simile a quella del tripode di tale tomba palesa l'impugnatura in steatite pure già menzionata (v. sopra, nota 20), trovata nella Tomba XVII dei più antichi scavi della medesima necropoli jalisia. Quest'altra tomba conteneva invece almèno 10 seppellimenti, con abbondanti suppellettili funebri, di cui alcune hanno aspetto assai più ricco, e di un periodo migliore che non quelle della tomba sopra citata; solamente i vasi più avanzati invece hanno una decorazione stilizzata e irrigidita, assomigliante ai vasi della Tomba LXVII (v. *Annuario* 6-7, p. 117 ss.; cfr. in questa tomba anche un sigillo di tipo siro-ittito, simile a quello trovato nella tomba LXVII, *ibid.*, 127, fig. 47). Ora il Furumark classifica questa tomba più ricca nel Miceneo III C 1 (*Chronol.*, p. 74; cfr. anche altre tombe simili, p. 74 s.); e, data l'evidente lunga durata della tomba, i vasi più recenti non possono appartenere alla fase più arcaica di questo periodo, ma debbono estendersi anche nella seguente, cioè al sec. XII.

34. Vedi *AJA* 49 (1945) 270 ss.

però dal Museo di Candia prima della sua pubblicazione e di cui m'era
stata data notizia dall' amico eforo St. Xanthoudides. L'anello ellittico,
di fine lavoro, donde deriva la cretula di H. Triada, non può scendere
molto sotto agli inizi del Tardo-Minoico.

Ma un'altra cretula cretese, pubblicata dopo il mio studio più
recente, cioè una delle cretule di Sklavokambos (fig. 3)[35] è venuta
a confermare brillantemente la mia ipotesi. Essa rappresenta con
tutta chiarezza un animale fantastico, questa volta del tutto simile al
"drago di Babele," col suo corpo tubiforme estremamente allungato,
le zampe grosse e tozze che sembrano terminare proprio in artigli, il
lungo collo su cui posa il piccolo muso appuntito; il corpo appare

Figure 3. Cretula cretese da Sklavokampos: Animale fantastico presso a un
cespuglio di papiri.

coperto di scaglie, quali riscontriamo in Oriente per es. nel cilindro
di Kish e più tardi nel fregio di mattoni smaltati sulla porta di Ishtar
a Babele,[36] e anche qui probabilmente l'ambiente esotico è suggerito
da un cespuglio che sembra di papiro.

Credo che si possa inoltre riconoscere il medesimo soggetto nel
cilindro di ematite rinvenuto in una tomba del cimitero minoico
di Haghia Pelaghia — un porticino a Ovest di Candia — in associazione a materiali ceramici che non permettono di farlo discendere più
in giù degli inizi del Tardo-Minoico III.[37] I contatti con l'Oriente in
questo caso si palesano già nella forma e nello stile del sigillo, che è
un'evidente imitazione locale di una categoria di cilindri ciprioto-
micenei, imitazione tuttavia trasformata al solito da un'immediata
interpretazione e rielaborazione da parte dell'indipendente spirito
artistico cretese. Anche qui la dea, in veste campanata minoica,
cavalca seduta di fianco sull'animale, volto verso destra, ma non nel-

35. Vedi Marinatos, *Ephemeris* 1939-41 (pubblicato nel 1948), tav. 4, n. 11.
36. Cfr. *AJA, loc. cit.*, 271, fig. 3 e, p. 276, fig. 6.
37. Evans, IV, 497, fig. 436; Demargne, *op. cit.*, 82, fig. 2.

l'atteggiamento della dea che riceve l'adorazione dei fedeli, a braccia
sollevate, come nel sigillo di H. Triada, bensì oramai nella naturale
posizione della cavalcatrice, appoggiandosi con una mano sul collo
dell'animale e ritirando indietro l'altra mano verso la coda. Le piccole
proporzioni dell'animale rispetto alla donna, la lunga coda e il muso
appuntito hanno fatto suggerire all'Evans, in forma dubitativa, la
sua identificazione con una volpe. In realtà anche questa volta la lunga
coda snodata, la prominenza del muso a becco acuminato, la posizione

Figure 4. a-b) Laminetta in pasta vitrea da Dendra: Dea cavalcante un animale
o mostro fantastico.

delle zampe, lo fanno assomigliare al "drago" della cretula sopra citata
di H. Triada, come ai due mostri dell'altra cretula gemella in cui un
ambiente nilotico o straniero è suggerito da ciuffi di papiro, nonchè
al mostro di un sigillo pittografico minoico, studiato in associazione
alla cretula stessa: anche nel cilindro di H. Pelaghia, invero, il mostro
trotterella, su un terreno roccioso, in mezzo ad alti steli di papiro,
precedendo un personaggio maschile, vestito dei calzoncini cretesi,
che tiene sollevato sulle spalle un altro essere mostruoso, un grifo.
Presso a poco contemporanea alla rappresentazione del cilindro é infine
quella (fig. 4), ripetuta su otto molto logore piastrelle in pasta
vitrea blu rinvenute nella Tomba Reale di Dendra, con la dea, vestita
di kaunakes e di polos, cavalcante questa volta un animale che sembra
un toro, dea di nuovo rappresentata nell'atteggiamento di accogliere
l'adorazione dei devoti a braccia sollevate.

La statuetta di Kharvati, abbiamo visto, è notevolmente posteriore
alle rappresentazioni sopra nominate; ma in compenso essa ci offre
per la prima volta nel mondo cretese-miceneo l'immagine della dea
cavalcante proprio un cavallo. Che questa volta si tratta di un cavallo
e non di un animale fantastico ci è garantito da una sola occhiata alla

seconda statuetta proveniente dal medesimo ritrovamento, quella del cavaliere in arcione: identica è la forma e l'atteggiamento dei due animali, mentre in quello della dea è conservata inoltre la coda di natura chiaramente equina; il confronto si può estendere del resto a un gran numero di statuette micenee coi cavalli attaccati a cocchi. Ma il cavaliere in arcioni nel mondo cretese-miceneo è una rarità anche maggiore che non quella della dea seduta su un animale. Trattando della cavalcatrice sulla cretula di H. Triada ho già avuto occasione di tracciare un rapido sunto delle nostre cognizioni sull'equitazione presso agli antichi. Il cavallo è stato probabilmente importato a Creta dall'Oriente, attorno alla metà del II millennio a.C., circa contemporaneamente alla sua importazione nell'Egitto:[38] quasi una vera e propria, suggestiva illustrazione dell'arrivo del cavallo nell'isola, contemporanea circa all'età dell'importazione, ci è offerta dalla famosa cretula di Cnosso in cui vediamo uno splendido esemplare di cavallo su una nave di tipo minoico, quasi simbolo del prezioso carico della nave. Ma nella civiltà cretese-micenea, come in quelle del prossimo Oriente donde vi è pervenuto, il cavallo è servito solo per tirare i cocchi dei re e dei principi, in guerra e in caccia: uso di cui un'abbondante serie di rappresentazioni ci è conservata, in anelli d'oro e sigilli, in affreschi, sulla ceramica, sulle stele di Micene. Il cavallo per uso di cavalcatura non ci era conosciuto finora, nè per scopo di guerra nè per diporto, se non proprio alla fine di tale civiltà, cioè nella rappresentazione rozzamente dipinta sul cratere di Moulianà, in epoca tarda micenea o forse già sub-micenea, in una necropoli precisamente in cui la penetrazione a Creta di costumi — e con tutta probabilità anche di ceppi etnici — stranieri è attestata dall'apparire del nuovo rito, non minoico, della cremazione del defunto, e del nuovo metallo, il ferro.[39] Anche nei poemi omerici, inquantochè essi descrivono la civiltà micenea, i guerrieri non combattono mai a cavallo, mentre solo i principi e nobili incedono sul cocchio di guerra; neanche gare di equitazione vi sono menzionate. Se Ulisse e Diomede saltano in groppa ai cavalli di Reso che rapiscono di notte dal campo troiano, è solo perchè per prudenza non hanno potuto portare con sè il carro (Il. X, 513); e se altrove il poeta (Il. XV. 679 ss.)[40] si giova come di confronto dell'immagine d'un abile cavaliere che salta in groppa a quattro cavalli che spinge simultaneamente nella pianura, egli descrive già usanze del suo proprio tempo. Egualmente nell'Egitto e nell'Oriente

---

38. Vedi Evans, IV, 827 s.

39. Vedi Xanthoudides in *Ephemeris* 1904, 21 ss., tav. III: Doro Levi, "Arkades," *Annuario* 10-12, 640 ss.; per gli inizi dell'arte del cavalcare in genere, Evans, IV, 830 s.

40. Cfr. anche *Od.* V, 371.

asiatico la cavalleria entra come un corpo distinto nell'esercito assai tardi, non prima dell'età del ferro, e in genere anche le rappresentazioni di cavalieri precedentemente sono rarissime. Facendo astrazione da un paio di esempi isolati di monumenti forse risalenti alla XVIII dinastia,[41] in Egitto figure di cavalieri appaiono solo nel XIV sec., ma non rappresentanti guerrieri egiziani, sibbene messi, nemici volti in fuga, schiavi senz'armi e semi-ignudi, tipi di asiatici, che probabilmente confermano la provenienza dall'Oriente anche di questo costume di cavalcare a dorso di cavallo. Infine la dea sira Anath appare, tutta vestita, seduta di fianco sul cavallo, in un'opera della XIX dinastia nel Grande Tempio di Karnak,[42] e un'altra volta, in simile posizione e tenendo sollevato l'arco, in uno schizzo su un frammento di calcare al Museo di Berlino.[43] Ma egualmente in Siria il costume di andare a cavallo ci è testimoniato assai tardi, e da principio in misura insignificante rispetto all'uso del cocchio. Da prima, per l'età circa in cui abbiamo visto apparire le sporadiche rappresentazioni nel mondo egizio, apprendiamo da alcuni testi cuneiformi di Boghasköi[44] che i re ittiti talora solevano montare a cavallo, e sentiamo citare cavalli da cavalcatura, e messi a cavallo; più tardi le fonti ci informano di nuovo che sotto Nebukadnezar I (1170 a.C.) vengono importati in Babilonia cavalli da cavalcare.[45] Ma rappresentazioni di cavalieri non risalgono aldilà dell'alba del I millennio a.C. Forse è un cavaliere armato quello che ci appare su un sigillo siro-cappadocio degli inizi del millennio;[46] poco dopo si moltiplicano le rappresentazioni di cavalieri sui ben noti rilievi neo-ittiti e siriaci di Marash, Sendjirlì, Karkemish, Tell Ahmar, Tell Halaf e via dicendo. Veri e propri corpi di cavalleria nell'esercito babilonese ci appaiono sotto Assurnasirpal II (860 a.C.), di solito armati di arco, più di raro di lancia, corpi di cavalleria per cui il re Salomone disponeva già di ben 12000 cavalli. E' ben vero che, migliaia d'anni prima di tutti i monumenti citati poco sopra, ancora nella

---

41. Cavaliere galoppante, entro la testa intagliata a giorno di un'ascia bronzea al Mus. Britannico, Budge, *Archaeologia* 53, tav. III, 2: W. Max Müller, *Asien u. Europa*, 301, nota 4, suggerisce che si tratta di un asiatico. Sulla dubbia autenticità e la data (XVIII o XIX dinastia) della statuetta lignea del Museo Metropolitano, cfr. *Bull. of the Metrop. Mus.*, 1916, 85.

42. Lepsius, C. R., *Denkmäler aus Aegypten u. Aethiopien*, 6, Abt. III, tav. 145.

43. Wiesner, J., "Fahren u. Reiten in Alteuropa u. im alten Orient," *Der alte Orient*, 38, Heft 2-4 (1939) tav. II, 1.

44. Vedi Götze, A., *Kleinasien* (in I. Müller's *Handb. der Altertumswissenschaft, Kulturgeschichte des alten Orients*, III, 1), 111, nota 7; 117. Cfr. anche id., *Hethiter, Churriter und Assyrer*, 85 s.

45. Cfr. Thomsen, s.v. "Pferd" in Ebert's *Reallexikon der Vorgeschichte*, 10, 109 ss.

46. Delaporte, *Cat. des Cylindres orientaux du Louvre*, tav. 96, 1: ma l'animale qui rappresentato, con muso corto e lunga orecchia, non si presenta sicuramente come un cavallo, e il cavaliere sembra montare di fianco, alla maniera femminile.

civiltà elamitica del IV millennio a.C., un paio isolato di rappresentazioni di cavalieri, persino con briglie e con una specie di sella o cuscino
sul dorso dei cavalli, è stato recentemente segnalato, su un gruppo di
istrumenti d'osso grafiti rinvenuti a Susa;[47] ma la concorde testimonianza negativa, letteraria e monumentale, per tutte le civiltà
passate in rassegna, esclude la diffusione del costume dell'equitazione
avanti agli inizi del I millennio a.C.: assenza di monumenti tanto più
esplicita per Creta, la cui arte più di ogni altra si compiace di molti-
plicare le rappresentazioni di ogni genere di esercizi ginnici e di
bravure sportive.

La nostra statuetta micenea ci rappresenta dunque la più antica
immagine di cavaliere nella civiltà cretese-micenea, sensibilmente
anteriore — assumendo la verisimile contemporaneità con la statuetta
della dea a cavallo — all'immagine finora considerata tale, cioè alla
rozza pittura del sopra citato cratere di Mouliana, confermandone
nello stesso tempo l'interpretazione di cavaliere, assai spesso posta
in dubbio.[48] A fianco a quest'ultima rappresentazione si sono messe
recentemente altre statuette fittili di cavalieri rinvenute negli scavi
d'Asine,[49] evidentemente classificabili proprio verso la fine dell'età
tardo-elladica o nel periodo di transizione al protogeometrico; il corpo
dei cavalieri è assai rozzamente modellato, ma la loro testa è sormontata da un'alta sporgenza, che sembra con tutta verisimiglianza un
elmo; gli occhi sono a dischetti schiacciati contro il volto.[50] Anche
queste statuette, che precedono le numerose immagini di cavalieri
dell'età geometrica, modellate in bronzo o argilla, dipinte su vasi o in-
cise sulle fibule beotiche,[51] hanno in comune con la nostra la posizione
del cavaliere, a cavalcioni sul dorso nudo del cavallo, e che si tiene
saldo semplicemente afferrandosi al collo, alla criniera o agli orecchi
del cavallo; le gambe di questi cavalieri si presentano assai corte, non
scendendo sotto all'orlo del ventre dell'animale, giustificando pertanto
la mancanza di indicazione delle gambe umane sul cratere dipinto di

---

47. *Mém. de la Mission archéologique de Perse* 25, 1934, 199, fig. 30, nn. 24-25;
Wiesner, *op. cit.*, tav. I, 1. Parallelamente, dalla testimonianza dei testi non
risulta con sicurezza che la sella sia esistita in Mesopotamia nell'epoca arcaica:
cfr. H. de Genouillac *Tablettes sumériennes archaïques*, 1909, XLV.

48. Ancora recentemente dal Furumark, *Mycenaean Pottery*, 200.

49. *Asine*, 309, fig. 213, 4.

50. Una rozza statuetta fittile maschile, conservante tronconi di gambe divaricate e di braccia tese in avanti (cfr. Schliemann, *Mykenai*, 83, tav. XIX, n. 110),
suggerisce la posizione del cavaliere; ma la mancanza di gran parte del corpo
come del cavallo rende l'interpretazione assai dubbia. Anche meno sicura è
l'interpretazione di un cavaliere nel frammento di un tardo piatto miceneo con
figurazione dipinta in bianco su fondo nero, v. Furtwängler-Loeschcke, *Mykenische
Vasen*, tav. XL, n. 417.

51. Sulle rappresentazioni di cavalieri nell'arte greca geometrica e orientalizzante cfr. Hanfmann, "Horsemen from Sardis," *AJA* 49 (1945) 570 ss.

Moulianà. Finora dunque, dai monumenti superstiti, non appare che alla fine dell'età del bronzo l'uso delle briglie sia stato trasportato dai cavalli attaccati al cocchio ai cavalli da cavalcatura: nè invero l'uso di briglie è ricordato ancora da Omero.

Ma un altro elemento del tutto nuovo e sorprendente nella statuetta della dea a cavallo è la sella:[52] altro oggetto che nel mondo antico appare assai tardi. Da prima, la vera e propria sella con armatura di legno, foderata di cuoio o di stoffa, è stata per lungo tempo preceduta dalla semplice coperta da cavallo, designata anch'essa col nome più tardi usato per la sella, ἐφίππιον. Ma i cavalieri greci assai a lungo hanno cavalcato semplicemente sul dorso nudo del cavallo: così vediamo saltare in groppa, incedere o trotterellare snelli e dritti sui loro cavalli, senz'aiuto di staffe o di sella o coperte, gli efebi ateniesi sul fregio del Partenone. Solamente Senofonte nei suoi trattati sulla cavalleria comincia a nominare l' ἐφίππιον, che non considera per altro come un elemento costitutivo della bardatura, ma piuttosto come un lusso, dal quale anzi si deve stare in guardia per non disabituarsi alle regole della severa equitazione. Dall'età di Alessandro in poi l'uso della coperta si estende, anche in questo caso con tutta probabilità per influenza dell'Oriente. Solo in ambiente orientale infatti, assai prima di questa età, ci appaiono nell'arte greca alcune isolate rappresentazioni di cavalieri su cavalli forniti di coperte, in vasi e sarcofagi clazomenii e in vasi arcaici dell'ambiente ionico egizio,[53] quindi fin dalla prima metà del VI sec. a.C.: un'anfora arcaica a figure nere da una piramide di Saqqarah ci rappresenta dei cacciatori tutti armati a cavallo, mentre su un frammento clazomenio incontriamo una donna che cavalca non più seduta di fianco ma in arcioni. Nell'ambiente orientale invero era proverbiale la passione per le ricche coperte da cavallo, che, secondo gli scrittori greci, i Persiani possedevano con maggior profusione che non le coperte pei loro letti; e cavalli con ricche coperte ci appaiono spesso nelle rappresentazioni dei rilievi assiri. Ma finalmente, su un rilievo di Berlino,[54] vediamo il cavallo da caccia di Assurbanipal bardato di una vera e propria sella. Alla periferia del mondo greco cavalli sellati ci appaiono, sin dal IV secolo, sui preziosi oggetto d'oro, d'argento e d'avorio, d'arte greco-scitica, rappresentanti la famosa cavalleria scita.

---

52. Su questo oggetto cfr. A. Schlieben, "Die Reit- und Packsättel der Alten" in *Annalen des Vereins für nassauische Altertumskunde*, 20 (1888); Daremberg-Saglio, s.v. "ephippium," "equitatio," "sella equestris"; *RE*, s.v. "ἐφίππιον," "ἀστράβη"; P. Thomsen, s.v. "Pferd" in Ebert's *Reallexikon der Vorgeschichte*, X, p. 113, s.; Günther, W., s.v. "Sattel," *ibid.*, XI, p. 212 ss.

53. Vedi Pfuhl, *Malerei u. Zeichnung der Griechen*, fig. 145; Edgar, *Cat. gén. du Caire, Greek Vases*, n. 32377, tav. V, ecc.

54. Ebert's *Reallex. d. Vorgesch.*, VII, tav. 152 b.

E' del tutto probabile che l'introduzione di una vera e propria sella da cavaliere sia stata preceduta dall'uso del basto, necessario per fissare il carico sulla schiena di cavalli, come di asini e muli. Infatti una vivace rappresentazione di una mula che, tutta sola, incede verso sinistra con una balla di mercanzia fissata al basto ci appare già nell'interno di una kylix a figure rosse attribuita al Maestro di Antiphon:[55] il basto posa sopra una coperta, ed è fornito di due forti prominenze davanti e di dietro, com'è nella nostra statuetta, forma ancora usata in tutto il Prossimo Oriente; nella tazza è accuratamente indicata l'intera bardatura della mula, con le redini e le cinghie incrociantisi attraverso al ventre. L'uso del basto *(ἀστράβη)* anche per comodità di cavalcare è attestato nella letteratura, per es. in un'espressione spesso ripetuta dagli oratori attici: *ἐπ' ἀστράβης ὀχεῖσθαι:*[56] *ἀστράβη* che è conosciuta soprattutto, nel mondo greco e poi in quello romano (dove si chiama *clitellae*), come sella da viaggio e da donne. Nel repertorio figurato essa ci appare, provvista per di più di uno schienale posteriore e perfino di uno sgabello per riposo dei piedi — dunque esattamente coi dettagli che abbiamo creduto di riconoscere nella nostra statuetta micenea — in un monumento relativamente tanto antico quale un'oinochoe a figure rosse di stile severo da Cervetri al Museo Britannico, in cui ci troviamo in ambiente orientale, con un Persiano o uno Scita a dorso di mulo.[57] Sempre su un monumento di ambiente asiatico, cioè nell' heroon di Gjölbaschi-Trysa,[58] una delle lastre a rilievo ci raffigura questa volta una donna a cavallo su tale comoda cavalcatura, col mantello sbattuto dal vento che forma il prediletto schema, protrattosi tanto a lungo nell'arte antica, dell'arco che incornicia tutto attorno la testa.

E' probabile che la scarsezza delle rappresentazioni di cavalli e muli bardati sia dovuta alla frammentarietà della documentazione archeologica, e che il moltiplicarsi delle nuove scoperte nel mondo egeo e nel Prossimo Oriente presto riempirà molte delle lacune tuttora aperte. Certo si è per altro che nella civiltà cretese-micenea il basto non era generalmente usato, come si potrebbe pensare, dal momento che la ben nota figurina fittile da Phaistòs rappresentante un cavallo carico di due anfore, a cui si è aggiunta recentemente un'altra simile

---

55. Hartwig, *Griechische Meisterschalen*, 563 ss., tav. LXIII, 1; Beazley, *Attic Red-figure Vase-painters*, 231, n. 26.

56. Cfr. Lysias, 24, 11, 12; Demosth., *c. Mid.*, 133, ecc.

57. Walters, H. B., *JHS* 41 (1921) 129, n. 2, tav. VIII.

58. Benndorf-Niemann, tav. 13; Günther, *loc. cit.*, tav. 54 b.

da Jaliso,[59] ci mostrano il carico appoggiato al dorso nudo dell'animale. A ogni modo anche per questo costume, dunque, il gruppo di trovamenti di Kharvati ci offre un'immagine che, a mia conoscenza, precede di lunga data le più antiche testimonianze finora a noi accessibili.

59. *Mon. Ant.* 12 (1902), col. 118, fig. 47 = Maraghiannis, *Antiquités crétoises*, 1, tav. XV, 2; *Annuario* 13-14, Tomba LXXIII, p. 293 ss.; figg. 35 e 39, tav. a colori XXII.

MYCENAE

Mycenae, city rich-in-gold, when within thy ruins I stand,
And my prayers ascend through the quiet air like incense for thy land,
Or when on the fallen fragments of thy palaces I sit,
Reading the Iliad reverently as a man reads Holy Writ,

Perchance—who knows—on reading o'er those rhapsodies sublime,
I'll see heroic shades rise up from tomb of olden time—
See first of all the phantom chief of the Achaean host,
Noble and proud, but head bowed low, weep thee, his glory lost.

Soteris Skipis

Translated by
John B. Edwards

ΔΙΟΓΕΝΕΙΣ ΒΑΣΙΛΗΕΣ

Spyridon N. Marinatos
University of Athens, Greece[1]

The archaeological discoveries of the Minoan-Mycenaean world have brought considerable improvement in our appreciation of Greek civilization. Cornerstones to our knowledge have been laid by Sir Arthur Evans and Professor Martin P. Nilsson. Their work enables us to see more and more clearly how many elements of Hellenic religion and mythology are derived from the Minoan-Mycenaean civilization. The sciences of linguistics and art are groping in the same direction, and the scope of scholarly investigation will evidently be further extended in the future. It is unnecessary to emphasize particularly how much our understanding of Homer has been improved by the Minoan-Mycenaean discoveries.

At this point I would like to emphasize another view which offers a wide horizon to scientific research: that all the great civilizations of the Eastern Mediterranean form, in one way, a single unit in which the mutual influence and the common cultural elements must have been much more important than appears at first sight. Many have already observed that the periods of rise and decline of these cultures coincide.[2] In the eastern Mediterranean the appearance of the purely Greek civilization inaugurated a new epoch in the history of human thought and spirit. But before the emergence of that civilization, the preceding ones, namely the Sumero-Babylonian, the Egyptian, the Minoan-Mycenaean, the Hittite, the Phoenician, and even the early Greek culture, constituted a fairly homogeneous and integrated unit. Their mutual inter-borrowings in the field of art are known, but investigation may show that there is even greater interdependence in intellectual and spiritual matters, such as religion, mythology, magic, folk tales, and folk medicine. Some of these elements, for example folk medicine and medical superstitions, spread as far as central

---

1. I wish to express my thanks to Dr. Constantine G. Yavis, Assistant Professor of Classical Languages and Archaeology at St. Louis University, for the translation into English of the original manuscript.

2. See for example Wilhelm Weber, *Die Staatenwelt des Mittelmeers in der Frühzeit des Griechentums* (1928). This phenomenon can be observed in detail in virtually every area of the world. This alternation of high civilization and decline, which our generation in Europe can appreciate more fully than ever, is chiefly the result of wars. But this is not always necessary. It could be shown that there is no historical justification for the usual opinion that culture advances continually. Instead humanity passes through alternating periods of progress and regression. Cf. the correct views of Albert Hyma, *An Outline of Ancient History*, 3 ff.

Europe, surviving even today.[3] The early Greek civilization is deeply imbued with these elements from preceding civilizations. Future investigation of the new evidence continually being brought forth by the spade of the excavator will, I am sure, reveal further connections. Obscure passages of Homer are constantly becoming more clear. The fragments of the laws of Rhadamanthys or of Pittheus are becoming constantly more intelligible against the background of the great Oriental law codes, such as the codes of Hammurabi and of the Jews, where the *jus talionis* dominates: "an eye for an eye and a tooth for a tooth." I feel that the common-sense admonitions of Hesiod are reflected on representations of Minoan-Mycenaean work of art, and his system of theogony is now much more understandable, since the cuneiform inscriptions have revealed to us the oriental views on cosmogony. Authors previously considered unreliable or otherwise neglected acquire new importance because of the discoveries made in various excavations: Manetho for Egypt, Berossus for Babylonia, Diodorus for Crete, and, since the discoveries at Ugarit (Ras-Shamra), Philo of Byblus and his Phoenician History.

In particular there are reasons to believe that very early the Achaeans or the Danaoi of Greece, or however else they should be called, sought to earn their livelihood as mercenaries. I hope that I shall be able to show that the treasures of the shaft-graves at Mycenae have such an origin. These treasures can not, at present, be considered plunder from Crete at such an early date; there is no proof that Crete was invaded about 1600-1500 B. C. On the contrary, at that time the Sekenen-Re and the Pharaohs of the 18th dynasty expelled the Hyksos and then created the Empire. Gold was always considered an Egyptian metal, and we know that the Pharaohs rewarded brave deeds with gold. Egyptian warriors, such as the Ahmes of El Kab, inscribed this in their tombs. Unfortunately the princes of Mycenae did not know how to write, and so were unable to inscribe on the stelai their exploits and the amount of their gold reward. It remains for us to prove this on the basis of the Egyptian elements which were brought to Mycenae and of the Minoan-Mycenaean elements which we find in Egypt at exactly this time. A little later, written evidence exists: already Amenophis III and then Rameses II, Mernephtah, and Rameses III regularly had European mercenaries. This tradition merely was maintained with the Psammetichs and Necho of the twenty-sixth dynasty, who had Ionian mercenaries.[4] This assumption of the existence of

---

3. Erman-Ranke, *Aegypten und aegyptisches Leben*, 418 ff.

4. On mercenaries in Egypt see in general Breasted, J., *A History of Egypt* (French edition, Paris Vromant) 434 ff., 485 ff., 531 ff., 571 f. On contacts of the rulers of the shaft graves of Mycenae with Egypt, cf. Persson, A., *The New*

mercenaries can, I believe, explain many aspects of the common cultural tradition of the Orient. In the realm of art our research has
shown definite relationships. But the intellectual elements are more
fluid and they have not provided us with physical remains. It is easier
to trace an artistic motif from Egyptian to Minoan-Mycenaean art
and vice versa, than to trace an intellectual element. Of the latter it
is possible that some have escaped us forever, and their probative
force is weak, unless we indicate also their probable manner of migration. One such manner, I think, is the migration through mercenaries.
It is easy for such persons to transplant from country to country
myths, military stories, popular superstitions, and even religious
elements. The Roman legionaries later transmitted religious beliefs
of Mithraism and other Oriental religions to their homeland and as
far as Germany.

The tale of Rameses III was transported to Greece as the myth of
Trophonios and Agamedes and was localized at the beehive tomb of
Hyrieus at Aulis. Wilamowitz attributed its spread to the Telegoneia
of Eugammon of Cyrene, while Herodotus preserved the Egyptian
version with the name of Rameses.[5] The myth of the wooden horse
of Troy seems to me to be simply a similar variation on the stratagem
of the general Thutiy in the time of Thutmose III at the siege of Joppa.
This general succeeded in capturing Joppa by secretly introducing his
soldiers into the town hidden inside baskets which were carried on
donkeys. This tale was very popular in Egypt, and had become for
many centuries a folk tale, just as other traditions pertaining to the
expeditions of that great Pharaoh.[6] His son Amenhotep was, it appears, a person of great physical strength and the tale of his bow
became another subject of folk tales. He repeatedly boasts in his inscriptions that no one else was able to bend his bow—and this very
bow is now extant, having been found in his tomb. We know that
Herodotus echoes this tradition when he mentions that Cambyses was

---

Tombs of Dendra, 176-196, where, along with interesting points given before by
Evans and Nilsson, are offered additional information and an interesting point of
view. In a forthcoming study I deal with the subject more fully especially from
the point of view of fundamental cultural and religious ideas and thoughts which,
as I believe, appear suddenly in Mycenae and which are of unquestionable Egyptian origin.

5. See Meyer, Ed., *Geschichte des Altertums*₂, 2, 1, 266, 595 with note 2. Meyer
feels that this tale is connected with Rameses III and his storehouses of treasures
at the temple and palace complex at Medinet Habu. The linguistic form Rampsini-
tus, which he considers unexplainable, can I believe, be interpreted by the name
of Rameses-Nacht, who was high priest of Ammon during the time of the reign
of the Ramessides. See Breasted, *op. cit.*, 514.

6. Breasted, *op. cit.*, 322, observes that the tradition is still preserved today in
the story of Ali-Baba and the forty thieves.

unable to bend the bow of the king of the Ethiopians.[7] Nor can we dissociate from this cycle the famous bow of Odysseus, as told in the Odyssey. Homer's mention of Ethiopians and his knowledge about the existence of Pygmies are easily explained by the intermediacy of mercenaries.[8] Many mercenaries must have reached Nubia before their later descendants, serving under Psammetichus II, carved their Greek inscriptions at Abu Simbel on the colossus of Rameses II. Without the knowledge of the mentality of such mercenaries, it is impossible to understand the odd simile in which the courage of Menelaus, when he is defending the fallen Patroclus, is compared to that of the fly.[9] For this also is an Egyptian view. In that land flies and fleas are a scourge because of their great numbers and harassing persistence, as ancient Egyptians and modern Egyptologists mention frequently.[10] The fly was considered a model of courage and bravery: a special decoration, "the Golden Fly," was awarded by the Pharaoh to those who had displayed bravery on the field of battle.[11] Only in the light of this concept can we understand why Menelaus was not ridiculed in the simile of the poet, as would be the case in Modern Greek, where the appellation fly is given to cowardly and worthless persons. Blind minstrels, such as Demodokus and even Homer, cannot be fully understood without the wonderful reliefs of Egypt whose inhabitants, both ancient and modern, suffer from blindness more than by any other people in the world.[11a]

Within the range of these thoughts, I shall attempt a more searching examination of the concepts of the Homeric world concerning the divine ancestry of kings. In this way we can recapture the original significance of Zeus as the father of the great rulers of the Minoan-Mycenaean period. It is clear that in Homer there is not a shadow of insult or of any adverse implication when it is clearly stated that the father of a given hero is not the person assumed by the people, but Zeus or some other god. The Greeks of later times did not understand completely what was involved. From misunderstanding to misunderstanding Zeus through the comic writers finally was transformed into a humorous personage. Lucian, for instance, represents him as an

---

7. *Ibid.*, 338, the fact is observed.

8. There is a well-known account of the Old Kingdom about a pygmy who was captured alive and was being led by the general Harkuf from central Africa to the young Pharaoh Pepi II, *ibid.*, 141. Numerous representations of pygmies are to be found in Egyptian art.

9. *Iliad*, XVII, 570.

10. Erman-Ranke, *op. cit.*, 417.

11. *Ibid.*, 133, 631. Breasted, *op. cit.*, 232, 311.

11a. See Erman-Ranke, *op. cit.*, 284 and 283, fig. 123 (blind singers from the Aton temple of El Amarna).

Olympian Casanova, a dabbler in unlawful love, and a pursuer of the wives of others.

In every primitive society the king, as the creator of law and order, as the person who brings success in wars, and also as the possessor of all the land (which actually belongs to the God according to the Babylonian view) is considered to partake of the divine himself. The Sumerian kings of the pre-dynastic cemetery of Ur were considered gods and only they were buried with human sacrifices.[12] The tombs of the common mortals lie thick about those of the kings, because the king after death is a god and he is able to insure life and happiness for his faithful subjects.[13] According to Sumerian beliefs the first king of the world "was created by the gods inside the body of his mother." It is certain that the statues of kings such as Ur-Nina and Gudea were set up in temples and were worshipped. It is likewise known that certain kings (for instance, Naram-Sin) were considered gods even before their death. For this reason they wore the horned tiara, which is the emblem of divinity, and the determinative "god" was placed before their names. The supreme god Enlil was considered the father of these god-kings. Goddesses (for example, Anunit, Innina) were considered occasionally as their wives. Temples are set up for them while still alive, but especially after death they are worshipped with regular sacrifices, and oracles are sought by their statues.[14] It is nevertheless true that after the time of Hammurabi this custom fell into disuse, because the kingship declined, and the barbarian Kassite kings occupied the throne of Babylonia for many centuries. But occasionally, and in the course of every period, we meet with this belief.

In Egypt we observe corresponding practices. The mighty kings of the Old Kingdom are considered gods. About the great pyramids are crowded the tombs of the faithful, the mastabas, as was the case in Sumeria. Only after kingship was weakened were the tombs of the nobles placed at a distance from that of the king. The Pharoah is regularly designated in his titles as the son of Re, who is the supreme god of Egypt. After the rise of Thebes, in the New Kingdom, Ammon also rose in power and became the supreme god. That is why Ammon is the god whom the Greeks identified with Zeus.

In Egypt of the time of the Theban New Kingdom, which is the time at which the Minoan-Mycenaeans became acquainted with Egypt, the Pharaoh was considered a god in actuality and not merely in title. That is, it was believed that on certain nights Ammon would come in

---

12. Woolley, Sir L., *Ur und die Sintflut*, 42.
13. *Ibid.*, 23 f.
14. On all these matters see Meissner, B., *Babylonien und Assyrien*, I, 46 f.

person to the queen in the form of her husband. Thus the new Pharaoh was considered a real son of Ammon.[15]

Let us now come to Mycenaean Greece. The kings generally had divine ancestry and were often descended from the supreme god, as is proven by their regular title "Zeus-born," *Διογενεῖς*. It is from this fact that they drew their power and their authority in law-giving, formulating laws, and in passing judgment.[16] This is so well known that it is unnecessary to dwell any longer on this question, on which there is an extensive bibliography.[17]

Great kings such as Minos and Aiakos had direct divine origin and had exceptional privileges. Minos ascended every nine years to meet his father and could speak with him familiarly. Homer for this reason calls him *ὀαριστής* of great Zeus.[18] Aiakos had the same privileges. In time of great drought all Greeks pleaded with him to intercede with Zeus. Only he could do this effectively, and indeed beneficent rain was sent in response to his prayer.[19]

This beneficial relationship with the father-god who was the lord of meteorological phenomena existed, I believe, for Minos as well. In the above-mentioned passage of the Odyssey he is called *ἐννέωρος*. The meaning of this word remains obscure, although much has been written about it. The etymology is clear. Nine hours means nine years or at least nine seasons. Fick tried to interpret the word as indicating a correlation between the lunar and the solar year.[20] Others have given different explanations, but the view of Plato and of Strabo still prevails, according to which reference is made to the tradition of the meeting between Minos and Zeus every nine years. But no satisfactory explanation has yet been given of the fact that Homer applies this same epithet to the ox, the pig, and to animal fat. It is now known that there exists the so-called eleven-year rainfall cycle, which is associated with the periodic appearance of sunspots. This observation has been considered one of the great achievements of modern meteorology. But at the same time it has also been found that the existence of such a cycle was known empirically to the inhabitants of Ceylon and other tropical areas. Investigation further showed that the cycle is not strictly regular, since it ranges from eight to thirteen years, and that very often it approximates nine years. Extensive observations preserved from Egypt pointed to the existence of such a cycle of

---

15. Erman-Ranke, *op. cit.*, 58-63.
16. Cf. *Iliad*, I, 238 f.: *Δικασπόλοι, οἵ τε θέμιστας| πρὸς Διὸς εἰρύαται.*
17. See, for instance, Hermann, *Lehrbuch der griech. Antiquitäten*, 1 (sixth ed. by Thumser) 59 f.
18. *Odyssey*, XIX, 178 f.: *Μίνως| ἐννέωρος βασίλευε Διὸς μεγάλου ὀαριστής.*
19. Pausanias, II, 29, 7.
20. Fick, A., *Hattiden und Danubier*, 40 f.

approximately nine years (8.33), and recent observations in Greece have led to a similar result (9.13 and 9.86).

In years of abundant rainfall crops are good and animals and plants develop more fully. Now it has been observed that Theophrastus in speaking of the exceptionally good reeds from which flutes were constructed, says that they grew in Lake Kopais every nine years at the time of ἐπομβρία, that is, more abundant rainfall. The ancients knew therefore of this phenomenon, and we are informed of the appropriate term, which should also be adopted into modern scientific terminology. The above evidence led me to the supposition that in Crete, where the land is fertile but ever-thirsty, perhaps the phenomenon of *epombria* was known and was connected with the visit of Minos to his father, the lord of rain. The same fact was preserved also in continental Greece but in a more obscure tradition; we hear that Aeacus interceded once with his father in the same manner. This interpretation is the only one which covers all the Homeric uses of the word ἐννέωρος: oxen and pigs become fat in wet years, in the years of ἐπομβρία, and then the fat is abundant and of good quality.[21]

In Crete Rhadamanthys and Sarpedon were considered sons of Zeus. In the usual tradition they were considered brothers of Minos but were kings in independent dynasties which correspond respectively with the palaces of Phaestos and Mallia.[22] Other genealogies of them are also mentioned without divine ancestry, but in the Homeric tradition they are of divine descent. Many and perhaps all Minoan-Mycenaean kings received heroic honor and worship. In Crete we know at least one temple-tomb for the king or for a number of kings of Knossos. The Pharaoh of Egypt possessed his sepulchral temple. In the Old Kingdom that temple was attached to the eastern side of the Pyramid. In the New Empire the sepulchral temple was built at some distance from the rock-hewn tomb, because the valley of the kings was so narrow that it could not accommodate it. The temple-tomb of Knossos is composed of two parts, of the burial grotto and of the temple that is attached to the east side of the grotto.[23] And so Diodorus, who, in describing the tomb of Minos in Sicily, speaks of the main grave that was "hidden" and of the attached temple that was open to view, is proved correct.[24]

---

21. It would carry us too far afield to develop this aspect fully. I have communicated my interpretation of the word ἐννέωρος to Dr. Vasilios Aiginites, Professor of Physics and Meteorology at the University of Athens, who has been working on this subject, and he has included it in his study "Meteorological Periods" in the *Scientific Annual of the University of Athens*, 1946-47, 1-51.

22. On this see my special study in *Mélanges Charles Picard*, 699.

23. Evans, *Palace of Minos*, IV, 692 ff.

24. Diodorus, IV, 79 3.

We may now note that Zeus does not visit beautiful women of any social standing, but, in absolute preference, only the daughters of kings and princes; and this is a very characteristic detail that will help us understand the original significance of his legendary relations. Sometimes he assumes the form of an animal or bird. Here we may be dealing with the Minoan-Mycenaean idea of the divine epiphany especially when we find the God assuming the form of a bird, as was the case in the story of Leda. In the case of Danae, gold, an inanimate article, assumes the important role. In the case of Alcmene the Theban-Egyptian form of the myth is preserved in its original form, because in that case Zeus assumes the form of the absent Amphitryon. From the divine union are born kings famous for wisdom and justice —Minos, Rhadamanthys, Aeacus—or famous heroes or twins—Perseus, Sarpedon, Dioskouroi, Zethus and Amphion. That the most important son of Zeus, Heracles, was not a king is explained by Homer as having resulted from the superficiality of Zeus which was exploited by the jealous Hera. The real explanation perhaps must be sought in the relations of Mycenae and Tiryns, cities which were situated so near each other and were so magnificent that they could not have served as the capitals of two independent kingdoms. Tiryns was evidently an annex or a second seat of the kingdom, Mycenae being the first, just as in Assyria and later on in Persia we find more than one capital. Now Heracles, in spite of the fact that he was also considered a Theban, was chiefly connected with Tiryns at the time that Eurystheus was reigning at Mycenae. Some temporary jealousy between two strong personalities residing in Mycenae and Tiryns seems to be hidden behind the myth of the hostility between Eurystheus and Heracles. The former prevailed, since he was the king of the mighty Mycenae, the first capital of the kingdom. The same tradition is still to be found in the Iliad: Agamemnon is superior to many great heroes— Diomedes, Ajax, Achilles, etc.—; they are simply $\beta\alpha\sigma\iota\lambda\epsilon\tilde{\iota}\varsigma$, but Agamemnon is $\beta\alpha\sigma\iota\lambda\epsilon\acute{\upsilon}\tau\alpha\tau o\varsigma$.[25] The additional myths of Heracles and his labors are part of a much broader mythological cycle.[26]

War is certainly the most compelling circumstance which forces leaders of men to present themselves as sons of gods. In the Homeric poems, the Olympian Gods, both superior and inferior, are presented by this necessity as the fathers of warriors. Poseidon, Hermes, Ares, and others have their sons with mortal women. The river Spercheios also has a son, the general Menesthius, of the mortal woman Polydora,

---

25. Nestor calls him so, *Iliad*, IX, 69.

26. On this question see Nilsson, M., *The Mycenaean Origin of Greek Mythology*, 187 f., and especially 207 ff. Homer, *Iliad*, XI, 100 f., relates the myth which explains the reason why Heracles was not born king.

daughter of Peleus.[27] It is also added in characteristic manner, without any connotation of censure against the woman, that Menesthius was officially a son of her lawful husband Borus.

Achilles is a descendant of Zeus only indirectly, through Peleus-Aeacus, but he does have a divine mother, just as in Babylonia goddesses are wives of kings. This is a frequent occurrence in the Mycenaean world and Hesiod drew up a catalogue of great men from mortal fathers and immortal mothers.[28] These are evidently parallel developments, derived from the need of peoples for mortal chiefs of divine descent. The original idea, as the title $Διογενής$ shows, is that Zeus normally is the father of kings, just like Enlil in Babylonia and Ammon-Re in Egypt.

After the Homeric period this concept fades, not only because kings cease to exist, but also because Greek mentality develops independently of the Oriental attitudes. Proof lies in the fact that in Classical times very rarely do we hear that a family traces its descent back to a god. Certainly most Greeks, influenced as they were by the searching spirit of philosophy, would react ironically to such an idea, which so little accorded with the new democratic ideals. The kings of Sparta were Herakleids and no more; but in the Orient and especially in Egypt, as certain events of the Graeco-Roman period show, the idea of divine descent of kings never died. At a suitable time the idea reappeared again. Alexander the Great, after the conquest of Egypt, must needs become son of Ammon. The final act is to be found in the deification of the Hellenistic and Roman Emperors and in the construction of temples in their honor. This is the last gleam of the spirit of the Orient harking back four millennia.[29]

----

27. *Iliad*, XVI, 175.

28. Hesiod, *Theogony*, 967 f. (Rzach).

29. This is the general outline of the question which, I believe, is the only possible one. I am, of course, aware that in the details more opinions are possible; as, for instance, that the deification in Hellenistic times was rather due to Greek ideas. See Ulrich Wilcken "Zur Entstehung des hellenistischen Königskultes," *Sitzungsber. der Akad. der Wissenschaften, Phil.-hist. Klasse*, 28 (1938) 298 f.

LE MUR PELASGIQUE DE L'ACROPOLE ET LA DATE DE LA DESCENTE DORIENNE[1]

JEAN BÉRARD
Université de Nancy

Dans une première étude sur la chronologie mycénienne, il y a trois ans, nous avons été conduit, par un examen d'ensemble des données archéologiques et des données de la tradition relatives à la fin de l'âge du bronze en Grèce, à la conclusion qu'on a tort d'attribuer une valeur qu'elle n'a pas à la chronologie ératosthénienne, qui ne s'est que tardivement imposée, et qu'une chronologie considérablement plus haute que celle d'Ératosthène doit être adoptée pour l'âge héroïque, si l'on veut tenter de retrouver des correspondances précises entre données archéologiques et données de la tradition.[2]

Nous annoncions dans cette étude que nos prochaines recherches auraient pour objet de préciser, autant que faire se peut, la date du Retour des Héraclides, c'est-à-dire de la descente dorienne dans le Péloponèse, événement qui marque pour la Grèce le terme de l'âge des héros, mais sur lequel subsiste beaucoup d'incertitude et de confusion. A cette fin il convenait de découvrir, pour ce moment de l'histoire grecque, un monument ou un fait archéologique qui, d'une part, fût datable archéologiquement de manière précise, et sur lequel, d'autre part, la tradition nous fournît une indication non moins précise. Ce repère nécessaire, on le cherche en vain à Mycènes et à Tirynthe, pour lesquelles les données de la tradition ne sont pas assez explicites. On peut en revanche le trouver dans la fortification mycénienne de l'Acropole d'Athènes.

L'Athènes de l'époque mycénienne, si obscure pour nous jusqu'à ces dernières années, commence à nous être un peu mieux connue, grâce à des travaux comme l'étude céramique de F. H. Stubbings,[3] grâce surtout aux derniers résultats de l'exploration archéologique. Cependant que les fouilles du Céramique ont apporté une documentation essentielle pour le passage du mycénien au protogéométrique et pour les débuts de l'âge du fer,[4] celles de l'Acropole et de ses pentes,

---

1. Communication faite à l'Académie des Inscriptions et Belles-Lettres le 31 Mars 1950.

2. *Recherches sur la Chronologie mycénienne*, Communication du 11 Octobre 1946 à l'Académie des Inscriptions et Belles-Lettres (*Comptes rendus de l'Académie des Inscriptions*, 1946, 519-523), Paris, 1950.

3. Stubbings, F. H., "The Mycenaean Pottery of Attica," *BSA* 42 (1947) 1-75 (étude entreprise parallèlement à celle, plus générale d'A. Furumark, *The Mycenaean Pottery*, et *The Chronology of Mycenaean Pottery*, Stockholm, 1941).

4. W. Kraiker-K. Kübler, *Die Nekropolen des XII. bis X. Jahrhunderts*; Kübler, K., *Neufunde aus der Nekropole des XI. und X. Jahrhunderts*. Parmi les comptes-

pour ne rien dire ici des découvertes de l'Agora, nous ont fourni de précieuses indications pour la période antérieure. Les recherches italiennes sur le versant méridional de la colline ont mis au jour principalement des vestiges prémycéniens.[5] Les fouilles américaines, grecques et allemandes sur les côtés Nord, Est et Ouest ont eu pour résultat de préciser notre connaissance de la fortification de l'Acropole à l'époque mycénienne, c'est-à-dire du mur cyclopéen généralement appelé mur pélasgique.

Les travaux d'excavation exécutés sur l'Acropole de 1885 à 1890 avaient depuis longtemps permis de reconnaître le tracé général de cette enceinte; et plusieurs études lui avaient été consacrées depuis lors, ainsi qu'à l'ouvrage avancé qui la complétait à l'Ouest.[6] Mais jusqu' aux dernières fouilles des archéologues grecs, américains et allemands nous ne possédions pas de données chronologiques précises à son sujet.

L'un des résultats des recherches américaines de 1937 sur la face septentrionale de l'Acropole dans la région de l'Erechtéion fut la découverte d'une fontaine mycénienne. Cette découverte a été publiée par Oscar Broneer, au long article de qui nous renvoyons pour le détail notre lecteur.[7] Il s'agit d'une source à laquelle on accédait directement depuis le sommet de l'Acropole par un passage souterrain au moyen d'un escalier et, à l'origine, par ce passage seulement. Les nombreux fragments de poterie recueillis au cours de l'exploration de ce puits d'accès ont permis de reconstituer l'histoire de cette fontaine. L'escalier, extrêmement abrupt, descendait à une profondeur de 40 mètres en huit étages pour atteindre le niveau de l'eau. Il fut construit en pierres soutenues par un poutrage de bois; pour cette raison sa solidité dès l'origine dut être précaire. Cet escalier, de fait, s'effondra partiellement et le fond du puits fut alors comblé, seule

---

rendus, voir en particulier celui de Ch. Picard, *RA* 15 (1940) 128-131. Voir aussi sur les débuts du protogéométrique: Desborough, R., "What Is Protogeometric," *BSA* 43 (1948) 260-272.

5. *Annuario* 13-14 (1930-31, [1940]) 411-498.

6. Pour la bibliographie jusqu'en 1931, voir Judeich, W., *Topographie von Athen²*, 113 sqq. Citons en particulier: O. Jahn et A. Michaelis, *Arx Athenarum³*. Köster, A., *Das Pelargikon* (Cf. Pfuhl, dans *Berl. phil. Woch.* 1911, 299 sqq. et Dörpfeld, dans *AM* 1911, 71-72). Heberdey, R., *Das Westtor der Akropolis*, *JOAI* 13 (1910) 1-4. Wide, S., "Il pomerium e il pelargicon," *Ausonia* 7 (1912) 177-184, également publié en suédois. Holland, L. B., "The Strong House of Erechtheus," *AJA* 28 (1924) 142 sqq. Wrede, W., *Attische Mauer*. Keramopoullos, *Tò Πελαργικόν*, *Praktika Ac. Athens* (1932) 110-124. Cf. *Ephemeris* 1934-35, 86-116. La courte étude de F. Dirlmeier, "Die Pelasgermauer der Akropolis," dans J. O. Plassmann, *Kleine Kostbarkeiten der Kunst*, 37-43, n'a pu tenir compte de toute la documentation la plus récente.

7. Broneer, O., "A Mycenaean Fountain on the Athenian Acropolis," *Hesperia* 8 (1939) 317-429. Voir aussi, de même auteur, *AJA* 52 (1948) 111-114.

la partie supérieure de l'escalier étant restaurée par la suite pour
servir d'accés à la pente Nord de l'Acropole. Les tessons de poterie
recueillis d'une part dans ce qui fut retrouvé de la maçonnerie de
l'escalier primitif, d'autre part au fond même du réservoir de la source
et au pied du quatrième étage, et en troisième lieu dans le remplissage
du puits d'accès, permettent de déterminer l'époque de la construction,
celle de l'utilisation et celle de la destruction de cette fontaine. Parmi
ces tessons, quelques-uns, peu nombreux, antérieurs à la période
mycénienne, n'ont pas de valeur indicative pour la datation. Mais
les moins anciens, qui sont aussi les plus nombreux, et qui peuvent
fournir un *terminus post quem*, appartiennent à une phase tardive du
Mycénien Récent et, sauf dans les couches supérieures du remplissage,
ne vont pas au delà. Dans cette poterie mycénienne tardive on ne
relève pas de différences bien sensibles entre les trois groupes apparte-
nant respectivement à l'époque de construction, à celle d'utilisation
et à celle de destruction; et le remplissage du puits d'accès, sur une
hauteur de 15 mètres depuis le fond, n'est en aucune manière stratifié,
certains fragments d'un même vase ayant été retrouvés à des hauteurs
très différentes. Il en résulte que construction, utilisation et effondrement de l'escalier, suivi du comblement partiel du passage souterrain,
se succédèrent en un laps de temps très restreint, le tout se situant
vers la fin de l'époque mycénienne. Ces tessons mycéniens tardifs se
classent dans le Mycénien III C; ils appartiennent aux types du *Panel
Style*, du *Close Style* et du *Granary Style*, c'est-à-dire à la poterie qui
précède de peu l'incendie et la destruction de Mycènes. Les tessons de
l'époque postérieure à cet incendie sont peu nombreux: ils rejoignent
les trouvailles les plus anciennes du Céramique et n'appartiennent
pas à la première phase du remplissage; ce qui indique que le comblement du puits d'accès se poursuivit pendant un certain temps après
une première opération rapide et massive au lendemain de l'effondrement de l'escalier.[8] L'effondrement de l'escalier, après une utilisation
qui dura fort peu,[9] est-il dû au fait que rapidement les poutres se
pourrirent, comme le pense O. Broneer? Ou, comme il l'a encore
supposé, faut-il y voir l'effet d'un tremblement de terre? A l'appui
de cette dernière hypothèse, O. Broneer invoque un passage du *Critias*

8. *Hesperia* 8 (1939) 317-429, notamment p. 346 sqq. et 416 sqq.; *AJA* 52
(1948) 112. Pour des exemplaires comparables de poterie mycénienne trouvés sur
la pente Nord, voir *Hesperia* 2 (1933) 356-363; et 6 (1937) 539-557. *AJA* 44
(1940) 252-256. Cf. Stubbings, *op. cit.*, 58-60 et 72. Furumark, *Myc. Pott.*, 658,
Motive 7; *Opuscula Arch.* 3 (1944) 231 (vases catalogués comme Mycénien III
C 1 a, et Mycénien III C 1 a-c).

9. Broneer pense que 25 ans "is a generous estimate" [*Hesperia* 8 (1939) 346];
ailleurs [*AJA* 52 (1948) 112], il parle de moins de 50 ans. En fait il semble que
l'utilisation fut très courte et que l'effondrement suivit presque aussitôt la construction.

de Platon, où il est dit qu'il y eut jadis une source sur l'Acropole, qui fut détruite par de violentes secousses sismiques.[10] Ce texte, en vérité, se rapporte à une époque beaucoup plus reculée et nous conduit en plein mythe, puisque Platon y parle du temps où l'Acropole était considérablement plus étendue, en un âge "antérieur au troisième déluge avant celui de Deucalion." Ce texte n'a donc aucune valeur probante ; et, s'il est possible qu'un séisme ait été pour quelque chose dans l'écroulement de l'escalier, cet effondrement doit être bien plutôt attribué à une construction défectueuse et à une insuffisante solidité.

Il s'ensuit que, durant la dernière phase de l'époque mycénienne, dans les décades qui précèdent la destruction de Mycènes au moment même où à Mycènes comme à Tirynthe des mesures étaient prises pour assurer l'approvisionnement en eau de la citadelle en cas de siège,[11] à Athènes des dispositions identiques eurent pour objet d'aménager un accès dérobé à une bonne source, à l'abri d'éventuels assiégeants. Au demeurant, comme on va voir, cette construction de la fontaine mycénienne n'est qu'un élément d'un vaste plan destiné à mettre l'Acropole en état de défense en la dotant d'une puissante fortification.

Sur le même côté Nord de l'Acropole, les recherches antérieurement entreprises par Leicester B. Holland d'après les fouilles de Kavvadias de 1885-90 avaient conduit à reconnaître en cet endroit deux enceintes successives nettement différenciées. Dans la plus ancienne de ces enceintes, le mur n'était épais que de 1 mètre à 1 m, 50 et il était percé d'une porte, à laquelle conduisait une rampe assez raide. La seconde enceinte, beaucoup plus puissante, est le mur pélasgique de l'Acropole, épais de 3 à 5 mètres. Cette seconde enceinte, à la différence de la première, n'avait pas de porte Nord.[12] Des fouilles américaines plus récentes dans cette zone il résulte que la porte Nord ne fut condamnée que vers la fin de l'époque mycénienne au moment de la construction du mur pélasgique ou un peu avant. L'approche de la porte, en contrebas du mur, fut ensevelie sous un dépôt datant de l'époque mycénienne tardive, qui a été retrouvé intact ; et de petites maisons de la même époque se construisirent sur la pente, certaines sur l'emplacement même de l'ancienne rampe d'accès. Ces maisons furent très brusquement abandonnées par leurs occupants et détruites ; l'abandon fut si soudain que de nombreux objets furent retrouvés en place, n'ayant pu être emportés par leurs propriétaires. La poterie mise au jour dans ces maisons nous reporte sensiblement à la même époque

10. Plat. *Critias*, 112 d. Cf. *Hesperia* 8 (1939) 429.

11. Karo, *AJA* 38 (1934) 123 sqq. Wace, J. B., *Mycenae*, 98. Müller, K., *Tiryns*, III, 61.

12. Holland, L. B., *AJA* 28 (1924) 142-169, notamment p. 146-151.

que la construction et l'effondrement de l'escalier de la fontaine mycénienne, c'est à dire vers le moment de la destruction de Mycènes. Les maisons détruites ne portent pas de traces d'incendie ni de pillage. Elles ne furent pas reconstruites et réoccupées par la suite.[13]

Pourquoi ces maisons extérieures au mur pélasgique furent-elles abandonnées? Si, bien que le fait ne soit en aucune manière établi, l'effondrement de l'escalier de la fontaine fut déterminé par un tremblement de terre, il se peut que l'abandon soudain et la destruction de ces maisons ait eu la même cause. Mais le danger imminent devant lequel s'enfuirent les occupants de ces maisons, n'est-il pas plutôt la menace extérieure même contre laquelle l'Acropole avait été si puissamment fortifiée? On serait d'autant plus porté à le croire que les maisons ne furent pas reconstruites et réoccupées; ce qui, en tout cas, semble indiquer une menace extérieure sérieuse et persistante.

La date de la construction du mur pélasgique lui-même a pu être précisée grâce aux sondages effectués à l'angle Sud-Est de l'Acropole par Walther Kolbe. Les recherches de W. Kolbe avaient pour objet primitif, non pas l'étude de cette muraille, mais celle des fondations du Parthénon. En essayant de déterminer quand furent commencés les travaux du Parthénon et quel était l'état des lieux à cette époque, W. Kolbe a été conduit à constater qu'au milieu du Ve siècle, lorsque les travaux du Parthénon commencèrent, ce qui subsistait du mur pélasgique de ce côté n'était pas plus haut que ce qui en a été retrouvé de nos jours, et que cette ruine avait déjà perdu toute valeur militaire.[14] De plus les sondages qu'il a effectués derrière le Petit Musée dans la maçonnerie même du mur pélasgique, ont permis de recueillir, parmi la terre ayant servi de mortier des tessons de poterie mycénienne, qui fournissent pour la construction du mur un élément de datation certain: les plus récents de ces tessons, qui sont aussi les plus nombreux, nous procurent un *terminus post quem*. Ils appartiennent à la dernière période de la poterie mycénienne et sont à peu près contemporains de ceux recueillis dans la fouille de la fontaine mycénienne de la face Nord.[15]

Il en résulte que la construction du mur pélasgique de l'Acropole n'est pas antérieure aux dernières décades de l'époque mycénienne et se situe peu de temps avant l'incendie de Mycènes, c'est à dire au

---

13. *Hesperia* 2 (1933) 350-372; 8 (1939) 424. *AJA* 52 (1948) 111-112.

14. *Ephemeris* 1937, 363-366. *Bericht über den VI. Int. Kongr. f. Arch.*, Berlin, 1940, 344-346. *Forschungen und Fortschritte* 15 (1939) 393-394, et 427-429; *Problems of the Acropolis, Research and Progress* 6 (1940) 259 sqq. *AA* 1939, col. 227-236. Kolbe, W., "Akropolisfragen."

15. *AA* 1939, col. 235-236. Cf. Broneer, *Hesperia* 8 (1939) 423; *AJA* 52 (1948) 111.

moment même où Mycènes et Tirynthe renforçaient leur système de
défense.

Cette date a été confirmée par les fouilles exécutées sous l'avancée
du temple de la Victoire Aptère, à l'angle Sud-Ouest de l'Acropole,
par Nicolas Balanos et Gabriel Welter. Ces fouilles, en permettant de
recueillir des tessons de la même époque qu'à l'angle Sud-Est, ont
confirmé que le mur pélasgique n'est pas antérieur à la dernière période
de l'époque mycénienne.[16] Elles ont en outre mis au jour de ce côté
un puissant bastion cyclopéen. Ce bastion semble en rapport avec la
défense de l'entrée principale de la citadelle, qui dès cette époque
sinon plus tôt déjà était à l'Ouest,[17] et avec un ouvrage avancé construit sur le versant occidental de l'Acropole, dans lequel on peut reconnaître l'*ennéapylon*.[18]

L'utilité de cet ouvrage avancé a pu être triple. Elle dut être
d'abord de protéger l'Acropole du côté où sa défense naturelle était
la moins forte et où s'ouvrait la porte; elle put être en second lieu
d'accroître l'aire comprise dans l'enceinte, si toutefois cet ouvrage
était de quelque étendue; elle put être, en troisième lieu, d'assurer un
approvisionnement en eau aux occupants de la citadelle en cas de
siège. C'est en effet de ce côté qu'au pied de l'Acropole sourd la fontaine Clepsydre, dont la récente exploration par les archéologues
américains a précisément montré l'utilisation en cette fin de l'époque
mycénienne.[19] L'inclusion de cette source dans l'enceinte était d'autant
plus utile à partir du moment où la fontaine mycénienne de l'Acropole
avait été rendue inaccessible par l'effondrement de l'escalier. Or,
comme nous le verrons plus loin,[20] il est possible que la source
Clepsydre ait été incluse dans cet ouvrage avancé.

Résumons ces différentes données archéologiques en dégageant
la signification. Vers la fin de l'époque mycénienne, au moment même
où Mycènes et Tirynthe renforçaient et agrandissaient leurs enceintes
et assuraient leur approvisionnement en eau en prévision d'un siège
à soutenir, et fort peu de temps avant que Mycènes et Tirynthe ne
succombassent avec les autres établissements mycéniens du Péloponèse,
Athènes de son côté conçut et réalisa un vaste plan de fortification
de son Acropole: le mur pélasgique est alors construit, pour remplacer
une muraille plus ancienne beaucoup moins puissante; dans cette nou-

---

16. Welter, G., "Vom Nikepyrgos," *AA* 1939, col. 1-22, principalement 1-10 et
14. Cf. Picard, Ch., *RA* 15 (1940) 257. Kolbe, W., *AA* 1939, col. 235.

17. Cependant que Köster, *op. cit.*, pense que primitivement il n'existait pas
de porte du côté Ouest, Heberdey, *op. cit.*, a soutenu avec vraisemblance l'opinion
contraire.

18. *AA* 1939, col. 7-10.

19. *Hesperia* 10 (1941) 7-8.

20. Voir ci dessous, p. 150.

velle enceinte la porte Nord fut supprimée, mais l'accès de la grande porte de l'Ouest fut solidement défendu par un ouvrage avancé; vers le même moment, un escalier souterrain fut construit pour conduire à une source utilisable même en cas de siège; mais cet escalier s'étant effondré, peut-être la source Clepsydre fut-elle comprise dans l'ouvrage avancé de l'Ouest pour fournir d'eau la citadelle. Le fait que les maisons de la pente Nord ne furent pas reconstruites et réoccupées après avoir été très soudainement abandonnées et détruites semble indiquer que même pour Athènes la menace fut alors très effective et sérieuse.

La date de cet ensemble de faits archéologiques, groupés en un laps de temps très restreint qui ne saurait excéder vingt-cinq ou trente ans si on en juge par la céramique, peut-elle être déterminée dès à présent avec exactitude? Des opinions divergentes ont été émises au cours des douze dernières années sur l'époque à laquelle il faut situer la céramique du Mycénien III C. Pour trancher le débat, examinons tout d'abord le résultat des fouilles de Tarse, qui nous ont apporté un repère assez précis.

Dans la couche supérieure du Bronze Récent mise au jour à Tarse, en Cilicie, par les sondages de Hetty Goldman, des tessons de céramique mycénienne ont été recueillis, qui appartiennent au style du *Granary* au sens large, c'est-à-dire à la première partie du Mycénien III C, et qui se situent dans la période précédant immédiatement la destruction de Mycènes. Au-dessus de cette dernière couche du Bronze Récent, épaisse de 0m,75, venait la première couche de l'âge du fer, qui en était bien distincte et nettement différenciée. Cette première couche de l'âge du fer ne contenait plus aucun tesson mycénien; elle a fourni en revanche de la poterie chypriote du début de l'âge du fer.[21]

---

21. Goldman, H., "Excavations at Gözlü Kule, Tarsus, 1936," *AJA* 41 (1937) 262-291, notamment p. 279 sqq. Relativement à cette poterie mycénienne de la couche supérieure du Bronze Récent, voici, d'après l'article de H. Goldman, quelques indications du rapport de J. F. Daniel, qui prit part aux fouilles: "The painted pottery found between the 15,15 and 15,90 meter levels in the southern half of Section B at Tarsus is almost without exception imported Mycenaean of the so-called Granary Class. . . . Three varieties of the Granary Class were found at Mycenae. Most common was a light ground ware decorated with very simple patterns in a vaguely lustrous black or brown paint. The second group consists chiefly of open bowls, painted dark inside and out, sometimes with a horizontal reserved band around the outside. The Third group is the well known Close Style, which is generally better finished than the first two classes and is decorated in an elaborate and minute style, often with highly stylized birds or octopods. The second class has not yet been found at Tarsus, but the other two are well represented, with a marked predominance of the simple linear style. . . . The relative date of the Tarsus Pottery is indicated by the absence of the second group and the scarcity of the third. . . . The similarity of style and shapes of the pottery of Tarsus and Mycenae suggests the possibility of complete identity." *AJA* 41 (1937) 281-283. Voir également Daniel, *AJA* 52 (1948) 108; Cf. Schaeffer, *Stratigraphie comparée . . . aux IIe et IIIe millénaires*, 263-265; Furumark, *Myc. Pott.*, 659, bas de la page, Motive 19, où un de ces vases de Tarse est catalogué

Or, dans la partie inférieure de cette dernière couche du bronze, à
0m,15 au-dessus de la couche antérieure, un silo creusé dans le sol a
été retrouvé intact. Ce silo avait été comblé dans l'antiquité en une
seule fois, puisque deux fragments d'un même vase mycénien du type
Panel Style ont été retrouvés l'un en bas, l'autre en haut du dépôt.
Il contenait notamment une tablette hittite du XIVe ou XIIIe siècle
et des bulles hittites, dont l'une portait une inscription au nom de la
reine Pudu-Hépa, femme du roi hittite Hattousil III (1295-1260
environ). Connue déjà au temps du traité égypto-hittite signé en la
21e année du règne de Ramsès II, en 1278, Pudu-Hépa survécut de
quelques années à son mari et en tant que reine-mère semble avoir
exercé la régence au début du règne de son fils.[22] Il en résulte que ce silo
fut comblé au plus tard dans le troisième quart du XIIIe siècle, sinon
déjà dans le deuxième. D'autre part la fin de l'âge du bronze à Tarse
et dans toute cette zone se présente comme sensiblement contemporaine
de la destruction d'Ugarit, où, sans être massées sur une période aussi
courte et tardive que dans la dernière couche du bronze à Tarse, les
importations mycéniennes furent abondantes dans le niveau supérieur
du bronze, au XIVe siècle et encore au XIIIe;[23] et de même que la
destruction d'Ugarit elle doit être mise en rapport avec la grande
migration des Peuples du Nord et de la Mer. Cette migration, qui est
arrêtée aux frontières de l'Egypte par la victoire de Ramsès III en
l'an VIII de son règne, en 1191, a dû déferler en Cilicie et dans la
partie septentrionale de la région syro-palestinienne dès avant 1200,
ou au plus tard dans les toutes premières années du XIIe siècle, en

---

dans sa classification Mycénien III C 1 early (c'est à dire antérieur à la destruction de Mycènes), et est rapproché par lui d'un vase de la fontaine mycénienne
de l'Acropole mentionné à la page précédente, Motive 7.

22. *AJA* 41 (1937) 281 et 289-291.

23. Schaeffer, Cl., *Stratigraphie comparée*, 263-265. La céramique découverte
dans les premières fouilles d'Ugarit-Ras Shamra sera prochainement publiée dans
Ugaritica II par Cl. Schaeffer.

Des deux dates de 1250 et 1200 entre lesquelles Cl. Schaeffer a hésité pour la
destruction d'Ugarit (*Stratigraphie comparée*, 39), la seconde plutôt, croyons-
nous, doit être retenue. En effet, la première grande bataille livrée par Mineptah
en 1227 contre les Peuples du Nord et de la Mer alliés aux Libyens, se déroule du
côté occidental, non du côté asiatique, du delta. Elle indique que des déplacements
de populations se sont produits par mer jusqu'en Libye dès ce moment, ou même
sans doute bien avant (puisque les gens du Nord établis en Libye ont adopté déjà
les coutumes indigènes et sont circoncis). Mais ce sont les Libyens qui sont
présentés comme les principaux adversaires du pharaon. Du côté asiatique, d'autre
part, Mineptah est bien amené à intervenir également; mais il apparaît que, de ce
côté, les Peuples du Nord et de la Mer n'ont pas encore envahi la région syro-
palestinienne et il n'en est pas encore question. Aussi bien l'effondrement de
l'Empire hittite n'est-il pas antérieur aux dernières années du XIIe siècle. La
grande migration des Peuples du Nord et de la Mer, telle qu'elle est décrite de
manière saisissante dans les documents égyptiens du règne de Ramsès III, ne
semble donc avoir déferlé sur la Syrie et la Palestine que dans les années qui
précèdent immédiatement la bataille de 1191, c'est à dire vers 1200 environ.

entraînant l'effondrement de l'Empire hittite. La dernière couche du bronze à Tarse, dont la durée semble avoir été assez brève, se situe donc entre le milieu du XIIIe siècle et 1200 approximativement; et elle ne saurait guère descendre au delà.[24]

Il s'ensuit que la céramique du Mycénien III C antérieure à la destruction de Mycènes commence approximativement dès 1250, et que la destruction de Mycènes se situe vers 1200 ou très peu après.

On parvient aux mêmes dates, nous semble-t-il, si l'on prend comme repère la poterie dite philistine. Cette céramique philistine, d'inspiration mycénienne, paraît avoir son point de départ dans la poterie du Mycénien III C qui précède la destruction de Mycènes, plus précisément dans le *Close Style*. Or cette poterie philistine, qui est postérieure au règne de Séti II, et qui se développe sous le règne de Ramsès III, est manifestement en rapport avec la grande migration des Peuples du Nord et de la Mer. Elle commence donc dans les premières années du XIIe siècle, et son début doit suivre de très peu la destruction de Mycènes; car il ne semble pas que les modèles mycéniens dont elle s'inspira, aient sensiblement précédé cette destruction.[25]

---

24. Voir déjà en ce sens Goldman, H., *AJA* 41 (1937) 281. C'est à tort, selon nous, qu'on voudrait abaisser cette date parce que la couche qui se trouve au dessus de ce dernier niveau du bronze à Tarse, contient du matériel du début de l'âge du fer chypriote. Ce début du fer en Chypre, en effet, semble aujourd'hui plus ancien qu'on ne l'avait dernièrement pensé. En outre un certain laps de temps a pu s'écouler entre la fin du dernier niveau du bronze à Tarse et l'apparition de la première poterie chypriote de l'âge du fer. Voir déjà en ce sens Goldman, *AJA* 41 (1937), 263, et Schaeffer, *Stratigraphie comparée*, 264.

25. Furumark, qui a annoncé son intention de revenir sur le problème de la poterie philistine, a proposé, dans sa dernière étude, "The Mycenaean III C Pottery and Its Relation to Cypriote Fabrics," *Opuscula Arch.* 3 (1944) 194-265, des dates plus basses encore que dans sa *Chronology of the Mycenaean Pottery* publiée en 1941, dont les dates déjà nous semblent avoir tendance à être trop basses, sans faire entrer en ligne de compte l'important repère fourni par les fouilles de Tarse (voir à ce sujet nos indications ci-dessus). Nous croyons que le début du Mycénien III B doit être situé dès le commencement, et non à la fin seulement, du règne de Seti Ier vers 1315, et que le commencement du Mycénien III C se situe vers le milieu du XIIIe siècle, comme il résulte de ce qui a été dit plus haut. Dans la poterie du Mycénien III C antérieure à la destruction de Mycènes, le Close Style apparait comme une branche particulière d'une facture plus soignée, qui est fabriquée dans certains ateliers seulement et a son centre en Argolide. Il s'est développé à côté d'une poterie de style plus simple jusqu'à la destruction de Mycènes. Dans l'étude des rapports entre le Close Style et la poterie philistine, il faut songer que la poterie enfouie dans la couche de destruction du Granary de Mycènes a, dans ses formes les plus récentes, précédé immédiatement cette destruction; cal il n'y a pas lieu de compter avec un intervalle plus ou moins long entre la fabrication et l'enfouissement comme lorsqu'un vase est trouvé dans une tombe. Il faut songer aussi que la poterie philistine put avoir comme point de départ non les formes les plus précoces, mais des formes attardées du Close Style. Furumark pense que "the earlier Philistine ware corresponds to the pottery of the Mycenaean III C 1 b phase, to a mature stage, when the Mainland Close Style was already fully developed. But it is earlier than the end of the phase, the late traits noted above as characteristic of its later stage being absent. Now the earliest Philistine Pottery is well dated to one or two decades after 1200 B. C." (*Opusc. Arch.* 3, 260). Et plus loin: "Disaster was inevitable and Mycenae fell.

La construction du mur pélasgique de l'Acropole et la réalisation
du plan de fortification dont elle faisait partie, se situeraient donc
dans les deux ou trois dernières décades du XIIIe siècle, ou au plus
tard dans les premières années du XIIe, ainsi que l'avaient admis
O. Broneer, W. Kolbe et G. Welter en suivant la chronologie établie
par Mackeprang pour la céramique mycénienne, non dans la première
moitié du XIIe siècle seulement, comme il résulterait des plus récentes
propositions d'A. Furumark.[26]

Comment interpréter cet ensemble de faits archéologiques ainsi
datés? Une interprétation en a été proposée par Oscar Broneer dans
sa publication de la fontaine mycénienne de l'Acropole, et a été reprise
par lui dans un article de synthèse intitulé: *What happened at Athens,*
rédigé pour faire partie d'une étude plus générale sur l'invasion
dorienne.[27] Examinons-la tout d'abord.

Partant des dates données par Eratosthène pour la guerre de Troie
(1184) et pour le Retour des Héraclides (1104) sans mettre en question leur valeur, O. Broneer commence par exclure l'idée qu'il peut
s'agir du Retour des Héraclides et de l'établissement des Doriens dans
le Péloponèse; et il pense que ces faits doivent être mis en rapport
avec la première tentative héraclide contre le Péloponèse sous la con-
duite du fils d'Héraclès, Hyllos, 100 ans avant la dernière et victorieuse
tentative du Retour des Héraclides; il mentionne également la bataille
que Codros dut livrer sur les bords de l'Ilissos contre les Doriens, tout
en estimant qu'on n'en saurait trouver la trace dans les données
archéologiques de l'Acropole même. Sa conclusion est que l'invasion
dorienne doit être considérée non comme une campagne militaire
organisée sur une vaste échelle, mais plutôt comme une série d'invasions barbares s'échelonnant sur plusieurs décades, et selon lui la
tradition implique que l'insécurité dura environ un siècle.

Précisément parce que nous avons suivi O. Broneer dans sa minutieuse description des données archéologiques de l'Acropole, il nous
semble impossible de le suivre maintenant dans cette interprétation,
qui ne répond pas au témoignage des fouilles et résiste mal à l'examen.

The ceramic evidence tells us that this happened before the end of Mycenaean
III C 1 b, when the Close Style had just reached its apogee, i. e. c. 1150 B. C.
or perhaps a little earlier" (*ibid.* 263). Si nous suivons la minutieuse et précieuse
analyse stylistique d'A. Furumark, cette date de 1150 qu'il propose pour la
destruction de Mycènes paraît trop basse d'une quarantaine d'années. Comme
nous l'avons dit, il semble qu' A. Furumark ait été porté à abaisser à l'excès
toutes les dates archéologiques de la fin de l'époque mycénienne, sans doute sous
l'influence de la chronologie ératosthénienne qui l'a conduit à appeler le Close
Style, pourtant immédiatement antérieur à la destruction de Mycènes, "The Palace
Style of Agamemnon."

26. *Hesperia* 8 (1939) 422. Voir note précédente.
27. *Hesperia* 8 (1939) 425 sqq.; *AJA* 52 (1948) 111 sqq.

Le point de départ même en est arbitraire, puisque, comme nous l'avons déjà montré,[28] la chronologie ératosthénienne de l'âge héroïque n'a qu'une valeur bien douteuse et ne paraît pas pouvoir être retenue. Par ailleurs la tentative d'Hyllos explique mal les mesures de défense prises à l'Acropole comme à Mycènes et à Tirynthe en vue d'un siège, étant donné qu'Athènes ne fut, selon la tradition, ni menacée, ni, moins encore, attaquée par Hyllos, qui tout au contraire passait pour avoir trouvé en Attique aide et refuge,[29] non plus que par les Péloponésiens. De plus la bataille livrée par Codros sur les bords de l'Ilissos ne se situe dans la chronologie d'Eratosthène ni au début du XIIe siècle, — ce qui est un lapsus manifeste[30] —, ni même une centaine d'années après la tentative d'Hyllos, comme le dit ailleurs O. Broneer,[31] mais à la veille de la migration ionienne vers l'Asie mineure, 59 ans après le Retour des Héraclides, soit 159 ans après la tentative d'Hyllos. La bataille livrée par Codros ne peut donc se rapporter qu'à des événements considérablement postérieurs à cette tentative d'Hyllos. Enfin il résulterait de cette interprétation que la destruction de Mycènes et des établissements mycéniens du Péloponèse, qui suit de quelques années la construction du mur pélasgique de l'Acropole, serait attribuable à l'attaque d'Hyllos, dont la tentative pourtant passait pour avoir échoué[32] et surtout elle se situerait avant le règne d'Agamemnon et le sac d'Ilion, qui dans la chronologie traditionnelle est de 20 ans postérieur à la tentative d'Hyllos; or c'est là ce qu'il est impossible d'admettre à moins de considérer que les traditions relatives à l'âge héroïque sont sans valeur aucune, auquel cas il faudrait résolument prendre son parti de n'en tenir aucun compte. Pour la même raison il faut écarter l'interprétation proposée par H. T. Wade-Gery dans un autre article de la même série consacrée à l'invasion dorienne,[33] en ce qui concerne la destruction du palais mycénien à Pylos de Messénie, qui est contemporaine de la destruction de Mycènes et ne saurait en conséquence être mise en rapport avec la guerre d'Héraclès contre les Pyliens.

28. Voir nos *Recherches sur la Chronologie mycénienne* déjà citées.

29. Eur. *Her.*, 31 sqq. Diod. IV, 57. Paus. I, 32, 6; cf. I, 42, 2.

30. *Hesperia* 8 (1939) 425; "in the early part of the twelfth century." L'article du Pauly-Wiss., cité à l'appui, indique des dates beaucoup plus tardives.

31. *AJA* 52 (1948) 113.

32. Selon une version de la tradition (Ps. Apoll. *Bib.*, II, 8, 2), les Héraclides se seraient maintenus un an dans le Péloponèse après quoi ils auraient dû se retirer; selon l'autre version plus généralement admise (Schol. ad Pind. *Ol.* X, 39 sq. Paus. I, 41, 3; cf. VIII, 53, 10, etc.), l'échec aurait été immédiat et Hyllos aurait été tué par le Tégéate Echémos avant de franchir l'isthme de Corinthe.

33. "What Happened in Pylos," *AJA* 52 (1948) 115 sqq. La destruction du palais de Pylos de Messénie est donnée par les fouilleurs américains comme sensiblement contemporaine de celle de Mycènes (*AJA* 43 [1939] 563 et 569).

Si l'on veut tenter d'interpréter nos données archéologiques à l'aide des données de la tradition, il convient de procéder de manière plus méthodique; et la première question qu'il faut se poser est de savoir si la tradition nous fournit ou non une indication précise relativement à la date de la construction du mur pélasgique de l'Acropole dans le cadre de l'histoire traditionnelle de l'âge héroïque.

Il se trouve que, de fait, un ensemble de textes anciens nous fournit sur la construction de cette muraille des indications complémentaires les unes des autres, qui nous permettent de reconstituer la tradition antique à son sujet; tradition qui jusqu'à présent a été négligée.

Le mur le l'Acropole qui aujourd'hui encore est appelé pélasgique, doit ce nom au fait qu'on l'identifie, avec raison d'ailleurs, au Πελασ-γικὸν τεῖχος dont nous parlent les auteurs anciens. Sur cette vieille muraille de l'Acropole une nombreuse série de textes nous renseigne, qui s'échelonnent depuis Hécatée, cité par Hérodote, et Hérodote lui-même, jusqu'à Lucien et Pausanias et jusqu'à l'époque byzantine même, en passant par Thucydide, Aristote et Strabon.[34]

Le témoignage le plus ancien, celui d'Hérodote se référant à Hécatée, est aussi le plus explicite et le plus détaillé. On y lit, à propos de l'expulsion des Pélasges de Lemnos par Miltiade le Jeune, peu avant les Guerres Médiques, que ces Pélasges avaient auparavant habité l'Attique et qu'ils y avaient reçu des Athéniens des terres situées au pied de l'Hymette comme prix du mur qu'ils avaient construit pour eux autour de l'Acropole; puis qu'ils furent chassés d'Attique, soit, selon Hécatée, injustement et parce que les Athéniens avaient envie de reprendre des terres que les Pélasges avaient su rendre fertiles, soit, selon la version athénienne, à juste titre, parce que les Pélasges se conduisaient avec arrogance et complotaient de s'emparer d'Athènes. Par la suite, après être revenus de Lemnos pour ravir les femmes athéniennes à Brauron et après le crime qui s'ensuivit, ces Pélasges s'étaient engagés à céder aux Athéniens Lemnos où ils s'étaient établis lorsque le vent du Nord pousserait en un jour un vaisseau de chez les Athéniens à Lemnos; ce qui se réalisa quand Miltiade vint attaquer Lemnos depuis la Chersonèse de Thrace.[35]

Les textes anciens qui nous parlent de cette enceinte pélasgique, portent tantôt la forme *pélasgicon*,[36] tantôt la forme *pélargicon*.[37]

---

34. On trouvera le plus grand nombre de ces textes commodément réunis dans O. Jahn et A. Michaelis, *Arx Athenarum*³, 3-4 et 79-80; et moins complètement dans l'étude déjà citée de Wide, S., *Ausonia* 7 (1912) 195-197.

35. Her. VI, 136-140.

36. Ainsi: Her. V, 64; VI, 137. Thuc. II, 17(?). *Marm. Par.* 45. Strab. IX, 2, 3. Paus. I, 28, 3. Lucian. *Bis Accus.*, 9; *Pisc.*, 42 et 47. Pollux VIII, 101. Hesych. Suid. s.v.

37. Ainsi: *IG*, I suppl., 27 b, p. 59, lignes 55-57 ed. min. I, 76; Ditt.³, I, 83.

Par là le plus souvent ils désignent explicitement un mur,[38] mais parfois ils désignent ou semblent désigner un emplacement,[39] et ils nous donnent *ennéapylon* comme un autre nom de cette enceinte.[40] La construction, ou l'occupation, en était attribuée par eux à des Pélasges,[41] aussi appelés Pélarges,[42] ou à des Tyrrhènes,[43] ayant pris en Attique un de ces noms.[44] Il est notamment question de ce *pélasgicon* au moment où Hippias y cherche refuge avant d'être expulsé d'Athènes, et durant la Guerre du Péloponèse, à l'occasion de son occupation par les campagnards réfugiés dans la ville, ou à l'occasion d'interdictions à son sujet; mais il apparaît que dès cette époque le *pélasgicon* n'était plus qu'une ruine; il en restait cependant encore des vestiges au temps des Antonins.[45] Que peut-on tirer de ces différentes indications?

Avant de nous demander quand fut construit ce mur, il convient de résoudre plusieurs questions préalables et de rectifier diverses erreurs d'interprétation relativement à ces indications des auteurs anciens.

1° Des deux formes *pélasgicon* et *pélargicon*, quelle est la plus ancienne? Est-ce *pélargicon*, comme on le pense souvent encore,[46] et en ce cas s'agirait-il d'un "mur des Cigognes," ainsi appelé parce qu'y nichaient des cigognes, et dont par un jeu de mots la construction aurait été attribuée tardivement à des Pélasges? Contrairement à ce qui a été dit, c'est la forme *pélasgicon* qui se présente comme la plus ancienne. La forme *pélargicon* est attestée de manière certaine de l'époque de la Guerre du Péloponèse par l'épigraphie comme par la tradition littéraire: elle revient alors à trois reprises dans une inscription attique; elle figure dans un fragment de Cleidèmos ainsi que dans un bon manuscrit de Thucydide, le Laurentianus C; et dans les *Oiseaux* d'Aristophane il est clair qu'elle évoquait pour un Athénien l'idée de Pélarges-Cigognes.[47] Mais la forme la plus anciennement

Clid. fr. 22, *FHG* I, 363; Aristoph. *Av.*, 832; et Schol. ad 832, 836 et 1139. Thuc. II, 17(?). Arist. *Ath. resp.*, 19. Dion Hal. *RA* I, 28. *Etym. Magn.* Phot., s.v.

38. Ainsi: Her., Arist., Marm. Par., Dion. Hal., Paus., Schol. ad Aristoph. *Av.*, Hesych., *locc. citt.*

39. Ainsi: *IG*, Thuc. et Schol. ad loc. Strab., Pollux *locc. citt.*

40. Clid. Suid. *locc. citt.* Cf. Polem. fr. 49, *FHG* III, 130.

41. Her. Strab., Paus., Schol. ad Thuc. *locc. citt.*

42. Strab. V, 2, 4, et IX, 1, 18. Cf. IX, 2, 3.

43. Callim. apud Schol. ad Aristoph. *Av.*, 832; cf. 1139. Hesych. Cf. Philoch. *FHG* I, 384, fr. 5.

44. Myrsil. apud Dion. Hal. *RA* I, 28. *Etym. Magn.* Phot. s.v.

45. Voir ci-dessous, Thuc. et *IG*, *locc. citt.* Pollux, VIII, 101. Lucian, *locc. citt.*

46. Ainsi: Köster, *op. cit.*, 5. Judeich, *op. cit.*, 113.

47. *IG*, I suppl., 27 b, p. 59, lignes 55-57 (ed. min., I, 76; Ditt. I, n. 83. Clid. *FHG* I, 363, fr. 22. Thuc. II, 17 (les autres manuscrits portent Πελασγικόν). Aristoph. *Av.* 832, cf. 1139.

attestée est *pélasgicon:* c'est elle qui est donnée par Hérodote et par
Hécatée qu'il cite, le contexte dans le principal passage d'Hérodote
et dans Hécatée excluant la possibilité de toute erreur de copie.[48] Fait
essentiel confirmation de cet ordre d'ancienneté nous est fournie par
une indication d'Hésychius, à tort négligée jusqu'à présent par ceux
qui se sont occupés du mur pélasgique de l'Acropole: la forme *Πελαστικόν* attestée par Hésychius pour le *pélasgicon* d'Athènes, outre qu'elle
nous apporte une donnée précieuse pour résoudre l'énigme du nom
des Philistins, implique que le nom *pélasticon-pélasgicon* est l'appela-
tion primitive et que *pélargicon* est une appellation secondaire.[48a]
Le jeu de mots s'est donc fait dans le sens *pélasgicon-pélargicon,*
et il ne s'est imposé qu'à une époque relativement récente, dans la
seconde moitié du Ve siècle, sans toutefois réussir à évincer la forme
pélasgicon. Il doit être rapproché du fait que, selon les Atthido-
graphes les Pélasges, ou d'après Myrsile, les Tyrrhènes, en raison de
leurs nombreuses migrations, avaient reçu en Attique le nom de
Pélarges ou Cigognes.[49]

2° Les deux mots de *pélasgicon* et de *pélargicon* sont-ils inter-
changeables? Ou, comme le pense S. Wide,[50] faut-il voir dans le
pélasgicon le nom d'une muraille, et dans le *pélargicon* celui d'un
quartier d'Athènes? Contrairement à l'opinion de S. Wide, il apparait
que les deux mots ne sont que deux formes d'un même nom et s'em-
ploient indistinctement. En effet, à propos d'un même événement,
l'expulsion d'Hippias, et pour désigner la même enceinte, la forme
pélasgicon est donnée par les meilleurs manuscrits d'Hérodote, dont
la leçon est confirmée par un autre passage de son oeuvre, et elle est
attestée de manière certaine par l'épigraphie dans le Marbre de Paros,
cependant que dans la *Constitution d'Athènes* d'Aristote c'est la forme
pélargicon qui est donnée par le papyrus comme par un fragment que
nous possédions déjà antérieurement.[51] De plus, tandis que dans
Aristote et Denys d'Halicarnasse *pélargicon* désigne un mur, dans
Strabon *pélasgicon* désigne expressément un quartier; et il n'y a pas
lieu de corriger Lucien, non plus qu'Aristote comme le propose S.

---

48. Her. V, 64 (où les manuscrits les plus nombreux et les meilleurs portent
Πελασγικῷ); VI, 137-140 (où il est longuement question des Pélasges).

48a. Hesych., s.v. *Πελαστικόν.* Cf. Schol. ad *Iliad.,* XVI, 233. Sur les rapports
qui sont à établir entre le nom des Pélastes-Pélasges et celui des Philistins, voir
notre étude *Philistins et Préhellènes* à paraître dans un prochain fascicule de la
Revue Archéologique.

49. Strab. V, 2, 4; IX, 1, 18. Myrs. apud Dion. Hal. *RA,* I, 28, 4; cf. I, 23-24
(*FHG,* IV, 457 fr. 3 et 456 fr. 2). Cf. Phot., *Etym. Magn. Anecd. Bekk.* 299, 16.
Eustath. ad Dion. Per., 347.

50. *Ausonia* 7 (1912) 189.

51. Her. V, 64; cf. VI, 137 (voir ci-dessus nos remarques). *Marm. Par.* 45.
Aristot. *Ath. resp.,* 19. Cf. *FHG* II, 111, fr. 17.

Wide[52] car ce ne seraient pas les seuls textes à corriger. Ajoutons enfin que le scholiaste de Lucien[53] indique que le mot πελασγικόν s'écrivait aussi avec un ϱ.

3° Qu'entendait-on au juste par *pélasgicon* ou *pélargicon?* Hérodote indique qu'il s'agit d'un mur construit par les Pélasges autour de l'Acropole; de même Cleidèmos, Myrsile dans Denys d'Halicarnasse, et Pausanias disent que le mur entourait l'Acropole.[54] En revanche Thucydide désigne sous le nom de *pélargicon* un emplacement situé sous l'Acropole, et il résulte semblablement de deux passages de Lucien que le pélasgicon se trouvait au pied des escarpements de l'Acropole, notamment sous la grotte de Pan.[55] Dans les trois passages où il parle du *pélasgicon,* Lucien ne dit pas clairement s'il s'agit d'un emplacement ou d'un mur; dans l'un d'eux, toutefois, le fait qu'il montre son personnage occupé à pêcher les pierres du *pélasgicon* du haut de l'Acropole semble impliquer que là du moins il s'agit d'un mur en ruines. Faut-il donc supposer, comme l'ont pensé E. Curtius et Th. Davidson,[56] que le *pélasgicon* est non pas un mur couronnant l'Acropole, mais une enceinte beaucoup plus vaste, cernant une bande de terrain plus ou moins large tout autour de son pied? Cette hypothèse est aujourd'hui abandonnée avec raison. Elle ne suppose pas seulement une conception des fortifications qui serait anachronique pour une enceinte réputée si ancienne; mais elle est en contradiction aussi avec une indication de Cleidèmos, qui rapporte que l'Acropole fut aplanie en même temps qu'elle fut entourée du mur pélasgique; en contradiction encore avec les indications d'Aristote et de Photius, surtout d'Aristophane et de Pausanias, qui nous montrent cette enceinte comme le mur de défense de l'Acropole même et bâtie à son sommet.[57] Elle est en contradiction aussi avec deux passages de Lucien, qui nous montrent une partie du *pélasgicon* au pied même des escarpements de l'Acropole et immédiatement au-dessous de la grotte de Pan.[58] Enfin elle est en contradiction avec les résultats des fouilles, qui nous ont révélé une enceinte cyclopéenne couronnant l'Acropole,

---

52. Aristot. *loc. cit.* Dion. Hal. *RA* I, 28, 4. Lucian. *Bis. Accus.,* 9; *Pisc.,* 42 et 47. *Ausonia* 7 (1912) 190 sq.

53. Schol. ad Lucian., *Bis Accus.,* 9.

54. Her. VI, 137. Clid. *FHG* I, 363, fr. 22. Dion. Hal. *RA* I, 28, 4. Paus. I, 28, 3, etc.

55. Thuc. II, 17. Lucian. *Bis Accus.,* 9; *Pisc.,* 47; cf. 42.

56. Voir à ce sujet Judeich, *op. cit.,* 114.

57. Clid. *FHG* I, 363 fr. 22. Aristot. *Ath. resp.,* 19. Phot. s.v. Aristoph. *Av.* 832 (où τῆς πόλεως désigne l'Acropole, comme le spécifie la scholie; Cf. Thuc. II, 15) et 836 (d'où il résulte que le mur repose sur les rochers; voir Scholie). Paus. I, 28, 3.

58. Lucian. *Bis Accus.,* 9; *Pisc.,* 47. Il est clair en effet que jamais une muraille défensive n'a pu être construite tout autour d'une acropole au pied même de ses escarpements.

mais ne nous ont livré absolument aucune trace de la grande muraille imaginée par E. Curtius et Th. Davidson. En fait, on peut aplanir l'apparent désaccord des auteurs anciens en considérant que tantôt ils désignent une muraille au sommet de l'Acropole, dont la construction était attribuée aux Pélasges, tantôt un emplacement au pied de l'Acropole, qui aurait dû son nom au fait que ces Pélasges y avaient habité.[59] On peut aussi songer à l'expliquer par le fait que la fortification pélasgique de l'Acropole se complétait à l'Ouest, du côté de l'entrée, qui était le plus vulnérable, par un ouvrage avancé qui s'étendait sur le versant occidental de la butte. Cet ouvrage avancé est à identifier avec *l'ennéapylon*, qu'il faut concevoir non comme un mur percé de neuf portes différentes, ce qui eût été un inutile élément de faiblesse pour l'enceinte, mais comme une entrée à plusieurs portes successives. L'un des deux passages de Lucien déjà mentionnés indique peut-être que cet ouvrage avancé venait se greffer sur les escarpements de l'Acropole, du côté Nord-Ouest, un peu à l'Est de la grotte de Pan, et, en ce cas, la source Clepsydre s'y serait trouvée incluse. Mais si le tracé du mur pélasgique couronnant l'Acropole peut être retrouvé sans peine, le dessin et l'étendue de cet ouvrage avancé du côté Ouest restent encore fort problématiques, faute de vestiges comparables à ceux du sommet de la butte, et risquent de le rester toujours.[60] Il est difficile de dire à l'heure actuelle si cette fortification de l'entrée était très restreinte, comme il est fort possible, — auquel cas il faut admettre l'existence d'un emplacement extérieur à l'enceinte portant aussi le nom de *pélasgicon* —, ou au contraire beaucoup plus vaste, — auquel cas l'emplacement au pied de l'Acropole aurait été compris à l'intérieur de l'enceinte. Peu importe, toutefois, pour notre recherche, de connaître au juste le tracé de cet ouvrage avancé ou l'étendue de cet emplacement sur le versant Ouest de l'Acropole; car

---

59. En ce sens cf. Schol. ad Thuc. II, 17 (expliquant le nom du *pélasgicon* sous l'Acropole par le fait que des Pélasges avaient habité là et rapportant que le lieu ne devait plus être habité par la suite) Schol. ad Lucian. *Bis. Accus.*, 9 (qui explique semblablement le nom du *pélasgicon* sous l'Acropole par le fait que les Pélasges y avaient habité) Paus. I, 28, 3 (où il est dit que les Pélasges constructeurs du mur de l'Acropole avaient habité sous l'Acropole). De même Strabon (IX, 2, 3) rapporte que le nom du quartier appelé *pélasgicon* à Athènes serait dû à des Pélasges, mais il fait habiter ces Pélasges sous l'Hymette. Hérodote (VI, 137), lui, nous disait que des terres leur avaient été concédées sous l'Hymette tout en rapportant qu'ils s'approvisionnaient en eau à *l'ennéacrounos* dont la localisation est malheureusement encore discutée.

60. Non seulement, en effet, les vestiges antiques ont pu disparaître plus complètement en cet endroit; mais il se peut que, dans cette partie, le mur ait subi des réfections plus ou moins importantes, notamment au temps des Pisistratides. Sur quelques traces de réfections à l'Acropole même, voir *AA* 1939, col. 9-10, et déjà *AM* 48 (1923) 193. A en juger d'après les résultats des dernières fouilles *AA* (1939, col. 1-10), il semblerait que cet ouvrage avancé ait été relativement peu étendu.

il nous suffit de savoir, ce qui résulte clairement des textes, que le mur cyclopéen, encore aujourd'hui appelé pélasgique, de l'Acropole constituait la partie principale, sinon la totalité de la fortification dont la construction était attribuée aux Pélasges.

4° Quels étaient donc ces Pélasges qui sont donnés comme les constructeurs du vieux mur de l'Acropole? S'agit-il des plus anciens habitants de l'Attique, comme on a tendance à le croire aujourd'hui encore;[61] et en ce cas nous trouverions-nous devant une tradition bien obscure et lointaine, à laquelle à bon droit on hésiterait à se fier? Hérodote connait bien, en effet, la tradition selon laquelle des Pélasges furent les premiers habitants de l'Attique, et selon laquelle la population de l'Attique tout entière, pour autant qu'elle passait pour autochthone, était regardée comme d'origine pélasgique.[62] Mais, lorsqu'il parle de la construction du mur pélasgique, c'est à une tout autre tradition et à d'autres Pélasges qu'Hérodote, à la suite d'Hécatée, fait allusion. Il s'agit des Pélasges, également appelés Tyrrhènes, qui habitèrent Lemnos et Imbros jusqu'à la conquête des deux îles par Miltiade à la fin du VIe siècle, et dont Thucydide comme Hérodote savait qu'ils avaient habité l'Attique avant d'occuper Lemnos, puis de se retirer dans l'Actè de Chalcidique; par là s'explique le nom de Tyrrhènes également porté par les constructeurs du mur de l'Acropole comme par les Pélasges de Lemnos.[63] Hérodote présente ces Pélasges qui construisirent le mur de l'Acropole et qui d'Attique s'en allèrent à Lemnos, non comme le fond ancien de la population, mais comme un élément étranger peu nombreux, accueilli en Attique lorsque la population en était déjà comptée parmi les Grecs, et y ayant obtenu des terres à condition de construire ce mur, puis expulsés d'Attique après un séjour apparemment très limité.[64] Nous savons par ailleurs que d'autres contingents étrangers passaient semblablement pour avoir été accueillis en Attique.[65]

5° Dernière question: l'histoire de ces Pélasges de Lemnos telle que la rapporte en détail Hérodote, leur expulsion d'Attique, puis la promesse conditionnelle qu'ils firent pour obéier à un oracle, après avoir perpétré le rapt de Brauron, n'auraient-elles pas été inventées

---

61. Judeich., *op. cit.*, 52 sqq. et 113 sqq.

62. Her. I, 56 sq.; VII, 161; VIII, 44.

63. Her. VI, 137; cf. I, 57, et II, 51. Thuc. IV, 109. Sur le double nom et sur l'histoire de ces Pélasges-Tyrrhènes de Lemnos, voir notre article dans la *Revue des Études anciennes*, 1949, 224 sqq.

64. Her. VI, 137; cf. II, 51.

65. Outre les Néléides et la population achéenne qui les suit, c'est ainsi que les Ioniens d'origine pélasgique de la côte septentrionale du Péloponèse (Cf. Her. VII, 94, et I, 145), passaient pour y avoir été accueillis au moment du Retour des Héraclides, c'est-à-dire, comme nous allons voir, vers le même moment que les constructeurs du mur de l'Acropole.

pour justifier la conquête de Miltiade, et, à l'appui de cette hypothèse, comme ont tenté de le prouver certains érudits allemands, ne faut-il pas attribuer la conquête de l'île à Miltiade l'Ancien plutôt qu'à Miltiade le Jeune, puisque la tradition était déjà connue d'Hécatée? Cette hypothèse ne résiste pas à l'examen. En effet, nous avons déjà montré dans une précédente étude, à laquelle nous renvoyons le lecteur,[66] que l'attribution de la conquête de Lemnos à Miltiade l'Ancien est exclue par les témoignages antiques les plus formels et les plus autorisés, notamment par celui d'Hérodote. De plus, non seulement Hécatée connaissait déjà cette tradition; mais il en connaissait une version qui n'était pas la version athénienne et qui en différait sur un détail, ce qui implique que cette tradition n'était pas une invention athénienne. Nulle part, au demeurant, il ne nous est dit que cette tradition fut contestée par les Lemniens, comme ils n'auraient pas manqué de le faire s'il s'était agi d'une invention athénienne; tout au contraire certains récits impliquent qu'ils ne la contestèrent pas. Enfin on voit mal comment une invention athénienne aurait pu faire naître de rien une tradition qui, comme nous verrons, a de lointaines résonnances jusque sur l'histoire de la Laconie, de la Triphylie et de la colonisation dorienne de l'archipel.[67]

Ces faits étant établis, il convient de chercher à quel moment la tradition ancienne situait le séjour des Pélasges-Tyrrhènes en Attique et la construction du mur pélasgique de l'Acropole. Lorsqu'on examine attentivement les textes, on constate qu'ils nous fournissent à ce sujet un ensemble d'indications complémentaires et concordantes, qui, une fois rapprochées les unes des autres, donnent une date très précise, bien qu'elle n'ait pas été jusqu'à présent remarquée.

D'une part, en un tout autre passage de son oeuvre que celui où il relatait la construction du mur de l'Acropole, et à propos de la colonisation dorienne de Thèra, Hérodote fait allusion aux Pélasges qui, chassés d'Attique à Lemnos, en revinrent pour perpétrer le rapt de Brauron, c'est-à-dire précisément aux constructeurs du mur pélasgique. Ces Pélasges, nous dit-il, expulsèrent de Lemnos partie au moins de ceux qui occupaient l'île avant eux, et qui étaient considérés comme des Minyens parce qu'on faisait remonter leur origine au passage des Argonautes à Lemnos. Ces Minyens cherchèrent refuge en Laconie, où ils furent d'abord bien accueillis par les Doriens de Lacé-

---

66. "Tyrrhènes de Lemnos, Tyrrhènes d'Etrurie et l'expédition de Miltiade," *REA* 1949, 224 sqq.

67. Faut-il ajouter que cette tradition ne saurait être non plus une invention destinée à expliquer le nom de pélasgique porté par cette muraille? Outre qu'il faudrait, même alors, justifier ce nom de quelque manière, cette hypothèse est exclue notamment par le fait que, dans certaines versions de la tradition seul figure le nom de Tyrrhènes, sans qu'il soit question de Pélasges.

démone. De là, peu de temps après, à la suite de difficultés survenues avec les Lacédémoniens, quelques-uns repartirent avec Thèras coloniser Thèra, tandis que d'autres s'établissaient en Triphylie. Cette tradition est également rapportée par Strabon, Pausanias et une scholie d'Apollonios de Rhodes.[68] Or des indications d'Hérodote il résulte que Thèras colonisa Thèra 20 ans au moins, 30 ans au plus après le Retour des Héraclides : Thèras, relate-t-il, en effet, oncle maternel des deux fils jumeaux d'Aristodème, Eurysthénès et Proclès, en fut le tuteur jusqu'à ce qu'ils eussent atteint l'âge d'homme ; Aristodème passait pour être mort aussitôt après la naissance de ses deux jumeaux, peu de temps après l'établissement des Doriens en Laconie, ou, selon certains, au moment même de cet établissement, et Thèras serait allé coloniser Thèra parce qu'il ne pouvait se résoudre à ne plus commander après avoir goûté du pouvoir.[69] Parallèlement Pausanias situe cette colonisation une génération, c'est à dire environ 30 ans avant la migration ionienne vers l'Asie Mineure,[70] elle-même de 60 ans postérieure au Retour des Héraclides. Il la situe donc une trentaine d'années après ce Retour. En conséquence, l'expulsion des Minyens de Lemnos par les Pélasges chassés d'Attique date de moins de trente ans, et peut-être de moins de vingt après le Retour des Héraclides.

Cette place de l'occupation de Lemnos par les constructeurs du mur pélasgique d'Athènes dans la chronologie traditionnelle de l'âge héroïque, est confirmée par la date d'un événement se rapportant au début de l'histoire de ces Pélasges-Tyrrhènes à Lemnos : la participation de certains d'entre eux, ou, selon une variante de la tradition, des enfants qu'ils eurent des femmes athéniennes ravies à Brauron, à la colonisation dorienne de Mèlos et de la Crète, postérieurement au rapt de Brauron ; colonisation qui, dans Pausanias se situe au temps de la guerre des Hilotes, et dans Conon à la troisième génération après le Retour des Héraclides, au même moment que la migration ionienne vers l'Asie Mineure et que la colonisation dorienne de Rhodes, c'est-à-dire 60 ans environ après le Retour des Héraclides.[71]

---

68. Her. IV, 145-148 (contrairement à ce qu'ont compris certains traducteurs, le texte ne signifie pas que le départ des Minyens de Lemnos se situe après le rapt de Brauron, mais seulement qu'il s'agit des Pélasges qui perpétrèrent ce rapt ; cf. Her. VI, 137). Strab. VIII, 3, 3, et 19. Paus. VII, 2, 2. Schol. ad Apoll. Rhod. IV, 1764.

69. Her. IV, 147 ; et VI, 52.

70. Paus. VII, 2, 2.

71. Plut. *Quaest. graec.*, 21 ; *De mul. virt.*, 8 (— *Moralia* 296 B et 247 A). Cono *Narrat.*, 36 et 47. Cf. Polyaen. VII, 49 ; *FHG* I, 237, fr. 18 (Eph.), et III, 375, fr. 36 (Nic. Dam.). Il est douteux que ce soient ces Pélasges qui sont mentionnés comme occupant la Crète à côté des Doriens dans le vers interpolé de l'*Odyssée* (19, 177). Bien que ces récits contiennent des contaminations avec l'histoire des Minyens de Lemnos qui accompagnèrent Thèras, il ne semble pas cependant

En ce qui concerne le séjour des Pélasges en Attique, Philochore précise, en les désignant sous le seul nom de Tyrrhènes, qu'il fut de courte durée, avant qu'ils en fussent chassés vers Lemnos, d'où ils revinrent pour perpétrer le rapt de Brauron.[72] Par là se trouve confirmé le récit d'Hérodote, qui semble impliquer lui aussi que ce séjour fut bref.[73]

Enfin, en ce qui concerne la date de l'arrivée en Attique des constructeurs du mur pélasgique, Strabon, sans doute d'après Éphore, nous fournit une indication précise. C'est en Béotie, rapporte-t-il, qu'avant de venir en Attique habitaient les Pélasges qui donnèrent leur nom à un quartier d'Athènes et qui habitèrent sous l'Hymette. D'où il résulte qu'il s'agit bien des mêmes Pélasges auxquels Hérodote attribue la construction du mur pélasgique de l'Acropole et qui, d'après lui, reçurent précisément des terres au pied de l'Hymette. Ces Pélasges, ajoute Strabon, furent chassés de Béotie par le retour des Béotiens qu'eux-mêmes et des Thraces avaient auparavant évincés, lorsque ces Béotiens revinrent de Thessalie au moment du départ de la migration éolienne vers l'Asie Mineure.[74] Nous ne reviendrons pas ici sur la question de la provenance immédiate et de l'origine plus lointaine de ces Pélasges-Tyrrhènes d'Athènes, que nous avons déjà étudiées en un autre endroit.[75] Contentons-nous de relever ce qui seul nous importe pour le moment: la date qui résulte de Strabon pour leur arrivée en Attique. Si cette arrivée est conséquence du retour en Béotie des Béotiens, dont Thucydide nous donne la date précise par rapport au Retour des Héraclides,[76] et si elle est contemporaine de la

---

qu'il y ait lieu de confondre les deux épisodes. Voir à ce sujet nos remarques dans *REA* 1949. Pareti (*Storia di Sparta Arcaica*, 1, 125 sqq.) pense que ces récits sont dérivés d'Ephore; mais le fait ne semble pas prouvé.

72. *FHG* I, 384, fr. 5. Le fragment 6 de Philochore attribue à tort le rapt de Brauron aux Sintiens de Lemnos, confondus avec les Pélasges-Tyrrhènes, en vue de donner du nom des Sintiens une explication étymologique qui n'a pas plus de valeur que celle donnée ailleurs par Hellanicos (*FHG* I, 59-60, fr. 112-113). Mais le témoignage du fr. 6 ne saurait contrebalancer celui du fr. 5 et du reste de la tradition antique.

73. Her. VI, 137.

74. Strab. IX, 2, 3. Hérodote (V, 57 et 61) de son côté rapporte l'immigration en Attique, apparemment au même moment, d'autres habitants de la Béotie, les Géphyréens, descendants des compagnons de Cadmos chassés de Tanagra par l'établissement en Béotie des Béotiens. Voir aussi Thucydide (I, 12). De Strabon et de *l'Iliade* il semble resulter que l'occupation de la Béotie par les Pélasges et les Thraces se situe non seulement après la Guerre des Epigones, mais encore après la Guerre de Troie. Bien que Thucydide paraisse ignorer la première éviction des Béotiens de Béotie et justifie de manière moins satisfaisante les indications homériques, il nous semble clair contrairement aux inférences de Th. W. Allen (*The Homeric Catalogue of Ships*, 42 sqq.), qu'une même tradition est à l'origine des indications de Strabon, de Thucydide, et aussi d'Hérodote.

75. Voir notre article de la *REA* 1949, 224 sqq.

76. Thuc. I, 12.

migration éolienne vers l'Asie Mineure, elle se situe vingt ans avant le Retour des Héraclides.[77]

Les trois renseignements que nous avons recueillis sur l'arrivée, le séjour à Athènes et le départ des constructeurs du mur pélasgique d'Athènes sont donc parfaitement concordants. Ces Pélasges, arrivés en Attique vingt ans avant le Retour des Héraclides, y restèrent peu de temps, et de fait ils en repartirent moins de trente ans après ce Retour.

Si, comme le rapporte Hérodote d'après Hécatée,[78] ces Pélasges obtinrent des terres en Attique à condition de construire le mur de l'Acropole, la construction de ce mur se place au début de leur séjour, c'est-à-dire dans les vingt ans qui précèdent le Retour des Héraclides. Or l'examen des données archéologiques nous avait conduit à la conclusion que cette construction du mur pélasgique et la réalisation du vaste plan de défense de l'Acropole devaient être datées de la fin du XIIIe siècle ou des toutes premières années du XIIe. Si cette construction a immédiatement précédé le Retour des Héraclides, comme nous venons maintenant de l'apprendre, ce Retour serait en consèquence à dater de 1200 ou des premières années du XIIe siècle.

La tradition que nous avons analysée ne saurait, naturellement, être acceptée sans être au préalable confrontée d'une part avec les autres indications chronologiques de la tradition, d'autre part et surtout avec les données archéologiques elles-mêmes; car il est évident qu'un simple examen de critique interne ne peut suffire.

Pour ce qui est des indications chronologiques de la tradition, la date du Retour des Héraclides ainsi fixée est assurément en désaccord avec la chronologie ératosthénienne, qui situait l'événement en 1104, et avec toutes les chronologies basses, qui le plaçaient vers ce moment ou même plus tard. Parmi les chronologies hautes, celle de Timée et sans doute aussi celle de Douris, qui n'hésitaient pas à repousser la Guerre de Troie jusqu'en plein XIVe siècle, ne situaient le Retour des Héraclides que vers le milieu du XIIe, si Timée, comme Clitarque et comme sans doute Douris, comptait 820 ans de l'expédition d'Ale-

---

77. Velleius Paterculus (III, 1) de son côté situe vers le moment du Retour des Héraclides, sans autrement préciser, l'arrivée à Athènes de Pélasges, qui sont peut-être ces Pélasges chassés de Béotie, mais peuvent être aussi les Ioniens de l'Aegialée, d'origine pélasgique. La première interprétation est suggérée par le fait qu'aussitôt après avoir parlé de l'arrivée à Athènes de ces Pélasges, et dans la même phrase, Velleius parle de l'établissement en Thessalie des Thessaliens, qui par l'intermédiare des Béotiens chassés de Thessalie par eux, sont à l'origine du départ des Pélasges de Béotie: la seconde est suggérée parallèlement par le fait qu'immédiatement avant, et aussi dans la même phrase, il parle de la migration de Laconie en Achaïe, auparavant appelée Aegialée, des Achéens qui en expulsent les anciennes populations d'origine pélasgique.

78. Her. VI, 137.

xandre à ce Retour.[79] Il n'en est pas de même, en revanche, pour les chronologies d'Hérodote, de Thucydide et du Pseudo-Hérodote.

Hérodote, en effet, comptait un peu plus de 800 ans entre l'époque où il vivait, c'est-à-dire le milieu du Ve siècle, et la Guerre de Troie, qu'il situait en conséquence vers 1280-1270.[80] Or il acceptait la tradition qui comptait cent ans ou trois générations, entre la tentative d'Hyllos et la conquête dorienne du Péloponése,[81] c'est à dire quatre-vingts ans entre la Guerre de Troie et le Retour des Héraclides, qu'il situait en conséquence vers 1200-1190. De son côté Thucydide rapporte, sans toutefois la prendre à son propre compte, une tradition mélienne, d'après laquelle la colonie dorienne de Mèlos, en 416, existait déjà depuis plus de 700 ans.[82] Or cette colonisation dorienne de Mèlos, ainsi que nous avons vu, était donnée comme d'une soixantaine d'années postérieure au Retour des Héraclides[83] qui se situerait donc vers le début du XIIe siècle. Enfin, d'après la *Vie d'Homère* à tort attribuée à Hérodote, la fondation de Smyrne serait de 622 ans antérieure à la bataille de Salamine, et postérieure de 168 ans à la prise de Troie,[84] qui se placerait en conséquence vers 1270. Or, si l'auteur de la *Vie d'Homère* compte 168 ans entre la Guerre de Troie et la fondation de Smyrne, c'est qu'il suit la chronologie qui comptait quatre-vingts ans entre la Guerre de Troie et le Retour des Héraclides, qui serait en conséquence à dater selon lui de 1190.

La date à laquelle nous sommes arrivé par l'étude du mur pélasgique pour le Retour des Héraclides, s'accorde donc parfaitement avec celles des chronologies hautes qui, comme les chronologies d'Hérodote, de Thucydide et de la *Vie d'Homère* attribuée à Hérodote, situaient l'événement vers le début du XIIe siècle.

Pour ce qui est des données archéologiques, rappelons-en maintenant le témoignage. Il résulte de leur examen que:

1° Le mur pélasgique de l'Acropole et l'aménagement d'une source accessible depuis la citadelle même font partie d'un plan de fortification exécuté au moment même où Tirynthe et Mycènes se mettaient semblablement en état de défense en renforçant et agrandissant leur enceinte et en assurant leur approvisionnement en eau, ce qui indique

---

79. Tim. apud Clem. Alex., *Strom.* I, 403, *FHG* I, 232, fr. 153. Cf. Dur., *FHG* II, 472, fr. 11. Voir nos "*Recherches sur la Chronologie mycénienne,*" 44.

80. Her. II, 145.

81. Her. VI, 52; VII, 204; VIII, 131 et IX, 26.

82. Thuc. V, 112; cf. 84. Le texte n'indique pas combien d'années s'écoulèrent en plus des sept siècles; apparemment il ne faut pas compter plus d'une ou deux décades.

83. Voir ci-dessus, p. 144.

84. Ps. Her. *Vita Hom.*, 38.

que les établissements mycéniens de Grèce se préparaient à repousser une rude attaque et même à soutenir un siège.

2° Mycènes, Tirynthe et d'autres établissements mycéniens du Péloponèse succombent simultanément, très peu de temps après la construction du mur pélasgique, cette catastrophe entraînant l'effondrement de la civilisation mycénienne. Athènes, elle, ne succombe pas et on n'y relève pas de traces de destruction.

3° Toutefois pour Athènes la non-réoccupation des maisons de la pente Nord situées en dehors de l'enceinte après un abandon précipité semble indiquer que la menace fut sérieuse et effective, et qu'Athènes elle aussi fut attaquée.

Si la construction du mur pélasgique se situe dans les deux décades avant le Retour des Héraclides, dans quelle mesure les données de la tradition répondent-elles à ces données archéologiques?

1° Au moment du Retour des Héraclides la menace pèse bien effectivement sur Mycènes, Tirynthe et les autres établissements achéens du Péloponèse, et il s'agit bien pour toutes les citadelles mycéniennes non seulement de repousser un assaut, mais encore de se préparer à un siège. Ajoutons que la tradition ne gardait souvenir d'aucune autre attaque aussi générale, ni d'aucune autre période d'insécurité aussi grande vers cette époque.

2° A ce moment la tradition veut que les établissements achéens du Péloponèse aient effectivement succombé coup sur coup aux attaques des Doriens, mais non Athènes; et le Retour des Héraclides marquait la fin de l'âge des héros.

3° Sur ce dernier point la tradition, à première vue, semble en désaccord avec les données archéologiques. Mais en vérité, elle y répond une fois encore parfaitement. Athènes en effet est restée d'abord à l'écart de la vague d'invasion dorienne, et la mort de Codros lorsqu'il repousse l'attaque des Doriens contre Athènes, n'est située que quelque cinquante-neuf ans après le Retour des Héraclides. Toutefois, au moment même du Retour, Athènes, qui a accru sa population en accueillant des émigrés du Péloponèse, doit repousser une attaque venue non des Doriens, mais des Béotiens établis depuis une vingtaine d'années en Béotie; et c'est à un des émigrés qui venaient de se réfugier chez elle, au Néléide Mélanthos, père de Codros, que selon la tradition elle dut son salut.[85]

Cette indication relative à Mélanthos, au demeurant, paraît jeter une lumière sur les découvertes archéologiques qui ont été faites près de Pylos de Messénie. Car, s'il est clair que les vestiges mycéniens mis au jour en cet endroit ne peuvent correspondre à ceux de la Pylos

85. Eph. *FHG* I, 239, fr. 25. Strab. IX, 1, 7. Joann. Ant. *FHG* IV, 539, fr. 19.

de Nestor telle qu'elle est décrite dans *l'Iliade* et *l'Odyssée*,[86] la tradition voulait que Mélanthos fût venu de Messénie.[87] N'est-ce pas de
cette Pylos de Messénie, détruite précisément alors, que ce Néléide de
branche cadette partit vers Athènes au moment du Retour des Héraclides?

Par ailleurs le Retour des Héraclides, ainsi daté du début du XIIe
siècle, ne répond pas seulement aux données archéologiques de Grèce,
il cesse d'apparaître comme un événement isolé et accidentel pour
reprendre sa place et son sens dans l'histoire générale du Proche-
Orient méditerranéen à la fin de l'âge du bronze. L'invasion dorienne,
qui amène la seconde vague des Hellènes en Grèce, se présente désor-
mais comme une manifestation ou du moins comme un contre-coup
des grandes invasions venues du Nord qui bouleversent au même
moment tout le Proche-Orient méditerranéen depuis les Balkans
juqu'aux frontières de l'Egypte. Ces invasions déferlent dès les
dernières décades du XIIIe siècle sur l'Asie Mineure, où elles entraî-
nent l'effondrement de l'Empire hittite et où, vers le même moment,
ou plutôt un peu avant, pour autant qu'on en peut juger par les
comptes-rendus préliminaires de la mission américaine, elles ont pour
conséquence à Troie l'apparition de la céramique à mamelons dans le
niveau VII B proprement dit. Dans l'histoire égyptienne les envahis-
seurs sont appelés Peuples du Nord et de la Mer, et c'est sur eux que
Ramsès III remporte sa victoire de 1191.

Ainsi, la date de 1200-1190 environ que nous avons pu établir pour
le Retour des Héraclides et l'identification de ce Retour avec la destruction générale des établissements mycéniens du Péloponèse, vien-
nent confirmer et préciser une interprétation des données archéologiques mycéniennes, qui se présentait déjà comme vraisemblable; et
en revanche elles vont à l'encontre d'hypothèses récentes qui n'étaient
pas sans soulever des difficultés.

---

86. Comme le reconnait H. T. Wade-Gery, *AJA* 52 (1948) 115 sqq. Voir déjà
à ce sujet Bérard, V., *Les Navigations d'Ulysse*. 2. 157 sqq.

87. Au moment du Retour des Héraclides, Mélanthos, descendant du frère cadet
de Nestor, Périclymène, cherche refuge en Attique avec les autres Néléides du
Péloponèse. Le fait que Mélanthos est donné comme venant de Messénie (Hellan.
et Demo. *FHG* I, 47, fr. 10; et 378, fr. 1. Paus. II, 18, 7. Cf. Her., I, 147) n'est
pas en soi-même significatif pour autant que la tradition (cf. Paus. *loc. cit.*) en
faisait venir aussi les autres Néléides. Mais Strabon qui était partisan de localiser
la Pylos de Nestor en Triphylie et non en Messénie, rapporte qu'au moment du
Retour des Héraclides, Mélanthos était roi de la Messénie, qui relevait de Ménélas
au moment de la Guerre de Troie (Strab. VIII, 4, 1; cf. XIV, 1, 3, et IX, 1, 7).
Or non seulement Mélanthos est présenté comme suivi de Pyliens (Strab. XIV,
1, 3), mais il est donné lui-même comme Pylien (Her. I, 147, cf. V, 65; Joann.
Ant. *loc. cit.*). Et ne serait-ce pas cette origine messénienne de Mélanthos, devenu
célèbre après son accession à la royauté d'Athènes, qui conduisit à identifier la
Pylos de Nestor avec la Pylos de Messénie?

Bien des points, assurément, restent encore à étudier, sur lesquels nous espérons avoir l'occasion de revenir. Pour ce qui est de la conquête dorienne du Péloponèse elle-même, il apparaît qu'elle s'est déroulée, comme le voulait la tradition, de manière rapide et brutale, et qu'elle porta le coup de grâce à la civilisation mycénienne. Il apparaît aussi qu'elle eut d'abord des résultats surtout négatifs, ruinant une civilisation déjà décadente sans lui en substituer aussitôt une autre.[88] Mais il reste encore à préciser comment s'est formé le style protogéométrique, comment s'est développé le rite de l'incinération, comment enfin s'est répandu l'usage du fer dans le cours du XIIe siècle. En ce qui concerne l'ensemble de l'âge héroïque, nos recherches évidemment ne résolvent pas tous les problèmes chronologiques; car elles ne tranchent pas la question de savoir quel intervalle sépare la Guerre de Troie du Retour des Héraclides. Mais elles semblent confirmer qu'il faut en chercher la solution dans le sens d'une chronologie considérablement plus haute que la chronologie d'Eratosthène; conclusion à laquelle nous avions été déjà conduit par notre précédente étude.

La présente recherche aurait néanmoins atteint son objet, si nous avons contribué, pour la catastrophe qui marque la fin de la civilisation mycénienne, à établir une date archéologique, et si, surtout, nous sommes parvenus à identifier de manière certaine le Retour des Héraclides avec la destruction générale des établissements mycéniens du Péloponèse; certitude qui se présenterait comme la première pour cette période reculée de l'histoire grecque.

---

88. Voir déjà Picard, Ch., *RA* 15 (1940) 128-131.

PREHISTORIC SARDIS

GEORGE M. A. HANFMANN
Harvard University

PLATES 5 AND 6

Among the many fields of Classic civilization which have profited by the pioneering efforts of the scholar to whom this volume is dedicated is the study of ancient Asia Minor. Throughout his career, Professor David M. Robinson has made major contributions to Anatolian archaeology. Since he has had an important share in the exploration and publication of the capital of Lydia, I venture to offer to him as a token of gratitude some notes on the archaeological problems of Prehistoric Sardis prompted by a visit which I made to the site in the spring of 1948.[1]

Nowadays the electric train from Izmir makes the 110 kilometers to Sardis seem a short stretch.[2] The railroad follows the course of the Hermus up the valley through which the Lydian cavalry rode down to the sea and the Greek colonists pushed up toward the interior.[3] The plain is lush and green, but the mountains on both sides, which are still heavily wooded, are difficult and often forbidding territory. Shortly before Manisa (Magnesia ad Sipylum, 66 km from Izmir) the valley narrows to a gorge. Here one would look for the earliest natural frontier between the archaic Greek settlers and the Lydians. Then the soil turns red; so do the clay huts of red-mud brick which are probably not too different from those built in the time of Croesus.[4] The same short-headed dogs that dash beside the chariots on the terracottas from Sardis now dash beside the electric train; and a donkey scratching himself catches the eye in the same posture that he strikes on some Ionic vases.

---

1. I am indebted to the authorities of Harvard University for the grant of a Clark Fellowship for the year 1947-8 in connection with my work on Sardis, and to Dr. George H. Chase for his invitation to participate in the publication of the pottery from Sardis and for his permission to use his records of this material. Dr. Chase also very kindly read the manuscript of this article.

2. This is the official railroad distance. Butler, H. C., *Sardis*, 1921, gives the distance as 150 km.

3. On geography and history of Lydia cf. Deeters and Keil in *RE*, *s.v. Lydia*, 26, 1927, 2122 ff., with a good map, repeated in Bossert, H. Th., *Alt-Anatolien*, pl. vii. Bittel, K., *AFO* 13 (1940) 186, points out that Roman milestones attest the use of this road, even though the Itineraries list a roundabout way through Thyateira (Akhisar). On the geography and geology of Sardis cf. also Butler, H. C., *Sardis* I, 15 ff. and Warfield, W., "The Geology of Sardis," *ibid.*, 175 ff.

4. There was apparently a definite contrast between the Greeks, who settled in towns and clung to the valleys, and the Lydians, who had retained the pattern of village life to a very high degree. Cf. Deeters and Keil, *op. cit.*, 2124.

After Manisa the valley widens steadily until near Sardis it becomes a plain—the Lydian Plain or *Sardiane*.[5] Far away to the left
(toward the north) against a low ridge rise the mounds of the Royal
Cemetery of Bin Tepe, never systematically mapped or explored.[6]
Southward, to the right, two striking and bizarrely shaped peaks
hold guard over a valley which rises rapidly into the wooded slopes
of the Tmolus range. The gold-bearing Pactolus has cut this short
and steep decline in its downward path. The contrast of the bright
red peaks at the entrance into the valley and the green of the wooded
upper slopes combined with the sweeping vistas across the valley
create a setting of haunting beauty.

The Sardian Mountains may have contained caves suitable for
habitations of earliest men. The Lydian tombs are rock-cut and many
of them have outlasted two and one half thousand years. On the
other hand, many landslides have occurred, even during the historic
era, so that such caves cannot have afforded too much safety. I do
not know, if any Prehistoric caves have been recorded in the immediate vicinity of Sardis.[7]

The site was, however, ideal for the early agricultural settlements.
The Pactolus and the Hermus provided water for all needs of the

---

5. Cf. Buerchner, s.v. *Sardiane*, in *RE* 2, 2, 1920, 2479 f.

6. Four attempts to excavate Bin Tepe have been made. The first and the
only one which resulted in a map of the site and in something approaching an
excavation report was that by H. Spiegelthal in 1853-4. Cf. Curtius, E., *AZ* 1853,
148 ff. Olfers, *Abh.Akad.Berlin*, Phil. Hist. Kl. 1858, 539-556, with map pl. 1
showing the location of the village of Sardis, Bin Tepe, and Gygaean Lake
(Marmara Göl), repeated in F. Schachermeyr in Ebert, *Reallex.* 14, 1929, pl.
61 x, and Bossert, *op.cit.*, fig. 153. A brief exploration was made by Choisy. Cf.
RA 32 (1876) 73. For the excavations of G. Dennis made in 1882, cf. Butler,
Sardis 1, 8 ff., a letter from Francis H. Bacon to Charles Eliot Norton describing Dennis' exploration of three mounds, all allegedly re-used in Roman times.
Some more tumuli were investigated by Butler and Shear in the campaign of
1914 but only preliminary notices have been published. Cf. *Sardis* 1, 154 ff. (two
mounds opened; cf. also *AJA* 18 [1914] 431 f.), and pp. 10 f., several
tumuli described briefly, with the view of one of the tumuli opened earlier on p.
157, and the interior dromos and chamber of another, in fig. 3. A good detailed
survey of all tumuli in the vicinity of Sardis (*Sardis* 1, 157, tumuli in the
Pactolus valley and others "three or four miles west of the Pactolus," in addition
to those of Bin Tepe) with all tumuli carefully mapped is urgently needed. It
would also be desirable to ascertain whether all of them were really sepulchral
mounds; in other parts of Asia Minor some of the supposed tumulus burials
turned out to be habitation sites.

7. On the systematic survey of caves in Turkey, cf Şevket Aziz Kansu, "Stone
Age Cultures in Turkey," *AJA* 51 (1947) 227 ff. No Palaeolithic sites appear
on M. Pfannstiel's map in this area; *Die altsteinzeitlichen Kulturen Anatoliens*
(Istanbuler Forschungen XV), 1941, repeated in Bossert, *op.cit.*, 101. I have
not been able to use Pfannstiel's publication. For a Lavalloisian find from Phry-
gia, Alpanus, south of Eskisehir, cf. Chaput, E., *Phrygie* (Institut Français de
Stamboul) 1, Geologie, 1941, pl. 5. For other recent finds and bibliography; cf.
Kansu, Ş. A., *Belleten* (Türk Tarih Kurumu), 9 (1945) 293 ff. Bittel, K.,
Grundzüge der Vor- und Frühgeschichte Kleinasiens, Ch. II, Map 1, supersedes
Pfannstiel's survey.

household and of the craftsmen and guaranteed fertile crops. There
were woods then as now to supply materials for buildings and boats.
And the curiously "fattish" red clay lent itself readily to brick-mak-
ing and the production of pottery. Finally, there was the Hermus
valley, a natural road leading from the coast into the interior and
eventually destined to become part of the Royal Road. Another road
led northward to Thyateira (Akhisar), while southward a more
arduous climb enabled the traveller to reach the Cayster valley
(Küçük Menderes Nehri).[8]

Was there an early agricultural settlement at Sardis? And if so,
where should it be looked for? The excavations of 1910-1914 and
1922 centered on the area of the temple of Artemis which is located
fairly high up the Pactolus valley.[9] No systematic search for prehistoric relics was undertaken, although a few were found. In my
opinion, the natural position for an agricultural settlement would
be one as close as possible to the confluence of the Pactolus and the
Hermus, yet far enough from the lowest part of the valley to escape
the danger of floods. The area of the later Roman town and the slopes
of the hills below—toward the north and west—would seem to satisfy
these requirements best. There is some evidence which lends substance
to this conjecture. When the modern railroad was being built, numerous polished stone implements came to light.[10] The railroad runs somewhat above the trough of the valley on the incline that slopes gradually from the foot of the Acropolis Hill. Here the earliest prehistoric settlement of Sardis may have stood.

---

8. Cf. *Harta Genel Direktorlügü* 1936, Izmir, also *Sardis* 1, fig. 18, and pl. 1.
It is pretty clear that the road to the south, to Hypaepa, cannot have been an
important one. For the Ionian march up the Cayster valley and across the
Tmolus in 499 B.C. as a movement to achieve tactical surprise, cf. Bittel, *AFO* 13
(1940) 188, n. 16.

9. Another important aspect was the exploration of the Lydian tombs cut
into the towering Necropolis Hill on the other (south) side of the Pactolus. I
disagree with Butler on the presumable location of the Lydian city. In *Sardis*
I, p. 21, he said that he looked for it within the Pactolus valley because of
Euripides, *Bacchae* 462 f., where Sardis is said to be encircled by Mount Tmolus.
In *Sardis* II, 2, Butler conceded that the large area just to the west of the Roman
ruins might be considered. Various tests were made by Shear in 1922, along the
torrent beds which descend into Pactolus north of the Artemis temple. This is
still higher upstream than the location I have in mind. Other promising areas
were the northward extension of the excavation into the "First" torrent gulch
(wady) and the southeastern end of the Acropolis, near the breach in the
medieval wall, both of which held out promise of good Lydian levels. Cf. Shear,
Th.L., *AJA* 26 (1922) 401 ff. The appearance of tombs about the base of the
Acropolis within the Pactolus valley is in my opinion another argument against
assuming that the center of Sardis was in that region. Cf. *Sardis* I, 35.

10. The railroad crosses the Pactolus just before the station of Sart. According to Butler, *Sardis* I, p. 16, the distance to the Necropolis Hill is about a mile.
On the stone implements found cf. Buerchner, *RE* II, 2, 2478, "beim Bau der
Eisenbahnlinie fand man eine grosse Anzahl neolithischer Beilchen, aehnlich
denen die auch in der Naehe von Sardis am Gygeischen See gefunden wurden."

Unfortunately, the finds made during the building of the railroad were not recorded, but polished stone implements from Sardis similar to those found during the building of the railroad exist in the collections of the Museums in London, St. Germain, and Mainz. These implements are so numerous that they point toward some area with abundant surface finds. They may, of course, belong not to one but to several villages.[11] Thus Spiegelthal and Sayce reported that they saw traces of at least two pile-dwellings in the Gygaean Lake[12] (Marmara Göl) which lies just north of the Royal Cemetery of Bin Tepe and some six or seven miles north of the site of Sardis.[13] Celts alleged to have come from these lake-dwellings have been published in *Festschrift zur Feier des 75 — jaehrigen Bestehens des Roemisch-Germanischen Zentralmuseums Mainz*, 1927, p. 99.[14] Buerchner, however, spoke of some polished celts of nephrite in his possession as coming from an "uralte Nekropolis" south of the Gygaean Lake.[15] A lake-dwellers' culture in Lydia would be a sensational matter—and we should remember that ancient authors regarded the lake as artificial, or at least as artificially expanded.[16] The site of the alleged lake-dwellings should repay investigation.

11. Smith, Reginald A., "The Sturge Collection," British Museum, 1937, 81 f. *Id. Guide to the Antiquities of the Stone Age*, 174. Bittel, K., *Praehistorische Forschung in Kleinasien*, 132, no. 133 (abbrev. below as *Praehist. Kl.*). St. Germain: Arne, T. J., "Den aldsk bebyggelsen vid Bosporen," *Förnvannen*, Meddelanden fran K. Vitterhets historie och Antikvitets Akademien, 7, (1922) 117, n. 4, from collections made by P. Gaudin (a flint axe). On this piece cf. also K. Bittel, *Kleinasiatische Studien* (Instanbuler Mitteilungen, Vol. 5), 1942, 153 n., who says that this flint axe and that of the Protesilaus Tomb (Troy I period) is of non-Asiatic, South Eastern European form.

12. Sayce, A. H., *JHS* 1 (1880) 87 f.

13. For the approximate situation of the Gygaean Lake cf. Spiegelthal's map referred to in n. 6, above. For its geology, Butler, *Sardis* 1, 21 and Warfield, *Sardis* 1, 178, who explains the lake as a result of the windings of the Hermus river during the process of elevation. The Lake called in ancient times *Gygaie Limne* and *koloe* is now officially called Marble Lake (Marmara Göl) and is shown on the *Harta Genel Direktorlügü*, Sheet Izmir, 1936. The famous temple of Artemis Coloene was near this lake, but its location is not as clear as Spiegelthal's map would lead one to believe. Cf. Shear, T. L., *AJA* 26 (1922) 408: "some foundations came to light and one or two late inscriptions were found but nothing that could be certainly connected with Coloe."

14. Smith A., *The Sturge Collection*, 81. Behn, F., in the *Festschrift* reports the acquisition of these celts from the Badisches Landesmuseum, Karlsruhe, which in turn had received them from the Stützel Collection. He reproduces the pieces and states cautiously that they are alleged to have come from the lake dwellings in the Gygaean Lake. The two basic types are "dreieckiges Beil mit walzenförmigem Querschnitt und ein flaches trapezoides Gerät." I am indebted to R. J. Braidwood and the Library of the University of Chicago for making this publication available.

15. *RE*, s.v. *Gygaie Limne*, 14, 1912, p. 1956: "im Sueden befindet sich eine uralte Nekropolis. Von ihr stammen polierte Nephritbeile (mehrere in meinem Besitz)." Cf. *Id.*, *RE* 2, 2, 1920, p. 2478.

16. Cf. the references given by Buerchner, *loc.cit.* Note, however, that geologists assume that the lake existed long before historical times. Ancient tradi-

Through the courtesy of the Department of British and Medieval Antiquities, I am enabled to reproduce here (pl. 6a) the photograph of the twenty stone implements from Sardis which are in the Sturge Collection of the British Museum. Of these, only one piece has been published previously.[17] Other stone implements from Sardis in the British Museum include the following items, which were sketched and described for me by Mr. E. M. M. Alexander, Assistant Keeper of the Department[18] (fig. 1).

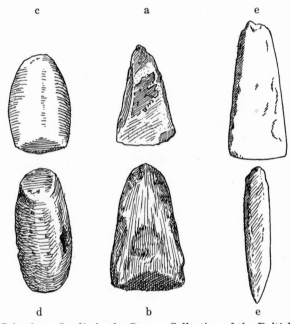

Fig. 1. Celts from Sardis in the Sturge Collection of the British Museum

Fig. 1a. No. 2403. Triangular celt of dull green serpentine. The surface partly polished. Marks of sawing on the sides. L. 2.2″.

Fig. 1b. No. 57-11-28-1. Haematite celt. Sides battered and worn. L. 2⅝″.

---

tion, therefore, refers probably to some kind of regularization and flood control instituted by the Lydian Kings.

17. I am indebted to Mr. C. F. C. Hawkes, then Keeper, for his permission to publish this material and to Messrs. E. M. M. Alexander and T. W. Brailsfold for information. The piece previously published is described by R. A. Smith, *The Sturge Collection*, no. 878. "Subtriangular celt of black volcanic stone, with straight cutting edge, oval section, and rounded butt polished all over. L. 2′."

18. Mr. Alexander's pen sketches were redrawn by Mr. Walter G. Hodsdon of Harvard College who has also drawn the profiles in Fig. 4. The drawings for Fig. 3 were made by Mr. J. P. Leeper.

Fig. 1c. No. 2404. Oval celt with rounded surface polished all over. L. 2½".

Fig. 1d. No. 4067. Pierced axe-hammer of dark grey stone. L. 6".

Fig. 1e. Narrow flat implement of close-grained sedimentary stone. L. 2⅞".

What conclusions can we draw from this material for the history of Sardis? Arne and Bittel have pointed out that small polished stone implements of this sort occur throughout Western Asia Minor and extend into Thrace.[19] They have been found on other Lydian sites as well as in Larisa on the Hermus and Izmir, and quite recently in the quicksilver mine of Çakmak near Karaburun on the Erythraean Peninsula which forms the western limit of the Gulf of Izmir.[20] Implements of this type continued to be used well into the Bronze Age, but a considerable concentration such as appears to have occurred in Sardis would not be likely to occur after the end of the third millennium.[21] For the time being, we may assume that a "Chalcolithic" village existed in the third millennium near the site of Sardis, while another settlement appears to have been made near the Gygaean Lake.

On such slender evidence little can be said about the cultural affiliation of the early settlers of Sardis. Years ago, Hogarth likened some mottled vases from Spiegelthal's excavations to the Vasiliki

19. Arne in *Förnvannen* 7 and Bittel in *Praehist.Kl.* Cf. Smith, *Guide to the Antiquities of the Stone Age₃,* 174.

20. Schefold, K., *Larisa am Hermos* 3, 1942, 7 f., pl. 1, 5-6 and 1, 23-24. *AA* 1934, 392 ff. figs. 16-17 (Late Troy II-V). Izmir: British Museum, nos. 1354-1359. George E. Mylonas informs me that he found three celts near Izmir and its suburbs known as Paradiso and Bayrakli in 1922. Çakmak: Hamit Zübeyr Koşay and Hakki Gültekin, *Türk Tarih Arkeologya ve Etnografya Dergisi* 5 (1949) 16 ff., figs. 4 ff. Cf. *AJA* 51 (1947) 197 f., pl. 40,e. Cf. also the celts from Philadelphia (Alaşehir) in the Ashmolean Museum, Bittel, *Prähist. Forsch.,* 120, n. 7, Magnesia ad Sipylum (Manisa), *ibid.,* 130, n. 114, and Ephesus, *ibid.,* 121, add British Museum Asia 1-2 (two celts). On the area in which these polished stone celts occur cf. Bittel, *ibid.,* 42 ff., pl. 18, 1-6 (Troy II). Smith, *Guide to the Antiquities of the Stone Age₃,* 174. Bossert, *Altanatolien,* figs. 18-37 (Kadiköy).

21. Burkitt, M., *LAAA* 26 (1939) 54 ff. observed that polished celts were infrequent at Mersin compared with the wealth of obsidian. He noted that they occur along the entire coast of Asia Minor from Cilicia to the Troad (Ridgeway Collection in the Museum of Archaeology, Cambridge). He also posed the question whether polished stone celts found in "Halafian" context at Mersin can really be three thousand years earlier than those of Swiss lake dwellings. There may be a time lag betwen Central Europe and Asia, and, to a lesser degree between Syro-Cilician cultures of the Amuq and Mersin and those of Western Anatolia, but I feel persuaded that the widespread use of these polished celts— and the frequency of surface finds indicates such use—cannot have lasted much into the Bronze Age in Western Anatolia. I am grateful to R. J. and Linda Braidwood for their enlightening remarks on this matter. For the Copper Age cf., for example, the gold-sheathed club from Alaca. Bittel, K., *AA* 57 (1942) 92 f., fig. 7. *Id., Prähist. Forsch.,* 45 (Troy VI).

ware of Crete;[22] subsequently, after the American excavations had taken place, he saw in the prehistoric sherds from Sardis resemblances to the Cycladic culture.[23] Neither suggestion can be maintained in the light of the advance in our knowledge of Prehistoric Asia Minor. In his courageous but premature attempt to reconstruct the trade routes of Prehistoric Asia Minor, Dussaud had assumed that Sardis was a center of overland trade already in the third millennium B.C. and that Lydia might have been in contact with the Mesopotamian civilization. The present state of our knowledge does not permit us either to affirm or to reject this theory.[24]

Since we lack the material to determine the cultural affiliations of Sardis proper, it may be well to consider briefly the material of the Hermus valley and beyond that of the entire region known later as Lydia. Only two sites have been excavated, both in the Hermus estuary and therefore belonging to the coastal region, where the cultural development may have diverged from development of the sites farther inland. The material found at Larisa on the Hermus (Burunçuk) seems to parallel in time the Trojan cultures from late Troy II on, but the prehistoric settlement continued until the arrival of the Greeks. Schefold points out certain resemblance of some vases to the Trojan and others to the Bithyno-Phrygian group (Demirci Hüyük) but notes that in general Larisa appears to have been a fairly poor village.[25] Bittel omits it altogether from his most recent map of prehistoric sites.[26] Old Smyrna (Bayrakli) is in process of excavation. The excavators state that "the place was first settled near the beginning of the third millennium B.C. about the same time as the first city of Troy, with which its culture was closely connected."[27] Other sites somewhat nearer Sardis have produced only isolated finds. Thus near Magnesia ad Sipylum (Manisa) two spouted jugs (Schnabelkannen) of the Yortan type have come to light and material of the Yortan culture was also found at Thyateira (Akhisar) to the

---

22. Butler, H. C., *Sardis* 1, 13. Did he mistake the historic Lydian vases for Prehistoric ones?

23. Hogarth, D. G., *Cambridge Ancient History* 3, 1925, 506.

24. Dussaud, R., *La Lydie et ses voisins aux hautes époques*, 20, 58 f., 99, 109 f., and pl. 1 (map) = Bossert, *Altanatolien*, Map X. Dussaud maintained that Sargon had reached the Ionian coast in Lydia; that a copper trade route went across Lydia to Troy; and that certain seals which he termed "Proto-Lydian" belonged to the third millennium. The evidence consists of lead idols (cf. Troy II) found at Thyateira (Akhisar) north of Sardis. Dussaud, *op.cit.*, 71 ff., fig. 11.

25. Schefold, K., *op.cit.*, 3. 6. Bittel, *Praehist. Forsch.* no. 32 (map).

26. *Grundzüge*, Map 3.

27. Cook, J. M., *Illustrated London News*, Nov. 1949, 775, brought to my attention by G. Kirk, and *JHS* 67 (1947) 42, where four Prehistoric layers are mentioned. They contained burnished pink and tan monochrome wares and a "fair admixture of grey ware." For some reason, the latter is rare at Larisa.

north of Sardis[28] Bittel has indeed suggested that the Yortan culture of Mysia, which is known so far only through burials, extended
to the Tmolus and Sipylus mountains, i.e. to the southern edge of the
Hermus valley.[29] In this case, Sardis would be included in the territory of the Yortan culture; but this hypothesis, though plausible,
needs to be tested by systematic survey and excavations.

Future exploration and research will have to answer many questions. Did the early inhabitants of Sardis come from the coast or
from the Central Plateau?[30] If they came from the coast, did they
arrive from the north, as representatives of the Yortan-Balikesir-
Troy types of culture, from the south, which is as yet unexplored, or
from the islands closest to the coast such as Samos and Chios?[31] Did
they trade only with their neighbors or did the Hermus valley already

28. Manisa: Özgüç, T., Türk Tarih Kurumu, *Belleten*, 1946, 605. A curious
double vase from Manisa is shown in Bossert, *Altanatolien*, fig. 119, who con-
jecturally assigns a marble idol, 23, fig. 133, to the same region. Thyateira
(Akhisar) : Bittel, *Prähist. Forsch.*, 120, n. 5, and *AFO* 13 (1939) 21, fig. 17,
Other Yortan sites near the Lydian region: Murdugan on the Erythraean
Peninsula: Bossert, *Altanatolien*, fig. 109. Bittel, *AFO* 13 (1939) 21, fig. 18. On
the Yortan culture and its date, cf. Bittel, *Grundzüge*, 21 f., fig. 52, Map 3
(extends into Europe, begins at the same time as Troy I, c. 3200 B.C.). Özgüç,
T., "Oentarihte Anadolu Kronolojisi," *Belleten* 9 (1945) 341 ff., (begins 3200
B.C.), and *Id.*, *Die Bestattungbräuche im vorgeschichtlichen Anatolien* (Veröf-
flentl. der Univ. Ankara 14, 5, 1948), pp. 12 ff., 25 ff., 61 ff., 76 ff., 149 ff., where he
considers that it ran parallel to Troy I and II and that its carriers may have
represented the intermingling of two racial stocks. Stewart, J., *Handbook to the*
Nicholson Museum₂, Sidney, 1948, pp. 79 f., dates the Mysian Culture of the
Balikesir Plain parallel to Troy I-II, but suggests that the Yortan culture might
fall between Troy II and Troy VI.

29. *Kleinasiatische Studien* (Istanbuler Mitteilungen V), 1942, 170 f.

30. Schefold considers that people from the plateau may have infiltrated
Larisa. On the relations of Central and Western Anatolia cf. Özgüç, *Artibus*
Asiae 10 (1947) 312 ff.

31. On Samos cf. Bittel, *Kleinasiat. Studien*, 127 ff., esp. 186 ff. *Grundzüge*,
27 f, Weinberg, S., *AJA* 51 (1947) 178 f. Bittel states that the oldest culture
of Samos cannot as yet be clearly affiliated. He sees some resemblances with
the Phrygian-Pisidian (Isparta) culture of Asia Minor. Weinberg points out
far flung connections with Crete, Cyclades, Troad, and Macedonia. He seems
to date at least part of the "Samian Neolithic" in the same period as early
Troy I (c. 3200 B.C.). For Neolithic finds on Calymnus cf. Brown, T. Burton,
JHS 67 (1947) 128 ff. Milojçic, V., *BSA* 44 (1949) 302 ff., compares the Tigani
material on Samos with Late Cretan Neolithic of Phaistos, and sees on Samos
a development parallel to that in Syro-Cilicia (Mersin VII, Tell Judeideh XI),
as well as Kum Tepe, Troy and Alishar I. He assumes (p. 286) a common
(Mesolithic) background for Serbia and South-Western Asia, and conjectures
further that the Vinça culture of Serbia may have had its origins in cultures
of Asia Minor which preceded Troy and have so far remained undetected. More
cautious views were expressed by J. Gaul in his summary on Anatolian relations with Bulgaria. Gaul, J. H., *The Neolithic Period in Bulgaria* (American
School of Prehistoric Research, Bulletin XVI), 1948, pp. 26 f., 76, 104 ff., 224
(brachycephals in Bulgaria and Alishar) pp. 229 ff. ("we cannot find in the
earliest occupation of Bulgaria any traits to relate the Early Neolithic period
with . . . . Anatolia") I don't quite understand Milojçic's statement that burials
corresponding in time to his dating of Vinça culture are "unknown to us in
Western Asia Minor." Cf. n. 28, above.

serve as a channel for overland trade? Do all the stone implements represent village cultures beginning about 3000 B.C., or was there an earlier Neolithic phase in this region?[32] Did people of this area participate in a movement into the Greek islands and Greece, as many students of Aegaean archaeology have supposed?[33] Finally, we must seek to clarify the relation of Western Anatolian agricultural communities to those of Eastern Anatolia and Cilicia. Bittel has recently maintained that the Eastern Anatolian (Sakçegözü) and Cilician (Mersin) village cultures preceded those of Central (Alaca, Alişar, Demirci Hüyük) and Western Anatolia (Troy, Yortan), by almost a thousand years (c. 4000 B.C. for Mersin against c. 3200 for Troy).[34] It would seem strange, however, if inventions as fundamental as those which caused the agricultural revolution should have failed to surmount natural barriers for such a long period of time. And it is not at all impossible that this formidable time-lag will have

---

32. Bittel has argued that a Neolithic culture, as yet not discovered nor defined, must be postulated as the ancestor of the Troy-Yortan and the Phrygian-Pisidian cultures of Asia Minor. He regards Western Anatolian, Cycladic, and Helladic cultures as descendants from that common Neolithic ancestor. The linguistic similarities between the pre-Greek names of Greece and Asia Minor would thus be the result of a common background in the Neolithic Age. *Kleinasiat. Studien*, 186 ff., and *Grundzüge*, 28. Cf. Angel, J. L., "Neolithic Ancestors of the Greeks," *AJA* 49 (1945) 258 ff., for the South Anatolian component among the Neolithic Greeks.

33. Cf. Goldman, H., *Hesperia*, Suppl. 8 (Commemorative Studies in Honor of T. L. Shear) (1949) 165 f., 169: "toward the middle of the third millennium there was apparently a movement of people from Anatolia to Greece and Crete . . . . one would have expected emigration to have taken place from the west coast of Anatolia."

34. The earliest pottery known in Asia Minor seems to be represented by the burnished wares of the lowest levels of Mersin, parallelled in the mounds near Antioch (Amuq). In Mersin, and perhaps also in Tarsus, these monochrome wares were followed by painted pottery affiliated with "Tell Halaf" painted pottery and other painted wares; for parallels with Hassuna, cf. Perkins, A. L., *Comparative Archaeology of Early Mesopotamia*, (Oriental Institute Studies 25 [1949] 15). The "Halafian" painted wares appear to have centered in the region of the "highlands" between Syria and the Caucasus (upper Tigris, Khabur, Balih valleys), with the Taurus and the Anti-Taurus as their western frontiers. Cf. Bittel, *Grundzüge*, 13, Map 3, and for the western frontier the valuable field survey by Ahmet Dönmez and W. C. Brice, *Iraq* 11 (1949) 44 ff., Map fig. 1. The dating of the Eastern Anatolian and Syro-Cilician painted wares rests upon analogies with Mesopotamia, not only in the Halaf, but also in the Ubaid phase. What is in doubt is not the correlation itself, but the duration of the "Halafian" phase and the dating of its lower limit. Bittel, *Grundzüge*, 10, concedes that especially in Cilicia this limit should be placed around 3000 B.C. Garstang, J., *AJA* 51 (1947) 375 ff. discusses the Mersin parallels with Halaf, Samarra, Ubaid, and Uruk, and dates the last two phases of Mersin Chalcolithic, c. 3500-3100 B.C. The reduction of dates for Troy (Kum Tepe Ia, 2900 B.C.), Troy I, 2700 B.C. and other Aegean and Anatolian sites proposed by Milojçic, *op.cit.*, 303 f., 299, entails a lower dating for the end of the painted wares at Mersin (3000-2900?), but does not affect the problem of the time lag between Eastern and Western Anatolia.

to be reduced by a thorough-going compression of dates for the early Syro-Cilician, and North Mesopotamian cultures.[35]

Beyond these archaeological questions, a very much better knowledge of the material culture of Lydia is needed before we can even speculate intelligently about the relation of the archaeological material to the early languages of Asia Minor. It would be of paramount interest to know whether the Lydian tongue of historic times was descended from a language spoken already in the third millennium, whether resemblances of names of gods indicate any early relation between the inhabitants of Cilicia and those of the West coast, and, finally, whether the prehistoric inhabitants of Lydia belonged to the same linguistic family as the carriers of the Early Cycladic and Early Helladic cultures in Greece. But only systematic exploration of sites, which on philological grounds might belong to this early stratum of languages, holds out prospects of progress.[36]

The polished celts from Sardis reflected presumably a culture of the third millennium. The few fragments of prehistoric pottery from

---

35. The discovery of a Neolithic obsidian industry at Ilica Punar near the Salt Lakes on the plateau (Acituz Göl) indicates a possible source for the obsidian of the lower levels at Mersin. In order to secure obsidian, Cilician agriculturists would have to traverse the Taurus barrier. Bittel, *AA* 57 (1942) 87 ff., fig. 4-5. Another indication that early agriculturalists might have penetrated westward beyond the boundary of painted wares is given by Dönmez and Brice, who have found burnished wares of the earliest Syro-Cilician type in the Elbistan Plain, on the road to Kayseri. *loc.cit.*, 49 ff., figs. 1-2, pl. 30. It does not seem very likely that a long period would pass between the establishment of settlements in the Elbistan Plain and those within and around the Halys bend.

36. The resemblance of pre-Greek place names and place names of Asia Minor and Greece was first observed by P. Kretschmer. For some of the examples cf. *Glotta* 28 (1940) 250 ff. Kretschmer's most recent views on the stratification of pre-Greek languages appear in *Glotta* 28 (1940) 275; 30 (1943) 84 ff.; 152, 31 (1948) 1 ff. and 126. For the region of Lydia, the following sequence is proposed by Kretschmer: 1. The earliest (?) linguistic stratum is "South Anatolian." Its carriers, called Leleges by Greek writers, were responsible for the Early Helladic and the Early Cycladic cultures. They inhabited the entire West coast of Asia Minor as well as Chios and Samos. They were related to the speakers of Proto-Hattic.

2. A migration from the North of the Balkans brought the speakers of the "Proto-Indoeuropean" or "Pelasgo-Tyrrhenian" languages to Asia Minor. They should be associated with the archaeological material of *Bandkeramik* cultures. They reached Lydia in the late third millennium.

3. The Indo-European Luvians entered the region in the early second millennium.

4. The historic Lydians arrived after 1200 B.C., at the same time as the Phrygians, Mysians, and Carians, and invaded Lydia from the east.

Kretschmer's articles demonstrate the great range and complexity of linguistic evidence. They also illustrate the difficulty of correlating controversial theses of linguistic scholarship with equally controversial theories of archaeologists. We need more detailed and systematic exploration of sites with "pre-Greek" names, with a correlated linguistic and archaeological map of Asia Minor as the objective. Cf. the attempt of Haley and Blegen, *AJA* 32 (1928) 141 ff., to devise such a map for Greece.

Sardis may well belong to the Bronze Age. They were found in three different areas of the excavations.

A complete vase (fig. 2) was found by T. L. Shear[37] on May 4, 1922, "on the South Slope of Ahmet's Hill, in the third Wady (ravine) behind the location of the pot of gold, three meters below surface." The "third Wady" is the third torrent bed to the north of the Temple

Fig. 2. Prehistoric Vase from Sardis

of Artemis which is shown as the second dotted line north of the excavation on the map in *Sardis* I, pl. 1. The location of the "pot of gold" with thirty staters of Croesus was on the north side of the same Wady, cf. Shear, *AJA* 26 (1922) 396 ff., fig. 6. The prehistoric vase (Inv. No. 0-247, P. 66) is described in Shear's notes as follow: "one-handled pot of coarse purplish clay, burned black on the outside. H. 10.3 cm, maximum diameter, 11.7 cm; diameter at rim, 7.3 cm." The drawing indicates that the handle was broken off.

Somewhat similar shapes occur at Troy (VI-VII b), Alishar, and Gordion.[38] Without a knowledge of the original, we cannot be too certain about its date. Small vases of crude black-burned clay occurred even in historical Lydian context.[39]

A number of prehistoric sherds were found below the archaic basis of the Temple of Artemis. "In the deep excavation below the basis,

37. The late Professor Shear generously gave me permission to use his notes and his drawing of the vase.

38. For example, Schliemann, H., *Ilios*, no. 1469. Schmidt, H., in E. Dörpfeld, *Troja und Ilion* 1, 301, Beil. 41, 1 and 44, 3. *Alishar* 3, fig. 51 (grey kitchen ware). Körte, G., *Gordion*, 1904, 65, nos. 25 f., p. 122, fig. 108.

39. Pithos and small vase of black-burned clay were found at a depth of 2 metres, west of the location of the pot of gold, with Lydian sherds. Shear, T. L., *AJA* 26 (1922) 400.

carried on by means of trenches over three metres deep layers of sand and gravel *mixed with small pieces of very ancient pottery*, and a few fragments of bone including a camel's tooth constituted the upper strata, and sand and gravel the lower on the level of the river."[40] Some of these fragments from the basis are reproduced in pl. 5 and fig. 3.

Coarse Ware:

a: Pl. 5, b, 2 ("Base a"), fig. 3 a. Piece from a bowl with rounded base. Handmade. L. 5.3 cm., H. 1.8 cm. Th. 0.04 cm. Clay light tan to pink. Many small mica particles. Heavy grit, with quartz, small pebbles, sand. Outside black, exterior and interior unsurfaced. Two incised lines (visible in the photograph) on the inside.

b: Pl. 5, b, 1 ("Base b"), fig. 3 b. Somewhat less coarse than a. Handle and Rim of a Jar? L. From rim to break of handle 6.4 cm., W. of handle 4.3 cm., L. of rim preserved 7.5 cm., Th. 0.07 cm., diameter at rim, c. 5.5.—6.0 cm. Clay brownish red to grey. Medium concentration of heavy grit with white crystalline particle. Exterior brown to black. Interior wet-smoothed. Rim perhaps wheeled. Stick traces on handle. 40% of the core underfired.

c: Pl. 5, b, 4 ("Base c"), fig. 3 c. Fragment of a slightly curving vase with the lowest part of a flat hand-handle. On the handle a shallow cavity suggestive of a thumb mark. L. 11 cm. W. of handle 5 cm. Th. of wall 0.5-0.6 cm. Clay, texture, firing like fragment "b" except that the core of "c" is black. In the profile drawing fig. 3 c, this fragment is interpreted as part of a jar, but R. J. Braidwood suggests that the fragment might come from a shallow bowl with three spreading feet. In this case the drawing should be turned ninety degrees.

Fragments "b" and "c" are certainly of the same ware and perhaps from the same vase. The two handle fragments might be the upper and lower part of the same handle.

Very Coarse Ware:

To the fragments of plain wares found below the base must be added a fragment of which the location is not definitely known.

Inv. P. 1, Pl. 6, b, A, fig. 4 a. This fragment seems to have belonged to a rather steep-walled large cooking pot with angular shoulder and a short vertical curved bandhandle, which is surmounted by a knob. H. 9.7 cm. W. 10. cm. Th. of wall, 1.1-1.3 cm. W. of handle 3.2 cm. Handmade. Micaceous clay varying from tan to grey and burned black on the outside. There is almost less clay than grit, as the vase consists of pebbles and small stones held together by clay. Exterior has been summarily treated; some finger marks and stick-marks are visible. Surface is blackened (by smoke?). Interior appears more even (wet-smoothed?).

Technically, this is the most primitive piece known from Sardis.

Grey Ware, Wheel-Made, Plain:

e: Pl. 5, b, 3 ("Base e"), fig. 3 e. Part of bottom and wall of medium-deep bowl with flat base. L. 10.5 cm. H. 4.1 cm. Dm of base ca. 15 cm. Th. of wall 0.6 cm. Clay buff to grey, levigated, micaceous. Very little grit.

---

40. Butler, *Sardis* 1, 76. Chase, G. H., *AJA* 18, 437 f. Butler, *ibid.*, 428, speaks of plain black and grey wares as coming from the same stratum as painted Geometric. For other sherds of this kind cf. *Sardis* 1, 148, "pottery of very great age" discovered in excavating the foundations of the archaic temple. For the archaic sandstone basis, apparently of the time of Croesus, cf. Butler, *Sardis* 2, 23 ff., 77 ff., and p. 101, where Butler says that no remnants of older structures were found, although numerous deep pits have been sunk below the foundations of the present building. Apparently no attempt was made to dig under the so-called Lydian building, which is probably the altar of the Croesan temple. Cf. Butler, *Sardis* 2, 4 f., E. Buschor and Schleif, *AM* 58 (1933) 207.

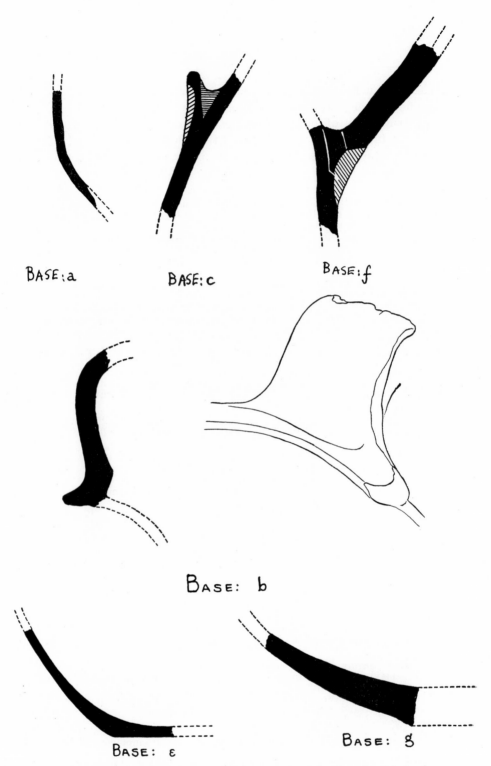

BASE: a   BASE: c   BASE: f

BASE: b

BASE: e   BASE: g

Fig. 3. Sherds from below the Archaic Basis of the Temple of Artemis

Pockmarked with "bubbles" perhaps due to disintegration of limestone particles. Fairly even fired. Exterior wet-smoothed, interior slightly "ribbed," clear wheel-marks.

Grey Ware, Wheel-Made Burnished:

f: Pl. 5, b, 6 ("Base f"), fig. 3 f. Slightly curving ribbon handle with adjoining piece of slightly curving wall. Deep "hollow" on the lower outer part of handle near juncture with wall. L. of handle 9.5 cm. W. of handle 4.4 cm. Th. of handle 1.3 cm. Th. of wall 0.7 cm. Clay pink to grey, fairly large particles of mica and grey impurities. Hard fired, metallic feel. Both surfaces slipped and burnished. As shown in drawing, the piece seems to belong to a jar with vertical band handle, but wheel-marks on the inner surface run as if the piece were from a lid with a large curving horizontal handle.

g: Pl. 5, b, 5 ("Base g"), fig. 3 g. Lower part of a shallow thick-walled bowl, possibly with ring or disk-base. W. 8.5 cm. Th. of wall at top 0.9, at bottom 1.5 cm. Clay micaceous, slightly reddish to even grey. Burnished on both sides; interior cross burnished, exterior burnished horizontally.

To these fragments of grey-burnished ware must be added a fragment of which the location is not definitely known.

Inv. X-1, Pl. 6, b, B, fig. 4 b. Part of wall curving outward from a vertical band handle, of which the upper part is preserved. The vase seems to have had a flattened rim; a bit of the rim is preserved on the inside. Perhaps from a goblet resembling those of Troy II-V. H. 9 cm. W. of handle 4 cm. Th. of wall 0.7 cm. approximate diameter at lower part of fragment 15-17 cm. Clay levigated. In cross-section it appears stratified in three layers, the outer layers black, the core light grey with light brown edges. Little grit, small limestone fragments, numerous "bubbles" (airpockets). Interior and exterior surfaces dark grey, burnished horizontally.

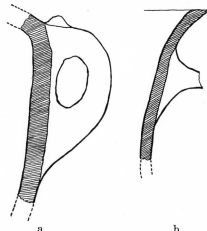

a   b

Fig. 4. Sherds from Sardis.

According to G. H. Chase, several other techniques could be distinguished among the fragments of grey to black vases which were found around and under the base. It should be noted that "from the base" is not necessarily the same as "under the base"; fragments from the former location may be in part contemporary with painted Lydian wares, which were found in the excavation of the same area.

According to Chase's notes the following varieties were represented:

"1. Coarse black clay, containing particles of quartz and other small stones. Surface smoothed but not polished.

2. Coarse buff clay containing particles of quartz and other small stones. Covered with slip of coarse black clay. Surface smoothed.

3. Coarse red and black clay in layers, black at center, then red on each side, covered with slip of coarse black clay. Surface smoothed.

4. Very coarse brown/black clay, containing pieces of quartz and other small stones. Surface smoothed but not polished.

1-3 are similar in clay slip, 4 is similar to 1 in texture of surface but not in color.

5. Close grained, light grey clay, surface smoothed but unpolished.

6. Same as 5, but with surface carefully polished.

7. Same as 5, but with slip of finer clay, carefully polished and ranging in color from light to dark grey.

8. There are also two specimens which are painted with black glaze. One has close-grained grey clay, the other reddish buff clay, with slip of fine-grained grey clay."

It will be seen that Techniques 1-4 correspond to the Coarse Wares and Techniques 5-7 to the Grey wares of the fragments described above. We are thus certain that two major types of "prehistoric" pottery occurred in the deepest stratum uncovered in the Temple Precinct. Information on shapes is not too extensive: large cooking pots, large and medium sized bowls, and possibly goblets with one or two vertical band handles were used.

Strictly speaking, the record of the excavation in and under the base proves only that these wares were in use before the construction of the archaic temple about the middle of the sixth century B.C. Additional indications for their dating are provided by the only part of the excavation which yielded a regular stratified sequence. This sequence was observed in the extension made in 1914 from the main excavation area uphill into the first Wady.[41] The following Table has been reconstructed on the basis of Butler's and Chase's accounts.[42]

---

41. Butler, *Sardis* 1, 150 ff., 167, 169, 171, and map III. *Id.*, *AJA* 18 (1914) 427 ff. This extension of the main excavation is seen in the upper right corner of Map III, marked "Level 108." It appears as the upper left extension of the excavation in the photograph *Sardis* 1, fig. 171. Shear, T. L., *AJA* 26 (1922) 400 f., also remarked on the clear character of the stratification and noted that in 1922 "at a depth of 1.40 m below the Graeco-Roman deposit Lydian wares of very early appearance were brought to light, the best preserved vase being of the cylix shape with an incised line about the circumference of the bowl." To this day, it is one of the few places on the site where sherds can be found easily.

42. Butler, *Sardis* 1, 151 f. Chase, G. H., *AJA* 18 (1914) 346 f. I omit the actual levels from the table. They are given by Butler as follows: Lydian, upper limit, 6.00. From Lydian, lower limit to first Geometric level, 1.30, first Geometric level to second Geometric level 1.00 plus. Chase distinguishes three Geometric levels, the first ca. 1.60 m. below the Lydian, the second ca. 1.80 below the Lydian, the third ca. 2.20 below the seventh century Lydian. This is, of course, the same level as Butler's second Geometric, at a depth of 2.30 below the historic Lydian. Only Butler mentions the trial pits dug to ca. 1 m. below the lowest Geometric level, but Dr. Chase confirms that they existed and were dug in the very last days of the campaign.

DATE	POTTERY
Roman	
Hellenistic	
Lydian VII-VI (?)	Lydian Wares. Found ca. 6.00 m below surface.
Lydian Geometric	a. "Streaked" scyphi. Yellow-white slip Geometric.
	b. Black and grey wares. Matt-black on orange Geometric. Increased yellow-white slip Geometric.
	c. Black and grey wares. Matt-black on orange Geometric. Few coarse yellow-white slip sherds.
Prehistoric	Coarse red, black, grey wares found in trial pits made at the end of the 1914 campaign, c. 0.60-1.00 m below the Geometric levels.

An approximate date for the early phase of the historic Lydian wares is provided by the Horsemen Vase published in *AJA* 49 (1945) 570 ff. which may be dated ca. 650-625 B.C.[43] It is not improbable that this phase distinguished by great productivity and foreign contacts corresponds to the rise of the dynasty of the Mermnads (687 B.C.).

The duration of the Lydian Geometric is a matter of guess-work. On stylistic grounds, we can distinguish an earlier phase which is untouched by Greek influence, and a later phase in which such influence is clearly present. Since the earliest Greek fragments found in Sardis are still Geometric and not later than 700 B.C., we cannot place the beginning of Lydian Geometric wares later than 750 B.C. It is, however, quite possible that they began much earlier.

The stratification at Sardis proves that "Prehistoric" monochrome wares definitely preceded the painted Geometric wares.[44] On the other hand, the separating layer was relatively shallow. We may, therefore, conclude that the monochrome wares of the Stratified Trench and the fragments found under the base in the Temple of

---

43. The vase apparently came from the level described as "seventh century Lydian level" by Chase. To the statement quoted in *AJA* 49 (1945) 581, add Butler, *Sardis* 1, 153, where he states that the horseman vase was found in one of the deeper levels in the eastern end of the trench together with a large jug in jet black clay without lip but with curling handle. The only other identifiable vase from that level is the scyphus adorned with a frieze of gazelles, probably the one in the Metropolitan Museum 16.75.12. (imitation of Rhodian).

44. Butler, *Sardis* 1, p. 152, "pits dug below the lowest level of the trench were yielding small bits of red, grey, and black pottery, apparently hand-made." Cf. above n. 42.

Artemis represent the culture immediately preceding that of the Lydian Geometric wares.

It is a general feature of the Early Iron (and Late Bronze) Age in Asia Minor that monochrome wares are succeeded by Geometric painted pottery.[45] In the Hermus estuary to the west of Sardis, Greek Geometric wares replace "native" monochrome cultures at Larisa on the Hermus and at Old Smyrna[46] without any intervening phase of native Geometric wares. On the plateau, to the east of Sardis, painted "Phrygian," or, more cautiously, "Post-Hittite" wares are found from Gordion all the way into South Eastern Anatolia.[47] In these sites, too, an earlier phase of predominantly monochrome wares is succeeded by painted wares definitely native in character, although elements of Hittite derivation, elements pointing toward the region of Van and Northwestern Iran, and elements derived from the "Cypriote" pottery of Cilicia and North Syria contributed to the formation of this style.[48] Despite the excellent work done on many Phrygian sites, the

---

45. Cf. Bittel, *ABB* 1935, Phil.hist.Kl. no. 1, 12 ff. *Id., Kleinasiat. Studien,* 110, where Bittel contends that the same change may be observed in all border regions of the Eastern Mediterranean. Also, *Grundzuege,* 69, 71. Hanfmann, *AJA* 52 (1948) 148 ff., with bibliography. T. Özgüç, *Ausgrabungen in Karahöyük* (Turk Tarih Kurumu Yayinlarindan Ser. V., No. 7, Ankara), 72 ff.

46. Schefold, K., *Larisa am Hermos* 3, 1942, 5 f., 58 ff., 192 f. Cook, J. M., *JHS* 67 (1947) 42. Cook mentions for Old Smyrna Protogeometric pottery in conjunction with the burnt levels which represent the end of the local monochrome culture. He seems to date some of the Greek sherds in the ninth century B.C. On the general problem of the dates of Greek colonies in Ionia cf. Hanfmann, *AJA* 49 (1945) 580 f. and 52 (1948) 144 ff. Cook, J. M., *JHS* 66 (1946) 67ff., on the dating of Proto-Geometric, Desborough, V., *BSA* 43 (1948) 264 ff.

47. Bittel, *Kleinasiat. Studien,* 109 ff. *Grundzuege,* 71 f. "the painted Geometric style develops east of the Sangarios." Hanfmann, *AJA* 52 (1948) 149 f. Add Koşay, H. Z., *Ausgrabungen von Alaca Hüyük,* (Veroeffentlichungen der Türkischen Geschichtskommission, V. Series, No. 2a), p. 1, pl. 3, and Özgüç, T., *op.cit.* who points out that painted pottery is common only in the two upper strata of Karahöyük (Elbistan Plain) but is not represented in the two earlier levels of the Post-Hittite period. At Karahöyük it never exceeds 10% of the pottery found. He suggests that the monochrome phase should be dated from the late second millennium to the late eighth century B.C. He seems to assume, however, that there was an earlier phase of "Phrygian" painted pottery which is not sufficiently represented at Karahöyük. The Phrygian vase imported to Karkhemish (Woolley, L., *LAAA* 26 [1939-40] 17 ff., pl. 12 c) and apparently dated in the ninth century suggests that "Phrygian" painted wares can hardly have begun later than 800 B.C. Cf. *AJA* 52 (1948) 150, n. 69. For the eastward extension of the Phrygians cf. the Phrygian signs found at Hama, Riis, P. J., *Hama, Les Cimitières,* 202 f.

48. The Hittite component has been emphasized by Bittel. On connections with Van cf. Özgüç, *op. cit.,* 83. On the inter-relations of Cypriote pottery with those of Syria and Cilicia cf. the detailed investigations by Gjerstad, E., *The Swedish Expedition* IV, 2, pp. 242 ff., with map fig. 53, and conclusions 311 ff, 434 ff, e.g., p. 446: "from Cilician harbours . . . . Cypriote goods were distributed inland . . . . as far as *Alişar Hüyük."* Gjerstad assumes that Cypriote trading "factories" existed in the Amuq plain and in Tarsus. Cf. also Riis, *op.cit.,* 110 ff., 203 f. Hancar, *AFO* 1944, and Stewart, J., *Handbook Nicholson Museum*₂, 95 ff. on parallelism of Anatolia, North Syria, Tepe Sialk B.

beginning of the painted pottery in Phrygia and Eastern Anatolia cannot be dated with any certainty. In contrast to my earlier opinion, I am inclined to believe now that the appearance of painted pottery in Central Anatolia (e.g. Gordion, Boghazköy, Alishar) took place not later than 800 B.C. and that an even earlier formative phase should perhaps be assumed for the Eastern area of Late Hittite states, a phase which would be analogous to the first phase of late Hittite sculpture successfully defined by E. Akurgal.[49]

The sources of Lydian painted Geometric are not too easily determined. A closer study of painted Iron Age wares of Asia Minor shows that the Sardian vases have a strong regional character of their own, and similarities to Phrygian wares are much less marked than photographs or reproductions might lead one to believe. There is also present in their decorative vocabulary an Aegean component. I should hesitate, however, to derive these "Aegean" elements directly from the Cypro-Cilician or from Greek Geometric wares. Perhaps these influences came to Lydia through some intermediary school located in Southwest Asia Minor and as yet undetermined. On the other hand, some connections with the plateau cannot be denied. Other changes in Lydian culture point in this direction and there are literary references to the Phrygian domination of this area.[50] On the whole, I am inclined to believe that some kind of cultural change was associated with the rise of the painted pottery in Lydia.

The prehistoric vases of Sardis, then, would represent an earlier Western Anatolian culture of the Late Bronze Age. Here, as at Larisa and Old Smyrna, this native culture may well have spanned all of the second millennium as well as the early part of the first. Particularly the grey wares appear to be a characteristic manifestation of the regions along the west coast of Asia Minor.[51]

This tentative conlusion may not sound impressive, yet it has significant implications for the history of Lydia. Various theories have been advanced concerning the culture of that region during the Bronze Age. The first theory postulated that Lydia came within the

---

49. Akurgal, E., *Spaethethitische Bildkunst*, 139 ff.

50. Cf. Bittel, *Grundzuege*, 62 ff. Cf. Strabo XII, 4, 6 (565) and XII, 8, 3 (572).

51. The fragments from Sardis reminded J. Sperling of Troy VII and VIII, while R. J. Braidwood recalled some of the wares in Boghazköy and North Syria of the period from 1500-1200 B.C. Cf. Lamb, W., *JHS* 52 (1932) 1 ff. Concerning Troy, Dr. C. Boulter remarks in a letter: "The Trojans of Troy VIII were still making that grey ware which had been the principal feature of their répertoire for a thousand years." For grey ware at Old Smyrna, cf. Cook J. M., *JHS* 67 (1947) 42. It should perhaps be noted that at Sardis the grey ware and other monochrome native techniques continued into the historical Lydian phase, but on a reduced scale.

orbit of the Mycenaean settlers who colonized the Ionian coast.[52] As
I have stated before, no Mycenaean or Sub-Mycenaean objects have
been found in Sardis.[53] The term "Sub-Mykenaian" was used in the
early reports to indicate that some patterns of early Lydian Geometric
wares showed a general resemblance to Proto-Geometric decorative
vocabulary, but it was never intended to be taken as a reference to
any actual Mycenaean objects. A second theory proposed by Dussaud
attempted to reconstruct a highly civilized Lydian culture distinguished by close relations to Mesopotamia. Dussaud's book remains
remarkable for the mastery of historical material found in Classical
authors, of results of Near Eastern philological material, and of
purely archaeological data; however, the intensive research in all
these fields during the past twenty years has failed to produce material substantiating his theories.[54] There is more substance to the
third theory according to which the Hittites may have extended their
influence into Lydia. Rock-cut reliefs and inscriptions of the time of
the Hittite Empire have been found at Karabel and on Mount Sipylus.[55] They have been interpreted as indications of the existence of
outposts designed to guard important roads, or as triumphal monuments for victorious campaigns.[56] Although the majority of scholars
regard them as monuments of Hittite Kings, it is perhaps too early
to rule out the possibility that they might be monuments of local
Kings or princes. In any case, they do not prove any continuous occupation of Lydia by the Hittite Kings. Significantly, genuine Hittite pottery does not seem to occur in regions to the west of a line
running from Bolvadin (between Afyon Karahissar and Akşehir)
to Kusura.[57] The scattered metal objects found between the plateau
and the West coast are mostly of uncertain origin and are in any case

52. The most recent treatment is by Bittel, *Grundzuege*, 55 ff. and map 5.
Bittel is inclined to assume Mycenaean colonies for Miletus, Colophon, and
Caria; to place the Akkhiawa State in Ionia and Caria (as well as on Samos
and Rhodes), and to assume contact between Mycenaeans and Hittites some-
were in Lydia.
53. *AJA* 49 (1945) 579 and 52 (1948) 153.
54. Dussaud, P., *La Lydie et ses voisins aux hautes époques*, 1930. Dussaud's
"Proto-Lydian seals," pp. 43 ff., are a very uncertain matter as is the seal
Bossert, *Alt-Anatolien*, 64, figs. 679 f. allegedly from Lydia. His attempt to
claim these seals for Lydia is rejected by Goetze, *Kleinasien*, 63, n. 9. H. Frank-
fort, *Cylinder Seals*, pl. 41 h, places one of them in his First Syrian group. Dr.
E. Porada writes that in her opinion Dussaud's Proto-Lydian seals show more
affinity with Mitanni than with anything Anatolian. She dates them in the
fifteenth century B.C.
55. Goetze, *op.cit.*, p. 165 and map. Bossert, *Alt Anatolien*, p. 58, figs. 557-562.
I. Gelb, *Hittite Hieroglyphic Monuments*, (Oriental Institute Publications XLV,
1939), pp. 15, 19, pl.
56. Bittel, *AFO* 13 (1940) 193 suggested that the reliefs might commemorate
the invasion of Assuwa by the Hittite King Tudhaliya IV (c. 1260-1230 B.C.).
57. Bittel, *op.cit.*, 192 f.

unreliable witnesses.[58] It is perhaps worth noting that a bronze bull from the Tmolus appears to resemble products of Late Hittite states.[59]

The theory which would best accord with archaeological data may be described as a "native" theory. It would seek to show that Lydia corresponded at least in part to the country Assuwa mentioned in the Hittite archives of the second millennium—hence the occurrence of the name Asia for a part of historic Lydia in late times.[60] A substantial part of population of the second millennium would have survived to form the historical Kingdom of Lydia.[61] We may picture this region in the Bronze Age as the habitat of mountaineers still substantially in the village rather than in the urban stage, strong in war and capable of keeping the Hittite Kings at bay, yet relatively uninfluenced by commerce and trade either from the coast or from the Hittite interior.

If this theory be correct, the final question to be answered concerns the end of this Prehistoric Lydian culture and the impact of the so-called Age of Migrations (1200-800 B.C.) upon Lydia and Sardis. Here again a number of linguistic and historical data pose problems which cannot yet be satisfactorily solved. The suggestion has been made that Sardians were involved in the great migrations to the extent of participating in the late thirteenth century in the famous raids upon Egypt.[62] The suggestion rests upon the interpretation of Sardana as Sardians rather than Sardinians. I see, however, in the representations of the Sardana considerable resemblance with Sardinians and none with Sardians.[63]

58. Metal objects were still precious at that stage and likely to travel widely. For finds in the region cf. Przeworski, S., *Die Metallindustrie Anatoliens* (Intern.Archiv fuer Ethnographie, Suppl. Vol.) Leiden, 1939, pp. 67 f. on alleged early fibulae from Ephesos, c. 1000 B.C., and *ESA* 10 (1936) 82 ff. A *Griffzungenschwert* of the Late Bronze Age was found in the excavations of the Roman Agora in Izmir. Bittel, *AA* 55 (1943) 202 f., fig. 3.

59. Cf. Przeworski, *op.cit.*, 119 f., fig. 36, who compared a statue from the region of Ankara in the Louvre. Cf. Bossert, *op.cit.*, fig. 610, from Karkhemish.

60. Radet, *La Lydie*, 68. Bossert, H. Th., *Asia* 1946. Cf. Herodotus IV, 45; a phyle of Sardis was called *Asias*.

61. Goetze, *Kleinasien*, 11, 49 ff., 193 ff. For Kretschmer's views cf. *supra* note 36. Bittel, *Grundzuege*, 81, says that Lydians are not immigrants of the migration period but "altkleinasiatisch."

62. Schachermeyr, F., *Etruskische Fruehgeschichte*, 75. Bonfante, G., *AJA* 50 (1946) 261.

63. Breasted, J. H., *A History of Egypt*, 467, 477 f., fig. 173. The horned helmets are a very conspicuous feature of Sardinian armor, but so far as I know not represented in the archaeological material from Asia Minor. The entire character of Sardinian culture appears to me to be Western Mediterranean and the contacts with the Mycenaean world, with Cyprus, and with Syria seem to fall in the period of migrations from ca. 1200- ca. 700 B.C. Cf. Ducati, P., *Italia antica*, 44 ff. Porro, *Atene e Roma* 18 (1915) 145 ff. Taramelli, U., *MonAnt*

The alleged emigration of the Etruscans from Lydia to Italy receives more support from linguistics and general historical considerations than from the archaeological material found in Lydia.[64] Future explorers may, however, keep in mind that this emigration must have taken place before 750 B.C. and may well have occurred during the "Prehistoric" phase of Lydian culture.

The arrival of the Heraclidae in Lydia is dated traditionally about 1192 B.C. This event is often interpreted as the arrival of foreign invaders, who ruled Lydia until they were ousted by the Mermnads. The Mermnads appear to have names related to names of the second millennium[65] and their rise might indicate the resurgence of "native" elements in Lydia.

Another problem is posed by the notice that Sardis was founded "after the Trojan wars" and the fact that *Hyde* mentioned by Homer was thought by ancient commentators to be another (native?) name for Sardis.[66]

Finally, there is the famous problem of the Maeonians, who are located by Homer on the Hermus[67] and near the Gygaean Lake, in the region of Sardis. Homer does not mention Lydia or Lydians. If the Lydian language goes back to the second millennium, and if Lydians are "People" (*ludva*)[68], the Maeonians might have been invaders who ruled the region under the dynasty of "the Sons of Heracles." It would not be implausible to suppose them to be Phrygians or relatives

---

24 (1931) *Id., Guida Cagliari and Studi Etruschi* III, 43 ff. Mueller, V., *AJA* 36 (1932) 9 ff. Taramelli, *Bull.paletn.ital.* 1933, 111 ff.

64. Schachermeyr, *op.cit.*, 103 ff. Hanfmann, *Journ.Amer.Soc.Archit.Hist.* 2 (1942) 7 ff. and *AJA* 47 (1943) 94 ff. Pallottino, M., *L'Origine degli Etruschi,* Rome, 1947, considers the different aspects of the evidence. He argues that the character of the Etruscan language presupposes the arrival of Etruscans in Italy in the third or second millennium B.C. At the opposite end, Akerström, A., *Der geometrische Stil in Italien,* 1943, puts the arrival of the Etruscans at ca. 675 B.C. *AJA* 53 (1949) 222 f. For the linguistic evidence cf. Kretschmer's articles quoted in n. 36, above, and the review of the major theories by Pallottino, *op.cit.*, 57 ff.

65. On the date cf. Dussaud, *op.cit.*, 15. Hogarth, D. G., *CAH* 3, pp. 501 ff. prefers 1185 B.C. There is also a story that Heracles took the double axe from the Queen of the Amazons and gave it to the legendary Lydian Queen Omphale. Plutarch, *Quaest.Graecae,* 45. Dussaud, *op. cit.*, 88 ff., with references. On the similarity of names (Maduwattash, Sadyattes) cf. *AJA* 52 (1948) 152, n. 81. Attention has also been called to the fact that King Kandaules had another ("native"?) name, Myrsilos, which compares with the Hittite Murshilish. Herodotus I, 7. Cf. n. 69, below.

66. Strabo XIII 4, 5 (625): "Sardis is a great city, and, though of later date than the Trojan times is nevertheless old." Cf. Bittel, *Kleinasiatische Forsch.*, 67. On Hyde cf. Strabo XIII, 4, 6 (626): "Some call Sardis Hyde, while others call its Acropolis Hyde." Cf. *RE, s.v. Hyde,* XVII, 1914, p. 43.

67. *AJA* 52 (1948) 151 f.

68. Bürchner, *RE, s.v. Lydia,* 2122.

of the Phrygians.[69] They might have constituted an upper class ruling
over a substantially "native" Lydian population.

These references, which cannot be taken as a very reliable tradition, seem to indicate changes in the twelfth century (Heraclidae,
"foundation" of Sardis) and possibly in the eighth or ninth century
B.C. (Phrygian domination, emigration of the Etruscans).

How do these indications given by the literary tradition compare
with the archaeological data? Excavations at Sardis give evidence
of several changes which may have connection with changes in population of Lydia.

1. Not later than the eighth century (800 B.C.?) the pottery
changes from West Anatolian monochrome to painted Lydian Geometric.

2. Not later than 700 B.C. rock-cut tombs make their appearance
and develop into chamber tombs with funerary benches.[70]

3. Not later than the seventh century B.C., royal and princely burials are made in *tumuli*, mounds containing burial chambers. The
huge (355 meters in diameter) mound which contained the tomb
of King Alyattes (605-560 B.C.) is probably a late example.[71] It is
not at all impossible that burial in mounds was already a Royal prerogative during the dynasty which preceded the *Mermnads*. Butler had
counted seventy-two mounds and had estimated the original number
of mounds in the cemetery of Bin Tepe as close to one hundred.[72] It
is doubtful that any of them were erected after the capture of Sardis

69. Bürchner, *RE*, s.v. *Sardis*, 2163, 2166. Strabo XIII, 1, 8 (586) says that
the plain of Thebes was colonized by Lydians then called Maeonians; XIII, 4, 11
(628) he reports that the Katakaumene is called also Maeonia. He also reports
an opinion that Lydians and Maeonians are somehow confused with Phrygians
and Mysians, XII, 3, 20 (550) and XII, 8, 3 (572). Strabo's critical discussion
of earlier Homeric scholars shows that they possessed practically no information on the Maeonians beyond the verses in Homer—at most the knowledge that
the regions mentioned above were called Maeonia.

The famous verse of Hipponax (fr. 1) indicates that the name Kandaules
was Maeonian, not Lydian as alleged e.g. by Mentz, A., *Glotta* 29 (1942) 152,
in a discussion of a Lydian god Kandaules. The verse says *Herme Kynankha
Meionisti Kandaula*. *Kandaules* has been interpreted as "Dog-Throttler," although others have preferred "son of Kanda" (e.g., Olmstead, A. T. E., *Anatolian Studies Presented to Sir W. M. Ramsay*, 192 ff.). At any rate, it is arguable
that the name Kandaules was Phrygian-Maeonian, while the King's other name
Myrsilos may have been traditional and derived from Lydian titles of the second
millennium B.C. On the use of double names in Asia Minor as an old "native"
custom cf. Sundwall, J., "Die einheimischen Namen der Lykier," *Klio*, Suppl.
11, 265 f.

70. This date seems to be indicated by the earliest vases found in the tombs.

71. Olfers, *ABB* 1858, 549 f., 556, pl. 5, 2 and description under pl. 5, 3. A
Protocorinthian lecythus with dot rosettes seems to date ca. 650-625 B.C., while
the other vases from the sepulchral chamber date ca. 600 B.C., cf. pl. 5, 1-9.
On the relief with does, allegedly from the tomb of Alyattes, cf. Barnett, R. D.,
JHS 68 (1948) 18, pl. 11, c.

72. Butler, *Sardis* 1, 9. Dennis estimated there were one hundred and thirty.

by the Persians in 547 B.C. Since a cemetery of such size presumably represents quite a number of generations, the earliest of the mounds may go back to the eighth century.[73]

Archaeological evidence thus provides no clues for any changes in Lydia during the twelfth century B.C., but does indicate a far-reaching transformation during the eighth century. The introduction of new burial rites for Kings and nobility and the appearance of an entirely new taste in pottery are certainly indicative of changes in social structure and commercial relations. Since the nearest parallels for mounds, funerary chambers, funerary benches[74] appear in the Phrygian sphere on the plateau, we may interpret these changes as resulting from an infiltration of Lydia by people coming from the interior. These archaeological data are not inconsistent with the theories concerning the domination of Lydia by the Phrygians or the Maeonians.

In concluding this sketch of Prehistoric Sardis, I should like to summarize the indications provided by our scant material. They must be regarded as working hypotheses to be tested by future explorers and excavators.

1. "Agricultural revolution" spread to the Hermus valley in conjunction with a village culture which may have resembled the Yortan culture of the third millennium B.C. These villagers had apparently established settlements at Sardis and on the Gygaean Lake. Future research in this region must also take into account the possibility of an earlier "Neolithic" phase.

2. In the Bronze Age, a native West Anatolian culture similar to those discovered at Larisa and Bayrakli appears to be attested at Sardis. It may have survived until ca. 800 B.C.

3. The carriers of this Bronze Age culture were probably the ancestors of the population who spoke Lydian in historical times.

4. In the eighth century B.C., newcomers from the plateau helped transform the native Lydian culture into a more highly organized

---

73. Bittel, *Kleinasiatische Studien*, 70 f., seems to think that some of the tumuli of Bin Tepe might be of the same period as the Carian tumuli of the Budrum peninsula which he dates in the eleventh century B.C. He has given a detailed survey of tumuli and rock-cut architecture of Asia Minor and other regions (Thrace, Scythia). In general, he takes the position that neither rock-cut architecture nor tumuli burials can be used to prove any foreign immigration, because they develop in the eighth century as a result of social and religious conditions and then spread as transferable cultural traits.

74. Bittel, *op.cit.*, 79 comments on the resemblance of funerary benches in the Phrygian tomb of Arslan Tash and the Lydian tombs.

society. The change may have come about as a result of a change in ruling houses or ruling classes.

A thorough survey of Prehistoric sites in Lydia and systematic excavation of the royal cemetery of Bin Tepe would go far toward solving the problems of Prehistoric Sardis.

ADDENDA

On Bayrakli, see now E. Akurgal, "Bayrakli, Erster Vorläufiger Bericht," *Zeitschrift Philos. Fakultät d. Univ. Ankara* 8 (1950) 52 ff., pl. 8. Akurgal discusses Prehistoric pottery of Bayrakli and mentions pottery of the third millennium found at Sertkaya near Manisa during a recent survey.

For the Maeonians and their possible participation in the events around 1200 B.C., cf. Albright, W. F., *AJA* 54 (1950) 168 ff. Goetze has suggested that the people Masa of Hittite and Egyptian documents may have been Maeonians. A ritual battle between men of Hatti and men of Masa is usually interpreted as commemorating an early phase of Hittite conquests in Asia Minor. Cf. Gaster, Th. H., *Thespis* (N. Y., 1950) 379. Bossert, *Altanatolien,* 42, fig. 384. On this theory, Maeonians (Masa, "who fight with weapons made of reeds" against bronze-armed Hittites) might be identified with the "native" element in the West Anatolian culture of the third and second millennium B. C. The Lydians, then, would be later invaders. However, neither the linguistic equation "Maeonians" = "Masa" nor the location of Masa in the geographical ambient of Lydia can be regarded as certain.

EGYPT AND THE AEGEAN

†John Devitt Stringfellow Pendlebury

This article was left in my keeping by my husband, John Pendlebury, before he went to Crete in 1940, and it represents his considered views up to the time of his departure. His reputation as an archaeologist is known and his fame as a soldier in Crete has been recorded by N. G. L. Hammond and T. J. Dunbabin.[1] I am sure that he would have been happy to offer this article—to which a few footnotes have been added—in honor of David Moore Robinson whom he first met at Olynthus in 1928.

Hilda Pendlebury

The contacts between Egypt and the Aegean, particularly during the Bronze Age, are of the greatest importance for the archaeology of the latter district. The results of a generation's excavations have given us a great deal of information about the civilization and the comparative, internal chronology of Crete, Greece, and the islands. But since we are so far unable to decipher such inscriptions as have come down to us, we must look elsewhere for our positive chronology in terms of years B. C., and, I would add in parenthesis, that even when we do decipher them we shall probably not have advanced much farther, for not one has the appearance of a historical document. It is, therefore, the more fortunate that from the earliest times some part of the Aegean at least was in touch with Egypt, a country on whose chronology all are now more or less agreed.

Our evidence may be divided into three classes. It may be direct; that is to say a Cretan vase found in Egypt, for the ancients were not, on the whole, in the habit of obtaining "antikas" as souvenirs[2] or of accepting such imports as oil in out of date containers. Unfortunately, however, our earliest pieces of evidence are in the shape of vases of hard stone, and these are the most dangerous things in the world on which to rely. They are practically indestructible and always useful. Three examples may show how they can be preserved out of their context. At Tell-el-Amarna a Middle Predynastic vase of porphyry was found in an Eighteenth Dynasty house; in St. Mark's in Venice today one of the ritual vessels is a syenite vase of late Predynastic date set in silver; in the Eski Museum at Constantinople is a

---

1. See *John Pendlebury in Crete*. Cambridge University Press 1948 (privately printed).
2. There is an apparent exception here in the scarabs of certain Egyptian kings, regarded as amulets of power, the manufacture of which continued for generations.

diorite bowl which had been mounted in bronze and used as a lamp in one of the mosques. Thus such vases are useless for dating the deposit in which they were found.

Secondly the evidence may be indirect; by this is meant the imitation of an Egyptian shape or pattern in Crete, or some obvious Cretan influence on Egyptian art. Such evidence is usually very good since people do not copy things which have ceased to exist. But again it is necessary to be quite certain that the objects in question cannot be due to any purely local development and we must also remember that peoples in a similar stage of culture often solve problems in exactly the same way and quite independently. Likenesses are great pitfalls, and he would be a rash man who would trace any connection between Neolithic Thessaly and modern Mexico, though the vase shapes and painted patterns are hard to distinguish.

Thirdly there is literary evidence; in this is included not only the mention of the other country in inscriptions but also representations of Cretans in Egyptian tombs or of Egyptians on Cretan objects.

Our first concern must be with Crete since that island was the first part of the Aegean to be in contact with Egypt. It is a mountainous country, split up by great blocks of hills, the White mountains, Mount Ida, and Dikte. Only the Eastern half concerns us since, until the Iron Age, the Western half—west of Mount Ida—was practically uninhabited, probably owing to the presence of virgin forests which prevented the advance of civilization; the various districts must have been practically independent of one another until there was some regularization of communications.

The landmarks, however, are good. The hill of Modhi shows the way to the harbors of the East coast; Dikte is visible soon after you leave the Southern Cyclades; Kophinos and Ida lead the traveller to the beaches of the fertile valley of the Messara, and Juktas, fantastically like the head of a recumbent man, shows the way to the harbor town of Knossos.[3]

The first inhabitants entered the island toward the end of the Late Stone Age. They came, it seems, from South West Anatolia[4] and were a sea-faring people, for they landed at various points on the island; but some terror, which we can no longer determine, drove them inland. You find regularly small miserable remains at one or two points on the coast, but the more flourishing settlements radiate inland from these. There are a few sherds at Zakros, but inland you find several settlements; there are a few sherds at Komo, but the immigrants

3. Pendlebury, *The Archaeology of Crete; An Introduction*, 1.
4. Evans, *Palace of Minos*, II, 4-5 and 268; Pendlebury, *op. cit.*, 42.

pushed forward at once into the Messara. Again from Amnisos and
Mallia settlements radiated up to the hills,[5] where the most usual place
of habitation was a cave.[6] Yet the largest of their settlements was
at Knossos where they were already building houses whose foundations were of stone,[7] covering a greater area than the later palace.[8]
Culturally their connections were Asiatic for there are sherds from
Megiddo[9] which are indistinguishable from Cretan fabrics. But direct
overseas connections were entirely with Egypt.

Numerous fragments of vases of hard stone have been found in
Cretan Neolithic strata, several of them apparently copied from vases
of Middle-Predynastic type found unstratified at Knossos.[10] These do
no more than indicate that Crete was inhabited at that period; but
there were also found fragments of late Predynastic vessels and even
of a protodynastic kohl pot and mace head.[11] And before the end of
the period in Crete appears a chalice-shaped vase whose nearest
parallels are the miniature copper vases from the tomb of Khasekhemui of the IInd Dynasty at Abydos.[12] We can therefore provisionally put down the end of the Neolithic period to somewhere in the
region of 3000 B. C.

The Early Minoan I period is better described as sub-Neolithic and
as far as one can see the population was increased by men of the same
Asiatic origin, who spread from the same parts.[13] But a new element
was entering southern Crete which predominated in that district
during the succeeding period; and this element was Libyan. It has
been suggested that the intrusion of this element was due to the disruption of the Libyan kingdom of the Western Delta. Originally this
disruption was associated with the first conquest by Menes, and so the
beginnings of Early Minoan I were pushed back some three hundred
years; but we have seen that Second Dynasty influence was visible
before the end of the Neolithic period, and it is far more probable that
the event with which we must connect the appearance of Libyan
features is the reconquest by Khasekhemui.[14] What the features were
must be described under E. M. II. It is sufficient to say that their
rudiments have already appeared. There is no direct evidence for this

5. Pendlebury, *op. cit.*, 35.
6. *BSA* 36, 23.
7. Evans, *P. of M.*, II, 18.
8. Pendlebury, *op. cit.*, 37.
9. Pendlebury, *op. cit.*, 42.
10. Pendlebury, *Aegyptiaca*, 21, nos. 22 and 23.
11. *Ibid.*, no. 24.
12. Pendlebury, *Archaeology of Crete*, 42.
13. *Ibid.*, 53.
14. *Ibid.*, 281.

period and for the date of its end we must depend on synchronisms for E. M. II which, as we shall see, seems to begin somewhere about the Fourth Dynasty.

In Early Minoan II the civilization of the Early Bronze Age in Crete attained its apex. Fine houses were built; the potter's art reached a very high standard, and the gold jewellery rivals even Twelfth Dynasty Egyptian work.[15] But our concern is with foreign relations.

In the south of Crete the universal custom of burial was communal interment in circular tombs built of stone.[16] These have been sometimes considered as beehive tombs, vaulted over like the famous tholoi, the Treasury of Atreus and others, at Mycenae. The fact, however, that they are built out in the open and are free standing implies that lateral pressure would be too great, and we are compelled to believe that they were either thatched over or not roofed at all. More interesting, though, is their resemblance to tombs in Eastern Libya, of somewhat uncertain date, explored by McIver and Wilkins. These were shaped like the circular Libyan huts, the mapalia as the Romans called them, and one might even liken them to Kaffir Kraals.

Besides these we find figurines of ivory and stone very like Predynastic figures found by Flinders Petrie at Nagada and generally recognized as Libyan.[17] Furthermore arrowheads of a Libyan type are found, and in the earliest representations of the human figure in Crete we can recognize two Libyan characteristics, locks flowing down on either side of the ear and arranged in curls over the forehead and the loin cloth with projecting cod-piece.[18]

Egypt itself was more closely connected with the Eastern end of the island. Among the amazingly rich contents of the tombs at Mochlos, a small island off the East end of the North coast, was a quantity of stone vases.[19] These were made locally of the most brilliant, variegated stones, many of the shapes resembling Egyptian examples, some of them admittedly Pre- and Proto-Dynastic, but the majority being imitations of Fourth to Sixth Dynasty vases. Early Minoan II is roughly parallel with Dynasties Four to Six.

Early Minoan III shows a distinct decline in almost every art, but a new feature suddenly makes its appearance, the engraving of seals. These come mainly from South Crete and are most frequently of ivory.

---

15. Evans, *P. of M.*, I, figs. 67, 68, 69.

16. Pendlebury, *Archaeology of Crete*, 64, fig. 8 and Pl. V. 2.

17. Evans, *P. of M.*, I, 84.

18. Evans, *P. of M.*, II, 34 ff.

19. Seager, R., *Mochlos;* Evans, *P. of M.*, I, fig. 58; Pendlebury, *Archaeology of Crete*, Pl. X, 3.

In many ways they resemble Egyptian seals of the First Intermediate period, i. e. Seventh to Eleventh Dynasties.[20]   Almost every linear design is common to the two areas as well as many of the figures of animals which form the handles of the signets.[21]

A further parallel is found in anthropomorphic vases of which very good examples were found at Rifeh[22] in Egypt, at Mochlos[23] and in the south of Crete. Unfortunately we still lack Minoan imports of this date in Egypt; but no doubt one day they will be found and provisionally we can equate E. M. III with the First Intermediate period.

Thus we have the following provisional dates for the Early Bronze Age. E. M. I: Sometime in the Second Dynasty to sometime in the Fourth; 3000-2800 B. C.

E. M. II: Fourth to Sixth Dynasties; 2800-2500 B. C.

E. M. III: First Intermediate Period; 2500-2200 B. C.

Now the thing which strikes a student of Aegean archaeology is this; we know we cannot get away from these synchronisms and the equations must stand: we know too that things moved very slowly in ancient times: but the dates are too high. We have not got the material to fill out 800 years; therefore we must consider very seriously Scharff's endeavor to bring down the date of Menes to about 3,000 B. C. and correspondingly to lower the other dates.[24]

With the Middle Minoan period a new age began in Crete. The center of power swung away from the East and was concentrated on the great sites of Knossos and Phaestos; at both these sites, as well as at Mallia, a little east of Knossos, great palaces were founded. At first these consisted, as far as we can see, merely of a number of isolated blocks built round a central court. Gradually, however, the barriers between them were broken down, the old alley ways roofed over and the blocks were linked up into a gigantic whole. This process took many centuries.[25] Knossos and Phaestos were like medieval cathedrals, old parts being replaced by, or incorporated into newer structures, and it will be best to leave them for the moment until the beginning of the Late Bronze Age when they reached their final form.

During the Middle Bronze Age we are fortunate, unlike the contemporary population, in that there occurred a number of violent earthquakes which sealed in deposits, at Knossos in particular, giving us a

---

20. Pendlebury, *ibid.*, 89 and note 5.

21. Pendlebury, *ibid.*, 88, fig. 12 and Matz, *Die Frühkretischen Siegel, passim.*

22. Evans, *P. of M.*, II, 257, fig. 152.

23. Evans, *P. of M.*, II, 258, fig. 153.

24. Scharff, *Journal of Egyptian Archaeology* 14, 275 and *Der Historische Abschnitt der Lehre für König Menikare*, 54.

25. Pendlebury, *A Handbook to the Palace at Knossos with Its Dependencies; with a foreword by Sir Arthur Evans*, London, 1933.

very clear series of strata which have enabled us on that site to divide each of the three main periods into sub-divisions "a" and "b." Yet at this point one word of warning is needed. Middle Minoan II is confined to Knossos and Phaestos; the rest of the island continues in the Middle Minoan I stage of culture until the beginning of Middle Minoan III. We must, therefore, not be surprised if we find Egyptian objects of precisely the same date in M. M. II strata at Knossos and in M. M. I strata elsewhere. For example Egyptian scarabs were found in Middle Minoan I votive deposits such as were still being made in the round tombs of South Crete,[26] which had by now fallen into disuse as burial places. Most of them are of Twelfth Dynasty date and one seal is perhaps Eleventh Dynasty. That these are contemporary imports from Egypt is practically proved by an amethyst scarab[27] of Twelfth Dynasty date found in the Diktaean Cave, the legendary birthplace of Zeus. The earliest deposit in this cave is Middle Minoan Ib and a Minoan artist has inscribed the scarab with a number of Middle Minoan hieroglyphs. Accordingly it may be said that Middle Minoan I begins about the Eleventh Dynasty, and in most parts of the island continues down at least into the Twelfth. In a Middle Minoan IIb stratum at Knossos there was found the lower part of a diorite statue of one "Ab-nub-mes-wazet-user, the deceased."[28] The date of it has been disputed. Hall maintained that so rococo a name was typical of the Thirteenth Dynasty; but Evers[29] has shown conclusively that the details of style, the throne, the method of cutting, etc., are typical of the early part of the Twelfth Dynasty, and he would confidently put it down to the reign of Amenemhat I. The object is interesting as being the only example of a personal possession found in the Aegean, and it can only mean that User or some member of his family actually came to Knossos. Scarabs and other objects could be bought as souvenirs by Minoan sailors but never a private statue.

Middle Minoan IIa pottery has been found at Haraga[30] in Egypt in a deposit of rubbish from the town built for the better class of men connected with the construction of the pyramid of Senusert II. A stele bearing the name of this Pharaoh was found in the deposit and the absence of any object bearing the names of his successors Senusert III and Amenemhat III, which are so common elsewhere, seems conclusive proof that the deposit did not extend into their reigns. A vase of a type transitional between M. M. IIa and M. M. IIb was found in a tomb at

26. Pendlebury, *Archaeology of Crete*, 121.
27. Evans, *P. of M.*, I, 199.
28. *Ibid.*, 18; Pendlebury, *Aegyptiaca*, 22, no. 29, Pl. II.
29. Evers, *Staat aus dem Stein*, II, 96.
30. Evans, *P. of M.*, II, 211 ff., 228; Pendlebury, *Archaeology of Crete*, 144.

Abydos[31] which besides objects of typical Twelfth Dynasty fabric contained cylinders of glazed steatite bearing the names of Senusert III and Amenemhat III.[32]

From the town of Lahun,[33] built for the workmen engaged on the pyramid of Senusert II, came a number of M. M. IIb sherds and it looks very much as if the change from M. M. IIa to M. M. IIb came somewhere in his reign though on the evidence of the Abydos tomb we might put it a little later, since Lahun was not immediately deserted though the rubbish heaps contained nothing of a date later than the Twelfth Dynasty.

We therefore provisionally make Middle Minoan I begin with the end of the First Intermediate period, say 2200 B. C., and go on right down to the end of the Twelfth Dynasty, or the beginning of the Thirteenth, except at Knossos where Middle Minoan IIa begins somewhere about 2000 B. C. and ends about 1875 B. C. or a little later, while Middle Minoan IIb carries on to some date between 1800 and 1750 B. C.

Middle Minoan III was a time of great prosperity in Crete and as usual in such times the art of vase painting lapsed. No doubt that accounts for the absence of M. M. III sherds abroad. At Knossos, however, in a M. M. IIIa deposit was found an alabaster lid inscribed with the name of Khyan,[34] the Hyksos Pharaoh, whose date is somewhere in the first half of the 17th century B. C. Great theories have been woven about this lid, which has been taken, in conjunction with a lion bearing Khyan's name found near Baghdad, and with his title "Embracer of Territories," to indicate a world empire. On such evidence I myself could claim that distinction, for undoubtedly relics bearing my name could be found in Egypt, Mesopotamia, and Greece, and I could even claim the Peloponnese, Macedonia, and several of the Greek islands. But it does show that intercourse with Egypt continued, as is further proved by alabaster vases of a second Intermediate shape found in a deposit of the same date at Isopata.[35]

Middle Minoan IIIb is connected less directly with Egypt, but equally surely. In the tomb of Queen Aahhotep, mother of Aahmes, the first king of the Eighteenth Dynasty, was found an axe blade decorated with a griffin.[36] The pattern on the wings of the griffin, the notched plume as it has been called, is found on the Miniature frescoes

---

31. Evans, *P. of M.*, I, 31, and Fig. 199a.
32. *Ibid.*, Pl. IV. Seltman, *CAH Plates* i, 104; Pendlebury, *op. cit.*, Pl. XXI, 2.
33. Evans, *P. of M.*, I, 266.
34. Evans, *P. of M.*, I, 18; Pendlebury, *Aegyptiaca*, 22 and Pl II.
35. Pendlebury, *Archaeology of Crete*, 172.
36. Evans, *P. of M.*, I, 548 f., fig. 402; Fimmen, *Die Kretisch-Mykenische Kultur*, 204, fig. 197.

at Knossos[37] and on two votive arrows[38] from the Temple Repositories which all date from M. M. IIIb.

We can, therefore, provisionally date M. M. IIIa from some time in the first half of the eighteenth century B.C. to about the middle of the seventeenth, and M. M. IIIb from then until about 1600 or 1500 B. C.

With the Late Minoan Period the power of Crete reached its height. The life of Crete was extremely peaceful, a fact well illustrated by the Late Minoan site of Gournia[39] in East Crete. It was built on a low knoll, close to the sea. There are no fortification walls and the houses cluster round the mansion of the lord of the manor which, with its tiny garden, lies on the hill top. It is one of the most fascinating sites in the world, and as you walk along the cobbled streets you are reminded of an English North country village with the steps leading up to the front doors.

But the most impressive building of the age was the great Palace at Knossos which in the Late Minoan period reached its final form as a gigantic rectangle of about 120 metres square. Its plan reflects its gradual growth, and one can see how it falls naturally into blocks which were once isolated, round the great central court. It has been so often and so fully described[40] that no more than a few brief points need here be made, but they are concerned with such things as might have surprised Egyptians as well as other ancient visitors to the Palace.

In the colonnade at the side of the North Entrance there has been placed the reproduction of a painted relief which once stood there. It represented a charging bull.[41] This magnificent relief stood for centuries after the destruction of the Palace still guarding the sea gate—and who shall say how much color it lent to the legend of the Minotaur, for without doubt the Palace was the original Labyrinth. At all events the Palace was evidently regarded as haunted and uncanny ground, for, although all round it later remains lie thick, in the Palace itself no later building was erected save one small shrine.

From the south corridor of the Palace one may still look toward the great trunk road which has been traced right across the island from the south coast. It skirts the low hill to the South of the Palace and runs below a building which was a kind of "Caravanserai"[42]

37. Evans, *P. of M.*, I, 550, fig. 401.
38. Evans, *P. of M.*, I, 548, fig. 399 a.
39. Pendlebury, *Archaeology of Crete*, Pl. V, 4; and Bossert, H. T., *The Art of Ancient Crete*, 25.
40. Evans, *P. of M. passim.*; Pendlebury, *Handbook to Palace at Knossos;* Bossert, *op. cit.*, 22 f.
41. Bossert, *op. cit.*, fig. 257.
42. Evans, *P. of M.*, II, 116 ff.

with a bathing pool and arrangements for the supply of hot water, and for stabling. It was then carried round the edge of the ravine, which lies between the southern hill and the Palace, on a viaduct, the massive piers of which with their stepped culverts let through the water from the springs above.[43] The road was then brought up under a great stepped portico to the South West porch of the Palace itself.

So elaborate a road, paved and guarded by stations[44] right across the island, implies considerable traffic to the south, and, of course, with Egypt and Libya. Indeed there is evidence of the employment by the Minoans of African mercenaries which figure on a contemporary fresco of a smart young Minoan subaltern leading a squad of Sudanese troops at the double.[45]

Egyptian imports into Crete during the Late Minoan I-II period are many, alabaster vases and scarabs forming the bulk. Most important of all is a circular seal bearing the name of Queen Ty, wife of Amenhotep III.[46] And now there occur a number of Minoan imitations of Egyptian objects, one of the most interesting of these being a pot in which not only the shape of an alabastron has been copied but the veins in the stone original have been represented in paint.[47] This vase is of Late Minoan Ia date. The idea caught on but very soon the wavy lines are formalized into regular chevrons.

On the Egyptian side too we begin to find monumental literary evidence in tombs at Thebes. Firstly in the tomb of Senmut, architect of Queen Hatshepsut, an unnamed folk, obviously Minoans, are bringing presents.[48] They bear metal vases of Late Minoan Ia shape. So do similar figures, called islanders, in the tomb of User Amen, vizier in the earlier part of Thothmes III's reign.[49] User Amen's nephew Rekhmire succeeded him in office and figures in his tomb are labelled "men of Keftiu and the Islands." Their contributions are of Late Minoan Ib date and their kilts are of the new Late Minoan Ib fashion.[50] On one figure the artist seems actually to have realized the change in fashion while doing the picture and has added a new flap to the old Late Minoan Ia type of loin cloth. Rekhmire's son Menkheperra Senb was High Priest of Amen at the end of Thothmes III's reign. There

43. Pendlebury, *Archaeology of Crete*, 184 and Pl. XXIX, 1.
44. Evans, *op. cit.*, 77-78.
45. Evans, *op. cit.*, 756 and Pl. XIII.
46. Evans, *P. of M.*, IV, 24, note 4; Paribeni, *Monumenti antichi*, 14, 735, fig. 33; Pendlebury, *Aegyptiaca*, Pl. I, 10.
47. Pendlebury, *Archaeology of Crete*, Pl. XXXIII, 1.
48. Bossert, *Art of Ancient Crete*, figs. 536-537.
49. Bossert, *op. cit.*, fig. 538.
50. Fimmen, *Die Kretisch-Mykenische Kultur*, p. 182, fig. 175.

again Late Minoan Ib vessels are brought by Keftians, including bull's head rhytons to which we have an exact parallel from Knossos.[51]

Among the Cretan vases of this period found in Egypt is one which is perhaps the most beautiful surviving vase they ever made. It is generally known as the "Marseilles" vase, an oinochoe in the Late Minoan Ib style of painting with marine decoration.[52] Unfortunately its exact provenience is unknown.

We are now in a position to consider the question of dates. Quite evidently the Late Minoan I period falls throughout the Eighteenth Dynasty and we may safely, from the tomb of Rekhmire, put the change from the end of Late Minoan Ia to Late Minoan Ib fairly early in the reign of Thothmes III, say about 1500 B. C.; and the end of L. M Ib sometime—certainly early, as we shall see—in the reign of Amenhotep III, about 1400 B. C. Parallel with the latter part of L. M Ib is the Knossian Palace style of pottery called Late Minoan II. It must be observed that this style of pottery is even more locally restricted than Middle Minoan II, being confined to Knossos only, while the rest of the island continues the L. M Ib style until the great and overwhelming disaster which caused a complete break before Late Minoan III.

At the end of the L. M Ib—L. M II period the power of Crete was suddenly destroyed. Knossos, Phaestos, Palaikastro, Mochlos, Agia Triada, Pseira, and all the other important towns went up in flames and ever after Crete was a backwater in the world.

Now this sudden destruction at the height of her power needs some explanation. It was certainly not an earthquake as has been suggested. There had been plenty of these before, which had wrecked the palaces, and these had only spurred the Minoans to fresh efforts. Besides, the first to go in an earthquake would have been the Great Staircase at Knossos, where five storeys were supported on wooden columns. Yet that staircase, we know, stood for a good two hundred years later. Nor was it the result of a mere raid of pirates. Scattered bands of "Vikings" could never have beaten a world power. Nor was it for the sake of colonization since no foreign influences appear in Late Minoan III. No, it must have been the result of a deliberate organization having the avowed object of destroying the political and economic power of Crete. And I think we can see why it happened. It is suffi-

---

51. Bossert, *ibid.*, figs. 541-544.

52. Bossert, *ibid.*, fig. 559. Cf. Robinson, *AJA* 54 (1950) 5 and note 27. On loan in the Metropolitan Museum is a similar LM oenochoe, almost a duplicate of one found at Pseira, said to come from Egypt, though it is difficult to prove it. Dinsmoor, in *PAPS* 87 (1943) 96, fig. 23, calls it "an importation from Crete about 1500 B. C."

cient to study the maps[53] of the sites in Crete and on the mainland where Egyptian objects of a date prior to the destruction of Crete have been found, comparing these with sites where objects made subsequent to the disaster occur. While only two sites in Crete provide one object apiece of a date subsequent to the disaster, on the mainland finds abound. Furthermore the earliest Egyptian objects found on the mainland in Late Helladic III times bear the names of Amenhotep III and Ty,[54] proving that it was in their reign that the disaster occurred.

Cretan exports to Egypt ceased completely but mainland vases literally flooded the Egyptian market. It does seem as though there occurred an organized expedition by the men of mainland Greece designed to break through a monopoly of the Egyptian trade held by Crete.

Bearing in mind all the evidence from archaeology and legend which can help us, I would present as a possible sequence of events the following theory.

During Late Minoan I-II Crete had what in practice amounted to an overseas empire. The mainland was completely Minoanized, and we remember the tradition that Minos tyrannized over the Saronic Gulf, the Argolid, Athens, and the Islands. The dreaded monster, the Minotaur, to which a yearly tribute of youths and maidens had to be sent, is surely a memory of the Bull-ring at Knossos, where athletes of both sexes played their part in the dangerous game of bull leaping, a game which seems to have partaken of the nature of a religious ceremony. What better method could be devised for keeping down the stock of the local vassals on the mainland than to do them the honor of selecting their best blood for it?

At the same time the Mainland dominions seem to have been debarred from the rich Egyptian trade, and we have perhaps an echo of their efforts to find another market in the legend of the Argonauts and their attempt to open up the Black Sea.[55] Yet these dominions were powerful and had perhaps gradually become largely independent. At all events they must have decided that Crete must go. No doubt the scandal of the yearly tribute of youths and maidens could be used to inflame the minds of some, but the ultimate reason was economic.

Now there is one man who is always associated, if not with the sack of Knossos, at least with the slaughter of the Minotaur and the rescue of the mainland from the tyranny of Minos, and that man is

---

53. Pendlebury, *Aegyptiaca;* Maps at end.
54. *Ephemeris*, 1887, 169; *ibid.*, 1891, 18; *ibid.*, 1888, 156; Pendlebury, *Archaeology of Crete*, 222, note 4.
55. Some authorities have, however, sought to date the Argonaut legend much later.

Theseus. According to legend, preserved in the yearly ceremony at Athens, he sailed in late April or early May. Observe that by a queer chance fate has preserved for us the time of year, though not the year itself, of the destruction of Knossos. On the Western facade of the Palace are the marks of fire where the great blazing beams fell during the final sack. The smoke from them was carried almost horizontally northwards by an extremely violent south wind. Now a south wind of such force is practically unknown in Crete except in late April or early May. The true tale we shall never know; perhaps it was written on some of those Amarna tablets which were pronounced forgeries and allowed to be ground to powder. Was there a great sea battle in the Roads of Candia? Was there treachery and the love of a King's daughter for the invader? Who can tell? But for the last scene of all we have the most dramatic room on any ancient site, the Throne Room at Knossos where Minos' throne still stands guarded by its painted griffins.[56] When it was excavated it was found in a complete state of confusion. Evidently some ceremony had been going on at the moment of the sack. A great oil jar lay overturned in a corner: ritual vessels lay scattered about. It looks as if Minos was hurried here when things became desperate and the press of spears was already in the Palace to undergo some last dreadful rite to save his people. Did he wear—as on occasion he seems to have done—a mask in the shape of a bull's head? Was it into this room that Theseus burst? Theseus and the Minotaur?

With the downfall of Crete direct intercourse with Egypt was confined to traffic between it and the mainland, where Egyptian imports became more usual, while at Gurob, Thebes and particularly at Tell-el-Amarna vases of Late Helladic III date are common. But at the same time the influence of Crete is not yet done. As far as can be seen the sack of the Cretan cities acted in much the same way as did the sack of Constantinople by the Turks; for hundreds of fine artists must have fled overseas, to Egypt. Here their ideas made such an impression on the young king Akhenaten as actually to revolutionize Egyptian art.

According to a fairly recent and probable theory the Minoans belong to a class of people, commoner in primitive times than today, known as "eidetics."[57] You know that when you look at a window and then look away suddenly at a blank wall you can still see the outline of the window. The "eidetic" however can call up at will such a picture. He can develop on a blank background an image latent in his mind, and, according to modern experiments, all he has to do is to draw

56. Bossert, *Art of Ancient Crete*, fig. 225.
57. Snijder, *Kretische Kunst*, 135 ff.

round the outline of what he sees. This theory would account for the extraordinarily subjective, individualistic nature of Cretan art, as exemplified, to take a single picture, by the fresco of a hunting cat from Agia Triada.[58]

Now Egyptian art had hitherto revealed the very opposite ideas. The artist translated his impressions into a form generally understood. He was objective and universalist. But suddenly, at Amarna, all this was abandoned and a purely Minoan outlook took its place. The Egyptians were not as a race liable to "eideticism" as were the Minoans: it is the kind of thing that seems to run by race, like some types of disease. But, whether Akhenaten was himself an "eidetic" or not, the frescoes from the North Palace[59] at Amarna show the new interest in nature with the almost photographic representation of birds and a desire to show the setting of the picture. But a tendency so foreign to the native art could not be anything but short-lived.

Meanwhile Egypt and the mainland of Greece and the Islands—we can now call it the Mycenaean Empire—traded together peacefully enough for over a hundred and fifty years, until 1223 B. C., in the reign of Merenptah. Then suddenly, with no warning at all the Peoples of the Sea, the Achaeans, the Shakalsha, and the Danauna raided Egypt in conjunction with a Libyan invasion.[60] They were beaten back[61] but thirty years later, in the reign of Rameses III, a more serious invasion took place. The people of the sea had already settled in North Syria, as we know both from documents and the evidence of excavations, and these folk, aided by their cousins from the Mycenaean Empire itself passed southwards as a great migration into Egyptian territory by land and sea.[62] But the Pharaoh "came upon them like a full flame" as he says. Their ships were trapped by the Egyptian fleet and their army was attacked simultaneously by the Egyptian troops among whom were numbered many of their own people, the Shardana.[63] A crushing defeat followed.

This sudden reversal of policy on the part of the Aegean peoples coincides exactly with the traditional date of the rise of a new ruling class at Mycenae, the house of Atreus; and now that Atreus has become a historical character we may see in him the leader of the first raid, and in Agamemnon his son the leader of the second. The results of these raids were disastrous to the Mycenaean Empire. The Egyp-

58. Bossert, *op. cit.*, fig. 246; Pendlebury, *Tell-el-Amarna*, Pl. VIII, 2.
59. *The Mural Paintings of Tell-el-Amarna*, Egypt Exploration Society 1929, Pl. III-VI.
60. Breasted, *A History of Egypt*, 467.
61. *Ibid.*, 468.
62. *Ibid.*, 476.
63. *Ibid.*, 447.

tian market was naturally closed; after 1200 B. C. no more Egyptian imports are found in Greece and no pottery of Late Helladic IIIb style has been found in Egypt. Where were the Achaeans to turn? Perhaps they remembered the tales of the wealth of the Black Sea which they had tried to tap when, two hundred years before, Egypt had been a closed country. But now Troy, which had been an insignificant city in the fifteenth century B. C., had grown powerful and lay across the way to the Black Sea, as Crete had years before lain across the way to Egypt. And so history repeated itself and an "Armada" sailed to Troy. Again we have a sentimental reason for an economic war, the Rape of Helen, which according to legend took place when Menelaus was raiding Egypt. And the traditional date of the Trojan War was 1194-1184 B. C.

So ended the Bronze Age connections between Egypt and the Aegean. Our last picture is given us in the Odyssey when at the mere sight of a sail on the horizon the Delta levies are called out and even old Pharaoh comes in person.

Five hundred years were to pass before the countries were again to establish peaceful relations.

November 22nd, 1937.

DAS AEGYPTISCHE FIGURALKAPITELL

EUGEN V. MERCKLIN
Hamburg

Tafeln 8-10

In der Geschichte des antiken Figuralkapitells nimmt das ägyptische eine Sonderstellung ein. Obwohl zeitlich an der Spitze stehend, ist es so gut wie ohne Einfluß auf die nachfolgenden Bildungen dieses Architekturgliedes in den klassischen Ländern geblieben. Das berechtigt dazu, es hier gesondert zu betrachten.[1]

Der häufigste und doch wohl schon für das Mittlere Reich gesicherte Typus ist das Hathorkapitell,[2] das auch in Tempeln anderer weiblicher Gottheiten verwendet worden ist.[3] Ludwig Borchardt hat die Säule mit Hathorkapitell als "Symbolsäule" erklärt,[4] als ein ins Monumentale gesteigertes Sistrum,[5] das der Himmelsstütze gleichzusetzen sei, so wie auf einem Fayence-Anhänger in Berlin neben dem Gotte Schu zwei Sistren den Himmel stützen.[6] Dagegen sieht F. W. v. Bissing[7] in ihr "einen Pfeiler, gegen den das Kultbild gelehnt ist"; er betont dabei, daß gerade an den ältesten Sistren der Frauenkopf fehlt, dagegen die ältesten Kapitelle keinen Naos über den Köpfen tragen, was nachgeprüft werden müßte (s. unten). Ueberdies verweist von Bissing auf das kleine, auf einer Stufenbasis stehende säulenförmige Kultsymbol der Göttin aus Dêr el-bahari,[8] dessen Aufbau als Vorbild für die Hathorsäule gedient haben könnte.

In der Regel besteht das Hathorkapitell aus zwei rückseitig mit-

---

1. Für weitgehende Belehrung und Beratung in ägyptologischen Fragen habe ich F. W. Fhr. v. B i s s i n g, G. R o e d e r und A. S c h a r f f herzlich zu danken.

2. Ueber Hathorkapitelle allgemein: Perrot-Chipiez I 560ff. (deutsche Ausg. 508ff). — Drexler bei Roscher, *ML.* I 2, 1867 (s.v. Hathor). — R. Pettazzoni, *Ausonia* 4, 1909, 185. — G. Jéquier, *Manuel d'archéol. égypt.* [1] *Les éléments de l'architecture.* Paris 1924, 184ff. — G. Lefèbvre, *Rites égyptiens* 67ff. — Ibr. Noshy, *The Arts in Ptolemaic Egypt.* Oxford-London 1937, 73f.

3. Liste bei L. Borchardt, *Die ägyptische Pflanzensäule.* Berlin 1897, 55f. Anm. 1. Die Bubastis-Kapitelle werden von ihm ins Neue Reich gesetzt. (Sein Zitat: Naville, *Bubastis* Taf. 33 a und b; Taf. 34 b muss in Taf. 23 a und b; Taf. 24 b geändert werden.)

4. Borchardt, *Pflanzensäule* 55f.

5. Ueber das Naossistrum: K. Sachs, *Die Musikinstrumente des alten Aegyptens* (*Mitt. aus der ägypt. Slg. Berlin* III, Berlin 1921) 29ff. — L. Klebs, AZ 67, 1931, 60f. — G. Jéquier, *Mém. Inst. Franç. Caire* 47, 1921, 79ff.

6. Borchardt, *a.O.* 56 Abb. 86. — Ausführl.Verz. (1899) Nr. 6611.

7. F. W. v. Bissing bei Springer, Michaelis, Wolters, *Handb.* I_{12} 32. — Ders., *Handb. d. ägypt. Kunstgesch.* 1, 152f. 2, 121f.

8. H. E. Winlock, *Metr. Mus. Bull. Egypt. Exped.* 1922/23, 39 Abb. 34 (18. Dyn.).

einander verbundenen oder aus vier nach allen Seiten blickenden Köpfen der kuhohrigen Göttin.[9] Ueber den Köpfen pflegt, wie beim Sistrum, der Naos mit den seitlich anschlagenden Spiralen zu sitzen, die Sachs[10] überzeugend aus den Kuhhörnern der Hathor hergeleitet hat. Nur selten fehlt der Naos;[11] in einigen Fällen ist sein Fehlen durch den Erhaltungszustand bedingt, wie z.B. an dem späten Exemplar im Hildesheimer Pelizaeus-Museum aus griechischer Zeit (Taf. 8, a mit freundlicher Erlaubnis von G. Roeder).[12] Hier führt die technische Zurichtung der viereckigen Oberseite des Blocks zur Annahme eines Naos von gleicher Ausladung wie die jetzt das Kapitell abschließende Hohlkehle, was tatsächlich ptolemäischen Beispielen entsprechen würde.[13]

Dem bisher meines Wissens stets ohne Naos abgebildeten, von Maspero und Jéquier irrig ins M.R. datierten Hathorkapitell aus Mendes,[14] das vielmehr in die Ramessidenzeit gehört, ist im Museum von Kairo der zugehörige Naos wieder aufgesetzt worden.[15]

Unentschieden ist die Frage bei den vermutlich ältesten Hathorkapitellen, die wir bisher besitzen. Sie fanden sich im großen Tempel von Bubastis[16] und wurden von E. Naville für das M.R., und zwar

9. Ueber die apotropäische Bedeutung der "nach den vier Winden" gerichteten Hathorköpfe: P. Perdrizet, *Mont.Piot*, 25, 1921/22, 377, mit Hinweis auf zwei Asylie-Inschriften aus Batn-Harit, *Annales du Service des Ant.* 19, 1920, 40ff. Taf. 1. 2.

10. Sachs, *a.O.* 30.

11. Tempel der Ipet in Karnak: Jéquier, *Les temples Ptolémaiques et Romains* (Paris 1924) Taf. 7,2; ders., *Manuel* 191 Abb 116. Marburger Phot. 86605, 86607. Die Hathormasken sind in versenktem Relief gegeben; den sie umgebenden Grund als Naos aufzufassen (so Jéquier, *Manuel* 191 Anm. 1: "la tête seule dans l'édicule"), halte ich für verfehlt. — Kapitelle der Hathorpfeiler in Serabit-el-Khadim (s.u.).

12. G. Roeder, A. Ippel, *Denkmäler des Pelizaeus-Mus.* 83 (mit Abb. 21 auf S. 76) Nr. 1885. Viereckiges, 3-4 cm tiefes Dübelloch in der Mitte mit etwa 1 cm tiefem Gußkanal nach der einen Ecke zu. Zu den Rosetten im Haar vgl. ein Kapitell im Louvre, Phot. Giraudon 25, Époque égyptienne.

13. Z. B. Dendera, unten Anm. 37.

14. E. Naville, *Archaeol.Report* 1892/93, 3f. mit Abb. S 8. — Maspero, *Gesch. d.Kunst in Aegypten* (deutsche Uebers. v. A. Rusch)₂, Stuttgart 1925, 98.— G. Jéquier, *Temples Memphites et Thébains* (Paris 1920) Taf. 17, 5. — Wenn Jéquier, *Manuel* 186 behauptet, "il ne reste aucune trace du couronnement", so übersieht er die ausdrückliche Erwähnung des Naos bei Naville, *Ahnas el Medineh* 18f. Auch seine Ansicht, das Haar der Hathorköpfe stecke in einem "couvre-tête en étoffe," kann ich nicht teilen.

15. Freundliche Auskunft von H. Gauthier. — Richtige Datierung: v. Bissing, *Handb.* 2, 122 § 10 e.

16. E. Naville, *Bubastis.* London 1891. — B e r l i n : *Ausführl. Verz.* (1899) 116 Nr. 10834, Abb. 23. — H.Schäfer, *Von ägypt.Kunst* 1919. II Taf. 49, 5.— *Führer durch die Staatl.Mus.zu Berlin. Die ägypt. Slg.*₂, 1933, 53. — B o s t o n : Naville, *Bubastis* 11, Taf. 9 und 23, A. — Jéquier, *Manuel* 185 Abb. 109.— J. Capart, *L'Art Egypt.* (I) *L'architecture.* Brüssel 1922, Taf. 75. — v. Bissing, *Handb.* Abb. 533. — Bd 'A.2.ser.1, 1921/22, 493 Abb. 4. — L o n d o n : *Brit. Mus. Guide to the Egypt. Galleries (Sculpture)* 1909, 212 Nr. 768. — A. W. Shorter,

für die 12. Dynastie, in Anspruch genommen. Diesen Ansatz hat gegenüber einer von verschiedenen Seiten vorgebrachten Spätdatierung zuletzt auch von Bissing vertreten.[17]

Die acht Kapitelle von Bubastis, aus rotem Granit und mit Farbspuren, die nach der Auffindung sofort verblaßten, bestehen aus je zwei Köpfen mit der für das M.R. charakteristischen Schneckenzopffrisur. Die vier größeren (Berlin, Boston [Taf. 9, b], London, Paris) sind reicher ausgestattet als die vier kleineren: Zwei von ihnen tragen an den Seitenflächen die Wappenflanze von Oberägypten, die beiden anderen die von Unterägypten. Darunter ist nachträglich die Kartusche mit dem Namen Osorkon II. eingemeißelt, der auch auf den glatt gelassenen Seitenflächen der kleineren Serie wiederkehrt. Außerdem sind die großen Kapitelle durch zwei sich zu beiden Seiten des Hathorkopfes über dem Halskragen aufbäumende Uräen, die an gleicher Stelle auch an Sistren der Spätzeit vorkommen,[18] und durch einen Uräenfries über der Hohlkehle ausgezeichnet, der an beiden Enden von einer nach innen eingerollten Spirale abgeschlossen wird.

Diese vier großen Kapitelle nun tragen auf der Unterseite, das Exemplar in Berlin auch auf der Oberseite, Reste von Inschriften.[19] Zur Zeit der in den Inschriften genannten Herrscher, Osorkon I. und eines Königs, dessen Name unvollständig erhalten, aber wahrscheinlich auf Ramses II. zu beziehen ist, müssen die Kapitelle so verbaut gewesen sein, daß ihre Unterseite (bezw. Unter- und Oberseite) zur Anbringung von Reliefs und Inschriften verwendbar war. Der Schluß Shorters, sie seien aus Mauerblöcken eines Gebäudes aus der Zeit der eben genannten Herrscher erst unter Osorkon II. hergestellt worden, ist abzulehnen, da der Stilcharakter und besonders die von Bändern zusammengehaltene Schneckenzopffrisur[20] der Hathorköpfe durchaus für eine Entstehung im M.R. sprechen; ein Archaisieren, mit dem man bei Shorters Annahme zu rechnen hätte, ist für die Zeit der 22. Dynastie noch nicht nachweisbar.[21] Allerdings wird der Schneckenzopf an Werken der 22. und der folgenden Dynastie zu-

---

BMQuarterly 10, 1936, 172ff. (mit Datierung in die 22. Dynastie unter Osorkon II.). — P a r i s: Naville, *Bubastis* Taf. 24, B. — Jéquier, *Temples Memph. et Théb.* Taf. 17, 4. — Ch. Boreux, *Mus.Nat.du Louvre, Département des Antiqu. Egypt. Guide-catal.somm.* I, Paris 1932, 60f. Ein Stück der kleineren Gruppe im Museum von Sydney: Naville, *Bubastis* 12 Taf. 23, B.

17. v. Bissing, *Handb.d.ägypt.Kunstgesch.a.O.* (vgl.oben Anm 7).

18. Sachs, *Musikinstrumente* Taf. 3, 58.64.

19. Naville, *Bubastis* Taf. 41, A.B.C. und Shorter, a.O. — Berlin, *Ausführl. Verz.* 115, G 377.

20. Vgl. z. B. Capart, *L'Art Egypt.* 2.sér. (1911) Taf. 132. — H. G. Evers, *Staat aus dem Stein* I Taf. 74: Königin Nofret, aus Tanis. Kairo, Museum.

21. Käthe Bosse, *Menschl.Figur* (*Aegyptol.Forsch.*1,1936) 95ff.

weilen angewandt, doch ist er dort ungegliedert.[22] Osorkon II. hat
die Kapitelle aus ihrer Verbauung befreit und sie ihrer ursprünglichen
Bestimmung wiedergegeben, wobei seine Kartusche in die Seiten-
flächen eingemeißelt wurde.

Bei dem geschilderten Schicksal der Bubastiskapitelle ist es an sich
durchaus möglich, daß sie ursprünglich einen Naos getragen haben,
der jetzt überall weggebrochen ist oder bei ihrer Wiederverwendung
abgearbeitet wurde. Aus solchen Erwägungen heraus wird H.
Schäfers Wiederherstellungsversuch entstanden sein, den er in Gips
im Berliner Museum hat vornehmen lassen (Taf. 8, c).[23] Einer Aenderung bedürfte dabei nur der Uräenfries, dessen erwähnte End-
spiralen fehlen. Vielleicht brächte eine neue Untersuchung der oberen
Fläche an allen vier Exemplaren dieser Gruppe eine endgültige Ent-
scheidung in der Frage, ob die Kapitelle von Bubastis mit einem
Naos ausgestattet waren oder nicht. Auch ihre Stützengattung ist
unbekannt: Naville[24] vermutet Pfeiler, Schäfer nimmt in seiner
Wiederherstellung eine Säule an.

Zu Beginn des Neuen Reiches (18. Dynastie) tritt das Hathor-
kapitell wieder auf. Der zweiköpfige Typus ist beibehalten, doch ist
die Spirallockenfrisur durch die gerade herabfallende und in gleicher
Höhe mit dem Halse waagerecht abgeschnittene Haarmasse ersetzt.
Als Beispiel diene das "Southern Speos" im Hathorheiligtum des
großen Tempels von Dêr el -bahari, dessen erste Halle sechzehnkantige
Säulen und viereckige Pfeiler mit Hathorkapitellen, die zweite runde
Hathorsäulen und sechzehnkantige Säulen hatte.[25] Die Angabe der
Haarmasse,[26] die sich nach untenhin verschmälert, und der sie zu-
sammenhaltenden Bänder setzt sich auf die Nebenseiten fort, in
deren Mitte eine Papyrussäule aufwächst. In den Aediculae über den
Hathorköpfen erscheinen zwei Uräen mit Sonnenscheibe und Kuhhörnern nebeneinander; an den Nebenseiten deutet Naville an gleicher
Stelle einen Osiris an, den Jéquier in seiner Wiedergabe der Naville-
schen Zeichnung fortläßt.

An den Säulen von Dêr el-bahari entspricht die Höhe des Schaftes

---

22. Bosse, a.O. 66, Nr. 180, Taf. 10a. — Sphingen der Schep-en-upet in Kairo
(Cat.gén., G. Legrain, Statues et statuettes III Nr. 42201 Taf. 9) und Berlin
(Ausführl.Verz. 246 Nr. 7972 Abb. 51).

23. Nach Vorlage, die ich der freundlichen Vermittlung von A. Scharff verdanke.

24. Bubastis 12.

25. Baedeker, Aegypten, 1928, 311. — E. Naville, The Temple of Deir el-Bahari
3 Taf. 68, vgl. 6, 24. — Jéquier, Manuel 186 Abb. 110 (die Originale sind alle
zerbrochen).

26. Jéquier, Manuel 186 glaubt auch hier, das Haar stecke in einem "couvre-
tête" (vgl.oben Anm. 14).

annähernd der des Kapitells (Kopf und Naos zusammengenommen).
Etwas gestreckter sind die Proportionen an einer Hathorsäule in dem
von Amenophis III. seiner Gemahlin Teje geweihten Tempel von
Sedeinga (Nubien).[27] Hier fällt die Haarmasse der beiden Hathor-
köpfe senkrecht herab, wodurch das Kapitell, das allseitig über den
Schaft herausragt, den Charakter eines Würfels bekommt. Der
Schaft hat 34 Kanneluren und zwei flache mit Hieroglyphen bedeckte
Streifen, die jeweils unter dem Kinn der Hathor ansetzen. In der
Mitte der Nebenseiten auch hier eine Papyrussäule. Der Naos ist
niedrig und breit.

In Napata am Gebel Barkal, das im 7. Jahrhundert v.Chr. Residenz
eines unabhängigen äthiopischen Reiches wurde, zeigen die zwei noch
aufrechtstehenden Hathorsäulen in dem von Taharka dem Amon-Rē
und der Mut erbauten Tempel immer noch eine verhältnismäßig
gedrückte Form.[28] Allerdings ist der Naos, mit einem Uräus in der
Aedicula, aus einem liegenden zu einem stehenden Rechteck geworden;
die Haarmasse der Hathorköpfe wird wie in Dêr el-bahari nach
unten zu schmäler, so daß der Absatz gegen den Schaft weniger
schroff erscheint als in Sedeinga. Dieser, aus mehreren glatten
Säulentrommeln aufgebaut, ist nach Sachs eine späte Reminiszenz
an einen Papyrusstengel als Sistrumgriff.

Aus der Zeit Amenophis' III. stammt das älteste Beispiel für die
Anbringung eines einzigen Hathorkopfes an der Säule. Dieses und
andere verwandte Beispiele seien hier mit angeführt, obgleich es sich
dabei nicht um Kapitelle im eigentlichen Sinn handelt. Im kleinen
Tempel von El Kab[29] ist den vier sechzehnkantigen Säulen an der
nach dem Inneren des Raumes weisenden Seite eine Hathormaske mit
niedrigem Naos angearbeitet, unter der ein breiter hieroglyphen-
bedeckter Pfeiler vorspringt; der eigentliche Gebälkträger bleibt
dabei die Säule.

Wie in El Kab, sind in der Halle des kleinen unterirdischen Tempels
von Abu Simbel[30] aus der Zeit Ramses' II. (19. Dyn.) die sechs Pfeiler

---

27. Lepsius, *Denkm.* I 115. Text 5, 228.

28. Sachs, *Musikinstrumente* 30 Abb. 26.

29. J. J. Taylor u. S. Clarke, *Wall Drawings and Monuments of El Kab.,* *The*
Temple of Amenhetep III. London, 1898, Frontispiece. Längsschnitt Taf. 14.
Querschnitte Taf. 15. — Jéquier, *Temples Memph. et Théb.* Taf. 73, wonach
Manuel 188 Abb. 113. — Capart, *Art ég. Architecture* (1922) Taf. 98. S. Clarke
u. R. Engelbach, *Ancient Egyptian Masonry,* Oxford 1930, 139 u. Abb. 150. —
Perrot-Chipiez I 408 (deutsche Ausgabe 377) Abb. 233; die Säule allein ebda. 552
(bzw. 501) Abb. 330 und 563 (bzw. 510) Abb. 342. — Borchardt, *Pflanzensäule*
56 Abb. 85. — Naville, *Bubastis* 13 irrt, wenn er El Kab zum zweiköpfigen Typus
rechnet.

30. Perrot-Chipiez I 419 (bzw. 387) Abb. 244. 546 (bzw. 495) Abb. 324. —
Lepsius, *Denkm.* III 192, wonach Jéquier, *Manuel* 189 Abb. 114.

nur auf einer Seite mit dem "Sistrum" ausgestattet, dessen Hathorkopf die Schneckenfrisur ohne Bänder trägt. Mit ähnlichem Schmuck
sollte die Fassade des Speos Artemidos, eines unter der gemein-
samen Regierung der Hatschepsut und Thutmosis' III. erbauten
Felstempels der Göttin Pachet, in Beni Hasan ausgestattet werden;
hier sind die "Sistren" auf der Vorderseite der acht Pfeiler unvoll-
endet geblieben.[31]

Vereinzelt steht der Pfeiler aus dem Grabe eines Nefer-Hotep im
Museum von Kairo (18. Dynastie), an dem der Hathorkopf mit Naos
über dem Djedzeichen erscheint. In der Aedicula ein Uräus, beider-
seits von ihm, auf der Wandfläche des Naos, je eine Isis in versenktem
Relief.[32]

In der Saitenzeit erreicht der Schaft zwei Drittel der Gesamthöhe,
wofür die monolithe Granitsäule des Apries in Kairo (26. Dyn.) ein
Zeugnis abgibt.[33] Diese Proportion hält sich weiterhin.

Eine grundlegende Neuerung erfährt der Aufbau des Hathorkapitells in der Ptolemäerzeit: Es wird nun vierköpfig gebildet.[34] Die
unten gerade abgeschnittenen Frisuren der einzelnen Köpfe ragen
über den Säulenschaft heraus und sind voneinander durch eine
Furche getrennt. Der Naos, mit dem Uräus in der Aedicula, kann die
niedrige breite Rechtecksform bewahren (z.B. Philae, s. Anm. 36),
oder er kann von gleicher Höhe mit dem Hathorkopf sein und auf
seiner geschlossenen Fläche Opferszenen in Relief tragen (Dendera,
Pronaos, s. Anm. 37, Taf. 9, c) Häufig, aber nicht immer,[35] wird das
Hathorkapitell als eine Art Abakus auf das Kapitell einer Pflanzensäule gesetzt, wie z.B. in der von Ptolemaios Philadelphos neu her-
gestellten Halle des Nektanebos (Taf. 9, d) im "Geburtshaus" von

31. Jéquier, *Temples Memph. et Théb.* Taf 27. — W. Wreszinski, *Bericht über
die photogr. Exped.* usw. (*Schriften der Königsberger Ges.Geisteswiss. Kl.* 4, 2,
1927) Taf. 14 A.

32. Perrot-Chipiez I 563 (Deutsche Ausg. 510) Abb. 343. — Borchardt, *Pflanzensäule* 56.

33. Jéquier, *Temples Ramessides et Saites* (Paris 1922) Taf. 78, wonach
Manuel 187 Abb. 111.

34. Erwähnt seien hier auch einige Kalksteinmodelle für vierseitige Hathorkapitelle: *Collections Lambros et Dattari, Vente Drouot,* Paris 17. — 19. 6. 1912,
Nr. 387 Taf. 42, mit Säulenansatz (H. 27 cm.). — Berlin, Schäfer-Andrae, *Kunst
des alten Orients,* 6.-10. Tausend, Taf. 427, 4 (H. 16, 3cm).

35. Tempel der Ipet in Karnak, s.oben Anm. 11. — Kapitelle in Dendera, s.
Anm. 37. — Kiosk von Kertassi (Nubien). G. Roeder, Debod, bis Bab Kalabsche,
(*Les temples immergés de la Nubie.* Le Caire 1911) I 153f., II Taf. 57 a, 50 , 51.
52.54.56. 136. — S.148: Datierung in ptolemäische oder auch noch frührömische
Zeit. — Tempel von Dêr el-Medina, Antenpfeiler. Lepsius, *Denkm.* I 88. — Jéquier,
Temples Ptol. et Romains Taf. 13, wonach *Manuel* 165 Abb. 92. — Kalksteinfenster
aus Dendera, London, Brit. Mus. E. A. Wallis Budge, *Egypt.Sculptures in the
Brit. Mus.* London 1914. 22 Taf. 49 (Nr. 972), wonach Capart, *L'Art ég., Architecture* Taf. 191. — J. H. Breasted, H. Ranke, Gesch.Aegyptens (Phaidon-Ausg.
1936) Abb. 324. Um 150 v.Chr.

Philae[36] und, neben einfachen "Sistrumsäulen" an der Nordfassade, in Pronaos, Neujahrskapelle und Dachtempelchen, im Säulensaal des Hathortempels von Dendera (1. Jahrhundert v. Chr.).[37] Der Hathorkopf allein, ohne Naos, erscheint über einem Pflanzenkapitell im Tempel der Ipet in Karnak (s. Anm. 11).

Entgegen allen ausserägyptischen Kopfkapitellen ist das Hathorkapitell eine von jedem vegetabilischen Beiwerk frei gehaltene Zusammensetzung von Köpfen, die selbst bei der Kombination mit dem Pflanzenkapitell von einer Vermischung und Durchdringung beider Elemente absieht.

Provinziellen Charakter tragen die von Flinders Petrie im Tempel von S e r a b i t   e l - K h a d i m   i m   S i n a i g e b i e t aufgefundenen Hathorpfeiler.[38] Einige von ihnen sind mit Inschriften Thutmosis' III. (Petrie Abb. 104), Amenophis' II., Thutmosis' IV. (?) und Amenophis' III. (Petri Abb. 95, in wiederaufgerichtetem Zustand) versehen. Die Pfeiler sind rechteckig, die älteren annähernd quadratisch, die jüngeren gestreckter. Die vier Pfeiler in Raum A (vgl. Plan 4 bei Petrie), auf Basen, die an Vorder- und Rückseite über sie hinausragten, trugen nur einen der Mittelachse des Raumes zugekehrten Kopf der Göttin. Gleiche Pfeiler und Bruchstücke wurden in den Räumen D (Petrie Abb. 95), E, G und J gefunden. An ihnen trägt die Göttin die unten glatt abgeschnittene Frisur. Aelter sind die Beispiele mit Schneckenzöpfen in Raum K, N und im Hof (vgl. Petrie 86). Der Wechsel muss zwischen Amenophis II. und Thutmosis IV. vorsichgegangen sein, in einer Zeit, in der auch sonst ein stilistischer Wechsel bemerkbar ist.

---

36. Kiosk des Nektanebos: Maspero, *Gesch.d.Kunst in Agypten₂*, 226 Abb. 430. 227 Abb. 431. — Perrot-Chipiez, deutsche Ausg. I 516 Abb. 349. — Capart, *Art ég., Architecture* (1922) Taf. 167. — G. Steindorff, *Die Kunst der Aegypter* (1928) 163. — Ibr. Noshy, *The Arts in Ptolemaic Egypt* 78 Taf. 9, 3.
Geburtshaus: Maspero, a.O. 227 Abb. 432. 232 Abb. 441. — Jéquier, *Manuel* 192 Abb. 117. — Schäfer, Andrae, *Kunst des alten Orients* (1925) 408; dass., 6.-10. Tausend, 426. — Steindorff, a.O. 165. — *Handb. d. Archäol.* I Taf. 102, 5.
37. Nordfassade: Jéquier, *Temples Ptol. et Romains* Taf. 55. 56, 1. — Ch. Boreux, *L'Art ég.* (1926) Taf. 15. — Steindorff, a.O. 159. — S. Clarke u. R. Engelbach, *Anc.Egypt.Masonry* (1930) Abb. 205. — E. Chassinat, *Le temple de Dendara* I. Le Caire 1934. Taf. 1-5. 21-24. Vorhalle (Pronaos): Maspero, a.O. 221 Abb. 421. — Capart, *L'Art ég.* (1909) Taf. 95; ders., *Architecture* (1922) Taf. 171. — Jéquier, *Temples Ptol. et Romains* Taf. 59. 60.61. — *Handb. d. Archäol.* I Taf. 102, 3. — H. Fechheimer, *Plastik der Aegypter* Taf. 11. — Springer, Michaelis, Wolters, *Handb.*₁₂ 415 Abb. 788 (eine Säule). — Wurz, *Plast. Dekor. des Stützwerkes* 14 Abb. 8. — Chassinat, a.O. Taf. 31-36. — Ibr. Noshy, *The Arts in Ptolemaic Egypt.* 74 Taf. 8, 1. Neujahrskapelle: Jéquier, a.O. Taf. 65, 2. — Chassinat, a.O. Taf. 37.38.IV (1935) Taf. 300.303. 305. Kiosk auf dem Dach: Maspero, a.O. 221 Abb. 420. — Capart, *L'Art ég., Architecture* (1922) Taf. 170. — Jéquier, a. O. Taf 66, 1. — Chassinat, a.O. I Taf. 40-42. Säulensaal: Baedeker, *Aegypten₆* (1928), 254. Eine Abbildung ist mir nicht bekannt geworden.
38. W. M. Flinders Petrie, *Researches in Sinai.* London 1906. 75ff.

Vier Hathorpfeiler enthielt der geräumige Brunnenraum (Hana-fiyeh-Petrie Abb. 99-104 und 111. — Jéquier, *Manuel* 190, Abb. 115). Sie stammen aus der Zeit Thutmosis' III.[39] An ihnen beabsichtigte der Steinmetz ein vierköpfiges Kapitell zu geben (Taf. 9, e) ; statt jedoch die vier Hathorköpfe einem rechteckigen Kern aufzulegen, schneidet er in die dem Haarkontur folgenden geschwungenen Seiten-flächen eines zweiköpfigen Kapitells die beiden übrigen Köpfe in kleinerem Format in flachem Relief ein: Also ein völliges Missachten des strengen Aufbaues, der im ägyptischen Mutterlande durch Jahr-tausende unverändert geblieben ist. Man mag diese Kapitelle mit Jéquier als Vorläufer des ptolemäischen und späteren vierköpfigen Typus betrachten.

An allen Hathorkapitellen von Serabit fehlt der Naos. Die Köpfe sind nur von einer Hohlkehle bekrönt, auf deren Abschlussplatte die zur Deckenkonstruktion gehörenden Steinbalken lagen.

Zu einer achteckigen Säule hat ein roh gearbeitetes Einzelkapitell gehört (Petrie Abb. 142, 5, vgl. S. 135), das Petrie auf Grund der vorauszusetzenden Säulenform ans Ende der 11. Dyn. anzusetzen und einem Bau Mentuhotep's III. (vor 2000 v.Chr.) zuzuweisen geneigt ist. Es wäre dann das älteste bekannte Hathorkapitell überhaupt. Angesichts der geringen Qualität dieser provinziellen Arbeit scheint es aber geratener, auf eine Datierung überhaupt zu verzichten.

Hingewiesen sei schliesslich auf die in einem Bau der IV. Stadt von tell el-Hesi (L a c h i s) in Südwest-Palästina eingemauerten Sandsteinplatten (H. 1, 20 m), nach Thiersch[40] halbierte Seiten von Pfeilerköpfen mit in flachstem Relief angelegten, schematisch ge-zeichneten Hathorkapitellen. Der Bau, vielleicht ein Hathorheilig-tum, gehört zu der von Josua um 1200 v.Chr. zerstörten Kananiter-burg des Königs Japhia. Die Ausbreitung des Astarte-Hathorkultes über ganz Palästina schon zu jener Zeit wird durch Funde gleich-artiger Votivterrakotten an verschiedensten Orten bewiesen.

Entlehnungen des Hathorkapitells oder seiner Elemente durch die k y p r i s c h - p h o e n i k i s c h e K u n s t,[40a] die sich teils durch Import kunstgewerblicher Erzeugnisse aus dem Nillande, teils durch kultliche Gründe erklären mögen,[41] sind nicht selten.

---

39. v. Bissing, *Handb.* 2, 122 lässt, mit Verweis auf Petrie 105, die Möglichkeit offen, dass, wenn ich ihn recht verstehe, gerade diese Pfeiler noch in die 12. Dynastie gehören könnten.

40. W. M. Flinders Petrie, *Tell el-Hesy* (Lachis) London 1891 Taf. 4. Thiersch, *AA* 1908, 21ff. Eine der Platten ebda 22 Abb. 12, das Gebäude 19 Abb. 11, links. Vgl. auch v. Bissing, Anteil der aeg.Kunst am Kunstleben der Völker, München 1912, 76.

40a. Ueber das kyprische Hathorkapitell allgemein: F. W. v. Bissing, *StEtr.* 2, 1928, 29ff.

Auf Kypros selbst kommen, z.T. aus Astarteheiligtümern stammend, Stelen in Betracht, unter denen zwei Typen zu scheiden sind:

1. Die Uebernahme beschränkt sich auf den Hathorkopf mit involutierten Haarenden, der entweder als Mittelmotiv in das kyprische "Iris" kapitell (Abb. 1) aufgenommen wird,[42] somit an derselben

Abb. 1. Kyprisches Kapitell mit Hathorkopf.

Stelle erscheint, an der an den Stücken aus Athienu[43] zwei Sphingen symmetrisch an einem heiligen Baum emporklettern, oder den dreieckigen Volutenzwickel darunter füllt (Taf. 10, a, b).[44] Für die Stücke aus Athienu ist die Datierung von Bissings[45] "nicht älter als 5. Jahr-

41. Im N. R. haben ägyptische Priester auf Kypros zelebriert. Freundliche Mitteilung von E. Zyhlarz.

42. a. New York, Metr.Mus. Cesnola Collection. — Myres, *Handbook of the Cesnola Coll.* (1914) 250 Nr. 1419. — *Descriptive Atlas of the Cesnola Coll.* I Taf. 22, 50. — Perrot-Chipiez III 535 Abb. 361. — Ohnefalsch-Richter, *KBH.* 192 Abb. 161. — *Ausonia* 4, 1909, 207 Abb. 39. — Bd' A. 2 ser. I 1921/22, 496 Abb. 14. Aus Golgoi. Etwa 550-500 v.Chr.

    b. Ebenda Nr. 1414. *Atlas* I Taf. 18, 27. Etwa 600-550.

    c. Ebenda Nr. 1415. *Atlas* I Taf. 18, 26. — Doell, *Sammlung Cesnola* Taf. 13, 21 (828). ". . Human head derived from the Hathor-type, but influenced by the Greek Medusa." Etwa 400-350.

43. a. New York, Metr.Mus. Cesnola Coll. — Myres, *Handbook* 250 Nr. 1418, mit Abb. auf S. 249. — *Atlas Cesnola Coll.* I Taf. 99, 671. — Ohnefalsch-Richter *KBH.* Taf 26, 1. Taf. 117, 4 Taf. 159, 1. — Perrot-Chipiez III 217 Abb. 152. — *RA.* N.S. 29, 1875 I 23 (Abb.). — Durm, *Baukunst d.Griechen*₃ 305 Abb. 284 ("Archaistisch"). — Cesnola, Stern, *Cypern* Taf. 20, 2. — *JdI* 35, 1920 Taf. 2, 4. — Etwa 550-500 v.Chr.

    b. Ebenda Nr. 1417. *Atlas* I Taf. 100, 672. — *KBH.* Taf. 26, 2. Taf. 117, 7. Taf. 159, 3. — Cesnola, Stern, *Cypern* Taf. 20, 1. — Etwa 500-450 v.Chr.

    c. Ebenda Nr. 1420. *Atlas* I Taf. 100, 673. — *KBH.* Taf. 26, 3. Taf 117, 2. Taf. 159, 2. — *JdI.* 35, 1920 Taf. 2, 5. (Das Zitat bei Myres: "Perrot fig. 361" ist irrtümlich; es bezieht sich auf Nr. 1419). Etwa 550-500 v.Chr. — Zur ganzen Gruppe vgl. Studniczka, *JdI.* 26, 1911, 75.

44. a. Berlin, *Skulpturensammlung.* Nr. 1849. Aus Idalion. Der Hathorkopf sitzt über der Mondsichel, die mit der Sonne darunter, auf anderen Stelen aus

hundert v.Chr." sicher richtig. Mit ihnen sind die bereits im 9.-8. Jahrhundert von phoenikischen Künstlern geschaffenen Elfenbeinreliefs aus Nimrud zu vergleichen, auf denen addossierte Greifen in Schalenpalmetten stehen,[46] und auf einem etwa gleichzeitigen Elfenbeintäfelchen aus Samaria sitzt, von einwärts geschwungenen Voluten gerahmt, Harpokrates auf einer Lotosblüte.[47]

2. Kopf und Naos werden übernommen. Die Kuhohren der Göttin sind verschwunden. Den Vertretern dieses Typus (Stelen aus Larnaka [Taf. 9, f] und Amathus)[48] ist in der Führung der Umrisse ein unfertiges Stück aus dem Mittelhof des Palastes von Vuni zu vergleichen,[49] doch glaube ich nicht, daß hier, woran man denken könnte, aus dem auf jeder Seite eingemeisselten weiblichen Kopf ein Hathorkopf, aus dem oberen Teil der Stele ein Naos werden sollte. Eine rechteckige Einarbeitung in der oberen Fläche zur Aufnahme eines querlaufenden Holzbalkens liess die Ausgräber an den Rest einer geplanten, aber infolge der Zerstörung des Palastes nicht mehr ausgeführten Schöpfvorrichtung für Wasser aus der Zisterne im Hof denken. Von einem Vorläufer dieser Vorrichtung, aus Holz, sind noch

Idalion allein den Zwickel füllt, vgl. etwa *KBH* Taf. 58. — H. 71, 5 cm. Br. der oberen Leiste 1 m. Dicke 19-19, 5 cm. Hier Taf. 10, a mit freundlicher Erlaubnis von Zahn nach alter Aufnahme von Ohnefalsch-Richter.

b. Leipzig, Grassi-Museum (Sammlung Weisbach). Aus Idalion. Im Dreieckszwickel der Hathorkopf allein. Taf. 10, b, nach alter Aufnahme.

45. Anteil 80.

46. Zwei Exemplare im Brit. Museum: Das eine durchbrochen gearbeitet: F. Poulsen, *Orient und frühgriech.Kunst* 48 Abb. 37. — Hogarth, *Excav. at Ephesus* 183, 4. Taf. 29, 1. — Layard, *Niniveh* I Taf. 90, 22; das zweite mit Resten einer Einlage von Lapislazuli und der Vergoldung der Stege: Poulsen a.O. 49 Abb. 39. — Perrot-Chipiez II 535 Abb. 249, wonach *Studi e Mat.* I 173 Abb. 6. — Layard I Taf. 90, 21. — Dieulafoy, *L'Art ant.de la Perse* III 50 Abb. 50. — Ohnefalsch-Richter, *KBH.* Taf. 116, 5. — *Handbuch d. Archäologie* I Taf. 194, 4. — Vgl. v. Bissing *StEtr.* 2, 1928, 29.

47. E. L. Sukenik, *AA.* 1933, 111, Abb. 18, vgl. 105. — J. W. und G. M. Crowfoot, *Palest.Explor.Fund, Quarterly Statement* 1933, 14f. Taf. 1, 1. — Reste eines zweiten Exemplares ebda. 17, F, vgl. Juli 1932, Taf. 3, 1. Crowfoot datiert um 860 v.Chr. (*PQS* 1933, 22).

48. a. Paris, Louvre. Aus Larnaka (Kition). — Ohnefalsch-Richter, *KBH.* Taf. 200, 1. 2. — Vorderansicht allein (nach *KBH.* Taf. 200, 1) *Ausonia* 4, 1909, 208 Abb. 42. — Bd' A. 2. ser. I 1921/22, 496 Abb. 13. — *JdI.* 35. 1920 Taf. 2, 7. — Meurer, *Vergleichende Formenlehre des Ornaments u. der Pflanze* 58 Abb. 7. Diese Abbildung ist darin richtiger als die im *JdI.* veröffentlichte, dass sie den Hathorbüsten am Naiskos keine Andeutungen von Armen gibt, die sie, nach freundlicher Nachprüfung Dussauds, am Original nicht haben. — *Handb. d. Archäol* I Taf. 204, 1 nach Phot. Alinari 23839.

b. Berlin, *Vorderasiat.* Abt. 2715. Aus Larnaka. — *KBH.* Taf. 200, 3. — *Ausonia*, a.O. Abb. 41. — Bd' A. a.O. Abb. 12. — *AA* 1934, 89, Abb. 8.

c. Berlin, *Antiquarium M. I.* 8171. Aus Amathus. — *KBH.* Taf. 200, 4. — *AA.* 1934, 91 Abb. 9.

49. *The Swedish Cyprus Exped.* 3, 238 Nr. 289 Taf. 94, 7. — *Corolla Archaeol.* (Skrifter *Svenska Inst. Rom.* 2, 1932), Gjerstad, *The Palace at Vouni,* Taf. 2, oben. — *Antike* 9, 1933, 271 Abb. 5. Kalkstein. H. 1, 75 m.

Spuren gefunden worden.[50] Eine Umbildung dieses zweiten Typus
bedeutet ein gleichfalls aus Vuni stammendes Kalksteinkapitell (Taf.
8, b), wahrscheinlich von einer Peristylsäule des Mittelhofes.[51] Hier
sind vom ägyptischen Vorbild nur die Hathorfrisur mit ihren drei
Bandverschnürungen an den auf beiden Seiten befindlichen Köpfen
und der Naos mit dem Uräus in der Aedicula übriggeblieben. Die
Hathorfrisur ist nur eine Zutat, denn der Kopf, den sie als äusserster
Streifen umrahmt, hat sein eigenes Haar und trägt darüber ein Dia-
dem. In den Ohren sitzt Rosettenschmuck. Goetherts Behauptung,
der Kopf stelle eine behelmte Athena dar,[52] beruht auf einem Irrtum.
Das Kapitell gehört ans Ende von Gjerstads Stil II B, ist also gegen
450-440 anzusetzen.[53]

Die Stelen des ersten Typus sind keine architektonischen Stützen,
sondern freistehende Votive gewesen, vielleicht Sinnbilder des heiligen
Baumes, der Aschera. Freie Aufstellung möchte ich auch, entschiedener als Julie Braun-Vogelstein,[54] für die Stelen des zweiten Typus
annehmen. Dafür spricht m.E. allein schon die Verschiedenheit in
der Ausschmückung des naosartigen Aufsatzes an Vorder- und Rückseite.

Gegenüber dem strengen Aufbau des ägyptischen Vorbildes mit
seinen stark betonten Senkrechten und Waagerechten, der sogar noch
in dem Kapitell von Dendera, das um Jahrhunderte jünger ist, als
das kyprische Taf. 9, f, zur Wirkung kommt, zeigt die kyprische Stele
ein stärkeres Schwingen des Umrisses, das Vorherrschen der ge-
krümmten Linie anstelle der Waagerechten und eine Bereicherung
der seitlichen Spiralen am Naos durch einheimische Pflanzenmotive.
Selbst das Bubastiskapitell (Taf. 9, b), das durch die Spiralfrisur
dem kyprischen Stück noch näher steht, ist trotz seines bogenförmigen
unteren Abschlusses geschlossener im Umriss, gemässigter in den
Kurven, und besitzt im Uräenfries eine stark betonte Waagerechte.

Eine Grabstele aus Hadrumetum (Sousse) im Louvre[55] und ein
Stelenbruchstück aus Karthago in der Bibliothèque Nationale[56] sind
Beispiele für die Wanderung des Hathormotivs in das w e s t -
p h o e n i k i s c h e   G e b i e t. Auf der Reliefstele von Hadrume-

---

50. *Swed.Cypr.Exped.* 3, 171 Abb. 109 und S. 166.

51. *Swed.Cypr.Exped.* 3, 155 und 238 Nr. 290 Taf. 57. — Harter weisser Kalkstein. H. 100, 7 cm. Gr. Br. 79, 5.

52. *AA.* 1934, 93.

53. *Swed.Cypr.Exped.* 3, 266. 289.

54. *JdI.* 35, 1920, 20f.

55. *Gaz.Arch.* 9, 1884, 51ff. Taf. 7 (Ch. Berger). Perrot-Chipiez III 461, Abb.
337. *Ausonia* 4, 1909, 194 Abb. 13. *Rom u. Karthago*, 158, Taf. 12 (Herbig).

56. Perrot-Chipiez III, 54 Abb. 16. Ohnefalsch-Richter *KBH.* 426, Taf. 85, 4.
CISem. I 2, Taf. 29, Nr. 1571. *Ausonia* 4, 1909, 194 Abb. 14.

tum stützen zwei kannelierte Säulen, die vom Oberkörper einer weiblichen Gottheit bekrönt werden, das Gebälk. Sie ruhen auf mehrgliedriger Basis, ihren Ansatz umhüllt ein Akanthuskelch.[57] Das vierzonige Gebälk zeigt in der geflügelten Sonnenscheibe und dem Uräenfries darüber deutlichen ägyptischen Einfluß. Die Göttin hält in ihren vor die Brust gelegten Armen eine Mondsichel und darin eine kleine Rundscheibe. Eine weitere Scheibe bekrönt ihr Haupt. Schneckenzopffrisur, gewiss vom Hathortypus übernommen, wenn auch die Bedeutung der Göttin hier eine andere ist: Tanit oder sonst eine phoenikische Gottheit.[58] Ober- und Unterarme bilden zusammen eine Dreiecksform; die waagerecht verlaufenden Unterarme geben diesem "Säulenkopf" die nötige Ausladung und dem weiteren Aufbau eine breitere Basis.

Von der Stele in Karthago ist nur ein Teil der linken Hälfte erhalten. Die Büste der Göttin mit der Schneckenzopffrisur ist unten abgerundet, was m.E. eher eine Reminiszenz an den Halskragen der ägyptischen Hathor als eine Mondsichel sein dürfte.[59] Dieser Kopf krönt das "äolisierende" Kapitell eines kannelierten Pfeilers. Rechts vom Kopf eine Rosette, vielleicht der Beginn eines Frieses wie auf der Stele von Hadrumetum; zuoberst ein Eierstab als Abschluß. Von der Inschrift nur wenige Reste im Felde rechts (Weihung an Tanit?).

In Gliederung und Verzierung des Aedicula-Gebälkes stimmt mit der Grabstele von Hadrumetum ein Marmorrelief des Museums in Kairo[60] überein, das augenscheinlich aus den Ruinen von Memphis stammt. Die Darstellung läßt sich zu einer Kulthandlung zu Ehren einer thronenden Göttin ergänzen, die innerhalb eines Naiskos von zwei Männern ausgeübt wird. Die Säulen des Naiskos sind von Hathorkapitellen bekrönt; die Göttin hat Kuhohren und Schneckenzopffrisur; der Halskragen besteht aus vier ornamentierten Zonen; auf den Schultern sitzen als Verschlußglieder nach außen blickende Falkenköpfe.[61] In der Türöffnung des Naos erscheint der von der Sonnenscheibe bekrönte Uräus. Noël Aimé-Giron kommt in seiner ausführ-

---

57. Vgl. die dem Melkart geweihten zwei Cippen im Malta und im Louvre, *CISem.* I 1, Taf. 24, Nr. 122 und 122 bis. Das Stück in Malta auch: Ohnefalsch-Richter, *KBH.* Taf. 81, 1 u. Perrot-Chipiez III 79 Abb. 28.

58. Ein Gegenbeispiel: Auf einem ägyptischen Relief des N.R. in Berlin wird die Göttin Kadesch in der Form der Hathor mit dem Naos dargestellt, H. Bonnet, *Aegyptische Religion (Bilderatlas zur Religionsgeschichte* hrg. v. H. Haas, Lief. 2-4, 1924) Abb. 55.

59. Ebenso Pettazzoni, *Ausonia* 4, 1909, 206 Anm. 4 und Noël Aimé-Giron, *Bull. Inst.franç.d'archéol. orient.du Caire* 25, 1925, 195 Anm. 1.

60. Nr. 43081. G. Daressy, *Rec. de trav.* 35, 1913, 46ff. Taf. 1. — Noël Aimé-Giron, *a.O.* 191ff. Taf. 1. 2.

61. Vgl. Originale wie H. Carter, *Tut-anch-Amun* 2₅ Leipzig 1928 Taf. 81, 1. Goldmaske des Tut-ench-Amun ebda. Titelbild und Taf. 73.

lichen Behandlung des Reliefs dazu, in diesem in außerägyptischem Material gefertigten Stück ein syrisches Werk zu erkennen. In der thronenden Göttin sieht er Astarte, deren Verehrung durch die Φοινικαιγύπτιοι gerade für Memphis bezeugt ist.[62] In der Datierung in hellenistische Zeit (3.-2. Jahrh. v.Chr.) folgt er Edgar[63] und setzt sich damit in Widerspruch zu Daressy's überzeugenderer Ansetzung des Stückes in die Kaiserzeit,[64] in deren Anfang es auch von Bissing zu gehören scheint.

Unter den ägyptisierenden Kapitellen des k a i s e r z e i t l i c h e n R o m, die, wenn es sich auch in keinem Falle beweisen läßt, aus Heiligtümern ägyptischer Gottheiten[65] stammen müssen, erscheint auch das Hathorkapitell.

Ein marmornes Säulenkapitell (Taf. 10, c) im Garten des Antiquarium comunale (1933 war es nicht mehr aufzufinden)[66] verbindet in einmaliger Weise Lotosblüten, Uräen und Hathorköpfe zu einem Ganzen. Ueber einem schweren Wulst ein Kranz aufrechtstehender Lotosblüten, unterbrochen von zwei darauf gesetzten Hathorköpfen mit Schneckenzopffrisur und doppeltem "Halskragen." Auf dem Hathorkopf (Gesicht fortgebrochen) Lotosknospe, hinter der nach beiden Seiten hin abwärts gebogene Stengel herauswachsen, die sich an den Enden kolbenartig zu Knospen verdicken. Zwischen den Hathorköpfen jederseits sieben Uräen, die in den Zwischenräumen zwischen den Lotosknospen aufsteigen. Auf der einen Seite ist ihr ganzer oberer Teil durch eine Stückungsleere, auf der entgegengesetzten nur der mittlere Uräus durch eine quadratische Einarbeitung zerstört. Zwischen dem 2. und 3. Uräus von aussen steigt in flachem Relief je ein gerundeter Stengel auf, der nach aussen umbiegt und anscheinend ebenfalls in einer grossen Knospe endete (links auf der Abb. zu erkennen). Leicht konvex geschwungener zylindrischer Kalathos; Abakusleiste bestossen. In der Mitte des Oberlagers ein quadratisches Dübelloch (7 cm Seitenlänge, 3 cm Tiefe) mit Guss-

62. Soc.Ital.di Firenze, *Papyri greci et latini* 5 Nr. 531. Wilcken, *Urkunden der Ptolemäerzeit* 37f.

63. *Bull. Soc. Arch. d'Alex.* Nr. 19, 1923, 114.

64. *Rec. de trav.*, a.ob.Anm. 60 a.O.

65. Eines der zahlreichen Heiligtümer der Isis und des Serapis hat bekanntlich der dritten Region der Stadt ihren Namen gegeben. Architekturglieder aus dem Iseum der neunten Region, hinter S. Maria sopra Minerva: Kapitell und Teil des Schaftes einer Papyrussäule aus Marmor: *Ann. Inst.* 24, 1852, tav.d'agg. V, wonach Köster, *Die ägypt. Pflanzensäule der Spätzeit* 26 Abb. 4. 5. Ferner Reste reliefgeschmückter Säulen: *Le recenti scoperte dell 'Iseo Campense descritte ed illustrate.* Roma 1883 Taf. 6 (SA. aus *Bull. Com.* 2, 1883). Settimo Bocconi, *Musei Capitolini, Pinacoteca e Tabularium.* Roma 1925, 44f.

66. Fot. Röm.Inst. 5384, wonach Mercklin, *AA.* 1925, 162 Abb. 1. H. 29, größter erhaltener Dm. oben 48 cm.

kanal, ausserdem, nach der Seite mit der Stückungsleere hin, ein quadratisches Stemmloch.

Ein zweites Kapitell (Taf. 9, a) der gleichen Sammlung (Saal IX), jetzt (Mai 1950) im Garten des Nuovo Museo Capitolino,[67] aus ziemlich feinkristallinischem, gräulichen, von hellbräunlichen Schichten durchzogenem, wohl ostgriechischem (kleinasiatischem?) Marmor gehört, zusammen mit dem Bruchstück einer römisch-ägyptischen Statuette und einem Sarapisrelief zu den Funden in Via Bocca della Verità. Es verbindet Elemente des korinthischen mit denen eines Hathorkapitells. Unten an den Ecken vier breite Blätter mit abgesetztem, 6-7 mm breitem Wellenrand (nicht überall erhalten) und weich ineinandergehendem Lappen; breite Mittelrippe und je drei weiche Seitenrippen. In den Zwischenräumen, auf jeder der vier Kapitellseiten, ein Hathorkopf, der bis zur Kalathoslippe reicht; darüber Blüte (in einem Fall Aussparung für Anstückung ihrer oberen Hälfte). Die Göttin hat Kuhohren und an fünf Stellen durch Querbänder zusammengehaltene Schneckenzopffrisur. Iris durch Absetzen der Fläche plastisch angegeben, Pupille vollrund eingetieft. Vor dem Halse der Göttin kreuzen sich die Schwanzenden zweier Uräen, die mit ihren geschuppten Leibern über den Blättern paarweise emporwachsen und deren abgebrochene Köpfe einst an Stelle der Voluten gesessen haben. Der Zusammenhang zwischen dem Schlangenleib und dem dazugehörigen Schwanzende lässt sich nur einmal klar verfolgen; gewöhnlich ist er durch das Blatt unterbrochen. Fast gar keine Verwendung des Bohrers. Wohl hadrianisch.

Die Häufigkeit ägyptisierender Motive an Kapitellen der Thermen von Lepcis (Leptis Magna) wird von P. Romanelli, *Leptis Magna*, Roma 1925, 80 hervorgehoben, der gleichzeitig auf das Vorkommen verwandter Formen an anderen Orten des antiken Tripolitanien, wie Sabratha, Gigthis und Girzah hinweist. Ob sich darunter ausser dem mir allein bekannten Kapitell aus dem Frigidarium der Thermen von Lepcis, das im Folgenden beschrieben wird, weitere Hathorkapitelle finden, entzieht sich meiner Kenntnis. Das eben erwähnte Kapitell[68] ist sehr verstümmelt, trägt auf der einen Seite als Schmuck in seinem oberen Teile einen Adler mit ausgebreiteten Flügeln und seitwärts gedrehtem Kopf, auf der anderen einen Hathorkopf "incorniciato da una folta capigliatura ritorta in tre grosse trecce

67. H. 49, 5, Br. etwa 62, Dm. oben 58, unten 35 cm. Oben rechteckiges Dübelloch. — *A A.* 1936, 471, 1940, 459 (wo als Kopfschmuck versehentlich ein Uräus statt der Blüte genannt wird); 1941, 499. — G. Lugli, *I monum. ant. di Roma e Suburbio*. Supplm. Roma 1940, 155. — Phot. Röm.Inst. 1937, 506. A. M. Colini gestattete freundlichst die Veröffentlichung.

68. R. Bartoccini, *Le Terme di Lepcis* (Africa Italiana IV) 1929, 45, Abb. 50.

a spirale per ciascun lato e, sul vertice del capo, le spoglie dello
sparviero" (Bartoccini). Bartoccini erkennt in diesen und in ver-
wandten Beispielen einen starken Einfluss der orientalisch-alexandri-
nischen Kunst, der eher durch Handelsbeziehungen als durch eine
wirkliche Uebertragung von Bildhauerschulen nach Tripolitanien
hervorgerufen worden sei.

Neben dem Hathorkapitell verwendet die ägyptische Baukunst in
selteneren Fällen das B e s k a p i t e l l.

Als Schutzgott der Gebärenden hat Bes seinen Platz in den "Ge-
burtshäusern." In Edfu[69] und Dendera[70] z.B. sind die Abaci über den
Pflanzenkapitellen mit Relieffiguren des Gottes geschmückt, der in
Dendera mit beiden Händen eine ihn umrahmende Lotosgirlande hält.
Die beiden Gebäude stammen aus dem Ende des 2. vorchristlichen
Jahrhunderts bezw. aus augusteischer Zeit.

Statt der ganzen Figuren ist in Philae[71] der Beskopf allein auf den
vier Seiten eines würfelförmigen Aufsatzes auf einem Pflanzenkapitell dargestellt.

Ein Doppelbes aus Kalkstein (Taf. 10, d) im Museo Egizio in
Florenz[72] ist von Rosellini als Rest eines Kapitells gedeutet worden,
was Schiaparelli als unwahrscheinlich zurückweist. Dass das Stück
als Stütze irgendwelcher Art gedient hat, ist durch eine quadratische
Einarbeitung auf der oberen Fläche gesichert. Die Einarbeitung, mit
verschmiertem Dübelloch (?), wird durch querlaufende Eintiefungen
durchschnitten, was auf besonders starke Befestigung eines darüber-
liegenden Werkstückes zu weisen scheint.

Vom Rest eines spätäthiopischen Tempels in Ben Naga aus der
Zeit um Christi Geburt stammt ein Aufbau, bei dem das Hathorkapitell
über einem Bespfeiler sitzt.[73] Dieselbe Kombination — Hathorkopf
über Besfigur — liegt an einem marmornen Tischfuss aus Porto im

---

69. *Ann.Inst.* 9, 1837, tav. d'agg. F, 21. — F. Ballod, *Prolegomena zur Gesch.
der zwerghaften Götter in Aegypten.* Münchener Diss. Moskau 1913, 65, Abb. 79.
— Jéquier, *Temples Ptolém. et Rom.* Taf. 22, 3. 33. 34. 35. — Chassinat, *Le
Mammisi d'Edfou* Taf. 2-4.

70. Ballod, a.O. Abb. 80. — G. Steindorff, *Kunst der Aegypter* 161. — Jéquier,
a.O. Taf. 68. 69; ders. *Manuel* 193, Abb. 118. — E. Chassinat, *Le temple de Dendara* I. Le Caire 1934. Taf. 13. 14. 16. 17. 20. — Ohnefalsch-Richter *KBH.* Taf.
101, 10 u. 138, 10.

71. Lepsius, *Denkm.* I 108.

72. Inv. 448. Schiaparelli, *Catalogo* 109 Nr. 869. — H. 64 cm. Spuren gelber
Bemalung. — Alinari 31123. 31123 a. — Die hier Taf. 10, d wiedergegebene Zeichnung verdanke ich der Güte A. Mintos.

73. Lepsius, *Denkm.* I 139.

Museo Torlonia vor[74] und wiederholt sich an einer von v. Bissing behandelten Gruppe römischer Sistra.[75]

Schon Borchardt[76] hat davor gewarnt, die uns nur in Flächendarstellungen, Malerei oder Relief, überlieferten Säulen allzu wörtlich als Abbilder der Wirklichkeit aufzufassen. Daher seien die Fälle, in denen an solchen Säulen T i e r e i m A u f b a u d e s K a p i t e l l s erscheinen, hier nur kurz erwähnt.

Prisse d' Avennes hat im ersten Band seiner *Histoire de l'art égyptien* mehrere Tafeln dieser zumeist gemalten Architektur gewidmet. Auf seine Zeichnungen gehen fast alle späteren Veröffentlichungen zurück.

Im Grabe des Ken-Amūn in Qurna (Nr. 93, früher Nr. 13) wachsen an gemalten, aus Holz zu denkenden Säulen zweier Baldachine über einem Winden- und einem Nymphaea- caerulea-Kapitell[77] nach drei Seiten blickende Löwenköpfe auf; einen vierten wird man sich dazu ergänzen müssen. N. Davies sieht in ihnen die Köpfe der Sachmet und des Löwengottes Bes,[78] worin man ihr nach v. Bissings Urteil (mündlich) nur im Falle des Bes wird beipflichten können. Löwen erscheinen auch an einer gleichfalls gemalten Säule im Grabe Nr. 58 (usurpiert von Amenemône, 20. Dyn.) der Nekropole von Theben.[79] Drei Falkenköpfe in gleicher Anordnung zeigt ein gemaltes Kapitell aus dem Grabe des Horemheb, königlichen Schreibers unter Thutmosis IV.,[80] zwei Köpfe desselben Raubvogels kommen, nach aussen blickend, auf einer Wandmalerei im Grabe des Nefer-Secheru (späte 18. oder 19. Dyn.) in Zâwijet el- Mêtîn[81] vor.

Eine Kompositsäule in Relief und eine in Wandmalerei in zwei

74. *Il Museo Torlonia* Taf. 5, 20. — Reinach, *RS* II 566, 3 zieht diese Zusammensetzung in Zweifel. Den Hinweis verdanke ich K. Lehmann-Hartleben.

75. v. Bissing, *Bull. Soc. d'Arch.Alex.* Nr. 31 (N.S. 9, 2) 1937, 211ff., besonders Abb. 3 d., 9, 9c, 11, 12.

76. Borchardt, *Pflanzensäule* 2, vgl. auch G. Foucart, *RA* 1896 II, 316.

77. Windenkapitell: Prisse I 363, IV, 6. Taf. 20, 6 (nach handschriftl. Numerierung des Exemplars der Staatsbibliothek München). — Borchardt *a.O.* 51, Abb. 83. — Ch. Chipiez, *Hist. des origines et de la formation des ordres grecs.* Paris 1876. Abb. 18. — Jetziger Zustand: N. Davies, *The tomb of Ken-Amun at Thebes*, New York 1930, Taf. 43. — Nymphaea-caerulea-Kapitell; Prisse, 363, IV, 4. Taf. 20, 4. — Davies, *a.O.* 22 Taf. 11 und farbig: Tafelband 11, A. — Lepsius, *Denkm.* III 63 a, wonach Borchardt a.O. 14 Abb. 24. — Chipiez, *Ordres grecs* Abb. 17. — Perrot-Chipiez V 512 Abb. 323.

78. Davies a.O; ausführlicher *Bull. Metr. Mus., Suppl.Egypt.Exped.* 1916-17, March 1918, 19f. m. Abb. 26.

79. Jéquier, *Manuel* 169 Abb. 93.

80. Grab 78 nach Porter-Moss. Prisse 363, III, 3. Taf. 19, 3. — J. Capart, *Propos sur l'Art ég.* (1931) 15 Abb. 10 rechts. — Heute nicht mehr erhalten, wie aus U. Bouriant, *Mém.Miss.franç.Caire* 5, 2. 1891 Taf. 4 hervorgeht.

81. Prisse 362, I, 5. Taf. 17, 5. — Capart, *L'art ég., Architecture* (1922) Taf. 152, 2.

Gräbern in Theben (18. Dyn.)[82] fügen in ihren reichen Aufbau die Protomen zweier Antilopen ein.

Hängende Uräen mit der Sonnenscheibe stellen an einer gemalten Bukettsäule im Grabe des Sennedjem (Porter-Moss Grab 1, 20. Dyn.) die Verbindung zwischen den beiden obersten Elementen des Aufbaues, einem "Lilien"-und einem Papyruskapitell, her,[83] und aus der Zeit Sethos' I. (19. Dyn.) stammt ein Grab, in dem das oberste, papyrusähnliche Kapitell einer gemalten Bukettsäule von zwei aufsteigenden Uräen umfasst ist.[84]

Das erste Beispiel derartiger Säulen in der wirklichen Architektur brachten die Ausgrabungen des Oriental Institute der Universität Chicago in Medinet Habu. Dort fanden sich als Reste einer Nischenumrahmung in einem der Räume des westlichen Hohen Tores der Tempelanlage Ramses III. (20. Dyn.) zwei Halbsäulen aus Kalkstein, 1,15 m hoch, mit reichlichen Farbspuren. Lotos-, Papyrus- und Lilienkapitell sind hier übereinandergesetzt; aus dem Lotoskapitell ragen, das schmalere Papyruskapitell flankierend, zwei Uräen mit Sonnenscheibe empor. Neben dieser Bündelsäule steht, der Nische zugekehrt, jeweils eine schlanke Säule, ein einzelner Papyrusstengel, auf dessen Blüte wiederum ein Uräus mit Sonnenscheibe thront.[85]

---

82. Prisse 362f. I, 4 u. III, 2. Taf. 17, 4 (Relief) u. 19, 2 (Malerei). — G. Foucart, *RA.* 1896 II, 314 Abb. 24. — Springer, Michaelis, Wolters, *Handbuch* I$_{12}$, 37 Abb. 92. — Capart, *L'Art ég. Architecture* (1922) Taf. 152, 1; ders., *Propos* Abb. 10 links.

83. Chipiez, *Ordres grecs* Abb. 9. — Borchardt *a.O.* 19 Abb. 34. — KiB$_2$ Taf. 13, 10. — Jéquier, *Manuel* 264 Abb. 172. — Eine ähnliche aus dem Grabe des Priesters Aïchesi in Theben: Prisse 363, III, 1. Taf. 19 Mitte, wonach Capart, *Propos* Abb. 10 Mitte.

84. Prisse 363, II, 3 Taf. 18, 3, wonach Capart, *Architecture* (1922) Taf. 152, 4.

85. U. Hölscher, *Medinet Habu* (*Morgenland*, Heft 24, 1933) 33 Taf 11 Abb. 18 a. b; ders., *Architectura, Zts. f.Gesch.d.Baukunst* 1, 1933, 45 Taf. 9. — H. H. Nelson und U. Hölscher, *Oriental Inst. Communications* Nr. 18. Chicago 1934, 97ff. Abb. 53.

DAS PELIKAN-MOTIV IN DER ALTAEGYPTISCHEN LITERATUR

Eberhard Otto

Göttingen

Die Wertschätzung der antiken Ueberlieferung als Quelle für die altägyptische Kultur schwankt naturgemäss im Hinblick auf die Schicht. Ich möchte dieses Bild gebrauchen: Der Strom der Volkszeugenbericht eines Herodot wird immer als zeitgenössisches Zeugnis eines Ereignisses oder einer Einrichtung seinen Wert behalten. Anders, wenn es sich um die Ueberlieferung von nur Gehörtem aus älterer Zeit handelt, wo sich sachliche Entstellungen und sprachliche Missverständnisse eingeschlichen haben können und es auch getan haben, wobei der Fehler nicht immer auf Seiten des in Aegypten Fremden zu liegen braucht. Anders wieder liegt der Fall, wenn es sich darum handelt, den Ursprung einer Einrichtung oder Sitte, eines künstlerischen oder literarischen Motivs, eines Gedankens oder einer religiösen Vorstellung als ägyptisch nachzuweisen, sei es dass die Alten einen solchen Ursprung ausdrücklich behaupten oder nicht. Denn die Dinge nehmen ein anderes Gesicht an, wenn sie uns im orientalischen Gewand entgegentreten, ein anderes, wenn sie vom Abendland rezipiert sind.

Nun hat neuerdings von Bissing[1] anlässlich einer Einzelfrage die nach dem Ursprung der Tierfabel aufgerollt und kommt zu dem Schluss: "Die Griechen haben ägyptisches Gut übernommen, es seines religiösen Charakters entkleidet und die Fabel so ausgebildet, wie sie dann in der Weltliteratur erscheint. Bis neue Funde den Gegenbeweis bringen, darf Aegypten als Geburtsland der Fabel gelten." Die Schwierigkeit, die von ägyptologischer Seite besteht, durch Hinzufügen von Einzelthemen und -motiven diese These zu erhärten, sind vorwiegend in der Einstufung dieser Literaturgattung, der Tiererzählungen im weitesten Sinne, seitens der Aegypter selbst begründet:[2] in die uns erhaltene *Kunst*literatur reicht die Tiererzählung in der älteren Zeit offenbar garnicht, in der jüngeren selten hinauf und in

---

1. Eudoxos von Knidos, *Forschungen und Fortschritte* Okt. 1949, 225ff. vgl. auch Max Pieper, *Die ägyptische Literatur, Handbuch der Literaturwissenschaft* hg. v. O. Walzel 1928, 84 5.

2. Es fehlt weitgehend an einer klaren Scheidung des Materials nach seiner Form, die zur literarischen Klassifizierung entscheidend ist. Im demot. Leidener Papyrus ist die Erzählung vom Löwen und der Maus eine Tierfabel. Im gleichen Papyrus wird der Mythus vom Sonnenauge in ein Kunstmärchen mit Tiergestalten eingekleidet. Umgekehrt ist im Pap. d' Orbiney (Märchen von den zwei Brüdern) ein alter Tier*mythus* in ein Kunstmärchen umgestaltet.

der religiösen Literatur spielt der Tiermythus die gleiche Rolle als Glied einer volkstümlichen, der offiziellen Theologie entfremdeten Schicht. Ich möchte dieses Bild gebrauchen: Der Strom der Volksvorstellungen und -erzählungen wird nur am Anfang and am Ende der ägyptischen Geschichte von dem sich über ihm erhebenden Bogen der Hochkultur berührt; dass diese Hochkultur auch in den dazwischen liegenden Zeiten von den uns fast unbekannten niederen Schichten gespeist wird, offenbart sich uns fast nur an den Wendepunkten und in den Krisenzeiten der kulturellen Entwicklung.

Um ein Beispiel dafür zu geben, wähle ich die bekannte Erzählung vom Pelikan, der sich um seiner Jungen willen die Brust aufreisst und seine Brut mit seinem Blut wiederbelebt. Ob die Voraussetzung, er habe sie auch selbst getötet, schon ägyptisch vorhanden war, vermag ich nicht nachzuweisen. Als christliches Symbol der Selbstaufopferung begegnet dieses Motiv ebenso in der Literatur wie in der bildenden Kunst.[3] In den naturgeschichtlichen Sammelwerken der Spätantike wird die Erzählung mehrfach gegeben, so beim Physiologus und in den sogenannten Koiraniden. In der letztgenannten Sammlung lautet sie folgendermassen: Ῥάμφιος πτηνόν ἐστι παρὰ τὸν ποταμὸν Νεῖλον ἠπταμένον λεγόμενον πελεκᾶνος, καὶ ἐν τῇ λίμνῃ τοῦ Αἰγύπτου διαιτώμενον, οὕτως φιλότεκνόν ἐστι πάνυ. Ὅταν οὖν γεννήσῃ νεοσσούς, καὶ ὀλίγῳ αὐξηθῶσι, τύπτουσιν εἰς τὸ πρόσωπον αὐτῶν. Ἐκεῖνοι μὴ ἀνεχόμενοι κολαφίζουσιν τὰ τέκνα καὶ ἀποκτείνουσιν αὐτά. ὕστερον δὲ σπλαγχνίζονται ἐπ' αὐτοὺς καὶ πενθοῦσι τά τέκνα ἅπερ ἐφόνευσαν. Τῇ οὖν αὐτῇ ἡμέρᾳ ἡ αὐτῶν μήτηρ ἐλεεῖ τὰ ἴδια τέκνα καὶ τὰς ἑαυτῆς πλευρὰς περιτίλασα ἀναπτύσσει, τὰ δὲ αἵματα στάζοντα ἐπί τὰ νεκρὰ σώματα αὐτῶν τῶν θανόντων τέκνων ζωογονεῖ αὐτά καὶ ἐγείρονται φυσικῷ τινι τρόπῳ. Fast wörtlich stimmt damit die Fassung des Physiologus überein, allerdings[4] mit der Erwähnung einer wohl auf christliche Anregung zurückgehenden Trauerzeit von drei Tagen zwischen Tod und Wiederbelebung. Für beide Sammelwerke hat man mit guten Gründen Alexandrien, das Sammelbecken orientalischer, antiker und christlicher Ströme als Ursprungsort genannt,[5] und zwar das vorchristliche Alexandrien. Isidor von Spanien erzählt die Geschichte ebenfalls mit Bezug auf Aegypten:[6] fertur, si verum sit, eam occidere natos suos,

---

3. Luther kennt die Erzählung wie auch Wolfram von Eschenbach. vgl. Grimms *Deutsches Wörterbuch s. v.* Pelikan. RGG *s. v.* Symbolik. ferner Cheyne-Black, *Encyclopaedia Biblica* Sp. 3645.

4. de Mély, *Les lapidaires de l'antiquité*, II, 96.

5. *RE s. v.* Kyraniden; ferner Hommel, *Die äthiopische Uebersetzung des Physiologus*, Leipzig 1877, Einleitung pass.

6. XII, 7=Hopfner, *Fontes religionis aegyptiacae* 725.

eosque per triduum lugere, deinde se ipsam vulnerare et aspersione sui sanguinis vivificare eos. Diese Form wird auf Augustin[7] zurückgehen, der teilweise wörtlich hiermit übereinstimmt: Dicuntur hae aves tanquam colaphis rostrorum occidere parvulos suos, eosdemque in nido occisos a se lugere per triduum; postremo dicunt matrem seipsam graviter vulnerare et sanguinem suum super filios fundere, quo illi superfusi reviviscunt. Und er fügt vorsichtig hinzu: Fortasse hoc verum, fortasse falsum sit. Aehnliches berichtet Horapollo[8] vom Geier, während er vom Pelikan[9] das Motiv der Selbstaufopferung zwar ebenfalls bezeugt, aber in einer anderen Form: Die Eier des Vogels würden mit trockenem Kuhmist bedeckt und dieser angezündet; der Pelikan verbrenne beim Versuch das Feuer zu löschen seine Flügel und falle so den Jägern in die Hände; weil er auf diese Weise für seine Kinder sich opfere, sei es den Priestern verboten, ihn zu essen. Eine naturwissenschaftliche Erklärung der Fabel bringt Aelian (*nat. hist.* 23): Storch, Reiher und Pelikan nährten ihre Jungen, wenn Mangel an Futter bestünde, dadurch, dass sie das am vorigen Tage Gefressene auskröpften und ihnen zur Nahrung gäben. Er kennt also wohl die Fabel, ohne sie als solche zu erwähnen, hebt jedenfalls die Mutterliebe der Tiere ausdrücklich hervor. Bei Aristoteles und Plinius findet sich nichts, was mit der Erzählung in Verbindung gebracht werden könnte.

Gibt uns die ägyptische Literatur Hinweise an die Hand, dass ihr diese oder eine ähnliche Fabel mit dem Motiv der Mutterliebe bekannt war?

Zu den heiligen Tieren im eigentlichen Sinne gehört der Pelikan offenbar nicht.[10] Dennoch wird er in der älteren religiösen Literatur mehrfach genannt.[11] Bereits in den Pyramidentexten geschieht des Tieres einmal in bezeichnender Weise Erwähnung.[12] Der Spruch ist einmal in der Onnos- und zweimal in der Tetipyramide aufgezeichnet. Er ist aus mehreren Stücken kompiliert: Der Tote erscheint als Schlange und seine Herrschaft über die Götter wird beansprucht.

---

7. *Enarratio in Psalmum* CI, ed. Migne IV 1299.

8. I, 11=Hopfner, a. a. O. S. 580.

9. I, 54=Hopfner, a. a. O. S. 587/88.

10. Der Pelikan wird weder bei Zimmermann, *Aegyptische Religion nach der Darstellung der Kirchenschriftsteller*, Paderborn 1912, noch bei Hopfner, *Der Tierkult der Aegypter, Denkschr. Wien. Akad.* 1913 genannt.

11. Hier sind nur die Stellen behandelt, die für unsere Frage aufschlussreich sind. In ihnen heisst der Vogel durchweg ḥn.t oder ḥnw.t. Die daneben auftretende Bezeichnung (ḥm) pśd.ti. scheint weniger ein Name als ein Appellativum des Tieres zu sein und charakterisiert ihn in einer uns wohl nicht mehr fassbaren Erzählung.

12. *Pyr. Texte* ed. Sethe, § 511 vgl. dazu Sethe, *Kommentar* II. 362ff. Ausserdem wird der ḥn.t-Pelikan noch § 278 genannt, an einer Stelle, die mit unserem Thema nichts zu tun hat.

Aber nur eine von den drei Fassungen, u.zw. die ältere aus der Tetipyramide, hat den inhaltlich völlig entbehrlichen Einschub: "Meine Mutter ist der Pelikan; ich bin ihr Sohn" (in der Niederschrift ist statt der ursprünglichen 1. Person der Name des Königs eingesetzt). Wir haben in diesem Passus nicht etwa eine gelehrte theologische Anspielung auf einen uns unbekannten Mythus, sondern ein sicherndes Zurückgreifen auf eine Volksvorstellung. Es soll damit ausgedrückt werden: Der Tote hat eine Mutter, deren Fürsorge sprichwörtlich ist. Eine solche Bedeutung des Einschubs kann nur dann erhärtet werden, wenn der Pelikan auch sonst wegen seiner Mutterliebe genannt wird. Das geschieht eindeutig in einem Sargtext,[13] wo der Tote einem dämonischen Türhüter im Jenseits zuruft: "O jener Grosse mit lauter Stimme! Ich bin der Pelikan, der auf dich schaut. Ich bin gekommen auf der Suche nach meinen Nestlingen" (der Text ist ebenfalls in der 3. Person niedergeschrieben). Das soll bedeuten, die Berechtigung zum Eintritt in ein bewachtes Tor holt sich der Tote durch die Gleichsetzung mit jenem Vogel, der für seine Mutterliebe bekannt ist und sich im Augenblick auf der Suche nach seinen Nestlingen als einem ihm unbedingt zugehörigen Teil befindet.

Komplizierter, aber für uns am meisten ausschlaggebend ist ein Spruch derselben Sammlung,[14] von dem nicht weniger als 10 Niederschriften bekannt sind, die z.T. nicht unerheblich voneinander abweichen (Abb. 1). Die Uebersetzung lautet:

    a. Ich bin der Pelikan, der auf deine Brut schaut.
    b. Ich bin gekommen, um meine Nestlinge zu revidieren.
    c. Ich fordere das Gehirn (?) von dem "Brustbeisser."
    d. Ich bin der Pavian und also bin ich stärker als du.

Die Uebersetzung bedarf einiger erläuternder Worte: Zunächst gehört der letzte Satz deutlich nicht in den Zusammenhang. Die Zusammenfügung von Textsplittern zu Totensprüchen bedarf keiner Glaubhaftmachung. Ueber die schwache Möglichkeit diesen Textteil in die Interpretation hineinzuziehen, s. u. S. 6. Der dritte Satz weist mehrere Varianten bezüglich der Personalsuffixe auf. Fünf Texte haben die oben zugrunde gelegte Form. Drei Texte schreiben "der in *seine* Brust beisst"; bei einem Text ist das Suffix an "Brust" zerstört. Das Wort "Brust" in seiner korrekten Form als fem. haben vier Texte; fünf Texte schreiben *m k; b.f.* d. h. "in seinem Inneren," offenbar eine Verderbnis, die zu Lasten des Schreibers geht. Der Ausdruck lautet klärlich "der in die Brust beisst" ohne Personal-

13. Gardiner — de Buck. *The Egyptian coffin texts* III, 393.
14. *Ibid.*, III S. 330-31 = Lacau. *Textes religieuses* Nr. 47.

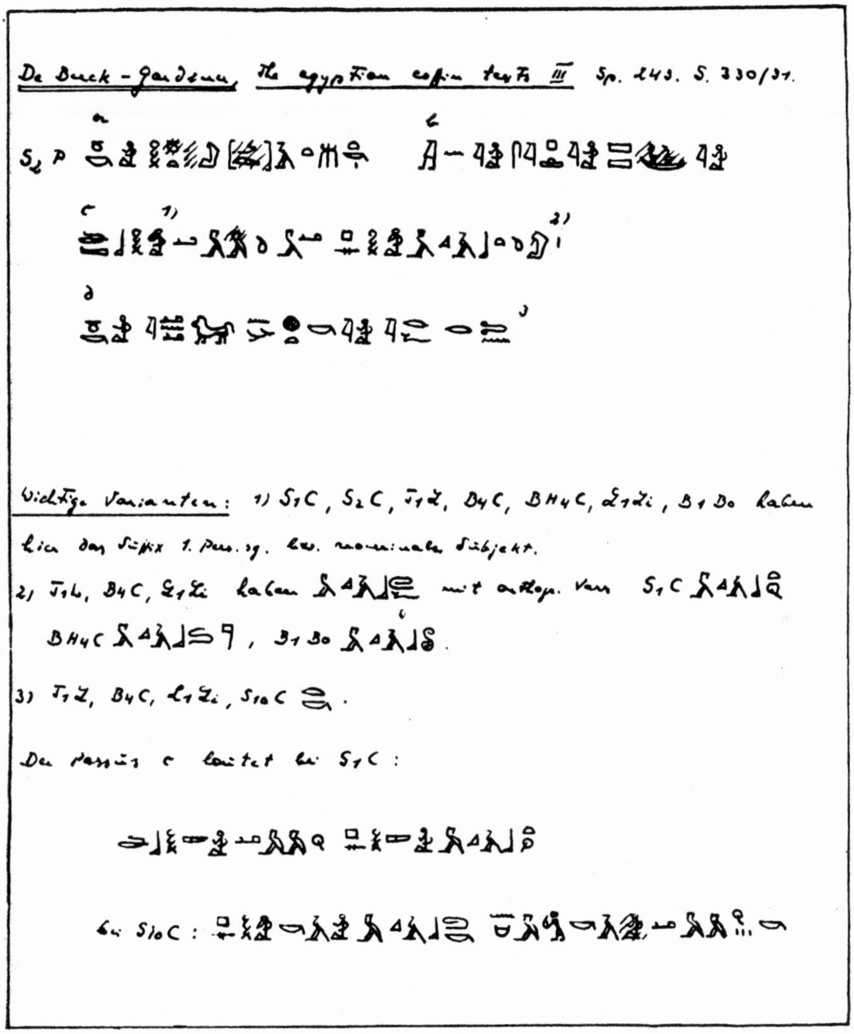

De Buck - Gardiner, *The egyptian coffin texts* III Sp. 243. S. 330/31.

Wichtige Varianten: 1) S₁C, S₂C, T₁L, B₄C, BH4C, L₁Li, B₁Bo haben hier das Suffix 1. Pers. sg. bzw. nominales Subjekt.

2) T₁L, B₄C, L₁Li haben [...] mit anthrop. Var. S₁C [...] BH4C [...], B₁Bo [...].

3) T₁L, B₄C, L₁Li, S₁₀C [...].

Das Passiv c lautet bei S₁C:

bei S₁₀C: [...]

Abb. 1.

suffix; er ist nach Analogie zu bekannten festen Wendungen wie
"der das Gesicht öffnet" = aufmerksam, "der die Hand ausstreckt" =
freigebig u.a.m. als *ein* Wort zu übersetzen "der Brustbeisser." So,
als Appellativum, fassen es offenbar zwei Texte auf, die die gesamte
Phrase mit dem Gottesdeterminativ versehen (S2P, BH4C). Schliesslich hat eine Niederschrift (S10C) den dem Aegypter selbst wohl
nicht sehr klaren Passus völlig verändert: "Dann beisse ich in deine
Brust und nehme dein Gehirn (?) weg." Geringer ist die Aenderung
bei S1C: "Ich fordere das Gehirn (?), ich beisse in die Brust." Die
Bedeutung "Gehirn" für das Wort ‛mm ist neuerdings von Iversen
aus anderen Stellen erschlossen.[15]

Die Interpretation des Textes ist nicht einfach, umso weniger, als
dem Aegypter selbst der Zusammenhang offenbar nicht ganz klar
war; das zeigen die zahlreichen Abwandlungen deutlich. Vom Zweck
des Spruches ausgehend lässt sich folgendes sagen: Der Tote tritt
einem nicht genannten Wesen gegenüber und will einen ihm wichtigen
Körperteil (Gehirn?) von ihm fordern. Die Berechtigung soll durch
die Behauptung gestützt werden: Ich bin der Pelikan. Dann bedeuten
die ersten beiden Sätze: Er ist der Vogel, der um seiner Mutterliebe
willen berühmt ist. Er hat somit ein natürliches Recht, seine Nestlinge als das ihm wesentlich Zugehörige zu "revidieren" d.h. etwa für
sich in Anspruch nehmen." Er blickt in dieser Gestalt auf die Brut
des Angeredten. Das ist eine Bedrohung in dem Sinne, dass jener
verdächtigt wird, möglicherweise einen der Pelikan-Nestlinge wider-
rechtlich weggenommen zu haben. Nach dieser Einschüchterung folgt
das eigentliche Anliegen: Der Toten will sein Gehirn (?) und zwar
scheinbar von einem Wesen, das Brustbeisser genannt wird. Das Ge-
suchte, worauf der Tote seinen Anspruch richtet, tritt anstelle der
Nestlinge, auf die der Pelikan ein Anrecht hat. Weiterhin werden in
Parallele zueinander gesetzt der Körperteil, den der Tote beansprucht,
mit dem Körperteil, den der Pelikan gegeben hatte, ohne dass des-
wegen beide einander genau entsprechen müssten. Hier erhebt sich
aber eine Unstimmigkeit: Nach den gesprochenen Worten will der
Tote seinen Körperteil *von* dem "Brustbeisser" fordern.

Ich glaube, mit einer verhältnismässig geringfügigen Textverän-
derung lässt sich diese scheinbare Unstimmigkeit beseitigen. Die
Präposition "von" *m‛* liegt lautlich und graphisch dicht neben der
Präposition *m* "als," sodass ein Verhören oder Verschreiben nicht aus-
serhalb des Möglichen bleibt. Wenn wir dies aber als Fehler unterstellen, ergibt der Satz den klaren Sinn: "Ich bin der Pelikan . . . .
ich fordere das Gehirn (?) *als* der Brustbeisser." Hier ist die den

---

15. Iversen, *JEA* 33, 47ff.

Vogel kennzeichnende Tätigkeit als Begründung des Anspruchs auf den Toten selbst übertragen, der sich ja am Anfang als Pelikan vorstellt. Die Veränderung der (ursprünglichen) Präposition "als" in die ähnlich klingende "von" kann unter dem Eindruck des Verbums "fordern" entstanden sein in Analogie zu anderen Totensprüchen, wo der Tote Körperteile oder Gerätschaften von anderen Wesen fordert oder nimmt. Die eine unserer Niederschriften kommt im Sinne der als möglich erachteten Form nahe, indem sie den Passus formuliert: "Ich fordere das Gehirn (?), (denn) ich beisse in die Brust." In diesem Falle ist die Identität Toter = Pelikan = Brustbeisser klarer gewahrt. Einen anderen Versuch, allen Schwierigkeiten aus dem Wege zu gehen, unternimmt die oben erwähnte Variante S10C: "Dann beisse ich in deine Brust und nehme dein Gehirn (?) weg." Hier ist der innere Zusammenhang mit der Pelikanerzählung weitgehend aufgegeben und die vom Tier an sich selbst begangene Handlung, die die Berechtigung erweisen soll, wird als Bedrohung gegenüber dem Angeredeten verwendet.

Schliesslich besteht noch eine Schwierigkeit grammatischer Art: Der Ausdruck "Brustbeisser" ist durchweg als Masculinum geschrieben, während der Name des Pelikan ebenso eindeutig ein Femininum ist. Es ist aber daran zu denken, dass uns die Pelikanerzählung als solche ja nicht hier erhalten ist; in ihr kann der offenbar alte und feststehende Begriff "Brustbeisser" auf einen maskulinen Namen des Tieres bezogen gewesen und von dort unverändert übernommen worden sein. Wenn auch zusammengesehen die vorgeschlagenen Veränderungen und Deutungen vielleicht zunächst etwas gekünstelt erscheinen, so bleibt doch zu erwägen, dass die inhaltliche und textliche Redaktion der Sargtexte uns fast nirgends ein glattes Uebersetzen und Verstehen des Textes erlaubt. Ferner ist immer vorausgesetzt, dass eine Fassung der Pelikanerzählung bestand, die sich in allen wesentlichen Punkten mit der uns bekannten deckte. Abweichungen von ihr, die uns nicht fassbar sind, mögen zum guten Teil ebenfalls Ursache sein, dass uns diese Anspielung auf die Fabel, denn mehr ist es nicht, nicht ohne weiteres verständlich wird.

Der Gedankengang des Aegypters war — zusammengefasst — folgender: Der Spruch soll dem Toten den Anspruch auf einen unentbehrlichen Körperteil sichern. Die Sicherung geschieht, wie so oft, durch Heranziehen eines allgemein bekannten Präzedenzfalles. Die Zusammengehörigkeit Toter — Gehirn (?) entspricht der zwischen dem Pelikan und seinen Nestlingen. Nun folgt ein Gedankensprung: Hat der Pelikan einen eigenen Körperteil hingegeben, der keineswegs das 'mm zu sein braucht, und kann ihn also jederzeit mit Recht zurückfordern, so ebenso der Tote, wenn er als Pelikan auftritt. Die innere Unlogik ist typisch, die darin liegt, dass das Begehrte mit verschiedenen Dingen gleichzeitig gleichgesetzt wird die — das ist für die Aegypter das ihnen Gemeinsame — alle rechtmässig beansprucht werden, d.h. in unserem Falle zuerst mit den Nestlingen, dann mit einem nicht genannten Körperteil des Vogels.

An sich würde der Text noch eine andere Deutungsmöglichkeit zulassen, nämlich unter Einbeziehung des letzten Satzes mit dem Pavian. Nimmt man an, es solle darauf angespielt werden, dass der Pavian den Pelikan in die Brust gebissen und einen Körperteil weggenommen habe, so liefe der Text: "Ich bin der Pelikan . . . . ich fordere das Gehirn (?) von dem Brustbeisser, ich bin der Pavian." Dann aber hätten wir einen schwer verständlichen Wechsel der Maske; der Tote ist erst der Pelikan, der etwas erlitten hat, dann der Pavian, der das Leid zugefügt hat. Daher scheint mir diese Auflösung, die noch verschiedene sprachliche Schwierigkeiten hat, nicht glücklich zu sein. Es wäre der innere Zusammenhang zwischen der Mutterliebe des Tieres, der Selbstaufopferung und dem darin begründeten Anspruch völlig zerstört.

In der Art, wie in dem behandelten Text eine als bekannt vorausgesetzte Tierfabel einem bestimmten Zweck zuliebe benützt worden ist, liegt etwas für die ägyptische Literaturgeschichte Beispielhaftes. Es erscheint mir darum nicht nur wesentlich, die Existenz dieser Literaturgattung durch ein indirektes Beispiel aus bemerkenswert früher Zeit wahrscheinlich zu machen, sondern auch darauf hinzuweisen, dass die Erzählung nicht in religiösem Gewand als Tiermythus existierte. Der Pelikan ist keine "Göttin," von der ein Mythus erzählt wird. Er ist vielmehr ein handelndes Tier geblieben, dem freilich — das ist die Voraussetzung zu Fabel und Märchen — menschliches Vorstellungsvermögen nur menschliche Empfindungen unterstellen konnte. Aber Tier und Handlung gehören der "Märchenschicht" an, die in der geistigen Entwicklung der Frühzeit eine nachweisbare Entwicklungsstufe dargestellt hat und die in historischer Zeit als Teil einer unter der offiziellen Theologie und Literatur befindlichen nicht-literarischen Schicht weiterlebt. Aus ihr leiht sich in unserem Falle der in den Sargtexten ja für eine breitere Menge wirkende "Schreiber" ein Motiv, um eine bestimmte Situation in ein allgemein bekanntes Bild einzukleiden und ein bestimmtes religiöses Anliegen wirkungsvoll vorzubringen. Dieser Vorgang ist beachtenswert. Zeigt er doch die Freiheit, mit der der Stoff zweckentsprechend behandelt wird, und die geheimnisvoll andeutende Ausdrucksart, die dem funerären Charakter des Textes entspricht. Denn nun erhebt sich natürlich für uns die Frage, ob nicht in manchen anderen Fällen, wo wir eine uns unverständliche gelehrte Anspielung vermuten möchten, ebenfalls solche volksmässige, untheologische Erzählungen vorauszusetzen sind. Gerade in der Fülle der Sargtexte, deren Kompilation im wesentlichen in die tiefste Krisenzeit der ägyptischen Geistesentwicklung fällt, ist ein Zurückgreifen auf Motive und Vorstellungen einer bisher nicht zu Worte gekommenen Schicht am ehesten zu erwarten.

Freilich zeigt das behandelte Beispiel auch recht eindringlich die Grenzen der Erkennbarkeit. Der Stoff wird als bekannt vorausgesetzt; anders bleibt der Text unverständlich. Zu dieser Kenntnis kann uns — und damit kehre ich zum Ausgangspunkt der kleinen Betrachtung zurück — auch die antike Ueberlieferung verhelfen. Nicht nur wenn sie Selbstgeschautes berichtet, steht sie dem alten Aegypten unmittelbar und zeitgenössisch gegenüber. Auch wo sie aus dem Strom der kontinuierlichen Volksüberlieferung schöpft, die dem Auf und Ab, dem rascheren Werden und Vergehen der Erscheinungen der Hochkultur weniger unterworfen war, leitet sie, wie im besprochenen Falle, als unmittelbares Bindeglied eine Tradition des alten Aegypten in die christliche Welt hinüber.

THE EASTERN MEDITERRANEAN ABOUT 1060 B. C.

W. F. ALBRIGHT
Johns Hopkins University

Since the Report of Wen-Amun was first published by the late Wladimir Golénischeff in 1899, many scholars have emphasized its importance.[1] It is true that some have treated it as a mere romance, but this is a complete misunderstanding of its character. Since there are no superhuman exploits or incredible adventures and since the only skill shown by the hero is occasionally in speech, there is nothing *a priori* against its substantial authenticity. Moreover, the loss of face suffered by Wen-Amun at every turn, together with the total lack of prestige enjoyed by Egypt and Egyptians in Syria, suggests a rather honest report of the failure (?) of a mission. Moreover, Wen-Amun belongs to essentially the same category as the Story of Sinuhe, which I formerly regarded as a historical romance, but now recognize as substantially true to fact.[2] One difference is that the Story of Sinuhe is a literary expansion of an autobiography which may well have appeared in the tomb of an historical prince Sinuhe about the middle of the twentieth century B. C., whereas the Report of Wen-Amun looks like a literary expansion of the Egyptian envoy's own official account of his mission. Discovery after discovery has confirmed the general reliability of the narrative, while the speeches may certainly be taken as typical, though scarcely as verbatim transcripts of what actually was said. When Wen-Amun mentions names and places, political and economic details, etc., we may safely follow his guidance; when he pictures himself favorably or claims to have succeeded in some ruse, we may remain prudently aloof, exercising the historian's duty to suspect an autobiographer of human vanity.

There is no comparable document from the world preceding Herodotus. Nowhere else do we have in such compact space so many interesting details about men and customs not belonging to the folk of the narrator. John A. Wilson has recently added an extremely important new detail, that a previously unexplained word occurring in ii: 71 is to be read *mw'd* and identified with Hebrew *mô'ēd*, "assembly."[3] This

---

1. First published in hieroglyphic transcription and translation, *Recueil de Travaux*, XXI (1899) 74 ff. Since then it has been extremely well edited in transcription by Sir Alan Gardiner, *Late Egyptian Stories* (1932), pp. 61-76. The most recent and best translations are by Elmar Edel in Kurt Galling's *Textbuch zur Geschichte Israels*, 36-43, and by John A. Wilson in J. Prichard's *Ancient Near Eastern Texts*, 25-29.

2. Cf. Albright, *Archaeology and the Religion of Israel*, 62 f.

3. *JNES* 4 (1945) 245. Gardiner's objection to Wilson's interpretation is based on the unusual spelling. However, in foreign words just such strange spellings

word was thus applied in Phoenicia about 1060 B. C. to the senate of a city, consisting of the "elders" of the community. The latter were called *shibūti* in the Accadian of an Amarna letter from Phoenician Arce;[4] they appear as *parshamūtu* in the treaty between Esarhaddon and Baal of Tyre;[5] they are called γερουσιασταί in the treaty between Hannibal and Philip V of Macedon.[6]

Before turning to certain details which have hitherto remained unrecognized, we may briefly describe the content of the Report. It consists of 142 long lines, somewhat damaged between lines 23 and 37, and lacking the end, whose length cannot be estimated. In translation it occupies about 1200 words. In the period between the XXth and XXIst Dynasties, either just before or more probably just after the death of Ramesses XI, Ḥriḥor, high-priest of Amun at Thebes and later king of Upper Egypt, sent a certain Wen-Amun to Byblus in order to obtain cedar beams for rebuilding the ceremonial bark of the god Amun. The date of Wen-Amun's departure from Thebes is fixed in the fifth year of an era which is almost certainly to be brought closely together with the accession of Smendes, head of the XXIst Dynasty at Tanis in the northeastern Delta.[7] The studies of M. B. Rowton[8] have restored a considerable amount of Manetho's lost respectability, and the beginning of the XXIst Dynasty may thus be placed 130 years before the accession of Shishak, head of the XXIInd Dynasty, cir. 935 B. C.[9] Wen-Amun's mission may, therefore, be dated about 1060 B. C., which is somewhat later than the dates usually given.

From Thebes our envoy made his way down the Nile to Tanis, capital of Smendes, which had been rebuilt after a previous destruction.[10] Smendes and his consort Tanet-Amun received the envoy and

---

became more frequent in this period. He does not dispute the perfect sense given by this Hebrew word in the context.

4. Knudtzon, J. A., *Die El-Amarna-Tafeln*, No. 100: 4, from ʿIrqatu = Ἀρκη.

5. See most recently E. A. Weidner, *Archiv für Orientforschung*, 8 (1932) 31.

6. See most recently Elias Bickerman, *TAPA* 75 (1944) 87-102.

7. On the historical situation of Ḥriḥor see A. Kees, *Nachrichten der Gesellschaft der Wissenschaften in Göttingen* (Phil.-Hist. Klasse, Fachgruppe 1, N. F., II, 1 [1936], pp. 1-20). Ed. Meyer's treatment of Wen-Amun is much better than that of Kees, who calls the Report "ein historischer Roman" (p. 3); see his *Geschichte des Altertums*, II, 2₂ (1931) 12-17.

8. *JEA* 34 (1948) 57-74.

9. On the date of Shishak's accession cf. a forthcoming discussion, based primarily on Manetho and on my dating of Shishak's invasion of Palestine cir. 918 B. C. (in agreement with the Tyrian annals as reported by Josephus); meanwhile cf. especially *Bulletin of the American Schools of Oriental Research*, No. 100, pp. 16 ff.

10. Cf. Montet, P., *Le Drame d'Avaris*, pp. 159 ff., 173 ff., 179 ff., and for additional evidence, *Festschrift für Alfred Bertholet*, pp. 13 f.

his letter from the god Amun favorably and sent him on his way north with a Syrian shipmaster named *Mngbt*, i. e., *Manqabt*, "The Hammer."[11] The term used for "ship" in this passage is as almost invariably elsewhere *br*, Greek βᾶρις (Ionic βάρις).[12] More than six centuries later Herodotus describes the *baris* in some detail (II:96). The word occurs frequently in Egyptian documents after the XIIIth century B. C. and it already appears in a Ugaritic list of ships about 1400 B. C.[13]

Though Wen-Amun must have stopped more than once on his way along the Egyptian caravan road from Tanis to Gaza, as well as at the Philistine ports, nothing happened until he reached Dor, modern Ṭanṭûrah, south of Carmel. Here was a town of the Tsikal (Tjikar), who had settled the coast north of the Philistines at the time of the irruption of Sea Peoples about 1175-1170 B. C.[14] Whether this people is to be identified with the Sikel of Homer, the later Sicilians, is still uncertain; the name of the chief of Dor, *Bdr/l*, does not help as yet. At all events, a member of the ship's crew stole all or part of the gifts which had been brought along from Egypt in order to compensate the prince of Byblus for the cedar which he was expected to deliver. Unfortunately the following text is damaged, but the chief of Dor seems to have advised Wen-Amun to recoup his losses by "borrowing" from another ship. Since he proceeded after leaving Tyre (i: 28) to board and rob a Tsikal ship, he earned for himself the bitter hostility of the latter people.

Most of the narrative is devoted to the varying fortunes of his prolonged stay at Byblus, whose prince, Zakar-Baʿal, bears a good Phoenician name. For a month after Wen-Amun's arrival, the prince of Byblus sent him daily requests to leave. Finally one of Zakar-Baʿal's old retainers went into an ecstatic trance[15] and demanded that the Egyptian envoy and the god Amun-of-the-Road (who accompanied Wen-Amun) be brought up to the palace, since he was the authentic messenger of the great Egyptian deity. The first interview was very

---

11. By the eleventh century the syllabic orthography had become virtually meaningless. For Eg. *g* = Semitic *q* in loanwords and transcriptions of this age cf. *ngb* for *naqb*, "mine" (*Archiv für Orientforschung* 12 [1939] 385; *mangabt* corresponds to Heb. *maqqébet*, "hammer," without assimilation of *nun*, as dialectally common in Northwest Semitic.

12. See my remarks, *Festschrift für Alfred Bertholet*, 4 f., n. 3.

13. Here it is flanked by several other words for "ship" which were already known from contemporary Egyptian (*loc. cit.*). It is noteworthy that at least half of the words for "ship" now known in early Northwest-Semitic dialects are loanwords from Egyptian, thus proving the primacy of Egyptian barks in Mediterranean navigation.

14. Cf. my remarks, *AJA* 54 (1950) 169 ff.

15. For the historical setting of this episode cf. my comments, *From the Stone Age to Christianity*, 232 ff.

unsatisfactory; Zakar-Ba'al angrily reproached the envoy for having left the validating documents from Amun and Ḥriḥor with Smendes and Tanet-Amun in Tanis. Zakar-Ba'al goes on to taunt him for not being able to keep the ship which Smendes had given him or its Syrian crew, and suggests that Smendes had turned him over to a Syrian shipmaster for the purpose of getting rid of him ("so that he might kill thee and that thou mightest be cast into the sea"—i: 55 f.). The following lines have been slightly misunderstood; *ente nīm* should be rendered "on account of whom"; the translation then runs: "On account of whom would the god [Amun-of-the-Road] be sought, and on whose account wouldst thou be sought?"[16] In other words, Wen-Amun was so unimportant and his god was so insignificant that no one would have taken the trouble to hunt for him if he failed to turn up. To demonstrate Wen-Amun's insignificance further, the Byblian went on to say that there were twenty ships (*mnshw*, larger than the *baris* vessels) in the port of Byblus (at the moment?) which were in *hubūr* relation with Smendes, and that even in Sidon, which Wen-Amun passed after leaving Tyre, there were fifty *baris* vessels in *hubūr* relationship with *Wr/lktr/l* and sailing for the latter's house (ii: 1 f.).[17] It is scarcely surprising that the Egyptian was silent (ii: 2 f.) after such a contemptuous reception. When the conversation was resumed the Byblian again tried to humiliate Wen-Amun by pointing out how very little he was bringing in comparison with what previous Pharaohs had sent to pay for the cedar which they wanted. Then follows a most instructive colloquy on the subject of the relative power of Amun and Baal, and the relation of Amun to Phoenicia.[18] Here the Egyptian was able to give his eloquence free rein—doubtless considerably heightened in the present literary form of the narrative. Finally a compromise is reached: Wen-Amun writes to Smendes and his consort asking for a further contribution; a ship is loaded with cedar beams and sent with the Byblian prince's own messenger to Tanis.

In due course the latter returned to Byblus, bringing a rich load of gifts in payment for the cedar which was to come; the shipment included 500 rolls of papyrus, which must have been in great demand

---

16. Ranke (1926) and Erman (1923, 1933) render *ente nīm*, "bei wem," but we should rather follow the meaning of the same preposition (written in both places *m-dr*) in Wen-Amun, ii: 67, where it appears in the passage "on account of the sad words which had been spoken to him." Sf. also Spiegelberg, *Zeitschrift für Aegyptische Sprache*, 60 (1925) 60.

17. "House" does not mean "residence" here but "family, estate, organization," as common both in Egyptian and Semitic.

18. On this passage cf. briefly my remarks, *From the Stone Age to Christianity*, 164.

in such a busy commercial city as Byblus.[19] Three hundred men and
as many oxen were then sent up into Lebanon to fell cedar logs, which
were allowed to lie on the ground for several months and were then
dragged down to the shore, where they were loaded on *baris* ships to
be transported to Egypt. Meanwhile eleven *baris* ships of the Tsikal
appeared off the shore in order to blockade the fleet of Wen-Amun
and prevent it from sailing. Zakar-Baʿal called a meeting of the assembly of elders (see above) and met with the chiefs of the Tsikal,
who explained their purpose in coming. It is a vivid commentary on
the comparative weakness of Byblus at this time that the Byblian had
to resort to treachery (or could be suspected of treachery by Wen-
Amun) in order to get rid of the Tsikal, whom he asked to lift their
blockade and permit the ships carrying the cedar beams for Wen-
Amun to leave port. "Afterwards," he is said to have proposed, "ye
may follow him in order to seize him" (ii: 74).

The last ten lines preserved give a tantalizing glimpse of political
conditions on the island of Cyprus (Egyptian *ʾr/ls*, cuneiform **Alasa-
Alashiya*),[20] whose queen bears the unexplained name Ḥtb. Wen-
Amun was driven by the wind (after escaping the Tsikal) to the coast
of Cyprus, directly northwest of Byblus, where the natives were about
to kill him. Luckily he found the queen as she was walking outside
her palace with her retainers. He found one who spoke Egyptian and
through him appealed to her sense of justice and hospitality, on the
one hand, and to her fear of Egyptian and Byblian retaliation, on the
other. She was impressed and took his side against her own people.—
Just at this interesting point the narrative breaks off.

---

19. It is true that Gardiner has expressed doubts about this rendering (in
Glanville's *Legacy of Egypt* [1942], pp. 54 f.), but other Egyptologists, including
most recently Edel, render "papyrus rolls" and it is very hard to square the
determinatives (scribal palette and roll) with any other meaning. On the great
antiquity of the use of βύβλος, βύβλινος in Greek in the sense of "papyrus, book"
cf. my discussion, *AJA* 54 (1950) 162 ff.

20. G. A. Wainwright (see his chief contribution on the subject, in *Klio*, 14
[1913], 1-36), followed by a few other scholars, continues to oppose the identification of Alashiya with Cyprus, but since there is absolutely no place on the North-
Syrian coast where it can be located, the hypothesis remains in the highest degree
improbable, like his identification of Eg. *Kftyw* and Caphtor with Cilicia instead
of with Crete and the Aegean islands. Meanwhile positive evidence for the identification with Cyprus has been steadily accumulating. The Mari archives of the
XVIIIth century B. C. have yielded many references to "copper of Alashiya (*erū,
siparru alashū*); cf. Dossin, *Syria*, 20 (1939) 111, and note that many additional references have turned up in the past decade according to personal information from M. Dossin. Evidence for a flourishing copper-mining industry in Bronze-
Age Cyprus from the third millennium on has been accumulating; cf. J. R.
Stewart, *Handbook to the Nicholson Museum* (Sydney, 1948), p. 131 and *passim*.
Since there never was any appreciable amount of copper mining in Syria, the consistent association of Alashiya with copper in cuneiform texts is very strong
evidence, even without the cumulative weight of data favoring the identification.
Jirku's paper in *Palestine Exploration Quarterly*, 1950, 40-42, adds little tangible
to the discussion.

The document swarms with interesting and important material. First are the ethnic data provided by many personal names. As might be expected, there are Egyptians in Byblus and Syrians in Egypt (besides Wen-Amun, an Egyptian interpreter and an Egyptian woman singer are mentioned). But most significant are the names *Wr/lktr/l, Wr/lt, and Mkmr/l.* The bearer of the first is mentioned on a level with Smendes, in order to depreciate the significance of Wen-Amun's mission; the name has been explained as a Canaanite *Brk⁾l* and attributed to some wealthy Canaanite merchant in Tanis.[21] But such a person could not be mentioned in the same breath with Smendes, and the combination is phonetically impossible. There cannot be the slightest doubt that the name in question is neither Semitic nor Egyptian. In that case it can scarcely be separated from the Sea Peoples, who were then in the heyday of their power, probably just before their conquest of Israel after the battle of Ebenezer.[22] The other two names appear in correlation (i: 15 ff.) with reigning princes: "Truly, the silver belongs to Amun-rē⁽, king of the gods and lord of the lands, it belongs to Smendes, it belongs to my lord Ḥriḥor and to the other grandees of Egypt, it belongs to thee, it belongs to *Wrt,* it belongs to *Mkmr,* and it belongs to Zakar-Ba⁽al, prince of Byblus." Neither of the names *Wrt* and *Mkmr* can be either Egyptian or Canaanite; they must then belong to the Sea Peoples, as indicated by their place with the name of *Bdr* himself between the Egyptians and the Canaanite Zakar-Ba⁽al. But since it is doubtful whether there was any other ruling prince of the Tsikal, and since omission of all Philistine names would be in the highest degree extraordinary (as the Egyptian envoy had to sail up the Philistine coast), we may rest assured that the names belong either to Philistine *serānîm*[23] or to chieftains of another Sea People settled in the Plain of Sharon, between the Philistine Pentapolis and the territory of Dor.

In the present state of our knowledge it is obviously impossible to attribute these names with certainty to any Anatolian or Aegean people, but it cannot be denied that *Wrktr* and *Wrt* may reflect good Asianic names from southwestern Anatolia. Since Graeco-Roman and Semitic *d* were regularly transcribed in Egyptian by *t,*[24] these names

---

21. For the most ingenious—and the wildest—combinations see Robert Eisler, *Zeitschrift der Deutschen Morgenländischen Gesellschaft,* 78 (1924) 61 ff.

22. For the archaeological and historical situation see *Tell Beit Mirsim* III, *AASOR* 21-22 (1943) 36 f., and Pelican, *Archaeology of Palestine,* pp. 113 ff.

23. Nothing has yet been found to invalidate the old suggestion of Klostermann that the word **ts-rán* (as the singular must have been pronounced at the time of its first use in Hebrew) is Greek τύραννος, which is unquestionably of pre-Hellenic origin.

24. Cf. *Festschrift für Alfred Bertholet,* p. 14, n. 4.

may reflect *Warka-dara and *Warda. The former may be compared
to such names as Amisōdaros (Lycian king in the Iliad, xvi: 328) and
Pixōdaros, etc. (common in both Caria and Lycia); in later Pisidian
we have Οναδαρας.[25] The first element of the name is presumably
the urqa of Sundwall; cf. Ορκαομανειτης, a Carian-Pisidian appellation of Zeus.[26] As for *Warda, it can scarcely be separated from Sundwall's urta for older *warda, which appears as Ορδος, etc., in Pisidian
and Carian.[27] Thanks to the progress of Hittite studies, it is now well
known that initial u tends to go back to older wa in various Anatolian
dialects of the last two millennia B. C. Mkmr is trickier; one can easily
find elements such as Cilician mu(n)k in Mukallu, Μογδατης, Μονγι-
λαρις, Μογγος (Sundwall, pp. 152, 155), and mura in Παδαμουρις,
Αζαμορα (Sundwall, p. 156 f.), but doubt will naturally persist. In
any case it is clear that the Asianic hypothesis is by far the most
probable in the present state of our knowledge. Obviously it suits the
writer's long-standing hypothesis that the Philistines came from the
eastern Aegean basin.[28] Though there have been a number of attempts
made in the past to identify some Philistine names,[29] the examples
which we know, such as Achish (properly Ekaush, or the like) and
perhaps Golyat (Goliath), have not been very helpful.

Another extremely interesting piece of evidence that emerges from
the Report of Wen-Amun is the role played by the ḫubūr, or trading
syndicate. Here we have specific mention of two; a ḫubūr of Smendes
with Byblus and another of a prince of the Palestine coast with Sidon.
The vocalization and etymology of the word are fixed by an unusual
combination of Accadian, Ugaritic, Egyptian, and Hebrew data.[30] The
basic meaning of the word in Accadian is "community"; it is given in
a vocabulary as a synonym of puḫru, "assembly." The derived
Ugaritic-Hebrew bt ḫbr (ḫbr)[31] means "granary," while in Accadian
bīt ḫubūri means "brewery"[32] and probably also "granary." The

25. See Sundwall, J., Die einheimischen Namen der Lykier nebst einem Ver-
zeichnisse kleinasiatischer Namenstämme (Klio, Beiheft 11, 1913), p. 64.

26. Ibid., p. 234.

27. Ibid., p. 235.

28. Cf. most recently AJA 54 (1950) 174.

29. E. g., Bossert, H. Th., Mitteilungen der Altorientalischen Gesellschaft, 4
(1929) 274 ff.; Alt, Albrecht, Zeitschrift für die Alttestamentliche Wissenschaft,
4 (1929) 250 f.

30. Cf. provisionally the writer's observations, Studies in the History of Culture
(Waldo Leland Anniversary Volume, Menasha, 1942), p. 36, n. 80; Annual of the
American Schools of Oriental Research, 21-22, 24, n. 9; Pelican, Archaeology
of Palestine (1949) p. 234.

31. Northwest-Semitic ḫ and ḥ fell together as ḥ not later than the tenth century B. C., at least in Phoenician and Hebrew.

32. Information from B. Landsberger, with regard to the inscription of the early
Assyrian king Errēshum discovered recently at Kültepe in Cappadocia. The mean-
ings "brewery" and "granary" are really closely related, since both employ grain.

Phoenician meaning, "partnership, syndicate," is preserved in the Maccabaean coins and the contemporary "Damascus Covenant" as ḥbr,[33] "community, commonwealth (κοινόν)." B. Maisler has pointed out late (post-exilic) Hebrew denominatives from it: in II Chron. 20: 35-37 we find ʾethabbar, "to be a partner in a trading syndicate with (ʿim)," ḥibbar, "associate oneself with another in a trading syndicate"; in Job 40: 30 ḥabbārîm means "merchants, i. e., members of a trading syndicate," parallel with kᵉnaʿnîm, "merchants (lit.: Canaanites)."[34] In Egyptian the word ḥubūra was borrowed before the end of the Bronze Age (though not actually found so early) and was changed by rule[35] to shbēr in Coptic, with the meaning "partner," originally "partnership."

The purpose of such a trading syndicate in the eleventh century is obvious. Commerce was growing rapidly and was almost ready to flower as it did in the tenth century with the reign of Solomon in Israel.[36] But expansion of commerce, especially where a heavy initial outlay of capital is necessary as in maritime operations, requires strong support from states as well as from wealthy individuals (who must themselves combine if they are to be successful). Moreover, the eleventh century was exceedingly insecure at sea. The Odyssey, which the writer would date in the first half of the tenth century,[37] abounds with allusions to pirates: Phoenicians, Taphians, Sicilians, etc. The chaos produced by the irruption of the Sea Peoples and the consequent breakdown of all established power could not be reduced to order inside of a century or a century and a quarter (the approximate interval between the critical invasions and the time of Wen-Amun), especially at a time when there were no strong political entities to keep order either at land or on the sea. Furthermore, the Report of Wen-Amun itself bears witness repeatedly to the insecurity of the times, in spite of the trading syndicates. Consequently, it became necessary for the heads of weak states to combine in syndicates which could be defended by force of arms as well as by the provision of capital.

There can be no question that the situation presupposed by the Wen-Amun Report antedates the period reflected by the composition of

---

33. Cf. n. 31.

34. See his important treatment of this material in *Bulletin of the American Schools of Oriental Research*, No. 102 (1946), pp. 9 ff.

35. See especially my discussion, *Vocalization of the Egyptian Syllabic Orthography*, 17 f.; my treatment of the word *ḥubūr* there is, however, incorrect, since the Asiatic word *ḥubūru* had not yet been recovered in its correct sense.

36. See my description of the expansion of Israelite trade at this time in *Archaeology and the Religion of Israel*, 131-138.

37. Cf. my paper "Some Oriental Glosses on the Homeric Question," in *AJA* 54 (1950) 163-166.

the Odyssey. The Sidonian state was still comparatively unimportant, and Byblus exercised some sort of hegemony over the Phoenician cities. Tyre did not play an important maritime rôle, as it had in the Late Bronze Age; there is no hint in our period of the astonishing development of Tyre, as capital of the Sidonian state, into the most important maritime city of the world. By the time of the Odyssey the conquest of Israel (about 1050 B. C.) and the entire hinterland of Tyre and Sidon by the victorious Philistines and their confederated Sea Peoples had taken place and had passed again into history with the triumph of David (about 990 B. C.).[38]

A substantial volume would be required to do justice to the interpretation of the Wen-Amun Report, which is still in some ways one of the most neglected historical sources of antiquity. Its importance for students of the Homeric question has been affirmed by various scholars, but has never been clearly brought out. This paper is only a hint of what the future historian will find in it of interest to students of Mediterranean antiquity.

---

38. On this subject see my forthcoming section on early Phoenician history in Vol. II of the new edition of the Cambridge Ancient History.

ANCIENT MAN IN SOUTHWESTERN ASIA

HENRY FIELD

Washington, D. C.

This area, known as the Middle East or Near East, may be defined as including that region bounded on the west by the Mediterranean and the Red Sea, on the south by the Arabian Sea and the Persian Gulf. To the north lies the Black Sea, the Caucasus Mountains and the Caspian. Afghanistan and Baluchistan form the eastern flank.[1] Southwestern Asia is the nursery of *Homo sapiens* and a cradle of civilization. Here we shall concern ourselves with the evidence for ancient man, his migrations and his cultures long before the dawn of the historical period some 4,000 years before Christ.

The sweep of history during the past six millennia from the earliest pictographic tablets to modern printing is relatively well-known. A few lacunae remain, but the main historical details are sharp and clear from large-scale excavations during the past fifty years.

With the exception of Doughty, who in 1875 found typologically Palaeolithic implements in the torrent bed of the Wadi Arabah at Petra in the Hashemite Kingdom of the Jordan (formerly Trans-Jordan), none of the early travelers in the Arabian Peninsula recorded evidence of early man. During the past twenty-five years our knowledge has increased very materially and as a result the general trends become less shadowy. To review in outline the data accumulated since 1925 it is more convenient to refer to each country, now a political entity. This geographical presentation will be followed by some deductions and hypotheses. Following the sun from east to west, our range is from eastern Afghanistan to southwestern Palestine. Our limits from north to south extend from the southern flank of the Caucasus to the Arabian Sea.

AFGHANISTAN AND BALUCHISTAN.—Evidence for Palaeolithic man and his cultures is lacking, although he probably migrated along the Makran coast from the "Land of the Five Rivers," the Punjab.

IRAN (Persia).—De Morgan[2] expected to find Palaeolithic or Neo-

---

1. *See* Field, Henry, "Early Man in North Arabia," AMNH, *Natural History,* 29, 33-44; "The Ancient and Modern Inhabitants of Arabia," *Open Court*, 46, 847-871; "The Cradle of *Home Sapiens*," *AJA*, 36 (1932) 426-430; "The Antiquity of Man in Southwestern Asia," *AA*, 35, 51-62, 1933; "Sulle caratteristiche geografiche dell' Arabia settentrionale," *BRSGI*, vol. 11, 3-13; "Contributions to the Anthropology of Iran," *FMNH*, 29, 1-706, Chicago, 1939.

2. De Morgan, Jacques, *La Préhistoire orientale*, 3 vols. Published posthumously by Louis Germain. Paris, 1925-1927.

lithic implements during his fourteen years of exploration. However, all stone tools were associated with copper so that he finally deduced (1927, vol. 3, p. 183) that "Iran, extremely cold on account of its altitude, barren, covered with deserts, salt lakes and arid mountains, could offer but few possibilities for existence. Consideration of these factors explain why throughout Persia, Trans-Caucasia and Armenia no trace of Pleistocene man has been found." On the other hand Herzfeld[3] writes that "the whole Near East, its plains and mountains, has been inhabited by man since the Stone Age, and compared with European sites of the same age the Oriental sites show a high degree of culture." Huntington[4] observes that the climate of Iran was ideal for human development and that Iran may have been the territory where *Homo sapiens* developed.

No prehistoric survey has yet been made, but the preliminary reconnaissances indicate that a wealth of data will be found in the near future.

To summarize our present knowledge:

(a) W. E. Browne, geologist and surveyor for the Anglo-Iranian Oil Company found on December 25, 1933, at Lat. 29°, Long. 53° flint implements of Middle Palaeolithic type, a classification accepted by the Abbé Breuil. They were collected twenty-seven miles from Lake Niriz at 8,000 ft. above sea level in sparsely wooded country with very large springs in the neighborhood. This may well have been a sweet-water lake in Palaeolithic times. The country in this region is not particularly adapted to general migrations, but many large valleys lead down to Shiraz.

(b) Browne recorded several twenty-foot raised beaches near shoe-shaped Daryacheh-i-Maharlu (Lat. 29° 18′ N. and 52° 45′ E.). He suggests that the lake level may have fallen suddenly during the past millennium.

(c) On August 28, 1934, Donald McCown and I visited two rock-shelters at the northwestern corner of Lake Maharlu. On the scree slopes lay hundreds of small flints, many of them microlithic in size. Dorothy Garrod expressed the tentative opinion that this culture resembled that from Iraqi Kurdistan.

(d) Carleton Coon during 1949 found Stone Age rockshelters at Behistun, at the southeastern corner of the Caspian and south of Qain in Seistan. His results will be published shortly.

(e) In 1950 at Konji cave near Khurrumabad in Luristan we found typologically Palaeolithic implements *in situ*. On the scree slopes

3. Herzfeld, Ernst, *Archaeological History of Iran.*
4. Huntington, Ellsworth, *Season of Birth. Its relation to human abilities,* 433-435.

outside two other rock shelters nearby lay flint flakes. For the first time we have evidence that ancient man dwelt in the great mountain complex of western Persia.

Thus, the new evidence from Iran links Seistan to the Mediterranean. Iran is, therefore, a key point for further investigation.

IRAQ (Mesopotamia).—No Palaeoliths have been found south of Baghdad. It is probable that in pre-Neolithic times the Persian Gulf extended far to the north, preventing any migrations south of the area where the Tigris and Euphrates bend together near the city of Baghdad.

(a) At Kish excavations were continued down to virgin soil, sixty ft. from the top of the mound. Below present water level a Neolithic facies was found. The flint implements were associated with black polished, red and incised pottery, with no trace of copper.

(b) In river gravels near Kirkuk Miss Garrod in March, 1928, found Mousterian implements[5]; later that year I also obtained a few from the same area. Miss Garrod excavated two caves during 1928 in the Sulaimaniya region: Zarzi yielded an Upper Aurignacian industry of Grimaldi type; Hazar Merd contained a Mousterian culture resembling that of caves in Palestine.

(c) In 1934, while leader of the Field Museum Expedition to the Near East, I visited Zakho, Aqra, Rowandiz, and Sulaimaniya—the four approaches from the Iranian Plateau to the Mesopotamian plain. At each point typologically Palaeolithic stone implements were collected on the surface. In Diyan cave on Jebel Baradost near Rowandiz animal long bones, split by the ancient hunters to remove the delicious marrow, were removed from beneath a thick layer of stalagmite.

(d) In May, 1949, Naji al-Asil, Director-General of Antiquities, visited a Megalithic monolith at Barda Balkha two miles northeast of Chemchemal.[6] Stone implements, including handaxes of Chellean type, were found nearby. In 1950 we collected a series for Harvard.

(e) On the surface of the high desert west of Baghdad toward the Jebel Tenf-Jebel Enaze boundary with the Hashemite Kingdom of the Jordan (formerly Trans-Jordan), from 1925-1928 and in 1934 I found many Stone Age surface stations, especially near Rutba Wells.

CAUCASUS.—Many caves and rockshelters, such as Devis Khvreli, Chiaturi, Gvardzhilas Khlde and Rudolf Virchow's Höhle, have been

---

5. Garrod, Dorothy, "The Near East as a gateway of prehistoric migration," *Early Man*, 33-40, ed. by George Grant MacCurdy. Philadelphia, 1937.

6. Naji al-Asil, "Barda Balka," *Sumer* 5 (1949).

excavated by G. K. Nioradze and his colleagues. Middle and Upper Palaeolithic cultures have been found over a widespread area.

TURKEY.—Palaeolithic sites have been located in Anatolia. In 1909, de Morgan collected obsidian implements of Mousterian type on the slopes of Mount Alagheuz, which lies about fifty miles north of Mount Ararat. Von der Osten also found implements of Palaeolithic types in Central Anatolia. In gravels near Ankara five Palaeoliths were found, according to a personal communication from Sir John Myres.

SYRIA.—Surface sites have been discovered east of the Aleppo—Damascus—Jebel ed-Druze line. At Deraa, in 1928, I found a superb series of handaxes of white, dehydrated flint. This site is similar to that of Ar-Rawafi in northeastern Sinai, located by Huzayyin, Albright, and myself in January, 1948, while members of the University of California African Expedition.

East of this arbitrary line Stone Age surface stations from Rouhaibe near Qataife to Abou Kemal have been located. During March, 1950, ten new sites were found in this area by the writer during the Peabody Museum-Harvard Expedition.

HASHEMITE JORDAN (Trans-Jordan).—The first stone implements between Allenby Bridge and Baghdad were found in 1925 by L. H. Dudley Buxton and myself at Royal Air Force Landing Ground "H," 128 miles east of Amman.

Many other surface stations were located by the Field Museum Expeditions of 1927, 1928, and 1934 from Qasr el-Azraq to Jebel Tenf and Jebel Enaze and in the triangle Al-Qatrani—Bayir Wells—Maan. The most significant discoveries were: (a) Lower Palaeolithic handaxes, choppers and scrapers from the Wadi Arabah at Petra collected by Doughty in 1875 and another series by the writer in 1927; (b) an Acheulean *coup-de-poing* excavated *in situ* from a depth of 11 ft. 6 in. in the gravel bed at Bayir Wells; (c) a deeply-patinated Mousterian point from the highest peak of Jebel Thlaithakhwat; and (d) a series of T-shaped implements from near Landing Ground "K," 150 miles east of Amman. Jordan is rich in surface sites and at Jebel Aweinat, southeast of Maan, rock drawings with animal figures, including an ibex, were found by Horsfield.

ISRAEL (Palestine).—Numerous surface sites have been found from er-Remtha to Rafah. At Tagba near the Sea of Galilee Turville-Petre found, in June, 1925, a fragmentary skull of Neanderthal type, associated with a Middle Palaeolithic culture and an extinct fauna.

At Shukbah cave on the pleasant slopes of Mount Carmel, Dorothy Garrod found in 1928 skeletons of Natufians with a Mousterian culture. The following year she excavated at Athlit a series of prehistoric skeletons of modern plus Neanderthaloid types together with a rich fauna and industry.

THE ARABIAN PENINSULA.—Since no organized search for Stone Age man and his cultures has been possible in Saudi Arabia,[7] the evidence for prehistoric occupation is confined to a few scattered data: (a) from the central part lying just north of the great sands of the Rub' al Khali a large handaxe was picked up by an oil geologist; (b) Bertram Thomas found a perfect flint arrowhead from the sands of Sanam; (c) Philby also brought back some flint implements from the "Empty Quarter"; (d) in June, 1950, I found typologically Mousterian and Aurignacian flint implements along the Trans-Arabian pipeline. On Tell Hibr near the Jordan frontier the superb quality of the honey-colored flint made this dominating hill a Mecca for Stone Age flint-knappers; and (e) in Aden and the Hadhramaut Miss Caton-Thompson collected stone implements and flakes, similar in technique and patina to those from eastern Jordan.

The search throughout this great Peninsula will undoubtedly prove the existence of widespread occupation in Palaeolithic times.

In the preceding paragraphs we have reviewed briefly and in outline the evidence for Stone Age migration and settlement in Southwestern Asia. Now taking this area as an unit, we see that Prehistoric man crossed and recrossed this region, the greater part of which is now relatively inhospitable. However, geological and archaeological evidence indicate a marked climatic change with an advancing wave of desiccation. Areas that were well-watered during the Palaeolithic Period are now wilderness or steppe. In recent times the Romans accelerated this desiccation by cutting down the cedars of Lebanon for shipbuilding and other construction.

In this area developed the beginnings of agriculture and the domestication of animals. The climate in prehistoric times was ideal for human development. For all these reasons I have called Southwestern Asia the "Nursery of *Homo sapiens*." When we glance at the surrounding territories, we see that man in various Palaeolithic phases of culture lived in the Punjab of northwestern India, in Soviet Central Asia from the Pamir Plateau to the Caspian Sea, along the Nile Valley, and in northeast Africa. As a result of studying the collections in the

---

7. See my forthcoming, "Reconnaissance in Saudi Arabia," *AJA* 55 (1951).

Coryndon Memorial Museum in Nairobi, it is clear to me that there were cultural links between northeast Africa[8] across the Strait of Bab el-Mandeb into Southwestern Asia and across Sinai[9] north of the Wilderness of Tih. However, the direction of migration was probably in both axes. Up to the end of the first quarter of this century, we believed that the "Cradle of Man" lay in Central Asia. Now it appears equally probable that there was another "Cradle" in Africa south of the Equator, probably in the Johannesburg region.

In conclusion, Southwestern Asia forms the focal point of the three continents termed Eurasafrica or Eurafrasia. Stone Age Man migrated into this pleasant land where he flourished for millennia. Here he learned new techniques. Here he allowed his inventive powers free rein. Here he had learned to domesticate reindeer and the members of the horse family. Here he learned to cultivate wheat and barley. Here he created the great civilization of the Tigris-Euphrates Valley with its temples, chariots, tablets, pottery, and other objects ranging from the dawn of writing to the beginnings of astronomy and scientific research which led ultimately to the use of atomic energy.

No other area in the world has yielded as much for the benefit of mankind, for from Southwestern Asia has flowed man's early knowledge of agriculture, the domestication of animals, the use of the wheel, writing, astronomy, scientific research, the first code of laws, as well as major contributions to architecture, irrigation, and human relations.

8. Field, H., "The University of California African Expedition: II, Sudan and Kenya," *AA* (1949) 72-84.
9. Field, H., "The University of California African Expedition: I, Egypt," *AA* (1948) 479-493. "Sinai Sheds New Light on the Bible," *Nation. Geog. Magazine* 1948, 795-815.

THE SUMERIAN SCHOOL: A PRE-GREEK SYSTEM
OF EDUCATION

SAMUEL NOAH KRAMER

The University Museum, University of Pennsylvania

The Sumerian school was the direct outgrowth of the invention and development of the cuneiform system of writing. Among the thousand-odd semi-pictographic tablets excavated by the Germans at Erech less than twenty years ago, tablets which date back practically to the very beginnings of writing, there were found several of the type generally known as "school" texts, that is, tablets inscribed with lists of objects for purposes of study and practice.[1] Thus we may assume, that as early as 3000 B. C., the date usually ascribed to these Erech semi-pictographic tablets, some of the scribes were already thinking in terms of teaching and learning. Moreover, these Erech "school" tablets are no isolated phenomena. Of the approximately 200 tablets excavated at Jemdet Nasr, not far from ancient Kish, which may date a century or two later than the Erech inscriptions, at least one is a "school" text.[2] In Ur, Woolley excavated some four hundred tablets and fragments from a period not much later than those of Jemdet Nasr, and among these were found over a dozen "school" tablets; several of these contain lexical material identical with copies made in earlier and later days.[3] And by the time we come to the so-called Fara tablets, which according to the new low chronology date from about the middle of the third millennium B. C.,[4] the numerous "school" tablets with their rich and varied contents indicate with reasonable certainty that there must have been schools throughout ancient Sumer where writing was formally taught.[5]

Turning to the second half of the third millennium B. C., and particularly to the so-called Ur III period, which may be dated roughly from about 2050-1950 B. C., there are now available tens of thousands of tablets, published and unpublished, which cover nearly every phase of the economic life and administrative organization of ancient Sumer.[6] The number of scribes who practiced their craft throughout

---

1. Cf. Falkenstein, A., *Archaische Texte aus Uruk*, 43 ff.
2. *Ibid.*, 45, and note 3.
3. Burrows, Eric, *Ur Excavation Texts II: Archaic Texts*, 2.
4. Cf. Kramer, *AJA* 52 (1948) 163-4 for a brief résumé of the problems involved and additional references.
5. Cf. in particular Deimel, Anton, *Schultexte aus Fara*, 1 ff.
6. Cf. now the list of publications in A. Leo Oppenheim, *Catalogue of the Cuneiform Tablets of the Wilberforce Eames Babylonian Collection*, 215-224, and add Legrain, Leon, *Ur Excavation Texts III: Business Documents of the Third Dynasty of Ur.*

those years ran into the thousands; there were junior scribes and "high" scribes, royal and temple scribes, scribes who were highly specialized for particular categories of administrative activities, and scribes who became leading officials in state and government. There is every reason to assume therefore that numerous scribal schools of considerable size and importance flourished throughout the land. But unfortunately we have no source material from this period relevant to the school and its activities. Almost no "school" practice tablets and but few literary documents have been recovered to date, although they must have existed in large numbers. Not even the Sumerian word for school é-dub-ba, literally "tablet-house," has been found in the available documents of this period,[7] which, except for relatively few short votive inscriptions, are entirely administrative and economic in character.

It is in the period immediately following the end of the Third Dynasty of Ur, that commonly known as the early post-Sumerian,[8] that we find considerable source material for the school and its organization and method of operation. It is from this period, which covers roughly the first four centuries of the second millennium B. C., that we have hundreds of tablets actually prepared by the pupils themselves and filled with all sorts of practice exercises; their script ranges from the sorry scratches of the first beginners, to the highly proficient inscriptions of the far-advanced students.[9] Indirectly, these school tablets reveal to some extent the method of teaching and the nature of the curriculum. But fortunately we have fuller and much more direct evidence for the school of this period and its educational activities. For, as will soon become evident, the school was the center of what we may term Sumerian creative writing; it was within its learned walls that the Sumerian writers and poets developed such varied literary types as myths and epic tales, hymns and lamentations, proverbs and "words of wisdom." Now one of their literary genres consisted of a group of compositions dealing with the activities of the school and scribe. Several of these have been recovered, to date. But with one exception the texts are still fragmentary and it is difficult to penetrate the real meaning of their contents. The exception mentioned is a document of ninety lines whose text is practically complete; it has been

7. Cf. now Oppenheim, *op. cit.*, 8; note that in Legrain, *op. cit.*, 52-3, *é-dub-ba* should read *é-kišib-ba*.

8. The period is usually termed "post-Sumerian," since Sumerian had now become extinct as a spoken tongue, although it continued in use as a literary and religious language and even to a certain extent as the language of current business and administrative documents.

9. Cf. for example Van der Meer, P. E., *Texts Scolaires de Suse*, and Syllabaries A, B, and B¹; Poebel, Arno, *Historical and Grammatical Texts*; Langdon, Stephen, *Sumerian Lexical Texts*.

restored from twenty-one tablets and fragments twenty of which are known to have been excavated in Nippur. Brief as this document is, its contents are particularly revealing since they consist in large part of a pupil's description, in his own words, of his daily school experiences and reactions. It is the recent restoration and translation of the text[10] which permit us to see in a new and clearer light the educational system of Sumer and its organization, and make possible the following sketch of the Sumerian school touching briefly on its aim and goal, its student body and faculty, its curriculum and teaching techniques.[11]

First, then, the aims of the Sumerian school. There seems to be little doubt that the original goal of the Sumerian school was what we would term "professional," that is, it was first established for the purpose of training the scribes necessary to satisfy the demands of the economic and administrative needs of the land, primarily of course, those of the temple and palace. This continued to be the major aim of the Sumerian school throughout its existence. However, in the course of its growth and development, and particularly as a result of the ever widening curriculum, it came to be the center of culture and learning in Sumer.[12] Within its walls flourished the "scholar-scientist," the man who studied whatever theological, botanical, zoological, mineralogical, geographical, mathematical, grammatical, and linguistic knowledge was current in his day, and who in some cases added to this knowledge. Moreover, rather unlike the present-day institutions of learning, the Sumerian school was also the center of what might be termed creative writing. It was here that the literary creations of the past were studied and copied; it was here, too, that new ones were composed.[13] While it is true therefore that the large majority of graduates from the Sumerian schools became scribes in the service of the temple and palace, and among the rich and powerful of the land, there were some who devoted their lives to teaching and learning. It seems reasonable to assume that like the university professor of today, many of these ancient scholars depended for their livelihood on their teaching salaries, and devoted themselves to research and writing in their spare time. And it is not uninteresting to note in this connection that the Sumerian

10. Cf. Kramer, "Schooldays: A Sumerian Composition Relating to the Education of a Scribe," *JAOS* 69 (1949) 199 ff.

11. For a sketch of the Sumerian school based on evidence available some twenty-five years ago cf. Meissner, Bruno, *Babylonien und Assyrien*, II, 324 ff.

12. It is described in the texts as "the place of learning (?)," and as "the house of instruction of 'the land,'" cf. "Schooldays" in *JAOS loc. cit.*, 11 and 17, and Stephen Langdon's *Sumerian and Semitic Religious and Historical Texts*, pl. 12, VI, lines 12-14.

13. Cf. note 28.

school, which probably began as a temple appendage,[14] became in time a secular institution; the teachers were paid, as far as we can see, out of the tuition fees collected from the students.[15] The curriculum, too, as will be seen later, was largely secular in character.

Turning now to the student body of the Sumerian school, it is of prime importance of course to know from which social stratum it derived. As is well known, society in the early second millennium was divided into three classes, the freeman, the "serf," who was deemed inferior to the freeman before the law, and the slave.[16] There is some evidence to show that these social and legal distinctions existed in much earlier days in Sumer.[17] In any case we may assume that throughout its existence, Sumerian society had its slaves and its many poor by the side of the relatively few rich and powerful who were usually described as *lú-gu-la* "big men."[18] *A priori* it seems reasonable to assume that the greater part of the student body came from the more wealthy families; the poor could hardly afford the cost and the time which a prolonged school education demanded.[19] Fortunately we have a considerable amount of detailed information relevant to this problem from the Sumerian documents of the Ur III period of about 2000 B. C.[20] From these texts we learn that the fathers of the scribes, that is, of the *é-dub-ba* graduates, were governors, "city fathers," ambassadors, high temple administrators, military officers, sea-captains, high tax officials, priests of various sorts, managers, supervisors, and foremen, scribes, archivists, and accountants.[21] Indeed the only high ranking individual not listed as the father of a scribe, as Schneider points out, is the *lugal*, "king;" no scribe is ever designated as "son of the king."

---

14. Cf. Deimel, Anton, *op. cit.*, 2-6 for the *sangu* as compilers of school texts; for the *sangu* as the temple administrative heads, cf. Schneider, Nikolaus, "Der *sangu* als Verwaltungsbehörde und Opfergabenspender der dritten Dynastie von Ur," *Journal of Cuneiform Studies*, 1 (1947) 122 ff.

15. Cf. particularly *JAOS*, *loc. cit.*, 206, lines 47-50 and Landsberger's comment, *ibid.*, 214.

16. Cf. Meissner, *op. cit.*, I, 373.

17. Cf. Falkenstein, A., *Archaische Texte aus Uruk*, 57.

18. Cf. in particular, Francois Thureau-Dangin, *Die sumerischen und akkadischen Königsinschriften*, 52.

19. Cf. particularly *JAOS*, *op. cit.*, 206, lines 51 ff.

20. Cf. Nikolaus Schneider's valuable article "Der *dub-sar* als Verwaltungsbeamter im Reiche von Sumer und Akkad zur Zeit der 3. Dynastie von Ur," *Orientalia*, New Series, vol. 15, 89 ff.

21. In several cases the "shepherd" is listed as the father of a scribe, cf. Schneider, *op. cit.*, 86; it seems likely, however, that the "shepherd" in these instances refers to a fairly high administrative official. Note, too, the interesting fact that among the more than 500 scribes listed by Schneider, there is not one bearing a woman's name; at least in the time of the Third Dynasty of Ur, therefore, the scribal occupation was probably practiced by men only; cf. Schneider, *op. cit.*, 84.

It is therefore obvious that at least at the time of the Third Dynasty of Ur, the student-body of the *é-dub-ba* derived to a large extent from the wealthy temple and palace officials. And what is true of 2000 B. C. in this respect is probably no less true of the centuries that preceded and followed.

Turning from the student-body to the faculty of the Sumerian school, it is primarily our new "Schooldays"[22] text which supplies the pertinent information. Head of the school was the *um-mi-a* ("professor" or "expert"), who was also called the *ad-da-é-dub-ba* "the school father." One of his assistants was the *šeš-gal* "big brother"; some of his duties were to write the new tablets for the students to copy, to examine the students' copies, and probably also to hear them recite their studies from memory and to punish them if they failed to do so correctly. In addition to the headmaster, that is, the "school father" and his assistant the "big brother," our "Schooldays" text lists the following personnel that we can more or less identify: "the man in charge of the courtyard," "the man in charge of drawing" or perhaps better "etiquette," the man in charge of Sumerian," the monitor who was in charge of attendance, and "the man in charge of the gate." Then there are several members of the school staff mentioned in the texts whose names are not intelligible at the moment; one of these may be "the man in charge of the whip," that is, the man primarily responsible for discipline.[23] At times also an *ugula* is mentioned; the word usually means "foreman" or "supervisor," but what his duties were relative to the school and student is at present not clear. We know nothing of the relative rank of the school personnel, except of course that the headmaster was the "school-father." Nor do we know anything about their sources of income; probably they were paid by the "school-father" from the tuition fees which he received.

If we now consider the curriculum of the Sumerian school, we find that we have at our disposal a wealth of data from the schools themselves which is indeed unique in the history of early man. For in this case there is no need to depend on the statements made by the ancients or on inference and deduction from scattered bits of information; we actually have the written products of the schoolboys themselves from the beginner's first attempts to the copies of the advanced student which were so well prepared that they were hardly to be distinguished from those of the professor himself. It is from these school-products that we realize that the Sumerian school's curriculum may be divided into two primary groups: the first may be described as semi-scientific

---

22. Cf. note 10. For the "big brother," cf. *JAOS*, *loc. cit.*, 207 ff.
23. Cf. Landsberger's comment in *JAOS*, *loc. cit.*, 214.

and scholarly, and the second as literary and creative. In considering the first, or semi-scientific group of subjects, it will be well to place it in its proper perspective by noting that it did not stem out of what we may call the scientific urge, the search for truth for truth's sake; rather it grew and developed out of the main school aim, which was to teach the scribe how to write the Sumerian language. For in order to satisfy this pedagogical need the Sumerian scribal teachers devised a system of instruction which consisted primarily of linguistic classification, that is, they classified the Sumerian language into groups of related words and phrases and had the students memorize and copy them until they could reproduce them with ease. In the course of the late third and early second millennium B. C. these lists became ever more complete and gradually grew to be more or less stereotyped and standard for all the schools of Sumer. Among them we find long lists of names of trees and reeds, of all sorts of animals including insects and birds, of countries, cities, and villages, of all sorts of stones and minerals. All in all these compilations show a considerable acquaintance with what might be termed botanical, zoological, geographical, and mineralogical lore, a fact that is only now beginning to be realized by historians of science.[24] In addition we find that our schoolmen prepared all sorts of mathematical tables, and many detailed mathematical problems together with their solutions.[25] In the field of linguistics we find the study of Sumerian grammar well represented in the school curriculum; among the school tablets a number are inscribed with long lists of substantive complexes and verbal forms which indicate a highly sophisticated grammatical approach.[26] Moreover as a result of the gradual conquest of the Sumerians by the Semitic Accadians in the last quarter of the third millennium B. C., our ancient professors prepared what are by all odds the oldest "dictionaries" known to man. For the Semitic conquerors not only borrowed the Sumerian script; they also treasured highly the Sumerian literary works and studied and imitated them long after Sumerian had become extinct as a spoken language; hence arose the pedagogical need for "dictionaries" in which the Sumerian words and phrases are translated into the Accadian language.[27]

---

24. Cf. B. Landsberger, *Die Fauna des alten Mesopotamien nach der 14 Tafel der serie HAR-RA = Hubullu;* R. Campbell Thompson, *The Assyrian Herbal; A Dictionary of Assyrian Chemistry & Geology.*

25. Cf. the works listed under the names Neugebauer and Thureau-Dangin in Neugebauer and Sachs, *Mathematical Cuneiform Texts,* 154 and 155.

26. Cf, e. g., Arno Poebel, *Grammatical Texts.*

27. These "dictionaries" are gradually being reconstructed by Benno Landsberger, now of the Oriental Institute of the University of Chicago; cf. especially his work on Mesopotamian fauna listed in note 24, and his *Die Serie ana ittišu.*

As for the literary and creative aspects of the Sumerian curriculum, it consisted primarily of studying, copying, and imitating the large and diversified group of literary compositions which must have originated and developed primarily in the latter half of the third millennium B. C. The number of these ancient works ran into the hundreds; they were almost all poetic in form, and ranged in length from close to a thousand to less than fifty lines. As recovered to date, they are seen to consist in the main of the following genres: myths and epic tales in the form of narrative poems celebrating the deeds and exploits of the Sumerian gods and heroes; hymns to gods and kings; lamentations, that is, poems bewailing the not infrequent destruction of the Sumerian cities; wisdom compositions including proverbs, fables, and sundry didactic types.[28] To date several thousand tablets and fragments have been recovered from the ruins of Sumer, and not a few are in the immature hand of the ancient pupils themselves.

As for the methods of teaching and its technique, there is relatively little information on the subject available. From our "Schooldays" texts[29] we learn that the student upon arrival in school studied the tablet which he had prepared the day before; that then the šeš-gal, the "big brother," that is, the teacher's assistant, prepared for him a new tablet, and no doubt the student spent much of his day studying and copying this new tablet. According to one passage he even took the tablet home with him and displayed his learning to his father, but this could hardly have been the daily practice. We are informed by one text that the "big brother" examined the student's tablet for possible errors; according to another text, the headmaster himself examined the student's tablets, found that his copy was unsatisfactory, and caned him. No doubt, memorizing played a great role in the student's work, but unfortunately the relevant passages in our texts are obscure.[30] Then, too, the teacher and the assistants must have supplemented the bare lists, tables and literary texts which the student was copying and studying with considerable oral and explanatory material. But these "lectures" which would no doubt prove invaluable for our understanding of Sumerian scientific, religious, and literary thought, were in all probability never written down and hence are lost to us forever.

One fact stands out from the "Schooldays" documents: the Sumerian

---

28. Cf. Kramer, *Sumerian Mythology;* "Sumerian Literature: A Preliminary Survey of the Oldest Literature in the World," *Proc. Am. Phil. Soc.* 85 (1942) 293 ff.; "Heroes of Sumer; A New Heroic Age in World History and Literature," *PAPS* 90 (1946) 120-130.

29. Cf. note 10 for the publication reference.

30. Falkenstein, Adam, "Der Sohn des Tafelhauses," *Die Welt des Orients,* 172 ff.

school was not tainted in any way by what we would call progressive education; particularly in the matter of discipline there was no sparing of the rod. While no doubt the teachers encouraged their students to do good work by means of praise and commendation, they depended primarily on the cane for correcting the student's faults and inadequacies, as is rather painfully evident from the "Schooldays" document. The student did not have an easy time of it. He attended school daily from sunrise to sunset; he must have had some vacation throughout the year, but we have no information on the point. He devoted many years to his school studies; one text states that he stayed in school from his early youth to the day when he became a young man.[31] It would be most interesting to know if, when, and to what extent the students were expected to specialize in one study or another. But on this point, as indeed on many other matters concerned with the school activities, our sources fail us.

In conclusion, just a word about the school building. In the course of several Mesopotamian excavations buildings have turned up which for one reason or another were identified as possible schoolhouses; one in Nippur, another in Sippar, and a third in Ur.[32] But except for the fact that a large number of tablets were found in the rooms, there seems little to distinguish them from ordinary house rooms, and the identification may be mistaken. However some fifteen years ago, the French who excavated Mari uncovered two rooms in a palace which definitely seem to show physical features that might be characteristic of a schoolroom; particularly they contain several rows of benches made of baked brick, capable of seating one, two, and four people.[33] Strangely enough however, no tablets seem to have been found in this room, and so once again the identification must remain somewhat uncertain.[34]

31. Meissner, *op. cit.*, II, 326.

32. Kramer, *Sumerian Mythology*, pl. 1; Scheil, Vincent, *Saison de Fouilles a Sippar*, 33; Woolley, C. Leonard, *AntJ* 11 (1931) 365 ff.

33. Parrot, André, *Syria*, 17 (1936) pl. III.

34. There is some hope that the new Joint Nippur Expedition of the Oriental Institute of the University of Chicago and the University Museum of the University of Pennsylvania will come upon a scribal school; as yet the uncovering of an area covered by private houses inhabited by scribes has been reported but no trace of a scribal library or school.

ZUR AUGENDARSTELLUNG AUF DER GESETZESSTELE DER HAMMURABI

LUDWIG SCHNITZLER
Freiburg i. Br.

Tafeln 6-7

Jüngst wurde geäußert,[1] die Reliefkunst der Hammurabi-, sogar die der akkadischen und neusumerischen Zeit hätte eine perspektivische Darstellung des menschlichen Auges zur Ansicht gebracht. Diese Meinung wurde erstmalig von E. Meyer vertreten,[2] dann in schärferer Fassung von B. Meissner erneut vorgetragen.[3]

Jeder, der der für die bildende Kunst elementaren Frage nach Entstehung und Entwicklung der perspektivischen Darstellungsweise Beachtung schenkt, wird von der Behauptung E. Meyers und der ihm folgenden Gelehrten überrascht sein.[4] A. Scharff hat das angebliche Vorhandensein der "perspektivischen Dreiviertelansicht" als "Wesensunterschied" der vorderasiatischen gegenüber der ägyptischen Kunst herausgestellt,[5] obwohl er bemerkt, es "bleibt diese perspektivische Augendarstellung, die wir in Aegypten erst viel später im Neuen Reich und auch da nur ganz vereinzelt antreffen,[6] auch

---

1. A. Scharff, *Wesensunterschiede ägyptischer und vorderasiatischer Kunst* (AO 42, 1943), 21 mit Anm. 76 u. 77; wichtigste Denkmäler: Hammurabistele, *HA.* VI, 1, Taf. 149, 1; *Encyclopédie photographique de l'art (Enc.)* I, 258-59; Ch. Zervos, *L'art de la Mésopotamie (AdM)*, 237; *Stelen gleicher Art: Enc.* I, 260, Zervos *(AdM) 243; 239; Relief aus Chafadschi:* Wilhelm II, *Das Königtum im alten Mesopotamien,* Abb. 4; Meissner, *Die babylonischen Kleinplastiken (Texte u. Materialien der Frau Prof. Hilprecht Collection),* Taf. 6, A 49; *neusumerische Stelen:* Berlin VA 2796, V. Christian, *Altertumskunde des Zweistromlandes I (AdZ),* Taf. 425; Zervos *AdM, 231; Stele des Naram-sin aus Diabekr:* E. Unger, *Sumerische und akkadische Kunst (SAK),* Abb. 38; Zervos *AdM, 164.*

2. *Abh. Ak. Berlin* 1906, 3, 14, 44; *Gesch. d. Altertums* I³, 642; M. spricht dies nicht direkt aus, aber aus seinen Worten (44: "Ueber die Technik bemerke ich gleich hier, daß bei den von links heranschreitenden Göttern [auf Berlin VA 2796] auch das Auge richtig im Profil gebildet ist, bei dem nach links gewendeten hinter dem Thron [Fragment nicht zugeörig! s. unten] dagegen nach alter Weise en face. Auf der Gesetzesstele Chammurabis ist bei beiden Gestalten das Auge richtig gezeichnet . . . .") geht hervor, daß er an eine perspektivische Erscheinung denkt. Die gleiche Formulierung gibt W. Andrae, *HA.* VI, 1, 696 u. *Prop. Kst. Gesch.* II⁴ *153* bei der Beschreibung der Hammurabistele.

3. *Grundzüge der babylonischen und assyrischen Plastik (AO* 15, 1915), 44, 59ff.; *Babylonien und Assyrien* I, 322.

4. Nur Unger, *OLZ* 37, 1934, 362 hat sich ohne näheres Eingehen auf die Frage gegen Meyers These gewandt; H. Schäfer spricht sich in einer schriftlichen Mitteilung gegen Scharff aus.

5. a. O. 22.

6. Das eindeutige Beispiel aus dem ägyptischen Bereich für eine perspektivische Augenwiedergabe, die von Schäfer, *Von ägyptischen Kunst*³ *(VäK*³), 381, Anm. 214b gebrachte Zeichnung (!) eines Paviankopfes fehlt bei Scharff.

in der babylonischen Kunst eine große Ausnahme." Aber diese Frage behält ihre wichtige Bedeutung selbst dann, wenn wir sie für Mesopotamien mit den denkbar größten Einschränkungen bejahen würden. Es bliebe nämlich die Tatsache, die mesopotamische Reliefbildnerei hätte in einem überraschenden Zuge ohne irgendwelche Vorstufen eine sehbildliche Darstellung schwieriger Art gemeistert; schon lange vor der griechischen Kunst, die doch die erste und einzige war,[7] die den überaus schweren und endgültigen Durchbruch von der Zwei- zur Dreidimensionalität im Flach- und Rundbild erkämpfte.

Vornehmlich sind es zwei Ursachen, die den Anschein einer perspektivischen Bildung des Auges an Reliefwerken Mesopotamiens hervorrufen können: die zum größten Teil unzulänglichen Reproduktionen[8] — auf sie ist auch heute noch die Forschung vielfach angewiesen — und die strukturelle Beschaffenheit neusumerischer- und altbabylonischer Reliefs. Die beiden Argumente sind zwar gänzlich verschiedener Art, bilden aber zusammen mit einem dritten für das vorliegende Problem den Schlüssel zum Erkennen des wahren Sachverhalts. Dieser dritte Punkt ist die Frage, ob es in der älteren Flächenkunst des Zweistromlandes Zeugnisse gibt, die eindeutig perspektivische Darstellungen überliefern.

Wer nun die Stele des Hammurabi an Hand von technisch durchschnittlichen Abbildungen betrachtet, der wird die Meinung Scharffs akzeptieren. In der Tat zeigt sich bei solchen Bildern[9] das Auge des Gottes und das des Königs in einer mit der Profilstellung des Kopfes in Einklang stehenden Ansicht. Es ist "verkürzt," d. h. nur sein äußerer Winkel ist sichtbar, der innere hingegen fehlt. Der Augapfel erscheint in seinem Umfang verringert und nimmt die Form eines Kreissektors an; Lider und Brauen erfahren gleichfalls die entsprechende Reduzierung.

Hingegen vermitteln die großformatigen und überaus plastischen Aufnahmen Enc. I 259 und Zervos *AdM* 237 (Taf. 7, b) ein gänzlich anderes Bild. Sie geben anschaulich wieder, daß die Augen in ihrer ganzen Ausdehnung ausgehauen sind, ihr Innenwinkel kräftig ausgebildet und somit auch deutlich sichtbar ist. Die für uns sehr nütz-

---

7. Schäfer *VäK*[3] passim; G. Krahmer, *Figur und Raum in der ägyptischen und griechisch-archaischen Kunst* (*28. Hallisches Winckelmannsprogramm*, 1931), 9.

8. In erster Linie ist der stark einfallende Schatten irreführend. Dafür lassen sich auch außerhalb der mesopotamischen Kunst viele Belege anführen; z. B. vgl. F. Sarre, *Die Kunst des alten Persiens* Taf. 29 mit F. Altheim, *Weltgeschichte Asiens im griechischen Zeitalter* I, Abb. 20; G. Contenau, *Manuel d'archéologie orientale* (Man.) III, Abb. 767 mit *HA*. VI, 1, Taf. 173, 2; Zervos, *L'Art en Grèce*, Aufl. 1936 (AeG), 315 mit Springer-Wolters[12], Abb. 533.

9. Wie Unger a. O. Abb. 62, HA. VI, 1, Taf. 149, 1, *Prop. Kst. Gesch.* II[2] 510=Scharff a. O. Abb. 31.

liche seitlich aufgenommene Abbildung Enc. 258 ist noch lehrreicher.
Der gleiche Bestand liegt auch bei anderen hier in Betracht zu zie-
henden Denkmälern vor. Für die Stele VA 2796 bringt Zervos, *AdM*
204. (Taf. 7, a) den Beweis. Ferner hat der Kudurru des Marduk-
apaliddin, der sichtlich auf der Bildform der Hammurabistele fußt,[10]
dieselbe volle Wiedergabe des Auges,[11] wie es Abb. 49 bei C. Bezold,
Babylon und Ninive oder HA. VI, 1, Taf. 173, 2 lehrt. Auch die
berühmte Kriegergestalt am Tore von Boğazköy stellt innerhalb der
"nordsyrischen und hethitischen Kunst" keine "bemerkenswerte Ausnahme"[12] dar. Die neuen Bilder H. Bosserts[13] (Taf. 6 d, 7 c) weisen
das volle Rund nach.

Die Behauptung, auf gewissen Reliefs Vorderasiens sei eine perspektivische Augendarstellung zum Vortrag gekommen, wird durch
die genaue Betrachtung dieser Denkmäler mit Hilfe guter Reproduktionen aufgehoben. Es ist aber erforderlich, eine andere, den Kern
treffende Aussage zu suchen; liegt doch hier ein Phänomen vor, das
innerhalb der "vorgriechischen" Kunst in so markanter Weise allein
dem vorderen Orient eignet, ein Phänomen, das mit Recht als "Wesensunterschied" der Formensprache der ägyptischen Flachbildnerei
konfrontiert wurde.

Alle hier in Frage kommenden Reliefs der altmesopotamischen
Kunst haben eine ausgesprochen voluminös-rundliche Struktur
ihrer Skulpturen. Sie ist so stark und so expansiv nach außen ge-
richtet, daß die Figuren Vollplastiken ähnlich werden. Dieser Zug
zu rundplastischen Formen ist ein sumerisches Erbteil,[14] den die
Reliefkunst bis zum Kassiteneinfall beibehielt. Er ist bereits in der
Djemdet Nasr-Periode ein dominierender Faktor.[15] Der von solchen
Formneigungen getragene Zweig der mesopotamischen Reliefbildnerei steht von seinem Ursprung an nicht der strengen Flächenkunst,

---

10. Andrae *a. O.* 729.

11. Dasselbe bei dem Kudurru des Marduk-zakir-shumi, *Enc.* II, 40; dem des
Nabu-pal-iddina, *Ars. asiatica* 11, Taf. 9, 3.

12. Scharff *a. O.* 43, Anm. 76.

13. *Altanatolien*, Abb. 476ff., 480; analog: Abb. 547; K. Bittel, *Die Ruinen
von Bogazköy*, Abb. 57.

14. Mit anderen Gründen ist er der stärkste Beweis für das Fortleben und die
Fortführung der sumerischen Form, der auch die akkadische Kunst verpflichtet
war. Auch im altbabylonischen Zeitalter erfolgt von ihr kein endgültiges Abgehen (so Scharff *a. O.* 21), wenn auch nominell von einer sumerischen Kunst
nicht mehr gesprochen werden kann. Eine eingehende Behandlung dieser Fragen
wird vorbereitet. S. auch *Bulletin of the Faculty of Arts Fouad I University*, 11
(1949) 161 ff.

15. Ueber die Reliefkunst dieser Zeit unterrichten am besten die skulptierten
Steingefäße (A. Moortgat, *Frühe Bildkunst in Sumer, MVAeG* 40, 3, 1935, 53ff.;
ZA., NF 11, 1939, 1ff.) ; z. B. E. Heinrich, *Kleinfunde aus den archaischen Tem-
pelschichten in Uruk*, Taf. 22-23; Moortgat, *Die Entstehung der sumerischen
Hochkultur* (AO 43, 1945), Taf. 24a; *Ars asiatica* 11, Taf. 3, 2.

also der Zeichnung und der Malerei nahe, wie es in Aegypten der Fall ist, nimmt auch keine Mittlerstellung zwischen Flächenkunst und Rundplastik ein, wie das griechische Relief, sondern steht der Vollplastik äußerst nahe. Gleich dieser wird versucht, für Mensch und Tier eine möglichst unmittelbare Verleiblichung zu finden. Eine Abstimmung auf die Reliefebene, die allein über den Weg einer merklichen Abschwächung des natürlichen Körpervolumens zu erreichen war, erfolgte nur in bedingter, der Flächenbreitung wenig gerechtwerdenden Weise. Deshalb fällt es bei manchen Bildungen schwer, sie noch als Reliefs im üblichen Sinne anzuerkennen.[16]

Es ist nun merkwürdig, daß Werken wie der Stele des Hammurabi trotz der scheinbar so bestimmten Festigkeit der massiven Gedrungenheit ihrer Skulpturen eine gleichmäßige Formgebung fehlt.[17] Die Figuren haben eine starke Leiblichkeit. Ihre fleischige Konstitution kommt massig, fast derb zur Sprache. Der Umriß entbehrt der linearen Festigkeit.[18] Dagegen herrschen runde, mehr oder minder kräftig gewölbte Bildungen vor. Figur und Einzelglieder sind zylindrischer Konzeption. Falten, Säume und Rüschen sind geglättet und abgeschliffen. Die Köpfe wirken wie Rundbilder, die genau im Scheitel gespalten, auf den Reliefgrund angeheftet wurden. Von der rechten Hälfte des Götterkopfes tritt das Horn der Krone mit seiner Spitze eben noch hervor (erkenntlich bei der Schrägansicht Enc. I, 258). Auch dieses besitzt trotz der unmittelbaren Nähe des Reliefgrundes eine fühlbare Plastizität. Sie beherrscht in hohem Ausmaß Nase, Augen, Ohr, Wangenbart und Haarschopf. Erst am herabwallenden Kinnbart kommt es zu einer Verflachung, angeregt durch die flächige Führung der Brust und ihre volle Ausbreitung in die

---

16. Im altmesopotamischen Zeitalter, vor allem während der "Meselim-Stufe" hat es ein zeichnerisch geradflächiges Relief gegeben, doch blieb es außerhalb jenes Zeitraumes gegenüber dem hochplastischen eine mehr sekundäre Erscheinung. Wie auf anderen Gebieten (darüber Moortgat, *Bildwerk und Volkstum Vorderasiens zur Hethiterzeit*, 8. *Sendschrift der Deutschen Orientgesellschaft*, 1934, 6) so scheint die elamische Kunst mit ihrem gleichmäßig in die Fläche gebreiteten Relief (*Enc.* I 269-70; 274; 275 [*Bronzerelief*]; *Felsreliefs:* Cheikh-Kan, Malamir, Contenau, *Man.* I, Abb. 47; IV, Abb. 1182; Kurangün, E. Herzfeld, *Archaeological History of Iran*, Taf. 2-3; *Reliefgefäß:* Contenau, *Man.* II, Abb. 629) eine Sonderstellung im vorderasiatischen Bereich einzunehmen. Dies dürfte in der stets hervorragenden Stellung der Malerei im Iran begründet liegen. In Mesopotamien selbst war es nur die assyrische Reliefbildnerei, die sich sehr eng an die Zeichnung anschloß. Daß aber auch ihr altes sumerisches Erbe innewohnt (Moortgat *a. O.* 30) beweisen u. a. die Stele Assurnasirpals aus Kalchu (Unger, *Assyrische und babylonische Kunst* [*ABK*], Abb. 39), die sogenannten Gilgameschfiguren (*Enc.* I, 304-05) und die geflügelten Genien (Contenau, *Les antiquités orientales* II, Taf. 8).

17. Für die babylonische Kunst allgemein vermerkt von H. Kees, *HA.* III, 1, 3, 1, 276.

18. Ausnahme: *Enc.* I, 247; dort auch eine für die mesopotamische Reliefkunst nicht häufige Unterschneidung (Adorant links).

Fläche. Die am Kopf so eindeutig durchgeführte Formung eines "halben Rundbildes"[19] wird aber nicht konsequent bei der ganzen Figur vorgetragen. Ursache dafür ist das Fehlen einer einheitlichen Schau, die hier eine geschlossene Seitenansicht entstehen lassen müßte. Wie die ägyptische und die griechisch-archaische, bei der sich aber schon verhältnismäßig früh, bald nach Findung eines mit Um- rißlinie arbeitenden Figurenstils die reine Profilansicht einstellt,[20] so ist auch die vorderasiatische Flächenkunst der "wechselansichtigen" Darstellung des Menschen unterworfen. Erst in der assyrischen Kunst kommt es zur häufigeren Darstellung der durchgehenden Sei- tenansicht.

Šamaš Oberkörper ist, wie schon vermerkt, in voller Ausdehnung in die Fläche gelegt, sein plastisches Hervortreten gegenüber dem Kopf merklich gedämpft. Dagegen sind die mit ihm verwachsenen Gliedmaßen, in erster Linie der vorgestreckte Arm (s. Schrägan- sicht) und die geballte Linke wiederum von kräftiger Leiblichkeit. An den Beinen mit dem aufgebauschten Gewand wird die halbrund- liche Modellierung wieder erreicht. Die Unstetigkeit der Formge- bung offenbart sich in gleicher Weise an der Gestalt Hammurabis. Kopf und Oberkörper stehen wiederum in formalem und komposi- tionellem Gegensatz. Das Zurücktreten der Plastizität des Ober- körpers wird etwas verschleiert durch den in Adorationsgeste vor die Brust gelegten Arm. Ferner bewirkt seine Haltung eine kugelige Herauswölbung des Schultergelenkes und zugleich eine stärkere Emporhebung und Abrundung gegen den Reliefgrund, während die andere Brusthälfte mehr zurücktritt. Die Arme haben ein röhrenar- tiges Aussehen. Der Unterkörper wird von einem langen, reich dra- pierten Kleid verdeckt. Seine anatomische Gliederung kommt außer der leichten Andeutung des Gesäßes nicht zur Geltung. Verschieden- artig fällt das Gewand herab; flächig im linken, gerundet im rechten Teil. Dieselbe Diskrepanz zeigt sich bei der Saumführung.

Wenden wir uns wieder der Wiedergabe des Kopfes zu. Es wurde festgestellt, daß gerade er weitgehend in rundbildlicher Art aus dem Stein gehauen wurde. Der Bildhauer konnte während der Arbeit seinen Standpunkt nach Belieben ändern. Er hat wie ein Rundbildner vielfach im Umschreiten die Köpfe modelliert, wobei ihm das Um- gehen durch die Wölbung der ganzen Stele[21] noch erleichtert wurde

---

19. Schäfer VäK[3] 76 für aus der Reliefebene frontal dem Betrachter zuge- wendete Figuren.

20. Krahmer *a. O.* 62.

21. Konvexer Form ist bereits die Löwenjagdstele aus Uruk, UVB. 5, 1933, Taf. 12-13; Christian *AdZ* Taf. 104; Scharff *a. O.* 22; die Stelen *Enc.* I 247, 260 sind kaum, Contenau, *Man.* II, Abb. 608 stärker gewölbt.

Er konnte seine Skulpturen von verschiedenen Seiten her angreifen, sie in der Relieftiefe fassen und gerade bei der Aushauung des Auges von vorne den Meissel ansetzen, sie wie bei einem freiplastischen Kopfe unter denselben technischen Voraussetzungen formen. Sein Verfahren — das natürlich schon den zitierten neusumerischen Stelen zugrunde liegt — stellt sich in den denkbar größten Gegensatz zu den inneren und äußeren Grundlagen der Flachbildnerei. Denn der Flach-bildner und noch mehr der Zeichner sind an ihren Standpunkt ge-bunden, nur geistig sind sie in der Lage ihn zu verändern.[22] Ihnen stehen durch den planen Charakter der Relief- bzw. Zeichenebene nur zwei Dimensionen, Breite und Höhe, für die Ausdehnung des Bildes zur Verfügung. Sie müssen sich erst durch eine gewaltige geistige Leistung, unter Anwendung von Hilfsmitteln, die in die Tiefe leitende Dimension schaffen. Demgegenüber tritt die Tiefenführung bei einer Gestaltung eines Reliefs von so starkem plastischen Volumen, daß es dem Rundbilde fast gleichkommt, ganz von selbst ein. Eine Perspektive bleibt vollkommen aus dem Spiel.[23] Die rundplastische Struktur des Reliefs veranlaßte, ja zwang den Bildhauer das Auge in eine Stellung zu bringen, in der es vom Betrachter nur in Seiten-ansicht gesehen werden kann. Formbedingt "verkürzt" sich das Auge streng von der Seite her betrachtet, gewinnt aber sofort an Ausdehnung, sobald es in einer schrägen Blickrichtung gesehen wird. Dieser, sowohl von der äußeren Gestalt der Reliefskulptur, als auch vom jeweiligen Standpunkt des Betrachters abhängige Wandel der Erscheinung ist gleich dem der Vollplastik. Auch ein im Profil gese-hener vollplastischer Kopf hat ohne jede perspektivische Linie das Auge "verkürzt." Ein durch die äußere Form erzeugter perspek-tivischer Effekt ist weder durch einen Willensakt entstanden, noch bewußt als künstlerische Ausdrucksweise angewendet worden. Viel-mehr ist er ein Spiel des Zufalls, das sich gerade an neusumerischen und altbabylonischen Reliefs gern einstellt. Solche scheinbaren Perspektiven, die aber im eigentlichen Sinne nicht raumbildend sind,[24]

---

22. Schäfer *VäK*³ 305.

23. Künstlerisch hat das Hochrelief der griechischen Klassik trotz der schein-bar gleichen äußeren Form nichts mit dem mesopotamischen gemeinsam. Trotz seiner starken Erhöhung und seiner teilweise äußerst weitgehenden Lösung der Figuren vom Grunde bleibt es ein Vertreter strenger Flächenkunst, wie Krahmer a. O. 58ff. herausgearbeitet hat. Doch ist nicht die Schrägstellung alleiniges Mittel für die Schaffung einer dreidimensionalen Gliederung (so K. 60). Aehnlich wie im Flachrelief wird auch im Hochrelief Schrägstellung in Verbindung mit Perspektive zur Festhaltung eines bewegungsreichen, raumergreifenden Vorgangs herangezogen. Die bei K. 59 abgebildete Parthenonmetope (S. 1) gibt dafür ein lehrreiches Zeugnis. Der Rücken des Kentauren ist nicht nur schräggestellt, sondern auch an seiner rechten Seite deutlich verkürzt.

24. Vgl. die treffliche Bemerkung an Hand etruskischer Reliefs v. Kaschnitz-Weinbergs, *RM* 41, 1926, 154.

können natürlich in jeder Reliefkunst auftreten, sofern sie stark gerundete Skulpturen vorträgt.[25]

Eine mächtige Relieferhöhung allein hat nicht unbedingt die den Gesetzen der Vollplastik folgende Bildung des Auges zur Folge. Das lehren Denkmäler wie das akkadische Stelenfragment *Enc.* I 212, die Stelen des Naram-sin aus Susa, *Enc.* I 214-15, Zervos *AdM* 165-67, und aus Diabekr, Zervos *AdM* 164, Christian *AdZ* Taf. 365, 3, die Reliefs auf der Basis der Ur-nin-girsu-Statue im Louvre, *Enc.* I 240-41, Contenau *Man.* II, Abb. 511, die Stele Berlin VA 2796. Das Auge Naram-sins auf seiner Siegesstele[26] ist in schräger Führung zur Nasenwurzel hin eingesetzt, behält aber ganz seine Vollansicht. Diese Art der Wiedergabe kehrt gelegentlich an anderen akkadischen und neusumerischen Monumenten wieder,[27] von denen die Stele aus Diabekr das bekannteste ist. Sie ist zugleich ein Beispiel, daß man sich gerne bei der Beurteilung der Augendarstellung eigener Voreingenommenheit hingab. Mit Recht betonen Ed. Meyer und Meissner,[28] daß das Auge in Vorderansicht gezeigt sei, während Scharff[29] von einem Beispiel "einer versuchten perspektivischen Augendarstellung" spricht.[30]

Derselben schrägen Einsenkung bediente sich auch die griechische Flächenkunst.[31] Allerdings verläuft dort die Reliefoberfläche gerade im Gegensatz zu den mesopotamischen Beispielen, denen selbst bei einer stärkeren Abflachung, wie sie eben an den genannten Werken vorhanden ist, immer eine gewisse Rundung innewohnt.

Auffallend ist die Figur auf dem Orthostaten von Sakçagözu, L. Delaporte, *Malatya* I, Taf. 39,[32] zumal eine formale Aehnlichkeit mit

25. Assyrisch: Contenau *Man.* III, Abb. 805; *AfO Beiheft* 4, 1939, Abb. 8; 13 (dazu Weidner 16); Abb. 23; persisch: Sarre *a. O.* Taf. 35; griechisch-archaisch: Zervos *AeG* 175; 178; Mendel, *Cat. Konstantinopel* II, 518.

26. Bei dem unter dem König liegenden Toten ist der Stein an der Augenpartie abgestoßen; ebenso u. a. bei H. de Genouillac, *Fouilles de Telloh* II, Taf. 99, 2c; Stele Zervos *AdM* 231; hethitisch: Moortgat. *Die bildende Kunst des Alten Orients und die Bergvölker*, Taf. 86, 2.

27. *Enc.* I 219 E; 243 C; irreführend AO 15, Abb. 77; auch die assyrische Kunst hat sich gerne dieser Bildung bedient.

28. *a. O.* 11, 44; AO 15, 25.

29. *a. O.* 42, Anm. 77 zu 22.

30. Dieselben sich widersprechenden Auffassungen bestehen auch über das Relief des Hammurabi in London (Unger *SAK* Ab. 60, *Prop. Kst. Gesch.* II,⁴ 511 oben): Meyer *a. O.* 14: "en face gezeichnet"; Bezold *a. O.* 164: ". . . . das Auge im ganzen richtig eingesetzt."

31. Relief: *Fouilles de Delphes* IV, Taf. 29, Zervos AeG 194; E. Langlotz, *Frühgriechische Bildhauerschulen*, Taf. 75b; H. Schrader, *Archaische griechische Plastik*, Abb. 58; Münzen: K. Lange, *Götter Griechenlands*, Taf. 68; K. Regling, *Die antike Münze als Kunstwerk*, Abb. 90; 115; Zervos AeG 251; verwandt in der mittelalterlichen Metallkunst wiederkehrend: H. Jantzen, *Ottonische Kunst*, Abb. 115 (von der Augsburger Domtür); Lange, *Münzkunst des Mittelalters*, 29, 31.

32. Im Mauerverband stehend: Bossert *a. O.* 883.

einer Gestalt auf einem um 530 in Samos entstandenen Fries[33] besteht. Eine Anlehnung des ionischen Werkes an kleinasiatische Reliefgestaltung ist bei aller Anerkennung der griechischen Eigenart nicht von der Hand zu weisen.[34] Dafür spricht die außergewöhnliche Dicke des Reliefs. Es wäre zu überlegen, ob der samische Fries nicht nach kleinasiatischem Vorbild unmittelbar am Fuße eines Bauwerkes lief. Die starke Relieferhebung zwingt nicht zu einer unbedingten Hochsetzung des Frieses an der Wand,[35] ist sie doch in gleichem Ausmaß außer auf kleinasiatischen Orthostaten auch an den Kroisossäulen in Ephesos vorhanden.[36] Sowohl auf der Platte von Sakçagözü, als auch auf dem Friesbruchstück ist der ins Profil gelegte Kopf so aus dem Stein gehauen, daß die abliegende Gesichtshälfte teilweise bei einer seitlichen Betrachtung (Delaporte a. O. Taf. 39) zum Vorschein kommt. Deutlich ist die innere Hälfte des Auges ausgemeißelt, das in gleicher Ausführung auch am samischen Werke vorhanden gewesen sein wird. Die Nase ist an beiden Denkmälern vom Grunde gelöst. Trotz dieser freien Anlegung des Kopfes behalten die Reliefs die absolute Geradflächigkeit. Somit wird auch das Auge gänzlich der Fläche angepaßt. Nur eine seichte Einsenkung des Innenwinkels erfolgte.[37]

Wenden wir uns wiederum mesopotamischen Reliefs zu. Bei dem Vergleich kahler und unbärtiger Köpfe mit bedeckten und bärtigen auf neusumerischen Stelen zeigt sich ein auffälliger Unterschied. Die Kahlköpfe sind flach gebildet, während die eine Bedeckung und Bart tragenden vielfach rundlicher Konzeption sind. Die Augenbildung ist diesem Wechsel der Relieferhebung unterworfen. An der Gudeastele

---

33. Buschor *AM* 58, 1933, 8, Abb. 3, Beil. 3, 2.

34. Allgemein zum Verhältnis Ionien-Vorderasien zuletzt Krahmer *a. O.* Anm. 30 zu 31; H. Thiersch, *Antike* 9, 1933, 203ff.; Pfuhl *JdI* 30, 1935, 10; H. E. Stier, *Grundlagen und Sinn der griechischen Geschichte*, 238; F. Schachermeyer, *Indogermanen und Orient* 86. Gerade in Samos scheint eine besondere Begünstigung östlicher Formen bestanden zu haben, wie dies vor allem die Hera des Cheramyes zeigt (Langlotz a. O. 120). Auch das Friesbruchstück offenbart den "flüssigen Kontur" und "spricht von einem geschmeidigen zarten Körper."

35. So Buschor a. O. 9.

36. Von den Griechen wurde manches unverändert aus dem Osten entlehnt. So hat der klazomenische Dichter Hipponax von phrygischen und lydischen Worten Gebrauch gemacht (W. Kranz, *Die Kultur der Griechen*, 113; D. M. Robinson, *AJA* 17 [1913] 362-368); Epimenides von Kreta entsühnte die Athener von der Hinmetzelung der Anhänger Kylons an den Altären der Eumeniden "nach einem, wie es scheint orientalischen Ritus" (W. Nestle, *Griechische Geistesgeschichte*, 51). Wir müssen also auch auf dem Gebiet der bildenden Kunst solche wortgetreuen Uebertragungen rein asiatischer Elemente unbedingt in Rechnung setzen. Ist die Rekonstruktion des Portals des Palastes vom Tell Halaf wirklich gesichert, so weisen sich die griechischen Karyatiden auch als im Prinzip ohne wesentliche Veränderung übernommenes Gut des Ostens aus.

37. Aehnlich: Orthostaten von Sendschirli, Moortgat, *Bergvölker*, Taf. 40; 43, 2.

in Berlin läßt sich jenes, von der unsteten äußeren Form hervorgeru-
fene Erscheinungsspiel gut verfolgen. Links der König mit kahlem,
flachgebildetem Kopf; sein Auge war sicher in die Fläche gelegt, wie
wir es aus vielen analogen Beispielen[38] entnehmen können. Der ihn
führende und der einen Stock haltende Gott hingegen tragen Krone
und Bart; ihr Kopf ist halb rundplastisch wiedergegeben. Die Augen
sind dementsprechend ausgeführt. Der ganz rechts stehende — aber
nicht in den Verband der Stele gehörige[39] — Gott hat trotz Krone und
Bart einen flächig wiedergegebenen Kopf mit en face gestelltem Auge.
Bemerkenswert ist auch ein Bildstreifen der Ur-nammu-Stele (Zervos
AdM 228, Prop. *Kst. Gesch.* II,[40] 506). Obwohl dort die thronende
Göttin eine Hörnerkrone und ein dichtes Haupthaar trägt, die beide
in kräftiger Plastik wiedergegeben werden, kam es nicht zu einer
flächigen Anlegung des Gesichtes. Eine Vertiefung der Augenhöhle
wie an den bärtigen Köpfen, wurde nicht vorgenommen.

Wie ist nun dieser merkwürdige Formengegensatz zu erklären?
Blieb die mehr rundbildliche Bildung der Köpfe, die einen perspektivischen Effekt zur Folge hatte, in erster Linie "Göttern, Königen
und anderen hochgestellten Persönlichkeiten vorbehalten"?[40] Eine
besondere Auszeichnung von Göttern und Königen kann nicht der
Grund dafür gewesen sein. Das somatische Aussehen der Köpfe gab
den Anstoß dazu. Geschorene und unbedeckte Schädel bieten keinen
Anreiz für eine plastiche Akzentuierung. Ihre völlige Blöße und
Glätte verleiht ihnen ein homogenes und monotones Aussehen, das —
abgesehen vom Gesicht und vom Ohr — keine besondere Gliederung
besitzt. Es ist daher naheliegend, sie in Form einer flachen, gegen
den Rand hin abgerundeten Scheibe darzustellen. Gänzlich anders
sind dagegen die Voraussetzungen für die Bildung von Köpfen mit
Hörnerkrone, Kappe und reichem Haar- und Bartwuchs. Sie bieten
ein wechselvolles, kontrastreiches Bild, das eine variantenreiche
Modellierung verlangte. Außerdem lockte die füllige Struktur
mancher Details, wie die Hörner der Götterkrone, die reifenartige
Krempe von Kappe und Krone, die Fülle des gleich prallen Trauben
hervorquellenden Haares, aus dem wiederum das Ohr in einer, seine
Fleischigkeit betonenden Weise herausgeschält werden muß, zu einer
plastisch-erhabenen Ausprägung; einer Lockung, der man durch die
Neigung zu stark gerundeten Formen gerne folgte.

Es zeigt sich auch auf dem Wege einer Untersuchung motivischer

---

38. Wie *Enc.* I 227; Christian *AdZ*, Taf. 427, 1.

39. Nach einer Moortgat verdankten Beobachtung "ist das Bruchstück mit dem
Gott rechts fälschlich mit den übrigen Fragmenten zusammengebracht worden.
Es gehörte ursprünglich einer anderen Stele an."

40. Scharff *a. O.* 44 Anm. 77 zu 22.

Eigenarten, daß von der äußeren Gestaltung des Reliefs allein die
Entstehung einer scheinbar perspektivischen Augendarstellung ab-
hängt. Wir müssen von dieser trügerischen Erscheinung, für die das
durch die antike und abendländische Kunst faszinierte Sehorgan des
heutigen Menschen eine geradezu fatale Schwäche hat, mit aller
Schärfe feststellen, daß sie in keiner Weise ein bewußtes Abgehen
von der "vorstelligen" Darstellungsform bedeutet.[41]

Der Kreis unserer Beweisführung verstärkt sich bei der Beant-
wortung der Frage nach dem Vorhandensein gelegentlich auftreten-
der Verkürzungen und Schrägansichten in mesopotamischen Flachbildern, wie sie ab und zu in ägyptischen[42] ohne genetische Vorstufen[43] plötzlich auftauchen. "Manchmal häuften sie sich" dort "so,
daß man glaubt, es hätte nur eines kleinen Ruckes bedurft zum
Durchbruch der Kunst zur sehbildlichen Darstellung."[44]

Eine Durchsicht der erhaltenen Denkmäler ergibt, daß die altme-
sopotamische Flächenkunst kaum,[45] die jüngere weniger solche Ab-

---

41. Schäfer *VäK*³ 274 meint, "ein scharf seitlich gesehenes Auge würde das
Wesen der Geradansichtigkeit ebenso wenig durchbrechen wie ein so gezeichneter
(Finger- oder Zehen-) Nagel," der auf ägyptischen Flachbildern meist in Seiten-
ansicht (darüber Schäfer *VäK*³ 278ff., 281ff.) festgehalten ist. Dem ist zu ent-
gegnen, daß die Nägel von Gliedmaßen im Gegensatz zum Auge in der inneren
Vorstellung eine nebensächliche und untergeordnete Stellung einnehmen. Sie
waren keine selbständige Vorstellungsformel wie das Auge. In den großen
Begriff "Fuß," "Hand" einbezogen, fanden sie keine spezielle Behandlung.
Werden nun die Glieder in Seitenansicht umrissen (über die Eigenarten der
ägyptischen Handdarstellung — für die es manche assyrische Parallele gibt —
Schäfer ebenda), die in Aegypten üblich war, ergab sich die seitliche Stellung
der Nägel ganz von selbst. Ein in der "vorgriechischen" Zeit verkürzt gezeich-
netes Auge (s. Anm. 6) bedeutet m. E. ein sehr beachtliches Abgehen von
der Geradansichtigkeit. Eine solche Darstellung stellt vielleicht den schärfsten
Bruch mit dem urtümlichen Denken dar. Nicht nur deshalb, da das Auge dinglich
in seiner vollen Ausdehnung im geistigen Bilde lebt (Schäfer *VäK*³ 273), sondern auch aus dem Grunde, weil es das hervorstechendste, in seiner Anziehungs-
und Ausdruckskraft packendste Punkt jedes Lebewesens ist. Seine Einmaligkeit
hat wesentlich dazu beigetragen, daß das Auge in der griechischen Zeichnung so
zähe die Faceansicht behaupten konnte, als schon verschiedene Verkürzungen
gegenständlicher und animaler Vorwürfe aufgekommen waren.

42. Schäfer *VäK*³ passim; OLZ 38, 1935, 76ff, 79; *JdI* 57, 1942, 172; *Nach.
Gött. gelehrt. Ges.* 1944, 105ff. mit Anhang 5.

43. Das Fehlen einer festen Entwicklungslinie, die zunächst eine beschränkte
Anzahl von Themen von primären Anfängen allmählich zu sinnfälligen perspektivischen Darstellungen führt, dokumentiert die Unstetigkeit und Unsicherheit
mit der die ägyptische, überhaupt jede "vorgriechische" Kunst Verkürzung und
Schrägansicht handhabte. In der griechischen Flachbildnerei, vor allem in der
Vasenmalerei, wurde schon früh der Keim zur "wahrnehmigen" Gestaltungsweise
gelegt, der einmal erwacht, kräftig, ohne Unterbrechung aufwuchs und in
ständiger Fortbildung blieb. Die unabweichliche, ja logische Folge seines orga-
nischen Wachstums war die endgültige Konstituierung der Dreidimensionalität.

44. Schäfer *VäK*³ 252.

45. Vgl. zum Folgenden auch die Ausführungen Andraes *a. O.* 781ff; das
leichte Herabziehen der Schulter der nackten Priester auf Weiheplatten aus
Nippur (Christian *AdZ* Taf. 277, Bezold *a. O.* Abb. 31) ist nicht, wie Bezold 164
meint, erfolgt, um "eine perspektivische Stellung zu geben." Die moderne Zeich-

weichungen von der "geradvorstelligen" Darstellungsweise kennt,
wie sie meteorhaft in der ägyptischen zum Niederschlag kamen. Wir
glauben die Gründe dafür zu erkennen: in der wahrscheinlich nicht
führenden Stellung der Malerei auf dem Gebiete der monumentalen
Flächenkunst,[46] in dem Bestehen zweier äußerst verschiedenartiger
Strömungen innerhalb der Reliefbildnerei, wobei durch lange Zeit
eine dominierende Neigung zu dicklich-runden Formen bestand, die
nur wenig an eine geradflächige Vorderebene gebunden waren; in
dem daraus resultierenden Zug zur Vollplastik, der das mesopotamische Relief erst spät zu einem Vertreter echter Flächenkunst werden
ließ. Schließlich dürfte der im Gegensatz zur ägyptischen und griechischen Kunst mehr in Unruhe und häufiger von außen gestörte Ab-
lauf der bildenden Kunst in Vorderasien ein wesentliches Moment
für das Ausbleiben perspektivischer Ansätze in der Flächendarstel-
lung gewesen sein.

Erwähnenswert ist die von der üblichen Art der Darstellung sich
abhebende Augenwiedergabe auf einigen assyrischen Reliefs der Zeit
Sargons II (Taf. 6, c). Das Auge ist in seinem vollen Umfang gezeichnet, gegen die Nasenwurzel eingesenkt. Aber im Gegensatz zur älteren
Weise wurde der Augenstern durch Ritzung effektvoll herausgearbeitet. Er erscheint jedoch nicht in Form eines Kreises, sondern als
hochgestellte Ellipse, die so weit an den Innenwinkel herangeschoben
wurde, daß sie dem Betrachter nur mit halber oder dreiviertel Fläche
sichtbar wird.[47] Der Augapfel ist an dieser Stelle stark vorgewölbt,
und läuft nicht wie am Außen- zum Innenwinkel spitz zusammen.
Bei solchen Darstellungen kann man von einer leisen Hinwendung
zur perspektivischen Bildungsweise sprechen. Hingegen ist es nicht
erlaubt, bei gewissen assyrischen Reliefs mit großzügigen Land-
schaftsschilderungen von einer Anwendung der optischen- oder der
Luftperspektive zu sprechen. Dieser Meinung Ungers[48] wurde schon

---

nung des Siegelbildes Berlin *VA* 8795 bei O. Weber, *AO* 17/18, Abb. 403 = *REV*
II, Taf. 172b legt die Annahme nahe, die Mündung des rechts oben befindlichen
Gefäßes sei zu einer schmalen Ellipse verkürzt. Die Photographie bei Moortgat,
Vorderasiatische Rollsiegel, Taf. 32, 235 gibt aber eine strenge Seitenansicht
wieder; dieselbe Erscheinung beim Siegelbild Contenau *Man.* I, Abb. 146 (Zeich-
nung) — *Enc.* II, 73, 41 (Photo). Eine verwandte Täuschung tritt sogar bei
Moortgat *a. O.* 236 auf. In der Freiplastik sind Abweichungen von der Geradan-
sichtigkeit ab und zu bereits in neusumerischer Zeit vorhanden (Christian *AdZ*
383ff.). Wie in Aegypten (Schäfer, *Das altägyptische Bildnis*, 29) sind diese
Ausnahmen in der Freiplastik häufiger als im Relief.

46. Die Behauptung Andraes *a. O.* 793 kann nach dem Bekanntwerden der
Malereien von Tell Uqair, Mari und ᶜAgarquf in ihrer alternativen Schärfe
nicht mehr aufrecht erhalten werden.

47. *Enc.* I, 312 (Abb. 5); Contenau, *Ant. orient.* II, Taf. 14 oben; Bezold *a. O.*
Abb. 107; Weidner *a. O.* Abb. 49.

48. *Die Reliefs Tiglatpilesars III, aus Nimrud* (*Publ. d. kais. osman. Museen*
5, 1917), 27, 29; ABK 42.

von mehreren Seiten widersprochen.[49] Ein Abweichen von der un-
perspektivischen Zeichnung zur "schrägvorstelligen"[50] führte zur
Vorstaffelung der Räder des einachsigen Wagens auf einem gegen
Ende des 1. Jahrtausends entstandenen phönikischen Siegelbilde.[51]
In aller Kürze sei noch ein Monument besprochen, das innerhalb
der vorderasiatischen Flächenkunst der einzige Vertreter einer ein-
deutigen und wissentlich ausgeführten perspektivischen Augendarstellung ist: das Magierrelief von Ergili.[52] Die Art der Wiedergabe
des Auges ist ein sicherer Anhaltspunkt für die Zeitbestimmung
dieses Stückes, das noch keine gesicherte Datierung fand.[53] Das Relief ist schwach gehoben, zart und ebenmäßig modelliert. Seine Entstehung und die strikte Anwendung von Grundsätzen strenger Flachbildnerei ist ohne die Anregung des klassischen Reliefs der Hellenen
undenkbar.[54] Auf den griechischen Einfluß geht ebenso die sehbildliche Wiedergabe des Auges (Macridy a. O. Abb. 4; hier Taf. 7, d)
und der Hürde zurück.[55] Die Seitenansicht des Auges wurde nicht
durch eine sehr kräftige Einkrümmung und Einsenkung gewonnen,
sondern durch den Fortfall der von der Schläfe abliegenden Teile;
ein Verfahren, das erstmalig griechische Zeichner nach unverdros-
senem und schwierigem, durch Jahrzehnte während Bemühen und
Experimentieren gegen 450 in die Flächenkunst einführten.[56] Die
rein zeichnerische Festlegung des seitlich gesehenen Auges ist in der
griechischen Reliefübung des 5. Jahrhunderts selten, vor seiner Mitte
mit Sicherheit nicht nachweisbar. Der Parthenonfries[57] und die

---

49. Contenau, *Man.* III, 121ff.; Moortgat, *Jahrb. d. preuss. Kunstsammlg.*
51, 1930, 141; Schäfer *VäK*³ 243, Anm. a.

50. Schäfer, *OLZ* 38, 1935, 76, Anm. 3.

51. *Morgenland* 23, 1932, Taf. 6, Abb. 15; dasselbe auf griechisch-archaischen
Vasenbildern: E. Gerhard, *Auserlesene Vasenbilder*, Taf. 95/96; *Brit. Mus. CV.*
III He Taf. 68, 1c (Rückstaffelung). Die Notiz Schäfers, *OLZ* 38, 1935, 79,
Anm. 1, in "vorgriechischen," also auch in ägyptischen Bildern kommen gestaf-
felte Räder überhaupt nicht vor, ist somit überholt.

52. *Istanbul, Mendel Cat.* III Nr. 1357; Macridy, *BCH.* 37, 1913, 348ff., Abb. 4,
Taf. 8; Ch. Picard, *Manuel d'archéologie grecque* I, Abb. 115; A. U. Pope, *Survey
of Persian art* IV, Taf. Taf. 103 B; Bossert *a. O.* Abb. 1218.

53. Mendel und Macridy: Ende 5. Jhdt.; Picard, *La sculpture antique* I, 199
ebenso; dagegen *Man.* I, 412: "à peine posterieur à la fin de l'archaisme";
Bossert: um 500; Casson in Pope *a. O.* I, 350 ohne feste Datierung; von G.
Rodenwaldt in *Sitz. Ber. Ak. Berlin* 1933, 1041 ist das Magierrelief bei der Besprechung des Fundes von Ergili nicht herausgehoben worden.

54. Dies hat Casson wieder betont; das von ihm vermerkte Vorherrschen
persischen Gutes beschränkt sich nur auf das Inhaltliche.

55. Auf ihre Gestaltung hat Casson zuerst hingewiesen.

56. Knappe Besprechung bei K. Reichhold, *Skizzenbuch griechischer Meister*,
59ff. und bei G. M. A. Richter, *Redfigured Athenian vases in the Metropolitan
Museum of art*, 29, 89.

57. *JdI* 45, 1930, 259, Abb. 52; 267, 72; 73; 271, 78.

Mädchenstele aus Paros in New York[58] überliefern die frühesten
sicheren Beispiele. In der Münzkunst hingegen tritt diese Bildung
nach Durchlaufen derselben Vorstufen,[59] die die Vasenmaler schul-
ten, schon früher auf.[60]

Außergewöhnlich ist auch die perspektivische Zeichnung der
Hürde. Die Schrägstellung länglicher und kantiger Gegenstände
kommt in der griechischen Flächenkunst erst im letzten Drittel des
5. Jahrhunderts[61] zur Anwendung.[62] Wieder ist die Zahl der Beispiele
nicht erheblich. Eine so weit in den Raum gedehnte Tiefenführung,
wie an unserem Relief, ist selbst am Nereiden-Monument in Xanthos[63]
und am Heroon von Gjölbaschi-Trysa[64] selten. Erst um 400 werden
lange Perspektiven beliebter.[65]

Die perspektivische Gestaltung von Dingen, die selbst griechischen
Künstlern des vorgeschrittenen 5. Jahrhunderts nur allmählich ge-
läufig wurden, zwingt zu einer zeitlichen Ansetzung des Magierreliefs
nicht vor 420. Das Nereiden- und das Monument von Gjölbaschi-Trysa
sind sicher vorausgegangen. Nur um 400 oder in den nachfolgenden
Jahren bis gegen 380 kann das Magierrelief entstanden sein. Durch
den Vergleich mit griechischen Werken wurde ferner ersichtlich, daß
wir nicht allein berechtigt, sondern geradezu verpflichtet sind, dieses
in den griechischen Bereich, soweit es Stil und Technik betrifft,[66] zu
stellen. Sein Meister war kein Asiat, der sich hellenische Art zu
sehen und zu bilden angeeignet hatte, sondern ein Grieche. Vielleicht
wurde er von Pharnabazos, dem Gegenspieler des jüngeren Kyros,
in seine daskylitische Residenz berufen.

58. F. Gerke, *Griech. Plastik* 147; P. Jacobsthal, *Die melischen Reliefs*, Abb.
41; G. M. A. Richter, *The sculpture and sculptors of the Greeks*, Abb. 205, 426;
dieses Merkmal spricht für eine Entstehung der Stele im Jahrzehnt 440/30.

59. Regling *a. O.* 35.

60. Z. B. M. Hirner, *Die schönsten Griechenmünzen Siziliens*, Abb. 2; 9;
Regling a. O. Abb. 352; 353, Lange a. O. Abb. 36; Regling a. O. 367; 396, Lange
a. O. Abb. 50; Regling, a. O. 386; 392.

61. E. Buschor in Furtwängler-Reichhold, *Griechische Vasenmalerei* III, 129;
vor 430: Gerhard a. O. Taf. 296 (Hermenschaft); *Oesterr. Jahresh.* 12, 1909, 166
(Schrein).

62. Stele der Philis aus Thasos, Brunn-Bruckmann, *Denkmäler griech. und
röm. Skulptur* 232a, *Enc.* III, 169; Bruchstück eines Reliefs aus Samos, Jacobsthal a. O. Abb. 38, W. H. Schuchhardt, *Die Kunst der Griechen*, Abb. 260; O.
Walter, *Beschreibung der Reliefs im kleinen Akropolismuseum Nr.* 42; H. Die-
polder, *Die attischen Grabreliefs*, Taf. 21; E. Kjellberg, *Studien zu attischen
Reliefs*, Taf. 17, 55; W. Hahland, *Vasen um Meidias*, Taf. 3, 11b; A. D. Trendall,
Frühitaliotische Vasen, Taf. 13a; 17a (mißglückt).

63. F. Winter, *Kunstgeschichte in Bildern* I, 265, 2; AM 52, 1927, Beil. 13, 5.

64. O. Benndorf - G. Niemann, *Das Heroon von Gjölbaschi-Trysa*, Taf. 12,
A 8; 16, A 3-4.

65. Hahland a. O. Taf. 16a; Trendall a. O. Taf. 29b; 30a; 32a; H. Süsserott,
Griech. Plastik des 4. Jahrhunderts, Taf. 16, 4; in der Frührenaissance galt die
Zeichnung über Eck genommener Gebäude auch als außergewöhnliche Leistung,
wie Vasari in der *Biographie des Masaccio* berichtet (*Ausg. Sammlung Dieterich*,
Bd. 39, 103).

66. Picard *a. O.* 299 spricht den Stil als ionisch an.

BUILDING MODELS AND THE ARCHITECTURE OF THE GEOMETRIC PERIOD

SIDNEY D. MARKMAN
Duke University

Plates 11-12

The "house" models discovered at the Argive Heraeum and Pera-chora[1] are well enough preserved, that inferences may be drawn as to the appearance of contemporary buildings, which without exception are known only from ground plans, very often fragmentary. The Argos model as reconstructed by Müller and Oikonomos, and the Perachora model as reconstructed by Payne, have been considered by these scholars and others as well to be representative of geometric architecture, both house and/or temple.[2] Such reasoning is based on two assumptions: first, that the "house" model is a more or less faithful replica of contemporary architectural forms; second, that the temple as the "house of god" already exists in the Geometric period and is structurally distinct from the private dwelling.

In order to appreciate fully the house models in the light of the extant geometric architecture, the following should be borne in mind: first, the model must be understood as an artifact of terra cotta displaying all the particular characteristics of that medium as distinguished from actual building construction; and second, the function of a temple as distinguished from that of the private dwelling must be defined. Temple and megaron, "god-house" and "man-house," have been generally accepted as one and the same architectural type, a type living on in Greece from one age to another, retaining much of its original form, but changing in function.[3] The "house" models from

---

1. *Argive Heraeum Model:* Müller, K., *AM* 48 (1923) 52 ff. Oikonomos, *Ephemeris* 1931, 1 ff.; dated, late geometric, second half of 8th century B. C. *Perachora Model:* Payne, *Perachora*, 34 ff.; dated first half of 8th century B. C.; *Cf.* footnote 46 infra.

2. Payne, *op. cit.*, 34, 41. Oikonomos, *op. cit.*, 25 ff., 45, figs. 16-20. Smith, *AJA* 46 (1942) 117. Lehmann, *Die Antike* 7 (1931) 44. Robertson, *Greek and Roman Architecture*, 54. Weickert, *Typen der archaischen Architektur*, 66. *Cf.* footnote 47 *infra*.

3. To mention a few examples: Weickert, *op. cit.*, 13. Robertson, *op. cit.*, 51 ff., with reference to Thermum. Lehmann, *op. cit.*, 38. Deubner, *ABA*, 1945/46, 1948, who supports the theory that the Anaktoron of the Eleusinian mysteries developed from the megaron located here. Dinsmoor, *AJA* 46 (1942) 370, in reference to pitched roofs and in the same connection, Smith *AJA* 46 (1942) 101. Dinsmoor, *AJA* 51 (1947) 109 ff., the megaron under the Hekatompedon on the Akropolis at Athens. Nilsson, *Minoan-Mycenaean Religion*, 405, temple of Athena at Mycenae built upon the ruins of the Mycenaean megaron, p. 406. In Athens, Hekatompedon, built on an older megaron, (*cf.* reference to Dinsmoor's article above) p. 406;

Perachora and Argos stand somewhere between the two extremes and represent after all our only concrete evidence of what the super-structure of the geometric house and/or temple may have looked like. The problem may be stated thus: to determine by what tokens, architectural and religious, the house and temple are differentiated, which physical features, if any, lend the house and/or temple each their particular character; and if the "house" models from Perachora and the Argive Heraeum do illuminate the problem of what is "house" and what "temple" in the geometric period.[4]

The reconstruction of the two models, though generally acceptable, leaves some details in doubt, particularly the prostyle porches—twin posts in either corner on the Perachora model, and single posts or columns on the Argive Heraeum model (pl. 11). However this much is certain. The Perachora model is apsidal in plan, has a pitched roof with an open gable, side walls ending in *antae,* and a porch, the reconstruction of which must remain conjectural because the upper portion is missing (pl. 11, d).[5] The Argos model is rectangular in plan, has a pitched roof, the front gable of which has a "window" opening, side walls ending in *antae,* and a porch, which by coincidence also lacks the upper portions and whose reconstruction must also remain conjectural (pl. 11, a, b, c).[6] We thus have illustrated two types of buildings: one, apsidal in plan; the other, rectangular in plan.

The *antae* of the Perachora model are quite clear, as are the stumps of the twin posts on one corner of the base (pls. 11, d, 12 a).[7] The *antae* of the Argos model, on the other hand, are slight indeed. Their presence can only be deduced from the markings left where the cross wall is broken off, showing that it did not come flush to the corner, but was set back a few millimeters. This feature is repeated at the other end of the side walls. Of the columns or posts in front of and in line with the *antae* nothing remains except the marking on the base where they were broken off.[8]

There is no difficulty in making out the floor plan of each porch— an area before the larger main room with vertical supports in the outside corners in front of and in line with the *antae,* open on three sides, the fourth side being the cross wall set back a bit from the

Greek temple over the megaron at Tiryns, quotes *AM* 30 (1905) 152, and *Tiryns* II, 2 (objected to by Blegen, *Korakou* p. 130), and p. 410. Argive Heraeum stands on hill once crowned by Mycenaean palace, quotes *AM* 34 (1909) 69.

  4. *Cf.* footnote 47 *infra.*

  5. Payne, *op. cit.,* 34 ff., pls. 8, 117.

  6. Müller, *op. cit.,* 52 ff., pls. VI, VII. Oikonomos, *op. cit.,* 1 ff., figs. 1-4, 11-15.

  7. Payne, *op. cit.,* pl. 8.

  8. Müller, *op. cit.,* 53, pl. VI 3.

corner so as to form slight projections or *antae*. To visualize the
elevation of the porches is a more complicated matter since the upper
portions are missing in both models. The unusual feature is of course
the prostyle porch.[9] The porch with columns or posts *in antis* is a
well known architectural feature in Greece before the geometric
period.[10] Actual building remains of the prostyle porch can in no
instance be dated before the 6th century B. C.,[11] yet in the case of the
terra cotta "house" models from the Argive Heraeum and Perachora,
we are confronted with examples of such porches in the 8th century
B. C.

While restoring the models, especially the porches, all three investigators relied too much on analogies with actual building construction and tended to overlook the technique of the potter's art.
Parallels are drawn from carpentry and masonry construction as if
the models presented problems similar to those one might expect in
the case of an actual building, and comparisons are made with buildings far afield in time and space.[12] Be they temples or dwellings,
buildings contemporary with the models are in so ruinous a state that
at most scarcely more than the ground plan can be restored with any
certainty. From the Geometric period ruins of both apsidal and rectangular buildings survive with which these models may be compared,
yet in no case do any of the existing material remains include evidence
for a prostyle porch.[13] Pendlebury does mention a single example,

9. Payne, *op. cit.*, fig. 7, pls. 9a, 117. Oikonomos, *op. cit.*, figs. 13, 14.

10. Müller, V., *AJA* 48 (1944) 342 ff., figs. 1 nos. 16, 19, 20. Robertson, *op. cit.*,
25, fig. 12. Anderson, Spiers and Dinsmoor, *Architecture of Ancient Greece*, 18,
fig. 4. Smith, *AJA* 46 (1942) figs. 15, 16, 36, 40. *BSA* 32 (1931/32) 42, pls. 18, 19
nos. 1, 2, 6; and numerous other examples quoted by the above mentioned scholars.

11. Temple of Athena at Sounion, and also a temple at Gaggera near Selinus
in Sicily, *cf.*, Robertson, *op. cit.*, 55, 325. Payne, *op. cit.*, 38. Oikonomos, *op. cit.*,
25. Weickert, *op. cit.*, 65, 117.

12. Müller, *op. cit.*, 61 ff., suggests walls of mud brick on a socle of stone, the
triangular holes in the side walls as a means of ventilation, columns and struts
of wood, carpentry technique throughout. Payne, *op. cit.*, 39, roof of thatch,
ventilation indicated by means of triangular depressions which, unlike those on
the Argos model, do not pierce the wall. Bagenal, H., *Perachora*, 42 ff, proposes a
system of crucks as support for the thatch. Robertson, *op. cit.*, 54, says the Argos
model represents half-timber construction. Oikonomos, *op. cit.*, 19 ff., discusses the
architectural type on the basis of analogies from as far off as Italy, Macedonia,
and Germany and from as far back as the Neolithic period down to classical Greek
times.

13. *A. Apsidal plans:*
    i. Antissa, Lesbos—*BSA* 32 (1931-32) 42 ff. Payne, *op. cit.*, 38.
    ii. Athens, Agora, circular house—*Hesperia* 2 (1933) 545 ff.
    iii. Eleusis, foundation underneath the Telesterion—*JHS* 1932, 239. *AJA* 37
(1933) 274 ff. Payne, *op. cit.*, 38.
    iv. Gonnos, Thessaly (7th century B. C.?)—*Praktika* 1910, 241 ff.; 1911, 286,
315. Scranton, *Greek Walls*, 167. Robertson, *op. cit.*, 55.
    v. Perachora, Temple of Hera Akraia—Payne, *op. cit.*, 27 ff.

the temple at Dreros, Crete, excavated by Marinatos,[14] but there is no evidence whatsoever in the actual remains to warrant Marinatos' restoration of a prostyle porch—including twin columns in the corners —which, by hypothesis, he insists must have been like the Perachora and Argos models.[15] Oikonomos' hypothetical reconstruction of a flat roof over the porch of the Argive Heraeum model (pl. 11, b, c) led Marinatos to the further hypothesis that the same was true at Dreros.[16]

Payne modifies the idea of a flat roof over the porch, and suggests instead that the building the Perachora model represents had inside the main room a ceiling which was carried over the porch too, the pitched roof enclosing both room and porch (pl. 11, d).[17] From the three square holes in the cross wall above the level of the door, which he interprets as windows, he deduces the presence of a ceiling inside

---

vi. Thebes, Temple of Apollo Ismenius (?)—Robertson, *op. cit.*, 322. Weickert, *op. cit.*, 10.

vii. Eretria, Temple of Apollo, and Ptoon—Weickert, *op. cit.*, 10 ff., includes these as possible apsidal buildings of geometric date.

B. *Rectilinear plans:*

i. Athens, geometric temple of Athena under the Hekatompedon—Dinsmoor, *AJA* 51 (1947) 109 ff.

ii. Corone, Longá Messenia—Robertson, *op. cit.*, 54, 322; Versakis, *Deltion* 2 (1916) 65.

iii. Cyprus, at Idalion—*SCE* I, 627. At Agios Jakovos, *SCE* I, 361 ff.

iv. Dreros, Crete—*BCH* 60 (1936) 214 ff. *Deltion* IV, par. II, 25. Pendlebury, *Archaeology of Crete*, 318.

v. Gortyna, Crete, Temple of Apollo Pythios—Pendlebury, *op. cit.*, 331, 342. *MonAnt* 1, 8; 3, 1; 18, 381.

vi. Karphi, Crete—Pendlebury, *op. cit.*, 306.

vii. Olympia, Heraeum A—Dinsmoor and Searls, *AJA* 49 (1945) 62 ff.

viii. Perachora, Temple of Hera Limenia—Payne, *op. cit.*, 110 ff.

ix. Samos, Heraeum—Buschor, *AM* 55 (1930) 1 ff.

x. Sparta, Artemis Orthia-Dawkins *Artemis Orthia*, 10 ff., fig. 13; Weickert, *op. cit.*, 11 ff. Robertson, *op. cit.*, 53 ff., 322, pl. II a. *BSA* 14 (1907-8) p. 1. *AM* 39 (1914) 254; 44 (1919) 175 ff.

xi. Thebes, Temple of Apollo Ismenius—Robertson, *op. cit.*, p. 322. *Deltion* 3 (1917) 33, 66 ff. *AA* 1922, 273. Weickert, *op. cit.*, 10.

xii. Thermum, Megaron B—Robertson, *op. cit.*, 51-53, 65 ff. *AntDenk* 2 (1902-1908). 5. *Deltion* 1 (1915) p. 225; 6 (1920-1) 158; 9 (1924-5) par. 4. *AM* 47 (1922) 43. Weickert, *op. cit.*, 7 ff. Lehmann, *op. cit.*, 38 ff., fig. 36.

14. Pendlebury, *op. cit.*, 318. Marinatos, *BCH* 60 (1936) 214 ff., pls. XXVI-XXVII.

15. Marinatos, *op. cit.*, 232 ff., 255, "L' édifice n'a qu'une seule pièce sans pronaos . . . . La seule chose qui semble donner un peu de grandeur à l'extérieur du bâtiment c'est le soubassement et le προστῶον que nous avons complétés par hypothèse. Cet élément met en rapport notre temple avec les reproductions en terre cuite de l'Heraion et de Pérachora."

16. *Op. cit.*, 250, proposes a combination flat and pitched roof. Over the hearth or ἐσχάρα inside he raises a pitched roof with gables and a ridge suported on posts, the rest of the area is covered with a flat roof, *cf.* his pl. XXVI.

17. *Op. cit.*, 39. In the drawing of the restoration pl. 96, the porch ceiling is omitted. The twin columns, however, are tied together by a beam or architrave, which Payne, p. 37, admits is conjectural because no evidence exists for the restoration of this member.

the building imitated in terra cotta. These windows provided a means by which the interior room, cut off from the open gable by the ceiling and loft above, could be lighted; furthermore they permitted air to enter and smoke from the hearth to escape. Following this same line of reasoning, he also explains the little triangular depressions below the eaves as a means of ventilation, noting that on the Argos model they actually pierce the wall.[18] He further points out that these holes or depressions are not decorative, even though such a feature is common at this time, because "they bear no sort of relation to the decoration, being in fact wilfully imposed on the pattern on one side." Actually the reverse is more correct. The pattern was imposed on the holes, for they must surely have been made before the painted decoration was applied. Payne is aware however that no analogies for this type of ventilation exist in Greek architecture.[19]

The problem of ventilation and escape for smoke has puzzled other investigators too. For example, E. Baldwin Smith in connection with the problem of the megaron roof postulates "some opening in its covering to take off the smoke," which if true, will bring about the association of the sloping roof with the fixed hearth, smoke from which could escape through the open gables.[20] Agreeing with Payne, Oikonomos, and Müller in regard to the gable openings, he accepts the present restorations of the Perachora and Argos models, except that he reduces the loft above to an interior gallery. The triangular depressions or openings help ventilate the interior and furthermore prove "that windows were not unknown on megaron structures."[21] Weickert too is concerned about the escape of smoke, and suggests hypaethral openings in the roof.[22] The reasoning of all these scholars is quite in keeping with the tastes of today, but not with what one would expect of a primitive agriculturalist in 8th century B. C. Greece.[23]

18. *Op. cit.*, 39. Müller gives the same explanation for the triangular holes, *op. cit.*, 61.

19. Since these triangular openings cannot be explained on architectural grounds, it would not be amiss to consider the possibilities of their serving either a decorative or symbolic function, or perhaps both.

20. *AJA* 46 (1942) 102, postulates B2 and B6.

21. *Op. cit.*, 117.

22. *Op. cit.*, 78.

23. In none of the private dwellings at Olynthus, Priene, Delos, Pompeii, and the tenement houses at Ostia is there any special device which might provide an escape for smoke. Vitruvius, 7, 3, 4, cautions the builder that in those rooms where fire and lamps are to be used cornices should be plain so that they may be the more easily dusted. In summer rooms more elaborate cornices may be carved since it is unlikely they will be blackened by smoke. He gives the same admonition again in 7, 4, 4. When fire is needed mainly for cooking and only occasionally for warmth the most common fuel is charcoal which, once well ignited, hardly smokes at all. Analogies to houses lacking chimneys or any other special devices for

Oikonomos' restoration of the terrace roof over the porch, which started the chain of comparisons, was itself based in part on an assumption of Müller, who visualized a hayloft under the eaves.[24] In juggling the roof, wall, and base fragments around, Oikonomos finds that the roof fragments are not long enough to cover main room and porch. He makes up for this discrepancy by fitting a single fragment of unexplained function into a terrace roof which as an extension of the interior ceiling projects in front of the gable.[25]

In the first place, there is no certainty that the side walls of the Argos model actually belong to the base they are set on now. Nor is it certain that the roof fragments fit the walls. Müller says that the fragments he is dealing with are a "roofless house" and a "houseless roof."[26] It might very well be that a third part should be added to the fragments, a "houseless base." Secondly, the curious lateral sills which have been reconstructed on either side of the porch between the columns and *antae* could very readily be interpreted as the spoors of missing walls on which the posts in the corners abutted.[27] It might therefore be possible that the original walls ran the whole length of the base, in which case the prostyle porch is eliminated! However, with regard to the Perachora model, the restoration of the prostyle porch cannot be challenged since the disposition of the twin columns in relation to the *antae* in the extant fragments is quite clear. But this is not so on the Argos model. A possible restoration of the porch plan would show an area before the main room enclosed by spur walls on either side, slightly thickened at the extremities in the form of posts, or *antae*. It may be that the potter was trying to reproduce the effect of mud-brick walls faced with planks or perhaps reinforced with roughly hewn squared timbers set at wall end to carry the point load of the partly closed gable above.

Müller reconstructs the two corner supports as round posts,[28] but Oikonomos correctly observes that the markings are rather squarish

letting out smoke may be culled from all those parts of the world where the climate is mild. There is no reason to suppose that the primitive farmer of geometric Greece had either the same aversion for smoke or love for fresh air as the modern city dweller. The simplest solution to the problem of the escape of smoke from the megaron and the geometric house and/or temple is to say that there was no problem, and that the smoke got out the best it could—through the open door, or if the roof was pitched, by filtering through the thatch.

24. *Cf.* footnotes 12, 18 *supra*.

25. *Op. cit.*, 9, figs. 10, 15.

26. *Op. cit.*, 58.

27. I have not been able to study the models except by means of photographs. A good photograph of the porch part of the base is given by Oikonomos, *op. cit.*, fig. 13.

28. *Op. cit.*, 59, pl. VI

in plan and restores them accordingly (pl. 11, b).[29] The markings may neither represent the spoors of round or square freestanding posts, but may indicate a change in material at the end of mud brick walls. If the side sills are continued up as walls, the posts may very well be thought of as rudimentary *antae* and suggest a plan well known in Greece before the Geometric period.[30]

The roof of the Argive Heraeum model is fashioned with a rim in the manner of eaves set at an oblique angle to the "rafters" or pitch (pl. 11 a, b, c). The covering material copied in terra cotta is supposed to have been thatch, and it may very well have been that the potter knew thatch as a roofing material.[31] In terms of pottery technique, however, the rim[32] gives the cover a surer fit on the top of the walls, allowing for discrepancies in the dimensions between the area enclosed by the walls below and that by the cover above. The roof and walls must be thought of as a cover and box of terra cotta. The rim however does suggest overhanging rafters too. To achieve this effect was no doubt the intention of the potter who made the Perachora model.[33] A detail overlooked before is the flare or widening of the walls of the Argive Heraeum model at the top.[34] This slightly concave flare may be interpreted as representing a moulding which runs around the top of the wall under the eaves. But on a model of terra cotta it also provides a wider surface where the precariously joined tent-like cover may be fitted securely.[35]

Oikonomos' flat roof over the porch results from his placing walls and roof together. Since the roof is not long enough to enclose the porch also, following Müller's hayloft idea he adjusts the piece of unexplained function as part of the rim over the porch (pl. 11, b).

29. *Op. cit.*, p. 11, figs. 13, 14, 15.

30. *Cf.* footnote 10 *supra*, except, of course, without columns *in antis*.

31. Payne, *op. cit.*, 39, suggests that the type of buildings represented by both models was probably covered with thatch. It is hardly likely that the rather crudely constructed and naively planned extant geometric buildings were roofed with terra cotta tiles, especially since none have been found. Weickert, *op. cit.*, 10, mentions the roof tiles discovered at Thebes from the Temple of Apollo Ismenius which was destroyed no later than the second half of the 8th century B. C. On the authority of Keramopoullos, *Deltion* 1917, 66 ff., *AA* 1922, 273, he claims these to be the earliest of Greek fabric, and to represent a survival of a Mycenaean tradition. Smith's proof of the sloping roof for the megaron, *AJA* 46 (1942) 99 ff., as seconded by Dinsmoor, *AJA* 46 (1942) 370 ff., on the basis of some terra cotta fragments identified as roof tiles of EH III, MH as well as LH dates, is refuted by Blegen, *AJA* 49 (1945) 35 ff., who points out that the material identified as roof tiles is not roof tiles at all.

32. Müller, *op. cit.*, pl. VI 2.

33. Payne, *op. cit.*, *pls.* 8, 119, 120.

34. Müller, *op. cit.*, pl. VI 3.

35. Judging from the photographs it is quite possible that the roof was fired separately from the walls below. The tops of the walls do not give the appearance of a break.

In keeping with its size, greater than the rest of the rim, it projects as a flat terrace in front of the gable, supported by the corner posts which are spanned by a hypothetical architrave.[36] The evidence from the extant terra cotta fragments does not warrant Müller's assumption, Oikonomos' restoration, Payne's comparison or Smith's deduction and places the restoration of the flat roof over the porch of the Argos model in doubt, and consequently the interior upper floor inside too, as well as any special devices for ventilation.[37]

A further incongruity in the restoration of the Argos model porch is the manner in which struts are shown connecting *antae* and columns. If based alone on a comparison with building technique, the struts should not be there. On one of the walls a short, jagged piece of terra cotta projects at right angles from the *antae* near the top of the wall.[38] Just what significance this feature may have in terms of pottery is difficult to say. In terms of construction technique, it is a most illogical manner of bracing the free-standing columns to the *antae*. Furthermore, there is absolutely no material evidence in the fragments from the two models to verify the present restorations of the beam or architrave on which rests either flat terrace or gable with window opening in the case of the Argos model or simply an open gable as on the Perachora model.[39] Buildings such as these suggest a construction technique far more sophisticated than is justified by the rather rudimentary planning revealed in the contemporary architectural remains on the one hand, and the general level of material culture in the geometric period on the other.

A simpler solution to the problem of restoring the superstructure of the porches must be sought, a solution more in keeping with what one would expect in this early period of the formation of Greek civilization. Granting that the plan of the prostyle porch has been correctly reconstructed on the Argos model as it most certainly has been on the Perachora,[40] and that Müller's and Payne's suggestions for the superstructure are in keeping with the logic of simplicity, nevertheless the cross beam which they conjecture as spanning the corner supports is quite unnecessary either in terms of an actual building roofed as suggested by the models, and most certainly not in terms of the terra cotta

---

36. *Op. cit.*, 6 ff., figs. 5-11; *cf. supra* footnotes 24 and 17 with reference to the conjectural restoration of the architrave of the Perachora model.

37. *Cf. supra*, footnotes, 14, 15, 16, 20 and 23.

38. Müller, *op. cit.*, pl. VI 3.

39. *Cf. supra*, footnote 17.

40. The *antae* of the Perachora model are quite clear, the side and cross walls are fashioned together with the latter set back a bit to form *antae*. The inside angle between the cross wall and the projecting side wall is concave. *Cf.* Payne, *op. cit.*, pls. 8, 9. The cross wall of the Argos model is missing, *cf. supra*, footnote. 8.

artifact, especially since no fragment which might serve this purpose exists. A simpler solution from the point of view of construction is that suggested by the porch of the well-known Melian cinerary urn, on which a pitched roof springs directly from the side walls without any cross beam running from one to the other.[41] The building suggested by both models must have had a ridge supported on posts.[42] In the Melian type of construction, really a double lean-to set on walls, the rafters exert no lateral thrust against the walls, thus precluding any need for cross beams to be used as collars to tie them in. This simple method of roof construction, taking into account too the lack of evidence in the actual terra cotta remains, rules out ceiling and loft in the building represented by the models.[43]

Summing up, it would thus seem that in some respects the models have been reconstructed in an anachronistic manner. Some of the restored details are not necessary either in terms of the terra cotta models or in terms of the extant remains of contemporary buildings. Among the features of the restorations which must be ruled out, and by analogy also in contemporary architecture, are the flat roofed porch, the ceiling in the main room and the upper story under the eaves; the interpretation as windows given the triangular patterns or openings in the walls, and the cross beams or architraves which span the corner supports of the porches. On the positive side, it must be noted that in these little models we have the only concrete evidence by means of which it is possible to visualize better than previously what geometric buildings were like. Apsidal and rectangular plans are known in the Geometric period, a fact borne out by the extant architectural remains.[44] Thatch-covered pitched roofs with openings in the gables may be deduced on the analogy of the models. However, of neither thatch nor tiles is there proof to be found in contemporary remains of buildings. Since no tiles have been found, it must be supposed that thatch or some other ephemeral material covered the slop-

41. Rider, *Greek House*, 52 fig. 4a. Anderson, Spiers, Dinsmoor, *op. cit.*, pl. IV. *AM* 50 (1925) 19 ff., fig. 1.

42. Payne (Bagenal), *op. cit.*, 47, suggests this method of support for the ridge.

43. The slightly curved shape of the Perachora model's roof led Payne to suggest that the cover material was thatch, which in turn led Bagenal to propose a system of crucks as the roof framing on which the thatch was laid. *Cf. supra*, footnote 12. Payne's earlier suggestion, *op. cit.*, 39, that the roof was supported at intervals by props resting on the tie-beams which also support the ceiling, is in keeping with his idea of a loft above the main room under the eaves. Payne's suggested roof framing, although simpler than Bagenal's crucks, *op. cit.*, fig. 8, is far too complicated a type of carpentry for the Geometric period. On the other hand, cruck framework is indeed far fetched in this connection for it is a system of framing developed in the Middle Ages in the British Isles, and to some extent in northern Europe. *Cf.*, Walton, *Antiquity* 22 (1948) 179 ff., "The Development of Cruck Framework."

44. *Cf.*, *supra*, footnote 13.

ing roofs of the buildings represented by the models.[45] The prostyle porches remain a unique and uncorroborated feature. The only explanation possible, and a weak one, is that the porches of contemporary buildings were of the same ephemeral materials as the roof, wood and thatch, requiring no special foundations as would the rubble stone or mud brick walls of the building proper.

There still remains the question of how these two building models may illuminate the problem of distinguishing between house and temple in the Geometric period, assuming of course that to make such a distinction, architecturally speaking, is already possible in the 8th century B. C.[46] Some scholars have identified the models as representations of temples. Others have suggested they are houses, while still others have chosen to leave the question unanswered.[47] One fact is certain: namely, the models do have a religious significance since they were found among other votive offerings within areas identified as sacred precincts. The identification of the areas as sacred is of course based on the presence of the *ex votos* in the first place. The Perachora model was found close by a little apsidal building identified by Payne as the temple of Hera Akraia, the older of the two temples dedicated to Hera at this site.[48] The other model is from the sanctuary of Hera at Argos. The condition under which it was found is unknown, nor was it included in the publication of the results of the excavations of the Argive Heraeum. Of the original 7th century B. C. structure of the Heraeum almost nothing is known, and even less about the building which may have existed in the 8th when the model was made.[49] That the two models are not common votive offerings[50] makes the problem of identification as temple or house all the more difficult. Dedications of temple models are known, but none are of geometric date.[51] Payne points out that the four or possibly five models repre-

45. Cf., *supra*, footnotes 31, 43.

46. Payne, *op. cit.*, 37, dates the Perachora model earlier than the middle of the 8th century B. C., possibly even in the 9th, but finally gives the date as 800-750 B. C. Müller, *op. cit.*, 57, dates the Argive Heraeum model in the second half of the 8th century B. C.

47. Cf., *supra*, footnote 2. Lehmann, *op. cit.*, 44, calls the Argos model a replica of the first temple of Hera. Müller, *op. cit.*, 59, believes house and temple are indistinguishable at this time. Robertson, *op. cit.*, 54, states that the Argos model may be a contemporary form of the Heraeum. Weickert, *op. cit.*, 66, refers to this model as a house. Payne, *op. cit.*, 41, believes that it is impossible to tell what the Perachora model may be, and believes that in this period house and temple were not distinct.

48. *Perachora*, 21, 27 ff., pl. 116.

49. Waldstein, *The Argive Heraeum*. Frickenhaus, and W. Müller, *AM* 36 (1911) 27. Robertson, *op. cit.*, 328.

50. Payne, *op. cit.*, 40.

51. Payne, *op. cit.*, 40 quotes Oikonomos, *op. cit.*, 46 ff., who mentions a number of examples. Müller, *op. cit.*, p. 58. *Cf.* also the limestone model from the Samian

sented by the fragments from Perachora are without question of Argive manufacture.[52] It can therefore be safely inferred that the use of models as an *ex voto* is rare indeed in the geometric period. The total number discovered to date consists of about six or possibly seven examples, all from but two sites, which furthermore are both in the same region of Greece.

By means of neither the architectural token, their unique prostyle porches, nor the religious token, their use as *ex votos*, are the building models from Argos and Perachora of help in determining if they were meant to represent temples, that is houses of the goddess, or to represent houses of devotees given as free-will offerings to Hera and thereby to win her favor as protectoress of their homes.[53] The type of religious symbolism implied by either alternative is of course too involved and perhaps even anachronistic. Judging by the variation in the orientation of buildings identified with cults, especially the two geometric temples of Hera at Perachora, one may infer that religious practices were not standardized in Greece in the geometric period.[54] Evidence from orientation alone is not enough to substantiate the conclusion that a particular building served to house a cult. Other tokens such as hearths, or pits for animal sacrifice,[55] and benches or ledges used

Heraeum, *AM* 55 (1930) 16 ff., Beilage IV, dated between the second half of the 7th and first half of the 6th century B. C. which Payne, *ibid.*, says is a model of a house.

52. Payne, *op. cit.*, 41 ff.

53. Payne, *op. cit.*, 41, thinks the models may be objects of personal reference, not to the god, but to the dedicator.

54. Buildings from the Geometric period, and even from the Orientalising, identified with a cult do not conform to a single scheme of orientation. At Perachora the apsidal shaped building identified as the Temple of Hera Akraia, Payne, *op. cit.*, 31, built in the 9th century B. C. and which stood until the third quarter of the 8th century B. C., is oriented East-West, while the nearby Temple of Hera Limenia, rectangular in plan, dated by Payne, *op. cit.*, 112, c. 750 B. C., is oriented North-South. Payne, *op. cit.*, 110 footnote 7, cites other examples of this type of orientation at Neandria, Calydon, Thermum, Eretria and even Phigaleia, to which should be added Dreros and Karphi in Crete, *cf. supra*, footnote 13.

55. Hearths or altars with ashes and animal bones were found in the Temple of Hera Limenia at Perachora, *cf.* Payne, *op. cit.*, 112, who mentions other examples in Crete, Rhodes, Lesbos, the Troad, and Sicily. Of particular interest is the hearth in the Cypro-Geometric temple at Agia Irini, where the change in the cult practices from the late Cypriote to the Cypro-Geometric is marked by the substitution of animal sacrifice instead of the earlier vegetable offerings, *SCE* II, 822. Nilsson, *Greek Popular Religion*, 72 ff., believes the fixed hearth was brought to Greece by the Greeks since it does not exist in Minoan houses. In *Greek Piety*, 11, he says the hearth or fire pit inside the shrine finds its way outside as an altar in later times. *Cf.* also Yavis, C., *Greek Altars*, 63, 77-78 *et passim*.

56. Ledges or low shelf-like benches used as offering tables were found at Dreros, Karphi, Perachora (Hera Limenia), Idalion and Agia Irini in Cyprus and Sparta (Artemis Orthia) to name but a few instances. *Cf. supra*, footnote 13 for bibliographical references. Nilsson, *Minoan-Mycenaean Religion*, 391, mentions this feature at Vroulia. *Cf.* Yavis, *op. cit.*, 86 f., 218 f., 242, 226, etc.

as offering tables or repositories for *ex votos*[56] are clearer indications of the religious function of buildings in the geometric period. In connection with the Perachora model, it is interesting that the nearby Temple of Hera Limenia, of rectangular plan, had such features in the interior.[57] Too little remains of the apsidal temple of Hera Akraia to decide whether or not a hearth and offering table were part of the interior arrangement. Unfortunately, not even the vaguest connection between the Argive Heraeum model and any contemporary building on the site where it was found can even be conjectured. At any rate, it would be pointless to try to deduce the presence of these religious tokens, hearth and offering table, in the terra cotta building models and thereby prove that they are representations of contemporary cult buildings.

If the definition of temple is to include the notion of a place of residence for the god, the absence of cult images in the Geometric period should cause one to hesitate to call contemporary religious edifices more than cult houses. The earliest sculptures which may be safely identified as cult images do not date before the orientalising period when monumental architecture and sculpture begin;[58] nevertheless one must presuppose an earlier tradition leading to this development. Just as the distinction between *ex voto* and cult image cannot always be made in the Geometric period, in a like manner it is not always possible to distinguish between house and temple, for the two had not yet begun to diverge in character in this early period. In the private house was performed a religious ceremonial ritual as

---

57. Payne, *op. cit.*, 112.

58. The many animal and human figurines found in the geometric strata at such important pan-hellenic sanctuaries as Olympia, Delphi, Delos, Argos, and others cannot be considered cult images. The origin and development of the "house of the god" and the plastic "image of the god" are bound together. V. Müller, *RE Suppl.* V, article of "Kultbild," p. 494c, would date the earliest temples and cult images at the end of the 7th century B. C. (cf. also his *Frühe Plastik in Griechenland und Vorderasien*, 225 ff.) when monumental sculpture, at least half life size, p. 496, and architecture begin. Gotsmich, *Probleme der früh-griechischen Plastik*, 8, is opposed to this view and agrees with Kunze, *AM* 55 (1930) 141 ff., that cult images existed in the Geometric period. It is an accepted fact that many of the religious practices of the Minoan-Mycenaean cults lived on in later Greek times, as for example the hearth and offering table in geometric religious buildings would indicate, *cf. supra*, footnotes 55, 56 also Lehmann, *op. cit.*, 12 ff., and Nilsson, *Minoan-Mycenaean Religion*, 385 ff., also his *History of Greek Religion*, 9 ff. Pendlebury, *op. cit.*, 306, 312, pl. XLI 1, 2, suggests that the bronze figurines of protogeometric date from the sanctuary at Karphi which display strong Minoan affinities may be cult images. But in a footnote, p. 312, note 2, he is more cautious saying that "the shrine at Karphi was built by a refugee Minoan population and cannot be reckoned as Hellenic." A figurine from Vroulia, Kinch, *Fouilles de Vroulia*, 101, pl. XIX, dated in the 7th century B. C., *cf.* Robertson, *op. cit.*, 323, may be a cult image according to V. Müller, *RE Suppl.* V, 496 e.

part of the daily round of household activities, a custom known to have been preserved in historical times as the cult of the hearth.[59]

The question of what is house and what temple, it would seem does not apply in the Geometric period, while the house models, though unique, may be accepted as a special type of *ex voto*, representative of the buildings in the 8th century B. C. in part known from and corrobated by the actual remains of contemporary architecture.

---

59. Blegen, *Korakou*, 98 ff. observes that in the ordinary private house at Korakou associated with the hearth are found "shaped pillar bases" which probably supported a baetylic pillar connected with the household worship. A base of similar shape was found in the Heraeum at Samos, *AM* 55 (1930) 15 ff., fig. 5, which the excavators took to be a column base from the "peristasis" of the geometric temple! It may actually be a base such as Blegen mentions, and if so, would point to the survival of a type of religious practice known in pre-hellenic times. *Cf.* also references to Nilsson in footnote 55, *supra*, in connection with the hearth around which family life and domestic religious worship revolved.

IL BRONZO NELLA GENESI DEL TEMPIO GRECO

PAOLO VERZONE
Politecnico di Torino

"I palazzi di Babilonia sono coperti di bronzo, ciò che li fa scintillare da lontano" scriveva Filostrato[1] e Polibio[2] della reggia di Ecbatana; "Quantunque tutta di cedro e di cipresso, nulla era scoperto ma le travi ed i soffitti e le colonne dei portici e dei cortili erano rivestiti di lastre di metallo .... e le tegole erano d'argento ...."

Gli scavi hanno confermato l'abitudine degli Orientali di difendere e decorare strutture lignee con rivestimenti metallici; ornamenti in rame sbalzato si trovano già in età remota nel tempio di Al'Ubaid[3] ma i rivestimenti più significativi si hanno in Assiria; dalle porte di Balawat (847) av. C),[4] dei templi di Khorsabad[5] e di Anu-Adad ad Assur[6] (tutte a striscie orizzontali figurate alternate a bande con rosette "di chiodatura") alla colonna scavata da Place nella zona dei tre templi ("Harem") di Khorsabad (imbricazioni in bronzo dorato).[7]

Testimonianze di rivestimenti e di coperture di bronzo dorato non mancano altresì per l'Italia etrusca e romana; Vitruvio, a proposito delle statue nei frontoni dei templi in travature lignee, sembra istituire un parallelismo fra lavori in terracotta ed in bronzo dorato in Etruria[8] e Plinio menziona l' "edicula aerea" eretta nel 304,[9] tegole e capitelli in bronzo.[10]

I ritrovamenti di Nemi ci consentono di farci un'idea della ricchezza dei lavori in bronzo dorato; alle tegole ricuperate colle navi[11] si aggiungono quelle del tempio di Diana e, particolarmente significativi i frammenti ornamentali[12] di questo santuario,[13] rivestimenti[14] ottenuti

---

1. *Apoll*, 1, 25.
2. *Le storie*, 10, 27.
3. Woolley e Hall, *Ur Excavations*, I, pls, V, VI, XXIX, XXX, XXXVIII.
4. King, *Bronze Gates of Shalmaneser III*, pass.
5. Place, *Ninive et l'Assyrie*, pl. 72.
6. *Wiss. Ver. d. Or. Ges.* 1909, pl. 33 (Andrae).
7. Perrot-Chipiez, *HA*, II, 213 fig. 72. Rivestimenti in bronzo di porte, ornate da rosoni, furono scavati anche a Susa: Perrot-Chipiez, *HA*, V fig. 353.
8. *De archit.*, 3, 3, 5—"Ornantur que signis fictilibus aut aereis inauratis earum fastigia tuscanico more."
9. *N.H.*, 33, 19.
10. *N.H.*, 32, 57 per le tegole del tempio di Giove Capitolino (l'oraziano 'Capitolium fulgens"); *N.H.* 34. 13 per quelle del tempio di Vesta, per i capitelli enei del Circo Flaminio e per quelli del vecchio Pantheon.
11. Ucelli, *Le navi de Nemi*, fig. 171.
12. Della Seta, *Museo di Villa Giulia*, 224.
13. La rozza pianta pubblicata in *Archeologia*, 50, pl. VIII e le notizie di NS, 1885, pp. 192ss. 428ss.—sono insufficienti per la conoscenza dell'edificio che pare avesse dimensioni discrete (metri 15, 90 x 30).
14. I pezzi superstiti offrono il bordo inferiore di una fascia di rivestimento

per fusione (spessore circa 1 cm.) e riccamente dorati (2/10 mm.) che ripetono nel metallo le forme e gli ornamenti di quelli di cotto del tempo (250 — 200 av. C.).[15]

L'uso di ornamenti in bronzo fuso risaliva tuttavia almeno alla seconda metà del sec. VI; l'Andrén[16] ha mostrato che certi pezzi in cotto (ornamenti penduli e cornici traforate) modellati con ricercatezza degna di cesellatore più che di figulino, ne copiano degli analoghi in bronzo nel gusto dei tripodi vulcenti e delle "appliques" dei vasi enei.[17]

Il Lazio ci ha restituito, inoltre, rivestimenti di un genere diverso, in lastra a sbalzo; si tratta dei frammenti di Palestrina (fig. 1), spessi 2 - 3 mm. e non dorati; lo schema decorativo permette di riferire al V sec. questi cimeli su cui ritorneremo.[18]

Anche la Grecia vide sorgere edicole e templi coperti o decorati col nobile metallo e viene il dubbio che vi fossero fra essi delle strutture antichissime, dell'età orientalizzante, veri elementi di raccordo fra le architetture di legno e metallo dell'Asia Anteriore e quelle in legno e terracotta della Grecia Arcaica e prototipi di queste ultime.

Pausania menziona il "Hieron" di Athena Chalkioikos a Sparta, la camera di Akrisios, il terzo tempio di Apollo a Delfi e due strutture, d'ordine dorico e ionico rispettivamente, nel tesoro dei Sicionii ad Olimpia[19] ma purtroppo ben poco è rimasto.

Esaminiamo brevemente i dati indiretti (a) e l'evidenza archeologica (b) a nostra disposizione.

TEGOLE — (a) — Erano notoriamente di due tipi, che si mantennero a lungo: leggermente incurvate ("laconiche") e piane coi bordi rialzati lateralmente ("corinzie"); i coppi coprigiunto, lunghi come le tegole, avevano nelle scuole della Laconia e dell'Asia Minore sezione semicircolare, nella scuola corinzia pentagonale.[20]

Ora certe caratteristiche sembrano accusare derivazione da tetti in lastra metallica; nella coperture "laconiche" le lastre sarebbero

---

con palmette a tre petali e dischi riuniti da spirali ad S, un tratto forse della zona mediana con una faretra, attribuito di Diana, ad alto rilievo, annodata da un panneggio ed, infine, un frammento del coronamento frontonale traforato; nulla è rimasto di altri numerosi pezzi "con bordatura a fave e fogliami in alto e con una rappresentanza figurata nella parte inferiore" (NS—1885, p. 429).

15. Ad esempio quelle del tempio dello "Scasato" a Civita Castellana. Cfr. NS 1895, p. 432, Andrén—*Architectural terracottas from Etrusco-Italic temples,* 384.

16. *Architectural terracottas,* CXXVII, CLIX.

17. *St. Et.* X, 16ss, Tavv. IIIss. (Guarducci).

18. Cfr. Andrén, *Arch. terracottas,* ill. 132 (Civita Castellana, V sec.), ill. 478 (Ardea, I metà V sec.).

19. 3, 17, 2; 2, 23, 11; 10, 5, 11; 6, 19, 2.

20. Robinson e Graham, *Excavations at Olynthus,* VIII, 233-4.

Fig. 1. Palestrina Frammenti di rivestimento in bronzo.
(A. M. De Marchi delin.)

state modellate su di un sottofondo di argilla disteso su di un tavo-
lato [fig. 2] (le tegole dell'Heraion d'Olimpia, in cotto, posavano
appunto su di un sottofondo del genere) mentre in quelle ad elementi
piani le lastre avrebbero acquisito funzionalità per i bordi rialzati,
fissati a listelli laterali (parrebbe che a Neandria le tegole fossero
distanziate appunto da un listello, e ciò per l'appendice della tegola
estrema) [fig. 3].

Significativo è poi il sistema dei perni che fissavano i coppi coprigiunto nell'Heraion d'Olimpia; tali perni sono necessari per le

lastre metalliche, leggere e quindi facili ad essere smosse dal vento, mentre di regola non si usano coi pezzi in cotto, pesanti.

Inoltre le forti dimensioni delle tegole nei tetti più antichi (Her. d'Olimpia cm. 120 x 59, Neandria 84 x 53)[21] possono ritenersi generate dall'imitazione dei tipi in lastra metallica.

I grandi pezzi in cotto sono difficili da essicare, si screpolano durante la cottura, sono pesanti e fragili e quindi di difficile messa in opera; le lastre metalliche si tengono invece di dimensioni forti per ridurre piegature, chiodature, sovrapposizioni e pericolo di fessurazioni nelle piegature.

Un'ultima, significativa, caratteristica di certe coperture è il color nero che le ricopriva in modo uniforme; neri sono coppi e tegole in

21. *RM* 30 (1915) 45ss, 10-11.

Fig. 2. Olimpia. Heraion III. Saggio di ricostruzione. (D. Ferrero delin.)

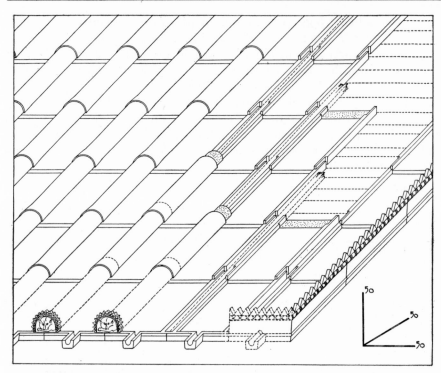

Fig. 3. Neandria. Ricostruzione della copertura. (D. Ferrero delin.)

molti edifici, ad es. nell'Heraion d'Olimpia e nelle fabbriche del tempio
d'Artemide Orthia a Sparta; perchè scegliere questo colore che
toglieva forza alle ombre e contrastava con le parti in pietra? La
ragione era la stessa che ha indotto tanti popoli dell'antichità a favo-
rire il color nero e le tonalità violacee nella ceramica, l'imitazione del
bronzo ossidato;[22] questo metallo costituiva il "non plus ultra" per
le coperture come per i vasellami.

(b) — Negli scavi della scuola inglese nell'area del "Hieron" di
Athena, "Chalkioikos" a Sparta, ricordato da Pausania come di bronzo
$(\chi\alpha\lambda\kappa\grave{o}\varsigma - o\tilde{\iota}\kappa o\varsigma)$ con diffusa descrizione dei soggetti rilevati nel
metallo nell'interno dell'edificio, furono trovati frequenti residui di
lastre di bronzo che portavano ancora infilati i chiodi che le fissavano;[23]
viene il dubbio che si trattasse delle lastre di copertura ma la defi-

22. Cfr. per l'esame dell'imitazione dei vasi di bronzo con la ceramica, specialmente corinzia, Payne, *Necrocorinthia*, 210ss, per gli effetti metallici nel bucchero
italico: Ducati, *Storia dell'Arte Etrusca*, 148; per l'imitazione, particolarmente
chiara, di modelli metallici nel bucchero "ad appliques": Ducati, *Ibid.*, 296.

23. *BSA*, 13 (1906-07) 137ss (Dickins) "On the other hand we discovered a
large number of bronze plates, mostly in the last stages of decay, and a great
quantity of heavy bronze nails, some still in position through the plates" (p. 139).

cienza di dati precisi impedisce di acquistare certezza. I resti dell'architettura, e altri frammenti di lamine bronzee su cui ritornoremo indicano la metà del sec. VI.[24]

SIME e CORNICI — (a) — L'esame delle terracotte architettoniche arcaiche fa pensare a tre scuole principali:

(1) Scuola laconica (o dell'Heraion) attiva solo fino al principio del VI sec. Offre sime frontonali a profilo pressochè verticale (per accordo con gli acroteri a disco, piatti) e decorazione geometrica a squame e linee parallele terminata da un piccolo guscio a linguette e da una fila di punte;[25] lateralmente non vi è spesso che un "portategole" orizzontale non decorato ed antefisse semicircolari; in qualche caso (Sparta)[26] vi era invece una cornice di profilo analogo a quello della sima, curioso pezzo sovrapposto alle estremità dei καλυπτῆρες per nasconderle.

La derivazione dai prototipi metallici è accusata dai colori scuri (nero, verde, rosso, azzurro) della decorazione, combinati in gioco fitto che richiama i riflessi delle patine del bronzo ossidato e più che tutto dalle punte del bordo superiore; queste appendici, fragili ed inutili in terracotta, avevano invece nei prototipi metallici una ben definita funzione, quella d'impedire agli uccelli di posarvisi ed insudiciare.

(2) La scuola corinzia[27] (fig. 4a), attiva a partire dalla fine del secolo VII in Grecia settentrionale e Sicilia e influente poi anche in Etruria, offriva in origine nel frontone una sima a cavetto egiziano sopra una fascia a matassa od a rosette "di chiodatura"; questa fascia continuava lateralmente sormontata ad intervalli da antefisse pentagonali nel bordo delle tegole che scaricavano liberamente. (Atene, Corinto, Egina, Kalydon).[28]

In certi casi la fascia si dilatò sulla testata di pietra del Geison ,ad es. a Kalydon,[29] Troizen[30] ed in Sicilia;[31] nell'isola prese un profilo particolare a C (ivi è chiamata "cassetta"), la matassa si raddoppiò nella tipica "doppia matassa," ed il cavetto frontale fu

---

24. *Ibid.*, 144.

25. Dawkins, etc., *Artemis Orthia*, 131, 139ss. pl. XXVI; fig. 97, 101.

26. *Ibid.*, fig. 98.

27. Payne, *Necrocorinthia*, 248ss.

28. Buschor, *Die Tondächer der Akropolis*, I e II, *pass.* e specialmente I pp. 8-10 (Sima I, III, IV, VII): II, p. 6ss, (Traufziegel II-VI); Van Buren, *Greek Fictile Rev. in the Archaic Period*, 100ss., 128ss.; Dyggve, *Das Laphrion der Tempelbezirk von Kalydon*, Taf. XXI p. 225ss.; Thallon Hill e King, *Corinth IV, I, Decorated Architectural Terracottas*, fig. 1.

29. *Ibid.*, Taf. XXII e p. 215ss.

30. Welter, *Troizen und Kalaureia*, 19 e Taf. 8 e 27.

31. *Archaic Fictile Rev. in Sicily and Magna Grecia*, pls. II, VI, VII, X.

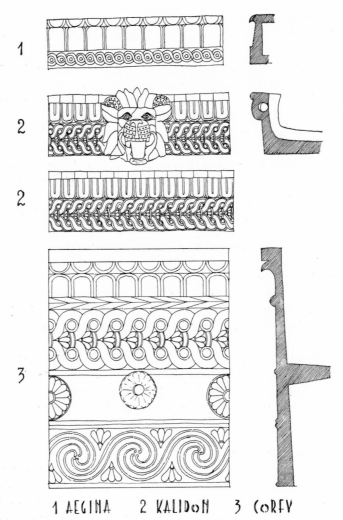

1 AEGINA   2 KALIDON   3 CORFV

Fig. 4. Sime e cornici in terracotta (Scuola Corinzia).
(D. Ferrero delin.)

continuato anche nei lati scaricando le acque attraverso tubi (Sicilia) [32]
o bocche coniche (Kalydon); questi organi di scarico in qualche
esempio, non furono aperti nel corpo del guscio terminale, ma in una
terza fascia, intermedia o sottostante alle altre due, decorata oltrechè
da doccioni, da rosette, ecc. (fig. 4). Nell'Etruria, di regola, al guscio

───────────

32. Cfr. MAL, XXV (Orsi) col. 370ss; Van Buren, *Archaic Fictile Rev. Sicily*,
pass.; MAL, XXXV (Gabrici) col. 138ss.

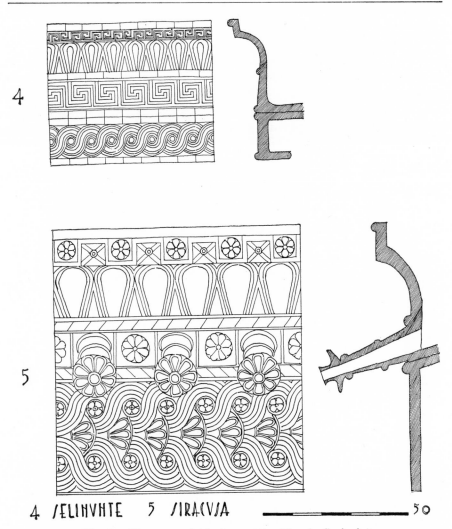

Fig. 4a. Sime e cornici in terracotta (Scuola Corinzia).
(D. Ferrero delin.)

sovrasta ancora un coronamento, traforato e terminato da punte o palmette.[33]

Nella seconda metà del secolo VI le sime e le cornici furono decorate invece dalla tipica decorazione a palmette e fiori di loto in doppia fila, rapidamente diffusa anche in Etruria che la modificò nei suoi "antepagmenta" fittili e bronzei in un gioco di palmette legate da nastri ad 8 (figura 1).

33. Andrén, *Architectural Terracottas*, p. CLXXXVIIIss.

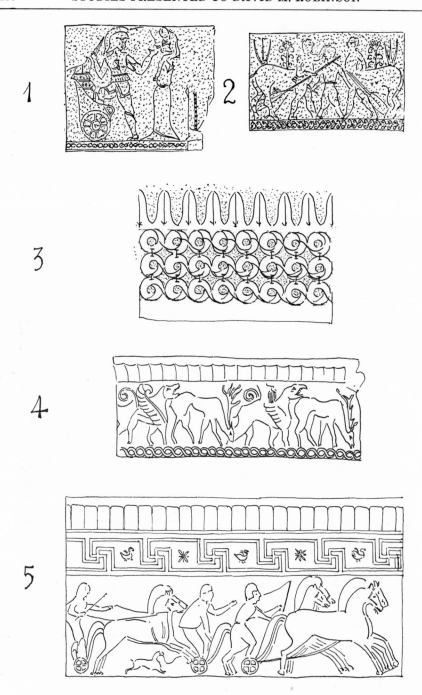

Fig. 5. Lastre in bronzo in Grecia. Sime e cornici in terracotta. Asia
Minore et Etruria. (A. M. De Marchi delin.)

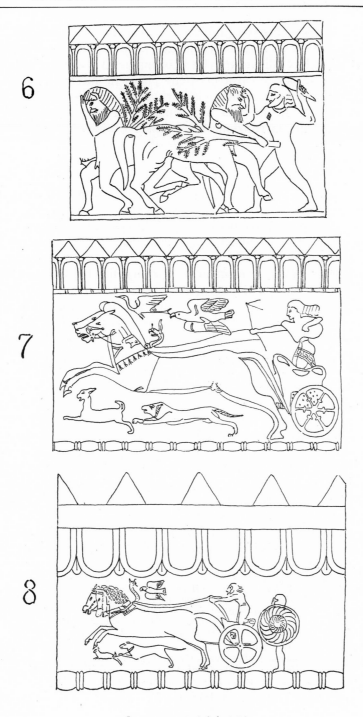

Fig. 5a. Sime e cornici in terracotta.
(A. M. De Marchi delin.)

Non è il caso di insistere qui sulla popolarità delle matasse e delle rosette nei lavori in metallo (chiodature delle porte assire) ; è però doveroso ricordare, di nuovo, che i coronamenti traforati, per la loro natura, oltrechè per le caratteristiche plastiche messe in evidenza da Andrén,[34] indicano chiaramente la derivazione da prototipi metallici e, qualora eseguiti in metallo (si tengano presenti quelli di Veio) mostrano evidente la funzione di "menisci"[35] cioè di punte destinate, con efficacia anche maggiore delle creste triangolari, ad impedire la sosta degli uccelli.

(3) — La scuola dell'Asia Minore dominatrice dell'Etruria nel sec. VI, offre anche scene a figure (fig. 5). Nell'Etruria si riconoscono in modo più chiaro le tre zone,[36] guscio a linguette superiore, fascia intermedia a meandri, squame o rosette, fascia decorativa inferiore, qui a scene di banchetto, cavalieri, cacce su carro, processioni di carri e cavalli, animali ad elementi identicamente ripetuti. Generalmente le lastre decorate in cotto formano sima sporgente nei frontoni mentre lungo i fianchi sono inchiodate nella trabeazione o sulla parete, sotto alle tegole che sgocciolano liberamente ; gli stessi soggetti (cacce su carri, centauri, processione di uomini e carri, animali, banchetti) si ritrovano nell'Asia Minore (Larissa),[37] ma qui di regola la fascia intermedia manca ed il guscio superiore a baccelli si trasforma in una fascia ad ovoli.

Insieme ai soggetti figurati si trovano nella stessa Asia Minore grosse teste di fiere variate oppure rosette quadrilobate[38] e la disposizione non è constante : talvolta la cornice continua nei fianchi la sima isolata, scaricando l'acqua da docce foggiate a coppo, altre volte passa sotto al bordo delle tegole, come in Etruria.

Le sime sono spesso sormontate da una cresta di triangoli isolati (Neandria, Larissa) (figs. 3, 5a) : ma quando le placche in cotto sono applicate sui lati, sotto le tegole, i triangoli sono espressi in semplice pittura (Larissa, Sardi)[39] (fig. 5a).

Tutto questo palesa rapporti di discendenza da prototipi in bronzo: delle creste a triangoli si è già parlato mentre i soggetti hanno evidente

---

34. *Ibid.* pp. CXVII, CLIX, CXCI.

35. Un'antefissa di Caere portava all'atto della scoperta ancora infisso il "meniscus" in forma di tridente. Cfr. Andrén, *Ibid.*, fig. 15 (testo) e fig. 65 (pl. 20) e p. CXXVII. In Grecia si hanno; fori per "menisci" nelle teste dell'acroteriosfinge di Kalydon (Dyggve, *Laphrion*, abb. 194) e delle statue archaic dell'Acropoli (cfr. Collignon, *Histoire de la sculpture grecque* I, 350).

36. Andrén, *op. cit.*, CXXXss.

37. Kjellberg-Akestrom: *Die architektonischen Terrakotten* (Larisa, II) Fries I-VIII; Shear, *Sardis*, X *(Architectural Terracottas)* pl. I, IV, V, IX, etc.

38. Kjellberg, *Larisa*, II, Fries IX; Shear, *Sardis*, X pl. VI, XI, XII.

39. Kjellberg, *Larisa*, II, fig. Fr. I-VI, orn. Fr. I; Shear, *Sardis* X pass.

parentela con le opere in metallo dell'Oriente. Gli elementi ripetuti nelle scene di caccia e di processioni di guerrieri e carri sembrano estratti da episodi delle geste reali espresse nelle porte assire, le rosette a quadrilobi si ritrovano oltrechè sui rilievi dell'Oriente su striscie in bronzo sbalzato;[40] la scena di banchetto, ripetuta su due lamine in bronzo Etrusche, ha un noto precedente in Oriente, nel rilievo conclusivo della campagna di Susa.[41]

(b) — Nel 1937 fu scavato in Olimpia un frammento (alt. cm. 10, 5, lungh. attuale 0,34) di rivestimento metallico lavorato con una doppia matassa[42] (due di disegno analogo, erano stati scavati pure ad Olimpia nel secolo scorso).[43]

La destinazione del pezzo del 1937, secondo Hampe, era una "sima." Noi, pur riconoscendo che la doppia matassa si ritrova nella fascia inferiore di sime e di cornici, data l'altezza di soli 10, 5 cm. l'abbiamo, in via di ipotesi, disposto su testata di mutulo (in realtà le due destinazioni si equivalgono poichè i mutuli possono considerarsi sezioni discontinue di geison) [fig. 2].

Lastre metalliche sbalzate con motivi analoghi a quelli figurati dell'Asia Minore e dell'Etruria, vennero alla luce in Olimpia: un frammento di carro guerresco (cm. 11 x 17, altezza origin. della scena cm. 20 circa), uno simile con partenza di guerriero (224 x 22 att.), un terzo con centauri (22, 5 h. x 33 cm.). [fig. 3].[44]

Oltre a questi pezzi, altri assai significativi vennero scavati in Etruria, a Palestrina; data la loro importanza, ne diamo notizia qui quantunque la loro data (sec. V), sia fuori dei limiti imposti a questo studio; si tratta (fig. 1) di quattro pezzi (alt. 23 cm.) di cavetto a linguette (qui completamente appiattito) e di un pezzo della sottostante fascia decorativa (una variante etrusca del motivo tipico corinzio della 2 metà del secolo VI della doppia fascia di palmette e fiori di loto[45] con palmette legate da linee ad S chiuse nei meandri di un nastro sinuoso).[46]

---

40. Payne, *Perachora*, pl. 47, 5; *Necrocorinthia*, fig. 104, E per la genesi dai prototipi orientali la fig. 54 a pag. 147.

41. Naturalmente la testa dal vinto re elamita Teumann appesa agli alberi circostanti, che costituiva la ragione d'essere del rilievo, non compare nelle vignette Etrusche o dell'Asia Minore. Speelers, *Les arts de l'Asie anterieure ancienne*, fig. 429; Perrot-Chipiez, *HA*, II fig. 27—8.

42. *JDAI* 52 (1937) [*I Bericht*] (Hampe, Jantzen) Abb. 43.

43. *Olympia*, IV, Taf. 42, n. 736a, e 738 (h. cm. 6 e 6, 3 rispettivamente).

44. *JDAI* 56 (1941) [*III Bericht*] Taf. 68; *JDAI* 52 (1937) [*I Bericht*] Taf. 30, 31, 26 p. 85ss.

45. Payne, *Necrocorinthia*, 261ss.; *Perachora* 92 e pl, A1.

46. Andrén, *Architectural Terracottas*, 378-9.

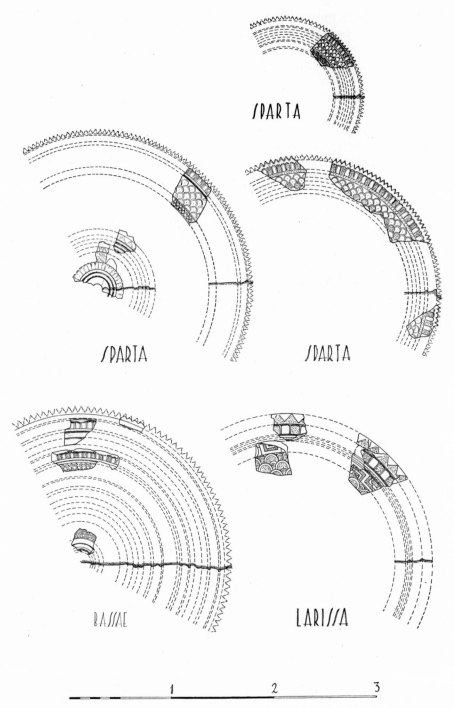

Fig. 6. Acroteri a disco in terracotta. (A. M. De Marchi delin.)

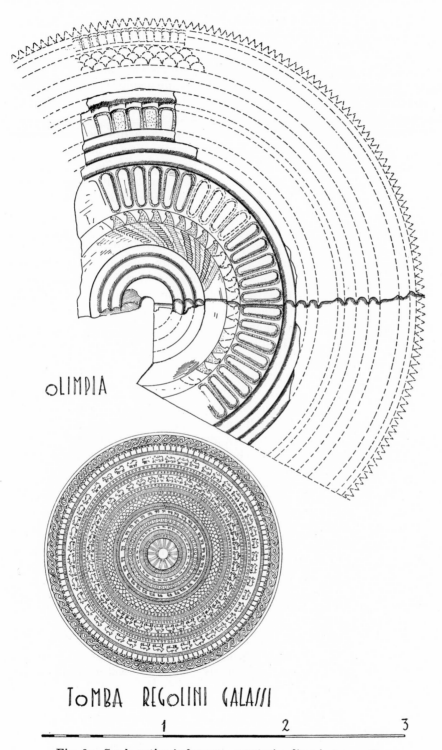

OLIMPIA

TOMBA REGOLINI GALASSI

1   2   3

Fig. 6a. Scudo votivo in bronzo e acroteri a disco in terracotta.
(A. M. De Marchi delin.)

ACROTERI—(a) Nel tempio arcaico gli estremi del frontone erano forniti di efficaci elementi profilattici, sfingi alate[47] (mostri che potevano con le ali coprire, difendere) figure gorgoniche (che "con la potenza della sguardo" disperdevano le influenze maligne)[48] oppure dischi, a gorgoneion od a semplice decorazione geometrica (figg. 6-6a).

Per la nostra disanima hanno particolare interesse i dischi, perchè, verosimilmente, imitano scudi votivi metallici.

L'uso di appendere scudi votivi ai templi era diffuso in Asia già nel sec. VIII; il tempio di Haldi nell'Urartu presenta, nel bassorilievo col saccheggio da parte dei soldati di Sargon (722-705), la facciata provvista di numerosi scudi ancora appesi mentre altri sono predati dai soldati che si agitano sul tetto (e sappiamo dall'inventario del bottino che sei di essi erano d'oro e dodici d'argento).[49]

Dall'Asia l'uso di appendere questi dischi metallici passò in Grecia ed in Etruria, regione dove acquistò particolare diffusione nei sepolcri monumentali;[50] si trattava evidentemente di elementi profilattici e questa caratteristica già insita nell'organo di difesa del guerriero veniva accentuata talora dai simboli rappresentanti al centro (nei più antichi esempi, come negli scudi d'Urartu[51] a dell'Antro Ideo a Creta,[52] teste di fiere; in quelli del sec. VI, come gli scudi scavati ad Olimpia[53] o quelli dipinti sui vasi, Gorgoneia, eliche rotanti, uccelli ad ali aperte.

E' quindi naturale che, come in età villanoviana si usavano riproduzioni in pietra di scudi a chiusura delle tombe a pozzo,[54] e in età classica si appendevano scudi bronzei agli intercolonni dei templi,[55] se ne siano collocati in età molto antica anche al vertice del frontone, tanto più se la materia si intonava ai rivestimenti enei della sima.

Degli acroteri a disco, quelli che risentono di più dei prototipi votivi

47—Van Buren, *Greek Fictile Revetments*, 166ss. (Egina, Atene, Korope, Kalydon, Corinto, Thermon, Halae, Tebe, Olimpia, etc.)

48. Cfr. Payne, *Necrocorinthia*, p. 79; BdA, 1922, p. 493 (Pettazzoni).

49. Riprod. in Perrot-Chipiez, *HA*, II, fig. 190 e cfr. Contenau, *Manuel d'Archeol. Orientale*, III, 1266ss.

50. La posizione nell'Archeologia degli scudi votivi etruschi si trova già definita nella monografia di Orsi in *Museo Italiano*, II, 97ss.

51. "Sei scudi d'oro che nel tempio di Haldia erano applicati e brillavano in modo scintillante, in mezzo ai quali sporgevano teste di cani ringhianti . . . dodici grossi scudi d'argento abbelliti di teste di dragone, di leone o di toro selvaggio . . ." Contenau, *op. cit.*, III, 1267-1268.

52. Halbherr e Orsi in *Museo Italiano*, II, 689ss.

53. Cfr. I Bericht (*JDAI* 52 [1937] Taf. 11-13) III Bericht (*JDAI* 56 [1941] 80ss.).

54. *Studi e Materiali*—II, Fig. 292-301; Ducati, *Storia dell'Arte Etr.*, 19, fig. 6.

55. Cfr. Daremberg, Saglio, "sub Clipeus"—Pare che scudi in metallo fossero appesi anche nelle case private. Vedi in Plutarco la descrizione della casa di Focione (nella "Vita" di lui).

in bronzo sono quelli della scuola laconica, resi famosi dal gigante dell'Heraion d'Olimpia (fig. 6a). Non solo il colore nero uniforme (Sparta) o le tinte delle decorazioni a striscie, a squame e matasse in rosso scuro, azzurro, viola (Bassae, Olimpia, Egina, Sparta)[56] si avvicinavano a quelli delle patine bronzee, ma il bordo esterno era percorso da punte isolate sporgenti che, inutili se eseguite in ceramica, impedivano se ottenute in lamine di bronzo sottile, agli uccelli di posarvisi ed insudiciare. Le stesse punte si ritrovano, in Asia Minore, ancora isolate, a Neandria, ed atrofizzate in triangoli dipinti entro il contorno circolare, a Larissa (fig. 6).

Anche lo schema decorativo di queste opere trova rispondenza in opere di bronzo a sbalzo: gli scudi votivi dell'Etruria (diam. 70-100 cm., data 650 av. C.) presentano appunto fasce concentriche di squame, matasse e linee geometriche opportunamente alternate (valga uno per tutti l'esempio degli scudi della tomba Regolini Galassi[57]) e costituiscono probabilmente coi loro contemporanei della Grecia Meridionale e dell'Asia Anteriore,[58] la chiave del sistema ornamentale in questione (fig. 6a).

Una diversa sensibilità, prevalentemente plastica presiedeva invece all creazione dei dischi acroteriali a Gorgoneion usati dalla scuola corinzia, attiva nel Nord della Grecia e in Sicilia, e talvolta limitati nelle dimensioni all'altezza della sima; a Kalydon, il Gorgoneion e ancora dipinto su di un disco piatto,[59] mentre quelli siciliani a grande rilievo si intonavano alle sime fortemente modellate.[60]

Una reminiscenza dei prototipi bronzei si ha a Capua ed a San Mauro[61] (fig. 6b); qui il simbolo profilattico (Gorgoneion ed elica a Capua) è al fondo di una corolla dove le punte radiali dei prototipi, come è stato riconosciuto, si sono trasformate in petali.[62]

ANTEFISSE—(a)—Vi era grande analogia funzionale fra acroterio apicale ed antefisse: queste terminavano i normali καλυπτῆρες e quello il καλυπτὴρ ἡγεμών. Tutte dovevano avere in origine funzione profilattica, quantunque in un secondo tempo certe scuola abbiano

---

56. Cfr. Van Buren, *Greek Fictile Revetments in the Archaic Period*, 179ss. *RM* 30 (1915) 1ss. (Koch); Dawkins, *Artemis Orthia*, 135ss.; per quelli neri uniformi *ibid.*, 137.

57. Mühlestein, *Die Kunst der Etrusker*, fig. 122-3 et *supra* nota (50). E' possibile che gli acroteri laconici avessero al centro una rosetta sporgente, di grandezza proporzionata; tali sporgenze che sembrano accennare, volumetricamente, alle teste di fiere di prototipi orientali si trovano negli scudi votivi etruschi.

58. Cfr. ad es. lo scudo di Van (Perrot-Chipiez *HA*, II, fig. 415). Cfr. Nota (50).

59. Dyggve, *Laphrion*, abb. 159.

60. *Mem. R. Acc. Lincei*, S. IV; V.I. (1925) p. 274ss. (Montuoro).

61. Koch, *Dachterrakotten aus Campanien*, 7ss. 73. Tav. XX e fig. 13—MAL, XX, col. 789, fig. 48 (Orsi).

62. Andrén, *op. cit.*, CLXIX.

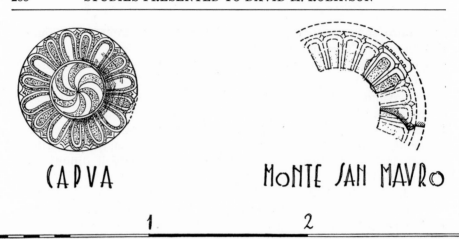

CAPVA   MONTE SAN MAVRO

1   2   3

Fig. 6b. Acroteri a disco in terracotta. (A. De Marchi delin.)

usato antefisse semplicemente ornamentali (ad es, la scuola corinzia con le caratteristiche palmette)[63] fors'anche perchè la funzione apotropaica era stata assunta dalle metope.

L'analogia si rifletteva nella forma (la curva rotonda delle antefisse era però interrotta dalla linea orizzontale della gronda su cui appoggiavano) e nella decorazione.

In certe antefisse troviamo il marchio della derivazione dai prototipi bronzei nelle punte radiali, che nel metallo erano isolate ed avevano funzione di "menisci";[64] queste punte sono modellate, isolate, a Neandria, o semplicemente dipinte come triangoli a Sparta ed ad Amicle, trasformate in una corona di foglie nell'Heraion d'Olimpia.[65]

I colori sono nella scuola laconica intonati alle tonalità scure del bronzo, al solito.

Gli "apotropaia," oltre al Gorgoneion, caratteristica creazione corinzia,[66] ed all'elica rotante di Sparta, sono coppie di sfingi (Kotylon e Bassae)[67] o teste di fiere (Neandria), motivi che ritroviamo tutti frequentemente nei rilievi bronzei arcaici.[68]

METOPE — (a) — Generalmente l'elemento determinante del fregio dorico (nelle più antiche strutture ioniche probabilmente al-

63. Payne, *Necrocorinthia*, 252ss.

64. Cfr. Nota (35).

65. Per Sparta Dawkins, etc., *Artemis Orthia*, fig. 92 e 95, per l'Amyclaion AM, 1927 (Von Massow) p. 71, Taf. 21 nn. 108-140. Per l'origine della corona di foglie cfr. Nota (62).

66. Payne, *Necrocorinthia*, 79ss.

67. Van Buren, *Greek Fictile Revetments*, 45 e 19 *RM* 30 (1915) [Koch 90].

68. Cfr. ad es. per sfingi affrontate *JDAI* 52 (1937) [I Bericht Olympia] Taf. 16-7; Payne, *Necrocorinthia*, fig. 102, pl. 45, 8. Per le teste di fiere *supra* note 51 e 52.

l'architrave era sovrapposta direttamente la cornice senza fregio intermedio) [69] è identificato nel triglifo sia esso considerato come testata di trave semplice[70] o composta[71], come pilastrino[72] o come finestra;[73] è verosimile invece che gli elementi essenziali del fregio fossero le metope, e che i triglifi fossero solo elementi lignei coprigiunto, dilatati per ottenere un più efficace effetto di ritmo e scanalati come ante o colonne per nascondere le screpolature od i giunti verticali.[74]

Comunque possiamo credere che nell'atmosfera magica che è propria dei primitivi e nel gusto essenzialmente plastico della scuola corinzia e delle colonie siciliane si sia sentito il bisogno di un poderoso sistema di simboli profilattici che affermasse il principio della difesa dalle maligne influenze più degli acroteri, attivi solo sulle fronti ed eventualmente delle antefisse di dimensioni troppo esigue. Chiare prove di questa interpretazione sono i grandi gorgoneia dipinti nelle metope di Kalydon e Thermon,[75] e più tardi quando i simboli apotropaici, erano stati inquadrati nel mito, le scene di caccia fortunata che sembrano riecheggiare ancora lo spirito augurale delle primitive civiltà, dal cacciatore di Thermon a quello di Kalydon, dal Perseo di Thermon che fugge col suo sanguinoso bottino all'uccisione della Gorgone del Museo Siracusano.[76]

Ed è significatico che le metope di Kalydon e di Thermon siano circondate da una fascia di rosette che fanno pensare a quelle "di chiodatura" comuni nei lavori in lamina bronzea a partire dalle porte Assire.[77]

(b) — I simboli profilattici, di significato più o meno evidente per noi, sono spesso esequiti in lamina di metallo sbalzato, specialmente sugli scudi[78] ma può darsi che, in qualche caso, ornamenti riferiti a scudi fossero invece applicati su metope.

Lasciando tuttavia indiscussi questi casi dobbiamo però ricordare

---

70. Vitruvio, *De Arch.* 4, 2, 10-20.

71. *Rendiconti Pont. Accad. Rom. di Archeol.* 18, 1941-2, p; 14 dell'estr. e fig. 9 (De Angelis d'Ossat).

72. Boetticher, *Die Tektonik der Hellenen,* 1874-81; *AJA* 21 (1917) 117, 158 e 1920, pp. 323-341 (Holland) e *Palladio* 1940, pp. 49-64 (Zancani Montuoro).

73. *AJA* 22 (1918) 434-37, 23 (1919) 33-49 (Washburn) ed ora *BCH* 55 (1931) 117-163 e 61 (1937) 421-438 (Demangel).

74. E' probabile che anche nei fusti lignei delle ante e delle colonne le scanalature siano state create per mascherare le fessure di essicazione e quelle, eventuali, di distacco per i vari pezzi se vi erano più travi unite; insieme. (Cfr. la struttura in più pezzi delle ante dell'Heraion d'Olimpia. Dörpfeld, *Alt Olympia,* abb. 42.

75. Dyggve, *Laphrion,* abb. 164; Payne, *Necrocorinthia,* fig. 23.

76. Dyggve, *Laphrion,* abb. 164; Woodward, *Perseus,* fig. 1, 2; cfr. anche la metopa del tempio C di Selinunte.

77. Le rosette metalliche usate nelle porte assire come ornamenti di chiodi continuarono in uso anche in età arcaica; ciò e dimostrato ad esempio da quella trovata nella grande lastra di Olimpia (*Olympia,* 4, Taf. 38).

subito che un rilievo metallico fu già identificato come metopa dall'Hampe ed è quello del grifone femmina col piccolo scavata ad Olimpia;[79] misura cm. 79, 5 x 80 ed una fitta chiodatura lungo il bordo prova che essa era fissata ad assi di legno. Essa fu giudicata troppo piccola per l'Heraion ma nella ricostruzione da noi tentata essa non sembra sfigurare tanto più se la si pensa affiancata o circondata da rosette metalliche (di chiodatura) (fig. 2) come quelle dipinte nelle metope di Thermon o Kalydon.

Probabilmente era proveniente da metope il Gorgoneion (cm. 37 x 33) scavato nell'area dello "Hieron" di Athena Chalkioikos di Sparta[80] (fig. 7), mentre si può affacciare l'ipotesi che il frammento di leone derivasse da una composizione frontonale.[81]

Ed è probabile che un accurato esame delle lamine arcaiche a sbalzo finora messe alla luce faccia scoprire altri elementi della serie.[82] In particolare lasciano incerti i grandi rettangoli metallici figurati, ad es. la "Signora delle fiere" (cm. 53 x 44)[83] scavata nel 1937 ad Olimpia. Questi pezzi sarebbero metope di tipo diverso, col metallo anche nel fondo e non solo nell'applicazione.

CAPITELLI—(a)—Certi capitelli dorici in pietra offrono inferiormente all'echino un anello lavorato che appare riproduzione di una corona di bronzo che mascherava il giunto fra fusto e capitello. E' anzi probabile che nelle antichissime strutture templari vi fossero fusti di legno (materiale leggero e non fragile che era di più comodo impiego per pezzi di tutta altezza) ma capitelli di pietra (materiale che per il suo monolitismo consentiva all'abaco di esplicare meglio la sua funzione di raccolta del carico degli architravi e di trasmissione

78. *JDAI* 52 (1937) [I Bericht], Taf. 11-13.

79. *Ibid.*, Taf. 34-35, p. 90-2.

80. *BSA* 26 (1923-1925) [Woodward] 266ss. pl. XXI (attribuito al 530-520 C.).

81. Composizione simmetrica con Gorgone fra leoni (*JDAI* 56 [1941] III Bericht, Olympia, Taf. 33) oppure "Signora delle fiere" (Nota 83); questo tipo di composizione con una figura maggiore e due minori simmetriche si trova notoriamente nel frontone di Corfù e nell'acroterio del vecchio tempio d'Athena ad Atene (*JDAI* 43 [1928] 54ss., abb. 14-15).

Il frammento potrebbe far parte anche di una composizione più semplice con due soli leoni (Payne, *Perachora*, pl. 50, 1; Olympia IV, Taf. LVII; *JDAI* 56 (1941) [III Bericht, Taf. 34-35] e su frontoni in pietra *JDAI* 43 (1928) (Schrader) Beil. 3 per l' "Urparthenon." Cfr. anche Lapalus, *Le fronton sculpté en Grèce*, 87ss.

82. Cfr. ad esempio fra i pezzi delle Tafn. 37-43 di *Olympia* IV, (Furtwängler) che potrebbero aver fatto parte di rivestimenti di edifici, l'arciere ritagliato della Taf. XL (n. 717), quello del n. 718, etc.

83. *JDAI* 52 (1937) [I Bericht Olympia], Taf. 32-3, p. 88-89. Cfr. anche la Taf. 29 (cm. 33, 5 x 37) con stambecco e serpente. Una grande lastra trapezia con varie striscie ornamentali fra cui una "Signora delle fiere" apparteneva secondo Furtwängler ad un supporto di arredamento. (*Olympia* IV, Taf. XXXVIII, n. 696 [cm. 86 x 35/25] p. 100-1.)

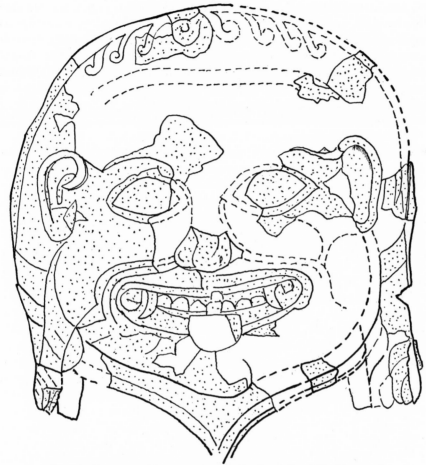

Fig. 7. Frammenti bronzei rinvenuti nel portico dello Hieron di
Athena Chalkioikos a Sparta.

al fusto) e che la corona rendesse meno sgradevole il divario fra le
diverse materie.

Le più significative di queste corone scolpite nella pietra portano
delle foglie, delle perline o dei festoni (capitelli di Xenvares a Corfù,
dell'Amyclaion,[84] del Tesoro dei Siracusani)[85] e talvolta, come nei
templi pestani,[86] sono doppie con una fila di foglie ed una di palmette
e fiori di loto (fig. 8).

---

84. Cfr. *AM* 52 (1927) 71 nn. 108-110.
85. Cfr. *Olympia* II, Taf. XXIV, Perrot-Chipiez, *HA*, VII, pl. XXVI.
86. Krauss, *Paestum*, Abb. 14-17.

Questi ornamenti che sembrano ricopiare elementi lavorati a sbalzo più che fusi, fanno addirittura pensare che anche i normali ornamenti alla base dell'echino dorico, cioè le scanalature concentriche (i vitruviani "anuli")[87] imitino un anello metallico, lavorato in questo caso con più semplicità di quelli sopra elencati; un capitello di Egina che offre una fascia, lavorata ad incisioni a spina di pesce,[88] sembra confermare questa deduzione d'indole generale.

(b) — Due frammenti di corona in bronzo lavorata a linguettine o foglie stilizzate con fascetta applicata a rilievo, furono scavati ad Olimpia nel 1937 e nei vecchi scavi.[89] L'Hampe le riferì all'Heraion III e noi, in questa supposizione, abbiamo cercato di adattarle ad un capitello in pietra (N. 8, cioè l' undecimo del lato Nord) dall'abaco rettangolare (cm. 140 x 131) che coronava un fusto monolitico[90] e che per la rozza lavorazione della parte inferiore ben poteva essere ornato da un fregio metallico (fig. 8).

Conclusioni

Mentre in genere è possibile intuire lo sviluppo iniziale di quasi tutti gli elementi del tempio, la storia delle terracotte architettoniche fino all'inizio del VI secolo è singolarmente oscura e caotica.

Si può rilevare anzi che le caratteristiche e le forme delle più antiche di esse, e specialmente delle sime e delle cornici, indicano uno stadio di vecchiezza più che di gioventù e tanto meno d'infanzia.

Dovremmo aspettarci che il cavetto egiziano, antesignano delle modanature di coronamento greche,[91] trionfasse, invece appare nelle terracotte laconiche con piccole dimensioni confuso in un complesso di ornamenti di gusto quasi geometrico e non compare in quelle dell'Asia Minore, coronate da ovoli e foglie.

La stessa disposizione dei pezzi nelle cornici è spesso illogica, il chè non è ammissibile per elementi di fresca creazione mentre è frequente in fase di vecchiezza, quando gli organi perdono la loro funzione trasformati in ornamenti. Così le fascie figurate della sima passano nei fianchi del tempio sotto alla gronda, inchiodate nelle pareti, nell'Asia Minore ed in Etruria; nella Grecia del Nord, contemporaneamente alle prime manifestazioni della scuola corinzia, che svilupperà secondo una logica impeccabile il suo gioco d'ornamenti

---

87. *De Arch*, 4, 3, 5.

88. *JDAI* 53 (1938) 18, Abb. 8, 9.

89. *JDAI* 53 (1938) Beibl. col 539; *Olympia* IV (Furtwängler) Tav. 53, n. 939.

90. Dörpfeld, *Alt Olympia*, Taf. p. 168. E' possibile che il fusto monolitico volesse riprodurre il predecessore in legno, cioe che nelle prime sostituzioni non si volesse allontanarsi troppo dal prototipo e si rimettessero in opera le corone bronzee.

91. Shoe, *Profiles of Greek Mouldings*, 91, pl. XL, L, LI.

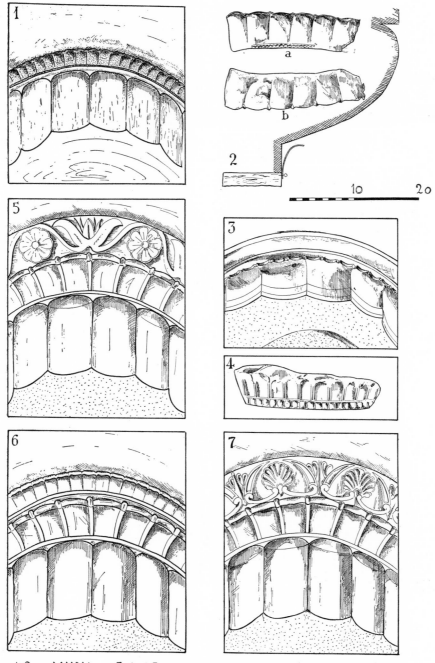

Fig. 8. Corone in bronzo ed in pietra dei capitelli dorici. (A. De Marchi delin.)

per tutto il sec. VI, troviamo cornici complicate come quelle di Delfi e Corfù.

Queste contraddizioni, e molte altre che lasciano interdetti gli studiosi della materia, possono agevolmente spiegarsi considerando le due scuole caduche (la laconica non continuò oltre l'inizio del sec. VI e quella "a figure" nell'Asia Minore e nell'Etruria si conchiuse entro il VI secolo) imitatrici delle forme delle architetture metalliche e la corinzia (unica vitale, anzi dominatrice delle ulteriori fasi della decorazione classica) creatrice originale nel campo dei rivestimenti fittili in terracotta.

Queste illazioni dánno forza alle considerazioni esposte ed ai dati raccolti in precedenza e ci spingono ad esporre quella che crediamo non una risposta definitiva al problema che ci siamo posti, ma una ipotesi augurandoci che nuovi dati di fatto diano presto quella sicurezza che, fors'anche per la rapacità umana che ha avuto sempre sete di metallo pel suo valore intrinseco, fa ancora difetto.

Fra i prototipi dei templi "dorici" vi sarebbero stati dunque degli edifici a struttura, oltrechè di pietra e mattoni crudi, di legno e bronzo. Il metallo sarebbe stato usato nelle lastre curve della copertura, nella sima quasi liscia frontonale, nell'acroterio "tipo scudo votivo" al vertice del frontone, nel bordo del portategole, nelle antefisse semicircolari oppure in una sima orizzontale laterale, nelle testate dei mutuli, nelle metope (in origine apotropaiche), ed, infine, nella corona delle colonne fra fusto di legno e capitello (ad echino e abaco in pietra); sima, cornici, acroterio ed antefisse a punte.

Fra i prototipi dei templi "ionici" vi sarebbero stati pure degli edifici di struttura analoga col bronzo nella copertura a lastre piane con bordo rialzato, nella sima frontonale composta di fascia figurata e soprastante cavetto a linguette, nell'acroterio centrale "tipo scudo votivo," nella fascia laterale a figure sormontata da tegole di gronda con antefisse profilattiche oppure da un cavetto con scarichi d'acqua a coppo, e, forse, nei rivestimenti dei capitelli e della base della colonna lignea. Anche qui sima, cornice, acroterio e antefisse a punte.[92]

92. Ho il dovere di ringraziare qui il prof. Minto per consigli sull'interpretazione profilattica degli scudi e le mie assistenti Dr. Ferrero e Dr. De Marchi per l'òpera prestata nella preparazione dei disegni.

HAUPTPHASEN IN DER PLANGESTALTUNG
DES DORISCHEN PERIPTERALTEMPELS

H. RIEMANN
Erlangen

Schon den ältesten griechischen Sakralbauten ist die strenge Proportionierung ihrer Grundrisse eigentümlich. Es spricht alles dafür, dass hier ein spezifisch griechischer Zug zum Ausdruck kommt. Denn Kenntnis der hochentwickelten aigyptischen Bautradition, die später in der Uebernahme der aigyptischen Bauelle[1] deutlich spürbar ist, kann unmöglich bereits für die Anfänge vorausgesetzt werden. Ebensowenig dürfte ein Erbe der kretisch-mykenischen Welt angetreten worden sein. In deren Kreis gab es keine monumentalen Sakralbauten, und die Untersuchung der Palastarchitektur auf die Anwendung bestimmter Proportionen hin stösst auf Schwierigkeiten wegen des auffallenden Mangels an Präzision in der Ausführung und an dem für diese Architektur charakteristischen Konglomeratbau, der die einzelnen Baukörper in einem vielgestaltigen Ganzen zusammenfasst. Fest steht nur, dass sich gewisse Einzelabmessungen wie z.B lichte Torweiten in Mykenai, Tiryns und anderwärts genau gleich wiederholen, dass man also mit runden Massen[2] gearbeitet hat; die bewusste Herausstellung bestimmender Proportionen jedoch lässt sich bisher nicht nachweisen. Den Griechen schon der geometrischen Zeit hingegen war die strenge Proportionierung ihrer Tempelbauten offenbar das Mittel, das Zufällige willkürlich gewählter Masse durch eine dem menschlichen Geiste immanente gesetzmässige Beziehung zu ersetzen. Hierin kommt ein besonderes Verhältnis zur Zahl als einer den Kosmos beherrschenden Ordnungsfunktion zum Ausdruck, wie es dem rationalen Denken der Griechen entsprach. Die Proportionierung eines Tempelgrundrisses erfolgt dabei so, dass sich die entscheidenden Masse stets in den Aussenkanten des Baukörpers, also bei der Cella meist im Toichobat, bei der Ringhalle im Stylobat finden. Proportionierung von Innenräumen kommt nur ganz ausnahmsweise und fast stets in Abhängigkeit von den Aussenmassen vor.[3] Das bedeutet, dass das gestaltende Interesse primär dem Baukörper, der plastischen Aussenerscheinung zugewandt ist, nicht dem Innenraum, dessen räumliche Gliederung erst im 5. Jhd. vom Parthenon an als ein weiteres vordringliches Problem architektonischer Durchformung begriffen wird.

---

1. H. Riemann, *Zum griechischen Peripteraltempel*, Diss.1935, Tafel der Masseinheiten, A. v. Gerkan, *Wien Jh.* 32, 1940, 145.
2. K. Müller, *Tiryns* 3, 1930, 71 Anm. 4.
3. Riemann, 14.124ff. (Tempel von Neandreia). 143ff. (Sog. Heraklestempel von Akragas). 204.

Der älteste griechische Tempel, über den wir uns ein Urteil bilden können, ein ringhallenloser Antenbau mit einer Innensäulenstellung in der Längsachse, ist das 1. Heraion von Samos, um 800 entstanden, ein langgestrecktes Rechteck von 20 : 100 Fuss. Nachträglich, noch in der 1. Hälfte des 8. Jhdts., wurde diesem Bau eine Ringhalle umgelegt, so breit, dass gerade eine Person zwischen Stützen und Wand passieren konnte.[4] Die Stützenzahl sicher zu bestimmen ist nicht mehr möglich; es ist nur gewiss, dass die Stützen aus Holz bestanden und zum Schutz gegen Feuchtigkeit auf niedrigen cylindrischen, sich nach oben leicht verjüngenden Steinbasen aufgestellt waren. Die äusserst gestreckte Proportion 1 : 5 entspricht dem Stande der geometrischen Bautechnik, die sich in keiner Weise mit der in kretisch-mykenischer Zeit erreichten Entwicklungsstufe messen kann. Die schwachen Bruchsteinmauern waren nicht geeignet, schwere Deckbalken zu tragen, und schlossen grosse Spannungen aus.[4a] Die Cella hat den beim griechischen Tempel später kanonisch gewordenen Typus des Antenmegarons, einer uralten und einheimisch-aigaiischen Bauform, die seit ihrem Vorkommen in Troia I A vor 3000 v. Chr. und in Thermi nicht mehr aus dem Norden hergeleitet werden darf, es sei denn, man verstehe darunter die nördliche Aigaiis. Aber griechisch ist der Gedanke, die Gestalt dieses Antenmegarons durch Proportionierung des Grundrisses zu bestimmen, und schliesslich, es durch Herumführung einer Ringhalle in gleicher Höhe wie die Cella selbst zu einem neuen architektonischen Gebilde umzuformen. Nicht dass der Gedanke einer umlaufenden Halle an sich neu gewesen wäre, die kretisch-mykenischen Paläste kannten solche Hallen in ihren Innenhöfen. Aber neu ist die Uebertragung dieses Gedankens auf den Aussenbau, auf den freistehenden plastischen Baukörper.[4b] Die Cellaproportion ist in den einfachen Zahlwerten von 20 : 100 Fuss

4. E. Buschor, *AM.* 55 (1930) 13ff. Beil. 2 (Grundriss) Abb. 5 (Basis). Buschor-Schleif, *AM.* 58 (1933) 150ff. Abb. 3-4 (verbesserter Grundriss).

4a. A. v. Gerkan macht mich darauf aufmerksam, dass die lagerhaften Kalksteinplatten, aus denen die Tempelwände erbaut waren, eine recht hohe Belastung vertragen und statisch sehr günstig sind; die lange und schmale Form der alten Tempel sei Stil und beruhe nicht auf mangelhafter Tragfähigkeit. Das wird für den Zeitpunkt des Entstehens des Heraions von Samos zutreffen, berührt aber kaum die Genesis: dass mit der submykenischen und protogeometrischen Zeit, also etwa ab 1150, ein Tiefstand des technischen Könnens verbunden war, dürfte nicht zweifelhaft sein; damals entstanden notgedrungen die schmalen langgestreckten Formen, die dann zur Zeit des Heraions und wohl auch schon etwas früher ins Stilbewusstsein übergegangen waren und nun ohne Notwendigkeit beibehalten wurden. Der kulturelle Zusammenbruch ist deutlich an dem Ersatzbau im Palastmegaron von Tiryns abzulesen, an dessen Deutung als Heratempel (A. Frickenhaus, *Tiryns* I 1912, 2ff.) ich gegen Blegens Einspruch (*Korakou* 1923, 133) mit K. Müller (*Tiryns* III 1930, 213ff.) festhalte.

4b. Der peripterale Tempel existierte bereits in Aigypten, ohne dort eine organische Entwicklung zu erfahren oder sich wesentlich im Bild der aigyptischen Gesamtarchitektur durchzusetzen. Der Totentempel Mentuhotep III. und IV. in

ausgedrückt. Runde Zahlen empfahlen sich von selbst, und die Zahl 100 wurde offensichtlich besonders geschätzt, denn der Begriff des Hekatompedons ist ja noch spät auf die Ostcella des Parthenons übertragen worden, auf die er den effektiven Massen nach nicht passt. Der Plangedanke, der diesem ersten bekannten Peripteraltempel zugrunde liegt, ist klar erkennbar: einem in sich proportionierten Kernbau, der Cella, ist ein Raumstreifen umgelegt worden, der an seinem äusseren Rande die Säulenstellung trägt.[5] Ein Spätling dieser Bauform ist der Apollontempel von Thermos in Aitolien, um 620 entstanden, mit einer Cella von 12 : 60 Ellen, deshalb für uns von besonderem Interesse, weil hier die Ringhalle ursprünglich noch keinen einheitlichen Stylobat besass, vielmehr jede Säule ein Fundament für sich hatte.[6] Die Säulenzahl, 5 : 15, ist zwar schon klar proportioniert, fällt aber durch die ungerade Zahl der Frontstützen, die der Mittelsäulenstellung der Cella entspricht, auf; der Enneastylos von Poseidonia[7] ist um 550 der letzte Vertreter einer Säulenanordnung, die zwar tektonisch sinnvoll ist, weil sie den Punkt der stärksten Belastung, die Giebelmitte, unterstützt, ästhetisch aber nicht befriedigen kann, da sie die Tempelmitte und damit den Eingang verstellt.

Weitere Spannungen liessen sich bewältigen, als die Zweischiffigkeit des Kernbaus durch die Dreischiffigkeit ersetzt wurde und man dazu überging, die Tempelwände statt aus Bruchsteinen in Lehmmörtel oder aus Lehmziegeln mit Holzankern aus soliden Quadern zu errichten. Dementsprechend erhielt die Cella im 6. Jhd. eine gedrungenere Gestalt, was in den Proportionsverhältnissen 1 : 4, 1 : 3½, 1 : 3, 1 : 2½ zum Ausdruck kommt.[8] Die Anwendung dieser ver-

Dêr-el-bahari wird auf 3 Seiten von zweischiffigen Pfeilerhallen umgeben; der Tempel Amenophis III. auf der Insel Elephantine war auf ein Podium gestellt, auf dem auf einer umlaufenden Brüstung an den Langseiten Pfeiler, an den Fronten zwischen ihnen Papyrosbündelsäulen standen, die auf der Eingangsseite, zu der eine Treppe hinaufführte, als Halbsäulen bis zum Umgang reichten. Aber diese Bauten der 11. und 18. Dynastie waren den Griechen, als sie den Peripteros zum 2. Male erfanden, natürlich unbekannt.

5. Masseinheit ist der Fuss zu 330mm. Umgangsbreite an den Fronten 2.00, an den Langseiten 1.50, was 6 und 4½ Fuss entspricht. Unterer Durchmesser der Säulenbasis 0.39. Es ist also schon bei diesem frühesten bekannten Ringhallentempel die Frontumgänge durch grössere Tiefe vor denen der Langseite ausgezeichnet worden.

6. G. Sotiriadis, *Ephemeris* 1900, 171ff. Plan S.175. C. Weickert, *Typen der archaischen Architektur* 1929, 50f. Es sind noch vier von den ursprünglichen Basisplinthen für die Holzsäulen mit angearbeiteter erhöhter kreisförmiger Standfläche erhalten (Sotiriadis 173). Riemann 115.

7. Koldewey-Puchstein, *Die griechischen Tempel in Unteritalien und Sizilien* 1899 Taf. 2.

8. 1 : 4 beim Heraion von Olympia und den Tempeln C und D in Selinus; 1 : 3½ beim Heraklestempel in Akragas und den Tempeln A und E in Selinus; 1 : 3 beim Tempel der Athena Pronaia in Delphoi, dem Enneastylos und Demetertempel in Poseidonia.

schiedenartigen Proportionen ist landschaftlich gebunden. Grossgriechenland und Sizilien halten an den gestreckteren Proportionen
selbst im 5. Jhd. fest, soweit die Tempelbauten nicht, wie die jüngeren
von Akragas, unter direktem mutterländischem Einfluss stehen.[9]
Umgekehrt hat die Cella des um 520 entstandenen peisistratidischen
Athenatempels, die wahrscheinlich schon früher mit einer oder ohne
eine Ringhalle existierte,[10] das extreme Verhältnis 1 : 2½, weil hier
die Cella ein vielteiliges Gebilde war, das offenbar Schatzkammern in
seinem westlichen Teil barg, wie ja selbst noch der Parthenon eine
für praktische Zwecke bestimmte Westcella hatte. Eine weitere un-
terscheidende Eigentümlichkeit beider Gebiete zeigt sich darin, dass
im Mutterlande fast ausschliesslich Peripteraltempel mit schmalem
Umgang vorkommen — die einzige Ausnahme bildet der an der
Peripherie gelegene Artemistempel von Korkyra[11] um 580 —, während in Grossgriechenland und auf Sizilien der Weithallentempel
üblich ist[12] und erst um 500, in Akragas und Selinus deutlich unter
mutterländischem Einfluss, in Poseidonia unabhängig davon, der
Schmalhallentempel sich durchzusetzen beginnt.

Beim Artemistempel von Korkyra ist um eine dreischiffige Cella
von 25 : 100 Fuss ein allseitig gleichbreiter Raumstreifen von 20 Fuss
Breite herumgelegt worden.[13] Das Entwurfsschema ist also noch
dasselbe wie beim 1. Heraion von Samos, nur hat sich die Proportion
geändert, und wir haben einen ausgesprochenen Weithallentempel
vor uns, der auf die Unterscheidung von Front- und Langptera ver-
zichtet. Zugunsten einer grösseren lichten Weite der dreischiffigen
Cella ist deren äussere Breite in der Ausführung um 2 Fuss auf 27
Fuss vergrössert worden. Solche Aenderungen des idealen Ausgangs-
entwurfs sind für das Verhältnis des dorischen Architekten zur
strengen Proportion symptomatisch; sie dient ihm als Richtschnur
und Wegweiser, aber er ordnet sich ihr keineswegs sklavisch unter,
sondern verändert sie vordringlicher Ausdrucksbedürfnisse halber.
Für die Untersuchung bedeuten solche Veränderungen, die sich im
Falle Korkyra ja auch auf die ganze Tempelbreite auswirken, die sich
automatisch ebenfalls um 2 Fuss vergrössert, eine bedeutende Er-
schwerung in der Erkenntnis der wirklich zugrundeliegenden Idee;
die tatsächlichen Abmessungen der Cella- und Ringhallenrechtecke
sind nicht nur oft, sondern fast immer das Ergebnis von Korrekturen
der ursprünglichen ganz einfach gehaltenen Idealplanung, und alle

---

9. Vgl. die Uebersicht Riemann 174ff.
10. *Ant.Denkm.* I Taf. 1. Th. Wiegand, *Die archaische Porosarchitektur der Akropolis* 1904, 1ff. W. H. Schuchhardt, *AM.* 60/1, 1935/6, 1ff.
11. G. Rodenwaldt, *Korkyra* I 1940 Abb. 56 und Taf. 22.
12. Riemann 206f.
13. H. Riemann, *JdI.* 58, 1943, 32ff. Masseinheit ist der Fuss zu 350mm.

Versuche, die Ausführungsmasse, die verändert und also abgeleitet sein können, als das schlechthin Gegebene hinzunehmen und von ihnen aus Vergleiche zu ziehen, müssen notwendig in die Irre gehen, da sie eben sekundär entstandene Formen für primär gegebene halten.[14] Welche Ursachen sind es nun, die den dorischen Architekten zu Aenderungen veranlassen, die von der reinen Proportion hinwegführen?

Das Schulbeispiel, an dem sich diese Aenderungen demonstrieren lassen, bildet das 2. Heraion von Olympia, der monumentale, mit einer Ringhalle versehene um 600 entstandene Bau, dem ein einfacher Antentempel vorausging.[15] Er nimmt in vieler Hinsicht eine besondere Stellung ein: seine Wände bestanden über einem sehr starken Mauersockel mit mächtigen Orthostaten aus Lehmziegeln mit Balkeneinlagen, waren aber vermöge ihrer Stärke und der Holzanker imstande, eine schwere Balkendecke zu tragen; die Spannung wurde mit Hilfe von Zungenmauern bewältigt, an deren Stelle erst später, bei einem Umbau, die normale Dreischiffigkeit getreten ist. Die Säulen waren, wie das gesamte Gebälk, ursprünglich aus Holz, wurden aber allmählich durch steinerne ersetzt; sie sind daher nicht einheitlich und zeigen die verschiedensten Schaftstärken und Kapitellformen vom ausladenden archaischen Tellerkapitell über das klassische Steilkapitell zu den toten geradlinigen Formen der hellenistischen und römischen Zeit. Die Ausgangsform lässt sich so rekonstruieren, dass eine Cella von 20 : 80 Ellen mit einer Ringhalle von 36 : 96 Ellen kombiniert worden ist, d. h. um die Cella ist ein gleichmässig 8 Ellen breiter Raumstreifen gelegt worden, dessen Masszahl so gewählt wurde, dass sich im Ringhallenrechteck wieder ein klares Verhältnis, 3 : 8, ergab.[16] Dass ist etwas Neues und ein Fortschritt; bisher liess sich lediglich die Breite des Umgangs zur Breite der Cella in ein Verhältnis bringen. In der Ausführung ist nun die Cella in der Weise verändert worden, dass man ihre Breite um denselben Betrag von 2 Ellen vergrösserte, um den man ihre Länge verkürzte; ihre Ausführungsmasse sind daher 22 : 78 Ellen. Der Sinn dieser Veränderung ist, den Umgängen eine verschiedene Breite zu geben; statt 8 Ellen, wie ursprünglich vorgesehen, messen die Frontumgänge nunmehr 9, die der Langseiten nur 7 Ellen.

Betrachtet man die uns bekannten dorischen Tempelgrundrisse archaischer und klassischer Zeit, so zeigt sich, dass weitaus die

14. Deshalb sind Verhältnislisten der Stylobatrechtecke wie die bei F. W. Schlikker, *Hellenistische Vorstellungen von der Schönheit des Bauwerks* 1940, 142 Anm. 52 irreführend und wertlos; sie treffen den Kern der Sache nicht.

15. H. Riemann, "Die Bauphasen des Heraions von Olympia," *JDAI* 61-2 (1946-7) 30ff.

16. Riemann 46ff. mit Tabelle I. Masseinheit ist die Elle zu 521mm.

meisten eine gleichartige Unterscheidung der Umgangsweiten aufweisen, und so ist der Schluss unausweichlich, in der Differenzierung
der Ptera die Ursache zu sehen, warum die festen Proportionen der
Ausgangsplanung nicht beibehalten werden können und man bei
jeder Planung zwischen einer Ausgangs- und einer Ausführungsform unterscheiden muss. Der Grund zu dieser Differenzierung der
Ptera ist leicht einzusehen. Die Cella ist ein Baukörper, der sich
meist an beiden Schmalseiten öffnet, an der Ostfront im Pronaos, aus
dem man in den Kultbildraum gelangt, an der Westfront im Opisthodom, der gegen den Hauptraum durch eine Querwand abgetrennt
ist, während die Langseiten geschlossene Wände zu sein pflegen. Die
Differenzierung der Ptera ist also Ausdruck einer Sinnbetonung
strukturell nicht gleichwertiger Teile. In der Tat finden wir eine
andersartige Differenzierung, wenn die Form der Cella von der eben
beschriebenen abweicht, wenn nämlich der Opisthodom nicht vorhanden ist und die Rückseite der Cella eine geschlossene Wand bildet.
Dann wird in der Regel die Umgangsbreite der Rückseite der auf
den Langseiten angeglichen und nur das Ostpteron durch grössere
Tiefe ausgezeichnet.[17] Die Differenzierung lässt sich nun auf zweier-
lei Weise durchführen, entweder, wie beim Heraion von Olympia,
durch Veränderung der Cellaproportion, oder, was weit häufiger ist,
durch die Veränderung der Proportion der Ringhalle;[18] daher darf
man schon bei archaischen Grundrissen nicht unbedingt erwarten, in
den Stylobatmassen den Schlüssel für die Beurteilung des Ganzen
zu finden.

Die archaische Zeit hat sich mit der Differenzierung von Front-
und Langptera nicht begnügt wie die klassische, sondern sie hat dar-
überhinaus das Pteron der Eingangsseite von dem der Rückseite
unterschieden. Am Heraion von Olympia wurde das dadurch bewerkstelligt, dass man die Cella in ihrer Längsachse um ½ Elle nach
Westen hin verschob, wodurch sich als Ausführungsmasse des Ost-
pterons 9½, des Westpterons 8½ Ellen ergeben (Abb. 1). Zum Wesen
des archaischen Grundrissentwurfs gehört es, dass die Jochweiten kein
Gegenstand der ursprünglichen Planung sind, sondern aus den Stylobatmassen des Tempels abgeleitete Grössen darstellen. Dagegen wird
die Zahl der Säulen und ihr Verhältnis an Fronten und Langseiten
wohl erwogen. Am Heraion entspricht die Zahl der Säulenkörper
in ihrem Seitenverhältnis der Proportion der Ringhallenmasse in den
Stylobataussenkanten; 6 : 16 Säulen entsprechen dem Ringhallen-

17. ebd. 19. 118 (Tempel der Athena Pronaia). 123 (Tempel zu Assos). 141
(Demetertempel in Poseidonia).

18. ebd. 19ff. 116f. (Peisistratidischer Athenatempel). 127f. (Tempel C). 131f.
(Tempel D).

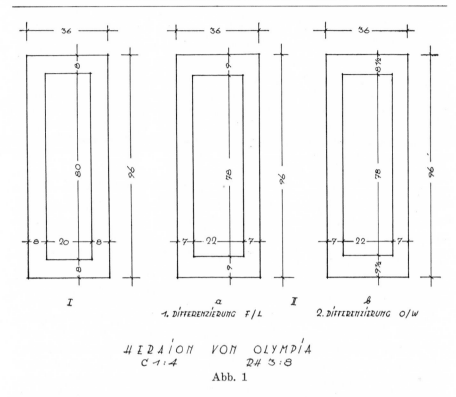

1. DIFFERENZIERUNG F/L

2. DIFFERENZIERUNG O/W

HERAION VON OLYMPIA
C 1:4   RH 3:8

Abb. 1

rechteck von 36 : 96 Ellen, beidemal liegt die Proportion 3 : 8 zugrunde. Geläufiger ist das Säulenverhältnis 6 : 15 (2 : 5), das beim
Apollontempel von Korinth und dem von Delphoi vorkommt; 6 : 12
Säulen hat der peisistratidische Athenatempel auf der Akropolis, 9 :
18 der Enneastylos von Poseidonia.[19] Bei diesem Verfahren, in fest-
gelegte Stylobatmasse Säulenstellungen hineinzukomponieren, ge-
langte man notwendig zu ganz zufälligen, rational nicht ausdrück-
baren und überdies an Fronten und Langseiten verschiedenen Joch-
massen. Beim Heraion von Olympia half man sich an den Fronten
mit Jochabstufung, indem man die Achsen der 2. Säulen in die Ver-
längerung der Toichobataussenkanten legte und das Mitteljoch weiter
als die anstossenden machte (Frontjoche zu 7, 6¾ und 6⅜ Ellen) ;
an den Langseiten wandte man das Verfahren an, das in archaischer
Zeit überhaupt das übliche war: man liess die Jochweiten um ra-
tionale Werte schwanken und verzichtete dabei auf präzise Masse
(Werte um 6⅜, 6¼, 6⅛ Ellen, Eckjoche zu 6 Ellen). Die Ungleich-
heit der Joche an Fronten und Langseiten — im allgemeinen sind sie
an den Fronten weiter, gelegentlich kommt aber auch das Umge-

19. ebd. 11 (Tabelle).

kehrte vor[20] —, und das Schwanken der Jochweiten an den einzelnen Seiten ist den archaischen Planungen eigentümlich.[21]

Die Unregelmässigkeiten der Säulenstellung müssen sich natürlich im Oberbau auswirken. Ein archaisches Triglyphon entbehrt notgedrungen der regelmässigen Anordung; eine strenge Proportionierung des Verhältnisses Triglyphe : Metope ist in diesem Stadium der Entwicklung unmöglich.[22] Daher offenbar erklären sich die Fälle, in denen das Triglyphon zur Erzielung einer gleichmässigen Durchgliederung von der Bindung an die Säulenstellung, wonach die eine Triglyphe über die Säulenachse, die folgende jedesmal über die Jochmitte zu stehen kommt, sich emanzipiert, wie bei der alten Tholos von Delphoi,[23] sogar noch bei der Antenfront des Athenerschatzhauses[24] ebenda, und möglicherweise hat man sich bei den Fronten des Heraions von Olympia in dieser Weise geholfen, um mit dem Problem der Jochabstufung fertig zu werden. So ergibt sich als Folge der proportionalen Festlegung der Stylobatmasse, dass dann eine vollständige Durchproportionierung des Oberbaus wegen der Unregelmässigkeiten in der Säulenstellung unmöglich ist.

Das Ziel, auf das die Entwicklung hinstrebte, war nun zweifellos die Durchproportionierung des Ganzen bis in seine kleinsten Teile, der Abbau des Unregelmässigen und Zufälligen. Der entscheidende Schritt auf dieses Ziel hin erfolgte am Ende des 6. Jhdts., als man auf die proportionierten Stylobatmasse verzichtete und dafür aus der Breite des Kernbaus das allseitig gleiche Joch, das sogenannte Normaljoch, entwickelte, damit die Ringhalle fest an die Cella band und die bisherige gleichwertige Unabhängigkeit beider Teile aufhob.[25] Das Schulbeispiel für die klassische Planung eines dorischen Tempelgrundrisses bietet der um 460 vollendete Zeustempel von Olympia[26] (Abb. 2). Aus dem Kernbau von 30 : 90 Ellen wird durch Dreiteilung der Breite das Normaljoch von 10 Ellen gewonnen, dementsprechend ein Raumstreifen von 10 Ellen Breite um die Cella gelegt, was Tempelachsmasse von 50 : 110 Ellen und eine Säulenzahl von 6 : 12 ergibt. Bei dieser Ausgangsplanung fallen die Achsen der 2. Säulen an den Fronten wie an den Langseiten in eine Linie mit den Toichobataussenkanten der Cella. Die Stylobatmasse sind bei einer solchen Planung vollkommen belanglos; sie ergeben sich durch Hinzurechnung der

20. Grössere Joche auf den Langseiten haben der Enneastylos von Poseidonia und die Tempel D und F in Selinus.
21. Riemann 8.
22. ebd. 31.
23. Weickert 82f.
24. J. Audiat, *Fouilles de Delphes*, II, *Le trésor des Athéniens* 1933 Taf. 9/10.
25. Riemann 13.
26. ebd. 56ff. Tabelle II. Masseinheit ist die Elle zu 521mm.

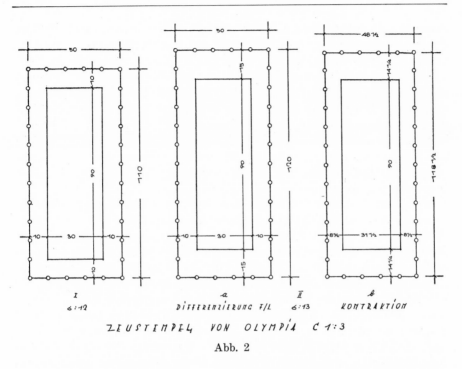

Abb. 2

Breite einer Stylobatplinthe zu den Achsmassen. Die Differenzierung der Ptera wird erreicht durch die Einschaltung eines weiteren
Joches auf den Langseiten, also die Einfügung einer 13. Säule. Die
Aussenkanten der Cellafronten fallen nun nicht mehr in eine Linie
mit den Achsen der 2. Säulen der Langseiten, sondern ihre Ver-
längerung geht jetzt durch die Mitten der 2. Langseitenjoche, so dass
sich nun die Umgänge der Fronten mit 15 Ellen Tiefe zu denen der
Langseiten mit 10 Ellen Tiefe wie 3 : 2 verhalten, von den Säulenachsen bis zum Cellatoichobat gemessen. Die von M. Theuer ge-
fundene Formel n : (2 n + 1) für das Verhältnis der Säulenzahl an
Fronten und Langseiten für den geschilderten Haupttypus des klassischen Tempels[27] drückt also die Tatsache der Differenzierung der
Ptera durch die Einstellung einer zusätzlichen Säule auf der Langseite aus. Damit geht die dem archaischen Tempel eigentümliche
Proportionierung der Zahl der Säulenkörper verloren. Man konnte
darauf verzichten, weil für den Blick in der Uebereckansicht diese
Unregelmässigkeit im Säulenverhältnis nicht wahrgenommen wird;[28]
eine die Achtzahl überschreitende Menge gereihter Säulen wird in

---

27. M. Theuer, *Der griechisch-dorische Peripteraltempel* 1918, 59. Riemann 11
Tabelle).
28. Riemann, *Gnomon* 19, 1943, 306f.

ihrer spezifischen Anzahl nicht mehr erfasst, wenn nicht betonte Ungleichmässigkeiten in der Reihung der Auffassung zu Hilfe kommen.

Die durch das Normaljoch bedingte Regelmässigkeit der Säulenstellung ermöglicht jetzt auch eine gleichmässige Durchgliederung des Triglyphons, für die am Zeustempel das klassische Verhältnis 2 : 3 zwischen Triglyphe und Metope gewählt worden ist. Während beim archaischen Bau die Dekoration der Traufsima keine Rücksicht auf die Jochgliederung nimmt,[29] ist die des klassischen Tempels auf diese abgestimmt; die als Wasserspeier dienenden Löwenköpfe sitzen über den Triglyphenachsen und in der Mitte zwischen ihnen über einem Mutulus.[30] So ist auf dieser Stufe die Durchgliederung des Ganzen bis in seine kleinsten Teile tatsächlich erreicht.

Neben der Differenzierung der Ptera wirkt aber beim klassischen dorischen Peripteraltempel noch ein anderer Faktor umgestaltend und massverändernd auf die Planform der Ringhalle ein, der ihm eigentümliche Ecktriglyphenkonflikt, der dadurch entsteht, dass die Breite der Triglyphe geringer ist als die des Epistylquerschnittes.[31] Dieser Konflikt wird am Ende des 6. Jhdts. deutlich spürbar, als man Triglyphe und Metope, die in ihren Massen ursprünglich einander stark angeähnelt waren und sich wie 8 : 9 verhalten konnten, stärker voneinander zu differenzieren anfing und zugleich der Epistylquerschnitt beträchtlich wuchs. Würde man die Ecktriglyphe über die Ecksäulenachse stellen, so bliebe nach aussen hin eine Restmetope als formal unbewältigter zufälliger Teil übrig, eine für den griechischen Architekten, der nach rationaler Einordnung der Gliederungen strebte, unmögliche Lösung. Wurde die Triglyphe nach aussen über die Säulenachse hinaus bis an die Epistylecke verschoben, so musste das archaische Auskunftsmittel einer leichten Verbreiterung der Ecktriglyphe in dem Augenblick versagen, wo der zu überbrückende Differenzbetrag zu gross wurde; dann entstand eine mehr oder weniger starke Dehnung der Eckmetope oder beider Metopen des Eckjochs, wenn man den Differenzbetrag zu seiner Milderung auf sie aufteilen wollte; auf jeden Fall wurde der gleichmässige Rhythmos des Triglyphons an seinen Enden in ästhetisch unbefriedigender Weise verändert. Der Dehnungsbetrag entspricht der halben Differenz zwischen Epistylstärke und Triglyphenbreite, $\frac{1}{2}(E - T)$. Die neue klassische Lösung erfolgt nun zugunsten der einheitlichen

---

29. Dem entspricht die Rücksichtslosigkeit, mit der die röhrenförmigen Wasserspeier der Marmorsima des alten Athenatempels auf der Akropolis (um 580) die eingeritzte Dekoration an beliebiger Stelle durchbrechen (*AM*. 60/1, 1935/6 Taf. 1 nr. 4, 13 nr. 3, 14 nr. 1, 15 nr. 1, 16 nr. 2, 17 nr. 1. 4. 7, 20 nr.2).

30. *Olympia, Ergebnisse der Ausgrabungen* Tafelbd. I Taf. 11.

31. Riemann 28ff.

Durchführung des Triglyphons, was dadurch ermöglicht wird, dass man die Ecksäulen um den nach der genannten Formel errechneten Differenzbetrag einrückt, das Eckjoch also verkürzt, kontrahiert; das hat den Vorteil, dass nun die Säulenstellung an ihren Enden stärker zusammengefasst erscheint. Immerhin ist die plötzliche Abbremsung des Jochrhythmos an den Ecken spürbar genug, und man hat deshalb im 5. Jhd. in Grossgriechenland und vor allem auf Sizilien die doppelte Kontraktion angewendet, welche auch auf die 2. Joche übergreift und so den Uebergang mildert; diese Jochabstufung hat bei gleichmässig durchgeführtem Triglyphon freilich die Folge, dass die Triglyphe über der 2. Säule nicht mehr in deren Achse stehen kann, sondern leicht nach aussen verschoben erscheint. Eine reine Lösung war nicht zu erzielen, und das Uebliche sind Kompromissbildungen, bei denen eine mässige Kontraktion des Eckjoches mit einer geringen Dehnung der Eckmetopen zusammengeht. Auf die Grundrissbildung wirkt sich die Eckkontraktion mit ihrer Verkürzung dahin aus, dass man nun im allgemeinen weder in den Achs- noch in den Stylobatmassen runde Zahlen erwarten darf.

Die beiden Hauptphasen in der Plangestaltung des dorischen Peripteraltempels, die archaische und die klassische, zeigen, wie diese Ausführungen ergeben haben, beide eine doppelte Abweichung von der streng proportionierten Ausgangsplanung, welche die endgültige Ausführungsform bedingt. Bei beiden handelt es sich zunächst einmal um die Differenzierung der Ptera, die beim archaischen Tempel in doppelter Weise erfolgt, zunächst als Unterscheidung der Front- von den Langptera, dann als eine solche der Frontptera untereinander; die Differenzierung der Ptera ist also beim archaischen Tempel das ausschliessliche Agens, das die Planabänderungen erzwingt.[32] Dagegen beschränkt sich beim klassischen Tempel die Differenzierung auf die Unterscheidung der Front- und Langptera, und als 2. Moment kommt hinzu die Eckkontraktion, die eine aus Rücksicht auf die gleichmässige Durchgestaltung des Oberbaus durchgeführte Veränderung des Grundrisses bedeutet.[33]

Grund- und Aufriss standen jedoch auch in archaischer Zeit nicht etwa beziehunglos nebeneinander, wenn wir auch für die Beurteilung der proportionalen Durchgliederung des Aufrisses in der Frühzeit sehr schlecht gestellt sind, da die Verwendung von Holz für den Oberbau uns meist jeden Anhaltes beraubt, und gewiss kann man sich urtümliche Verhältnisse vorstellen, in denen eine klare Beziehung zwischen Grund- und Aufriss tatsächlich noch nicht bestand. Vom

---

32. S. Taf. I (Heraion von Olympia).

33. S. Taf. II (Zeustempel von Olympia). Zur Erweiterung der Cellabreite um 1½ E. Cf. Riemann 59. 61f.

Heraion von Olympia haben wir wenigstens das Mass der Säulenhöhe, das die runde Zahl von 10 Ellen, also der halben Ausgangs-
breite der Cellafront, betrug. Für den Tempel C von Selinus, der
nach seinem Metopenschmuck um 520 vollendet gewesen sein muss,[34]
lässt sich wahrscheinlich machen, dass in der Ausgangsplanung die
Höhe der Ordnung, also Säule samt Gebälk ohne Giebel, der halben
Tempelbreite im Stylobat entsprach und das Gebälk sich zur Säule
wie 1 : 2 verhielt.[35] Ganz ähnlich liegen die Verhältnisse bei dem
etwas jüngeren Tempel D.[36] Die Höhe der Ordnung beträgt hier 25
Ellen, und das Gebälk verhält sich zur Säule wie 8 : 17, d. h. die
Proportion 1 : 2 = 8 : 16 wird im Sinne einer Erleichterung der
Last durch Vergrösserung der Säulenhöhe um eine Einheit verändert,
ein Verfahren, das wir in klassischer Zeit ganz ebenso angewendet
finden und das zeigt, in welcher Weise eine vom sich wandelnden
Stilgefühl bedingte Veränderung der reinen Proportion rational
durchgeführt wird.

Im Sinne der fortschreitenden Entwicklung, die freilich nicht einfach geradlinig verläuft, sondern vielfaches Vor und Zurück kennt,
ist die zunehmende Erleichterung der Last durch Verminderung der
Gebälk- und Anwachsen der Säulenhöhe; dem geht der oben schon
angedeutete Formwandel in der Gestalt der dorischen Säule parallel.
Am Tempel F von Selinus findet sich, schon nach 500, das Verhältnis
3 : 7 annähernd zwischen Gebälk und Säule;[37] der Demetertempel von
Poseidonia, um 500,[37] und der Zeustempel von Olympia, um 460,[38]
haben beide das Verhältnis 2 : 5, der Aphaiatempel von Aigina, um
480, sogar das Verhältnis 3 : 8.[39] An Stelle der verlorengegangenen
archaischen Bindung zwischen Ordnung und Tempelbreite tritt eine
solche zwischen Joch und Säule, die sich beim Tempel F annähernd,
beim Aphaiatempel und beim Zeustempel genau wie 1 : 2 verhalten.
Am Hephaisteion von Athen, um 440, ist die Höhe der Ordnung
gleich der Summe von 3 Normaljochen.[40] Wieder ist die alte archaische Aufrissproportion 1 : 2 der Ausgangspunkt; das Gebälk wurde
zunächst ein, die Säule 2 Normaljoche hoch angesetzt, aber in der
Ausführung hat die Säulenhöhe das Doppel des Normaljochs um 2

---

34. E. Langlotz, *Zur Zeitbestimmung der strengrotfigurigen Vasenmalerei*
1920, 37.

35. Riemann 183f.

36. ebd. 184.

37. ebd. 186 Tabelle.

38. ebd. 190 Tabelle.

39. ebd. 181f.

40. Die zugrundeliegende Masseinheit ist der Fuss zu 294mm. Meine Untersuchung über diesen Tempel ist noch unveröffentlicht.

Einheiten überschritten, und diese sind von der ursprünglichen Gebälkhöhe in Abzug gebracht.[41] Wir begegneten diesem für griechi-
sches Architekturdenken typischen Verfahren auch in der Grund-
rissgestaltung, bei der Veränderung der Cellaproportion des Heraions
von Olympia. Bei dem jüngeren Poseidontempel von Sunion, einem
dem Hephaisteion gleichzeitigen Bau, ist das Verhältnis 1 : 3 zwischen
Gebälk und Säule erreicht,[42] und das gleiche finden wir an dem um
420 vollendeten Apollontempel von Bassai.[43] Bei den beiden letztgenannten Bauten finden sich auch neue Beziehungen zwischen Grund-
und Aufriss: am Poseidontempel ist die Höhe der Säule gleich
der halben Achsbreite, beim Tempel von Bassai verhält sich die
Höhe der Ordnung zu dieser wie 3 : 5 Die extreme Schmalheit des
Poseidontempels ist freilich durch die Tatsache bedingt, dass es sich
bei ihm um einen Neubau unter möglichster Ausnutzung des von den
Persern zerstörten älteren Tempels handelt.

Auch im Aufriss kommen die beiden Hauptphasen klar zum Ausdruck. Die in jedem Falle verwendeten einfachen Verhältnisse
knüpfen beim archaischen Tempel an die Stylobatbreite, meist in der
Ausgangsform, an, beim klassischen an das Joch, später an die Achsbreite. Durch die Proportionierung entstehen einfachste geometrische
Rahmenformen, in welche der Aufriss hineinkomponiert erscheint,
ohne dass diese Rahmenschemata störend zum Ausdruck kämen; die
Gestalt der Säule entzieht sich der Einspannung in einen Raum-
kubus, und wo das Proportionsgerüst sie in ihrer Achse einbezieht,
sorgt die Eckkontraktion dafür, dass es zu keiner streng stereome-
trischen Festlegung kommt. Die Uebergangsformen vom schwereren
zum leichteren Verhältnis werden durch gleichhohe Zusatz — bzw.
Subtraktionsbeträge bewerkstelligt.

Die Tendenz zur Durchproportionierung des ganzen Baukörpers
hat nach dem 5. Jhd. weitere Fortschritte gemacht; der Mangel an
ausreichenden Publikationen für diese spätere Zeit ermöglicht heute
noch keinen klaren Ueberblick. Die Entwicklung führte offenbar
zum Akademischen, Komplizierten, allmählich Erstarrenden, zu
weiterer Entwicklung Unfähigen; das kommt in der Ablösung der
dorischen Ordnung im Tempelbau durch die ionische zum Ausdruck,
schliesslich auch in den rezeptartigen Bauvorschriften Vitruvs, wenn
diese auch wesentlich theoretischer Natur sein werden und selbst
mit späthellenistischer Bautradition nicht wirklich übereingestimmt
zu haben brauchen. Eine dritte den beiden behandelten Hauptphasen

41. Also (2 NJ + 2) : (1 NJ — 2).
42. Riemann 189.
43. ebd. 190.

ebenbürtige wird sich schwerlich aus der nachklassischen Entwicklung herausstellen lassen. Was nach der 1. Hälfte des 5. Jhd. im dorischen Tempelbau geleistet wird, liegt auf einer Linie, bedeutet Verfeinerung am Parthenon und am Poseidontempel von Poseidonia in der Anwendung der Kurvatur, die freilich prinzipiell schon im archaischen Stadium vorkam;[44] ebenso in der Anwendung des goldenen Schnittes in rationalisierter Form, so schon am Zeustempel von Olympia, wo die Säule mittlere Proportionale zwischen Gebälkhöhe und Achsbreite in der Ausgangsform ist (8 : 20 = 20 : 50). Die innere Struktur des klassischen Tempels hat sich jedenfalls in der nachklassischen Zeit nicht mehr geändert.

44. Apollontempel von Korinth und Artemision von Ephesos, Riemann 43.

THE ATHENIAN THEATER OF THE FIFTH CENTURY

WILLIAM BELL DINSMOOR
Columbia University

In recognition of Professor Robinson's leadership in both of the fields of classical archaeology and classical literature, I am tempted to dedicate to him an archaeological study which has some literary import, a restudy of the Athenian theater building in the fifth century. This may seem appropriate also because Robinson's own earliest publication dealt with the choregic inscriptions of Delos; and the theatre has not lacked representation among his later articles and reviews.

During the period of more than a half century since the publication of Dörpfeld's great work of 1896 on the Greek theater, practically everything that could conceivably have been said about the Athenian theater has been said, in one way or another. During the half century two great heresies developed, the Puchstein-Furtwängler heresy of 1901, and the Fiechter heresy of 1936, both with tremendous influence upon contemporary and subsequent scholarship. And despite the intensive investigations during the past three decades by Allen, Flickinger, Miss Bieber, Bethe, Frickenhaus, Bulle, Fensterbusch, Fiechter, Broneer, Schleif, Gerkan, Pickard-Cambridge, Anti, and Dilke—punctuated by Dörpfeld's periodic returns to the fray[1]—our present state of mind is still distracted by the variety of opinion as to the exact appearance of the theater in its successive periods. It is a question of steering a course through a maze of conflicting theories, and of attempting to view the development as a consistent whole, but with the discrimination that can result only from study of the actual remains. The following notes primarily record my reactions upon reading many of the modern investigations upon the spot in 1937, together with subsequent analysis.

In view of limitations of space, we must here dispense with problems of the present Lycurgan theater (338-326) and of the Hellenistic and Roman alterations, confining ourselves to the first century of the existence of the theater of Dionysus. Thus two distinct periods of the theater, those of the greatest importance as the setting for the master-

---

1. In view of restrictions of space, footnotes have been reduced to a minimum. Bibliographical references may be found in the comprehensive works of Miss Bieber (1939) and Pickard-Cambridge (1946), to which may be added the following: Anti, *Teatri greci arcaici da Minosse a Pericle* (1947). Dilke, *BSA* 43 (1948) 125-192. Reviews of Pickard-Cambridge by Miss Bieber, *AJP* 69 (1948) 97-100; Fensterbusch, *Gnomon* 21 (1949) 148-151. Reviews of Anti by Miss Bieber, *Art Bull.* 31 (1949) 61-63; McDonald, *AJA* 53 (1949) 412-414. For the general development see also Dinsmoor, *Architecture of Ancient Greece* (1950), pp. 119-120, 207-210, 264-249, 298-319.

pieces of dramatic art, are covered in this study. The first is that of
the theater of the early fifth century (500-421), the scene of the
dramas of Aeschylus and Sophocles (and part of those of Euripides),
the period which corresponds in structure, though by no means in
date, to period I of Fiechter and Miss Bieber (Solon), of Dörpfeld,
Frickenhaus, Fensterbusch, Schleif, Gerkan, Pickard-Cambridge, and
Anti (Thespis), and to periods I-IV of Bulle (Peisistratus, Thespis,
Aeschylus). The second period is that of the theater of the late fifth
century (421-415), the scene of the later dramas of Sophocles and
Euripides and of most of the comedies of Aristophanes that were not
produced in the Lenaion, again corresponding in structure, though
not in date, to Dörpfeld's and Gerkan's period II (Pericles), Schleif's
periods IIa-IIb (Pericles, with a preceding tentative phase), Pickard-
Cambridge's periods IIa-IIb (Periclean, early fourth century for the
stoa), Frickenhaus's and Fensterbusch's and Anti's periods II-III
(Aeschylus, Euripides), Fiechter's periods II-IV (Thespis, Aeschylus,
Pericles), Miss Bieber's periods II-IV (beginning, middle, and late
fifth century), and to Bulle's periods V-VI (Sophocles, Nicias). It will
be apparent that, apart from slight lowering of the dates, we are in
closest agreement with Dörpfeld; and perhaps the chief result of this
study is the corroboration of his discernment of the facts, as expressed
in his great work of 1896 and his sketchy revision of 1925.

I. The Theater of Aeschylus and Sophocles

The traces of the first theater, as detected by Dörpfeld in 1886, survive primarily in three fragments of the circumference of a circular
orchestra, an eastern arc of polygonal masonry of Acropolis limestone
(R = SM1), a shorter piece of masonry of diverse materials toward
the west (Q = J3), and a rockcut bed in the present east parodos (V).
For fifty years (1886-1936) the existence of this circular orchestra,
with a more or less hypothetical auditorium on the Acropolis slope at
the north, and the archaic Old Temple of Dionysus outside it at the
south, remained unchallenged. There were, to be sure, some qualms as
to the exact diameter of the old orchestra. From the longest surviving
portion of its periphery, the polygonal wall about 4 metres in length,
Dörpfeld estimated that the diameter was about 24 metres, while
Fiechter with the same evidence made it 24.30 m. Something of a
minor scandal developed when Dörpfeld admitted that, while speaking
of the diameter as 24 metres, he had silently drawn it as 26 metres
in order to include the two other traces, and that, in view of the difficulty of measuring the curved polygonal wall, it might even have been
as great as 27 metres. Meanwhile Petersen had noted that a so-called

"basic circle" *(Grundkreis)* described within the lower edges of the concave-fronted Augustan marble thrones and the corners of the Lycurgan paraskenia and the front of the Lycurgan scene wall foundation, that is, 26.86 m., would have been approximately identical with the diameter of the old orchestra; this was followed by Allen, Flickinger, and Fensterbusch, postulating for the old orchestra circle an exact diameter of 26.86 m. or, as measured by Fensterbusch, 27.02 m. Thus the old orchestra grew from 24 m. to 27.02 m., regardless of the fact that the so-called "basic circle" disagrees with the practice in other Greek theaters, is in itself an incongruously haphazard and inaccurate mixture of Lycurgan and Augustan elements, and is anachronistic when thrust back into the archaic period.

Then followed the disintegration of Dörpfeld's old orchestra circle. Fiechter argued that the little piece of wall (Q = J3) toward the west, only 1.85 m. in length, is not curved but is perfectly straight, and that the rock cutting (V) toward the northeast is too ambiguous and has nothing to do with the so-called orchestra circle. Thus disposing of two of the three elements of the circumference, he felt free to move the oldest orchestra center westward to the present north-south axis of the theater, and around this to develop an entirely new plan. The curved polygonal wall (R = SM1) now became part of a curved bow-shaped terrace outside the orchestra; and, though Fiechter himself had measured it as an arc with a diameter of 24.30 m., he restored it as an arc of a circle about 30 metres in diameter. Conversely, the western piece of wall (Q =J3), which he stated to be perfectly straight, was inconsistently restored as part of an inner orchestra with a diameter of only 20.40 m., a curve even more intensive than Dörpfeld had assumed. In spite of these inconsistencies in Fiechter's own argument, which leave me without confidence in his restoration, it has been widely accepted: "The wall [R = SM1] is not circular" and "of the circle of which this is supposed to be a part there are no other traces." "There is nothing in the ruins of the theater to indicate that . . . the earliest orchestra in Athens was of necessity circular; . . . Fiechter . . . rejected the evidence—and rightly—on which Dörpfeld built his early 'Orchestrakreis.'"

In his plan of the archaic theater Fiechter had shown at the north a circular well excavated in 1893, and 21 metres farther west a rectangular manhole excavated in 1927. The manhole descends to a tunnel with a terracotta water-pipe, and is evidently of classical date; but the bottom of the well, with no sign of an outlet, is 2.25 m. above the manhole tunnel, and was filled with Mycenaean and geometric pottery, evidently having been abandoned long before the beginnings of the theater. Nevertheless Fiechter in a forgetful moment connected them with dotted lines. Anti thereupon projected this hypothetical sub-terranean connection 6.50 m. up to the surface, employing it as the front of a trapezoidal archaic orchestra. The east side of this archaic orchestra is formed by the dotted prolongation of a drain built by Lycurgus in the fourth century. The back of the orchestra is formed by the curved polygonal wall, with the long suffering diameter now enlarged to 52 metres, twice Dörpfeld's final diameter. Such is the theater of Thespis as restored by Anti, recently greeted as demon-strating that "until the end of the fifth century the Greeks used rec-tangular, not rounded, auditoria." "The dogma of the originally circular orchestra has been more clearly challenged than ever before; . . . the dogma of the originally rectilinear orchestra has now been formulated, and perhaps already with more evidence than is available to support the other theory."

Though these two attacks on Dörpfeld's old orchestra have greatly shaken recent opinion, it would seem that both are totally devoid of foundation. The elements employed both by Fiechter and by Anti have been either distorted or misinterpreted. On the other hand, I still believe that the old orchestra circle, which Schleif alone has defended within recent years,[2] is quite capable of mathematical demonstration.

Returning to the arc of polygonal masonry (R = SM1), accepted by all though with differing diameters and interpretations, it is evi-dent that if we use it as part of a circumference of 24 or 24.30 m., as Dörpfeld and Fiechter had independently estimated, this circum-ference will pass within a metre of the short western wall fragment (Q = J3) and exactly parallel to it. It would be too much of a coin-cidence to suppose that this western fragment, in itself so short and defaced that a curve is not discernible, but appropriate in material, direction, and position, was anything else than part of the same circumference.[3] We are justified, therefore, in revising the calculation accordingly: connecting the extremities of the two pieces of wall by a chord 24.80 m. in length, we erect a diameter at right angles, and on this we ascertain by experiment that a circumference coinciding with both wall faces would require a diameter of 25.50 m., equivalent to

---

2. Dörpfeld and Flickinger never abandoned the old orchestra circle, as shown by their latest discussions (1926, 1932, and 1936 respectively), despite the inference of Pickard-Cambridge (1946, p. 8) that they had altered their position. Dilke (1948, pp. 126, 127) likewise still regards R = SM1 as part of a sixth-century circular orchestra.

3. The variation in material is no more than would be expected in this period; compare the similar use of poros intermingled with Acropolis limestone in the sixth-century (?) polygonal wall running up the west slope of the Acropolis, and also the retaining wall of 488 B. C. south of the Older Parthenon.

78 Doric feet,[4] the center (I) lying 12.60 m. southeast of the present orchestra center (IV), and 2.90 m. east of the present north-south axis.

The orchestra circle thus described would leave the rockcut bed (V) at the northeast just outside it; and perhaps this is just as well. Instead of attempting further adjustment, we may infer that the more sophisticated rock cutting, unsuitable for a polygonal wall, was an external addition either for a drain outside the orchestra or for a platform or head of a ramp ascending to the old orchestra from the east parodos. Similarly a long terrace wall (D = SM3) to the west of the orchestra, in a slightly later style of polygonal masonry, would apparently have supported the ramp forming the west parodos.

The plan of this first theater, with its circular orchestra and the traces of the parodos entrances at the west and perhaps also at the east,[5] would suggest that, if these parodos entrances were opposite one another, the axis differed greatly in direction as well as in location from that of the present theater. Its direction, veering so much more to the northwest, is perhaps corroborated by, and so might have caused, the peculiarly oblique orientation of the odeum of Pericles subsequently erected toward the east (446-442), so completely out of harmony with the present theater axis (cf. fig. 2).[6]

It seems impossible, however, to follow Allen in the geometrical construction which makes the above-mentioned west parodos wall determine the exact location of the front paraskenion corner of a wooden scene building of Lycurgan plan wrapped around outside the old orchestra, or Flickinger in his adaptation of the Frickenhaus-Fensterbusch geometry, prolonging the west parodos wall D = SM3 across the old orchestra and using it as the back wall of a wooden scene building erected on the orchestra itself. I believe that we must confess

4. The Doric foot (D.F.) was 0.32666 m. in the Lycurgan theater (as obtained from the orchestra diameter of 19.60 m. = 60 D.F.), and apparently 0.32689 m. in the fifth-century theater (as obtained from the revised column spacing of 2.8195 m. = 8 5/8 D.F. in the stoa, see note 22). As for my calculated radius of 12.75 m., based on Dörpfeld's careful plan, it may be noted that a direct calculation on the spot by DeJong, cited without enthusiasm by Flickinger (1926, p. 108; 1936, p. 348, note 2), gave a diameter of 25.26 m. (radius 12.63 m.), which may be regarded as satisfactory corroboration, especially if we make some allowance for the broken face of Q = J3.

5. Noack (1915) and Flickinger (1930) assumed that there was only one parodos, that at the west, against which Dörpfeld (1917, 1932) and Allen (1937) rightly protested.

6. The still incompletely excavated odeum is shown in *fig. 2* in accordance with my conjectural restoration. The length of the north wall is known, and also the positions of eight columns, two rows each of four in the north half of the east side. The spacing of the columns shows that nine are required to fill each side of the square, theoretically giving 9 x 9 = 81 columns. But 3 x 3 = 9 columns should be omitted at the center to permit an octagonal lantern (opaion), thus leaving 72 columns arranged in three rows all around the central space.

that the restoration of the temporary wooden scenes erected for Aeschylus and Sophocles between 465 and 458 B. C., presumably on the south edge of the old orchestra itself, lies beyond the bounds of our available evidence.

As for the date of the first theater, represented by Dörpfeld's rehabilitated old orchestra, a date which Fiechter placed as early as 600, Bulle about 560 (Peisistratus), Dörpfeld and Anti in 534 (Thespis), all these suggestions seem too early. Neither in the masonry nor in the scanty records of pottery can I discern any evidence that a theater existed in the precinct of Dionysus Eleuthereus before 500 B. C. And on the literary side we have explicit statements:[7] Photius says that the collapse of the bleachers *(ikria)* in the Agora was the immediate cause of the transfer of the theater to its present site; and, while Hesychius and Suidas omit the words "in the Agora," their allusions to the single poplar tree *(αἴγειρος)* which is known to have been in the Agora show that this is what they meant. Suidas definitely gives the date of the collapse of the *ikria* as the 70th Olympiad (500-497); his alternative date (458) is discredited not only because it is coupled with the myth of the murder of Aeschylus by the eagle, but also because at that time the theater of Dionysus was already in existence. We may, therefore, regard the old orchestra as a creation of Cleisthenes, a companion to the other great curved structure of that period, the first form of the Pnyx; and the old orchestra would have been the scene, not of the performances of Thespis, but of the dramas of Aeschylus and Sophocles, and of the earlier works of Euripides, down to the time of the Peace of Nicias (421), a period of approximately eighty years.

II. The Theater of Euripides and Aristophanes

It was originally assumed by Dörpfeld that the old orchestra circle continued to serve until the present stone theater was erected by Lycurgus (338-326). But in 1901 both Puchstein and Furtwängler argued that the present theater, or at any rate the scene building with the stoa behind it, dated back to the end of the fifth century; Furtwängler even supplied a definite date, to which we shall return, the last years of the career of Nicias (421-415). Furtwängler's argument was based not only upon the known interest of Nicias in the theater, as shown in his dedications mentioned by Plato (*Gorgias,* p. 472 a) and Plutarch (*Nicias,* 3), but also upon the superficial resemblance of the breccia theater foundations to those of the New Temple of

---

7. Passages gathered by Frickenhaus (*RE*, ix, 1914, 992-994) and Pickard-Cambridge (1946, pp. 11-12).

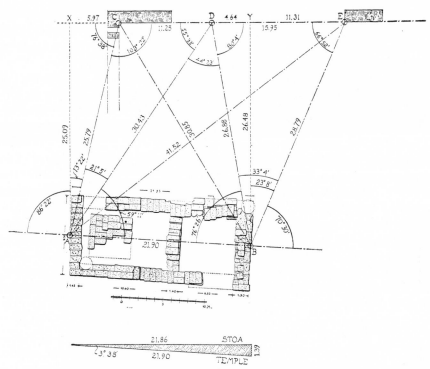

Figure 1. Divergent orientations of Theater, Stoa, and
New Temple of Dionysus.

Dionysus, built to contain the late fifth-century gold-and-ivory statue
of Dionysus by Alcamenes,[8] and plausibly attributed to Nicias himself,
and particularly upon the exact parallelism of the theater and the
temple. Furtwängler interpreted this exact parallelism as indicating
that temple and theater formed parts of a single prearranged building scheme; and this statement concerning their parallelism has been
taken as axiomatic in every book and article written about the theater
since 1901, even though some have argued that they need not be identical in date, that the temple may have been built parallel to a previously
existing theater, or that the theater may have been later, built parallel
to the temple.

Furtwängler's observation of parallelism was based on Dörpfeld's
restored plan, in which the temple was made parallel by a draftsman's
error. And while Dörpfeld's actual state plan shows a very different
situation, the statement was never corrected, perhaps because of the
embarrassing circumstances. Penrose, interested in the orientation of

8. Pausanias, I, 20, 3.

temples rather than in the theater, estimated that there was a difference of only 0° 42′ between the axes of the Old and New Temples; and
since I could measure directly a difference of 3° 56′ between the Old
Temple and the stoa, it seemed obvious that the New Temple likewise
formed a marked angle with the stoa and consequently with the theater
as a whole. But Penrose had made a minor mistake, while running his
line from the southwest to the southeast corners of the New Temple,
in failing to observe that the roughly projecting foundations required
an ear on each flank of the wider east porch. By means of a careful
series of triangulation measurements between the New Temple and
the stoa (fig. 1),[9] however, it has been possible to work out all the
angles of the resulting triangles and to demonstrate that the New
Temple formed an angle of 3° 38′ with the theater. The east front of
the temple is turned 1.40 m. too far south for exact parallelism. But
in spite of this marked difference we have done no more than to eradi-
cate one of the factors of recent argument; the orientation cannot be
cited either for or against their simultaneous date. Even if the theater
and temple were contemporary we could hardly, in the fifth century,
have expected exact parallelism, the former being governed by reasons
of location, the latter independently regulated by the cult. It is rather
upon more stable archaeological grounds than direction, and the superficial resemblance of the foundations, that it is necessary to test the
relationship.

The date of the westward shift of the theater axis, which Dörpfeld
had originally equated with Lycurgus (338-326) and Furtwängler
with Nicias (421-415), has varied greatly in more recent opinion,
Dörpfeld eventually proposing about 442-430, Bulle 458, Flickinger
465, Frickenhaus 472, Bethe and Fensterbusch 500 B. C., while
Fiechter, as we have seen, erroneously concluded that the old orchestra
already stood on the present axis as early as 600 B. C. It was at first
assumed that Lycurgus (Dörpfeld) or Nicias (Furtwängler) or Pericles (Schleif), or the theater builders of 472 (Frickenhaus) or 500
B. C. (Bethe and Fensterbusch), moved the orchestra center (I) to its
present location (IV), 12.60 m. to the northwest (by my calculation),
in a single sweeping change. Dörpfeld eventually suggested that there
was an intervening center (II) about 2.00 m. south of the present
orchestra center (IV), followed by Allen and Bulle, while Flickinger
and Gerkan placed this intervening center only 1.15 m. south (coinciding with the present auditorium center III). Fiechter, having

---

9. I owe these triangulation measurements to the kind cooperation of Miss
Evelyn Harrison (who also verified several other items) and Mr. John Travlos;
from the triangles thus obtained I calculated the various angles and the distances
from the temple axis at front and rear perpendicular to the toichobate of the stoa.

claimed that the oldest orchestra center (I) was already on the present north-south axis, argued that there were two intermediate shifts northward along this axis, to 6.00 m. south (of IV) in 534 B. C. and to 1.13 m. south (i. e., at III) in the Periclean age.

Together with the vacillation in the dates of the shifting orchestra centers has occurred a separation of the breccia foundations of the present scene building complex into two or more parts, in opposition to Dörpfeld's original supposition that all were uniformly of the fourth century, Puchstein's and Furtwängler's that they were all of the late fifth. Separating the foundations of the stoa from those of the scene building proper, for reasons which will be shown to be valid in spite of the superficial resemblance of the breccia material, Dörpfeld finally concluded that the stoa was the earlier of the two, dating from about 430 (followed by Schleif and Gerkan), while Pickard-Cambridge assigned it to the early fourth century, Miss Bieber to the early fifth, Anti to about 500, and Fiechter to 534 B. C. The scene building itself would be Lycurgan according to Dörpfeld (followed by Schleif, Gerkan, and Pickard-Cambridge), of about 420 according to Miss Bieber, of about 430 according to Anti, of 458 B. C. according to Fiechter. A curious reversal was proposed by Bulle: the scene building would have been erected first, in 458, and then rebuilt, in part on the same foundations, together with the stoa in 421-415 B. C.

The only logical date *post quem* for the westward shift of the theater axis is the construction of the odeum in 446-442 B. C., preventing eastward expansion of the theater. This same consideration, moreover, would appear to contradict Dörpfeld's final assumption that the odeum and the stone theater were portions of a single coordinated Periclean scheme; the group as a whole suggests rather that when the odeum was erected there was as yet no plan for a new theater. Otherwise, we should have expected better coordination between the two structures, probably with the theater rebuilt on the old site and the odeum located farther eastward. A date later than 442 B. C., moreover, is implied by the breccia material used for all portions of the foundations of the stone theater, a material which Dörpfeld had regarded as first used in the fourth century. The accumulation of evidence later convinced him that breccia was introduced as early as the last third of the fifth century; and this conclusion appears to be correct, inasmuch as its earliest appearance seems to be in the temple at Rhamnus (436-432), where it was not yet used for foundations (here of marble) but only experimentally as underpinning for floors. Probably its use in foundations was initiated by the economic stress of the Peloponnesian War, and the last quarter of the century would be the more suitable period for its introduction. With such a date *post quem,* we must eliminate all proposals to date the stoa as early as 534 or 500 B. C., an elimination which is corroborated by Kübler's analysis of the fifth-century pottery found beneath the foundations, as published by Fiechter in contradiction of his own hypothesis.[10] Such a date *post quem* would also eliminate the dating of the scene building proper as early as 458 B. C.

With regard to the date of the stone scene building, our first and most obvious evidence is the breccia foundation (C = aA) in the west parodos, intended to support a retaining wall of the auditorium before the present auditorium was erected. Dörpfeld had illustrated but had not discussed this foundation in his original publication; Puchstein in 1901 offered the proper interpretation of the sequence, which Dörpfeld accepted six years later, assigning wall C = aA to the Periclean period. That such is the proper sequence was shown by excavation: when the older parodos wall was demolished and replaced by the Lycurgan parodos wall farther north, the latter rested in part on the surviving four breccia courses of the older foundation. Frickenhaus and Fensterbusch, accepting Dörpfeld's late fifth-century date for wall C = aA, argued rightly that it could not, as an old parodos wall, be associated with the old orchestra circle, since its line would have passed so far to the north of the center (I) that a cavea surrounding the old orchestra would have occupied much less than a semicircle; consequently it must be associated with a theater farther west on the present axis, showing that the shift had taken place at least by the late fifth century. This older parodos wall, moreover, disagrees in position with the similar breccia foundations of the scene building, the paraskenia almost touching it so that the parodos would have been closed; the two elements are mutually contradictory. Frickenhaus avoided any difficulty of this sort by interpreting the scene building as a Lycurgan alteration, after the destruction of wall C = aA. But Fensterbusch, assuming that wall C = aA and the scene building foundations were erected simultaneously in the late fifth century, strove to escape the dilemma by arguing that there were originally no projecting paraskenia and that these were Lycurgan additions. And Bulle, likewise assuming that wall C = aA and the scene building foundations were contemporary, but as early as 458 B. C., attempted to solve the difficulty by arguing that the paraskenia originally had less projection (as later in the Hellenistic period) in order to permit reasonable entrances. Flickinger inferred, regardless of the material, that this older parodos wall formed the north side of a single and somewhat informal

10. Kübler, in Fiechter (1936 iii), 43-49.

west parodos of the old orchestra, even as early as Thespis (534), and that it was later combined with the orchestra shifted westward and with a wooden scene building of about 460 B. C., enframed by wooden paraskenia (essential to his argument) past which the audience could have squeezed only in single file, unless perchance it was already broken down as early as 460 B. C. (before this material came into use), which he admitted as a possibility. Fiechter, likewise without regard for the material, receded only to 500-497 B. C., assigning it to the reconstruction after the (first) collapse of the *ikria*. But this older parodos wall, being itself of breccia, is to be placed after 430 or 425 B. C.; and since the sequence of construction requires that the breccia scene building foundations, in order to avoid closing the parodos, should not have been laid out until after the older parodos wall had been demolished and replaced by the present parodos wall, it seems evident that the scene building foundations belong to the following period, the fourth century.

Under these circumstances, if the scene building could be separated from the stoa in point of time, the latter might have preceded the scene building and thus have been contemporary with the older parodos wall. Such separation appears to be corroborated by a second piece of evidence, the absence of any traces of bonding the four cross-walls of the scene building at their points of contact with the stoa behind. It would seem that the breccia footing wall backing the actual stoa wall was erected continuously from end to end, with no expectation that foundations would abut against its north face. The sequence here would have been (a) the stoa rear wall and (b) the scene building.

Our third piece of evidence is the homogeneous construction, not only of the breccia stoa foundations 2.05 m. wide and of the breccia footing wall 0.65/0.68 m. thick resting on their north edge, but also of the floor and walls of the stoa itself, as Dörpfeld, Furtwängler, and others had concluded, though with differing opinions as to whether the date should be the fourth century or the late fifth. That the breccia footing wall was independent in function rising no higher than the orchestra level, and that 0.715 m. was the total thickness of the stoa wall, was clearly perceived by Dörpfeld; Bulle's suggestion that such thickness is inadequate is disproved by contemporary analogies (Rhamnus 0.552 m., Athenian Temple at Delos 0.610 m., Erechtheum 0.652 m., Stoa of Zeus Eleutherius 0.702 m., Hephaesteum 0.761 m., etc.), and his restoration of a wall of 1.00 m. straddling the orthostates and the breccia footing wall is structurally impossible. Fiechter concluded that the poros toichobate and the poros orthostate backers with

Hymettian marble facing blocks (the latter missing except at the northeast corner, where a special marble block constitutes the entire thickness), occupying the southern portion of the rear wall foundation, were later replacements of the time of Lycurgus, having been preceded by an older heavy foundation (that of a "skenotheke") rising to the orchestra level and dating back to 534 B. C., the period to which he assigned the foundations and the footing wall. Anti accepted the theory but with a slightly later date (500-497), after the collapse of the *ikria*. But these early dates are impossible, as we have observed, not only for the breccia material of the foundation but also because fifth-century potsherds lay beneath them. Technically, moreover, there are insuperable objections both to the early date and the proposed restoration of a "skenotheke" at a higher level. Fiechter insisted that the poros toichobate and the orthostates, adapted to a lower floor level, were later alterations on the ground that they are in no way bonded with the breccia footing wall behind. If, however, we look along the line of the poros toichobate and the orthostate backers, we come to a point just short of the axis of the theater where the toichobate course once turned inward and passed northward through the breccia footing wall behind. A single poros block, exactly at the same level and with the same dimensions as the toichobate, is here imbedded in the breccia wall,[11] projecting slightly to make a tight joint with the toichobate; and the form of the anathyrosis joint indicates that the toichobate here turned at right angles, about 1.30 m. east of the axis of the theater, suggesting that it was once intended to leave a passage in width about 2 x 1.30 = 2.60 m. (probably 3.92 m. = 12 D.F. between the orthostates), at a low level through the rear wall to the orchestra, necessarily with a flight of steps because of the difference in level. It is evident that the poros toichobate was laid earlier (though perhaps only by a few days) instead of later than the footing wall, and hence that the floor was intended to be at this low level from the very beginning. There is no corresponding return of the toichobate west of the axis; evidently the plan was changed almost immediately, both the poros toichobate and the breccia footing wall being continued westward without interruption, and the flight of steps pulled southward so as to begin within the stoa itself, passing through the footing wall at the higher level of the great opening about 5.55 m. (17 D.F.) wide recognized by Fiechter. This change of plan does not, however, presume a difference of date; the breccia foundations and

---

11. The existence of this imbedded poros block, noted by Bulle (1928, p. 73, note 1) and, while not mentioned by Fiechter, shown in his illustrations (1935 i. fig. 7, Pl. 4), is rightly stressed by Broneer (1936, p. 597) as significant for the relation of the stoa wall and footing wall, though without interpretation.

footing wall, and the poros toichobate and poros orthostates faced by Hymettian marble, must all be contemporary with each other.[12] The breccia and Hymettian marble, though at first glance suggesting the fourth century, might be assigned to the end of the fifth, as Dörpfeld, Schleif, and Gerkan eventually agreed.

A fourth piece of evidence is the drain running diagonally beneath the stoa and the scene building, in two sections, with two sudden drops or waterfalls as it descends from the Lycurgan orchestra gutter. Wrede and Fiechter, who studied the drain in detail, insisted that both of these waterfalls were makeshift alterations, and that the whole upper section is earlier in date than the lower. Bulle and Wrede dated the upper section in 458, the lower in 420 B. C.; Fiechter and Anti placed them farther apart, the upper in 534 and the lower in 338 B. C.; Pickard-Cambridge compromised with about 430 and 390 B. C., respectively. The sequence of construction, however, appears to be exactly the opposite. The upper section has breccia walls, and eighteen of its twenty-five ceiling slabs are of Hymettian marble, a combination of materials which could hardly be earlier than the end of the fifth century, excluding such dates as 534 or 458 B. C.; and the seven other ceiling slabs, as well as the two northernmost wall blocks, are poros second-hand seat blocks with inscriptions of the late fifth century, implying that their reemployment here is not earlier than the fourth. The manner in which the north end of the drain combines with the Lycurgan orchestra gutter, furthermore, while awkward because of the differences in direction and depth, is of consistent construction and obviously contemporary.[13] The assumption of Bulle and Wrede, of Fiechter and Anti, that this upper section of the drain once con-

---

12. Thus we may reject the compromise offered by Allen (1941, p. 177) and Pickard-Cambridge (1946, pp. 16, 21-22, 27, 135, 266), following Fiechter to the extent of assuming that the footing wall was actually erected first, with the stoa shortly afterward. Allen dated these shortly afer 446/5 and in the period of Nicias, respectively, while Pickard-Cambridge preferred the period of Nicias and the first decade of the fourth century, respectively. Our analysis has shown that the actual process of erection was exactly the opposite.

13. Dörpfeld always consistently regarded the upper section of the drain as contemporary with the orchestra gutter, at first as Lycurgan (1896, p. 37) and finally in 1935 as Periclean (letter quoted by Fiechter, 1936 iii, p. 55, note 1), the latter with the consequence that the present tiers of seats must also be regarded as Periclean. Dörpfeld's new proposal with regard to the date of the gutter and auditorium was accepted by Schleif (1937) and Fensterbusch (1949); but it seems contrary to all the evidence. Fiechter's reason for separating the drain and gutter was merely the triangular shape of the northernmost marble ceiling slab, assumed to have been recut to this shape at a later date to admit the poros lintel forming the south side of the shaft descending from the Lycurgan orchestra gutter. But the marble slab might equally well have been trimmed to this shape immediately after laying; the irregularity of the trimming would be explained by the fact that it was done in situ, to fit the change of direction which it was impractical to calculate in advance.

tinued farther northward seems to be disproved by the fact that the floor at just this point is armored with Acropolis limestone slabs, running beneath the walls and so erected simultaneously, to resist erosion by water falling from the gutter above. Again, the upper section of the drain would hardly have been laid at such depth (2.19 m. to 3.11 m. below the orchestra) except for the purpose of passing beneath the scene building foundations, which, as we have seen, must have been later than the stoa and its footing wall. On the other hand, the above-mentioned investigators all assumed that the upper section once continued southward at the upper level; Fiechter and Anti would even have it pass through the breccia footing wall, which the former regarded as contemporary and the latter as slightly later than the drain, regardless of the fact that the breccia wall is here perfectly preserved without any possibility of a passage at the upper level. On the contrary, the passage at the lower level was obviously built simultaneously with the breccia stoa foundations and footing wall, with a Hymettian marble floor slab to withstand the falling water, and with poros wall slabs supporting a large poros lintel 2.03 m. long, which is bonded into the breccia footing wall and carries it across the drain. The junction of the upper and lower sections at this point is clearly an awkward makeshift, due in part to the diagonal direction of the drain;[14] but even here the evidence suggests that the breccia footing wall was already standing when the endmost marble ceiling slab of the upper section was precariously balanced with one corner set loosely into a pocket cut diagonally in the breccia wall and shored up with small stones. In other words, the sequence here was as follows: (a) the stoa with the breccia footing wall and the lower section of the drain (presumably once with a northward continuation at a much higher level, little below the surface level of the orchestra, with a sharp descent just behind the stoa wall), and (b) the present upper section dropped to a deeper level (but not as deep as the lower section) so that it would pass beneath the new scene building foundations.

The fifth source of evidence is the existence of the breccia platform (T) protruding northward from the breccia footing wall and erected simultaneously with it, as shown by the bonding of the foundations, and also of the five vertical sockets for heavy timbers on either side (two of them now obliterated by later patching). Both the projecting platform and the ten sockets would have been meaningless after the erection of the stone scene building; and Dörpfeld in 1907 admitted that they must have been intended for an earlier wooden scene build-

14. For the conditions here, see Fiechter's clear perspective drawing (1935 i, fig. 10), also Bulle (1928), Pl. 7, figs. 1, 7, 8.

ing,[15] which would have been contemporary with the older retaining wall C = aA in the west parodos. The evidence points to a moment when the background of action on the orchestra consisted of the stoa, faced by a removable wooden scene building. Fiechter, who had dated the stoa foundations and the breccia footing wall in 534, thought that the moment in question was the hypothetical reconstruction of 500-497 B. C. But it has been pointed out that this separation into two periods is needless, since the vertical timber sockets, while cut in the breccia footing wall after its erection, are really of the same period, later by only a few days rather than by a full generation. Thus Schleif, Gerkan, and Anti rightly made the wooden scene building and the stoa foundations contemporary; but Anti again dated them far too early (500-497), restoring in connection with them a second imaginary trapezoidal orchestra. Actually, as we have seen, the stoa and consequently the wooden scene building cannot be earlier than the last quarter of the fifth century, while on the other hand they must precede the breccia scene building foundations which cannot be later than Lycurgus (338-326).

Summarizing the evidence as to the sequence of erection, we find many elements belonging to a theater of a period intervening between the old orchestra circle and the fourth-century theater of Lycurgus. These earlier elements, all compatible with each other, include (a) the older parodos wall C = aA, the stoa with its poros toichobate and orthostates faced with Hymettian marble and backed by the breccia footing wall, the protruding platform T and the timber sockets, the lower section of the drain under the stoa (presumably with a continuation northward only slightly below the surface), and the second-hand poros seat blocks now built into the upper section of the drain. These earlier elements, including breccia and Hymettian marble, could not antedate the last quarter of the fifth century; nor could they, on the other hand, be placed as late as the first half of the fourth century, because of the late fifth-century inscriptions on the seat blocks. Later than all these in turn are the following (b) : the present west parodos wall A = wA and its eastern counterpart (oA), the breccia scene building foundations which are compatible with wall A = wA but later than the stoa with its breccia footing wall, the present upper

15. Dörpfeld (1896, pp. 61-62) had originally interpreted the timber sockets as preparation for a removable episkenion, the platform as a support either for a stairway or for theatrical machinery, all of the time of Lycurgus. For impossible interpretations, see Versakis (1909), pp. 223-224; Frickenhaus (1917), pp. 59-60, figs. 15, 21. For the revised opinion see Dörpfeld (1907), p. 231; (1909), p. 226; (1924), p. 89; (1925), 313; (1926), pp. 29, 32; (1927), 1487; (1932), 284; this attribution to a pre-Lycurgan scene building has been adopted as indisputable by Fiechter, Schleif, Gerkan, Miss Bieber, and Anti, though Miss Bieber (1939, p. 125) compromises by suggesting a later reemployment in Dörpfeld's original sense.

section of the drain reconstructed at a deeper level beneath the scene building, the present orchestra gutter which agrees in construction with the upper section of the drain, and the present auditorium which fits the orchestra gutter and the later parodos walls. These later elements, likewise with breccia and Hymettian marble but belonging to a second period of construction, would hardly be earlier than the fourth century (in order to leave time for the preceding structure of the late fifth century, and as implied also by the use of second-hand seat blocks with late fifth-century inscriptions in the upper section of the drain and in the west parodos wall A = wA), and so should be attributed to the theater of Lycurgus.

With this sequence, the wooden scene building assigned to the late fifth century and lasting down to the middle of the fourth—as corroborated by the allusion of Demosthenes in 348 B. C. (*Meidias*, 17) to boarding up wooden paraskenia[16] and followed directly by the theater of Lycurgus with its marble colonnaded paraskenia as correctly restored by Dörpfeld,[17] we find no excuse for the restoration of intervening scene buildings, either of wood or stone, such as have figured in most of the modern discussions.[18] Those who, like Puchstein, Furtwängler, Frickenhaus, Bulle, and Fensterbusch, disregarded the evidence for the vertical timbers of a movable scene building, or who, like Fiechter, Miss Bieber, and Anti, dated it too early, were obliged to bridge the gap between the early fifth century and the Lycurgan period by assuming that a stone scene building rested on the present breccia foundations during the Periclean age or the last quarter of the fifth century. Thus arose the modern theory, illustrated for example in restorations by Bulle and Fiechter, of two- or even three-storeyed towerlike paraskenia with solid walls, flanking a receding scene wall, such as never existed either in the fifth century or subsequently.[19] Fiechter assumed that not only this imaginary scene build-

16. Cf. Xenophon (*Cyropaedia*, VI, 1, 54), writing before 362 B. C. of the timbers of the tragic scene building.

17. The restoration of the third or Lycurgan theater lies outside the province of this article, though it should here be noted that Dörpfeld's restoration of the Lycurgan marble paraskenia, with columns on the fronts and both flanks, is quite correct. The various restorations with solid walls, or with prostyle columns only on the fronts (Fiechter, 1914), or with columns only on the inner returns facing the central axis (Fiechter, 1936), are certainly erroneous. The old argument advanced by Puchstein, Furtwängler, Petersen, Bulle, Fiechter, Schleif, Miss Bieber, and Anti, that the foundations are too heavy to have been erected primarily for the colonnades, is not a valid reason for regarding the foundations as earlier than Lycurgus.

18. The theory that the early wooden scene buildings of 465-458 were erected in connection with the present orchestra site (Frickenhaus, Fensterbusch, Flickinger) may be rejected, there being no evidence that the theater was shifted westward before the latter part of the fifth century.

19. Cf. Bulle (1928), 338, fig. 31; Fiechter (1936 iii), Abb. 36; repeated by Bieber (1939), figs. 712-174; and particularly the extraordinary restorations in

ing, but also most of the present auditorium, was of Periclean date, with a difference in the lowest rows of seats and in the endmost kerkides, supposed to have been curved in horseshoe form rather than in the straight U-shape now existing. He attempted to corroborate this Periclean scheme with strange and wonderful geometry, based on concentric circles with diameters of 19.34/19.52 m. (inner edge of stone curb), 20.46 m. (outer moulding of same), 24.40 m (raised step below proedria), and 27.28 m. (backs of earlier thrones).[20] These circles are not only imaginary, but some of them can even be disproved, as when he placed the hypothetical proedria thrones athwart the beautiful circumferential joint which was emphasized by the careful alignment of the radiating joints of the specially long blocks in the outer ring; the intention certainly was, not to conceal this arrangement beneath the thrones and a superposed step behind, but to make it count as an essential part of the design, albeit Lycurgan rather than Periclean in date.[21] The need of all such imaginary restoration, both of the scene building and of the orchestra and auditorium, is now obviated by the evidence that the wooden scene building itself dated from the last quarter of the fifth century, and, with its wooden paraskenia to which Demosthenes alluded, lasted down to the time of Lycurgus.

Thus we still have, I believe, sufficient evidence for the restoration of the second or late fifth-century theater, that of Euripides and Aristophanes (fig. 2). Here, at the south, is shown the New Temple

---

Bulle and Wirsing, *Szenenbilder zum griechischen Theater des 5. Jahrhunderts v. Chr.* (1950) 20-21, Pls. 2-12.

20. In a preliminary article (*Mélanges Navarre*, 1935, 181-189) Fiechter had estimated 20.20 m. instead of 19.34/19.52 m., 25.10 m. instead of 24.40 m., and 26.92 m. instead of 27.28 m., arguing that 20.20 m. and 25.10 m. formed a ratio of 4 : 5. Against such plane geometry see Gerkan, *Gnomon* 9 (1933) 151-152; (1938), 243; Schleif (1937), 36. It is unfortunate that Fiechter's theory so pervaded his publication as to cause him to neglect the really significant tangency of the Lycurgan orchestra circle of 19.60 m. with the line connecting the Lycurgan paraskenia.

21. Strictly speaking, Fiechter's argument is a little more complicated, assuming three stages: (1) Periclean, the proedria step at the orchestra level with the thrones forward (1936 iii, fig. 35); (2) Lycurgan, the present proedria step one course higher, with the thrones forward (1935 i, fig. 59 = 1936 iii, fig. 36); (3) Augustan, the same with the thrones pushed back (1936 i, fig. 58). It is the second of these which can actually be disproved. The circumferential joint has a radius of 12.03 m., and the fronts of the present thrones with a radius of 13.51 m. are 0.335 m. outside the circumferential joint at the middle (north) and 1.48 m. outside on either flank (owing to the displacement of 1.145 m. between the auditorium and orchestra centers), so that the joint is exposed throughout its length. But if the thrones were moved forward 0.53 m. (the radius to their backs reduced from 14.17 m. to 13.64 m. according to Fiechter), the circumferential joint would be overlapped by about 0.195 m. at the middle and exposed by only 0.95 m. on either flank; the gradual emergence of the circumferential joint would be unpleasant, and the use of the especially long stones in the second ring of the proedria step would be meaningless. With Fiechter's second stage thus eliminated, no ground exists for its hypothetical predecessor.

of Dionysus, shifted to its true position and orientation; and toward
the east is restored the odeum of Pericles. The southernmost portion
of the theater, the great stoa with a length approximately equal to the
square of the odeum, and placed as far south as possible so that it
actually overlapped the Old Temple, presumably had either a blank
wall or mere pilasters in the closed portion behind the Old Temple.
The open portion of the stoa, where Dörpfeld had restored a serried
row of twenty-six columns and Fiechter twenty-two, here receives only
sixteen columns with a wider spacing, fitting the regular jointing of
the euthynteria but showing three metopes per intercolumniation, as
in the stoa of Zeus Eleutherius on the Agora.[22] Within the stoa,
against the back wall, appears the necessary stairway and landing
giving access to the great doorway discovered by Fiechter, with the
stairway continuing to the top of the platform on the theater axis
north of the stoa.

This platform, apparently 6.53 m. (20 D.F.) in width and projecting
3.26 m. (10 D.F.) on the missing finished course at the ground level,
encasing the upper end of the stairway ascending to the orchestra
level, would have supported alternatively a wooden central pavilion
(prothyron or aedicula) or the movable ekkyklema of Euripides
(brought in through the great doorway from the stoa) ; for the latter,
wheels may have rotated in two deep holes left in the platform close
to the stoa wall. Or vertical timbers, about 0.368 m. (1 1/8 D.F.)
square and spaced 2.56 m. (7 5/6 D.F.) on centers, could have been
set up in the ten vertical sockets of the footing wall and on two corresponding points on the platform, a continuous row of twelve occupying a length of 28.16 m. (11 x 7 5/6 = 86 1/6 D.F.) on centers, their
faces flush with the face of the breccia footing wall. A second row of
twelve timbers, centered 2.56 m. (7 5/6 D.F.) in front of these, would
have their faces 0.027 m. (1/12 D.F.) within the north edge of the
finished platform, where the two central timbers would find ample
support and the others would rest on individual bases containing
sockets (as was afterwards the case at Pergamon).[23] A third row,

22. Dörpfeld (1896, 13, Pl. II) made the axial spacing 1.86 m., equivalent to
two euthynteria blocks of 0.93 m. (followed by Gerkan) ; and Fiechter (1936 iii,
pp. 19-20, Pl. 2 IV) disregarded the euthynteria spacing, estimating a column
spacing of 2.092 m. But both are too trivial in proportion to the size of the building, and also as compared with 3.018 m. in the contemporary Stoa of Zeus Eleutherius. Actually the euthynteria spacing is a little greater than Dörpfeld's
estimate, apparently averaging 0.9398 m. = 2 7/8 D.F. Three euthynteria blocks
(or triglyph spacings) would give a column spacing of 2.8195 m. = 8 5/8 D.F.
The greater column diameter thus resulting would agree better than Dörpfeld's
smaller columns with the great stylobate width of about 0.985 m. (estimated
from traces on the foundations observed by Miss Harrison).

23. Gerkan (1938), p. 239) rejected the restoration of a second row of free-
standing posts, arguing that in two instances (over R = SM1 and Q = J3) the

at a similar distance in front of the second and so with a total projection of 5.80 m. (17 3/4 D.F.) from the stoa wall, would probably have been utilized only for projecting lateral pavilions or paraskenia, each two bays in width, without intruding upon the area of the orchestra. In accordance with this scheme, we might assume that while the second row would have required five separate footings on either side of the central platform, the third row would have required only three at each end, a total of sixteen special footings. Whenever the whole scheme was in operation, the receding "proskenion" would have had seven bays, and each of the paraskenia two bays.[24]

The older west parodos wall C = aA and its presumable eastern counterpart converged on the north-south axis at a distance of 6.30 m. (19 1/4 D.F.) south of the present orchestra center (IV), or 16.00 m. (exactly 49 D.F.) north of the rear wall of the stoa.[25] The center (II) thus determined being 12.74 m. (39 D.F.) from the finished face of the prothyron or proskenion platform, the latter was tangent to a circle 25.48 m. (78 D.F.) in diameter, identical with the diameter of the old orchestra circle of the first theater. In its late fifth-century form this circle would presumably have coincided with the front edges of the proedria seats, just as subsequently, in the more constricted theater at Priene, the line of the overhanging edge of the front row of seats was marked out on the pavement by an engraved circle tangent to the face of the scene building. Within this circle would have been the circular arc of a shallow orchestra gutter, connecting at the southeast corner with the original upper section of the diagonal drain.

---

earlier masonry still rises to higher levels than the bottoms of the sockets in the footing wall. It so happens, however, that the remnant Q = J3 lies between post positions, not directly beneath, and in any case its top is 1.25 m. below datum (Gerkan's 0.85 m. refers to a later breccia block set on the wall), and the level 1.25 m. below datum given by Gerkan for R = SM1 refers only to its apex which likewise would not lie beneath a post. On the other hand, only a few of the sockets in the footing wall descend to the course level 1.33 m. below datum; the bottoms are at various levels, some 0.15 m. above the course line and so only 1.18 m. below datum. Thus Q = J3 and R = SM1 do not conflict with the conjectural plan of the free-standing posts.

24. Fiechter (1936 iii, Pl. 18) restored the paraskenia with the improbable width of three bays (which would intrude upon my proposed circle) and thus left only five bays for the recessed "proskenion" between them. Schleif (1937, fig. 2) followed Fiechter's plan but with the addition of an extra row of posts, giving four posts (rather than three) for the depth, in order to fill up part of his tremendous orchestra space.

25. This was Fiechter's method (1936 iii, Pls. 15, 18, 19), here retested on Dörpfeld's plan. Dörpfeld himself (1924, p. 89; 1926, p. 32) located center II only about 2.00 m. from IV, and was followed by Bulle (1928, Pl. 4 II). Gerkan (1938, p. 243) utilized center III, rejecting center II on the ground that it should lie north of, rather than in the plane of the parodos wall (despite the analogies of Oropos, Sicyon, Megalopolis, New Pleuron, and Ephesus, for instance). Schleif (1937, fig. 2) likewise ignored center II and utilized center IV with the timber scene building, thus obtaining an excessive depth for the orchestra area, even with his extra row of posts.

Of the late fifth-century auditorium we possess some significant
pieces, in addition to the older west parodos wall. Seven of the ceiling
slabs of the upper section of the drain were second-hand flat poros
slabs, 0.24 m. high and 0.65 m. (2 D.F.) wide, with inscriptions in
large letters and with vertical lines of demarcation on their front
edges. Bulle and Lehmann, as well as Anti, assumed that these had
formed a rectangular or at most a polygonal platform for the thrones
of officials; but these blocks, although tooled to have the ground rise
behind them nearly to their tops, were not dressed to rest on the
ground in front, nor would it have been practical to have the names
and the separating lines between the seats beneath the feet of the
spectators. As in the present theater, such indications should be
directly on the faces or upper edges of the seats themselves. The two
northernmost wall blocks of the drain are second-hand upright poros
blocks, 0.655 m. high, one likewise inscribed and showing lines of
demarcation; but for these no reasonable interpretation has been suggested. It is to be noted that the faces must originally have been buried
in the ground for about one third of the height, and that the lines
of demarcation and the letters are near the top, the individual spaces
apparently less commodious and the letters smaller, seemingly for
persons of lesser rank *([ὑπηρ]ετόν)*. The latter inscription recalls
another inscribed poros block, cut down to a height of 0.44 m. and
used upside down at the southwest corner of the present auditorium
wall (A = wA), with the letters *βολῆς ὑπηρετόν* (*IG*, 1² 879), but
probably once part of the same series. The letters on this last block,
with the Ionic lambda and eta, appear to be of the very late fifth century, awkwardly cut as if the scribe had worked under difficulties;
and those in the drain, though preserving no distinctive Ionic letters,
are probably of the same period.

Keeping in mind these differences between the two series of blocks,
it is easy to understand how they were employed (fig. 3). The flat
slabs were the actual seats of the first row, the proedria. The upright
slabs supported the seats of the second row; and since the seats were
here of movable planks, the names had to be inscribed on the stone
just below. Since wooden planks were of necessity straight *(ὀρθά)*,
their stone supports and likewise the lowest row of stone seats had to
be straight. The upper rows would have consisted merely of separate
stones imbedded in earth, for supporting movable planks, the *ikria*
upon which sat the audience whom Aristophanes pitied, in 410 B. C.
(*Thesmophoriazousai*, 395), for being obliged to add to their physical
discomfort by listening to Euripides. The wedge-shaped kerkides
were thus described about the 25.48 m. (78 D.F.) circle in the form

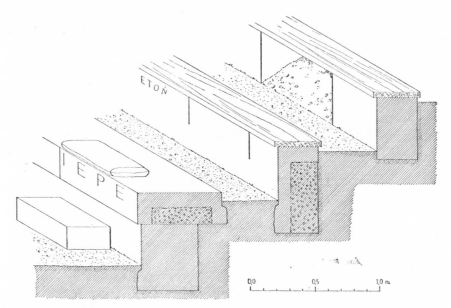

Figure 3. Seating arrangement in the Theater of Nicias.

of a polygon; and since we have no evidence of obtuse angles at the ends of the rows, we may assume that the rows of seats were square-ended, in the most natural manner, with the adjustment made in the intervening radiating aisles. Thus the auditorium, while literally polygonal as required by the material, was essentially circular, being tangential to a circle; and the orchestra would have been regarded as a circle.

Such would have been the scheme of the earliest formal auditorium, the central feature of the late fifth-century theater of which the date now remains to be determined. The evidence of the dramas, as reviewed by Bethe, led him to infer that important changes in methods of production occurred in 427 or 426 B. C. (the date adopted in 1914 by Fiechter for the present scene building foundations and the stoa) ; but such changes in production may well have been, not the results of the new plan, but the motives which dictated the reconstruction. On the other hand, the inscribed seat blocks imply that the erection occurred before the official adoption of the Ionic alphabet (403/2), and probably during the transitional stage of the alphabet some years earlier. Between these limits, the archaeological evidence suggests that the theater was erected simultaneously, despite the absence of parallelism, with the New Temple of Dionysus which is so plausibly attributed to Nicias (421-415). Thus it might well have been completed in 415 B. C., at the very moment when Aristophanes was writing the *Birds*, parodying the great schemes then permeating the air; perhaps we can imagine that Meton the astronomer was made to demonstrate his quackery on the auditorium itself:[26]

> "Applying here my flexible rod, and fixing
> My compass here,—you understand?
>
>   I don't.
>
> With the straight rod I measure out, that so
> The circle may be squared . . . just as from
> A star, though circular, straight rays flash out
> In all directions."

Our picture of the theater of Nicias is completed by its eastern neighbor, the odeum of Pericles, the conjunction of the two enabling us to visualize a memorable scene of the same year, when "Diocleides bent on wreaking harm" testified that on the night of June 7, 415 B. C., "he saw a number of men descending from the odeum into the orchestra. Feeling suspicious of them, he retired into the darkness and sat down between a column and a pedestal. . . . . From that position he saw that the men were fully three hundred in number. . . . He gave a list of those whom he claimed to have recognized, fifty-two in number. 'How did you recognize the faces of the Hermae-mutilators?' 'By the light of the moon.' But there was no moon at all when the deed was done."[27]

---

26. Aristophanes, *Birds*, 1002-1009 (trans. Rogers).

27. Phrynichus, ed. Kock, *Com. Att. Frag.* I, 385; Plutarch, *Alcibiades*, 20; Andocides, I, 37-38, 43. For the date see Dinsmoor, *Archons*, 337-338.

THE POROS TRIPODS OF THE ACROPOLIS OF ATHENS[1]

GORHAM PHILLIPS STEVENS
American School of Classical Studies, Athens, Greece

Plate 12

During the excavation of the Acropolis of Athens by the Greek Government in 1885 to 1890, ten poros blocks, all of about the same dimensions, came to light. As could be seen from their triangular shapes, from the small variations in their dimensions, and also from their cuttings for metal members, there was no doubt in the minds of the excavators, but that the blocks originally belonged to a series of fairly similar tripods. Six of the blocks were found built into the foundations of the south wall of the Acropolis, near the southwest corner of the Chalkotheke. There they still are, but buried so completely that they cannot be examined without a considerable amount of excavating. The four remaining blocks can, however, be readily studied. One block is built into the foundation of the north wall of the Acropolis, on the inside of the wall. The block is west of the House of the Kori, in a hole which the excavators of the Acropolis purposely left so that archaeologists might examine the interesting blocks which, at this point, make up the foundation of the wall. The tripod block in question was cut down somewhat to agree with the height of the course into which it was built. The block is so damaged, however, that it gives little information beyond the fact that it belonged to a tripod which must have antedated the Acropolis wall. Two other blocks of the series are about midway between the block just mentioned and the base of the Promachos. They fit each other (pl. 12, b). The fourth block is at the south end of the large flight of steps to the west of the Parthenon (pl. 12, c). The triangular plan of this block is larger than that of the blocks mentioned. But of special interest is the fact that the top of this block is cut to receive the bowl of a tripod (cf. pl. 12, c).

As the north wall of the Acropolis was erected shortly after the Persian sack of 480 B. C., we may be certain that the block built into the wall belonged to a tripod destroyed by the Persians. And we may say the same of the six blocks still in the south wall of the Acropolis. Further, we may claim the same for the three blocks represented in plates 12, b, c because of their similarity to the blocks built into the

---

1. The writer wishes to thank the Greek scholars in charge of the Acropolis, Mr. J. Threpsiades and Mr. N. Kotzias, for granting him permission to study the poros blocks, and for lending Acropolis workmen for turning the blocks over.

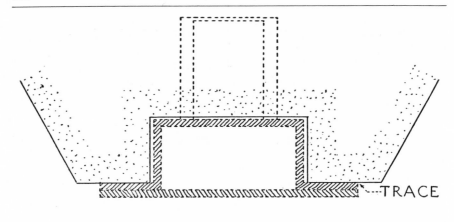

Fig. 1. Trace of overlap of metal leg upon the lower poros block of plate 12, b.

Acropolis walls. Thus we can assert that all the triangular blocks antedate the Persian sack of the Acropolis.

The poros stone used for the blocks is fine grained, has no fossils, and is yellowish straw in color. Traces of stucco appear on the blocks of plate a. The stucco is about as thin as a sheet of paper. The stucco may have been colored a uniform tint or even decorated with painted figures. Fine grained poros covered with color stucco is characteristic of Athenian works in poros—both architecture and sculpture—in the period before the Persian sack.

There are traces, in two places on the blocks of place 12, b, of the overlapping of a metal leg of the tripod (cf. fig. 1).

In 1908 Kawerau, one of the excavators of the Acropolis, published an article about the blocks.[2] He gives a restoration of the tripod which he supposed went with the block with the bowl shaped cutting. But his restoration is not satisfying, for the legs of his tripod are vertical, while the slots into which the legs were fitted and doweled are considerably inclined inward—tripods with legs inward are not uncommon.[3]

In attempting restorations of the tripods, we may proceed as follows:

2. *AM* 33 (1908) 273-278. Professor Rhys Carpenter kindly supplied the writer with this reference.
3. Compare *Olympia*, IV, pl. XLIX. Even more to the point are the archaic tripods with solid supports, which are sheathed with decorated bronze plates—the legs of these are invariably inclined inward (cf. *Olympia*, IV, pl. XXXVIII and the text going with the plate).

1. The visible metal portions of the tripods, following pre-Persian precedent, were of bronze.

2. Consider the two blocks which fit each other (cf. pl. 12, b and fig. 2, A). The top of the upper block is roughly dressed—it was cut down so that the block could be re-used (perhaps somewhere in the Acropolis wall). The writer believes that the top of this block was

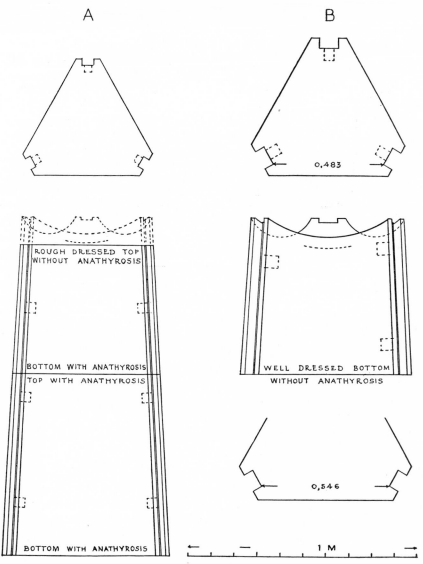

Fig. 2. Poros blocks of plate 12, b, c drawn to scale.

originally cut to receive a bowl, like the block shown in plate 12, c.
If this was the fact, comparatively little cutting would be needed to
dress the top of the block into a horizontal plane.

There is anathyrosis between the two blocks of plate 12, b—in both
the upper and lower blocks (cf. also fig. 2, A).

There is anathyrosis in the bottom of the bottom block of plate
12, b, an indication that there was a block beneath—apparently the
pedestal was composed of at least three blocks (cf. fig. 2, A). The
nature and the height of the third block is, of course, unknown. A
likely guess for the function of the third block is that the block was

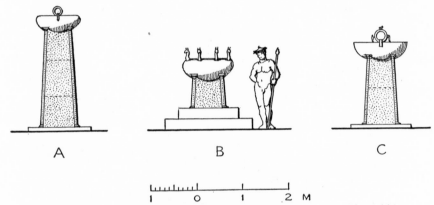

Fig. 3. Restoration of the tripods: with pedestals of three blocs (A),
one block (B), two blocks (C).

needed to elevate the bowl of the tripod for some specific reason. The
third block probably did not greatly differ in height from the blocks
above it. The restoration of the tripod thus becomes somewhat like
that shown in figure 3, A. In the drawing the monument seems high,
but if the tripod were surrounded by other votive offerings, an elevated
tripod would be a requirement.

3. Consider the block with the cutting for the bowl (cf. pl. 12, c).
The bottom is well dressed and has no anathyrosis (cf. fig. 2, B). The
pedestal may, therefore, have had but one block (cf. fig. 3, B).

4. When we remember that there were at least ten of the poros
blocks, possibly more, a type of restoration with a two block pedestal
cannot be excluded (cf. fig. 3, C).

Thus we see that, on the Acropolis of Athens, there was a series of
pre-Persian tripods with poros pedestals, varying from each other
in height. From the variation in height we deduce that the tripods

were not placed side by side. From the number of the tripods we gather that the type—a core of poros which gave solidity to the tripods and brought their centers of gravity so low that the highest winds even of the Acropolis could not overturn them—was popular on the Acropolis before the Persian sack of 480 B. C.[4]

4. For an important architectural inscription giving complete details for erecting tripod bases cf. David M. Robinson, *AJP* 28 (1907) 425-430.

IMMORTALITY

On Pentelicus Immortality
Sprang into life one rosy morn;
A gentle shepherdess came down the mountain
Through the Attic plain,
Seeking Athens, the violet-crowned.

Wherever she trod—there were jewel-bright flowers!
Pheidias, Ictinus, hastened to gather them,
To weave them in garlands, shining, glorious,
To offer their sovereign, radiant Beauty.

These are the Parthenons and Erechtheums;
Sceptres that Hellas holds, crowns that she wears.

Soteris Skipis

Translated by
John B. Edwards

"IDAEISCHE GROTTE" IN OLYMPIA?

Roland Hampe
Mainz

Tafeln 13-14

Σωτὴρ ὑψινεφὲς Ζεῦ, Κρόνιόν τε ναίων λόφον
τιμῶν τ' Ἀλφεὸν εὐρὺ ῥέοντα Ἰδαῖόν τε σεμνὸν ἄντρον
Pindar, *Ol.* V, 17f.

Diese Stelle des fünften, dem Pindar zugeschriebenen Siegesliedes ist nicht von allen antiken Erklärern auf die Idäische Grotte in Kreta bezogen worden. Die alten Scholien führen vielmehr drei Erklärungen an: Die eines Demetrios von Skepsis, der im 2. Jh. v.Chr. einen "Troikos diakosmos" in 30 Büchern verfaßte, wo er auch auf die gottesdienstlichen Verhältnisse in Elis zu sprechen kam. Dieser Demetrios setzte die im Gedicht erwähnte Grotte anscheinend in Elis an. Andere antike Interpreten haben dieser Ansicht widersprochen und nahmen an, der Dichter habe vielmehr die bekannte Idäische Grotte auf Kreta im Sinn gehabt. Ein Erklärer setzte sie sogar auf dem Ida in der Troas an.[1] Die Ansicht des Demetrios wurde von manchen neueren Pindarinterpreten übernommen,[2] von anderen verworfen.[3] Die Ausgrabungen in Olympia gaben dieser Frage neuen Auftrieb. Bei dem Bestreben, die antike Ueberlieferung mit den gefundenen Denkmalsresten in Uebereinstimmung zu bringen, stieß man wieder auf die angebliche "Idäische Grotte" in Elis. Die Erwähnung in einem olympischen Siegeslied, die Nennung neben Kronoshügel und Alpheios schienen für eine Ansetzung im olympischen Heiligtum zu sprechen und die Ansicht des Demetrios zu bestätigen. Es war nicht so, daß man in Olympia auf eine einwandfreie natürliche Grotte gestoßen wäre, die man nun hätte identifizieren müssen. Kronoshügel und Landschaft von Olympia sind vielmehr zur Grottenbildung denkbar ungeeignet.[4] Man konnte darum allenfalls an eine künstliche Grottenanlage denken und suchte sie unter den gefundenen Bauresten ausfindig zu machen. Bei dieser Fahndung nach einer Grotte in Olympia, welche a priori unwahrscheinlich und de facto nicht vorhanden war, verfiel man zunächst auf eine Notlösung: Man

---

1. Schol. vet. in *Pindari carmina*, ed. Drachmann, S. 149ff.
2. Zuerst von Boeckh, expl. Pind. p. 140ff.
3. Zuerst von Welcker, *Gr. Götterlehre* II 241.
4. Hierauf verwies schon Welcker, *Tagebuch e. gr. Reise* I 283ff. ". . . . keine Grottenbildung vorhanden, nur künstlich möglich. . . ." R. Menge bei L. Weniger, Olympische Forschungen *Klio* 7 (1907) S. 156, 5.

setzte den von Pausanias VI 20, 2 überlieferten Doppeltempel der
Eileithyia und des Sosipolis mit der "Idäischen Grotte" gleich und
nahm hierfür das winzige, schatzhausartige Gebäude unmittelbar
westlich des Sikyonierschatzhauses in Anspruch (Abb. 1 u. Taf. 13a).[5]
Den Grottencharakter erblickte man darin, daß an der Rückwand
dieses kleinen Gebäudes, das sich an den Hang des Kronoshügels

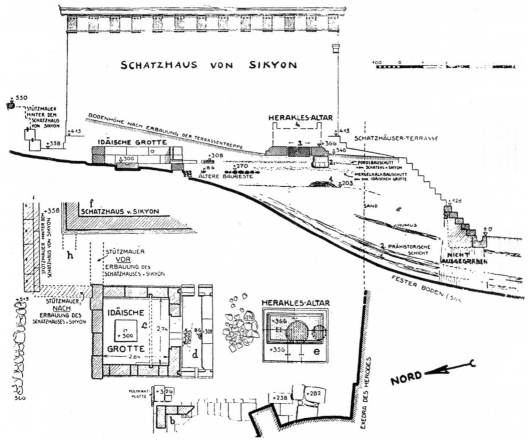

Abb. 1. Idäische Grotte in Olympia.

lehnte, der Werkzoll stehen geblieben war. Man mußte dabei annehmen, Pausanias habe sich "inkorrekt und mißverständlich" ausgedrückt, sich "in Bezug auf die Himmelsrichtung getäuscht." Man
konstruierte: der von Pausanias ausdrücklich als "einheimischer
Dämon" bezeichnete Sosipolis sei "eine Hypostase des Zeuskindes oder

---

5. Zuerst C. Robert, *Sosipolis in Olympia* AM 18 (1893) 37ff.; Weitere Lit.
RE. 35 (1939) 117 Nr. 8.

richtiger das Zeuskind selbst."[6] Man mußte darüber hinweggehen,
daß die von Pausanias geschilderte Kulthandlung in dem winzigen,
durch eine Schranke auch noch zweigeteilten Raum des kleinen
Häuschens unmöglich Platz finden konnte.[7] Ja, man ging so weit,
um den von Pausanias (VI 20, 3) erwähnten ναός der Eileithyia und
des Sosipolis mit dem archäologischen Befund in Einklang zu bringen,
ναός für synonym mit ἱερόν zu erklären.[8] Zustimmung und Widerspruch haben sich zum Worte gemeldet, bis Dörpfeld den Nachweis
erbrachte, daß das fragliche kleine Gebäude zur Zeit des Pausanias
längst unter der Erde lag, von ihm also nicht mehr gesehen und als
Tempel der Eileithyia und des Sosipolis beschrieben werden konnte
(*Alt-Olympia*, im ff. = *AO.*, 26-38 u. ö.).

Nach dem Grundsatz "semper aliquid haeret" blieb aber die Bezeichnung "Idäische Grotte" nun an dem kleinen Gebäude neben dem
Sikyonierschatzhaus haften. Seit Dörpfeld diese Benennung in *"Alt-
Olympia"* nicht nur im Text zu begründen suchte, sondern unbedenk-
lich auch in die Pläne übernahm, hat sie sich als scheinbar fest er-
wiesener Bestand eingebürgert. Man vergaß darüber, daß die Deutung der Pindarstelle auf eine Idäische Grotte in Olympia keineswegs
gesichert ist, somit auch die Bezeichnung "Grottenbau" bzw. "Idäische
Grotte" für den kleinen Bau neben dem Sikyonierschatzhaus auf
unsicheren Füßen steht.

Angesichts dieses Sachverhaltes gilt es, die philologischen und
archäologischen Grundlagen für diese Benennung nochmals zu überprüfen. Die einzige literarische Quelle, auf die man sich allenfalls
berufen kann, ist Pindar *Ol.* V. 17f. Dies Epinikion war in den ältesten
Sammlungen pindarischer Gedichte nicht enthalten, wurde erst nachträglich eingereiht. Aristarch hat es im 2. Jh. v.Chr. schon besprochen. Es ist, wenn auch vielleicht nicht von Pindar selbst verfaßt,
so doch als Schöpfung eines zeitgenössischen Dichters anerkannt
und darf daher als Zeugnis der pindarischen Zeit gelten. Von den
späteren Erklärern hat, nach unserer Kenntnis, nur Demetrios von
Skepsis, ein Zeitgenosse Aristarchs, die im Gedicht erwähnte Idäische
Grotte in Elis lokalisiert. Die anderen hielten sie für die auf Kreta,
einer setzte sie auf dem Ida in der Troas an, wo eine solche Grotte
ebensowenig wie in Elis sonst je überliefert ist. Stünde im pindarischen Epinikion lediglich Ἰδαῖον σεμνὸν ἄντρον, so würde kein
antiker und auch kein moderner Interpret diese Grotte anderswo
gesucht haben als auf dem kretischen Ida, dessen weiträumige Zeus-

---

6. S. Robert a.O.; dagegen richtig L. Ziehen *RE*. 35 (1939) 54ff.
7. Dies suchte vor allem E. Pfuhl *JdI* 21 (1906) 151ff. nachzuweisen. Dörpfeld
hat dies *Alt-Olympia* 109ff. widerlegt.
8. C. Robert *a.O.* 44ff.

grotte, wie die Fülle der ausgegrabenen Weihgeschenke lehrt,[9] eine
große Berühmtheit erlangt hatte. Da aber hier "Zeus, der auf dem
Kronoshügel wohnt," angerufen wird, welcher "sowohl den breit
strömenden Alpheios als die ehrwürdige Idäische Grotte ehrt," war
man versucht, auch diese in Olympia anzusetzen. Aber gerade die
Gegenüberstellung mit dem "Alpheios" macht eine solche Erklärung
unwahrscheinlich; denn der Alpheios wird bei Pindar und Bakchylides
oft erwähnt. Diese Erwähnungen haben wir zu überprüfen. Außer
Betracht lassen können wir hier die Stellen, wo etwa der Oberlauf
des Flusses Alpheios Ol. VI 34 58) gemeint ist oder der Flußgott
selbst, der auf der Insel Ortygia in Syrakus den Rastplatz fand
(N I, 1). Der Flußgott wird auch da gemeint sein, wo der Sage nach
Herakles die Altis absteckt und den Kult des Alpheios zugleich mit
dem der zwölf Götter stiftet (Ol. X, 48);[10] den Flußgott, dem ja beim
Fest in Olympia Opfergaben in die Flut gespendet wurden,[11] meint
wohl auch Bakchylides mit seinem Anruf: "Besinge Zeus, den Kroni-
den und den ἀκαμαντορόαν Ἀλφεόν und die Kraft des Pelops und
Pisa," von wo das Rennpferd Pherenikos einen Sieg nach Syrakus
brachte (5, 180). An drei Stellen, bei Erwähnung des Pelopsgrabes,
das am Alpheiosfluß liegt (Ol. I, 92), bei der Einsetzung des fünf-
jährig wiederkehrenden Festes durch Herakles "an den gotterfüllten
Hängen des Alpheios" (Ol, III, 22) und bei dem Anruf "O Pisas baum-
schöner Hain am Alpheios" kann tatsächlich der Flußlauf gemeint
sein. Aber es scheint auch hier schon etwas anderes mitzuschwingen,
was die übrigen, häufigen Erwähnungen des Alpheios kennzeichnet:
Dort wird der Alpheios nicht um seiner selbst willen, sondern als
Umschreibung für das Heiligtum von Olympia und die Olympischen
Spiele gebraucht. So wird bei einem Olympiasieger daran erinnert,
es liege noch von seinem Vater her" die glanzvolle Kunde von seinen
schnellen Füßen ἐπ' Ἀλφεοῦ ῥεέθροισιν Ol. XIII, 35). Oder es wird
ein Knabensieger gepriesen, der mit seinen Füßen siegend Ruhm
erlangte ἐπ' Ἀλφεοῦ προχοαῖσι (Bakch. 6, 3) d.h. in den olympischen Spielen. Einem isthmischen Wagensieger wünscht Pindar, es
möge ihm vergönnt sein, "auch noch von Pytho und aus den Olympien
mit ἐξαιρέταις Ἀλφεοῦ ἔρνεσιν den Arm zu umwinden (I. 1, 65),
wobei die "auserlesenen Reiser des Alpheios" eine Umschreibung für
die olympischen Siegeszweige sind. Pindar Ol. I, 20) und Bakchylides
(fr. 20 C 9 Snell) preisen den Sieg des Rennpferdes Pherenikos "am
Alpheios," d.h. in den olympischen Spielen. Noch deutlicher wird dies
in den Fällen, wo der Wettkampf 'am Alpheios' anderen panhelleni-

---

9. RE. 9 "Ida" 867ff.
10. Vgl. hierzu RE. 35 (1939) 54.
11. Vgl. RE. 35 (1939) 51.

schen Wettkämpfen gegenübergestellt wird. Die Stadt Opus "prangt
in Siegen an deiner, Kastalia, und des Alpheios Flut" (*Ol.* IX, 18),
d.h. in pythischen und olympischen Siegen. Der Faustkämpfer
Diagoras wird gepriesen, weil er "am Alpheios" und "an der Kastalia"
bekränzt wurde (*Ol.* VIII, 15), d.h. in Pytho und Olympia, wie ausdrücklich bestätigt wird: "Bringe eine Spende denen, die zu Olympia
und Pytho gesiegt" (v. 10). Bakchylides feiert den Sieg des Rennpferdes Pherenikos ᾿Αλφεὸν παρ᾿ εὐρυδίναν dem ein Sieg in Pytho
gegenübergestellt wird (5, 38; vgl. 3, 7). Ein Sieger hat zum ersten
Male Zweige errungen ἐπ᾿ ᾿Αλφεοῦ, während er schon fünfmal am
Isthmos bekränzt wurde (*N* VI, 18). Bei Bakchylides werden (8, 27;
11, 26; 13, 192) Siege am Alpheios solchen in Pytho, Nemea, am
Isthmos konfrontiert. Wie die Kastalia für Pytho und die pythischen
Spiele, so steht auch der Alpheios in allen diesen Fällen stellvertretend
für Olympia als Heiligtum und Stätte der olympischen Spiele. In
diesem umschreibenden Sinne werden wir auch den "breit strömenden
Alpheios" an der fraglichen Stelle *Ol.* V, 18) aufzufassen haben.
Bedeutet aber hier der Alpheios das olympische Heiligtum als Ganzes,
so kann die gleichwertig daneben genannte "Idäische Grotte" nicht
eine Lokalität innerhalb dieses Heiligtums sein; vielmehr werden
zwei berühmte Zeus-Heiligtümer einander gegenübergestellt, das in
Olympia und das auf dem kretischen Ida. Daß hier "Zeus Soter, der
auf dem Kronion wohnt" angerufen wird, beweist keineswegs, daß
die im folgenden genannte "Idäische Grotte" auch in Olympia zu
suchen wäre. So heißt es etwa *Ol.* II, 13ff.: "O Kronide, Sohn der Rhea
(Anspielung auf den kretischen Geburtsmythos), der du herrschest
über den Sitz des Olympos (in Thessalien) und den Sieg in den Kampf-
spielen (wohl allgemein zu fassen) und den 'Fluß Alpheios' (stellvertretend für Olympia und die dortigen Spiele), freue dich an den Ge-
sängen."[12]

Die philologische Ueberprüfung unserer Pindarstelle ergibt also,
daß man aus dem Wortlaut (*Ol.* V, 18) nicht auf eine Grotte in
Olympia, die auch sonst nirgends bezeugt ist, schließen würde — es
sei denn, daß in Olympia ein so grottenähnliches Gebäude gefunden
worden wäre, daß kein anderer Ausweg bliebe als — gegen die
philologische Wahrscheinlichkeit — die Pindarstelle auf dies Bauwerk
zu beziehen. Trifft dies für das kleine schatzhausartige Gebäude neben
dem Sikyonierschatzhaus zu, das Dörpfeld "Kapelle, kleinen kapellen-

---

12. Boeckh und Welcker wollten in den Nennung der "Idäischen Grotte" eine
Anspielung auf kretische Abstammung des Siegers Psaumis aus Kamarina er-
blicken. Kamarina war gerade von Geloern neu besiedelt. Gela selbst aber war
eine Gründung von Kretern (vgl. Welcker, *Gr. Götterlehre* II 241; Weniger, *Klio* 7
[1907] 155ff.). Da jedoch diese Abstammung nicht erwiesen ist, kann sie hier als
Beweismittel nicht verwendet werden.

artigen Bau, kapellenartigen Bau, kapellenartigen Grottenbau, Grottenbau, Grotte, Idäische Grotte" nennt (*AO.* 108ff.)?

Dörpfeld spricht (*AO.* 67) von der "Idäischen Grotte" in Olympia als einem "der berühmten, am kretischen Ida gelegenen Höhle nachgebildeten Heiligtum." Er verweist zwar (*AO.* 69) auf den Größenunterschied; aber in "Olympia wird eine kleinere, mehr künstliche Grotte angelegt." Die Idäische Grotte auf dem Ida in Kreta hat einen Vorraum im Freien mit einen großen, viereckigen Brandopferaltar, der aus dem anstehenden Fels gehauen ist. Die Grotte ist eine Naturgrotte. Der vordere Raum ist 25-31 m breit und sehr hoch. Der hintere Raum ist 22 m lang, 12 m breit, 4 m hoch. Die Grotte auf dem Ida hat also kolossale Ausmaße. Der kleine künstliche Bau in Olympia hatte mit der großen Naturhöhle keinerlei Aehnlichkeit. Ein kleiner tempelartiger Bau von 2,74 Breite und 2,84 Länge mit einer schmalen Vorhalle (Abb. 1 u. Taf. 13). Die Wände bestehen aus regelmäßigen, verschieden langen Quadern aus Mergelkalk von 0,50 Dicke. Die Quadern sind weder durch Klammern noch durch Dübel miteinander verbunden, die Anschlußflächen so gearbeitet, daß sich die Steine nur mit einer schmalen Kante berühren, eine Bauweise, die an die des jüngeren Heraion erinnert (*AO.* 109). Ebenso weist die in der Südwand befindliche Türöffnung Einarbeitungen zur Einlassung von Holzfassungen auf, wie sie in ähnlicher Weise bei den Parastaden des Heraion vorkommen. Im Inneren der kleinen Cella liegt noch der Unterstein für eine fast quadratische Basis von 0,91 Breite und 0,97 Tiefe, die sich etwas über den Kalk-Estrich des Fußbodens erhob. Zwischen Türwand und Basis war die Cella durch eine Schranke abgeteilt, die aus wagrechten, in die Seitenwände eingeschobenen, leicht entfernbaren Holzbalken bestand. Brandspuren um eines der Einlaßlöcher ließen vermuten, daß sie durch Feuer zerstört wurde. Die einstige hölzerne Tür der Kapelle war gegen die Einflüsse der Witterung durch eine Vorhalle geschützt. Diese Vorhalle war ursprünglich tiefer und wurde später verkürzt, was früher (Ol. II 45) noch nicht erkannt worden war. In der jüngeren Phase war diese Vorhalle 1,32-1,38 tief. Um wieviel tiefer die ältere Vorhalle war, ist nicht sicher auszumachen. In dem aus Mergelkalk bestehenden Bauschutt, der von der Errichtung dieses Bauwerkes herrührt, fand sich der Rest eines gebogenen, auf der konkaven Seite mit schwarzem Firnis überzogenen Dachziegels, der in seiner Machart an die Heraionziegel erinnert. Vielleicht war also das Gebäude mit solchen Ziegeln eingedeckt (*AO.* 110).

Bei der *zeitlichen Ansetzung* dieses kleinen Gebäudes, können wir die von Dörpfeld genannten absoluten Daten außer Acht lassen und

müssen uns an die von ihm aufgeführten Datierungsmerkmale halten:
"Unter dem 'Grottenbau' selbst steht der feste Sandboden an" (*AO.*
115). Er war, wie auch zum großen Teil die Fundamente des Heraion
(*AO.* 138) ein wenig in den Berghang eingeschnitten. Die untersten
Quaderschichten der Rückwand und der Seiten ruhten ohne Funda-
mentierung auf dem Sandboden auf. Dies gilt vermutlich auch für
die Türwand,[13] nicht aber für die Vorhalle. Sie ruht nicht auf ge-
wachsenem Boden. Bei Tiefgrabungen unter ihr fanden sich "eine
Bronzeschale und ein Stück einer eisernen Speerspitze . . . . ferner
Teile von Tieren aus Ton und Bronze und auch mehrere Scherben mit
Firnisüberzug" (*AO.* 116). Leider sind diese Fundstücke, zumal die
Bronzeschale und die Scherben, nicht mit abgebildet. Immerhin
widerrät dieser Befund einer Datierung vor dem 7. Jh. Andererseits
muß unser Gebäude seiner Fundtiefe wegen ein gut Teil älter sein als
das jüngere Schatzhaus von Sikyon, also vor dem 5. Jh. Innerhalb
dieses Rahmens wird man infolge der oben angeführten Aehnlich-
keiten mit der Bautechnik des jüngeren Heraion am ehesten in das
späte 7. oder das frühe 6. Jh. gehen.[14] Der Mergelkalk, aus dem das
sehr gut gebaute Mauerwerk besteht, ist nur wenig verwittert (*AO.*
40) was darauf schließen läßt, daß das Bauwerk nicht sehr lange Zeit
der Witterung ausgesetzt war.

Nun zur *Deutung* des kleinen Gebäudes: "Als das Gebäude bei den
Ausgrabungen zum Vorschein kam, glaubten wir zuerst, dasselbe für
eines der Schatzhäuser halten zu müssen, weil es ihren Grundriß hatte,
und auch mit ihnen in einer Reihe lag" (*Ol.* II, 1892, 45). Man
nannte aber das "kleine . . . . tempelartige Gebäude" darum nicht
Schatzhaus, weil Pausanias als erstes Schatzhaus das der Sikyonier
nennt, dieses aber inschriftlich gesichert ist. (*Ol.* I, 1897, 75.) Damals
war noch nicht erkannt, daß das kleine tempelartige Gebäude zu des
Pausanias Zeit schon längst unter der Erde lag (*AO.* 26. 38). Wäre
dies damals schon ganz klar gewesen, wäre vermutlich niemand auf
den Gedanken einer Idäischen Grotte in Olympia gekommen. So
aber mußte man nach einem Grottenbau Umschau halten. Womit
suchte man nun den Grottencharakter des Bauwerkes und die Deutung
auf eine Idäische Grotte zu erweisen?

1. Während die Quadern des Bauwerkes innen sorgfältig geglättet
sind, ist an den Außenwänden ein feiner, an der Rückwand — nament-

---

13. Unter der Türwand fanden sich um 40 cm nach S verschoben Fundamentreste aus kleinen runden Steinen, deren Zugehörigkeit zum "Grottenbau" nicht
ganz sicher ist. Wenn Dörpfeld sie zu "einer älteren Grottenanlage" zählt (*AO*
115), so ist dies äußerst kühn, zumal er selbst angibt, daß unter dem Grottenbau
der feste Sandboden ansteht.

14. Helen E. Searls — W. B. Dinsmoor "The date of the Olympia Heraeum"
AJA 49 (1945) S. 62ff.; Yavis, *Greek Altars*, 1949, S. 69, 120-121.

lich an den Ecken — ein dicker und rauher Werkzoll stehen geblieben, der darauf schließen läßt, daß "der Bau hier nie sichtbar gewesen sein kann." "Er war vielmehr wie ein Grottenbau in den festen Boden des Berges gleichsam hineingebaut" (*AO.* 109). Gewiß, das kleine Gebäude lehnte sich an den Berghang an, war nicht rings umgehbar, wie das Sikyonierschatzhaus. Seine Quadern ruhten auf keinem

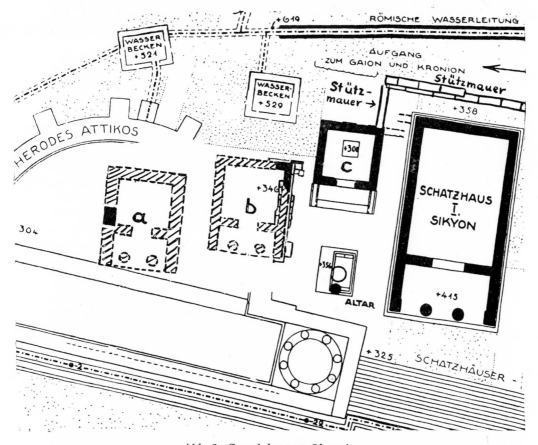

Abb. 2. Grundplan von Olympia.

Stufenunterbau sondern lagen direkt im Sandboden. Nur diese untersten Quaderschichten sind erhalten. Sie tragen an den Seitenwänden noch den feinen, an den hinteren Ecken einen groben Werkzoll. Im Süden lag die unterste Quaderschicht im Boden. Nach Norden stieg das Gelände an. Dort war vermutlich nicht nur die unterste, sondern auch die nächsthöhere Quaderschicht noch vom Sand bedeckt (vgl. Abb 1). Wie die höheren, aus dem Erdreich hervorragenden Quaderschichten bearbeitet waren, wissen wir nicht. Sie sind ja nicht erhalten. Sollen wir annehmen, daß Rück- und Seitenwände vom Erdreich bedeckt waren, um ein grottenartiges Gebilde vorzutäuschen? Diese Frage kann nach den Beobachtungen von Dörpfeld-Schleif klar verneint werden (*AO*. 111, u. Taf. 7). Die Ausgräber nahmen eine von der NO-Ecke des Grottenbaues abgehende "Stützmauer *vor* Erbauung des Schatzhauses von Sikyon" an (gemeint ist das jüngere Sikyonierschatzhaus; die Geschichte des älteren darunter liegenden und damit dessen Verhältnis zur sogenannten Idäischen Grotte ist noch ungeklärt). Anschlußflächen an der NO- und NW-Ecke des Schatzhauses zeigen, daß hier Stützmauern geplant waren (*AO*. Taf. 7 h; hier Abb. 1 u. 2). Ob sie tatsächlich ausgeführt wurden, ist ungewiß. Sicher ausgeführt wurde aber die "Stützmauer hinter dem Schatzhaus von Sikyon," von der zwei Schichten erhalten sind, eine dritte durch Dübellöcher gesichert. Von ihrem W-Ende führte eine Verbindungsmauer zur rückwärtigen NO-Ecke der "Idäischen Grotte." Dieser Befund lehrt eindeutig, daß mindestens die östliche Seitenwand der sogenannten Grotte nicht von Erde bedeckt war. Man suchte also nicht einen grottenartigen Charakter vorzutäuschen, sondern gerade im Gegenteil durch Errichtung von Stützmauern diesen Charakter möglichst zu vermeiden.

2. Dörpfeld erklärt, daß der in der Cella liegende Unterstein "sicher einst eine Basis für ein Kultbild getragen hat" (*AO*. 109). Dies ist indessen keineswegs sicher; Pausanias zählt VI 19 die zu seiner Zeit noch bestehenden Schatzhäuser in Olympia auf. Mehrere Schatzhäuser bargen im Innern außer sonstigen Weihgeschenken Standbilder, die zum Teil Götterbilder (nicht aber Kultbilder) waren. Im Schatzhaus IX von Selinunt ist die Basis noch in situ. Sie trug vermutlich das von Pausanias dort gesehene Dionysosbild. Im Schatzhaus von Gela befand sich, wie die neueren Untersuchungen geklärt haben,[15] die größte Basis von Olympia nach der des Zeustempels. Sie trug einst Götterbilder (nicht Kultbilder), die Pausanias schon nicht mehr sah. Die Basis in der Cella des "Grottenbaues" kann also sehr wohl ein Standbild getragen haben, welches kein Kultbild zu sein brauchte.

3. Dörpfeld hielt den unweit des "Grottenbaus" gelegenen Altar (Abb. 1) für zugehörig, glaubte, mehrere Vorstufen zu erkennen, was ein hohes Alter des Kultes zu erweisen schien (*AO*. 111ff.). Er nannte ihn Altar "des Herakles und der Kureten" (*AO*. 26) bzw. des "kretischen Herakles" (*AO*. 38 76. 107), setzte den Altar des Herakles, welcher den Beinamen "Parastates" trug (Paus. V, 14, 7) mit dem

---

15. H. Schleif — H. K. Süsserott, in *"Olymp. Forschungen"* I (1944) 83ff.

von Pausanias (V, 14, 9) dicht beim Sikyonirschatzhaus erwähnten Altare gleich (*AO*. 39. 46), womit sich der Ring zu schließen schien, indem nun der "Idäische Herakles" seinen Altar vor der "Idäischen Grotte" bekam. — Hiergegen muß entschiedener Einspruch erhoben werden: Pausanias führt (V, 7, 6. 9) eine Gründungslegende der olympischen Spiele an, nach welcher der "Idäische Herakles" mit seinen Brüdern den Daktylen bzw. Kureten zum ersten Male in Olympia Wettkämpfe abgehalten habe. Ihnen sei dann später, 50 Jahre nach der Deukalionischen Flut, vom Kreter Klymenos, einem Nachkommen des Idäischen Herakles, in Olympia ein Altar errichtet worden. Der an diesem Altar verehrte Herakles habe den Beinamen "Parastates" gehabt. Pausanias zählt etwas später die Reihenfolge auf, welche die Eleer bei den Opfern auf den olympischen Altären beobachteten (5. 14, 4ff). Dabei nennt er nochmals den Altar des "Herakles Parastates" und seiner idäischen Brüder (V, 14, 7). Seine Aufzählung ist ausdrücklich *nicht* topographisch (V, 14, 4. 10). Wo der Altar des Herakles Parastates lag, muß demnach offen bleiben. — In Elis hatte Herakles Parastates einen Altar im Gymnasion, etwa auch in Olympia im Gymnasion? — Außer diesem Altar des Herakles Parastates nennt Pausanias in eben dieser Aufzählung der Opfer- ordnung einen anderen Altar "in der Nähe des Schatzhauses der Sikyonier," der "entweder den Kureten oder dem Herakles, dem Sohn der Alkmene," gehörte (V, 14, 9), also entweder den kretischen Kureten *oder* dem thebanischen Herakles. Diesen, wie Dörpfeld tut, mit dem Altar des Herakles Parastates gleichzusetzen, ist ganz un- zulässig, eben weil beide Altäre in der Aufzählung der Opferreihen- folge jeder für sich aufgeführt werden. Bei diesem Altar erfahren wir durch Pausanias ungefähr, wo er lag: "In der Nähe des Sikyonier- schatzhauses." Es liegt nahe, den Altar vor dem "Grottenbau" hierfür in Anspruch zu nehmen. Doch könnte es sich ebenso gut um den Altar westlich des Metroon handeln.[16] Selbst wenn aber von Pausanias der vor dem "Grottenbau" gelegene Altar gemeint sein sollte, so bleibt offen, ob er dem thebanischen Herakles oder den Kureten gehörte. Ueber das Alter des Kultes erfahren wir von Pausanias nichts.

Die Ausgräber hatten sich zunächst so geäußert: "Nun wissen wir zwar nicht, ob der Altar zu unserem Heiligtum gehört, aber bei seiner

---

16. Daß der Altar westlich des Metroon gleichen Anspruch wie der vor dem "Grottenbau" hat, für den des thebanischen Herakles oder der Kureten zu gelten, hat schon Robert *a.O.* 41 ausgesprochen. — Diesen Altar, hinter der Rückssite des Metroon, auf das Metroon zu beziehen, ist eine sehr gewaltsame Lösung. Sie kann nicht damit gerechtfertigt werden, daß vor dem Metroon im O kein Platz gewesen sei, weil dort das Hippodameion gelegen habe wie Weniger *a.O.* 149 annahm; denn weder die genaue Lage noch der Umfang des Hippodameion ist bekannt. Vgl. auch *RE*. 35 (1939) 148, 26; Yavis, *Greek Altars*, S. 180, 209.

Stellung unmittelbar vor dem Eingang, ist die Zugehörigkeit sehr möglich, man kann sogar sagen wahrscheinlich" (*Ol. II,* 1892, 45). Der viereckige Altar liegt zwar vor dem "Grottenbau" aber in anderer Orientierung (Abb. 1). Während sich die Cella des Baues nach S öffnet, liegt die Standplatte des Altars im W, der Priester blickte also beim Opfern nach O. Da der Viereckaltar einen Rundstein umschließt (Taf. 13b), nahm man an, der Rundstein sei ein älterer Rundaltar, der später zu einem viereckigen umgebaut wurde. Hierin wurde man noch mehr bestärkt, als nach der Grabung eine Ecke der viereckigen Platte abfiel (Taf. 14, a) und darunter ein kleinerer Rundstein hervorkam, den Dörpfeld als ältere Altarphase wertete (*AO.* 111ff.). Dörpfeld unterschied nun folgende Perioden (wobei wir wieder die von ihm gegebenen absoluten Daten außer Acht lassen und uns an die Datierungsmerkmale halten) :

1. Frühe Altarstufe, erschlossen aus Humusschicht, welche "gerade unter dem Altar sehr stark war und Opferreste und auch einige vorhistorische Scherben enthielt" (*AO.* 112 Abb. 20; Taf. 7; hier Abb. 1). Hierzu ist anzumerken: Diese Fundschicht ist von den beiden prähistorischen Schichten durch eine 1,50 bis 2,00 m tiefe fundlose Sandschicht getrennt. Sie enthielt unter der Vorhalle des "Grottenbaus" eine Bronzeschale, eine fragmentierte eiserne Speerspitze, Teile von Tieren aus Ton und Bronze, mehrere Scherben mit Firnisüberzug und "weiter südlich," nämlich unter dem Altar, "auch vorhistorische Scherben und Steinwerkzeuge" (*AO.* 116). Es handelt sich also um eine frühgriechische nicht um eine vorhistorische Schicht (diese liegt ja um anderthalb bis zwei Meter tiefer). Sollte es sich bei den vorhistorischen Einsprengseln in dieser Schicht nicht um Stücke handeln, die vom Kronoshügel abgeschwemmt waren? Die Schatzhäuser nützten zunächst eine natürliche Erdwelle am Kronion aus, die erst später künstlich terrassiert wurde. In dieser Erdwelle häuften sich die Schwemmfunde dichter an als am Normalhang. Sollte sich die Funddichte unter Vorhalle und Altar nicht so erklären? Jedenfalls liegt über dieser Fundschicht wieder etwa 50 cm fundloser Sand bis zur Mergelkalkschicht aus der Zeit des "Grottenbaus"; mithin müßte mindestens eine längere Kultpause angenommen werden.

2. Grottenbau aus Mergelkalk, Mergelkalkschicht und Rundaltar aus Mergelkalk (Abb. 1 u. Taf. 13, b). Zeit des jüngeren Heraion, also rund um 600. Hierzu ist anzumerken: Der "Rundaltar" aus Mergelkalk (DM 0,64, Höhe 0,51) ist nur zur Hälfte ausgearbeitet. Die untere rauh gelassene Hälfte steckte nach Dörpfeld in der Erde, (dann hätte der Altar schon bei seiner Errichtung ein höheres Niveau gehabt als die "Grotte"). Dieser Altar müßte nach Dörpfeld sehr

lange in Gebrauch gewesen sein, nämlich von ca. 600 (nach Dörpfeld
ab 7. oder 8. Jh. oder auch noch früher (*AO*. 68) bis ins späte 5. oder
frühe 4. Jh. In dieser Zeit wuchs das Terrain erheblich, endgültig
bei Regulierung der Schatzhausterrasse. Altar 2, der ohnehin nur
ca. 30-35 cm aus dem Boden schaute, müßte in dieser Zeit von Erde
bedeckt worden sein. Ist er wirklich als Altar gesichert? Gibt es in
archaischer Zeit Rundaltärchen dieser simplen Art, ohne Unterplatte?
Sollte es sich nicht um eine unfertige, verworfene Säulentrommel eines
kleineren Gebäudes handeln, welche bei Errichtung des Viereckaltars
als Unterfütterung unter dessen Südseite gelegt wurde? Wir wollen
dies als Frage offen lassen und die nächste Altarphase Dörpfelds näher
prüfen.

3. Rundaltar 3 (Taf. 13, b, u. 14, a) ruht nicht etwa auf dem angeb-
lichen Vorgänger sondern auf Sand, schon fast auf dem Niveau der
regulierten Schatzhausterrasse (Abb. 1). Nach Dörpfeld braucht er
nur wenige Jahre älter sein als das Metroon, kann noch während oder
bald nach der Bauzeit des Metroon in ein Viereck umgeändert worden
sein (*AO*. 114). Im Gegensatz zu Altar 2 hätte dieser Altar 3 also
nur eine sehr kurze Lebensdauer gehabt. Bei der Umänderung in
einen Viereckaltar ist man nicht sehr pietätvoll verfahren. Im Gegenteil: Der Rundstein wurde an der Westseite rigoros abgearbeitet (Taf.
13, b, u. 14, a). Das Material ist Muschelkalk (Poros), dasselbe, was
in sehr verschiedenen Spielarten bei den Säulen des Heraion verwendet wurde (*Ol*. II, 27ff.; *AO*. 165). Der Durchmesser des Rund-
steines beträgt 0,95 bis 0,98 m (*Ol*. II, 164 Nr. 7; *AO*. 112), ein Durchmesser, welcher zu den oberen Durchmessern der Heraionsäulen gut
passen würde (vgl. die Tabelle *AO*. 168). Die Trommelhöhe der
Heraionsäulen schwankt zwischen 0,35 und 1,50 m je nach der Beschaffenheit des Steines, einer Steinart, die infolge ihrer Unregel-
mäßigkeit sehr schwer zu bearbeiten war. Daher wäre durchaus
verständlich, wenn auch bei Herstellung einzelner Säulen (und die
Heraionsäulen wurden ja nach und nach gegen hölzerne ausge-
wechselt) Fehler auftraten, einzelne Werkstücke verworfen wurden.
Könnte es sich bei Porosaltar 3 nicht um eine verworfene Säulentrommel des Heraion handeln? Müßte eine unfertige verworfene
Säulentrommel nicht Hebevorrichtungen aufweisen? Hebebossen
haben sich in Olympia bei Muschelkalkblöcken nirgends nachweisen
lassen.[17] Offenbar war der Muschelkalk dafür zu brüchig. Also
Hebelöcher? Nur die Trommeln der SW-Ecksäule sind in eigen-
artiger Weise zur Aufnahme eines Hebe-Schlüssels durchbohrt. Alle
anderen Trommeln haben ebenso wie die Kapitelle auf der Oberseite

---

17. Vgl. E. Kunze — H. Weber *AJA*. 42 (1948) 495, 12.

keine Hebelöcher (*AO.* 165ff). Die Versetzung der Heraionsäulen hatte ja ganz andere Vorraussetzungen als die sonst üblichen. Hier galt es, bei bestehender und hinderlicher Cellawand, Ringhalle, überkragendem Dach die Säulen unter ein bereits vorhandenes Gebälk unterzuschieben. Ein senkrechtes Herablassen war daher mindestens für die oberen Trommellagen nicht durchführbar. Nur ein seitliches Einschieben, etwa mittels irgendwelcher Rampen, war hier möglich. Daher dürfen wir auch an einer oberen Säulentrommel keine Hebevorrichtungen erwarten.

4. Der Viereckaltar (*Ol.* II, 1892, 164 Nr. 7 Taf. 95, 4 = Weniger, *Klio* 7. 154) ist von den Dörpfeldschen Altarphasen allein gesichert (Abb. 1, u. Taf. 13, 14a). Mit dem Vorbehalt daß eine Nachprüfung in Olympia selbst nicht möglich war, sei hier gegen Dörpfelds Theorie die Gegenthese aufgestellt: Es gab keine verschiedenen Altarphasen sondern nur *einen* Altar, den viereckigen. Eine verworfene, ursprünglich für das Heraion bestimmte, Porostrommel wurde wegen des in Olympia notorischen Steinmangels in diesen Altar verbaut und dabei rücksichtslos abgearbeitet. Die Viereckplatten des Altars wurden mit ⊢⊣-Klammern sorgfältig verklammert, weil man sie fundamentlos auf den Sandboden verlegte und ein Absacken einer der Platten verhindern wollte. Im Süden, wo das Gelände abschüssig war, wurden die Platten unter der Fuge mit einer kleineren, unfertigen Trommel aus Mergelkalk unterfüttert. So sind auch die Schatzhäuser (I, II, IV) an der Südseite sorgfältiger fundamentiert. Wo eine solche Vorsorge nicht getroffen wurde, senkte sich der Bau stark wie bei VII oder klafften die Fundamente nach starker Senkung auseinander wie bei VI. Diente die Mergelkalktrommel wirklich zur Unterfütterung, so würde dies für Anlage des Altars vor der endgültigen Regulierung der Terrasse sprechen, d.h. zu einer Zeit, wo das Gelände dort noch abschüssig war. Ob noch im 5. Jh. oder schon im 4. Jh. ist nicht sicher auszumachen, da die Klammerform eine genauere Datierung nicht zuläßt, nur etwa in diese Zeit weist. Pausanias mag diesen Altar noch gesehen haben. Vielleicht ist es der von ihm V 14, 9 beschriebene der Kureten oder des thebanischen Herakles, keinesfalls der des Herakles Parastates.

Als der Altar errichtet wurde, war das kleine Gebäude neben dem Sikyonierschatzhaus nicht mehr in Gebrauch. Es lag schon seit geraumer Zeit unter dem angewachsenen Niveau der Schatzhausterrasse. Für seine Deutung müssen wir den Weg von der "Idäischen Grotte" über "Grotte, Grottenbau, kapellenartigen Grottenbau, kapellenartigen Bau, kleinen kapellenartigen Bau, Kapelle" zum Schatzhaus zurückfinden. Als solches wollten die Ausgräber dies Gebäude

ursprünglich auch auffassen, wurden aber von dieser Ansicht abge-
bracht, da sie noch nicht wußten, daß dies Gebäude zu des Pausanias
Zeit längst unter dem Boden lag. Die Schatzhausreihe scheint sich in
der Frühzeit nach W in das Gebiet der späteren Exedra fortgesetzt
zu haben. So vermutete schon Lehmann-Hartleben 1927.[18] Die
neueren Ausgräber sind darauf zurückgekommen, wobei sie innerhalb
des Halbrunds der Exedra vorhandene archaische Fundamentreste
mitverwerten.[19] Abb. 2 soll veranschaulichen, wie man sich den W-
·Flügel der Schatzhausreihe in der Frühzeit denken könnte. Das kleine
Schatzhaus neben dem Sikyonierschatzhaus mag in der Zeit des jüngeren Heraion, also etwa rund um 600, errichtet sein. Kleine Schatzhäuser dieser Art gab es auch in Delphi.[20] Auf der Basis im Innern
mag wie in anderen Schatzhäusern ein Weihgeschenk gestanden haben.

Wie noch heute, so schwemmte auch im Altertum der Kronoshügel
nach jedem Regengusse Sand vom Hang herab. Das Niveau im Heiligtum stieg unablässig. In Rücksicht auf diese Sandabschwemmung
mußte man die Fundamente des jüngeren Heraion bereits höher legen.
In römischer Zeit lag aber die nördliche und östliche Ringhalle zum
guten Teile schon wieder unter Sand (*AO.* 161). Die Schatzhäuser
suchten sich zunächst durch einzelne Stützmauern hinter ihrer Rückwand gegen die Abschwemmung zu schützen, dann durch die große
durchgehende Stützmauer im N, die aber auch im 2. Jh. n. Chr. bereits
wieder von Erde bedeckt war (*AO.* 64). Diese große Stützmauer
endet beim Sikyonierschatzhaus. Als sie angelegt wurde, waren die
Schatzhäuser westlich des Sikyonierschatzhauses vermutlich schon
außer Kurs. Die kleinen Stützmauern zwischen Sikyonier- und dem
kleinen Nachbarschatzhaus ("Grottenbau") konnten die Sandmassen
nicht lange abhalten. Das Gebäude wurde ziemlich rasch verschüttet
(insofern unfreiwillig zu einem "Grottenbau"), worauf auch die
geringe Verwitterung der Quadern weist. Dörpfeld· erkannte im
Innern Brandspuren. Ob Brand die Ursache für die Aufgabe des
Bauwerks war, muß vorerst offen bleiben. Es wird vorgeschlagen,
dies Gebäude unter der Bezeichnung "Schatzhaus c" in die Literatur
aufzunehmen.

---

18. *Gnomon* 3 (1927) 328; vgl. C. Weickert *Typen der archaischen Architektur* 88, 1.

19. H. Weber in *Olymp. Forschungen* I (1944) 65, Abb. 10. 79, Abb. 18. 80ff.
Dörpfeld hat diese Fundamentreste vielleicht schon mit verwertet bei seiner
Rekonstruktion der Brunnenanlage, welche er *AO* 108 als "nachgewiesen" be-
zeichnet, während er AO 104 nur "vermutungsweise" ein altes Brunnenhaus
ergänzt. Brunnenanlagen an dieser Stelle sind durchaus möglich, aber für die
Frühzeit nicht erwiesen. Der Aufstellungsplatz des 'Wasserspeier'-Löwen aus
Kalkstein (F. Crome, *Mnemosynon Wiegand* 44ff.) ist nicht bekannt.

20. P. de la Coste-Messelière *Au Musée de Delphes* 64,2. 471.

Dies Ergebnis bedeutet weitgehend Resignation. Eine Resignation, die aber fruchtbarer ercheint als kühne Hypothesen, die doch nach einer gewissen Zeit als Kartenhäuser (bzw. "Grottenbauten") in sich zusammenfallen. Eine weitere Klärung kann nur durch Nachgrabung an den fraglichen Stellen[21] erwartet werden.

---

21. Grabungen wären nötig etwa zur Feststellung der Ausdehnung der fundreichen frühgriechischen Humusschicht am N-Hang des Kronion und in der Altis selbst. Ferner zur Klärung des älteren Sikyonierschatzhauses und seines Verhältnisses zum Schatzhaus c; ferner zur Klärung der älteren Phasen der Schatzhausterrasse sowie des Geländes im N der Exedra. Kann man behaupten, daß es einen älteren Meterkult nicht gegeben habe, solange unter dem Metroon des 4. Jh. nicht systematisch Tiefgrabungen vorgenommen wurden?

SHEPHERD'S SONG

To the woods on the hill over yonder
  Some day I'll be off and away;
And mine eyes I shall never turn back to
  The town and the cares of the day.

Flute notes of far falling water
  Will accompany my last song there;
A song that shall float out to freedom
  Like a leaf riding light on the air.

Miltiades Malakassis

Translated by
John B. Edwards

THE MAVROZOUMENOS BRIDGE IN MESSENIA

CARL ROEBUCK
University of Chicago

Plates 14-15

The district of Messenia bore in antiquity a well deserved reputation for the fertility of its central plains which is justified today by their garden crops and groves of fruit trees. The rich lower plain which was deemed to deserve the epithet, Macaria,[1] is largely the gift of the Mavrozoumenos and Pamisus river system which drains the plain land from the mountain barriers on the north, east, and west. In the upper plain the Mavrozoumenos River is formed by the junction of streams from the northwestern and northeastern parts of the plain which meet about one kilometer to the west of the modern town of Meligala.[2] The Mavrozoumenos flows from this point through the passage between the upper and lower plains at the west edge of which Mt. Ithome rises to serve as the nodal point of the district and guardian fortress of the rich plain land. The area served as a preserve of the Spartans; after 369 B. C., when the independent state of Messene was created, its citizens devoted their efforts to holding their rich land by a judicious policy of internal consolidation, fence-sitting, and political neutrality.

An important factor in this program of consolidation seems to have been the establishment of small towers to serve as observation and control points for the routes important to the new city.[3] The most vital of these routes was that which led northwards from the Arcadian Gate of Messene to provide a link with its Arcadian allies. This road, the course of which is followed by the modern mule path, descended through the foothills of Ithome to the junction of the streams which form the Mavrozoumenos River. At the point where the road leaves the hills a tower was constructed[4] and where the route crossed the rivers a bridge of unique plan was built, usually known as the Triple Bridge. The bridge was the focal point of Messenian communications through the plains and from the capital city. It con-

---

1. Strabo VIII, 4, 6; on this reputation and Messenian economy see Roebuck, C., "A Note on Messenian Economy and Population," *CP* 40 (1945) 149 ff.

2. The sketch map reproduced in M. N. Valmin, *Études Topographiques sur la Messénie ancienne*, is very useful.

3. Roebuck, *A History of Messenia from 369 to 146* B. C., 39-40; Valmin, *op. cit.*, 67-68, 70, 79-82.

4. Valmin, *op. cit.*, 70. The tower is dated to the same period as the walls of Messene.

tinued to serve that purpose in medieval times as an inscription cut by the feudal lords of Karytaina indicates,[5] in the Turkish period, and, to a limited extent, at the present time. The modern railway and highway, however, have been built farther to the east to make a more direct connection with Kalamata, the modern capital of the district.

The bridge attracted the notice of the early topographers and travellers, but, since the relegation of its roads to a position of secondary importance, it has been somewhat neglected so that its unusual plan and architectural features are comparatively unknown.[6] In this brief study I should like to draw attention to them although the structure merits a careful examination and architectural drawings to complement and correct those published by Blouet.[7]

The plan (pls. 14 and 15) of the bridge takes skillful advantage of the rivers to serve the needs of communication. Its three arms radiate from a large central pier set on the apex of land between the two streams. The southwestern arm (pl. 15, A) carries the road from Messene across the stream from the northwestern part of the plain, probably the ancient Leukasia River.[8] The northern arm (pl. 15, C) spans the low ground between the rivers which is subject to flooding and provided the start of the road to the religious center of Messenia: Andania and the Karnasion Grove,[9] and thence to Megalopolis. The southeast arm (pl. 15, D) spans the stream from the northeast, probably the Amphitus River.[10] In antiquity it possibly carried a road running from Pherai (Kalamata) on the Gulf of Messenia through the town of Thouria to this important junction. Below the bridge the united courses of the streams form the Mavrozoumenos River, the ancient Balyra.[11] While much of the construction of the piers and of the arches which carry the causeways is of medieval or later date, there are sufficient remains of the Greek masonry to show that this design was essentially the original one. It has, however, added certain features which necessitate some discussion.

A large part of the Greek masonry of the central pier is preserved,

5. The inscription is mentioned by E. Curtius, *Peloponnesos*, II, 151. It was still preserved when I last visited the bridge in 1939.

6. Bibliography is given by Frazer, *Pausanias*, III, 441-43 and by Reinach, *Voyage Archéologique en Grèce et en Asie Mineure*, 31.

7. Blouet, A. G., *Expédition scientifique de la Morée*, I, *Architecture*, Plate XLVIII. The plan is reproduced in plate 14, b.

8. Valmin, *op. cit.*, 86-88. Valmin reverses the usual identification.

9. Roebuck, *History of Messenia*, 6-11; Valmin has identified Andania and the Grove with the neighborhood of Polichne on the west side of the upper plain (*op. cit.*, 92 ff.).

10. Valmin, *op. cit.*, 86-88, cf. n. 8.

11. *Ibid.*, 82-86. The Mavrozoumenos becomes known as the Pamisus after the stream from Agios Floros joins it in the lower plain.

visible on its west side (pl. 15, C and E). This pier has been so over-
built with later work that its original form is difficult to recover
without some demolition. It seems, however, to have been a rectangular mass of masonry, measuring *ca.* 3.38 by 8.50 m. Its foundations
are of large rectangular blocks marked off from the regular coursing
of its sides by a string course (pl. 15, E). The north end of the pier
was probably set in a straight line, but blocks preserved under the
later coating at the south indicate that it was rounded on that end.
The pointed end and the retaining wall along the bank of the Amphitus
depicted in Blouet's plan (pl. 14, b) are a later addition. At the present
time the causeway to the north is carried by two arches to the higher
ground. It seems likely, although the point could only be settled by
excavation, that in antiquity there were no passage-ways for water
here, but that the causeway was built up solidly from the ground
below. In the first place this causeway did not span a stream; then,
there appears to be no ancient masonry in the pier which supports
the present arches; finally, as discussed below, the other passage-ways
for water were originally vaulted. In this arm the preserved end of
the central pier does not show any provision for a vaulted construction.

The southwestern arm across the Leukasia River is at present
carried on three archways with a narrower rectangular passage between the two westernmost (pls. 14, B and 15, A). The span at the
extreme west end does not appear to have been a part of the original
structure. Its construction does not seem to contain any ancient
masonry *in situ* and it is difficult to explain the function of the narrow
rectangular channel (pl. 15, F) in such an arrangement. Thus, the
original design apparently consisted of two passages, 5.00 m. in
width, to provide for the main flow of the river and, at the west end,
the rectangular passage, 1.20 m. in width, 2.15 m. in height, to carry
the overflow of the river at flood.

The main architectural interest of the bridge lies in the construction
of the passage-ways for the main stream as preserved in this arm.
They were apparently vaulted and supported in the center by a pier
built in midstream. Of the pier[12] only the foundation and string course
are Greek (pl. 15, C), but the preservation of the pier at the west
end (pl. 15, F, G) indicates the original existence of the vaulting.
The voussoirs have been removed and their place taken by later
masonry, but it is apparent that the cuttings on the ends of the blocks
against which they rested were made for this purpose. Further, the

---

12. Here again and in the southeastern arm the pointed ends of the piers are
later additions.

springer on which the voussoirs rested remains in place (pl. 15, G). Probably an examination of the stream bed below the bridge would yield some of the missing blocks to aid in the reconstruction of the arch. Since the span of this archway is the same as that of the adjoining one and as those in the southeastern arm it seems probable that they should be restored as vaulted passages also, although their preservation is less good.

Of the southeastern arm only the foundations of the piers are visible (pl. 15, D). It seems likely, since the Amphitus River is of similar size to the Leukasia, that it should be restored on the analogy of the southwestern arm—with two main passages and a narrow side channel. Again, excavation might clarify the problem.

The bridge, then, reveals not only a Greek vaulted construction which is unusual in itself at this period,[13] but one used for a purpose unusual in Greek architecture,[14] and more at home in Italy. The passage-ways which were formed were not unlike the city gates for which arches had been used before and about this period, as at Oiniadai[15] and in the Isthmian Gate at Corinth,[16] but the span is considerably greater. It is also a more ambitious undertaking than the vaulted passage-ways in the theaters of Sicyon and Eretria.

There is no specific evidence for the date of the bridge's construction so that we are forced to fall back on the style of its masonry and certain general considerations. The former has long been associated[17] with that of the walls of Messene, presumably built *ca.* 369 B. C., at the time of the refounding of the city, when immediate protection from Spartan reprisals was necessary. This association would seem justified, for in both cases the same type of masonry is used—isodomic ashlar employing large quarry-faced blocks.[18] There is a slight tendency to non-vertical joints in the blocks used in the pier holding the preserved part of the arch (pl. 15, G) as in parts of the Messenian

---

13. See the remarks of Robertson, *A Handbook of Greek and Roman Architecture,* 231-32.

14. Frazer (*op. cit.,* 442-43) mentions the bridge at Xerokampo in Laconia as a parallel (from Mure, *Journal,* II, 247 ff.). I have not visited it nor do I know of any good description or reproduction of its masonry. Frazer's conclusion that the vault of the Mavrozoumenos bridge was produced by corbelling is obviously incorrect. The courses of masonry do not protrude one above the other but are cut in a curve for the voussoirs; also, the existence of the springer is not noted.

15. Powell, B., *AJA* 8 (1904) 137 ff.; on the date of the fine polygonal wall at Oiniadai (mid-fifth century) see R. L. Scranton, *Greek Walls,* 60ff.

16. Parsons, A. W., *Corinth,* III, ii, pp. 107-13, 121-22; the gate is dated *ca.* 300 B. C.

17. Frazer, *op. cit.,* 442-43; Clarke, *Peloponnesus,* 240; Leake, *Travels in the Morea,* I, 479-80; *Peloponnesiaca,* 118 f.; Curtius, *Peloponnesos,* II, 150-51.

18. On the type see Scranton, *op. cit.,* 112-20.

fortification wall.[19] The same is true to a lesser degree in the masonry of the central pier, where a characteristic seems to be the occasional use of drafted edges at the joint (pl. 15, E). As a general consideration it might be argued that the building of the bridge would have been postponed until the fortifications of the city were substantially complete. Yet, its importance in the scheme of Messenian communications should have suggested the project either soon after the refounding in 369 B. C. or shortly after 338 B. C. when Philip II took steps to increase Messene's territory and consequently its revenues.[20]

19. Scranton, *op. cit.*, 112.
20. Roebuck, *CP* 43 (1948) 84-89.

DER "GARTEN DES HEPHAISTOS"

HERBERT KOCH
Halle

Dorothy Burr Thompson hat unter diesem Titel einen Aufsatz veröffentlicht, dessen Wert in der vorzüglichen Bekanntgabe und Analyse
eines sehr eigenartigen Ausgrabungsbefundes liegt.[1] Um so proble-
matischer bleibt alles, was nicht Beschreibung sondern Deutung ist.
Zu den hierbei aufgeworfenen Fragen Stellung zu nehmen fühle ich
mich durch meine jahrzehntelange Arbeit an dem Tempel berechtigt,
der heute von den meisten Gelehrten "Hephaisteion" genannt wird,
dessen wahrer Name jedoch bisher so wenig gesichert ist, wie vor
reichlich 100 Jahren, als Ludwig Ross seinen neugriechischen Aufsatz
"Τὸ Θησεῖον καὶ ὁ ναός τοῦ Ἄρεως" erscheinen ließ.[2] Ich gebe
diesen kleinen Beitrag um so lieber, als ich noch jetzt der gleichen
Universität angehöre, an der einst der Jubilar, David M. Robinson,
ein Sommersemester bei F. Blass, W. Dittenberger, E. Meyer, C.
Robert und G. Wissowa studiert hat, an das er gern zurückdenkt; in
der Tat war es eine Glanzzeit der klassischen Altertumswissenschaft
und des schönen Institutes, das seit Roberts Tode seinen Namen führt.

Was Th. als Mitarbeiterin an der amerikanischen Ausgrabung des
athenischen Staatsmarktes festgestellt hat, ist in Kürze folgendes.
Der Tempel ist im späten Altertum auf 3 Seiten (S., N., W.) von
Gartenanlagen umschlossen gewesen; daß auch vor seiner Ostfront
Sträucher oder gar Bäume gestanden hätten, ist dagegen höchst unwahrscheinlich: denn dort muß der Platz des Altares gewesen sein.
Von einem solchen ist zwar bisher nicht die geringste Spur gefunden,
doch würden die erhaltene Festordnungen für die Hephaisteia vollkommen genügen, um seine einstige Existenz zu beweisen.[3] Daß die
altherkömmlichen Tieropfer aufgegeben worden wären, nur um für
Sträucher Platz zu schaffen, wird wohl kaum jemand glauben.

Die sichersten und bezeichnendsten Spuren sind längs der Südseite
zutage getreten, weil dort der hoch anstehende Felsboden besondere
Vorkehrungen erfordert und bewahrt hat; doch kann auch die Fort-
setzung nach W. und N. nicht bezweifelt werden. Es handelt sich um
ansehnliche Ausschachtungen mit ungefähr senkrechten Wänden,
deren Oeffnung rund 0.90 m, deren Tiefe 0.65 m bis 0.90 m beträgt;
sie sind wenigstens teilweise nach den Säulenachsen orientiert. Der

---

1. *Hesperia* 6, 1937, 396ff., weiterhin einfach als Th. zitiert.
2. Athen 1838; umgearbeitet und erweitert: *Das Theseion und der Tempel des
Ares in Athen*, Halle 1852.
3. L. Deubner, *Attische Feste*, 212ff.; *IG* I 84, datiert 421 v.Chr.

typische Zustand der südlichen, vielleicht ältesten Hauptreihe (B bei
Th. Abb. 2) ist in Abb. 12 schematisch dargestellt: in eine etwa 0.31
m tiefe Schicht von mit Asche vermengter Erde (neugr. σταχτόχωμα)
ist ein Blumentopf von konischer, manchmal etwas bauchiger Form
eingesenkt; der Rest der Grube ist mit leichter, gelblicher Erde auf-
gefüllt; darüber liegt eine deutlich abgesetzte "byzantinische" Schicht.
Die Standfläche der Töpfe war glatt abgeschnitten, unten befand sich
ein kreisrundes Loch von größerem Durchmesser, als bei unseren
üblichen Blumentöpfen. Die Höhe betrug 0.17-0.185 m, die Oeffnung
von Rand zu Rand 0.23-0.25 m. Es gibt Exemplare von besserer und
von minderer Technik. Vor ihrer Verwendung sind alle Töpfe ab-
sichtlich zerschlagen worden; wo (in den zusätzlichen Reihen) Topf-
scherben fehlen, sind statt ihrer vielleicht Körbe aus leichtvergäng-
lichem Material gebraucht worden.[4]

Durch Schriftquellen — Cato, Columella, Plinius, die Geoponica
u.s.w. — die bei Daremberg-Saglio s. v. hortus und bei Pauly-Wissowa
s. v. Gartenbau fleißig gesammelt und natürlich auch von M. L.
Gothein in ihrer Geschichte der Gartenkunst ausgenützt worden sind,
läßt sich zur Evidenz erweisen, daß alle die seltsamen von Th. beschriebenen Vorkehrungen keinen anderen Zweck gehabt haben, als
die Niederbiegung von Absenkern. Daß künstliche Berieselung notwendig war, versteht sich von selbst, und in der Tat sind denn auch
verschiedene Bewässerungssysteme (Zisternen, unterirdische Kanäle
von der Pnyx her) entdeckt worden; als sie zu funktionieren auf-
hörten — vermutlich in der 2. Hälfte des 1. Jahr. n.Chr. —ist die
ganze Anlage eingegangen.[5]

Th. betont ausdrücklich und gewiß mit Recht, daß die nächste Um-
gebung unter Tempelschutz gestanden haben müsse;[6] ebenso ist das
geräumige Plateau im Süden[7] wahrscheinlich Tempelbesitz gewesen.
Hierbei denkt Th. natürlich an die Unterbringung von Pilgerscharen
beim Feste der Hephaisteia; daß man den Spieß auch umdrehen und
daran erinnern könnte, wie der Ueberlieferung nach gerade der
Theseusbezirk eine weite Fläche umfasst hat, die gelegentlich als
"Alarmplatz" diente, auf der die Thesmotheten Beamtenwahlen vor-

4. Th. 419 Abb. 16.
5. Th. 419: "Very probably for lack of water the garden died."
6. a.O. 398: "But the central area must have been left open under sacred jurisdiction."
7. das jedoch erst in der Bayernzeit ganz eingeebnet worden ist, wo es als Exerzierplatz diente; aus zeitgenössischen Bildern und Schilderungen (bes. bei E. Bréton, *Athènes décrite et dessinée*, Paris 1862) geht dies klar hervor.

nahmen, auf der bisweilen auch die **Βουλή** tagte,[8] ist ihr offenbar entgangen.

Zu den mancherlei Unstimmigkeiten, die sich bisher schon ergeben haben, kommt noch die Frage, weshalb denn ausgerechnet Hephaistos mit einem Tempelgarten bedacht worden sein soll. Der Hinweis auf Longos, *Pastoralia* 4, 2 befriedigt jedenfalls nicht, denn der Verfasser des späten Hirtenromanes schildert ja einen persischen Paradeisos, einen riesigen Wundergarten, in dessen Mittelpunkte nicht etwa ein Hephaisteion steht, sondern ein Dionysostempel und -altar; den Altar umrankt Epheu, den Tempel umgeben *κλήματα,* d.h. Absenker, vielleicht Weinreben. Eine Erinnerung an die um 6 Jahrhunderte ältere Phineusschale wäre am Platze gewesen. Von Hephaistos aber sagt Th. durchaus richtig: "The tree or plant associated with the god formed the essential character of the garden. . . . And Hephaistos seems to be the one god without a plant of his own."[9]

Sollte sich also nicht eine ganz andere Möglichkeit auftun, wenn man sich einmal von der verhängnisvollen Hephaisteion-Hypothese frei macht und die Dinge unvereingenommen betrachtet?

Mir war schon bei der ersten Lektüre des Th.'schen Artikels ein solcher Einfall durch den Kopf gegangen. Wonach wir suchen müssen, ist doch schließlich die religionsgeschichtliche Erklärung der seltenen Anlage, der Zusammenhang der Pflanzung mit dem Inhaber des Tempels, der Absenker mit einem irgendwie geheiligten Mutterbaume. Des Rätsels Lösung liegt nicht allzu fern.

Im Kult des Theseus haben bekanntlich das Geschlecht der Phytalidai und sein Ahnherr Phytalos eine bedeutsame Rolle gespielt;[10] dieser ist in der Legende ein Gartenbauer und Baumpflanzer, den Demeter mit der Feigenkultur beschenkt, weil er sie freundlich aufgenommen hat.[11] Pausanias hat das Heiligtum der Demeter und Kore, in dem auch Poseidon und Athene verehrt wurden, besucht; er hat das Epigramm auf den "Heros Phytalos" abgeschrieben. Der Stadtbezirk, der am heiligen Wege nach Eleusis lag, wurde *ἱερὰ Συκῆ* genannt.[12] Der fruchtbare Garten des Phytalos, in dessen Nähe der Mystenzug Halt zu machen pflegte, scheint sich bis ans Ufer des Kephisos ausgedehnt zu haben.

Nun berichtet Pausanias weiter:[13] "Geht man über den Kephisos,

---

8. vgl. W. Judeich, *Topogr.* 2. Aufl. 352, der im übrigen ein eifriger Verfechter der Hephaisteion-Hypothese gewesen ist.

9. a.O. 415.

10. das folgende in engem Anschluss an J. Töpffer, *Attische Genealogie* 247ff.

11. Paus. 1, 37, 2.

12. vgl. a. W. Judeich, *Topogr.* 2. Aufl. 411.

13. 1, 37, 4.

so ist da ein alter Altar des Zeus Meilichios; an diesem wurde dem Theseus durch die Nachkommen des Phytalos die Entsühnung zuteil, weil er unter anderen Räubern auch den Sinis getötet hatte, der ihm von seiten des Pittheus verwandt war." Daß die Tötung des "Pithyo-kamptes," des Poseidonsohnes Sinis, auf der zweiten Südmetope des Tempels dargestellt werden durfte, hat mich schon immer beunruhigt und an der "Hephaisteion"-Taufe irregemacht.

Bedarf es noch weiterer Hinweise? Gerade der "Garten des Hephaistos" macht es mehr als wahrscheinlich, daß die hochverdienten amerikanischen Ausgräber des Staatsmarktes, wenn sie ihn wiederer-stehen lassen, nicht Hephaistos, sondern Theseus eine Ehre erweisen werden. "Suum cuique, Theseum Theseo!"[14]

14. E. Curtius, *Commentatio de portubus Athenarum*, 1841, *Sententia controversa* V.
Nachtrag (Oktober 1950)
Die bald nach Wiederaufnahme der Agora Excavations aufgetauchten Reste von Ostgiebelskulpturen unseres Tempels, auf die mich Robinson zuerst brieflich hingewiesen hat, und die zweifellos von einer Darstellung der Einführung des Herakles in den Olymp herrühren, bestärken mich in der oben vertretenen Ansicht, daß der Tempel wirklich das Theseion ist. Euripides hat das vor Augen gehabt, als er die Verse 1324 ff. im Herakles Mainomenos dichtete.

A SECOND HEROON AT CALYDON

EJNAR DYGGVE
Copenhagen

Plates 16-18

By the excavation of the Leonteion at Calydon,[1] a clear picture developed, revealing a Hellenistic heroon constructed on an intricate and interesting plan, of a type nowhere better preserved than there. This heroon is often referred to in the literature, and its lay-out has proved most fruitful and inspiring, also for studies of the cult of the later—early Christian—period.[2] As is well-known, the structure consists of a two-storeyed mausoleum, fronted by an open portico (pl. 16 a), which was used for ritualistic agones and dances at annual celebrations. Such large edifices with courts for agonic contests, presumably formed one of the prerequisites of Vitruvius' hardly advanced ideas of the proper design for an amphitheater.[3]

Since it has now become possible to point to another Calydonian heroon, Heroon II, the remains of which were encountered by this author in 1935 during topographical research work in the territory fronting the outer walls of Calydon, this revelation of a second heroic memorial is, no doubt, deserving of attention. That is the place where spadework should be commenced, and until it can be undertaken the following preliminary observations should suffice:

The Laphrion hill, with its many shrines, projects from the western main gate of the town as far as the Calydonian plain. On either side of this long and narrow ridge, facing south, is a valley proceeding from the city wall in the north and terminating in the lowland. In the eastern valley, where a necropolitan development is discernible, the already published Leonteion was discovered, whereas Heroon II, discussed here, is situated as a pendant in the western valley,[4] where

---

1. Dyggve, F. Poulsen, Rhomaios, *Das Heroon von Kalydon; Kgl. Dansk. Vidensk. Selsk, Skrifter; Hist. og Filos.* Afd. 7. R., IV, No. 4, København, 1934.

2. Dyggve, *Das Mausoleum in Pécs. Ein christliches Heroon aus Pannonia Inferior.* Pannonia. Pécs, 1935. Dyggve, "Der Apsissaal des Leonteion," *Actes du XIVe congrès internat. d'histoire de l'art*, Bâle 1936, 198 ff. Dyggve, Egger, *Forschungen in Salona*, III, Wien 1939; Dyggve, *Gravkirken i Jerusalem*, København, 1941. Th. Klauser, *Vom Heroon zur Märtyrerbasilika*, Bonn 1942. Dyggve, 1941. Th. Klauser, *Vom Heroon zur Märtyrerbasilika*, Bonn 1942. Dyggve, *Dødekult, kejserkult og basilika*, København 1943. H. P. L'Orange, *Fra Antikk til Middelalder*, Oslo 1944. A. Grabar, *Martyrium*, I-II, Paris 1946 (Album 1943).

3. Vitruvius, I, 7, 1; V, 1, 1. cf. Dyggve, *Funktionalismen i Amfiteatret*, 67 f.

4. Cf. Dyggve: *Das Laphrion, der Tempelbezirk von Kalydon. Kgl. Dansk. Vidensk. Selsk. Arkaeol. — Kunsthist. Skrifter.* B. I, No. 2 København 1948. Taf. XXXVIII, Abb. 277.

a small torrent has been identified, by Poulsen and Rhomaios, as the mythical Kallirrhoë.[5]

In 1935 I made a rough survey of the said ruins of Heroon II, as far as it was accessible then (fig. 1). Other tasks at the place claiming my time, I was not in a position to make any closer investigations by digging or probing. It is difficult to tell whether the traces of evident

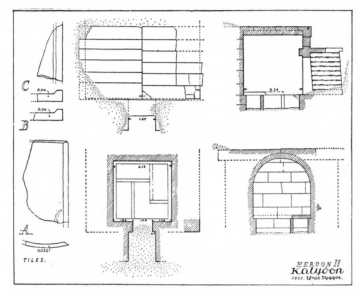

Figure 1. Survey of Heroon II in the "Kallirrhoë" valley, 1: 2000.

digging are the work of ordinary grave robbers, or whether, on some occasion or other, trial digging has been attempted. In 1908 Soteriades undertook various minor investigations at Calydon:[6] at the Acropolis of the town, at the Temple of Artemis, and at the Leonteion, and it is likely that this very badly preserved ruin was also touched, although the structure is difficult to see in the terrain (pl. 16, b). The building apparently consists only of a barrel-vaulted subterranean tomb. In form the sepulchral chamber proper, though bigger, comes close to the Leonteion hypogeum. However, being 3.15 m as compared with the 1.90 m of the Leonteion, this Heroon II should be classed between the large sepulchral chambers of Pydna (3.09 m) and Mal Tepe (3.18 m).[7] A Calydon mausoleum of a simpler design—in the hills behind the Leonteion, to the northeast—is 2.90 m wide (fig. 2) ; the

5 Fr. Poulsen, Rhomaios, *Erster vorl. Ber. über die dän. — griech. Ausgrab. in Kalydon*, 49 f.

6. *Praktika*, 1908.

thickness of the wall indicates to a certainty that the structure was not vaulted, and that for reconstruction it should be given an ordinary flat saddle-back roof.[8]

The walls of the tomb chamber in Heroon II are constructed of smooth-worked sandstone ashlars, about 0.50 m deep, with slight borders chiselled along the edges at the joints. The two lower ashlar courses project plinthlike from the face of the wall proper (to the west and north 0.16 m, eastward 0.20 m, and southward 0.17 m), and

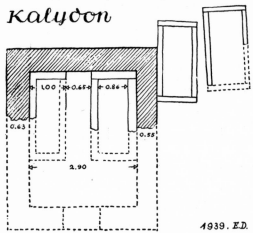

Figure 2. Hellenistic Mausoleum on the hill N. E. of the Leonteion.

at the same time form sides in the grave *klines* and beds for the *kline* covers. The other *kline* sides are made up of full-size flag-stones in the usual Hellenistic manner. In section the barrel vault is constructed of six blocks of stone, of which the upper two are broader than the others and meet in a joint at the axis of the vault, a most unusual fact. Longitudinally the joints are horizontal throughout, whereas a few of the vertical joints are oblique.

The dromos normally leading to a tomb chamber is absent here, but the doorway is flanked by two piers which project well in front of the opening and are joined at the top by a broad horizontal topstone. The two flanking piers are worked to an extremely dainty and re-strained style of rustication in specially select hard sandstone vein.[9] The bay of the chamber door slopes inwards towards the top, on the outside; and it is remarkable that there are no traces of any means for barring the opening.

7. *Das Heroon von Kalydon*, Abb. 111.
8. Cf. the small treasury buildings, *Das Laphrion*, Taf. XXXV.
9. *Op. cit.*, 16 ff. (concerning the building material at Calydon).

Above, on top of the grave chamber, there is a horizontal paving of long parallel flag-stones, on an average 0.60 m broad. The outside row of flag-stones, or rather blocks (being 0.52 m in thickness), had been fastened together by a type of cramp dating from the Hellenistic middle-period (of half-length 0.16 m, outside width 0.05 m, and inside width 0.035 m).[10] At this place a coarser sandstone had been used, and the surface is uneven (pl. 17, a). This level flagging resembles the substratum of the floor of the cella in the Calydon Artemision,[11] though here the paving is slightly more even and regular. The plane surface is only partly preserved; at this place, as everywhere in Calydon, later generations have heedlessly used the ruins as if they were quarries.[12] The remnants are enveloped in layers of alluvial soil. However, there was also heaped-up earth (cf. the aforesaid), and in this dug-up humus a few fragments of Hellenistic tiles were found (fig. 1). I have not succeeded in finding ceramic or other remains of buildings in the vicinity of this Heroon II, whence it may be assumed that the tiles derived from the latter.

As far as may be deduced from the treatment of the walls, the hole for the cramp, and the tile sherds, the structure should be of the period of the great stoa on the Laphrion hill and the Leonteion; hence II century B. C. With a knowledge of the local conditions, this approximate dating is not difficult. The difficulty is in forming a closer idea of the original appearance of the mausoleum, as long as the ruins remain uncovered.

At first glance, at any rate, it appears to be an isolated chambered tomb of the tumulus type. I have examined such tumular graves in Dobrudža, where, as also in Thrace, they are widespread. Plate 17, b shows a tumulus of this type from the vicinity of Mangalia. The mound proper has been removed leaving the bare chamber tomb under a regular barrel vault (seen from inside in pl. 17, c). It is worth noting that the rebate in the door-frame indicates the existence of a door intended to shut off the burial chamber from the earth packing. However, in a small tumulus of this description no dromos would be required, inasmuch as access to the grave chamber—if desired—might fairly easily be contrived by digging. The most essential difference between this chambered tumulus and the Heroon II at Calydon is the aforementioned level flagging carried by the walls of the tomb chamber, similar to the flag-stone flooring above the hypogeum in the Leonteion cult apsis.[13] The remains seem to have formed a floor, or

10. *Das Heroon,* Abb. 39; *Das Laphrion,* 260 ff.
11. *Op. cit.,* Abb. 46.
12. *Das Heroon,* 26. Cf. *Das Laphrion.*
13. *Das Heroon,* **Taf. VI.**

the foundation of a floor (cf. the above),[14] for a place of worship on top of the tomb chamber, either *sub divo* or, perhaps, covered over as at the Leonteion. To me, at any rate, it seems unlikely that work should be undertaken to build a barrow over this flagging after expending work on tieing up the outer row of flag-stones by means of cramps. Such a level flagging is not technically requisite for a tumulus (cf. pl. 17, b), nor is it essential for sepulchral rites, which, of course, might be performed with equal effect on top of the mound proper.

Against the idea of a tumulus is also the absence of any trace of means of obstructing the entrance; whose peculiar open architectural design, moreover, has nothing in common with the dromos of the usual chambered tomb, and whose delicate rustication obviously was intended to be seen. A hindrance to the application of the Leonteion type of this Heroon II is the fact that the entrance thereto is situated in the longitudinal axis of the tomb chamber. However, if actually no means existed for barring access to the entrance, the least conceivable protection must have been a wall surrounding the entire edifice. Should this be the fact, then the ground plan would perhaps approach a further simplification of the already much simplified specimen of the Leonteion type[15] pointed out by me among the ruins of the Temenos of Dodona.[16] The great uncertainty regarding the actual facts of the monumental structure might be overcome by carefully opening up the area down to virgin ground, for the purpose of discovering the original conditions of the terrain and possible traces of foundations and walls, from which a picture might be formed of the lay-out for the ritual observances at the tomb—the purpose of the structure being mainly to serve as a frame for the sepulchral ceremonies—which picture, or idea, should afford the most significant fruit of the research work.

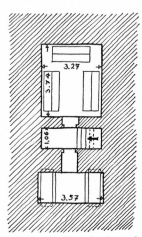

Figure 3. Sketch plan of staircase and chambers in the Heroon at the museum in Delphi.

In closing we may perhaps draw attention to the Heroon at Delphi, which exhibits many similarities to the structures discussed (pl. 18, a, b and fig. 3), and which, as far as I know, has remained unpublished.

14. At Calydon there are quite a number of buildings revealed by remnants of flagging of the same poor description; as e.g., *Das Laphrion*, Abb. 91 and 93.
15. For a further description cf. in particular, *Das Heroon*, 120 and Abb. 132.
16. Dyggve, *Dedonaeiske problemer. Arkaeol. og kunsthist. afh. tilegn. Frederik Poulsen.* København 1941, 96 ff.; Dyggve, *Cahiers Archéologiques;* Tome III, 10, Fig. 1.

VILLA OR PANDOKEION?

W. A. McDonald
University of Minnesota

Professor Robinson's excavations at Olynthus are unique in the light they have shed on the way the Greek people lived in a provincial town of the Classical period. The promptness and thoroughness of his publication of this material and his familiarity with the pertinent literary evidence and with the results of modern research and excavation cannot be too highly praised. Yet the number and variety of the finds and their intrinsic interest and importance is such that new interpretations on minor points are sure to appear as the *Olynthus* volumes are continuously used. It is, in fact, the hope of every scholar worthy of the name that his work may be significant enough to produce such reaction.[1]

The purpose of this paper is to suggest that the Olynthian building called by the excavators the Villa of Good Fortune[2] was designed and built not as a luxurious private house, but as a rather high-class inn, providing refreshment, recreation, and probably sleeping accommodations for a limited number of paying guests. The same theory apparently occurred to Dr. Robinson when the building was first uncovered,[3] but it is not mentioned in the final publication.[4] It should be admitted from the start that the evidence presented here is not entirely conclusive, but some new arguments are adduced which, when added to those cited by Dr. Robinson, make the identification a very real possibility.

We have ample literary evidence to prove that Greek towns normally possessed not only official public "hotels"[5] but also numerous

---

1. Dr. Robinson has demonstrated this principle by encouraging the preparation of the present article and by giving his permission to reproduce the plan which appears as figure 1.

2. Cf. the ground plan in figure 1, which must be referred to in the whole discussion to follow.

3. Cf. *AJA* 38 (1934) 505 f.n. 2.

4. Robinson and Graham, *Excavations at Olynthus*, vol. VIII, 55-63. Robinson's recent article on the Wheel of Fortune (*CP* 41 [1946] 207-216) shows, however, that he had not completely abandoned the idea. If the sale inscription (*TAPA* 65 [1934] 124-127) found on the surface above this building could be definitely associated with it, we would have to call it an οἰκίη. But the editors wisely do not press the connection. As far as I am aware, the pandokeion theory occurred to me independently while working over the material in Olynthus VIII in another connection.

5. Xenophon's term δημόσια καταγώγια (*On the Revenues* 3, 12) would probably apply to them. They were primarily the prytaneion, where important state guests were entertained; also shelters closely connected with religious shrines, particularly those of international importance visited by many pilgrims from distant

establishments (many of them with none too savory a reputation) owned and operated by private individuals who fed and housed strangers and their beasts and who provided for travellers and townsmen alike facilities for eating, drinking, gambling, and other perennially popular *divertissements*.[6] But in our preserved sources, there is practically nothing in the nature of a useful description of any of the buildings mentioned,[7] nor as far as I know has a single building from the Classical Greek period been identified as what we would call a privately operated inn, hotel, tavern, restaurant, casino, or roadhouse.[8] Probably there was little in location, general outward appearance, or even in ground plan to distinguish them from private houses, and the equipment and furnishings which would assist in the identifi-

---

points (cf. that at Plataea described in f.n. 7); and no doubt the leschai and public buildings of that sort on occasion.

6. The ancient Greek language, like others both ancient and modern, employs a wide variety of names for such places. Sharp distinctions in function are very difficult to establish from the names alone, since the same word (for example, καταγώγιον) may be used to designate a large public building of the class mentioned in f.n. 5 and a small privately operated concern. There was doubtless a considerable variety in the kind of services offered by the privately operated establishments, ranging from merely selling wine over the counter (οἰνοπώλιον, καπηλεῖον; cf. the *cauponae* of Pompeii) to the provision of a good many additional services for the patrons. The most usual designations seem to be these: πανδοκεῖον which Liddell and Scott translate "inn" and which was both semantically and in actual fact the most general and inclusive; κατάλυσις, κατάλυμα and καταγώγιον which L. and S. render "lodging" but which obviously connote not only the relaxation gained through a good night's sleep (apparently a rather rare actuality in these places) but also refreshment and recreation as a result of food (cf. restaurant) and entertainment. The term καπηλεῖον is equated by L. and S. first with "shop" and then with "tavern," but the probable connection with κάπη "manger" (κάπτω "gobble") would suggest that it may have experienced a parallel development to σταθμός, which first meant a "stopping-place" for animals and only later "inn" (cf. Boisacq, *Dictionnaire Étymologique de la langue grecque*, 408, 409, 901). For further information on the names and functions of buildings of this class, cf. Firebaugh, W. C., *The Inns of Greece and Rome*, 27-59 (a very superficial study); Daremberg-Saglio *Dictionnaire* s.v. *caupona* (Fr. auberge, cabaret); *RE* s.v. *caupona*, καταγώγιον, καπηλεῖον (G. Herberge, Gasthaus, Wirtshaus); Stephanus' *Thesaurus* under the terms given above; and the numerous primary authorities cited in these works.

7. Thucydides (III, 68, 3) has, indeed, left a few lines for which we are grateful, and I quote them in Jowett's version: "But they [the Spartans] afterwards razed the whole place [Plataea] to the very foundations and built near the precinct of Herè an inn *(καταγώγιον)* forming a square of two hundred feet; it had two stories, and chambers *[οἰκήματα]* all round. They used the roofs and doors of the Plateans; and of the brass and iron articles of furniture found within the walls they made couches which they dedicated to Herè; they also built in her honour a stone temple a hundred feet long." This will obviously have been a public hostel at a religious shrine on the order of those mentioned in f.n. 5; and while it is of assistance in identifying buildings of a similar function on sites like Olympia, Delphi, and Epidaurus, it must be used with the greatest caution in reference to the necessarily simpler and smaller private establishments which are our present concern.

8. Wycherley *(How the Greeks Built Cities)* barely mentions these buildings, not because they were not a typical element but because he is describing primarily what is known from archaeological discoveries. From prehistoric times we have the "caravanserai" of Knossos cf. Evans, Sir Arthur, *Palace of Minos*, II, 103-40.

cation were doubtless almost all of a perishable nature.[9] It would, therefore, be of real interest and some importance if we could identify an inn at Olynthus, where so many new facts about Greek "private life" have been uncovered.

To come to the Villa itself, the following are the main points on which I base the identification: the inscriptions and symbols in the

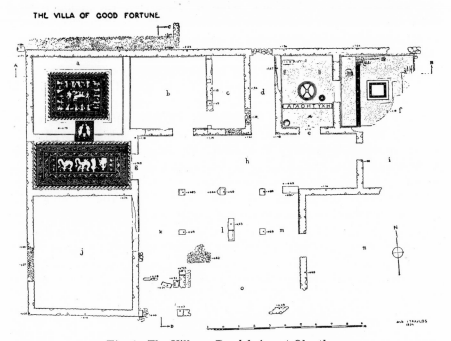

Fig. 1. The Villa or Pandokeion at Olynthus.

mosaics of rooms **e** and **f**; certain features of room **j**, particularly the capacity of the pithoi; the apparent absence of a bath-room on the ground floor; and various minor points which are quite inconclusive singly but have a certain amount of supporting weight in sum.

The use of most of the rooms on the ground floor is clear and typical (figure 1). Room **j** was apparently a storage chamber (see below); rooms **a** and **g** were dining-room (andron) and ante-room; rooms **b** and **c** were the *oikos* and kitchen; **l** is the courtyard with complete peristyle (porches **k, m, o,** and pastas **h**). The south-east corner

---

9. One has only to reflect how little would remain after a similar lapse of time to identify the modern χαφενεῖον, ἑστιατόριον, or even the moderate sized ξενοδοχεῖον. At Eleusis the late Dr. Kourouniotes brought to light a series of πανδοχεῖα immediately to the northeast of the sanctuary. Cf. also *Hesperia* 16 (1947) 241.

(called room **n**) is badly destroyed and the excavators do not theorize
as to its original purpose. Rooms **e** and **f** are in better shape and seem
essentially to repeat the andron-anteroom complex. It is possible that
they may have served on occasion for dining, though the inner room
lacks the distinctive raised border for the couches; but the evidence
points to a different primary purpose. As one entered room **e** he was
confronted with the inscription *ΑΓΑΘΗ ΤΥΧΗ* in the pebble mosaic
floor. Behind it are two circles or wheels with four "spokes," in the
larger forming a St. Andrew's cross, in the smaller a Roman cross.
On the long axis of the room are two single letters, an *A* near the doorway and a *Σ* near the back wall. In the north-west corner and approximately in line with the *Σ* are the letters *ΔΙΚΑΙΩ*.[10] Turning to
the right into room **f** one is confronted with another mosaic inscription in a single line reading *ΕΥΤΥΧΙΑ ΚΑΛΗ*, and in the center of
the room there is a rectangle around the border of which is written in
smaller letters *ΑΦΡΟΔΙΤΗ ΚΑΛΗ*. The mosaic floor is missing in
the south-east corner but there is a double axe symbol near the break,
and along the north wall a swastika.[11]

The praise or invocation of Tyche and Eutychia calls for no special
elucidation,[12] but for the Aphrodite inscription there are at least two
possible interpretations. The goddess' name may be used to extol the
delights of love[13] or the term may be a reference to the highest throw
in the rolling of knuckle-bones where "Aphrodite" signified that each
of the four astragaloi had turned up a different face.[14] If the second

10. Professor Robinson is probably right in insisting, *AJA* 38 (1934) 505, that
the mosaic is unbroken and that there were no letters connecting these with the *Σ*
(unless an *I* immediately after the *Ω*), although his photograph (*loc. cit.*, fig. 2)
gives the impression of a sloping line immediately to the left of the *Σ*. But with
this mosaic technique one is apt to imagine he sees letters or parts of letters in
various places. Similarly, the "ladder" and "hand" are probably fortuitous or
essentially meaningless.

11. Various similar symbols are found at Olynthus. Cf. especially the strange
mosaic in House A xi 9 (*loc. cit.*, Pl. XXXI). Dr. Robinson (*loc. cit.*, 503) believes
that the letter ⴲ is to be made out above the double axe.

12. They are well known personified abstractions and very popular in this
general period as well as later. It is quite unlikely that Aphrodite and Eutychia
refer to particular women living at the time the mosaic was laid.

13. The erotic theme would not be out of place in many a pandokeion, as we
gather from literature; but there is no open indication of this aspect here, as there
is in the seductive paintings and inscriptions in certain rooms of the *cauponae*
at Pompeii.

14. The clearest reference is Lucian, *Erotes*, 16: εἰ ποτε τὴν θεὸν αὐτὴν
εὐβολήσειε, μηδενὸς ἀστραγάλου πεσόντος ἴσῳ σχήματι – – – Ἀφροδίτην καλὴν
ἐκήρυσσεν. But there is every reason to believe that this, with some of the other
gaming terms like "Solon," goes back at least to classical Greek times. Cf. the
"Venus throw" among the Romans as early as the time of Plautus. For games
of chance played with knuckle-bones (ἀστράγαλοι, tali) and dice (κύβοι, tesserae)
cf. especially L. Becq de Fouquières, *Les Jeux des Anciens*,[2] 302-356—full references; also W. A. Becker, *Charicles* transl. by F. Metcalfe 3rd ed. 348-355; Becker,
Gallus, same translator 2nd ed. 499-504; Daremberg-Saglio, *Dictionnaire* s.v. *talus*,

interpretation is correct, the *A* in room **e** is very likely acrophonic for Aphrodite; and the *Σ* balancing it may well stand for the name of another throw beginning with that letter,[15] or possibly for the numeral eighteen signifying the three sixes or highest throw with three dice.[16] Then the ἀγαθὴ τύχη and the εὐτυχία καλή would take on a particular significance, an appeal to and praise for Lady Luck or Chance, the patroness of gamblers at all times and places. The wheel designs, like the inscriptions, are of course primarily decorative and are found in other Olynthian buildings. Dr. Robinson sees in them the "wheel of fortune" symbol,[17] which would fit in well with the inscriptions, the other good luck symbols (double axe and swastika), and the obvious emphasis in these rooms on wooing Dame Fortune. But, without losing this significance, they might also have served for the game of chance called ὤμιλλα, in which the aim was to have one's own counters stay in the circle and to try to dislodge those of one's opponents.[18] When these indications are all considered (even the finding of an inscribed bronze astragalos in the nearby pastas), it is difficult to avoid the conclusion that these two rooms were set aside primarily for games of chance; and it seems very unlikely that the owner of a private house would sacrifice so much space for this specific purpose.[19] The

---

tessera; RE s.v. ἀστράγαλος. Much of our information comes from Pollux *Onomasticon*, IX, 94-129, a section entitled Περὶ τῶν ἐν συμποσίοις παιδιῶν κτλ. Cf. especially for these and other references Robinson, D. M., *Olynthus*, X, 502-505; XII, 323-324.

15. Among the thirty-five possible combinations with four astragaloi, Becq de Fouquières (*op. cit.*, 388) lists six throws with names beginning with sigma. The best documented is the "Stesichoros" which counted eight. It was apparently less necessary to name the fifty-six possible combinations with three dice, since the usual method was simply to add up the counters showing; but the Romans called the three sixes "Venus," and no doubt the Greeks had earlier made the transfer.

16. The fully developed alphabetic scheme to express the decimal system seems not to have been in use before the third century B.C. There is some evidence to show that prior to this the areas using the Ionic alphabet of twenty-four letters employed them to express the numerals 1 through 24 (cf. Reinach, *Traité d'épigraphie grecque*, 220, 221; Larfeld, *Griechische Epigraphik* in Müller's *Handbuch* I, 5, 298; Smith, *History of Mathematics*, 51). Hence, *Σ* may very well have been employed to write 18 by fifth and fourth century Olynthians. It has also occurred to me that the *Σ* might stand for the imperative *Σ[ΕΙΕ]* from the verb σείω— shake (the dice), although the preposition διά is usually compounded in this sense.

17. *CP.* 41 (1946) 207-216.

18. For this game cf. Becq de Fouquières *op. cit.*, 118, 119 (le jeu de cercle); Daremberg-Saglio *Dictionnaire* s.v. *talus;* Stephanus' *Thesaurus* s.v. ὤμιλλα and references quoted there. The well known terracotta group in the Louvre (illustrated in Daremberg-Saglio), where two women throw astragaloi in a divided circle, attests the early popularity of the pastime. Cf. Robinson as cited *supra* and in *Olynthus*, XIV, where several terra cotta Olynthian figurines of astragalus players will be published.

19. It is true that ἀγαθὴ τύχη is a fairly common formula. It occurs in most of the inscribed deeds of sale found at Olynthus, but there it invokes Fortune on a particular venture, not with the generalized meaning of "God Bless Our Home." If the latter were the meaning of the formula, as Dr. Robinson suggests, one would expect it much more frequently in the preserved mosaic floors. I am aware,

impression is rather of organized commercial gambling and, although gambling was by no means confined to pandokeia, the connection is a likely one and they are often associated in literature.

Secondly, room **j** does not seem to have been the apotheke of a private house. It had an outside door, which reminds one of numerous Olynthian shops.[20] The wall between it and the portico (**k**) was not well enough preserved to indicate whether or not there was a door connecting this room with the interior of the building.[21] But the fact that at least five pithoi were scattered around the room is a strong argument against its use as a shop.[22] It would seem to have been used for storage, but the owner apparently found it advisable to have goods transferred directly from carts on the street to his containers in the "cellar." This fact in itself may well indicate that the quantity of goods handled was unusually great. The capacity and number of the pithoi further suggests that the consumption of supplies here was in excess of the needs of any ordinary family, for there were five (and perhaps more) very large jars with a calculated capacity of *ca.* three hundred gallons each.[23] Although too much confidence should perhaps

---

too, that elsewhere at Olynthus the good-luck symbols appear and that dice and astragaloi are commonly found. But there is in this one section of one building a striking accumulation of references and symbols pertaining to luck which can hardly be explained as mere coincidence. As for the *ΔΙΚΑΙΩ* inscription, I can add nothing to the suggestions made by Dr. Robinson nor can I choose from among them. The juxtaposition of Justice with Luck is not at all out of keeping with gambling sentiment.

20. None of the store-rooms discussed in *Olynthus*, VIII, 207-208, appears to have had a door opening on the street.

21. The editors assume that there was, although there is a difference in floor level of at least a meter. If so, the possibility that the room was a shop is lessened but not excluded, since some of the rooms identified as shops did connect with the interior of the houses (cf. *Olynthus*, VIII, 211-213). The fact that ten of the thirty-seven coins found in the building were concentrated in this room may perhaps favor the shop theory, but can be explained by the theory that drivers who replenished the pithoi were paid off in the room.

22. Three pithoi were *in situ* and there was no orderly arrangement apparent such as one would expect in a shop. Furthermore, there is no mention of the finding of pithoi in the rooms identified elsewhere as shops.

23. Cf. *Olynthus*, VIII, 313-316; XII, 183-206; XIII, 432-434; *TAPA* 69 (1938) 51. Their inscribed rims have been interpreted as indicating the cost of the jars rather than of the contents. They were quite expensive and no householder would be likely to buy and instal more than would supply his minimum requirements, whatever they were. It is very difficult to arrive at any trustworthy statistics since there are so many unknowns. But let us take as a norm the provisioning of the troops on Sphakteria during the truce (Thucydides IV, 16; for the feeding of a Roman soldier cf. Parker, *The Roman Legions*, 220). Each hoplite was allowed approximately one quart of barley and one pint of wine (plus a little meat), and the attendants half that amount. Let us estimate a large family at twelve and provide full rations for two free adults and half rations for ten children and slaves. We thus arrive at a figure of seven quarts of grain and seven pints of wine per day. Thus, the basic provisions for a full year for this family would have been about 600 gallons of grain and 300 gallons of wine, all of which could have been contained in three pithoi of 300-gallon capacity, leaving a very large available capacity. Moreover, the excavators believe that the fragments point to an even

not be placed in the bits of straw, olive pits, and pine bark found in them, they do suggest the three staples of diet, wine (resinated), olives or olive oil, and grain. The likeliest conclusion is that outsiders were supplied from here, that there was either retail trade over the counter or that supplies were stored for the preparation of an extraordinarily large number of meals served in the building itself. Other indications, as we have seen, point to the second as the more likely explanation.

Thirdly, the better Olynthian houses usually have a complex of three rooms, now identified as living room (οἶκος), kitchen, and bathroom.[24] The latter two are regularly side by side, occupying about one-third of the area of the complex, and opening onto the living room. In this building, however, while the *oikos* and kitchen are clearly rooms **b** and **c,** there is no sign of a bathroom in its usual place —or elsewhere on the ground floor[25] The kitchen is therefore larger by about one-third, which additional space would be particularly needed if meals were served commercially. But it is difficult to believe that if this elegant building had been a private house it would not have been provided with the usual "built-in" bathtub in a separate room on the ground floor. On the other hand, if it was an inn, the absence of the ground floor bathroom is easily explained. Olynthian bathrooms provided only those facilities which the name properly implies,[26] and the whole ground floor area of an inn would have been busy and more or less accessible to strangers and servants, so that guests or proprietors would have enjoyed a much more leisurely and private bath in a tub (scarcely of the built-in type) in a room on the second floor.

---

larger number of pithoi, and we have the likelihood of frequent refilling from carts in the street. The only Olynthian building where a comparative number of large pithoi was found is A xi 10, which had two in each of two rooms. Here too it is likely that some kind of commerce was involved.

24. Cf. *Olynthus*, XII, 369-398.

25. It is, of course, possible that a bathroom existed in the missing southeast corner, but the above-mentioned position is much the most usual. A few seem to have opened directly off the courtyard. It must also be kept in mind that in only about one-third of the houses excavated was a ground floor bathroom found. Mylonas has isolated a group of five houses which seem to have the usual oikos and kitchen unit, but no bathroom (*Olynthus*, XII, 389-393, 398). This perhaps weakens the present argument but it does not, I think, destroy it, since the built-in tub on the ground floor was clearly the most up-to-date arrangement in the "best" houses.

26. The ancients showed their sense of what is fitting in not combining in a single room the functions of a bathroom proper and a latrine. The latter would seem to have been a prime necessity here, to judge from the capacity of the pithoi, some of which presumably contained wine; but it appears that we are fated to remain essentially in ignorance on this intriguing point as far as Olynthian houses are concerned (cf. *Olynthus*, VIII, 205). Cf., however, Robinson's exhaustive treatment of the subject in *Olynthus, XII*, 178-180.

The minor supporting points in my argument are as follows: (I) The rear "service entrance" is unusual,[27] and its position adjacent to the kitchen is perhaps indicative of more than average activity there. This impression is strengthened by the two breaks in the kitchen walls, one along the corridor (d) leading from the rear entrance, and the other between the kitchen and the pastas (h). There may originally have been doors here, but they seem to have been filled in and the excavators suggest that there were windows or vents at these points. It is possible, however, that these openings (if such they were) served to facilitate the transfer of provisions from the rear entrance to the kitchen, from the storeroom to the kitchen through the pastas, and of cooked food from the kitchen to the pastas, and thence to the dining tables. Low walls with wide wooden shelves or counters surmounting them would have served admirably to speed up kitchen traffic.[28] (II) The beautiful mosaics in rooms a and g with their allusions to wine (Dionysos, the crater—the only clearly Dionysiac scenes in Olynthian mosaics) and love (Eros, satyrs and maenads) are of course quite appropriate to a private dining room. But, as Dr. Robinson has pointed out, they might be even better calculated to please diners-out who had their thoughts particularly centered on *carpe diem.*[29] (III) The preserved stairbase shows that in this alone among excavated Olynthian buildings the stairway ascended toward the south. This seems to indicate a more extensive second storey with a gallery all round the court and rooms opening off at least three sides of it. There would likely have been at least ten rooms, which seems more than ample sleeping accommodation for a single family.[30] (IV) The very size of the building (approximately one-half again as long as the usual Olynthian house and bigger than any other "private" dwelling found), the spaciousness of the rooms, and its free-standing position put it in a special category. (V) Finally, its location, surely

27. A second entrance occurs in at least four other buildings, but they are corner houses in the block system and so it was necessarily on the side.

28. It is possible that the rather puzzling foundations between kitchen and oikos in this and many other Olynthian buildings are to be interpreted similarly, with a low wall and broad flat shelf, usually between wooden pillars. This would have made the kitchen much more accessible and better lighted. It would also have helped to heat the oikos.

29. Similarly, the presentation of the armor scene in the vestibule may have been chosen with patrons among the military in mind.

30. There is also the distinct possibility that this large building, like several others at Olynthus, was provided with a wider entrance off the main street for cart traffic. The full peristyle and the altar in the middle of the courtyard and also the fact that the storage room had its own street door would suggest that this entrance would not have given onto the court. It may well have led directly into the large southeast corner area (n), which would have served admirably as a stable (cf. *Olynthus*, VIII, 210, 211). In that case, the building would have been well equipped to take care of all the needs of any traveler.

not far from the road to the port and probably outside the walls,[31] is a strategic one for an inn catering to sailors and tradespeople as well as to local residents who hankered for an occasional "night out with the boys" at a convenient distance from the domestic scene.[32]

Admittedly, the Villa of Good Fortune could have been the mansion of a very wealthy Olynthian with a large family of children and slaves; a man who perhaps owned a large farm; who stored and sold (maybe even processed) his wine and grain and olives in his home. But I believe it was open to the public. Olynthus must have had her pandokeia. Most of them were "dives" on the South Hill, no doubt, but there is nothing intrinsically unlikely about the existence of a prosperous and even luxurious hostel in a town that provided its citizens with living accommodations which seem to have been of more than average comfort.

31. The fact that there are signs of intense burning in the buildings of this area, while those on the hills show no signs of fire (*Olynthus*, VIII, 62), may indicate that Philip's men burned the suburbs before they had taken the city itself.

32. The eastern caravanserai was usually located just outside the city gates; and our own road-houses are very frequently built on the outskirts of a city or town, as were many of the taverns of pre-automobile days.

ADDENDUM

Since the manuscript of this article was submitted, the author received a letter from Professor John Travlos, who is now studying the public hostels (referred to in f.n. 5, 6, 7). It is gratifying to learn that he believes a case has been made out for the above interpretation of the evidence in connection with the Olynthus building.

DUSAE AD OLYMPUM
EIN TOPOGRAPHISCHER IRRTUM

Friedrich Karl Dörner

Tafeln 19-20

Die Tabula Peutingeriana verzeichnet im dritten Abschnitt von Segment IX[1] einen Ort, der *Dusepro Solympum* geschrieben ist; er liegt im Zuge einer Strecke, die in folgender Weise verläuft:

Nicomedia XVII[2] *XXIII Lateas XVIII Demetriu XIII Dusepro Solympum XXX* (Vignette einer Stadt) *XX;* es folgt der Lauf des *Sangarius fl.* (heute Sakarya) and jenseits des Flusses die Station *Manoris.*

Diese Strecke ist nach der Tabula Peutingeriana Teil einer großen West-Ost-Route, die von Nikomedeia nach Gangra führt; hier teilt sie sich. Der südliche Zweig geht — ganz wie es den geographischen Gegebenheiten entspricht — nach Amaseia, während die nördliche Abzweigung über Pompeiopolis nach Sinope verläuft, dessen Geschichte durch die grundlegende Arbeit von David M. Robinson vor mehr als vier Jahrzehnten so entscheidend aufgehellt worden ist.

So klar die Gesamtführung dieser Strecke im ganzen anmutet, so viel Schwierigkeiten macht sie, wenn man sich mit Einzelheiten, besonders ihrem Anfangsteil beschäftigt. Zunächst fällt auf, daß die Entfernung bis zum Sangarios mit *102 m.p.* bzw. *122 m.p.* (wenn man noch die *XX m.p.* für *Manoris,* die auf der westlichen Seite des Flusses stehen, hinzuzählt), d.h. mit 150 bzw. 180 km viel zu hoch gegriffen ist, während sie in Wirklichkeit nur etwa 45 km beträgt. Das Verhältnis der Strecke jenseits des Sangarios ist aber dann weit ausgeglichener und entspricht fast den tatsächlichen Verhältnissen. Während man bisher für die Ansetzung von *Lateas* und *Demetriu(m)* keinerlei sichere Anhaltspunkte hatte, zögerte man doch nicht, Bithynion-Claudiopolis in der nur mit einer Vignette dargestellten Stadt zu sehen.[3] Diese Stadt liegt zwar nach der Tabula Peutingeriana westlich des Sangarios, während sie sich in Wirklichkeit östlich des Flusses befindet, aber diese kleine Korrektur schien um so eher gerechtfertigt, weil Versehen dieser Art auf der Tabula öfter fest-

---

1. Nach der Einteilung von K. Miller, *Die Weltkarte des Castorius, genannt die Peutinger'sche Tafel.*

2. Diese Zahlangabe steht auf der Tabula ohne Namensangabe etwas über der folgenden Zahl *XXIIII.*

3. Anscheinend erfolgte diese Identifikation zuerst von K. Mannert in seiner *Geographie der Griechen und Römer* VI 3 (1802) 620; ihm folgte A. Forbiger im *Handbuch der alten Geographie* II (1844) 394 und die späteren Autoren.

zustellen sind.[4] Dann hätte man *XXX* m.p. westlich davon die Station *Dusepro Solympum* zu suchen. "Die Entfernungsangaben der Tabula Peutingeriana führen nach der alten Niederlassung Beiköi am Südrand der Ebene von Düsdsche",[5] von der man durch G. Perrot[6] und W. von Diest[7] Nachricht hatte. W. von Diest glaubte, hier *Dusai* πρὸς ᾿Ολυμπον gefunden zu haben; in dieser Form bzw. mit *Dusae ad Olympum* stellte man durch eine leichte Korrektur der Tabula Peutingeriana den Stadtnamen wieder her.[8] Außerdem hielt sich von Diest berechtigt, in dem Kardüz Dagh, der die Ebene von Düzce südlich abschließt, einen *mons Olympus* zu sehen, dem er den Beinamen: *Olympus Bithynicus*[9] verlieh, obwohl wir sonst keinerlei Nachrichten aus dem Altertum weder über diese Stadt noch über einen bithynischen Olymp besitzen. Alle Angaben über den *mons Olympus* im nördlichen Kleinasien beziehen sich vielmehr auf den Ulu Dagh,[10] die höchste Erhebung im westlichen Kleinasien, der, obwohl an der Grenze Bithyniens gelegen, den Beinamen *Mysius* führt.

Bei einer Forschungsreise, die ich im Herbst 1948 im nördlichen Kleinasien durchführte, beschäftigte mich auch die Frage der Existenz von *Dusae ad Olympum*. Nachdem ich längere Zeit im nördlichen Teil der Ebene von Düzce verweilt hatte, wo ich mit der

---

4. Vgl. die Ausführungen von K. Miller über die Darstellungen von Flüssen auf der Tabula Peutingeriana in der Einleitung seines Werkes *Itineraria Romana* 42f.

5. W. Ruge, *RE* V 1865 s.v. *Dusae* πρὸς ᾿Ολυμπον; in seinem Artikel unterstellt allerdings Ruge als Tatsache, daß *Dusae* 30 m.p. von *Claudiopolis* liegen müsse, ohne zu erwähnen, daß es sich nur um eine vermutete Zuweisung der Vignette an *Claudiopolis* handelt. Doch ist *Dusae* nicht von Ruge in der von ihm 1899 gemeinsam mit E. Friedrich herausgegebenen *Archäologischen Karte von Kleinasien* aufgenommen. Die älteren Autoren des vorigen Jahrhunderts wie z.B. Mannert *a.O.* 623 oder Forbiger *a.O.* 394 wollten in dem Ortsnamen Düzce (früher Düsdsche oder ähnlich, auch Tuske von älteren Reisenden geschrieben) ein Fortleben von *Dusae* feststellen (anscheinend teilt auch Miller, *It.Rom.* 667 diese Annahme); aber Düzce ist wohl eine rein türkische Bildung und von türk. düz = eben abzuleiten, verbunden mit dem Suffix — ce. An das Fortbestehen des alten Namens glaubt auch Schwarz, Quer durch Bithynien (vgl. S. 73 f.); die von Schwarz in Düzce gesehenen und für den Neubau eines Hauses bereit gelegten antiken Fragmente sind aber wohl kaum an Ort und Stelle gefunden; sie werden wahrscheinlich von Prusias hierher transportiert worden sein.

6. *Exploration arch. de la Galatie et de la Bithynie* 26.

7. *Peterm.Mitt.Erg.* 94, 1889, 86.

8. Als *Dusae ad Olympum* ist die über Beyköy (Beiköi) liegende Burg bei R. Kiepert, *Kleinasien*, Bl. A III (Zafaranboli) eingetragen (vgl. auch die Aeußerungen zu dem Problem der Streckenführung bei J. Sölch, *Klio* 19, 1925, 170 mit Anm. 3). Nicht recht verständlich ist die Bemerkung von Mannert a.O. 623: "Bis hierher (d.h. bis Dusae) reichte also dieser nördliche Olympus, welcher den Sangarius von den Flüsschen der Nordküste trennt".

9. Vgl. seine Karte der Ebene von Düzce auf Bl. II von *Pterm.Mitt.Erg.* 94, 1889, übernommen von R. Kiepert und ebenso von W. Ruge *RE* XVIII 313 s.v. Olympos nr. 15.

10. Bei Kiepert und den älteren Reisebeschreibungen wird das heute allgemein als Ulu Dagh, d.h. großer Berg, bezeichnete Massiv Keshish bzw. Keschisch Dagh genannt.

Aufnahme der Denkmäler und Inschriften beschäftigt war, die im Gebiet von Prusias πρὸς Ὕπιον neu gefunden worden waren,[11] untersuchte ich anschließend auch den Südteil der Ebene genauer. Zunächst gewann ich die Ueberzeugung, daß in und um Beyköy (Beiköi) nichts die Ansetzung einer antiken Stadt oder Siedlung rechtfertigt. Ich fand auch die von Perrot beschriebenen Architekturteile und Inschriften nicht mehr auf, die inzwischen zu Grunde gegangen sind.[12] Trotz intensiver Bebauung hat man hier keinerlei Funde aus antiker Zeit gemacht, so daß ich geneigt bin zu glauben, *Prusias ad Hypium* habe auch für die Gebäude in Beyköy, in denen Perrot antike Fragmente verbaut sah, ebenso das Baumaterial geliefert wie für das aufstrebende Düzce, wo z.B. das vor wenigen Jahrzehnten errichtete Minarett der neuen Moschee vollständig aus Steinen erbaut ist, die man aus antiken Baulichkeiten in Prusias holte; auch in anderen Dörfern der Ebene fand ich Steine und Inschriften, die man in Üskübü "gekauft" hatte, wie heute der kleine Ort heißt, der sich an Stelle der Akropolis von Prusias erhebt.

Die Untersuchung der "Kale" (Burg) am Südrand der Ebene von Düzce ergab, daß hier die spärlichen Reste der Anlage einer kleinen spätantiken Befestigung erhalten geblieben sind. Den Zugang zu der Burg gewinnt man von Süden her, wo das Gelände die Anlage eines Weges erlaubt, während auf den anderen Seiten der Burgberg steil abbricht, den der aus der Schlucht herausströmende Derdin Boghaz, in zwei Arme geteilt, umfließt. Die Aufnahme Taf. 19a läßt gut die Lage der Kale erkennen; sie liegt auf dem Hügel am Fuße des Kardüz Dagh unterhalb einer neuerbauten Volksschule, die sich auf der Spitze der folgenden Hügelkette erhebt und in der Mitte des Bildes als weißer Fleck deutlich wahrnehmbar ist. Das Bahngeleise im Vordergrund der Aufnahme wurde von der Forstverwaltung für den Abtransport von Holz angelegt und führt noch einige Kilometer in die Schlucht des Derdin Boghaz hinein.

Das kleine Plateau, auf dem die Burg steht, hat eine ganz unregelmäßige Form; die schmalste Stelle liegt im Süden, wo allein noch Teile des aufgehenden Mauerwerks anstehen. Taf. 19, b zeigt einen Blick von innen her auf die Südfront. In der Mauerlücke ist das Gestein zwar weitgehend abgebröckelt, aber auf der rechten Seite des Bildes, wo ein kleiner Turm gestanden hat, erkennt man noch den Ansatz zu einem Torbogen, den Taf. 20 von außen her zeigt. Die Mauer selbst ist aus unregelmäßig zubehauenen, kleinen Steinen unter

---

11. Ein Vorbericht über die Ergebnisse dieser Reise erschien im Anzeiger der Akad. der Wissenschaften in Wien 1949 Heft 12; die Gesamtpublikation in den *Denkschriften der Akademie* ist in Vorbereitung.

12. a.O. 26.

sparsamer Verwendung von Mörtel aufgeführt, deren Ungleich-
heiten man durch Einlage von Ziegelplatten ausgeglichen hat. Die
Dicke der Mauer schwankt um 1,85 m; sie zog sich ursprünglich
schützend um das ganze Plateau, dessen Durchmesser gut 50 m beträgt,[13] ist aber jetzt bis auf geringe Reste abgestürzt oder abge-
tragen. Irgendwelche Spuren der Anlage im Innern der Burg waren
ohne Grabung nicht mehr festzustellen.

Die Untersuchung zeigte deutlich, daß es sich bei der Anlage aus-
schließlich um ein byzantinisches Kastell handelt, das zur Ueber-
wachung des Südteils der Ebene angelegt sein mag, vielleicht auch
den durch die Schlucht des Derdin Boghaz führenden Uebergang über
den Kardüz Dagh nach Mudurlu sichern sollte.[14] Dieses Kastell nach
den Angaben der Tabula Peutingeriana mit *Dusae ad Olympum*
identifizieren zu wollen, scheint mir völlig unmöglich zu sein! Denn
es zeigt sich nach den bisherigen Untersuchungen, daß im Norden
der Ebene in spätantiker Zeit *Prusias ad Hypium,* inzwischen Bi-
schofssitz geworden und geschützt durch einen starken Mauerring,
fortbestand. Wer von Osten oder Westen her die Ebene durchzog,
wird natürlich sein Quartier, wenn er die Auswahl hatte, eher in
Prusias genommen haben als in einem kleinen Kastell, abgesehen
davon, daß dort vermutlich keinerlei Gelegenheit zur Unterkunft für
gewöhnliche Reisende bestand. Wenn aber das kleine Kastell für
eine Namengebung der Tabula Peutingeriana ausscheidet, wie erklärt sich dann der Name von *Dusae ad Olympum?*

Einen radikalen Lösungsversuch hat bereits W. M. Ramsay vorge-
schlagen; er glaubte, *Dusae pros Olympum* sei nur verwechselt mit
Prusa ad Olympum; außerdem sei die ganze Streckenführung der
Tabula Peutingeriana verderbt, die nicht in eine West-Ost-Route,
sondern in einen Verbindungsweg zwischen Prusa ad Olympum und
Nikaia bzw. Nikomedeia gehöre.[15]

Diese Hypothese ist allgemein abgelehnt worden,[16] und sie läßt sich
auch wohl nicht aufrecht erhalten; selbst der Hinweis von Ramsay
auf den bei Pachymeres erwähnten Ort Platanea[17] verleiht ihr nicht

---

13. Die Angabe bei von Diest *a.O.*86, die "Hochburg, ein ovaler Hügel" sei
"150 m lang", muß wohl auf einem Versehen beruhen.

14. von Diest *a.O.*86. A. M. Schneider verdanke ich den Hinweis, daß —
nach dem Mauerwerk zu urteilen — eine Erbauung erst in paläologischer oder
frühtürkischer Zeit wahrscheinlich sei; eine genauere Datierung ist aber sehr
schwer, so lange wir vom Innern Kleinasiens noch so wenig wissen!

15. *Hist.Geography of Asia Minor (Royal Geogr.Soc.Suppl.Papers* IV 1890)
64f.

16. So z.B. von G. Hirschfeld, *RE* I 2441 s.v. Antinoupolis; W. Ruge in den
phil.-hist.Beiträgen C. Wachsmuth überreicht S.25 und RE V 1865 s.v. *Dusae;*
vgl. auch die Eintragungen auf der Karte von Kleinasien durch R. Kiepert, Bl.
A III (Zafaranboli) und die Bemerkungen von J. Sölch, *Klio* 11, 1911, 408.

17. II p. 286 E (ed.Bonn p. 413,2).

mehr Wahrscheinlichkeit. Da auch die Kosmographia des Anonymus Ravennas einen Ort Platana[18] erwähnt und nach Plinius ein Fluß Plataneus[19] existierte, der nach dem Zusammenhang zu schließen, wohl in die Propontis unweit des Sinus Cianus mündete, muß man einen Ort dieses Namens wohl auch in der Gegend von *Prusa ad Olympum* suchen, ohne aber daraus folgern zu können, daß *Plateas-Lateas* oder ähnlich[20] nicht im Zuge einer Strecke von Nikomedeia nach Osten existiert haben könne.

Entscheidend aber ist für die Frage, was es mit *Dusae pro Solympum* in der Streckenführung der Tabula Peutingeriana für eine Bewandtnis habe, folgende Beobachtung: Zwar stimmt die Tabula Peutingeriana, wie an so manchen anderen Stellen, auch in diesem problematischen Teil mit den Angaben in der Kosmographia des Anonymus Ravennas im wesentlichen überein; aber es gibt doch einige wichtige Unterschiede, die am besten eine Gegenüberstellung aufzeigt:

TABULA PEUTINGERIANA (IX 2/3)	KOSMOGRAPHIA (II 19)
Calcedonia	Chalcedon
Livissa	Livissa
Nicomedia	Nicomedia
Lateas	Plateas
Demetriu	Demitriu
Dusepro Solympum	Druso prosipeo
(Vignette)	Claudopolis (sic)
Manoris	Mandris
Potomia Cepora	Potomi Cepora
Antoniopolis	Antoniapolis

Bei einem Vergleich dieser Gegenüberstellung erhebt sich sofort die Frage: Hat der Anonymus Ravennas seine Angaben der Tabula Peutingeriana entnommen oder haben beide ihre Kenntnisse aus der gleichen Vorlage geschöpft? Die neuen Untersuchungen von J. Schnetz über die Quellen der Kosmographia[21] lassen das erstere vermuten. Aber offensichtlich war das ihm vorliegende Exemplar der Tabula Peutingeriana noch besser erhalten als die auf uns gekom-

---

18. II 19 (Pinder-Parthey p. 109,5; Schnetz p. 31,5).

19. Plin. *N.H.* V 148.

20. *Plateas* hat die Kosmographia, *Lateas* die Tabula Peutingeriana (vgl. die Gegenüberstellung unten).

21. Untersuchungen über die Quellen der Kosmographia des Anonymen Geographen von Ravenna, *SB Akad.d.Wiss., phil.-hist.Abt.* München 1942, Heft 6. Schnetz gewann im Verlauf seiner Untersuchung auch für die Tabula Peutingeriana das wichtige Ergebnis, daß wir in *Castorius* den Verfasser der Tabula Peutingeriana zu sehen haben (vgl. S.54f. und besonders 85f.), ein Ergebnis, das K. Miller Zeit seines Lebens mit Leidenschaft gegen die Lehrmeinung vertreten hat, ohne aber damit eine allgemeine Anerkennung gefunden zu haben.

mene Kopie; vielleicht hat er selbst seine Vorlage der Tabula Peutingeriana auch nach einer anderen Quelle berichtigt, von denen er
II 16 mehrere angiebt.[22] Jedenfalls bin ich der Ueberzeugung, daß wir
den Angaben der Kosmographia vertrauensvoll folgen können, zumal
sie den geographischen Verhältnissen auf das beste entspricht. So
zögere ich nicht, die irreführende Angabe der Tabula Peutingeriana,
Dusepro Solympum nach der Kosmographia: *Duso prosipeo*, d.h.
Prusias pros Ipeo oder nach der offiziellen Schreibung in Προύσιας
πρὸς Ὕπιον richtigzustellen, und ich bin überzeugt, daß nach der
Kosmographia die Vignette der Tabula Peutingeriana richtig mit
Claudiopolis identifiziert worden ist,[23] zumal sich so auf das glück-
lichste die historische Ueberlieferung mit der bei meinem Besuch
dieser Stätte gewonnenen Ueberzeugung deckt, daß es nie einen Ort:
Dusae ad Olympum gegeben hat. Wenn durch dieses Ergebnis das
kleine Kastell am Südrand der Ebene von Prusias ad Hypium namen-
los bleibt, so wird die historische Forschung diese Einbuße ver-
schmerzen können.

---

22. Vgl. Schnetz, *Untersuchungen* 63f.

23. Die Uebereinstimmung zwischen Tabula Peutingeriana und der Kosmo-
graphia ist natürlich schon lange beobachtet und ausführlich zuerst von P. W.
Wesseling in seiner Vorrede zu der *Diatribe de Judaeorum archontibus ad in-
scriptionem Berenicensem* (1738) begründet worden, aber sie wurde im Sinne von
Dusae pros Olympum ausgewertet, zuletzt bei Miller, *It.Rom.* 667; vgl. die An-
führung der Stadt Prusias als *Prusa ad Hippium,* a.O. 670 (sic! wohl eine
Mischung aus Ptolem.V 1, 13 und der Eintragung des *fl.Hyppium* auf der Tabula
Peutingeriana, der als Flüßchen neben dem versehentlich zum zweitenmal einge-
zeichneten Lauf des *fl.Sangarius* in der Route entlang dem Pontos Euxinos eingetragen ist). Auf der richtigen Spur war allein J. H. Mordtmann, dessen *Athen.
Mitt.* 12, 887, 181 geäußerte Vermutung einer Gleichsetzung der Kosmographia
mit der Tabula Peutingeriana aber zugunsten von *Prusias ad Hypium,* unter
Ablehnung einer eigenen Existenz von *Dusae ad Olympum* nicht beachtet oder
abgelehnt worden ist. Die gesamte Ueberlieferung über *Prusias ad Hypium,* auch
alle Zeugnisse über ihre Namensform, habe ich in der *RE* s.v. zusammengestellt
(im Druck).

VIA EGNATIA AND THESSALONIKE

CHAR. I. MAKARONAS,
Thessalonike

Plate 21

Our knowledge of the *Via Egnatia*—the great military artery that, traversing Illyria, Macedonia, and Thrace, connected the Adriatic with the Aegean Sea—still is incomplete.[1] The relative sources are not altogether illuminating. We do not know, for instance, whence its name was derived, nor do we know exactly when it was constructed. Of course, the *itineraria romana* offer more or less clear and at times valuable information;[2] but they refer in the main to stations and to distances between them.

Strabo tells us that the *Via Egnatia* from Apollonia to Cypsela and the Hebros river was βεβηματισμένη κατὰ μίλιον καὶ κατεστηλω-μένη,[3] and this will mean that it had been measured with exactitude, and that at every mile a marble stele had been erected to indicate distances. These stelai, the *miliaria,* now form a supplementary but important source of historic and topographic information.

The length of the *Via Egnatia* between Apollonia and the river Hebros is known to us; we can therefore figure out that the *miliaria* which originally stood on it between these two points must have exceeded five hundred.[4] Of these only nine have survived, and all belong to later years; consequently, their discovery should not be attributed to a special favor of the fates. To this series of nine, given in his catalogue by P. Collart—the most recent scholar to study the problems of the *Via Egnatia*—we can now add another *miliarium,* the tenth, whose publication here will give us the opportunity to re-examine some topographical questions which deal with the section of the *Via* that is adjacent to Thessalonike and its environs.

The new *miliarium* was found accidentally in June 1949 to the north of Thessalonike, by the Langada road, exactly thirty meters to the west of the bridge that stands in front of the gate to the military barracks of Pavlos Melas. It was transported to and placed in the Museum of Thessalonike under the inventory number 1837 (pl. 21).

---

1. cf. the important study of Collart, P., "Une réfection de la via Egnatia sous Trajan," *BCH* 59 (1935) 394ff., where the pertinent bibliography.

2. Miller, K., *Itineraria Romana,* col. 516-527.

3. Strabo, *Geogr.* 7,322.

4. Strabo, *loc. cit.,* **Μιλίων δὲ ἐστὶ πεντακοσίων τριάκοντα πέντε** (from Apollonia to Cypsela).

Description: It is a cylindrical column of marble, ending irregularly on top in the form of a truncated cone. To a height of 0.28 m. from its lower end, its surface is worked grossly and irregularly. This will certainly indicate that the column up to that height was inserted in the ground. The rest of its cylindrical surface, that was exposed to view, has been worked more carefully and was smoothed. The *miliarium* bears inscriptions which start from its top and occupy almost half of the width of its cylindrical surface and a little more than half of its length. Above: after the first line a deep *rasura* exists in which was cut a later inscription of five lines. In the tenth line and between the fourth and the fifth letter a large *A* was inserted. Another *A*, equally large but of a different type, was inscribed below the last line. In general the lettering is careless and not clear.

Dimensions: Height, 1.85 m. Diameter, 0.35 m. Height of inscribed surface, 1 m. Distance from the last *A* to the lower end of the stone 0.73 m. Heights of the letters vary from 0.04 m. (l. 1) to 0.02 m. (l. 19) Height of the large *A* inserted in the tenth line, 0.08 m.; of the *A* at the end of the inscription, 0.075 m. The spaces between the lines are varied and irregular (pl. 21).

Transcription:

```
      Ἀ[γ]αθῇ Τύχῃ.
      Τῷ κυρίῳ ἡμῶν Αὐτο-
      κράτορι Καίσαρα (sic)
      Γ. Οὐαλ. Διοκλητιανοῦ  (sic)  Σεβ.
   5  καὶ Μᾶρ. Αὐρ. Οὐαλέριος
      Μαξιμιανός,  (sic)  ⟦[Θεσσα-]⟧
      λονικέων ἡ πόλις.
      Καὶ τοῖς ἐπιφανεστά-
      τοις ἡμῶν Κα<ί>σαρσιν
  10  Φλαβ- Α΄ - ίῳ Οὐαλερί-
      ῳ Κωσσταντίῳ
      κὲ Γαλερίῳ Οὐαλερίῳ
      Μαξιμιανῷ
      Σεβαστοῖς καὶ Φλ.
  15  Οὐαλ. Σεβήρῳ καὶ Γαλ.
      Οὐαλ. Μαξιμίνῳ, ἐπι-
      φανεστάτοις Καί-
      σαρσιν, ἡ Θεσσαλο-
      νεικέων πόλις.
  20        Α΄
```

The negligence in the cutting of the letters finds a parallel in the carelessness and syntactic inconsistency that is to be observed in lines 3-6, where instead of the required dative we find all the other cases except the vocative: Line 3: *Καίσαρα* instead of *Καίσαρι·* line 4: *Διοκλητιανοῦ* instead of *Διοκλητιανῷ·* lines 5-6: *Οὐαλέριος Μαξιμιανός* instead of *Οὐαλερίῳ Μαξιμιανῷ*. At any rate, our *miliarium* belongs to the type which R. Cagnat in his *Cours d' Épigraphie Latine*[4], p. 276, places in the eighth group; aside from the recorded number of miles, the rest of our inscription in every respect is similar to the honorary inscriptions to Emperors.

In addition to the epigraphic evidence, the fact two Emperors and four Caesars are mentioned at the same time proves that here too, as is the case in other *miliaria* especially of the late Imperial times, we have successive cuttings of inscriptions in different chronological intervals corresponding to the succession of these leaders.[5] We shall attempt to determine these successive inscriptions from the palaeographic and historic indications offered by our stone.

The *rasura* of lines 2-6 proves that lines 1 and 7 belong to the first inscription inscribed on the stone. It is not, of course, permissible to conjecture whether or not the erased name was that of the Emperor Numerianus—the predecessor of Diocletian—or that of an older Emperor, especially when we bear in mind the turbulent years of the Empire, the frequent succession and the short-lived stay on the throne of the Emperors who preceded Diocletian. To that first inscription must belong the large *A* of line 10, which indicates the first mile apparently from Thessalonike.

A difference is observed both as to the character of the letters and as to the spaces separating lines between lines 2 and 4 on the one hand and 5-6 on the other. Without doubt lines 2-4 were cut before Diocletian took Maximian as co-ruler. The fact that here the title *Σεβαστός* is not stated, permits the dating of these two lines to the year between Mars 1, 286 and September 17 or 19(?), 286, during which Maximian had only the title of Caesar.[6]

It should be noted that at the end of line 6 the letters: *Θεσσα-* were not cut again to complete the ensuing line: *λονικέων πόλις*.

Lines 8-13 belong to the period in which Constantius Chlorus and Galerius, taken as Caesars by Diocletian and Maximian, formed the first tetrarchy. We have of course a *terminus post quem*, the date of May 21, 293, when Galerius, after Constantius Chlorus, took the title of Caesar.[7] It seems that at the same time was cut at the end of the

5. *BCH* 59 (1935) 400-402.
6. Seston, W., *Dioclétien et la Tétrarchie I*, 60ff.
7. *Ibid.*, 93 ff.

inscription the second large *A,* which repeats the distance of one
mile from Thessalonike.

The different type of the letters of lines 14-19, the ligatures, the
compression of the lines, so that they would not run over the lat *A,*
indicate still another later period. Now we see added to the names of
Constantius[8] and Galerius the title *Σεβαστοῖς,* and we find inscribed
the names of the two other *ἐπιφανέστατοι Καίσαρες,*[9] of Severus and
Maximinus Daia, who with Constantius and Galerius formed the new
tetrarchy after the resignation of Diocletian and Maximian on the
first day of May 305.[10] These lines therefore must have been cut between the first day of May, 305, and the twenty-fifth day of July, 306,
when Severus took the title of Augustus.[11]

Summarizing our observations we may determine the chronological
sequence of the successive inscriptions of our *miliarium* as follows:

A.   1 *'Α[γ]αθῇ Τύχῃ.*
         -rasura 5 (?)
              lines   Before the accession of
                                             Diocletian Augustus:
      6   ⟦[*Θεσσα-*]⟧   17 (or 19) of September,
      7 *λονικέων ἡ πόλις.*   284.
     10   *Α′*

B.   2 *Τῷ κυρίῳ ἡμῶν Αὐτο-*   After September 17 (or
      3 *κράτορι Καίσαρα* (sic)   19), 284, and before
      4 *Γ. Οὐαλ. Διοκλητιανοῦ* (sic) *Σεβ.* March 1, 286.

C.   5 *Καὶ Μᾶρ. Αὐρ. Οὐαλέριος*   After March 1, 286 and
      6 *Μαξιμιανός.* (sic)   before September 17 or
                                            19(?), 286.

D.   8 *Καὶ τοῖς ἐπιφανεστά-*
      9 *τοις ἡμῶν Κα<ί>σαρσιν*
     10 *Φλαβ- ίῳ Οὐαλερί-*
     11 *ῳ Κωσσταντίῳ*   After May 21, 293 and
     12 *κὲ Γαλερίῳ Οὐαλερίῳ*   before May 1, 305.
     13 *Μαξιμιανῷ.*
     20   *Α′*

---

8. The form *Κωσστάντιος* on the inscription should be compared with *Κοστάν-
τιος, Κοστάντις* and *Κοσταντῖνος, Κωσταντινούπολις,* etc., in Pape-Benseler, *Wörterbuch d. griech. Eigennamen*[3].

9. The titles *ἐπιφανέστατοι Καίσαρες* and *ὁ κύριος ἡμῶν* (a translation of the
Latin *nobillissimi caesares* and *dominus noster*) were common especially during
the epoch of the tetrarchy (Sandys, J. E., *Latin Epigraphy*[2], 254).

10. Stein, E., *Geschichte des spätrömischen Reiches* I, 123.

11. *Ibid.* 125.

E. 14 Σεβαστοῖς καὶ Φλ.
    15 Οὐαλ. Σεβήρῳ καὶ Γαλ.
    16 Οὐαλ. Μαξιμίνῳ, ἐπι-   After May 1, 305 and be-
    17 φανεστάτοις Καί-   fore July 25, 306.
    18 σαρσιν ἡ Θεσσαλο-
    19 νεικέων πόλις.

*   *   *   *   *   *   *

The belief prevailing to date is that the *Via Egnatia* in the course of its run from the West entered the city of Thessalonike through the Golden Gate, and, following exactly the course of the modern street that bears the name Egnatia,[12] traversed the city from West to East. Thence, leaving the city through the Kassandrean Gate, continued its course toward the heights of mount Chortiates and, descending to the southern shore of the Langada Lake, continued to the straits of Rentina and the Strymonic gulf.[13] Against this hypothetical course that cannot be proved, a serious objection could be raised, an objection that could be presented in the form of the following questions: Why would the engineers who laid out the *Via* prefer this uneven course through mount Chortiates, when it would have been simpler and easier to by-pass from the north the heights lying to the northeast of Thessalonike and thence to approach the Langada Lake through the straits of Derveni? Why should this smoother and easier course, that is followed by the modern road of Thessalonike-Kavala, not have been preferred? Would it be because the *Via Egnatia* had to pass through the center of the city? But was this reason so important as to make the Romans disregard the essential disadvantages presented by a course through mount Chortiates: *i. e.* the greater expense involved in the construction of such a road, the

---

12. That street was and continues to be the largest and most important of the city, having formed, at least in Roman times, one of the basic axes of the city plan (cf. Schoenebeck, H. v., "Die Stadtplanung des römischen Thessalonike," *Bericht über den VI intern. Kongress für Archäologie*, Berlin 1940, 479 and 481 fig. 1). We know that it was called Λεωφόρος in Byzantine times ('Ιωάν. Καμενιάτης, Bonn, 500; Κωνστ. 'Αρμενόπουλος, Χειρόγρ. κῶδ. 'Αθηνῶν 2118, page 19b. in 'Α., Ξυγγοπούλου, Συμβολαὶ εἰς τὴν τοπογραφίαν τῆς βυζαντινῆς Θεσσαλονίκης, 9; Γρηγ. Παλαμᾶς Migne, *Patr. Gr.*, 151, 544.) In the years of the Turkish occupation it was officially called the "great street of Vardar," but the Greek inhabitants of the city called it "φαρδύν" or "μεγάλον δρόμον" while its popular Turkish name was "Djatéghyol" (Tafrali, O., *Topographie de Thessalonique*, 21, pl. 2.) After the great fire in 1917, in consequence of which the street was broadened, it was officially called Egnatia street.

13. Tafel, Th., *De via militari Romanorum Egnatia* [III]: *De viae Romanorum militaris Egnatiae parte orientali*, 4. cf. Tafrali, *op.cit.*, 21; Oberhummer, E., *RE* 11, col. 149; Schoenebeck, *op.cit.*, 479; Vakalopoulos, Ap., 'Ιστορία τῆς Θεσσαλονίκης, 12-13.

problems of maintenance it offers, and the greater difficulties it presents to the flow of armies and travelers?

We believe that these questions, which of their nature offer arguments that are at the same time logical but impossible to prove,[14] could be answered by a further study of the *miliaria* which provide definite evidence that will help the final solution of the problem. Following are the *miliaria* which were found in the district of Thessalonike.

1. The *miliarium* described above, now in the Museum of Thessalonike. We have seen that it bears the letter *A* that indicates the first mile from Thessalonike.

2. The *miliarium* in the collection St. George, Thessalonike, with the inscription: *a Thessalonica V.*[15]

3. The *miliarium* in the Louvre, bearing successive inscriptions in which, with the exception of the first, we find the letters [V]IIII *Θ*, i. e. nine miles from Thessalonike.[16]

Our first task will be to determine whether or not the distances from Thessalonike of the spots in which these three stones were found is in agreement with the miles inscribed on them. We must insist on this examination, because the positive establishment of this factor forms a *sine qua non* presupposition for the solution of our problem. For *miliarium* no. 1 we may state that such an agreement does exist, if we accept as starting point the Letean Gate, which marked the west

---

14. The opposite view is maintained by Bädeker, *Konstantinopel*, etc.[2], 102 (cf. Oberhummer, *l.c.*) and Collart, *op.cit.*, 411.

15. Collart, P., *op.cit.*, no. 2, p. 407ff., pl. XXVI, 2: Imp(erator) | Caes(ar), Divi Ner|vae f(ilius). Nerva Tra|ianus Aug(ustus), Germ(anicus), Dac(icus), | P(ontifex) m(aximus), trib(unicia) p(otestate) XI (sic) imp(erator) VI, co(n)s(ul) | VI (sic), P(ater) P(atriae), viam a Dyrrac(hio) | usq(ue) Neapoli(m) per pro|vinciam Macedo|niam longa inter|missione neglect(am) | restituendam cu|ravit, a Thessalonica | V.

16. Dain, Alph., *Inscriptions grecques du Musée du Louvre*, no. 24, p. 30ff; Lambrino, S., *Istros*, I, 157; Collart, *op.cit.*, 401 Note 1. It bears three inscriptions:

(i) Imp(erator) | Caesar, Divi | Traiani Parthici | fil(ius) Divi Nervae | nepos, Traianus | Hadrianus Aug(ustus), | Pont(ifex) max(imus), trib(unicia) pot(estate) | VIII, co(n)s(ul) III, a Thessal(onica) | m(ilia) p(assuum) | IIII.

(ii) Imp(erator) Cae(sar) F[l(avius)] | Val(erius) | Constantinu[s], | Pi(us), Invictus, | Aug(ustus) .... (4 lines erased) .... m(ilia) p(assuum) [V] IIII. *Καί Κλ(αύδιος) Κρίσπος, | καί Λι(κίνιος) Κλ(αύδιος), Λ[ι(κινίου) υἱός], | καί Κλ(αύδιος) Κωνσταντεῖνος, | οἱ ἐπιφ(ανέστατοι) Καίσαρες,* | [V]IIII *Θ*. The appropriate completion: [V]IIII, corresponding to the indication *Θ*, is due to S. Lambrino, who suggests that it is possible to complete the number IIII at the end of the first inscription, if the probability is excluded that between the epoch of Hadrian and that of Constantinus the *miliarium* was transferred from the first to the ninth mile.

(iii) Eight lines erased. Only some isolated letters can now be distinguished. Further down in line 9: ΠΟΛΙⳞ ΙΘΙ, where we can complete, I believe: *[ἡ] πόλις ἡ Θε[σσαλονικέων]*.

end of the modern street of Agios Demetrios.[17] Some difference arises
in the case of *miliarium* no. 2; because while it bears the number:
five miles, *i. e.* about 7.400 meters,[18] it was found, as Stanley Casson
states,[19] "near the 6th kilometre from Salonica, on the Salonica-
Serres road," on the road which today is known as the Langada road.[20]
Perhaps we can overlook this difference when we take into consideration a) that the information offered by Casson is not very clear; b)
that we do not know the exact course of the ancient road, which in
all probability was not as straight as the modern; and c) we do not
know the starting point from which distances on the modern road
were calculated in 1918.[21] Finally, about *miliarium* no. 3, that bears
the inscribed distance of nine miles, *i. e.* nearly 13.300 meters, from
Thessalonike, we get the following information from Dain's inscription: "Environs de Salonique. Trouvé sur la route de Monastir, pont
de Galico. Envoi du général commandant en chef les armées alliées
en Orient."[22] The bridge of the Galico (Echedoros) river is to be
found today on the 11th kilometer from the Vardar Square of Thessalonike. Here again we have some difference between the inscribed
distance and the distance from Thessalonike of the place where the
stone was found. Again, however, we can overlook this difference, if

---

17. Tafrali, *op.cit.* pl. 2.
18. If we figure the mile at 1480 meters.
19. *BSA* 23 (1918-1919) 39.
20. Collart, *op.cit.*, 411, accepts without discussion that this *miliarium* "a sans
doute été decouvert en place: la route moderne de Salonique à Serrès, au bord
de laquelle it était, commence par suivre le tracé de la Via Egnatia jusqu' à la
depression de Langada que longeait alors la route romaine pour se diriger vers
le golfe d'Orfano et vers Amphipolis." This conception of Collart is correct,
although it is obscured by his preceding vagueness (p. 396): "Nous la suivons
(via Egnatia) pas à pas . . . . jusqu' à Thessalonique, ou elle touchait une pre-
miere fois à la Mer Egée; puis au-delà c o u p a n t l a C h a l c i d i q u e, etc."
cf. Collart, *Philippes, ville de Macédoine*, 491. Our purpose is to prove that conception which, offered in a casual way, did not aim at the solution of a topographical problem—that, indeed, was not Collart's objective—a problem, posed
since the days of Tafel, that remained unsolved since the solution offered in those
days and generally accepted until now is not correct. At any rate it is essential
at the very beginning of the discussion of the problem to prove whether or not
the *miliarium* was found in its original position. And this has to be done in an
objective manner and not by a deductive process, that is by the *a priori* acceptance "as self evident," or "given that the conceptions cited above can be considered correct."
21. I was informed by the authorities, who are responsible for the construction and repair of the roads of the Thessalonike district, that the milestones of
today are not placed in the same positions which they held during the first
World War. It is probable that then the point where the Langada-Serres road
was crossed by the road to Asvestochori was considered as the starting point of
the former. The distance of that point from the Vardar square, which today is
considered the starting point of the Langada road, covers a considerable part
of the difference noted between the number inscribed on the *miliarium* (*a Thessalonica V*) and the distance of the place in which it was discovered.
22. Dain, *op.cit.*, 30.